Leviticus
and
Numbers

TEACH THE TEXT COMMENTARY SERIES

John H. Walton
Old Testament General Editor

Mark L. Strauss
New Testament General Editor

When complete, the TEACH THE TEXT COMMENTARY SERIES *will include the following volumes:*

Old Testament Volumes

New Testament Volumes

To see which titles are available, visit the series website at www.teachthetextseries.com.

TEACH the TEXT
COMMENTARY SERIES

Leviticus
and
Numbers

Joe M. Sprinkle

Mark L. Strauss and John H. Walton
GENERAL EDITORS

ILLUSTRATING THE TEXT

Kevin and Sherry Harney
ASSOCIATE EDITORS

Adam Barr
CONTRIBUTING WRITER

BakerBooks
a division of Baker Publishing Group
Grand Rapids, Michigan

© 2015 by Joe M. Sprinkle
Captions and Illustrating the Text sections © 2015 by Baker Publishing Group

Published by Baker Books
a division of Baker Publishing Group
P.O. Box 6287, Grand Rapids, MI 49516–6287
www.bakerbooks.com

Printed in the United States of America

Library of Congress Cataloging-in-Publication Data

Sprinkle, Joe M.
    Leviticus and Numbers / Joe Sprinkle ; Mark L. Strauss and John H. Walton, general editors; Kevin and Sherry Harney, associate editors ; Adam Barr, contributing writer.
        pages cm. — (Teach the text commentary)
    Includes bibliographical references and index.
    ISBN 978-0-8010-9233-6 (pbk.)
    1. Bible. Leviticus—Commentaries. 2. Bible. Numbers—Commentaries.
I. Title.
BS1255.53.S67 201
222′.1307—dc23   2015015878

15   16   17   18   19   20   21   7   6   5   4   3   2   1

Contents

Welcome to the Teach the Text Commentary Series

Why another commentary series? That was the question the general editors posed when Baker Books asked us to produce this series. Is there something that we can offer to pastors and teachers that is not currently being offered by other commentary series, or that can be offered in a more helpful way? After carefully researching the needs of pastors who teach the text on a weekly basis, we concluded that yes, more can be done; the Teach the Text Commentary Series (TTCS) is carefully designed to fill an important gap.

The technicality of modern commentaries often overwhelms readers with details that are tangential to the main purpose of the text. Discussions of source and redaction criticism, as well as detailed surveys of secondary literature, seem far removed from preaching and teaching the Word. Rather than wade through technical discussions, pastors often turn to devotional commentaries, which may contain exegetical weaknesses, misuse the Greek and Hebrew languages, and lack hermeneutical sophistication. There is a need for a commentary that utilizes the best of biblical scholarship but also presents the material in a clear, concise, attractive, and user-friendly format.

This commentary is designed for that purpose—to provide a ready reference for the exposition of the biblical text, giving easy access to information that a pastor needs to communicate the text effectively. To that end, the commentary is divided into carefully selected preaching units, each covered in six pages (with carefully regulated word counts both in the passage as a whole and in each subsection). Pastors and teachers engaged in weekly preparation thus know that they will be reading approximately the same amount of material on a week-by-week basis.

Each passage begins with a concise summary of the central message, or "Big Idea," of the passage and a list of its main themes. This is followed by a more detailed interpretation of the text, including the literary context of the passage, historical background material, and interpretive insights. While drawing on the best of biblical scholarship, this material is clear, concise, and to the point. Technical material is kept to a minimum, with endnotes pointing the reader to more detailed discussion and additional resources.

A second major focus of this commentary is on the preaching and teaching process itself. Few commentaries today help the pastor/teacher move from the meaning of the text to its effective communication. Our goal is to bridge this gap. In addition to interpreting the text in the "Understanding the Text" section, each six-page unit contains a "Teaching the Text" section and an "Illustrating the Text" section. The teaching section points to the key theological themes of the passage and ways to communicate these themes to today's audiences. The illustration section provides ideas and examples for retaining the interest of hearers and connecting the message to daily life.

The creative format of this commentary arises from our belief that the Bible is not just a record of God's dealings in the past but is the living Word of God, "alive and active" and "sharper than any double-edged sword" (Heb. 4:12). Our prayer is that this commentary will help to unleash that transforming power for the glory of God.

The General Editors

Introduction to the Teach the Text Commentary Series

This series is designed to provide a ready reference for teaching the biblical text, giving easy access to information that is needed to communicate a passage effectively. To that end, the commentary is carefully divided into units that are faithful to the biblical authors' ideas and of an appropriate length for teaching or preaching.

The following standard sections are offered in each unit.

1. *Big Idea*. For each unit the commentary identifies the primary theme, or "Big Idea," that drives both the passage and the commentary.
2. *Key Themes*. Together with the Big Idea, the commentary addresses in bullet-point fashion the key ideas presented in the passage.
3. *Understanding the Text*. This section focuses on the exegesis of the text and includes several sections.
   a. The Text in Context. Here the author gives a brief explanation of how the unit fits into the flow of the text around it, including

reference to the rhetorical strategy of the book and the unit's contribution to the purpose of the book.
   b. Outline/Structure. For some literary genres (e.g., epistles), a brief exegetical outline may be provided to guide the reader through the structure and flow of the passage.
   c. Historical and Cultural Background. This section addresses historical and cultural background information that may illuminate a verse or passage.
   d. Interpretive Insights. This section provides information needed for a clear understanding of the passage. The intention of the author is to be highly selective and concise rather than exhaustive and expansive.
   e. Theological Insights. In this very brief section the commentary identifies a few carefully selected theological insights about the passage.

4. *Teaching the Text*. Under this second main heading the commentary offers guidance for teaching the text. In this section the author lays out the main themes and applications of the passage. These are linked carefully to the Big Idea and are represented in the Key Themes.

5. *Illustrating the Text*. At this point in the commentary the writers partner with a team of pastor/teachers to provide suggestions for relevant and contemporary illustrations from current culture, entertainment, history, the Bible, news, literature, ethics, biography, daily life, medicine, and over forty other categories. They are designed to spark creative thinking for preachers and teachers and to help them design illustrations that bring alive the passage's key themes and message.

Abbreviations

Old Testament

Gen.	Genesis	2 Chron.	2 Chronicles	Dan.	Daniel
Exod.	Exodus	Ezra	Ezra	Hosea	Hosea
Lev.	Leviticus	Neh.	Nehemiah	Joel	Joel
Num.	Numbers	Esther	Esther	Amos	Amos
Deut.	Deuteronomy	Job	Job	Obad.	Obadiah
Josh.	Joshua	Ps(s).	Psalm(s)	Jon.	Jonah
Judg.	Judges	Prov.	Proverbs	Mic.	Micah
Ruth	Ruth	Eccles.	Ecclesiastes	Nah.	Nahum
1 Sam.	1 Samuel	Song	Song of Songs	Hab.	Habakkuk
2 Sam.	2 Samuel	Isa.	Isaiah	Zeph.	Zephaniah
1 Kings	1 Kings	Jer.	Jeremiah	Hag.	Haggai
2 Kings	2 Kings	Lam.	Lamentations	Zech.	Zechariah
1 Chron.	1 Chronicles	Ezek.	Ezekiel	Mal.	Malachi

New Testament

Matt.	Matthew	Eph.	Ephesians	Heb.	Hebrews
Mark	Mark	Phil.	Philippians	James	James
Luke	Luke	Col.	Colossians	1 Pet.	1 Peter
John	John	1 Thess.	1 Thessalonians	2 Pet.	2 Peter
Acts	Acts	2 Thess.	2 Thessalonians	1 John	1 John
Rom.	Romans	1 Tim.	1 Timothy	2 John	2 John
1 Cor.	1 Corinthians	2 Tim.	2 Timothy	3 John	3 John
2 Cor.	2 Corinthians	Titus	Titus	Jude	Jude
Gal.	Galatians	Philem.	Philemon	Rev.	Revelation

General

ca.	circa	lit.	literally
cf.	*confer*, compare	mg	margin
chap(s).	chapter(s)	p(p).	page(s)
col(s).	column(s)	rev.	revised
e.g.	*exempli gratia*, for example	s.v.	*sub verbo*, under the word
esp.	especially	v(v).	verse(s)
ibid.	*ibidem*, in the same source		

Ancient Texts, Text Types, and Versions

LXX	Septuagint
MT	Masoretic Text

Modern Versions

CEV	Contemporary English Version
CJB	Complete Jewish Bible
ESV	English Standard Version
HCSB	Holman Christian Standard Bible
KJV	King James Version
Message	The Message
NASB	New American Standard Bible
NCV	New Century Version
NEB	New English Bible
NET	New English Translation (The NET Bible)
NIV	New International Version
NJPS	*Tanakh: The Holy Scriptures: The New JPS Translation according to the Traditional Hebrew Text*
NKJV	New King James Version
NLT	New Living Translation
NRSV	New Revised Standard Version
REB	Revised English Bible
RSV	Revised Standard Version
TEV	Today's English Version

Greek and Latin Works

Diodorus

Bib. hist.	*Bibliotheca historica* (*Historical Library*)

Herodotus

Hist.	*Historiae* (*Histories*)

Josephus

Ant.	*Jewish Antiquities*
J.W.	*Jewish War*

Pliny the Elder

Nat.	*Naturalis historia* (*Natural History*)

Porphyry

Abst.	*De abstinentia* (*On Abstinence*)

Secondary Sources

ABD	*Anchor Bible Dictionary*. Edited by D. N. Freedman. 6 vols. New York, 1992
BDB	Brown, F., S. R. Driver, and C. A. Briggs. *A Hebrew and English Lexicon of the Old Testament*. Oxford, 1907
CAD	*The Assyrian Dictionary of the Oriental Institute of the University of Chicago*. Chicago, 1956–
HALOT	Koehler, L., W. Baumgartner, and J. J. Stamm. *The Hebrew and Aramaic Lexicon of the Old Testament*. Translated and edited under the supervision of M. E. J. Richardson. 4 vols. Leiden, 1994–99
IDB	*The Interpreter's Dictionary of the Bible*. Edited by G. A. Buttrick. 4 vols. Nashville, 1962
ISBE	*International Standard Bible Encyclopedia*. Edited by G. W. Bromiley. 4 vols. Grand Rapids, 1979–88
NBD	*New Bible Dictionary*. Edited by J. D. Douglas, N. Hillyer, and D. R. W. Wood. 3rd ed. Downers Grove, IL, 1996
NIDB	*New Interpreter's Dictionary of the Bible*. Edited by Katharine Doob Sakenfeld. 5 vols. Nashville, 2006–9
NIDOTTE	*New International Dictionary of Old Testament Theology and Exegesis*. Edited by W. A. VanGemeren. 5 vols. Grand Rapids, 1997
TDOT	*Theological Dictionary of the Old Testament*. Edited by G. J. Botterweck, H. Ringgren, and H.-J. Fabry. Translated by J. T. Willis, G. W. Bromiley, and D. E. Green. 15 vols. Grand Rapids, 1974–2006
TLOT	*Theological Lexicon of the Old Testament*. Edited by E. Jenni, with assistance from C. Westermann. Translated by M. E. Biddle. 3 vols. Peabody, MA, 1997

Introduction to Leviticus

Leviticus is among the least appreciated books of the Christian canon. Nonetheless, it is essential for biblical theology. In particular, Leviticus speaks of the concept of the holiness of God and the need for atoning sacrifice for sin. That in turn provides the conceptual framework for understanding the atoning work of Jesus Christ.

Title

The title "Leviticus" is derived through the Latin Vulgate from the early Greek translation, the Septuagint, that labels this book *Leuitikon*, "Pertaining to Levi" (i.e., the priestly tribe). This is somewhat misleading because much of the book is in fact addressed to the laity. The title in Hebrew is *wayyiqra'* ("and he called"), the first word of the book in Hebrew.

Setting

The book of Leviticus continues the story of Exodus. Exodus ends with Israel at Sinai having built the tabernacle. Leviticus tells Israel how to use the tabernacle they just built. Narratives in Leviticus take place at Mount Sinai, where God gives Moses further instructions.

Outline of Leviticus

Leviticus can be outlined as follows:

1. Sacrificial system (Lev. 1–7)
2. Priesthood (Lev. 8–10)
3. Impurity system (Lev. 11–15)
4. Day of Atonement (Lev. 16)
5. Laws of holiness (Lev. 17–27)

John Walton has proposed an outline based on the concept of preserving and maintaining sacred space.[1] In this outline certain procedures and qualifications maintain the divine equilibrium of sacred space against sin and impurity: sacrifices, priesthood, purity regulations for the camp, and the Day of Atonement ritual that resets the equilibrium annually (Lev. 1–17). Regulations that disqualify people, priests, and animals from the sacred space contribute to preventing Israel and its sacred space from being set out of equilibrium (Lev. 18–22), and regulations establishing religious festivals promote that equilibrium (Lev. 23). Other regulations maintain equilibrium between the human and sacred space (Lev. 24–27).

1. Divine equilibrium (Lev. 1–23)
   a. Equilibrium of sacred space: maintenance procedures and qualifications (Lev. 1–17)
      i. Sacrifices to maintain the holiest center zone (Lev. 1–7)
      ii. Priests set up to maintain enclosure zone (Lev. 8–10)
      iii. Purity regulations to maintain the camp zone (Lev. 11–15)
      iv. Yom Kippur, which resets the holiness of the entire sacred compass annually, features the priest moving into the center, bringing the accumulated impurities out and, finally, sending them outside the camp (Lev. 16)
      v. Maintaining holiness from outside the camp (Lev. 17)
   b. Equilibrium of sacred status: disqualifications from sacred space (Lev. 18–22)
      i. Disqualification of people from the camp (Lev. 18–20)
      ii. Disqualification of priests from the enclosure (Lev. 21–22:16)
      iii. Disqualification of animals for use in the center (Lev. 22:17–33)

The Israelites are camped around Mount Sinai when God reveals the instructions to Moses that are recorded in Leviticus. This view of Saint Catherine's Monastery at the foot of Mount Sinai shows the Wadi el Deir spreading out below it. Open areas like this would have provided a place for the Israelites to pitch their tents.

c. Equilibrium of sacred times: sacred festivals (Lev. 23)
2. Human equilibrium (Lev. 24–27)
   a. Human equilibrium in sacred space (center zone) (Lev. 24:1–9)
   b. Human equilibrium in status (in the camp) (Lev. 24:10–23)
   c. Human equilibrium in setting times (outside the camp) (Lev. 25)
   d. Establishing or disrupting equilibrium across the zones (Lev. 26)
   e. Sacred objects vowed to Yahweh (movement through zones) (Lev. 27)

Authorship

The authorship of Leviticus is anonymous, but Moses plays a key role in it. Although critical scholars typically deny to Moses any role in writing the Pentateuch, the traditional view among Jews and Christians is that Moses wrote it. Jesus's statements support a role for Moses's writing the Pentateuch (Matt. 8:4; 19:8 [cf. Deut. 24:1–4]; Mark 7:10 [cf. Exod. 20:12, 17]; John 5:46). In Leviticus and Numbers Moses is repeatedly said to have received laws from Yahweh for Israel. Any view must take into consideration the following observations. Moses could not have written the account of his own death (Deut. 34). Genesis, which is part of a continuous narrative with Exodus, Leviticus, and Numbers, mentions geographic and ethnic terms that probably were unknown in Moses's day (Arameans, Chaldeans, Dan [the city], Philistines). The statement about Edomite kings reigning "before any Israelite king reigned" (Gen. 36:31) seems to imply a perspective after kings reigned in Israel (i.e., after David and Solomon).

Most of the laws were given to Moses (e.g., Lev. 1:1; 4:1; 5:14; Num. 1:1; 3:5), though a few laws were given only to Aaron (Lev. 10:8; Num. 18:1, 8, 20), and some were given to both Moses and Aaron (e.g., Lev. 11:1; 13:1; 14:33; 15:1; Num. 2:1; 4:1). Presumably, Moses and Aaron wrote down the laws given to them. Those Mosaic (and Aaronic) materials could then be incorporated into the book, making the final product essentially Mosaic. And it is not just laws. Numbers 33:2 indicates that Moses wrote down an account of the stages of the journey. Exodus 17:14 says that Moses recorded its narratives. It is entirely possible that Moses wrote narrative accounts of many events in the wilderness even if the text does not explicitly say so.

In the Pentateuch Moses is described in third-person narration (he, him) rather than first person (I, me). Is that incompatible with Mosaic authorship? Referring to oneself in the third person is not unknown in ancient writings. Moses could have adopted third-person narration about himself as a literary style.[2] Alternatively, third-person narration may indicate that someone took the Mosaic laws and other archival materials from Moses and Aaron and finalized a narrative for them.

The Pentateuch, including its narratives, could still be essentially Mosaic even if a later editor put Moses's materials in their final form. The view adopted in this commentary is that Leviticus and Numbers are essentially Mosaic but not purely Mosaic. Moses (with Aaron) received and wrote down the laws and is responsible for other materials in the Pentateuch; however, these writings have been edited and updated for a later audience, creating the present Pentateuch.

Theological Themes

There are many important theological themes in Leviticus.

1. *Holiness.* Holiness is the key theme of Leviticus. Holiness involves being set apart to God or the realm of the divine. Thus priests and all items associated with God's sanctuary were holy. God by definition is holy, and he expected his people likewise to be holy (Lev. 19:2); that is, they were set apart from other nations through the covenant as God's special possession (Exod. 19:5–6) and were to maintain moral and ritual purity out of respect for God's holiness. Holiness was conveyed by righteous laws, sacrifices, and the purity system that helped Israel be uniquely dedicated to God. Violation of God's holiness could be severely punished, as happened when Nadab and Abihu encroached on the sanctuary improperly (Lev. 10). The laws of purity (Lev. 11–15), among other things, underscore the holiness of God.

2. *Purity: life and death.* The laws of purity (Lev. 11–15) concerning unclean animals, childbirth, skin diseases, and sexual discharges symbolically associate impurity with death and purity with life. One purpose of these laws was to promote life and to encourage avoidance of that which is associated with death.

3. *Worship.* Israel's worship differed from Christian worship in that it was centered on the tabernacle (later the temple), with its priesthood and animal sacrifices, and involved holy days no longer obligatory under the new covenant. There were

Most of the laws recorded in Leviticus were given to Moses by God. This section from the sarcophagus of Agape and Crescenziano (AD 330–60) depicts Moses receiving God's commandments.

no congregational "church services" as we have today. Despite his holiness, God wanted to have fellowship with his sinful people. The sacrificial system (Lev. 1–7; 16) made it possible for Israel to remain in the presence of the holy God. Worship involved special holy days and festivals (Lev. 23). It could involve vows that dedicated animals or persons to God (Lev. 27). Rituals played an important role in Israel's worship.

4. *Mercy, love, and grace.* The sacrificial system (Lev. 1–7) graciously allowed undeserving sinners to be forgiven. The fact that God planned to receive them back after their violation of the covenant (Lev. 26:40–45) also showed God's mercy.

5. *Priesthood.* Leviticus conveys lessons about spiritual leadership as represented by the priests. Priests were chosen by God (Lev. 8–9) and had to show proper holiness (Lev. 21–22). Failure of priests to maintain holiness could be deadly, as in the case of Nadab and Abihu (Lev. 10). Priests were subject to sin and defilement like anyone else, so they had to seek to avoid impurity (Lev. 21–22) and had to purify themselves before conducting rituals to purify others (Lev. 4:1–12; 6:19–23; 16:3–4).

6. *Morality.* Leviticus contains many abiding moral lessons. It condemns incest (Lev. 18; 20), which Paul applies to a specific case (1 Cor. 5:1). "Love your neighbor as yourself" (Lev. 19:18) is cited by Jesus as one of the two greatest commandments (Matt. 22:39). The laws of holiness (Lev. 17–27) give moral instruction about the poor, the foreigner, the slave, children, justice, honesty, sexual purity, integrity, and keeping one's promises.

7. *Typology.* The writer of Hebrews sees in the tabernacle, priests, and sacrifices of Leviticus a foreshadowing of Jesus Christ (Heb. 5:1–6; 7:11, 26–28; 8:1–6; 9:1–14, 23–28; 10:10–14).

The Burnt Offering

Big Idea *God is receptive to the petitions of those totally consecrated to him.*

Understanding the Text

The Text in Context

Leviticus continues the story of the book of Exodus. Eleven and a half months after the exodus, Israel completes the tabernacle, and the "glory of the LORD" takes up residence there (Exod. 40:1, 17, 34–38). Leviticus instructs Israelites on using that tabernacle for burnt offerings (Lev. 1), grain offerings (Lev. 2), fellowship offerings (Lev. 3), sin offerings (Lev. 4:1–5:13), and guilt offerings (Lev. 5:14–6:7). It then instructs priests about these same offerings

(Lev. 6:8–7:38). All this underscores the importance of sacrificial worship for ancient Israel.

Historical and Cultural Background

Israel's neighbors conducted animal sacrifices similar to Israel's. The prophets of Baal in their contest with Elijah prepared a burnt offering (1 Kings 18). Mesha of Moab offered his son as a burnt offering (2 Kings 3:27). Ugarit in the thirteenth century BC utilized burnt offerings, labeled *shrp* ("[totally] burnt"). Worshipers sacrificed fellowship offerings on altars to pagan gods (2 Chron. 34:4). Though disputed, the cognate for "fellowship offering" probably

Rituals involving offerings, sacrifices, and altars were common to the cultures of the ancient Near East. Pictured here is the large, round stone altar at Megiddo dated to the Early Bronze Age.

is used for sacrifices at Ugarit and in Phoenician/Punic.[1] Archaeologists found what appears to be an altar dating to the Bronze Age at Canaanite Megiddo.

Food gifts contributed to the "care and feeding of the gods," gifts that gods ate and drank (Deut. 32:37–38), though Mesopotamia lacked Israel's "blood consciousness"—blood rituals or a sense of blood's power.[2] But since Yahweh does not actually eat or drink offerings (Ps. 50:12–13), the sacrifices of Leviticus do not feed him in the way pagans thought they were sustaining their gods. Nonetheless, the text uses the language of sacrifice as God's food (Lev. 3:11; 21:6; cf. Mal. 1:7) or as a "food offering" (Lev. 1:9; 2:2; 3:3; 7:5). The tabernacle's table, plates, dishes, cups, bowls, and bread set before God's presence (Exod. 25:23–30; 1 Kings 7:48–60) have the look of a royal banquet. Symbolically and metaphorically, the sacrifices appear to be cultivating Israel's relationship with God by presenting him with covenant meals (cf. Lev. 24:5–9: "lasting covenant").[3]

Interpretive Insights

1:2 *When anyone among you brings an offering to the* LORD. Leviticus begins with a general introduction to sacrifices. This introduction applies to both burnt offerings and fellowship offerings (Lev. 3), both of which are voluntary sacrifices. The "tent of meeting" is the just-completed tabernacle, so named because God has promised to "meet" there with worshipers (Exod. 29:42–43). Teaching about sacrifice is not limited to priests because lay Israelites can voluntarily offer this sacrifice when they wish. Animal sacrifices are permitted from livestock or from birds (Lev. 1:14). From the livestock the choice is limited to the "herd" (cattle) or the "flock" (sheep or goats). This excludes all other mammals (e.g., donkeys, camels, deer).

1:3–17 Now come rules specific to the burnt offering, or holocaust. The text is organized on the basis of more-expensive bulls (vv. 3–9), to medium-expensive sheep/goats (vv. 10–13), to less-expensive birds (vv. 14–17). Every "you" in this section (though not vv. 1–2) is literally "he" or "his." The NIV adjusted the renderings for gender neutrality since women could also offer the various sacrifices (cf. female Nazirites [Num. 6:2, 12–15]).

1:3 *a burnt offering from the herd*. A burnt offering must be a male. Males are expendable: only a few bulls are needed to sire calves, while cows have additional value for milk. Moreover, bulls are aggressive, so having fewer of them aids in herd control. Only animals "without defect" are eligible for the altar (Deut. 15:21), whether for burnt offerings as here or for fellowship offerings, sin offerings, or guilt offerings (cf. Lev. 3:1; 4:3; 5:15). Offering blemished animals on the altar would show contempt for God, a practice bringing prophetic condemnation (Mal. 1:7–8). The animal is presented at the entrance to the tent of meeting in the presence of God in the tent. This is as close as a layperson can come to God's presence. "So that it will be acceptable to the LORD" could also be rendered, "to gain favor on his behalf before the LORD."[4]

Key Themes of Leviticus 1:1–17

- Show total consecration to God.
- Seek God's favor.
- The burnt offering is a substitutionary sacrifice.

The procedure for bringing a burnt offering from the herd includes laying a hand on its head and slaughtering it before the Lord. Cutting the throat, as illustrated in this painting from the tomb of Djeserkareseneb (Thebes, 1422–1411 BC), was the most humane method.

1:4 *lay your hand on the head.* "Lay" (*samak*) connotes "lean on" with pressure. What does this symbolize? It could refer to a transfer of sin as in the Day of Atonement offering (Lev. 16:21–22), though there two hands are laid on the animal, whereas only one hand is laid here. The laying of one hand is also required for the fellowship offering that is nonatoning for sin (Lev. 3:2). Perhaps the use of two hands represents the transfer of something, whether sin (Lev. 16:21–22) or authority (Num. 27:23), whereas using one hand implies identification between the person and the sacrifice.[5] The leaning of a single hand on the animal indicates that the animal belongs to and is being offered on behalf of the worshiper.

and it will be accepted. This phrase should instead be rendered modally: "so that it can be accepted." Although God's acceptance requires proper ritual, final acceptance of the sacrifice by God depends on the moral/spiritual state of the offerer, not the worshiper's doing the mechanics correctly, for "the LORD detests the sacrifice of the wicked" (Prov. 15:8). On "atonement," see "Additional Insights" following the unit on Leviticus 4:1–35. The burnt offering, the sin offering, and the guilt offering are atoning sacrifices.

1:5 *slaughter the young bull before the LORD.* The layperson would "slaughter," or "cut the throat of,"[6] the animal, a relatively humane way of dispatching it. "Young bull" probably should be rendered simply "bull" (ESV, NRSV) because the Hebrew expression (lit., "son/member of the herd") does not indicate the age of the animal. See also "young pigeon" (v. 14). "Before the LORD" indicates before the tabernacle, his abode.

1:9 *a burnt offering, a food offering, an aroma pleasing to the LORD.* The priests are to "splash," or "dash" (cf. NRSV), the blood against the altar. On the importance of blood, see "Teaching the Text" at Leviticus 17:1–16. "Fire" (v. 7) often symbolizes God (Exod. 24:17; Deut. 4:24). The burnt offering, the grain offering, the fellowship offering, and the sin offering are each called a "food offering" (*'ishsheh* [1:9; 2:2, 3; 3:3; 5:12]). Traditionally, this word has been rendered "an offering made by fire" (KJV), but Hebraists increasingly prefer the rendering "food offering" (NIV).[7] "Pleasing" (*nihoah* [vv. 9, 13, 17]) could also be rendered "soothing" or "tranquilizing."[8] A pleasing sacrifice appeases any anger that God might have (see Gen. 8:21) and makes him favorably disposed to grant requests.

1:10–17 *sheep or goats . . . birds.* The sequence of bull → sheep/goats → birds is from most expensive to least expensive animals. The location, "north side of the altar" (v. 11), is less specific for the harder-to-control bull (v. 5). The dove (or turtledove [ESV]) and the young pigeon are snared and caged. Birds are not "slaughtered" with blood collected in bowls to be dashed on the altar, but their necks are wrung and their blood directly drained onto the altar. Removal of the bird's crop would serve to clean out the intestines, all of which would be discarded. Due to its small size, it is split open rather than quartered in preparation for burning on the altar.

Theological Insights

The burnt offering is intended to make God favorable toward the worshiper so that he will grant the worshiper's requests. It can also be used to quell God's anger. When human wickedness brings God's wrath on humankind through the flood (Gen. 6:5–7), God finds Noah's burnt offering a "pleasing" or "soothing" aroma (Gen. 8:20–21; cf. Lev. 1:9 above) that pacifies his anger and makes him inclined to grant favor. The burnt offering can also be used primarily to seek God's favor when no particular sin is in view (see below). All of this shows God's receptiveness to human petition.

Teaching the Text

With burnt offerings, the entire animal was burned to ashes. There were daily burnt offerings every morning and evening (Exod. 29:38–41), but Leviticus 1 describes a freewill offering.

The purpose of the burnt offering is not explicit here, except that it could "make atonement" for the offerer (Lev. 1:4). But its purpose can be deduced from various Scriptures.

1. *Show total consecration to God*. By leaning a hand on the head of the animal being sacrificed, the worshiper was identified with the animal (Lev. 1:4). Arguably, the animal represented the worshiper, and its being burnt to ashes symbolized the surrender of the person's life to God.[9] Support for this is seen in Paul's allusion to the burnt offering in Romans 12:1: "Therefore, I urge you, brothers and sisters, in view of God's mercy, to offer your bodies as a living sacrifice, holy and pleasing to God—this is your true and proper worship." Paul sees the identification with and total consumption of the animal in the burnt offering as representing total consecration of the worshiper to God. Just as the burnt offering was totally consumed on the altar, so the Christian should express total allegiance to God and his service. But unlike the burnt offering, we are to sacrifice ourselves totally to God while we remain alive.

2. *Seek God's favor*. The burnt offering seems to represent an appeal on the part of the worshiper for God's favor and appeasement. It made God favorably disposed to answer petitions and overlook any unaddressed sin that might prevent him from bestowing favor.

Several examples show how the burnt offering was used to entreat God for favor and appeasement. In 1 Samuel 7:9 Samuel uses the burnt offering to seek favor for a fearful Israelite army about to face the Philistines. God answers this appeal by granting them victory in battle (1 Sam. 7:10–11). Saul likewise uses the burnt offering to appeal for Yahweh's favor in battle (1 Sam. 13:12). Though the Israelites do not know why God has not favored them, they in remorse seek God's forgiveness and renewed favor through burnt offerings after he allows them to be defeated in battle (Judg. 20:26). The burnt offering is used for appeasement and forgiveness when David offers a burnt offering to stop God's wrath in the form of a plague (2 Sam. 24:21–25).

3. *The burnt offering is a substitutionary sacrifice.* Genesis 22 suggests that the burnt offering was a substitutionary sacrifice. God commands Abraham to offer up his son Isaac as a burnt offering. Abraham in faith sets out to obey God's horrible command. But when Abraham is about to slit Isaac's throat, God intervenes and provides a ram caught in the thicket as a substitute for Isaac (Gen. 22:12–14). That the burnt offering was substitutionary in nature goes along with the notion above that totally burning

Although difficult to see because of the deterioration of the reliefs, one of the registers on the White Obelisk of Ashurnasirpal (I or II) depicts a bull-offering scene similar to that described in Leviticus 1 (see detail).

the animal represented the worshiper's total consecration to God.

Although no New Testament text identifies Christ specifically with the burnt offering, the New Testament does (especially in Hebrews) see the whole Old Testament sacrificial system as pointing to the atoning work of Christ, a work often understood in terms of substitutionary atonement (see Rom. 5:8; 1 Cor. 15:3; 1 Pet. 2:24).

Illustrating the Text

Sacrifice was practiced throughout the ancient world.

Historical Artifact: The White Obelisk of Ashurnasirpal (I or II), now in the British Museum, shows, according to its inscription, a ritual for the goddess Ishtar (see the image). A person (the king?) stands before the goddess Ishtar sitting on her throne in a temple on a hill (left). Offerings were deposited on tables, and incense was burning before the king followed by a man (priest? servant?) (center). A man puts his hand on a bull's head, perhaps with the other men leading the bull to an altar for sacrifice. This whole scene is reminiscent of the bull offering in Leviticus 1:4.[10]

Our sacrifices to God must be wholehearted.

Scripture: Acts 5:1–11. This narrative tells of how Ananias and Sapphira sell some land and pretend to give all the proceeds to God, when in fact they have kept back a portion.

Hymn: "I Surrender All," by J. W. Van De-Venter. This older hymn (1896) might be used in its beautiful rendition by the contemporary Christian artist CeCe Winans.

We must seek God's favor by giving him what he asks for.

Literature: *The Lost Princess: A Double Story,* by George MacDonald. In this wise and convicting children's story (first published in 1875 as *The Wise Woman: A Parable*), George MacDonald, a great British writer whose works influenced C. S. Lewis, shows the importance of following God's commands. His godly heroine is the Wise Woman, who tries to teach two young girls the evil of their selfishness and direct them toward a different way. One of them, Rosamund, who is spirited away by the Wise Woman from her indulgent parents, is put through a series of disciplines that she can obey or disobey to her own good or misfortune. She is asked to do the things that the Wise Woman wants done, in the way the Wise Woman wants them. At one point she is left alone in a cottage and told to keep it clean in specific ways, or else she will be unable to eat. Because Rosamund does not do it according to the directions, she has to clean the rooms twice. The Wise Woman says to Rosamund, "Let me remind you that if you had not put it off, you would have found it not only far easier but by and by quite pleasant work. . . . More than that, you would have been glad to see me when I came back. You could have leaped into my arms instead of standing there looking so ugly and foolish."[11]

Grain Offerings

Big Idea *All people, rich and poor, can please God through giving their best.*

Understanding the Text

The Text in Context

Leviticus 1–7 gives Israel instruction concerning sacrifices at the tabernacle that Israel had just completed (Exod. 40).

The instruction about the grain (or cereal) offering follows the burnt offering probably because it could serve as the poor person's burnt offering. The sequence in the burnt offering is from more expensive to less expensive (bull, sheep/goat, bird). The cereal offering, in line with that sequence, is even less expensive. It is also an important sacrifice that is used to supplement both burnt offerings and other offerings in making an appeal for God's goodwill or expressing gratitude for his blessings.

Historical and Cultural Background

Sacrifices similar to Israel's grain offerings were not unknown outside Israel. Food offerings to gods were common in ancient Mesopotamia, though without burning. The cognate for "grain offering" (*minhah*), like the Hebrew word itself (see below), was used for "gift, tribute" in Late Bronze Age Ugarit. The cognate was used for gifts and sacrifices (stelae, temples, vegetables, food [cereal?] offerings) in Aramaic and Phoenician-Punic. Leviticus appropriated some customs well known among the surrounding nations in setting up

Throughout the ancient Near East, many different types of food were brought as offerings to the gods. This stele records a hymn to Osiris and Wepwawet and depicts the deceased and his wife standing in front of an offering table piled high with bread and other foodstuffs, not just animal parts (1850 BC).

Israel's sacrificial system, though always in a way compatible with Israel's unique covenant relationship with Yahweh.

Interpretive Insights

2:1–16 There are a variety of ways that a grain offering can be made: raw flour (vv. 1–3), cooked cakes or wafers (vv. 4–10), and crushed natural heads of new grain (vv. 14–16).

2:1–3 *When anyone brings a grain offering.* The simplest grain offering is raw flour mixed with oil and incense. "Grain offering" (*minhah*) means more generally a "gift, present" or sometimes even "tribute."[1] It could be used for the nongrain gifts of people (Jacob's gifts to Esau [Gen. 32:20–21]) as well as both animal and vegetable offerings to God (Gen. 4:3–5; 1 Sam. 2:17). However, here it refers to a gift of grain to God. Fine flour is made from wheat rather than the inferior barley cereal. This is because an offering to God should be of the finest quality. It is combined with olive oil, something that can be done to make a simple cake (1 Kings 17:12–13). Oil probably is a symbol of gladness, pleasure, and joy (cf. Ps. 45:7; Prov. 21:17; Isa. 61:3). Incense or frankincense is an expensive, fragrant gum whose sweet smell would help mask the smell of burning flesh on the altar and mark this offering as special. Not all grain offerings require it (e.g., Lev. 2:4–10 below), and when a grain offering substitutes for a sin offering, it is forbidden (Lev. 5:11). The layperson hands the offering over to the priests, who burn a portion of it on the altar (v. 2) as something that pleases God ("an aroma pleasing to the LORD") and keep the remainder as payment for conducting the ritual (v. 3a). The precise

Key Themes of Leviticus 2:1–16

- Accommodations are made for the poor.
- Give your best to God.

meaning of the Hebrew word rendered "memorial portion" (*'azkarah* [Lev. 2:2, 9, 16; 5:12; 6:15]) is uncertain. It is from a root that means "to remember, mention," but it is unclear what this offering memorializes or remembers or mentions. Other renderings include "representative portion" (NIVmg), "token portion" (NRSV), or "invocation portion."[2] This last view suggests that God's name was called out ("mentioned") or praised as part of the grain offering was offered to him. Anything "most holy" (v. 3b) must be eaten at the sanctuary by a ritually clean priest (Lev. 6:16–18; cf. Num. 18:8–10; Ezek. 42:14). Less holy offerings belonging to priests can be eaten elsewhere by other members of their families (Num. 18:11–13). On food offerings, see comments at Leviticus 1:9.

2:4–10 *baked in an oven . . . cooked in a pan.* Other grain offerings are cooked in various ways before being brought to the altar (vv. 4–7). Cooked grain offerings include olive oil, as would bread baked at a home, but no yeast (see v. 11). The lack of frankincense may be a deliberate concession to the poor who could not afford such an expensive item.[3]

2:11–13 *yeast . . . honey . . . salt.* "Yeast" or leaven is more precisely sourdough (fermenting dough). This normally was mixed with raw dough to make it rise as the yeast spreads and emits carbon dioxide bubbles. The yeast dies in cooking. But all yeast, dead or otherwise, is prohibited from the grain offerings. No reason is given for this prohibition, though perhaps the fermentation of yeast was considered a symbol of corruption and death inappropriate for the altar, which was the source of Israel's life. The New Testament makes leaven a symbol of false teaching and sin (Matt. 16:6, 11–12; 1 Cor. 5:7–8). The prohibition of yeast is not absolute, however. Although leavened bread and honey cannot be burned on the altar, they can be given to the sanctuary as a nonaltar gift in conjunction with an offering of firstfruits (v. 12; cf. Lev. 23:17) or in conjunction with a fellowship offering (Lev. 7:13). "Honey" (*deˢbash*) is not limited to bee's honey but includes other sweets such as date or grape syrup (Deut. 8:8 probably refers to date syrup). Like yeast, honey is subject to fermentation and decay (note mead, a honey wine). Perhaps that is why it is prohibited from the altar. Salt, on the other hand, is a symbol of preservation, used to keep meat from decaying. Accordingly, it is required for grain offerings. It symbolizes the incorruptible, lasting covenant between God and his people. The expression "covenant of salt" is also used for God's perpetual covenant provisions for the priests (Num. 18:19) and of his promise of a perpetual kingship for the line of David (2 Chron. 13:5).

2:14–16 *new grain roasted in the fire . . . oil and incense on it.* This case is similar to 2:1–3 in requiring incense, but similar to 2:4–10 in that it is cooked. A small portion is burned, the rest to be used by the priests. On an offering made by fire, see comments at Leviticus 1:9.

Theological Insights

Distinctive is the grain offering's acknowledgment of God as the provider of

Wheat is the plant required for the grain offering. Flour would be made by grinding the heads of wheat that remained after threshing and winnowing. The stones shown here were used as a hand mill. The worker would place wheat kernels on the larger stone and slide the smaller stone back and forth, crushing and grinding the grain.

Israel's food,[4] some of which is returned to God as "tribute" in the offering.

The grain offering's purpose overlaps with the purposes of the burnt offering (Lev. 1). That this least expensive of offerings could be substituted for the sin offering (Lev. 5:11) and probably also the burnt offering shows the mercy of God for the poor (see below).

Teaching the Text

Among the lessons of Leviticus 2 are the accommodations that the Bible makes for those who are poor and the need to give one's best to God.

1. *Accommodations are made for the poor.* Standing as it does after a series of burnt offerings in descending value—bull, sheep/goat, bird—the grain offering (Lev. 2) probably is to be considered akin to the burnt offering. A portion was, like the burnt offering, burnt to ashes on the altar.

Sacrifices were expensive. In Israelite society livestock represented one's wealth.

Most Israelites were not wealthy. To burn a bull on the altar represented tremendous sacrifice economically for most Israelites. For a person of modest means to offer even a lamb or a dove might be a significant sacrifice. The grain offering could function as the poor person's burnt offering. When offered without oil, it also served as the poor person's sin offering (Lev. 5:11), an option also given after listing more expensive animal options for the rich. Even a poor person who could not afford to offer God meat probably could afford to give a small bit of raw grain in petitioning God.

The laws require that grain offerings accompany the animal sacrifices (Exod. 29:40–42; Lev. 9:17; 14:20, 31; 23:18, 37; Num. 15:24; 28:13). For the rich person, this would not have been a problem. Richer Israelites could use the grain offering in addition to either a burnt offering or a sin offering or a guilt offering to fill out the divine meal (meat and bread). However, for the poor, who rarely ate meat, even the grain offering might represent a great sacrifice.

God is less impressed by the size of a gift than the depth of devotion that lies behind it. God could find a sacrifice pleasing whether the offering was an expensive bull or an inexpensive cake composed of flour and olive oil (Lev. 1:9; 2:4–9). Conversely, the expensive gift of a rich person might well be less highly regarded than the small gift of a poor person. Compare the poor widow who gives only "two very small copper coins" but whom Jesus commends for giving "more" than the rich (Mark 12:41–44; Luke 21:1–4). God takes into consideration the limitations of people's economic status. But regardless of economic status, all people can give gifts that God will find pleasing.

2. *Give your best to God*. In the case of grain offerings, one was to offer only "the finest [wheat] flour" (Lev. 2:1, 4, 5, 7) as opposed to the inferior barley flour. Those who could afford it were encouraged to choose a form of grain offering that included the addition of very expensive frankincense to enhance its pleasing aroma (Lev. 2:1–2, 15–16).

The principle behind these requirements is that Israelites were expected to give of their best to God. The same was true in the case of animals: Israelites were to offer only animals "without defect" (Lev. 1:3, 10). Lame or blind or sick animals were unworthy of God and so were forbidden from the altar (Deut. 15:21).

In Malachi's time, Yahweh castigates people for presenting fifth-rate offerings. Such offerings in fact show people's contempt for God. Yahweh says to his people,

You ask, "How have we shown contempt for your name?" By offering defiled food on my altar. But you ask, "How have we defiled you?" By saying that the LORD's table is contemptible. When you offer blind animals for sacrifice, is that not wrong? When you sacrifice lame or diseased animals, is that not wrong? Try offering them to your governor! Would he be pleased with you? Would he accept you? (Mal. 1:6–8)

One would never serve a fifth-rate meal to a chief of state, so how can people expect to impress and find favor from God when they are offering him a meal of sickly animals that they would never dare serve to anyone whom they regarded as important? They clearly have more respect for their human governor than for their divine King. God deserves the best, not the dregs.

Sacrifices are supposed to be costly. David, presenting burnt offerings to appease God for his sin, comments, "I will not sacrifice to the LORD my God burnt offerings that cost me nothing" (2 Sam. 24:24). A cheap sacrifice is really no sacrifice at all. God deserves and expects the best from us.

So the Christian's sacrifices to God today should be of his or her finest or best. We should strive to love God with all our heart and soul and strength (Deut. 6:5). We should be willing to sacrifice to God the finest things we have, be it our time, talents, or money. Sometimes that may mean going to minister to poor people rather than enjoying the comforts of affluence. Sometimes that may mean encouraging our children or grandchildren to serve God in distant places when we prefer that they stay close to home. Sometimes that may mean spending time in devotion and prayer to God when we would rather watch a ball game. God deserves our best. He receives honor and pleasure as we give our best to him.

No matter how the grain offering is prepared, only the finest flour may be used. Loaves may be thick or thin if baked in an oven, perhaps like the one used by an Egyptian in this tomb statue from Giza (2477 BC).

Illustrating the Text

The state of our heart is more important than the size of our gift.

News Story: The *New York Daily News* tells the story of Myles Eckert, an eight-year-old whose father was killed in the Iraq conflict. On his way into a restaurant, young Myles found a twenty-dollar bill in the parking lot. Most kids would have been looking for something new to buy, but Myles saw a better way to invest. When sitting down to eat, he noticed a uniformed soldier across the restaurant. Myles gave Lt. Col. Frank Dailey the money and a note that read,

> Dear Soldier, my dad was a soldier. He's in heaven now. I found this 20 dollars in the parking lot when we got here. We like to pay it forward in my family. It's your lucky day! Thank you for your service. Myles Eckert, a gold star kid.

Twenty dollars cannot cover the cost of putting one's life at risk. But the gratitude of such a young child can make it all worthwhile. The God who bought us with his blood does not require an extravagant gift. He looks for extravagant gratitude.[5]

We are called to give our best to God.

Literature: "The Gift of the Magi," by O. Henry. This short story spins a tale in which two lovers sacrifice their greatest treasure out of love of the other, though with an ironic twist.

James Dillingham and his lovely wife, Della, are deeply in love with each other, but money is tight. Della has no money to buy Jim a Christmas present. So she makes a great sacrifice. To get money to buy her husband a present—a fancy fob or chain for his prized pocket watch—she sells her beautiful, long hair to a wig maker. Jim, in turn, has no money to buy her a Christmas present, so he sells his prized pocket watch to buy her beautiful combs for her lovely hair. O. Henry concludes his story by underscoring the wisdom of this foolish gift giving:

> And here I have lamely related to you the uneventful chronicle of two foolish children in a flat who most unwisely sacrificed for each other the greatest treasures of their house. But in a last word to the wise of these days let it be said that of all who give gifts these two were the wisest. Of all who give and receive gifts, such as they are wisest. Everywhere they are wisest. They are the Magi.[6]

These two, out of the love of each for the other, sacrificed their best. And both realized more deeply than previously the degree of love expressed through the other's sacrificing of their best. So too in the Bible, love of God is most profoundly expressed by giving one's best to God, whether that is an Israelite giving to God the finest of flour or a Christian giving the best of his or her gifts, talents, and service to Christ.

We are to make accommodations for the poor.

Quote: In his book *Money and Power*, French philosopher, historian, and sociologist Jacques Ellul (1912–1994) writes,

> The Poor One and poor people in general are God's question to us. God gives us responsibility in the world by asking us a question which we have to answer. This question is constant, permanent, living, for "you always have the poor with you." We cannot sidestep this question, for we are always in contact with the poor, and each one of them puts God's big question in human flesh. The question is addressed to everyone. We do not have to understand theological explanations; we do not even have to be Christian to hear it. It is part of the silent interrogation that God is always carrying on.[7]

The Fellowship Offering

Big Idea *God's people should express joy and gratitude to God for his blessings.*

Understanding the Text

The Text in Context

Leviticus 3 continues Leviticus 1–7's instructions on sacrificial worship at the tabernacle. The fellowship offering (or peace offering) is the only animal sacrifice that has no atoning value. Its purpose is not to atone for sin but to deepen a person's relationship with God by expressing gratitude to God for various blessings. It is also the only animal offering that is eaten by the worshiper.

Historical and Cultural Background

On similar offerings among Israel's neighbors, see Leviticus 1.

Israel used breeds of sheep still known in the Middle East and Africa that had large, fatty tails and hind parts (see Lev. 3:9).

The ancient historian and traveler Herodotus commented on the breeds of fat-tailed sheep that he discovered in Arabia.

> There are also in Arabia two kinds of sheep worthy of admiration, the like of which is nowhere else to be seen; the one kind has long tails, not less than three cubits in length, which, if they were allowed to trail on the ground, would be bruised and fall into sores. As it is, all the shepherds know enough of carpentering to make little trucks for their sheep's tails. The trucks are placed under the tails, each sheep having one to himself, and the tails are then tied down upon them. The other kind has a broad tail, which is a cubit across sometimes. (*Hist.* 3.113)

Interpretive Insights

3:1 *If your offering is a fellowship offering . . . from the herd.* "Fellowship offering" is *zebah shᵉlamim* ("sacrifice of *shᵉlamim*"), an expression rendered variously "fellowship offering" (NIV), "peace offering" (KJV), "sacrifice of salvation" (LXX), and "sacrifice of well-being" (NRSV). At issue is the precise meaning of *shᵉlamim*. "Peace offering" comes from its similarity with *shalom* ("peace"), though this is doubly problematic: First, "peace offering" in common parlance refers to a gift offered to turn away anger. That is precisely what the *shᵉlamim* offering does not do. Moreover, the root *sh.l.m* has a range of meanings that include wholeness, completeness, and health, not just peace. "Sacrifice of well-being" reflects the use of this sacrifice to express gratitude for answers to prayers, for help through challenges, and the like (see below). The Septuagint (the Greek translation of the Old Testament) rendering "sacrifice of salvation" probably means "a sacrifice to celebrate God's deliverance." The NIV rendering "fellowship offering" is not literally what the term means, but it rightly expresses the effect: this sacrifice served to maintain and deepen one's fellowship with God, and to a lesser degree it fostered fellowship with people through the shared meal of meat that typically ensued (Gen. 31:54).

Fellowship offerings are limited to bulls or cows from the herd or a sheep/goat from the flock (see vv. 6–16 below). No provision is made for offering birds, perhaps because the amount of blood and fat is too minuscule to bother offering on an altar.[1] Unlike the burnt offering (Lev. 1:3, 10), the fellowship offering can be either male or female (v. 6). Like other offerings, the animal has to be without defect (v. 6) to be worthy of presentation before God.

3:2 *lay your hand on . . . your offering and slaughter it.* Leaning one hand (see comments at Lev. 1:4) cannot here transfer sin to the animal, since a fellowship offering is nonatoning. Instead, it implies that the

Fellowship offerings can be either male or female animals without defect from flocks or herds. The bounty of the land, including livestock, is on display in this scene from the Standard of Ur (Mesopotamia, twenty-fifth century BC). Two of the men in the procession have their hands clasped in prayer, so these animals may be part of a religious ritual.

Key Themes of Leviticus 3:1–17

- Take joy in the Lord.
- Give thanks for food.

animal belongs to and is being offered on behalf of the worshiper. "Slaughter" probably means "cut its throat" (see comments at Lev. 1:5), a relatively humane method.

the entrance to the tent of meeting. This is before God's throne, the ark.

splash the blood against the sides of the altar. Aaron's sons the priests complete the ritual by "splashing" (or "dashing") the blood against the sides of the altar as with the burnt offering (Lev. 1:5, 11), thereby giving it to God. On the importance of blood, see comments at Leviticus 17:11.

3:3–5 *bring a food offering . . . an aroma pleasing to the Lord.* On "food offering" (NIV 1984: "sacrifice . . . made by fire"), see comments at Leviticus 1:9. The fat or suet is specifically the fatty membrane surrounding the intestines as well as the kidneys with the fat on them and the fat covering the liver. Suet is edible—it is an ingredient in Christmas, plum, and kidney puddings—and in Roman times it was used to cure various ailments (see, e.g., Pliny the Elder, *Nat.* 28.38, 62, 67, 70; 30.34, 37). However, the suet of sacrificial animals is not to be eaten or used by people, but instead given to God (see v. 16). Metaphorically, "fat" can refer to the "best" or "choice" portion of something (rendered "best" or "finest" in Gen. 45:18; Num. 18:12; Deut. 32:14; Pss. 81:16;

When a sheep is offered as a fellowship offering, the fat tail must be included in the parts that are burned on the altar to the Lord. The breeds of sheep common in the Middle East, such as the ones shown here, store fat in their large, broad tails, which provide nourishment when food is scarce.

147:14). The breast and right thigh go to the priest as payment for his services (Lev. 7:33–35), and the rest to the worshiper for a meal celebrating how God has bestowed blessing (Deut. 12:7). The fat and kidneys and the covering or lobe of the liver are burned atop the morning burnt offering that smoldered throughout the day (Exod. 29:38–42; Lev. 6:9–13). In Mesopotamia hepatomancy—the examination of livers of sacrifices for divination purposes—was common (cf. Ezek. 21:21), though all divination was forbidden in Israel (Deut. 18:9–13). Burning the liver eliminates subsequent possibility of using it for divination. Why the kidneys are removed is uncertain. It may be no more than their association with suet or their having the color of blood, since suet and blood both belong to God (Lev. 3:16–17); or kidneys, like fat, may have been regarded as a delicacy and thus given to God (see Deut. 32:14, where "the finest wheat" is literally "the fat of the kidneys of the wheat").[2] This sacrifice, carried out in faith, produces "an aroma pleasing to the LORD," an anthropomorphism meaning that it delights him the way the smell of food cooking might please us.

3:6 *If you offer an animal from the flock as a fellowship offering.* Here, "flock" applies to both sheep (vv. 7–11) and goats (vv. 12–16a). The ritual for sheep is the same as that for cattle with the exception of the need to offer the fat tail (v. 9) as part of the fat burned to God. Israel used breeds of sheep that had large, fatty tails and hind parts (see above). Goats do not have fat tails, so their fellowship offering follows the same procedure as that for cattle (vv. 12–16a).

3:16–17 *fat . . . blood.* Fat and blood of fellowship offerings are not to be eaten because they are supposed to be given over to God. On "fat," see comments at verses 3–5 above. On eating blood, see "Theological Insights" below. This regulation would be "lasting" or "permanent" (ESV) so long as the sacrificial system remains in effect.

Theological Insights

It appears that in the early days of humankind, people were supposed to be vegetarians (see Gen. 1:29). Permission to eat animals was not given until after the flood:

"Everything that lives and moves will be food for you. Just as I gave you the green plants, I now give you everything. But you must not eat meat that has its lifeblood still in it" (Gen. 9:3–4). Now humankind could eat animal flesh, but with one stipulation: the blood must not be eaten (cf. Lev. 3:17).

But what does it mean to eat blood? Jewish tradition takes it to mean eating meat without draining the blood thoroughly. But all meat has some blood in it, even if the rules of kosher are followed.

In 1 Samuel 14:31–35 we have clarification about what it means to eat meat with blood. Here, the wrong way to get meat is to just kill an animal, cut out a steak, and cook it. That is eating with the blood. The right way is first to pour out the blood on an altar—in this case, a large stone designated by Saul to serve as a simple altar—before consuming the meat. In other words, eating the flesh with the blood means eating the flesh without first pouring out the blood to God through sacrifice on an altar. With wild game not eligible to be fellowship offerings on the altar, Israelites had to pour out the blood on the ground like water; failure to do this was to "eat the blood" (Deut. 12:15–16).

Through ritual slaughter Israelites acknowledged that God was the author and taker of life, and it was he who in Genesis 9 had given them permission to slaughter animals for food. For that reason, the blood had to be poured back to him as a way of saying thank you.

An Israelite would obtain butcher meat through the fellowship offering. The fellowship offering was an expression of gratitude to God for various blessings, but specifically for the meat itself. In pouring out the blood to God, the Israelite expressed gratitude for God's permission to eat meat.

Teaching the Text

Leviticus 3 gives ritual procedures, but the significance of the fellowship offering must be derived primarily from other passages.

1. *Take joy in the Lord*. There were three types of fellowship offering: the freewill offering, the vow offering, and the thanksgiving offering (see Lev. 7:11–16). A fellowship offering was an expression of gratitude and thanksgiving on the part of the worshiper for various blessings (Jer. 33:10–11). It could be used to praise God for his goodness (Ps. 54:6), or for his provision of material things (Deut. 16:10), or to celebrate a successful completion of a vow (Num. 6:14; Prov. 7:14). It could also be offered as a response to answered prayer (Ps. 50:14–15) or deliverance from danger on stormy seas (Ps. 107:22–29).

Joy was the key feature of this offering. Only a portion of this sacrifice was burned and/or given to the priest. Most of it was eaten by the worshiper "before the LORD" as an act of worship, gratitude, and joy. Deuteronomy 27:7 instructs worshipers, "Sacrifice fellowship offerings there, eating them and *rejoicing* in the presence of the LORD your God." Deuteronomy 12:7 states in regard to the place where they were to offer vows and freewill offerings, "There, in the presence of the LORD your God, you and your families shall eat and shall *rejoice* in everything you have put your hand to, because the LORD your God has blessed you."

The joy of this sacrifice went beyond the individual. This sacrifice was a prelude to having a meal with meat. The majority of people could afford to eat meat only on special occasions. This offering could be enjoyed at the sanctuary during one of the festivals (Deut. 12:6–7; 16:10) or at home, where the offering was shared with friends or relatives (Gen. 31:54; 1 Kings 3:15), thus combining the sacrifice's purpose of fostering fellowship with God with a fostering of fellowship with other human beings. When a large number of this type of sacrifice was offered, it meant a big feast or barbecue would take place (e.g., 1 Kings 8:63–65; 1 Chron. 29:21–22; 2 Chron. 7:5; 29:33; 30:24; Ezra 6:17; Neh. 12:43). The widespread eating of meat on these occasions allowed the whole community to express its joy and gratitude to God.

Christians should likewise worship God joyfully. Paul, writing from prison, encourages Christians to always rejoice (Phil. 4:4). As Israelites could enjoy the fellowship offering, so Christians can enjoy a meal designed to express gratitude to God, the Lord's Supper. The resurrection of Jesus has turned our mourning into joy (John 16:20). Christian worship should be joyful, not somber and sullen, just

as the fellowship offering was an occasion for joy.

2. *Give thanks for food*. One purpose of the fellowship offering was to supply meat for the table. Domestic animals eligible for the altar were supposed to be sacrificed as fellowship offerings with the blood poured out before God and the fat burned on the altar (Lev. 3:17) before the meat could be eaten as food. Doing this was a way of expressing thanks to God for the privilege of eating meat (see "Theological Insights" above). Although animal sacrifice plays no role for Christians under the new covenant, the principle of giving thanks to God for food still does. We too should regularly

Acknowledging that God permits the slaughter of animals for food is one of the purposes of the fellowship offering. When believers offer thanks before a meal, like the family in this painting by Cornelis Pietersz Bega (AD 1663), our grateful attitude should reflect an understanding of this same provision for us.

express gratitude to God for the food that he has graciously granted us to eat.

Illustrating the Text

God wants us to celebrate joyfully.

Human Experience: A small church in rural Georgia had the custom once a year of having a big barbecue meal. That meal served two purposes. Primarily, it was a fundraiser that attracted not only the members of the church, about forty people, but also friends, relatives, and neighbors who came to purchase a meal too. About eight hundred people showed up, allowing this small church to raise a significant amount of money for its programs.

But there was another reason for doing this. It was a lot of fun. A large barbecue pit allowed the members skilled at the task to cook hundreds of chicken halves in a very short period of time. There was fellowship, good food, and the joy that all of this was being done for the Lord. It was a festive occasion.

That is what the fellowship offering was for the Israelites: a time to enjoy a nice meal together with gratitude to God.

Joyless faith is dangerous.

Biography: If we fail to worship God with joy, it can affect others negatively. Consider this vignette about Oliver Wendell Holmes.

> Oliver Wendell Holmes, Jr., was a member of the U.S. Supreme Court for 30 years. His mind, wit and work earned him the unofficial title of "the greatest justice since John Marshall." At one point in his life, Justice Holmes explained his choice of a career by saying: "I might have entered the ministry if certain clergymen I knew had not looked and acted so much like undertakers."[3]

A certain minister's failure to worship God with joy may have cost the church one of the greatest minds of American history.

The same may be true if we fail to worship God with sincere joy. Does your worship attract people by its celebrative joy, or does it repel people by its grim somberness or its unenthusiastic lethargy? Not only is joyful worship a moral obligation, but also it is good for us. And it is good for others who may observe us worshiping.

The Sin Offering

Big Idea *There needs to be cleansing from sin before God.*

Understanding the Text

The Text in Context

The sin offering is the fourth in a series of five offerings found in Leviticus 1:1–6:7.

Why are the sin and guilt offerings not treated with the earlier atoning sacrifice, the burnt offering? Probably because unlike the burnt offering, the sin and guilt offerings are obligatory.[1] The burnt, grain, and fellowship offerings can be offered whenever one feels the need; sin and guilt offerings are mandatory whenever one commits certain offenses.

This passage is ordered from weightier to less weighty persons/groups: the more significant the person/group, the more expensive the sacrifice and the deeper into the holy place the blood was taken (see table 1).

Historical and Cultural Background

Leviticus 4 speaks of the "horns" of the altar (vv. 7, 18, 25, 30, 34). These were not literal horns but rather vertical extensions from the four corners of the altar that are clearly evident in altars found by archaeologists.

Table 1. Sin Offerings

Scripture	Person	Occasion	Sin Offering	Ritual
Lev. 4:3–12	High priest	Inadvertent sin	Bull	Blood sprinkled seven times in front of veil and on horns of altar of incense. Remainder drained at altar of burnt offering. Fat/kidneys burned on altar as with fellowship offering. Remainder dumped/burned outside camp.
Lev. 4:13–21	Whole community	Inadvertent sin	Bull	Blood sprinkled seven times in front of veil and on horns of altar of incense. Remainder drained at altar of burnt offering. Fat/kidneys burned on altar as with fellowship offering. Remainder dumped/burned outside camp.
Lev. 4:22–26	Leader	Inadvertent sin	Ram (male goat)	Blood on horns of altar of burnt offering. Rest drained at base of altar. Fat/kidneys burned on altar as with fellowship offering.
Lev. 4:27–35	Member of community	Inadvertent sin	Female goat or lamb	Blood on horns of altar of burnt offering. Rest drained at base of altar. Fat/kidneys burned on altar as with fellowship offering.

Note: Table after Gane, *Leviticus, Numbers,* 97.

Ritual manipulation of blood for cleansing rituals was also known among the second-millennium BC Hurro-Hittites. Their Zurki ("blood") rites used blood for expiation and sanctuary purification in a way reminiscent of Leviticus's use of blood.[2]

Interpretive Insights

4:2 *When anyone sins unintentionally and does what is forbidden.* This serves as an introduction to this section. "Sins" (*hata'*) means doing "what is forbidden in any of the LORD's commands." This verb can mean to "miss" a target (Judg. 20:16) or "fail to reach" a goal (Isa. 65:20) or "miss" or "veer from" a path (Prov. 19:2). Religiously, to sin is to deviate from God's norms. "Unintentionally" (*bishgagah*), or "inadvertently," includes offenses of ignorance (cf. KJV) and offenses of negligence—that is, not knowing something is wrong or accidentally violating what one knows to be unlawful. The

Key Themes of Leviticus 4:1–35

- Sin is a pollution that offends God.
- The sin offering is a remedy for sin.

opposite of unintentional sin is brazen and defiant sinning (sinning "with a high hand" [Num. 15:30]). For examples of sins of inadvertence, see comments at Leviticus 5:1. For a more complete discussion of unintentional sins and on how defiant sins can be forgiven, see "Teaching the Text" at Numbers 15:1–41.

4:3 *If the anointed priest sins.* "The anointed priest" is the high priest who has been anointed at his installation (Exod. 30:22–33; Lev. 8:12; 16:32). Representing Israel before God in the sanctuary, his sins can bring "guilt on the people," which is why his purification must be an expensive "young bull" (or "bull" [ESV]; see comments at Lev. 1:5). On "without defect," see comments at Leviticus 1:3.

sin offering. "Sin offering" and "sin" are the same word in Hebrew (*hatta't*),

Diagram of the Tabernacle

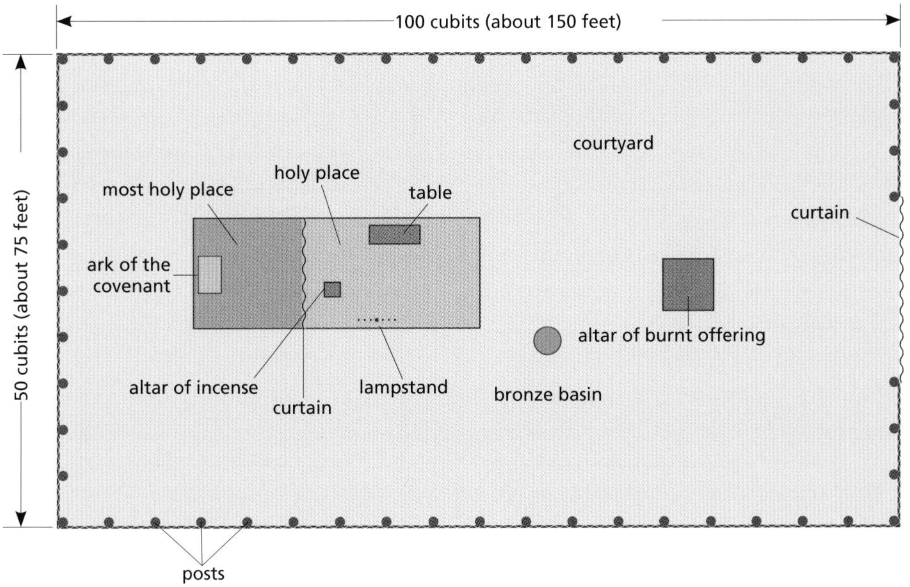

100 cubits (about 150 feet)

50 cubits (about 75 feet)

courtyard

holy place

most holy place

table

curtain

ark of the covenant

altar of incense

curtain

lampstand

bronze basin

altar of burnt offering

posts

Leviticus 4:1–35

denoting both the offense ("sin") and its remedy ("sin offering"). The Day of Atonement *hatta't* offering covers ceremonial uncleanness in addition to various transgressions and sins (Lev. 16:15–16). It is offered as part of a ritual for cleansing lepers (Lev. 14:19), for purification after childbirth (Lev. 12:6), for purification from an abnormal male or female genital discharge (Lev. 15:15, 30), and for purification after touching a corpse (Num. 6:9–11; 19; Ezek. 44:25–27). None of these are sins, though for each the purification involves the *hatta't* offering. For that reason, Jacob Milgrom has proposed calling this sacrifice the "purification offering" (cf. HCSBmg) rather than the "sin offering." Thus, while sin is one of the main reasons for this offering, as this chapter emphasizes, it is broader in scope.

4:4 *present the bull . . . lay his hand on its head*. The bull is presented and slaughtered like the burnt offering (see Lev. 1:3–5). On "lay his hand on its head," see comments at Leviticus 1:4; 3:2.

4:5–6 *the anointed priest shall take some of the bull's blood*. With the sacrifices for the priest and community, the blood is brought into the holy place and sprinkled "seven times" before the "curtain" or veil dividing the holy place from the most holy place. Blood serves as a purifying agent that purges the sanctuary of the priest's impurities. "Seven" derives an aura of holiness from God's seventh day of creation (Gen. 2:3).

4:7 *put some of the blood on the horns of the altar of fragrant incense*. The "altar of fragrant incense" (cf. Exod. 30:1–10; 37:25–28) is in the holy place and is different than "the altar of burnt offering," which is in the courtyard (see the diagram of the layout of the tabernacle). Dabbing blood on the four

corners of the altar purges the whole altar from defilement (Ezek. 43:20, 26).

4:8–10 *He shall remove all the fat*. The "fat," "kidneys," and "liver" are removed and burned in the same way as the ox of the fellowship offering (see comments at Lev. 3:3–5).

4:11–12 *the hide of the bull and all its flesh . . . he must take outside the camp*. The hide and carcass are burned at a "ceremonially clean place," not a dump, for this is a holy sacrifice. "He must take [the carcass] outside the camp" can also be rendered impersonally, as "someone must take," not necessarily the priest. This bull is not eaten by the priest, since it is a sin offering for him. Neither does he eat sin offerings for the whole community (see comments at vv. 13–21 below), since the priest is part of the community. But sin offerings for leaders or laypersons are eaten by priests (Lev. 6:25–29).

4:13–21 *If the whole Israelite community sins unintentionally and does what is forbidden*. These verses deal with purification for the whole community. The procedure for the whole community is the same as that for the high priest. The community could at first be unaware of the offense. For example, if a new moon has been missed so that a holy day is celebrated on the wrong day, the whole community might be inadvertently guilty.[3] In such a case, the elders as community representatives lay their hands on the bull for a sin offering (v. 15). Other aspects of the ritual for the whole community (vv. 16–21) resemble that of the high priest (vv. 5–12 above). On "make atonement" (v. 20b), see "Additional Insights" following this unit. And "they will be forgiven" (v. 20c) is better rendered "so that they can be forgiven," for sacrifices are effective only if God finds the sacrifice acceptable, something that depends on the heart attitude of the offerer, not the mechanics of ritual (Lev. 1:4; 7:18; cf. Gen. 4:3–5; Heb. 11:4).

4:22–26 *When a leader sins unintentionally and does what is forbidden.* This section deals with purification for leaders. "Leader" (v. 22) can refer to the twelve tribal leaders (cf. Num. 2:3–29), though it is used more broadly. A less expensive "male goat" rather than an expensive bull is specified for a leader (v. 23), since a leader is a less weighty figure than the high priest or the whole community. The blood is applied only to the "horns of the altar of burnt offering" (v. 25), not inside the sanctuary. Laypersons cannot enter the sanctuary. The principle seems to be that the blood is applied only as far as the person or group can go, but no further (see "Teaching the Text" below).

4:27–35 *If any member of the community sins unintentionally and does what is forbidden.* The text then turns to purification for members of the community. A "member of the community" (lit., "one of the people of the land"), meaning "a common person," who sins unintentionally (or "inadvertently" [see on v. 2 above]) is to bring a female goat (v. 27) or a female sheep (v. 32) for a sin offering. This use of female sin offerings should make Christian interpreters cautious about reading too much typology into the gender of atoning sacrifices. Perhaps the female was chosen

to differentiate this ritual from that of the leader that comes before. It may have been a more expensive offering than the male because females provided milk and offspring, whereas males were expendable; only a few males were required for breeding purposes. The other aspects of the ritual are the same as the previous case.

Theological Insights

Leviticus 4's teaching about sin, guilt, and the need for atoning sacrifice undergirds biblical teaching of that topic throughout the Bible. Sin offends God and makes him disposed to punish people. He cannot simply ignore sin. Sin, to be forgiven, must be purged and atoned for through sacrifice.

From the New Testament perspective, the sin offering foreshadows the purging of sin through the cross. Although the book of Hebrews denies that the blood of bulls and goats could actually take away sin (Heb. 10:4), it identifies Christ as the ultimate offering to do away with sin to which these sacrifices pointed: "But he has appeared once for all at the culmination of the ages to do away with sin by the sacrifice of himself" (Heb. 9:26). Peter too uses the language of sacrificial, substitutionary atonement in referring to the death of Jesus. Christians have been redeemed by the blood of Christ, who was "a lamb without blemish or defect" (1 Pet. 1:19), and "Christ also suffered once

Leviticus 4:1–35

for sins, the righteous for the unrighteous, to bring you to God" (1 Pet. 3:18).

The apostle Paul picks up on the Old Testament's sacrificial imagery as well. Twice he seems to use the word "sin" in the Old Testament sense of "sin offering." Romans 8:3 reads, "For what the law was powerless to do because it was weakened by the flesh, God did by sending his own Son in the likeness of sinful flesh *to be a sin offering* [margin: "for sin"]." The NIV's main rendering, "sin offering," indicates that Christ's death does for us what the sin offering did for Israel: it provides purification from sin and allows God to forgive us.

Similarly, 2 Corinthians 5:21 reads, "God made him who had no sin to be *sin* [or, "*a sin offering*"] for us, so that in him we might become the righteousness of God." Here the NIV margin's reading probably is correct, identifying Christ as the sin offering that provides the purification from sin that put us in right standing before God. Even if the other rendering, "to be sin," is adopted, the concept of the sin offering underlies the language.

Blood atonement is at the heart of Paul's gospel. In the Old Testament animals died for the sins and offenses of people so that those people could be forgiven. According to 1 Corinthians 15:1–3, "Christ died for our sin"; and this was not by chance but was "according to the Scriptures." Among the Scriptures according to which Christ died are the ones describing the sin offering. The sin offering provides the conceptual framework for understanding the meaning of Christ's death.

Thus our passage, far from being a bit of historical trivia concerning ancient Israel's rituals, turns out to undergird the Christian gospel itself. The gospel teaches that Christ has come to be our sin offering that purges our impurities before the presence of God, so that through his atoning death we can be forgiven.

Teaching the Text

1. *Sin is a pollution that offends God.* Sin is a distasteful subject. People do not like to admit that they are sinners. Leviticus 4 reminds us that we are. It deals with the problem of human sin and the need of its cleansing before the holy God. Sin is doing "what is forbidden in any of the LORD's commands" (vv. 2, 13, 22, 27). It produces guilt (vv. 3, 13, 22, 27), defiles the sanctuary, and offends God, so that the sinner needs to be "forgiven" by God (vv. 20, 26, 31, 35). The rituals of blood sacrifice that would have to be repeated many times over the years were an indication to Israel of how seriously God takes sin.

2. *The sin offering is a remedy for sin.* The sin (or purification) offering (*hatta't*) is the most important sacrifice for cleansing impurities in the Old Testament. The rendering "sin offering" is appropriate in Leviticus 4, which refers repeatedly to sin and sinning, though it also covers ceremonial uncleanness. It cleansed the unintentional or inadvertent (not high-handed) offenses of persons so that their impurities could be removed from the presence of God in the sanctuary and their offenses could be forgiven.

The sin offering purified the tabernacle from Israel's impurities. The thing onto which the blood is sprinkled indicates what the blood cleanses. Thus the sacrifice for the high priest cleansed the holy tabernacle with its incense altar. The offering for the community also cleansed the tabernacle and the incense altar because Israel's representatives, the priests, could go into the holy place. The sacrifice for individual leaders or common Israelites only went as far as the horns of the altar because that was as far as any nonpriest could go. "The principle is that the blood went as far as the particular person or collective group of persons could go and, therefore, decontaminated the tabernacle to that point."[4] In decontaminating the tabernacle, the sin offering allowed God not to be angry with the ones who produced the contamination defiling his abode, but rather to forgive them (Lev. 4:21, 27, 31, 35).

The purification offering thus served to teach Israel about the holiness of God. God's holiness was incompatible with Israel's impurities. For God to remain in Israel's midst, human impurities needed purging through the sin offering. The New Testament speaks of both the church and the Christian's body as God's sanctuary indwelt by the Spirit (1 Cor. 3:16–17; 6:19; Eph. 2:21–22). As the sacred space of the sanctuary had to be regularly purged of sin's pollution by the blood of sin offerings, so the sins of both the church and individual Christians need to be purged by the blood of Christ so that God's Spirit will not be grieved.

Illustrating the Text

Our sin offends God.

Food: One of the longest-running reality TV shows is *Fear Factor*. In the show, contestants must overcome common fears, such as fear of heights or bugs or fire, to complete challenges. One of the mainstays of the show is for contestants to be faced with unappetizing "foods" to eat. These often include live bugs, such as grasshoppers, or beetles, and other revolting ingredients such as scorpions or rat's hair or cow's blood. These segments are entertaining because of the repulsive nature of the foods, things most of us wouldn't ever consider eating. Our sin is even more repulsive to God, unpleasant and offensive in his sight.

Sometimes a person can violate societal norms unintentionally, an experience similar to "inadvertent sin" in the Levitical law.

Personal Experience: I went on a mission trip to Rwanda, East Africa, in 2010. When doing my laundry by hand, I hung my underwear along with my other clothes on the public clothesline where we were staying. Afterward, I was told that it is considered immodest to hang intimate clothing where it could be seen. Subsequently, I hung my underwear in my room.

The college-aged girls on the same trip discovered after arriving that shorts are an item of clothing considered indecent for women in Rwanda. Several of them had to cover up their shorts with skirts when they ventured out.

I violated another norm when I took a moto, the motorcycle taxi that is available all over Kigali. It is considered improper for the passenger to touch the motorcycle driver during a taxi ride. Not knowing this, and being quite nervous about riding a moto, I held the driver's shoulders. The driver, who knew little English, did not try to correct me. But I learned later that I had committed a social blunder.

In a similar way, we may unknowingly or unwittingly violate the norms of God. When we become aware of such offenses, we need to take corrective action.

Atonement

The exact meaning and derivation of the Hebrew word *kipper*, "to make atonement" (Lev. 4:20a), is disputed. The following is one take on it.

The verb *kipper* ("to atone") arguably is derived from the noun *koper* ("ransom, gift"), with an original meaning of "placate," "mollify," "satisfy," or "appease" an offended party by means of gifts. That is the meaning when Jacob tries to "pacify" or "appease" Esau by sending him presents (Gen. 32:20–21). A gift that turns away a god's anger is a propitiation (see, in KJV and NASB, Rom. 3:25; Heb. 2:17; 1 John 2:2; 4:10). The Septuagint regularly renders *kipper* with forms of *hilaskomai*, meaning "to propitiate, appease."[1] The sin, burnt, and guilt offerings could be considered gifts to placate or mollify God. This interpretation fits well with the traditional English gloss "atone," which denotes reconciling parties who are at odds, making them "at-one." The alternative means of atoning God's wrath is by punishing the guilty, as when Phinehas kills Zimri and Kozbi (Num. 25:5–15).

Sin and uncleanness are pollutions that create a rift between God and people, for God finds the pollution and persons producing the pollution offensive. To make atonement requires purging the offensive pollution that has created the rift. Accordingly, *kipper* has taken on a secondary meaning of "to cleanse, purge." The sanctuary and its objects are purged by the application of the blood of the sin offering (Ezek. 43:20; cf. Lev. 4:7). Whatever the blood is applied to is cleansed. To make atonement for people (Exod. 32:30; Lev. 1:4; 4:20; 16:24) makes it possible for their pollution to be forgiven (Lev. 4:20, 26, 31, 35; 5:10, 13). To make atonement for things—the altar (Exod. 29:36; Lev. 16:18), the tabernacle/tent/sanctuary (Lev. 16:16–17, 33)—is to purge those things from the human pollution of sin and uncleanness that offends God, whose abode is the tabernacle.

By carrying out God's instructions and using the blood and choice parts of the animal brought as the required sacrifice, the priests are able to make atonement (*kipper*) for sins that have been committed. A man carries a goat as his offering in this figurine from Susa (2450 BC).

Impurity is like uranium. When uranium reaches a critical mass, it produces a nuclear explosion. When impurity reaches a critical mass, God breaks out in wrath. But the sin offering was a ransom to God that appeased his anger and purged from his presence the offending human sin or uncleanness.

Contrary to the claims of nineteenth-century reference works, *kipper* is not a "covering" of sin derived from *kapar* ("to cover"). On the basis of this earlier interpretation it was argued that atonement in Old Testament times served to "cover" sins temporarily until the time that sin could be fully removed through Christ. However, *kapar* (the Qal form) does not mean "to cover" but rather means "to daub with pitch."[2] *Kipper* (the Piel form rendered "atone") is not derived from the Qal root but is probably derived from the noun *koper* ("ransom, gift") as argued above.

Thus *kapar*, "to cover," is one root and *kipper*, "to atone" represents an entirely unrelated root.

The whole atonement system in Leviticus is complex. According to Roy Gane,[3] it worked by first transferring impurity from the people to the sanctuary and then subsequently cleansing the sanctuary on the Day of Atonement. When people sinned or acquired impurity, they could transfer their sin or impurity to the sanctuary by making a sin offering. Then, once a year, on the Day of Atonement, the sanctuary itself was purged from the impurities that had accumulated throughout the year. If sin offerings were not offered or if the sanctuary itself were not purged, the equilibrium between God and the people would be disrupted and divine wrath would occur. For more details, see "Theological Insights" at Leviticus 16:15–34.

Cases Requiring Sin Offerings

Big Idea *Acts of omission, ignorance, oversight, and impulse can lead us to sin.*

Understanding the Text

The Text in Context

Leviticus 4 introduces the ritual of the sin or purification offering. That chapter makes clear that this offering applies to unintentional or inadvertent sins, not defiant, high-handed sinning. Leviticus 5:1–13 clarifies the previous chapter by providing some specific cases where the sin offering is required. In particular it shows that this offering applies to sins of omission, to offenses due to accident or negligence, and to rash or impulsive acts. It also makes accommodations for the poor by allowing them to substitute either birds or a grain offering in place of the usual female goat or lamb.

Interpretive Insights

5:1–6 Three cases illustrate the kind of situation that might require a sin offering.

5:1 *If anyone sins because they do not speak up when they hear a public charge to testify.* The first case is a sin of omission or ignorance where a person fails to respond to a public charge to testify. An announcement was made in public that anyone who has witnessed a particular crime or who has evidence relevant to a specific case in court is to appear and give testimony about that case. The "charge" (lit., a "curse, oath" ['*alah*]) warns that anyone who withholds relevant evidence will be under a "curse"; that is, God himself will hold such a person accountable and administer punishment for obstructing justice by withholding evidence. Someone who fails to show up becomes responsible for sin and thus needs a sin offering. The curse could have had the psychological effect of making anyone who was guilty of withholding evidence fear divine punishment, thus leading the person to make the offering. Why would a person refuse to come testify? One might simply have missed the announcement or been unsure whether his or her evidence was relevant. Or one might not want to take time to come to court because of other pressing duties. Or one might be afraid; the criminal or his cronies might come to hurt a witness. The accused might be a relative or a friend whom the witness was reluctant to incriminate. Regardless, it was the witness's civic duty to come forward to testify. If witnesses did not come, it would undermine the entire court system. A guilty person could be punished only if there were two or three witnesses (Deut. 19:15). Thus, justice can be served only if witnesses were (and are) willing to testify.

5:2–3 *If anyone becomes . . . unclean.* The second case involves ceremonial uncleanness. Anyone who contracts ceremonial uncleanness through touching animal (cf. Lev. 11:8, 24, 26–27, 31, 36, 39) or human uncleanness (cf. Lev. 15:5, 7, 10–11, 20–24, 27) is required to offer a sin offering. If uncleanness is due to neglect or inattention, this can still be considered a sin. However, it is not necessarily sinful. If an unclean animal has died in one's barn, it

Key Themes of Leviticus 5:1–13

- There are sins of omission, negligence, and impulse.
- God shows grace to sinners.

might be necessary to touch the carcass to remove it. That is not a sin, though it does require a "sin" offering. For such cases Jacob Milgrom's rendering "purification offering" is more apt than the traditional "sin offering."

5:4 *if anyone thoughtlessly takes an oath.* A third occasion requiring a sin offering is the case of a rash oath. An oath is a formal commitment in God's name to do something or to abstain from something, usually involving some sort of ritual performance. A rash oath is one in which a person promises "as the LORD lives" to do something that either he or she cannot do, or upon reflection ought not to do, or simply forgets or chooses not to do. Oaths are taken very seriously: "When a man makes a vow to the LORD or takes an oath to obligate himself by a pledge, he must not break his word but must do everything he said" (Num. 30:2). One need not make an oath, but oaths made must be fulfilled. Swearing falsely brings one under divine curse. That is why Ecclesiastes 5:5 says, "It is better not to vow than to make one and not fulfill it." Jesus discouraged oaths, instead promoting honesty even without oaths (Matt. 5:33–37). To make an

One example of an unintentional sin is the failure to provide known information when there is a call for public testimony. In contrast, this cuneiform envelope shows the seal impressions of ten witnesses who participated in the court case recorded on the cuneiform tablet (Alalakh, 1720 BC).

oath and not carry it out makes the person guilty and requires a sin offering. For a fuller discussion of vows and oaths, see "Historical and Cultural Background" at Numbers 30:1–16.

5:5–6 *when anyone becomes aware that they are guilty in any of these matters.* In any of these cases the person is required to do the following: (1) confess the wrongdoing, (2) bring a female lamb or goat to serve as a sin offering (cf. Lev. 4:27–35), and (3) participate with the priest in offering the animal as a sin offering. "Confess" is from a Hebrew root (*yadah*) that often means to "praise, thank" but in the context of sin means "confess." The concept that binds these two usages together is "to acknowledge" something: "either the delivering activity of God or one's own trespasses, one's own failures."[1]

make atonement. See "Additional Insights" following the unit on Leviticus 4:1–35.

5:7–13 Accommodations are made for the poor in regard to the sin offering.

5:7 *Anyone who cannot afford a lamb.* Just as the grain offering can serve as the poor person's burnt offering (see "Teaching the Text" at Lev. 2:1–16), so the poor are allowed to offer cheaper sin offerings.

two doves or two young pigeons. Perhaps to make up for using cheaper animals, the value of this offering is expanded by offering two sacrifices, one for a sin offering and the other for a burnt offering (v. 7b). The burnt offering, like the sin offering, is used to make atonement (Lev. 1:4), seeking God's favor or appeasement (see "Teaching the Text" at Lev. 1:1–17). The burnt offering also adds material substance to the otherwise meager offering of a small bird as a sin offering.[2]

as a penalty for their sin. Atonement ordinarily involves substitutionary death.

5:11 *If . . . they cannot afford two doves.* For those too poor to afford even a bird, a cereal offering consisting of a tenth of an ephah (= about two quarts) of fine flour serves as a substitute for his sin offering. On fine flour, see comments at Leviticus 2:1–3. Other cereal offerings can have incense (frankincense [Lev. 2:1–2, 15–16]), though incense is omitted here probably because it has a pleasing aroma and is symbolic of joy (Prov. 27:9), while a sin offering is not a pleasant or joyous occasion. Moreover, the poor could not afford it. See the similar omission in Numbers 5:15.

5:13 *they will be forgiven.* See comments at Leviticus 4:13–21.

Theological Insights

The writer of Hebrews comments, "The law requires that nearly everything be cleansed with blood, and without the shedding of blood there is no forgiveness" (Heb. 9:22), carefully pointing out that it is "nearly" everything. Despite the emphasis on blood in Leviticus (cf. Lev. 17:11), the very poor could get atonement with a bloodless sacrifice (Lev. 5:11–13). How was this possible?

Hebrews also states that even bloody sacrifices are not inherently able to purge sin (Heb. 10:4). Animals are inadequate substitutes for humans; only Christ was the perfect sacrifice for sin (Heb. 10:10). The usual emphasis on blood in the sacrificial system is important because it foreshadows the shedding of Christ's blood. But the Old Testament could allow a bloodless sacrifice for the very poor precisely because all the sacrifices were merely symbolic. The real sacrifice that achieves forgiveness is that of Jesus Christ.

So, were the Old Testament sacrifices effective? Yes and no. They were effective in that the worshiper genuinely received and experienced forgiveness; but they were not effective intrinsically, for the sacrifice per se did not in and of itself purge sin. What allowed forgiveness of sin was that to which these sacrifices (with their emphasis on blood) pointed: the sacrifice of Jesus Christ (more below).

Teaching the Text

1. *There are sins of omission, negligence, and impulse.* Sin is a major concern in Leviticus and Numbers, as well as the rest of the Old Testament. Sin can be against other people (1 Sam. 2:25), but the Bible overwhelmingly speaks of sin as an offense against God. Sin is doing "what is forbidden in any of the LORD's commands" (Lev. 4:2).

But one can sin in other ways. In Leviticus 5:1 a public proclamation goes out asking anyone who has been a witness to a crime to come forward to testify. Similar situations occur today. We witness a crime or an accident. We know that the right thing to do is to offer our eyewitness testimony to the investigating officers. Or we hear a coworker being slandered and know that what is being said is untrue or unfair. We know we should speak up on behalf of the person slandered. But often people walk away, not wanting to be bothered. The other two sins listed in Leviticus 5:1–13 are sins of neglect and impulse. In one case (vv. 2–3) a person has inadvertently contracted ceremonial uncleanness. In the other case a person has done something rash, making an inappropriate vow (v. 4).

One does not have to do something to sin; one can sin by doing nothing. James writes, "If anyone, then, knows the good they ought to do and doesn't do it, it is sin for them" (James 4:17). In the story of the good Samaritan, the priest and the Levite who pass by the man waylaid by robbers should have known that the right thing to do was to stop and help the man, but they do not do it (Luke 10:30–32). Similarly, in Leviticus 5:1 a witness to a crime who does nothing is guilty of sin. God holds us accountable not only for what we do, but also for what we do not do. We can do wrong even when we do not intend it. Neglect or inattention can cause us to do something bad. We may impulsively do or say something that we later regret and realize was wrong. Sin is subtle and can overtake us in many ways.

2. *God shows grace to sinners.* The problem of sin is universal and lifelong. Solomon remarks in dedicating the temple, "There is no one that does not sin" (1 Kings 8:46). David acknowledges that he has been a sinner since birth (Ps. 51:5). Still worse, sin can bring punishment from God. In Eden sin results in the estrangement of humankind from God (Gen. 3). Miriam's sin leads God to strike her with leprosy (Num. 12:9–15). Israel's sin leads God to condemn the nation to wilderness wanderings (Num. 14:11–12, 19, 34).

But God also responds to the problem of sin with grace. The sacrificial system itself was a gracious means that God provided for his sinful people so that they could be forgiven (Lev. 5:10, 13). It is not true that Israel was to merit forgiveness by doing enough good works; the sacrificial system assumes that Israelites could not earn forgiveness in this way. But God provided a means of forgiveness through the sacrificial system. One would confess one's sin and then through sacrifice seek God's purification, forgiveness, and grace (Lev. 5:5–6).

What must Christians do when they fall into sin? It is similar under the new

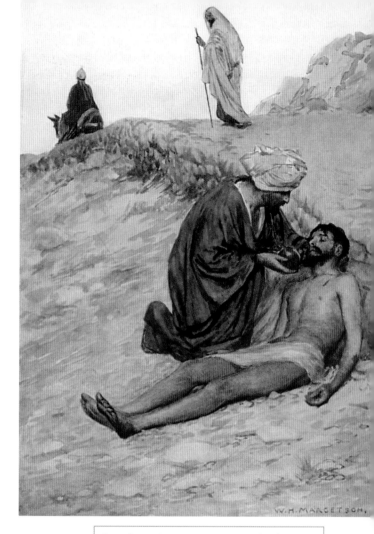

According to Leviticus 5:1, a witness who does nothing is guilty of sin. This would have been understood by the expert in the law to whom Jesus tells the parable of the good Samaritan. The Samaritan who shows mercy is obeying the law, unlike the priest and the Levite who hurry past. This illustration of the scene was created by William Henry Margetson (1861–1940).

covenant: "If we confess our sins, he is faithful and just and will forgive us our sins and purify us from all unrighteousness" (1 John 1:9). God still graciously provides a means of purification, forgiveness, and grace. That purification is through "the blood of Jesus, his Son," which "purifies us from all sin" (1 John 1:7b).

Illustrating the Text

First and foremost, sin is an offense against God.

Scenario: A single young adult decides to have a group of buddies over to see his new apartment. He serves gallons of Mountain Dew. The place is redolent with the scent of oven-baked hot wings and pizza pockets. The game-system, flat-screen, surround-sound combo is fired up like a visual spider web, catching all the guys in its addictive glow. At a certain point, the night gets a bit out of hand, and one of the young men, trying to hit a friend with a hard-thrown remote control, tosses it through the glass of the third-story window instead.

"Dude! I'm sorry," he apologizes. "I broke your window and remote!"

True. He might have to buy his friend a new remote. But his apologies about the window are aimed at the wrong party. The window, room, and entire building belong to someone else—the owner. Ultimately, that is who will be demanding payment.

All our sins, ultimately, are against God, who made, owns, and cares for this world.

Sin is subtle and sneaky.

Object Lesson: For this humorous illustration, use an enormous bottle of hand sanitizer (the bigger the better). Have the bottle positioned so that it cannot be seen by the congregation. With exaggerated drama, begin by talking about the dangers of living in the world. Everywhere we go, we are under attack. Whether we know it or not, an enemy is seeking to invade us, trying to infect us. But, thankfully, doctors and parents everywhere have found the secret to combating this dire threat. At this point, plop the hand sanitizer down for maximum dramatic effect. How in the world did we ever get along without this stuff? It is like the A-bomb of germophobes everywhere!

Whether we realize it or not, we are constantly under attack. Sin is not just the "big" stuff. It is all the small things that we do without even realizing it. We constantly need to seek cleansing in our lives.

The Guilt Offering

Big Idea *The guilt offering shows how to repent.*

Understanding the Text

The Text in Context

Leviticus 1:1–6:7 is addressed to the laity, giving them instructions about five types of sacrifices. It is organized around those that the layperson could voluntarily choose to offer (burnt, grain, and fellowship offerings), followed by those that the layperson must offer whenever certain offenses have occurred (sin and guilt offerings).

The guilt offering is meant to address offenses against holy things, whether done by directly desecrating a holy thing (Lev. 5:14–19) or by swearing a false exculpatory oath, thus desecrating God's holy name (Lev. 6:1–7). In both cases the remedy involves restitution of an item plus 20 percent and a guilt offering.

Historical and Cultural Background

The oath (Lev. 6:3) was also employed in Mesopotamia. A man accused of deflowering a maiden, or accused of fraud in the case of stolen goods, or accused of negligence in the case of a rented ox and who denied the charges could be forced to make an oath of innocence before a god (Sumerian Laws Exercise Tablet ¶8′; Laws of Eshnunna ¶37; Laws of Hammurabi ¶249). A witness who refused to take an oath was deemed false (Laws of Ur-Namma ¶29).[1]

Interpretive Insights

5:14–6:7 "Guilt offering," traditionally "trespass offering" (KJV), is from a root (*'asham*) meaning "to be/feel guilty." Others render it "restitution offering" (HCSB), "compensation offering" (Message), or "penalty offering" (NCV), all taking into consideration its associated restitution (Lev. 5:16; 6:5). The word *'asham* can mean "guilt" (Gen. 26:10), "guilt offering," or "penalty [for guilt]" (Lev. 5:6–7; Num. 5:7–8). This creates ambiguity: "as a penalty" in Leviticus 5:15b can be translated "as his guilt offering" (NASB). The word "sin" behaves similarly (see comments at Lev. 4:3).

5:15 *When anyone is unfaithful.* Both the NIV rendering and "commits a trespass" (KJV, NRSV) are too general for *ma'al*. Though it can mean "commit rebellion, treachery," in ritual texts it regularly means "to commit sacrilege"[2] as an offense against God. It is used to refer to illicit offerings of incense, idolatry, and defiling consecrated utensils and the temple (2 Chron. 26:16–18; 28:19, 22–24; 29:19;

36:14). Here one form of *ma'al* consists of desecration of Yahweh's holy things (Lev. 5:14–16)—that is, taking something sacred (belonging to God) and wrongly turning it into something profane and no longer appropriate for God (examples below). Another form involves swearing falsely in an exculpatory oath (Lev. 6:1–7). All these instances are acts of sacrilege.

sinning unintentionally in regard to any of the LORD's holy things. On sinning unintentionally, see comments at Leviticus 4:2. The "LORD's holy things" include the firstborn and firstfruits (Lev. 23:20; Num. 18:17), animals to be sacrificed (2 Chron. 29:33), things vowed to the sanctuary (Lev. 21:22; 27:21–23; Num. 5:9), grain offerings (Lev. 2:3), tithes (Lev. 27:30), and the meat of the fellowship offering (Lev. 19:5–8). Holy things are profaned by making them ceremonially unclean or by damaging them. This can also occur by eating holy food while in a state of ceremonial uncleanness (cf. 1 Sam. 21:4) or by eating a priest's food (Lev. 22:14–16). Such things require a ram as a guilt offering.

a ram . . . without defect. The offenses described above require a ram as a guilt offering. On "without defect," see comments at Leviticus 1:3.

of the proper value in silver, according to the sanctuary shekel. This may mean, as the NIV has it, that the animal must be of the proper value as appraised by the priest (cf. Lev. 27:8, 12). Alternatively, it could mean "convertible into silver"

- True repentance shows remorse.
- True repentance renounces sin.
- True repentance seeks to make restitution.
- Removal of guilt before God requires atonement.

(NRSV), whereby one can bring money (silver) instead of a ram, and the money is then used to purchase an animal from the priests. The sanctuary shekel is the standard weight kept at the sanctuary, roughly eleven to twelve grams,[3] though the exact weight varied by time and place.

5:16 *They must make restitution.* Restitution plus a 20 percent penalty goes to the priest, who suffers material loss by the desecration.

the ram as a guilt offering. This offering deals with the offender's guilt before God.

make atonement . . . and they will be forgiven. Better, "so that he can be forgiven" (see comments at Lev. 4:13–21). On "atonement," see "Additional Insights" following the unit on Leviticus 4:1–35.

5:17–19 *though they do not know it, they are guilty.* This may mean that they had not realized that they were committing sacrilege at the time. A guilt offering (implicitly with restitution and penalty) must be offered even if the offense was unintentional. Alternatively, "they do not know it" may mean that, unlike the

When sin has occurred with regard to the Lord's holy things, a guilt offering of a ram and the proper value in silver must be brought to the sanctuary. Shown here is a coil of silver, which would be cut into shekel weight pieces for payment.

Leviticus 5:14–6:7

previous case, they are uncertain whether a holy thing was desecrated. On this view, "they are guilty" means "they feel guilt,"[4] having psychological turmoil over the possibility of a sacrilege: the person suspects having been in a state of ceremonial impurity when a fellowship offering was eaten or suspects that the item vowed to Yahweh was not the item that was sent. To dispel such guilty feelings, a guilt offering is made. On this reading, the restitution requirement is dropped.

6:1–7 The law of the guilt offering for false oaths overlaps with the law of Numbers 5:5–10. Where evidence is insufficient to go to court, suspects can be required to swear (see Lev. 6:5) that they "did not lay hands on the other person's property" (Exod. 22:11). The guilt offering is the remedy for such a person who swears falsely but then repents.

6:2 *If anyone sins and is unfaithful.* On "sins," see comments at Leviticus 4:2. "Unfaithful" means "commits sacrilege" (see Lev. 5:15 above).

deceiving a neighbor. Or "lying to" a neighbor (NKJV). What follows are different ways of expropriating a neighbor's property. In the case of "something entrusted to them" (lit., "to him"), the neighbor leaves items for safekeeping with someone while the neighbor is away, but the keeper swears falsely to have had no possession of such a thing, or that it has been stolen or it has died and thus cannot be returned (cf. Exod. 22:10). "Left in their care" is better taken as "an investment" (HCSBmg), in which the culprit swears falsely that the deal had gone sour and all the money is gone. "Stolen" is better rendered "robbed" (cf. NRSV) because *gazal*

normally involves force. This is a case where the victim lacks legal proof that the suspect is the thief/robber.

cheat their neighbor. Or "extorted" (NASB, NKJV) or "defrauds/defrauded" (HCSB, NRSV). This term (*'ashaq*) is used of withholding wages of laborers (Deut. 24:14–15; Mal. 3:5) or withholding the pledges given for a loan (Ezek. 18:18 where *'ashaq 'osheq*, "did what was wrong" [NIV], is the opposite of returning collateral in Ezek. 18:7). Here the culprit admits to having confiscated the goods but swears falsely about the circumstances, claiming that confiscation is fully justified.

6:3 *find lost property and lie about it.* The rule of "finders keepers, losers weepers" makes sense where an owner of lost property cannot be found, but here the culprit refuses to return a lost item even after identifying the rightful owner and swears falsely to have owned it all along or else never to have found it.

swear falsely. In each of these cases suspects take an oath swearing that they are innocent of any wrongdoing. The oath brings the suspect under the direct divine judgment. An oath is used only in cases where evidence is insufficient to prosecute the accused in human courts.

6:4–7 *when they sin . . . and realize their guilt.* This is better rendered "when they . . . sin and feel guilty" or "when they feel guilty about having sinned."[5] N. Kiuchi's view that *'ashem* means "realize guilt"[6] (the view reflected in the NIV, ESV, NRSV) fails because the defrauder, embezzler, and robber would each be quite aware of having sinned all along. It is when they feel guilty and are willing to act on that feeling that this law applies (so HCSB: "acknowledge their guilt"). The human victim is redressed by the perpetrator returning whatever has been wrongfully taken or its monetary equivalent, with a 20 percent windfall on top as a penalty, and the sacrilege against God is redressed by giving the ram for a guilt offering that makes atonement and forgiveness available (cf. Lev. 5:16c above).

Theological Insights

It is possible to have true moral guilt before God and humans. It is also possible for that guilt to be removed and forgiven by repenting and turning to God.

Isaiah 53 describes the Suffering Servant and likens the work of that servant to a guilt offering. Isaiah 53:10 states, "Yet it was the Lord's will to crush him and cause him to suffer, and . . . the Lord makes [lit., 'you make'] his life a guilt offering" (NIV 1984). Here the servant does not offer a guilt offering but rather is offered as one by God. Just as the guilt offering dealt with offenses against God's holy things (Godward) and offenses against human beings (humanward), so "the Death of the Servant satisfied both the needs of sinful people before God and the 'needs'/requirements of God in relation to his broken law and offended holiness."[7] The prophecy of Isaiah 53 finds fulfillment in Jesus Christ. Christ's death not only removed sin before God like the Day of Atonement sin offering (Isa. 53:6; see Lev. 16:21) but also removed the guilt caused by offenses against God and other human beings.

Teaching the Text

The guilt offering was required for two types of sins: profaning God's sacred property (Lev. 5:14–19) and swearing a false exculpatory oath concerning lost or disputed property (Lev. 6:1–7). The former involved the sacrilege of ill treatment of a sacred object; the latter involved the sacrilege of taking God's name in vain by a false oath.

Sometimes people have a vague sense that they have offended God (Lev. 5:17–18). What can they do to remove that guilt, real or imagined? At other times people know that they have denied God by their acts. How do they go about having their sin and guilt removed? Our passage shows that deliberate sin, even things such as robbery and defrauding people of goods, can be forgiven through repentance and atoning sacrifice (Lev. 5:16, 18; 6:7).

What does Leviticus 5:14–6:7 teach about repentance and God's forgiveness?

1. *True repentance shows remorse.* The first step in repentance is remorse. A person must "feel sorry" or "feel guilty" for what he or she has done (see Lev. 6:4 and comments above).

Repentance involves the whole human personality: intellect, emotion, and will. One must not only "know" that one has done wrong; one must also "feel" the wrong that has been done and "act" to change one's behavior. The ritual of sacrifice was not enough. David writes in Psalm 51:16–17, "You do not delight in sacrifice. . . . My sacrifice, O God, is a broken spirit; a broken and contrite heart you, God, will not despise." "A broken and contrite heart," or remorse, is a key element that allows an atoning sacrifice to be effective in removing guilt. If you are to be forgiven, you must first feel the moral guilt of your offense.

Zacchaeus shows true repentance after coming to know Jesus by offering anyone he has defrauded fourfold restitution (Luke 19:8; cf. Exod. 22:1). In response, Jesus remarks, "Today salvation has come to this house" (Luke 19:9).

The requirement of restitution reminds us that sin is not just a religious offense against God; it is also an offense against other human beings that must be addressed.

4. *Removal of guilt before God requires atonement.* God does not take sin lightly. Sinful acts are made still more heinous when covered up by false religiosity, in this case a false oath (Lev. 6:1–7). Remorse, renunciation, and restitution might be enough to obtain forgiveness from another human being, but forgiveness by God required and requires expiation. The ram of the guilt offering served as the guilty party's atoning sacrifice that allowed God to grant forgiveness (Lev. 5:16, 18; 6:7). This requirement shows us something of the gravity of sin in the sight of God.

> For cheating a neighbor, once guilt is realized, restitution must be made. When Zacchaeus meets Jesus, he is convicted of his sin and says, "Look, Lord! Here and now I give half of my possessions to the poor, and if I have cheated anybody out of anything, I will pay back four times the amount" (Luke 19:8). These coins are Tyrian shekels typically used to pay the Jerusalem temple tax during the time of Jesus.

2. *True repentance renounces sin.* It is also not enough simply to feel sorry for a sin. To find release from guilt, you also need to renounce the sin that produced the guilt (cf. 1 John 1:9). The very act of making restitution to an injured party and coming to a priest to present a guilt offering was an admission of and renunciation of sin.

3. *True repentance seeks to make restitution.* Real repentance wants to right the wrongs done. That is why the law required making restitution with interest (20 percent) to the person whom one had wronged (Lev. 6:6). The interest would assure that the injured party was more than adequately compensated for the wrong done. A person who is unwilling to try to make right the wrongs that he or she has committed has not really repented.

Illustrating the Text

When we treat God's holiness lightly, we show contempt for him.

News: When Danish cartoonist Kurt Westergaard drew a controversial cartoon of Muhammad in September 2005, it set off violent Muslim protests around the world. On January 1, 2010, an attempt was made on Westergaard's life by a Muslim extremist who considered the cartoon blasphemous.[8] In January of 2015 two Muslim gunmen killed eight members of the staff of the French satirical magazine *Charlie Hebdo* for portraying Muhammad in cartoons. When a pastor of a small church in Florida merely threatened to burn a Qur'an in September 2010, it set off an international uproar that led President Obama to urge him not to do it.[9] Muslims find the desecration of their holy things deeply offensive.

Christians too find desecration of their holy things offensive. The work by California artist Enrique Chagoya portraying Jesus Christ in a sex act provoked outrage and protests among Christians when he displayed his art at a temporary exhibit at the Loveland Museum in Colorado in the fall of 2010.[10] Some fifty protestors picketed the museum to express their objections to using taxpayer money to fund this blasphemous exhibit, and one woman broke through the exhibit's protective casing and began to rip the painting apart.

But as much as people are offended by sacrilege, God is even more offended when his holy things are profaned. It is his displeasure that really counts. Deliberate desecration of the holy is an expression of contempt for God.

And yet all of us may inadvertently defile God's holy things. Not showing proper respect for the elements in taking the Lord's Supper could be an act of sacrilege: "For those who eat and drink without discerning the body of Christ eat and drink judgment on themselves" (1 Cor. 11:29). Christians too need to be careful about how they treat God's holy things.

Confession of sin can lead to true transformation.

Human Experience: The ritual of the guilt offering constituted symbolically a confession and renunciation of sin. Confession and renunciation are essential features of Alcoholics Anonymous (AA) meetings.

Psychologically, confession of sin to others and to God helps give the sinner the courage and the resolve actually to change. Among the "Twelve Steps" of the AA program is "Admit to God, to ourselves, and to another human being the exact nature of our wrongs" (step 5). One must also be ready to have God remove these defects of character and in fact ask God to remove these shortcomings (steps 6–7). It takes a great deal more courage to verbalize one's faults to others than simply to understand them within one's own mind. Consequently, the act of public confession is a means, psychologically, of bolstering and strengthening the will.

Another step of the AA program parallels the requirement for restitution in the guilt offering: one is to make a list of persons he or she has harmed and make direct amends to these persons wherever possible (steps 8–9).

Twelve-step programs have helped many people overcome alcohol addiction. Part of the program's effectiveness is that it mimics in significant ways aspects of the guilt offering.

The Priestly Portions of Sacrifices

Big Idea *God's ministers help people to worship, and they deserve to be paid.*

Understanding the Text

The Text in Context

Leviticus 1:1–6:7 discusses the five basic sacrifices from the layperson's point of view. Leviticus 6:8–7:38 changes the audience to priests: "Aaron and his sons" (Lev. 6:9, 25). This unit emphasizes portions of the sacrifices to be given to the priests. It anticipates Leviticus 8–10, on the ordination and duties of priests.

Historical and Cultural Background

A relief from Karnak in Egypt showing a man lifting up a food offering bears the inscription, "Come, O King, elevate offerings before the face (of the god) . . . Amen-Ra', Lord of the Thrones of the Two Lands [Egypt]." This relief may illustrate how the "wave" or "elevation" offering (v. 30) was presented.[1]

Interpretive Insights

6:8–13 *These are the regulations for the burnt offering.* These regulations are specific to the evening

burnt offering (see Exod. 29:38–39) that is kept going continually (v. 13) until morning (v. 9b), not freewill burnt offerings (Lev. 1) that are offered during the day. The ashes are, more specifically, the fat ashes. "Body" (v. 10) is literally "flesh," meaning

This Karnak relief illustration and inscription record an elevation offering that may have been similar to the wave offering described in Leviticus 7:30.

the genitals (cf. Lev. 15:3). The priest must maintain sexual propriety in worship (see Exod. 20:26; 28:42–43). Linen is a simple if rough fabric made from flax.[2] Disposal of the ashes does not require priestly garb (v. 11a). Ashes produced by ritual sacrifice cannot be disposed of at ordinary garbage dumps, thus the requirement for a ceremonially clean place (v. 11b).

6:14–17 *These are the regulations for the grain offering.* Leviticus 6:14–18 may be describing a raw grain offering that accompanies the regular grain offering (Lev. 6:20) rather than one of the general grain offerings of Leviticus 2. It must lack yeast, a symbol of decay and death (v. 17a; Lev. 2:11). "Most holy" (v. 17b) offerings of grain, like sin and guilt offerings, can only be eaten by priests in the sanctuary (see 6:26). Fellowship offerings, firstfruits, and food gifts have a lesser degree of holiness and so can be eaten by any member of the priestly family. On "memorial portion" (v. 15), see comments at Leviticus 2:1–3.

6:18 *Whatever touches them will become holy.* There is debate whether verse 18b should be rendered as in the NIV, indicating a kind of "sancta contagion,"[3] or as "Whoever touches them must be holy" (NIVmg, NKJV),[4] which would exclude the ceremonially unclean priests. Exodus 29:37; 30:29; and Leviticus 6:27–28 support the transferring-holiness-by-touch view. Thus utensils and vessels used by the worshiper to transport the offering would belong to God too. On "memorial portion" (v. 15), see comments at Leviticus 2:1–3.

6:19–23 *This is the offering Aaron and his sons are to bring.* This section describes a special grain offering for the priests (v. 20) prepared by the priest next in line

for the high priesthood (v. 22). This "regular" (*tamid*) or "continual" (NKJV) grain offering is always on the altar evening and morning like the continual burnt offering (Num. 28:3, 6), offered on a priest's behalf "beginning on the day he is anointed" (v. 20 NKJV). A tenth of an ephah ("about 3 1/2 pounds or about 1.6 kilograms" [NIVmg]) constitutes about two quarts of grain, the same as the poor person's sin offering (Lev. 5:11). On "fine flour," see comments at Leviticus 2:1–3. Priests eat other grain offerings (Lev. 6:16), but not offerings made for them, so they are required to burn this offering completely (v. 23).

6:25–26 *These are the regulations for the sin offering.* On "most holy" (v. 25b), see comments at 6:14–17 above. "Shall eat it" (v. 26) should be rendered "may eat it." It would have been physically impossible for a priest to eat every offering entirely.

6:27–28 *Whatever touches any of the flesh will become holy.* Clothing, vessels, and utensils used by the worshiper to process the meat belong to God and remain in the sanctuary. The alternative, "Everyone who touches its flesh must be holy" (NKJV) (see Lev. 6:18 above) is unlikely. Priests are already holy, and the context is about things, not persons.

wash . . . broken . . . scoured . . . rinsed. Holy things that have absorbed impurity from the sin offering must be cleansed, or if that is impossible, as with porous clay, destroyed (cf. Lev. 11:33, 35; 15:12).

6:30 *blood is brought into the tent of meeting.* This kind of sin offering is made for the priests themselves (Lev. 4:1–12) or for the nation including its priests (Lev. 4:13–21; 16:27), so it cannot be eaten by priests (see comments at vv. 19–23 above).

7:1 *These are the regulations for the guilt offering, which is most holy.* On "most holy" (v. 1), see comments at 6:14–17 above. The ritual is similar to that of Leviticus 3.

7:7 *The same law applies to both the sin offering and the guilt offering.* Ritually, sin and guilt offerings are similar in that the meat of both belongs to the conducting priest (see Lev. 6:25–26, 30).

7:8 *The priest who offers a burnt offering . . . may keep its hide.* Priests get the hides of burnt offerings. The hide of fellowship offerings presumably belongs to the worshiper, and hides of sin offerings for priests are burned (Lev. 4:11). It is unclear whether the priest or the worshiper gets the hides of regular sin and guilt offerings. Rabbinic tradition says that they went to the priests per verse 7b, but the text's mention of hides of burnt offerings perhaps implies a contrast. On disposal of unburned portions of grain offerings (vv. 9–10), see Leviticus 6:16–18.

7:11–36 There are three types of fellowship offering: for "thankfulness" (v. 12), at the completion of a "vow," and the "freewill" offering (v. 16). See "Theological Insights" below.

7:12–14 *If they offer it as an expression of thankfulness.* A thank offering (*todah*) is a fellowship offering made to express gratitude to God for answered prayer or deliverance (see "Theological Insights" below). Loaves round out the feast (v. 12). Yeast (vv. 12–13), as a symbol of corruption, is prohibited from the altar (see Lev. 2:11), but it can be eaten by

priests or worshipers otherwise (Lev. 7:13; 23:17). "Contribution" (*t*ᵉ*rumah* [v. 14]), traditionally "heave offering," probably is not from a root meaning "to be high," hence "heave offering," but rather from an Akkadian root meaning "to give,"[5] hence "contribution" or "tribute," the priest's stipend.

7:15 *eaten on the day it is offered.* Compare Leviticus 22:29–30. Like the Passover lamb, the ordination offering for priests, and possibly the ram of the Nazirite (Exod. 12:10; 29:34; Lev. 8:32; Num. 6:19), the thank offering must be eaten on the same day before decay can defile this now-holy sacrifice. All four of these offerings were mandatory and must be eaten by the offerer.[6]

7:16 *If . . . their offering is the result of a vow or is a freewill offering.* On the significance of vow and freewill fellowship offerings, see "Theological Insights" below. For freewill burnt offerings, see Leviticus 22:18.

anything left over may be eaten on the next day. The voluntary nature of the freewill offering—the offering is not required, and it can be eaten by others besides the offerer outside the sanctuary—explains why the time span for eating it is longer than for thank offerings (Lev. 7:12–14). Why the time to eat a vow offering is longer is less clear.[7] However, the worshiper accrues no benefit from God if the offering is eaten beyond the second day (v. 18).

7:19 *ceremonially unclean . . . ceremonially clean.* Only an undefiled fellowship offering can be eaten, and only the ceremonially clean can eat it. Defiled meat must be burned.

7:20–21 *cut off from their people.* See "Additional Insights" following this unit.

7:22–27 *Do not eat any of the fat . . . you must not eat the blood.* On "fat," see comments at Leviticus 3:3–5. The fat of livestock that have died apart from the altar can be used for making soap or lubricants, but not as food (v. 24). Livestock fat belongs to God, though eating the fat of animals not eligible for the altar (deer) is not prohibited (v. 25). On the proscription against eating blood, see "Theological Insights" at Leviticus 3:1–17 and comments at Leviticus 17:10–11.

7:28–35 *I have . . . given them to Aaron the priest and his sons as their perpetual share.* Laypersons ("Israelites" [v. 29]) must give priests the breasts and right thighs of fellowship offerings as stipends (vv. 30–35). "Wave offering" (*teⁿupah* [v. 30]) is derived from *nup*, a verb of motion used for offerings and consecration. Was the motion a lifting up of the gifts to God ("elevation offering" [NJPS]) or a back-and-forth motion ("wave offering")? Aaron's "presenting" (*nup*) the Levites before Yahweh as a *teⁿupah* (Num. 8:11, 13, 15, 21) cannot involve waving, only a consecration before Yahweh. The same could be true of other things designated *teⁿupah*. The HCSB's rendering, "presentation offering," captures the essential meaning without speculating on any gestures used.

7:37–38 *These, then, are the regulations . . . which the* LORD *gave.* These verses summarize Leviticus 1–7. On the "ordination offering" (v. 37), see comments at Leviticus 8:22.

The right thigh of the fellowship offering is given to the priest. In this relief from the tomb of Nes-peka-shuty (seventh century BC), the Egyptians are carrying cattle legs, including the thigh portion, as offerings.

Theological Insights

Leviticus 3 gives instruction about the fellowship offering, but the instruction in Leviticus 7:11–16 indicates that there are three subcategories:

The freewill offering (*nedabah*). Freewill offerings are spontaneous expressions of gratitude that also provide meat for the table. They praise God for material blessings (Deut. 16:10) and his goodness (Ps. 54:6). The usual requirement of an animal being unblemished seems to have been waived for the freewill fellowship sacrifice (Lev. 22:23). This probably was the most general and most common of all sacrifices.

The vow offering (*neder*). The vow offering is brought at the successful completion of a vow (Prov. 7:14; see Num. 6:14, 21) or as fulfillment of a vow-promise to worship God or give something to God should God provide help (Gen. 28:20–22; 2 Sam. 15:7–8; Jon. 2:9; cf. Judg. 11:30–31). For instance, at the completion of the Nazirite vow, a fellowship (vow) offering is prescribed (Num. 6:14, 21). If the vow has promised to dedicate to the sanctuary persons or things (Lev. 27; 1 Sam. 1:11, 21), they would be transferred to God at the time of the vow offering.

The thanksgiving offering (*todah*). The thanksgiving offering expresses gratitude to God (Jer. 33:11). It is made for answered prayer (Ps. 50:14–15) or after a safe traversal of stormy seas (Ps. 107:22–25). The "sacrifice of praise" in Hebrews 13:15 is an allusion to this sacrifice, though spiritualizing its application under the new covenant to an expression of one's lips without the animal sacrifice.

All fellowship offerings express joy: "Sacrifice fellowship offerings there, eating them and rejoicing in the presence of the LORD your God" (Deut. 27:7). Christians too should express joy and gratitude for God's blessings and answers to prayer.

Teaching the Text

God's ministers deserve the privilege of material support. One can give things to God by giving things to his ministers.

The duties of priests were many:

1. They maintained fire on the altar day and night (Lev. 6:9–13).
2. They offered continual grain offerings for themselves (Lev. 6:19–23).
3. They helped fellow Israelites offer sacrifice, making sure that proper procedures were followed.

But along with the priestly duties came privileges. One important privilege was that priests ate a portion of most offerings brought to God, including grain, sin, and guilt offerings (Lev. 6:16, 18, 26, 29–30; 7:6–7). The sin and guilt offerings were "most holy": only priests or their sons could eat of them and only at the sanctuary. Priests received the right thigh and breast of fellowship offerings (Lev. 7:31–32, 34), which

Offering regulations ensure that Israel's priests are well cared for. Depending on the sacrifice, portions of the offered grain and meat can be eaten in the sanctuary. The breast and thigh of fellowship offerings and the hide of guilt offerings are allotted to those serving as priests. Various aspects of the butchering process are depicted in this tomb relief (2350 BC).

could be eaten at home by any "clean" family member, including women (Lev. 10:14; Num. 18:11). Priests also kept the precious hide of burnt offerings (Lev. 7:8), and maybe that of sin and guilt offerings too.

The apostle Paul applies this to the need to pay ministers of the gospel. He says in 1 Corinthians 9:13–14, "Don't you know that those who serve in the temple get their food from the temple, and that those who serve at the altar share in what is offered on the altar? In the same way, the Lord has commanded that those who preach the gospel should receive their living from the gospel." Under the old covenant, priests earned their living by their priestly duties. Likewise, under the new covenant, ministers of the gospel should be supported from people's offerings to God.

Illustrating the Text

We can express gratitude to God in community.

Cultural Institution: The fellowship (Lev. 7:11–16) offering is like the American holiday of Thanksgiving. The American national tradition of celebrating the Thanksgiving holiday can, to some degree, be traced back to the celebration of the Pilgrims, who after good harvests or the like would declare days of thanksgiving. Subsequently, governors or officials from time to time did the same. The current holiday was formally designated to be on the fourth Thursday of November through the proclamations of Presidents Abraham Lincoln and Franklin Roosevelt.

Thanksgiving involves a feast with family and friends. Traditionally, roast turkey is the main course. Although for many people the holiday is primarily secular—a football game is often the big event of the day—many Christians still incorporate the spiritual element of this holiday by using this time to reflect on God's blessings in their lives.

The fellowship offering was akin to Thanksgiving. In it, a meal was eaten in the presence of God to express gratitude to God for his help and blessings. We can still do that both at Thanksgiving and throughout the year.

God's ministers should receive income.

Human Experience: One mark of maturity is a growing recognition of other people's effort. Each morning children wake up, come to the kitchen table, and eat breakfast. They get dressed, putting on clothes that were washed for them, grab a bag lunch already prepared for them, and then head to school. They go through their day, wondrously oblivious of how much people around them have worked to make their day possible. But as children age, we expect them to gain perspective, live in gratitude, and eventually come to appreciate all that parents do for them. This perspective becomes even more finely focused when they begin doing these things for their own children.

Sometimes immature or unaware Christians fail to realize what it takes to cultivate a healthy church. They might be tempted to think that pastors spend their days drinking coffee and thinking about God. They might imagine that the pastor wakes up on a Sunday and decides, "I think I'll preach out of Romans today." But the work that ministers do is intense, the responsibilities demanding, and the energy required immense. This is why, like the priests of the Old Testament, they should be financially supported in their service.

"Cut Off from One's People"

The precise meaning of being "cut off from one's people" has been debated. It has been taken to mean banishment, execution, or excommunication (cf. Lev. 22:3: "cut off from my presence"). But the most likely view is that this is a divine punishment rather than a human one.

Being cut off from one's people is the threatened punishment for cases of eating a fellowship offering while unclean (Lev. 7:20–21), eating a fellowship offering after three days (Lev. 19:5–8), eating the fat of the fellowship offering that belongs to God's altar (Lev. 7:25), and eating blood (Lev. 7:27; 17:10, 14). It is also threatened for sacrificing on an unapproved altar outside the camp where goat-demons are being worshiped (Lev. 17:4, 8–9), sacrificing one's children to Molek (Lev. 20:3–5), and turning to mediums and spiritualists (Lev. 20:6). It is threatened for working on the Sabbath (Exod. 31:14), for failing to fast on the Day of Atonement (Lev. 23:29), and for failing to keep the Passover (Num. 9:13). It also applies to incest and human sacrifice among other abominations (Lev. 18:29) and for intercourse with a menstruating woman (Lev. 20:18). More generally, it is the penalty for any flagrant, high-handed, or defiant sinning that represents blasphemous rebellion against God (Num. 15:30–31). All these are religious sins against God. Only incest and human sacrifice can be construed as crimes against other people.

The nature of a number of these cases—incest, sex with a menstruating woman, eating a fellowship offering after three days—is such that they would be difficult to detect and prosecute in a human court. In some cases God explicitly says that it is he who will do the cutting off (Lev. 17:10; 20:3, 6). This fact, combined with the primarily religious nature of the offenses, suggests that "cutting off from their people" likely denotes not banishment, human execution, or excommunication but rather divine punishment resulting in a person's separation from ancestors and/or descendants.

The precise nature of the divine punishment is not spelled out. It might involve premature death before bearing children (so Rashi [1040–1105]). Jacob Milgrom believes that "cutting off from one's people" may also include as an option separation from one's relatives in the afterlife, a view that explains why cases of Sabbath violation and of sacrificing to Molek involve both execution and (divine) cutting off (Exod. 31:14; Lev. 20:2–3).[1] A weakness in Milgrom's view is that evidence for belief in the afterlife is very limited in the Pentateuch. This is why the Sadducees can deny any belief in the resurrection (Acts 23:8). Baruch Levine, perhaps for this reason, has a more general understanding of such verses: "If the community failed to punish the offender or failed to uncover the offense, God would mete out punishment in

His own way and in His own good time."[2] However, in favor of Milgrom's view is the evidence later in the Old Testament for belief in an afterlife. Saul in 1 Samuel 28:8–20 seeks through a medium to consult with the deceased Samuel, and Samuel actually comes back and gives an accurate prophecy of Saul's impending death. Certain texts in the Psalms also suggest an afterlife (Pss. 16:10–11; 49:15; 73:24). The book of Daniel affirms a full-fledged doctrine of the resurrection of the just and the unjust (Dan. 12:2). Jesus argues that when Exodus 3:6 calls God "the God of Abraham, Isaac and Jacob," this implies that these patriarchs are still living in the afterlife since God is the God of the living not the dead (Mark 12:24–27). The warning that offenses against God can lead culprits to be "cut off from their people" by divine punishment is a reminder that no offense, even if hidden from human eyes, can escape the scrutiny of God. Those today who choose to sin defiantly in contempt of God and his demands may also find themselves "cut off from their people."

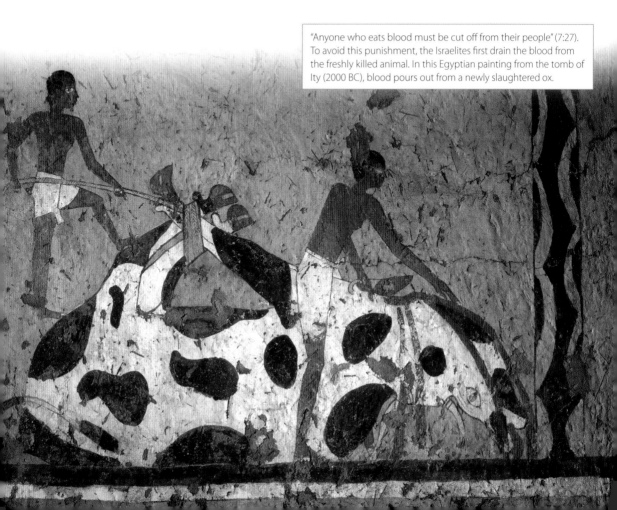

"Anyone who eats blood must be cut off from their people" (7:27). To avoid this punishment, the Israelites first drain the blood from the freshly killed animal. In this Egyptian painting from the tomb of Ity (2000 BC), blood pours out from a newly slaughtered ox.

The Ordination of Aaron and His Sons

Big Idea *Ordination to ministry conveys dignity to a vital profession.*

Understanding the Text

The Text in Context

The description of the various kinds of sacrifices in Leviticus 1–7 assumes the existence of the Aaronic priesthood as anticipated in Exodus 29. But these sacrifices cannot be performed until the priesthood is actually established. Leviticus 8–10 concerns the establishing of the Aaronic priesthood. Leviticus 8 describes the ordination

of the Aaronic priests, as God commanded Moses in Exodus 29 and 40. Leviticus 9 goes on to describe the initiation of formal worship in the tabernacle. Leviticus 10 follows with a cautionary tale for priests: the account of the death of Aaron's sons Nadab and Abihu, which warns priests to conduct their duties properly.

Historical and Cultural Insights

The ceremonial vestments of the high priest bestowed on him "dignity and honor" (Exod. 28:2). (See the image of those vestments in this unit.)

> In the ancient Near East, priests could be identified by special clothing or headdresses. This water basin excavated from the Temple of Assur depicts priests wearing fish-skin cloaks and hoods (704–681 BC).

The Hebrew word for "priest" (*kohen*), and its cognates in Ugaritic, Aramaic, and Phoenician,[1] could also be used of pagan priests (Gen. 41:45; 1 Sam. 5:5; 2 Kings 11:18; Jer. 48:7). In Mesopotamia and Egypt, cultic functionaries (loosely "priests") sometimes wore a headdress or other clothing indicating their status as such. Some also wore animal masks or costumes that symbolized the deity (see image of water basin). In contrast, Yahweh was not to be symbolized by any image.

Interpretive Insights

8:1–36 The ordination of the priests involves washings (v. 6), investiture (vv. 7–9, 13), anointing (vv. 10–12), various sacrifices (vv. 14–29), consecration with oil and blood (v. 30), eating consecrated food (vv. 31–32), and a seven-day waiting period at the entrance to the tent of meeting (vv. 33–36).

8:1–2 *The Lord said . . . "Bring Aaron and his sons."* The first verb in verse 1 probably should be translated as a pluperfect, "The Lord had said." This unit repeats what God has previously said in Exodus 29:1–4, then moves on to the fulfillment of these commands. "Their garments" refers to the priestly vestments. On the oil, bull, rams, and bread, see verses 14–32 below.

8:3 *gather the entire assembly.* The anointing and investiture of priests must be public. The "assembly" is probably a governing body of elders (cf. Lev. 4:13; 9:1–3), since it would have been impossible to gather to a meeting the whole population of six hundred thousand males (per the census of Num. 1–4).

the entrance to the tent of meeting. The rite is conducted at the tabernacle before

Key Themes of Leviticus 8:1–36

- It is good to ordain ministers and dedicate sanctuaries.
- Those going into ministry must maintain purity and dedication to God.

God's presence, where the priests will later perform their duties.

8:6–7 *washed them with water . . . clothed him.* Moses is the only functioning priest, so, using water, he must purify Aaron and his sons ritually for investiture with the holy garments. On the tunic, sash, robe, ephod, waistband, breastpiece, turban, and gold plate, see Exodus 28–29.

8:8 *Urim and Thummim.* These items in the high priest's breastpiece (Exod. 28:30) are used as a means of revelation from God. Thus in a sense revelation is on the high priest's heart. The words may mean "light(s) and perfection(s)" or alternatively "curses and innocence." A common view based on the Greek rendering of 1 Samuel 14:41 (LXX) is that they are sacred lots; the drawing of one indicates a negative answer ("curses"), the drawing of the other a positive answer ("innocence"). However, the terminology of lot casting is never used with these stones in the Hebrew Bible. Cornelis Van Dam argues for an alternative view, that God's revelation took the form of an appearance of a miraculous glowing of "perfect light" from these gems as a sign confirming that the message was from God.[2] That priests might be expected to have a revelatory function finds support in the Arabic cognate for Hebrew *kohen*, "priest," namely *kahin*, which means "soothsayer, seer."[3]

8:9 *the gold plate, the sacred emblem.* The gold plate on the turban marks the priest as "Holy to the Lord" (Exod. 28:36).

8:10–11 *Moses took the anointing oil . . . sprinkled . . . seven times.* Moses's anointing of the tabernacle and of Aaron repeats and fulfills the instructions of Exodus 40:9–13. Anointing oil is a blend of olive oil, myrrh, cinnamon, and cassia (Exod. 30:22–25) used to dedicate objects and persons to God's service. That priests are anointed like kings (e.g., 1 Sam. 10:1; 2 Sam. 2:4) indicates their high status.[4] The number "seven" has an aura of holiness derived from the seventh day of creation (Gen. 2:1–3).

8:13 *put tunics . . . tied sashes . . . fastened caps.* Aaron's sons wear simpler garb than their father, the high priest. They lack the high priest's robe, ephod, waistband, breastpiece, turban, and gold plate.

8:14 *presented the bull for the sin offering.* Alternatively, "sin offering" is "purification offering" (NIVmg) (see comments at Lev. 4). This offering cleanses the altar on behalf of the priests to purify it from any moral or ceremonial pollution that they might bring to it, to consecrate it for their use.

laid their hands on its head. This gesture identifies these soon-to-be priests with the sacrifice on their behalf. The ritual follows the directions of Exodus 29:10–14; Leviticus 4:3–12.

8:18–21 *presented the ram for the burnt offering.* This ritual follows the directions of Exodus 29:15–18. Burnt offerings appeal to God for favor or appeasement and symbolize total dedication to God (see comments at Lev. 1), something especially appropriate for priests.

8:22 *presented the other ram . . . for the ordination.* "Ordination" (*millu'im*) literally means "filling." It is derived from the

expression "to fill the hand" (Num. 3:3), an idiom for "to ordain." God "filled the hand" of the priests by giving them responsibility for carrying out the sacred rites. It may also hint at God's providing for their material needs.[5]

8:23–24 *ear . . . thumb . . . big toe.* Purification/consecration with blood of these body parts, all on the right-hand side, symbolizes that henceforth these priests shall listen, act, and go in accord with God's instructions. The right side is the side of favor and strength (Gen. 48:13–14; Exod. 15:6; Ps. 110:1).

8:26 *bread made without yeast.* Only this kind of bread is fit for the altar (v. 28). See comments at Leviticus 2:11–13.

8:27 *wave offering.* The ordination offering is also a wave offering; better, a "presentation offering" (HCSB). See comments at Leviticus 7:28–35. Wave offerings are fellowship offerings (Lev. 3:1–17; 7:11–21) expressing gratitude to God, in this case for being chosen as priests.

8:29 *Moses also took the breast.* Because Moses is functioning as the priest to ordain other priests, he takes a portion of the offering for his services. In other fellowship offerings, priests receive the right thigh (Lev. 7:32–33).

8:30 *took some of the anointing oil and some of the blood from the altar.* The oil and blood become more sacred by virtue of coming directly from the altar. Anointing with them is thus a potent symbol of the holiness bestowed upon these priests and their vestments.

8:31–35 *the meat . . . the bread . . . seven days.* The ordination ritual involving eating the consecrated food and remaining before God at the entrance of the tent of meeting for seven days fulfills Exodus 29:30, 35–37. On the number "seven" and holiness, see on verse 11 above. This waiting period allows the priests time to reflect on the gravity of the office that they are about to assume. Afterward they can begin serving as priests. The eating of holy food anticipates male priests eating holy offerings in the sanctuary as part of their priestly duties. Failure to obey God exactly can result in death (v. 35), which two sons of Aaron later discover (Lev. 10).

Theological Insights

Priests play an essential role in Mosaic religion. Priests (and other Levites) are guards of the sanctuary, maintaining its holiness and protecting it from encroachment (2 Kings 12:9; Jer. 29:26; Ezek. 40:45; 44:15). They alone can draw near to God in the tabernacle, wear the sacred vestments, enter the tent of meeting, and, with the Levites, attend to its sacred objects, the golden lampstand, the altar of incense, and the table of the bread of the Presence (Exod. 19:22; 27:21; 30:7; 31:10; Lev. 21:10; Jer. 33:18).

Priests serve as mediators between God and the people. They mediate the people's worship before God by conducting various rituals, including burning the fat on God's altar and sprinkling the blood of animal sacrifices before God on behalf of the people (Lev. 1–6). They receive gifts

> Sacred garments are made for Aaron and his sons so that they can serve the Lord as priests. Shown here is a manikin dressed in the clothing of the high priest, which stands inside the replica of the tabernacle at Timna.

dedicated to God from the people (2 Chron. 34:9). They also mediate revelation from God to the people. They keep the official copy of the law and teach it to the people (Deut. 17:18; 31:9–13; 2 Chron. 15:3; Jer. 18:18; Ezek. 7:26; Hag. 2:11; Mal. 2:7). They pronounce God's blessing on the people (Num. 6:23–27; Deut. 21:9). The high priest keeps the sacred Urim and Thummim (Lev. 8:8), used for revelation from God to the people (Num. 27:21; 1 Sam. 14:41; 28:6).

Aaron is a most important spiritual leader in Israel by virtue of his high priesthood. But as great as he and his office are, they are only a foreshadowing of the ultimate great high priest, Jesus Christ. Under the new covenant Christ, rather than the Aaronic priests, is the sole mediator between God and humankind (1 Tim. 2:5). Hebrews 7–10 celebrates the superiority of Christ's priesthood to that of Aaron. Jesus brings a perfection to the priesthood that Aaron could not (Heb. 7:11). Unlike Aaron, who died, Jesus becomes a priest forever (Heb. 7:23–24). The Aaronic priests were never totally morally pure, which is why sacrifices needed to be made on their behalf; Jesus, however, possessed and possesses absolute moral purity (Heb. 7:26–27). Christ also offered a better sacrifice: himself (Heb. 9:23, 26). So as we see the glorification of the Aaronic priesthood in this chapter, we should be reminded also of the glory of the priestly role of Christ.

The New Testament also tells us that the church of God has a priestly role. God's people constitute a holy and royal priesthood who serve God (1 Pet. 2:5, 9; Rev. 1:6; 5:10). As priests, Christians help to mediate God to the world. Therefore, inasmuch as the Aaronic priests were to be morally pure and dedicated to God, so too the church, both as individuals and as a body, should strive to be morally pure and dedicated to God so that Christians will be qualified to carry out their priestly functions.

Teaching the Text

The ordination of priests in the Old Testament and the requirement that they be pure show us what God expects of those who serve him in particular ways and therefore are analogous to the ordination of ministers today.

1. *It is good to ordain ministers and dedicate sanctuaries.* God commands Moses (v. 5) to conduct an ordination ritual appropriate to the dignity and gravity of the priestly office, and to perform it in public before all the assembly (vv. 3–4) so that all Israel can recognize that these men are set apart for God's ministry in the tabernacle. Not only are these new priests anointed with oil, but so too are the tabernacle and its objects (vv. 10–12), since this event not only ordains the new priests but also initiates the use of this structure for divine purposes.

What about today? There are no Aaronic priests or tabernacle under the new covenant, so direct application of this chapter is not appropriate. Nonetheless, from the ordination ceremony here we could well infer that it is appropriate to ordain church leaders and publicly dedicate sanctuaries for divine service with appropriate rites and ceremonies. The New Testament does not spell out a specific ritual for ordination other than that it involves the laying on of hands (Acts 6:6; 13:3; 1 Tim. 4:14; 2 Tim. 1:6). But although churches have considerable freedom in the details, some sort of ordination ceremony for ministers seems appropriate to underscore the dignity and importance of their positions, just as Israel ordained its priests. Likewise, it seems appropriate for Christians to dedicate church buildings, just as the Israelites anointed the tabernacle to dedicate it for its initial service. Although Leviticus 8 does not mandate such services for the church, it is suggestive.

2. *Those going into ministry must maintain purity and dedication to God.* Purity and dedication are symbolized in several elements of the ritual ordination of priests (Lev. 8:6, 12, 14–15, 18–21, 24). Those going into the priesthood need to be undefiled and totally consecrated and dedicated to God. Aaron and his sons are warned of the dreadful consequences of disobedience and are exhorted to follow God's commanded ritual exactly (vv. 35–36).

Purity and dedication should also be hallmarks of God's servants today. Elders or overseers in the New Testament were to show moral purity, fidelity, and dedication (1 Tim. 3:1–7; Titus 1:6–9). Those who serve as God's ministers both in Old Testament times and today must be people of integrity who firmly uphold God's word and live lives of purity consistent with its teaching. What is especially true of church leaders is also true of ordinary Christians, who also, in a sense, function as priests (see "Theological Insights" above). All Christians are called to moral purity (Matt. 5:8; 2 Cor. 6:6; Phil. 1:10; 2:15; 1 Pet. 3:2; 1 John 3:3). All Christians are called to be devoted fully to God and his people, to prayer, to God's word, and to doing good works (Acts 2:42; Rom. 12:1–2, 11; 1 Cor. 7:35; Col. 4:2; Titus 3:8, 14). Thus, the symbolic admonitions to Aaron and his sons to purity and dedication in Leviticus 8 are, by analogy, also admonitions to us.

Illustrating the Text

Though we do not live under the law, the practice of ordination has continued significance.

Cultural Institution: When a husband and wife are married, there is significance beyond the ceremony. In the exchange of vows, sharing of rings, and saying of prayers, much more than one marriage is celebrated. Marriage itself is affirmed. The couple is given a new place in the community. The community is asked to recognize, affirm, and support the new family unit. Many significant things take place, each of them pointing God's people to the God who keeps covenant.

In a similar way, the practice of ordaining leaders in the church is a community-building experience. As vows are made and prayers prayed, leaders are recognized and affirmed. More than that, leadership is affirmed. In calling out and recognizing elders and deacons, God's people remind themselves that the church is itself under the lordship of Jesus Christ.

We are called to dedicate all that we are to the Lord's service.

Hymn: "Take My Life and Let It Be," by Frances Havergal. The purity and dedication to God symbolized by the consecration of the priests' right ear, thumb, and big toe remind us of how we as God's royal priesthood ought to consecrate our whole being to God. The classic hymn "Take My Life and Let It Be," especially in its second and third verses, expresses that kind of sentiment. Our desire should be, like these priests, totally dedicated and consecrated to God, even down to the level of our body parts.

God calls ministers to set an example.

Education: In an article describing how young children learn, educational researcher Jeanne W. Lepper comments,

> In a natural, almost unconscious, process, children follow the examples set by others, modeling both behavior and the accompanying emotional tone. When children see their parents reading regularly, they want to read and be read to. When they see disrespectful or violent behavior, live or on television, they are just as likely to imitate it.[6]

The takeaway: example is highly significant. This is true not only for children but also for anyone who is learning how to do something new. People inevitably observe and imitate what they see done by those who are meant to be followed. This is something that pastors and church leaders, and all Christians, must never forget.

Aaron Begins His Duties

Big Idea *God uses imperfect ministers to lead his people to see and joyfully worship him.*

Understanding the Text

The Text in Context

In this passage Aaron and his sons are directed by God through Moses to commence sacrificing. Leviticus 9 continues the account of the inauguration of worship under the Aaronic priesthood that began in Leviticus 8 and goes through Leviticus 10. In Leviticus 8 the ordination of priests involves a seven-day ceremony. On the eighth day following this (Lev. 9:1), Aaron and his sons begin to function as priests by offering sacrifices. God shows his approval in the sight of the people by manifesting his glory and consuming the offerings. Hence Israel begins its sacrificial worship in the tabernacle under the Aaronic priesthood.

Interpretive Insights

9:1–4 *On the eighth day . . . the Lord will appear to you.* This follows the seven-day ordination ceremony of the previous chapter (Lev. 8:33–35). The "elders of Israel" (v. 1) represent the people both as witnesses and initiators of the sacrificial system. The sacrifices (vv. 2–4) include each of the general sacrifices except the guilt

As Aaron and the priests begin their ministry, they offer sacrifices for themselves and for the people of Israel. All this takes place in front of the tent of meeting, where the altar stands. This replica of the tabernacle at Timna in Israel shows the altar outside the tent of meeting in the courtyard of the tabernacle.

offering that is specifically for sacrilege (see Lev. 5:14–6:1–7). The Hebrew behind "bull calf" (v. 2) is literally "a calf a son [member] of the herd." It refers to a weaned, essentially mature male bovine, older than the yearling calf brought by the people.

9:5–6 *so that the glory of the* LORD *may appear to you.* The glory of the LORD manifests itself in the fire cloud (Exod. 16:10; 40:34–35; Num. 16:42). Its appearance is conditioned on obedience. For the fulfillment of this promise, see verses 23–24.

9:7–14 *sacrifice your sin offering and your burnt offering and make atonement.* Before the priests can make offerings on behalf of the people, they first must make atoning sacrifices for their own sins and impurities. The "sin offering," or alternatively "purification offering" (vv. 7–11), follows the ritual of Leviticus 4, except that it omits putting blood on the altar of incense (Lev. 4:7), perhaps because Aaron had not yet entered the holy place and so could not yet have contaminated it (see v. 23).[1] This sin offering is not for some specific sin on Aaron's part but rather to purge the sanctuary's altar of any inadvertent sin or impurity that priests might have brought into the tabernacle precincts. On the "burnt offering" (vv. 12–14), see Leviticus 1 for the ritual. It supplements the sin offering by being another means of making "atonement" (v. 7; cf. Lev. 1:4; 4:20) and appealing for God's favor. On "atonement," see "Additional Insights" following the unit on Leviticus 4:1–35.

9:15–21 *the offering that was for the people.* The text transitions from offerings for priests (vv. 7–14) to offerings for the people. Two are for atonement to purify the sanctuary from the people's defilements

Key Themes of Leviticus 9:1–24

- Even God's servants are subject to defilement.
- God appears to us in worship.
- God's servants obey his commands.

(sin offering) and to seek God's favor (burnt offering). The others express the people's gratitude to God (grain and fellowship offerings).

9:22 *lifted his hands . . . and blessed them.* The blessing is yet another of the priestly duties initiated here. When a priest blesses someone, he makes an indirect prayer for God to do good to him, saying something like, "May the LORD bless you." See also comments at Numbers 6:22–27 (the Aaronic blessing). Outstretched hands are a gesture of prayer (Exod. 17:11; Pss. 28:2; 141:2). Jesus uses this gesture when blessing his disciples before the ascension (Luke 24:50).

9:24 *Fire . . . from the presence of the* LORD *. . . consumed the burnt offering.* This happens on the first occasion that Aaron is allowed in the tent of meeting. Perhaps Aaron and Moses have gone into the tent to pray that God will fulfill the promise of showing his glory (v. 6). If so, God dramatically complies. By consuming the still-smoldering offerings on the altar, God expresses approval of the sacrifices for Aaron and the people. God similarly shows his approval by visibly consuming sacrifices at Elijah's contest with the prophets of Baal and at the dedication of Solomon's temple (1 Kings 18:38; 2 Chron. 7:1–3).

they shouted for joy and fell facedown. In response to the fire miracle, the people "shouted for joy." The Hebrew word *ranan* indicates singing or shouting for joy, often as an act of emotion-filled worship or praise (Pss. 51:14; 95:1; 145:7). They also "fell facedown." Literally, "they fell on their faces." This is an act of homage by a humble supplicant or admirer, whether of God (Num. 16:22; 20:6) or of kings (2 Sam. 14:4, 22). To fall facedown may mean that the worshipers kneel while looking down rather than that they are fully prostrated.[2] Sometimes people first "fall facedown" and then "worship/prostrate" (*shahah* [Josh. 5:14; Ruth 2:10; Job 1:20]), suggesting that the former precedes the latter. Alternatively, falling facedown and prostrating may be a hendiadys describing two aspects of the same complex body gesture.

Theological Insights

The appearance of the glory of the Lord in the sacred space of the tabernacle is a highly significant theological event. A similar thing happens at the end of the book of Exodus when the tabernacle had first been built. At that time God's glory is manifested when the fire cloud fills the tabernacle (Exod. 40:34–35). This is a visible sign that God approves of the newly constructed holy place and will indeed tabernacle in that place. This happens again when Solomon dedicates the temple. God's glory manifests itself and consumes the burnt offerings and sacrifices on the altar (2 Chron. 7:1–3). This too signifies God's approval of a newly built holy place.

In Leviticus 9:23–24 the manifestation of God's glory and God's public consumption of Aaron's offering on the altar similarly show God's approval. God is a consuming fire (Exod. 24:17). Had God disapproved, he could easily have used his fire cloud to consume the Aaronites and even the assembly around the tabernacle (see Lev. 10:1–2;

Num. 16:35). But God instead shows his approval of Aaron and the sacrificial worship of the newly installed Aaronic priesthood by shooting a flame out from his fiery presence to consume the smoldering sacrifices placed by Aaron on the altar on the occasion of his first act of worship as a priest (Lev. 9:24).

Teaching the Text

At first glance, this passage might seem to have little to say to Christians today. However, it teaches us about how God graciously uses flawed and fallible ministers to lead his people to worship him and see his glory.

1. *Even God's servants are subject to defilement.* Before Aaron can begin serving as high priest for the people, he first must offer atoning sacrifice for himself: "Moses said to Aaron, 'Come to the altar and sacrifice your sin offering and your burnt offering and make atonement for yourself'" (Lev. 9:7a). The reason for this is obvious: Even Aaron as high priest is subject to sin and defilement. To serve in God's holy presence in the tent of meeting requires a purging of Aaron's impurities, or else God's holy wrath might break out against him and/or the people.

There is an irony here in that the animal sacrificed to make atonement for Aaron is a bull calf (Lev. 9:2, 8). The term "calf" (*'egel*) was last used in the story of the golden calf (Exod. 32). In that story Aaron violates the second of the Ten Commandments by making an image of Yahweh in the form of a calf or bull, encouraging the people's idolatry (Exod. 32:2–4). It is almost as if he is making amends for that earlier idolatry by sacrificing the sort of animal used for that idolatrous image. It is a matter of God's grace that this earlier event did not permanently disqualify Aaron from serving in the priesthood. But God is able to redeem sinners and make them fit for his service.

The same is true today. Those who serve as church workers are themselves sinners. To be fit to serve God's people, a person must first experience cleansing from sins through Jesus Christ. That may involve a transformation from bad behavior to good behavior. Aaron exhibited some very bad behavior when he made the golden calf, but God purged his sins and made him qualified to serve as high priest. Similarly, in the church some of God's most effective ministers have been people who once lived in defiance of God's laws but who, like Aaron, came to repent of idolatry and turn to God. A servant of God must receive daily cleansings. Christians, including pastors, are still subject to defilement by sin and need, as Jesus put it, to have their feet washed even if so far as salvation is concerned they are already clean (John 13:8–10).

2. *God appears to us in worship.* When Moses and Aaron initiate worship in the tabernacle, God promises to manifest his glory (Lev. 9:6). The "glory of the LORD" appears as a fire cloud, and that in turn leads the people in awe, joy, and fear to fall on their faces and worship God (Lev. 9:23–24).

One of the purposes of the tabernacle is to allow Israel to take a little bit of the Mount Sinai experience with them as they move toward the promised land. On Mount Sinai they had seen a manifestation of God on top of the mountain (Exod. 19:18–20; 24:16). At the tabernacle they continue to see such manifestations of God. That in turn helps the Israelites revere and worship Yahweh (Lev. 9:24b).

Visible manifestations of God were unusual, however, even for Israel. Most of the time there was no overt, supernatural

Once again God makes his presence known by sending fire to consume the burnt offering at the tabernacle. The Israelites would have recalled the Lord's fiery descent on Mount Sinai recorded in Exodus 19:18. That traditional mountain location is Jebel Musa, shown here.

appearance of God in sacrificial worship, though the people no doubt could sense his presence hidden in the midst of the tent. But even without such miraculous manifestation, God promised to meet them in sacrificial worship and bless them (Exod. 20:24b).

The same is true of Christian worship. Although God can manifest himself dramatically and miraculously in our worship (e.g., Acts 2), it is unusual for him to do so. And yet as we obey God's commands to worship him (cf. Lev. 9:5), we can expect God to be invisibly present in our services (Matt. 18:20). One goal of worship services is to help God's people "see" in their mind's eye what God is like and worship him in awe and joy as Israel does in Leviticus 9.

3. *God's servants obey his commands.* This chapter emphasizes repeatedly doing what Yahweh through Moses "commanded" (Lev. 9:5, 6, 7, 10, 21). God has not only created his people, but he also gives instructions that he expects his people to follow. They are promised that if they obey God's command, they will see God's glory (Lev. 9:6).

Although the specific commands that God gives believers have changed since Old Testament times, obeying God's commands remains obligatory for Christians. Disciples are to be taught to obey everything that Christ has commanded (Matt. 28:20). Peter refers to Christian moral teaching as "the sacred command" and "the command given by our Lord" (2 Pet. 2:21; 3:2). The book of Revelation describes believers as those "who keep God's commands" (Rev. 12:17; 14:12). One expresses one's love of Christ and of God by keeping their commands (John 14:15, 21, 23; 1 John 5:3). God's love is made complete in those who obey

The glory of the Lord appears before the people of Israel because Aaron has followed God's commands. The fellowship offering God requests is an ox and a ram. This fifth-century BC relief fragment shows two priests with their animal sacrifices, one from the flock and one from the herd.

him (1 John 2:5). Like the Old Testament saints, we too must do "as the Lord has commanded."

Illustrating the Text

It is a privilege to approach God.

Quote: Charles Spurgeon. Spurgeon's words about approaching God strike a perfect balance, encouraging us to draw near to the throne of grace with reverent boldness:

> Beloved, the gathering up of all our remarks is just this,—prayer is no trifle. It is an eminent and elevated act. It is a high

and wondrous privilege. Under the old Persian Empire a few of the nobility were permitted at any time to come in unto the king, and this was thought to be the highest privilege possessed by mortals. You and I, the people of God, have a permit, a passport to come before the throne of heaven at any time we will, and we are encouraged to come there with great boldness; but still let us not forget that it is no mean thing to be a courtier in the courts of heaven and earth, to worship him who made us and sustains us in being.[3]

God invites us to experience his presence in worship.

Scenario: There is remarkable power in modern communications. Humans have graduated from using messengers and carrier pigeons, to the telephone, to the computer, to the smartphone. We have found amazing ways to connect with other people across great distances. However, nothing can replace face-to-face fellowship. In ways that cannot be replicated by pixels or sound waves, we experience deep connection through presence. God promises that he is present in real, tangible ways as we worship him.

True love will be proven through willing obedience.

Science: Many parents can still remember when they realized for the first time they would be having a baby. The memory is probably marked by a lot of cheering. Phone calls. Excitement. Trepidation. There are three words that probably do not stick out in the memory: human chorionic gonadotropin (HCG). But these three words describe the hormone that let them know about the pregnancy in the first place. Pregnancy tests depend on the detection of HCG, which appears when a woman is pregnant. Its presence says, "Baby is coming!"

One of the surest signs of true faith is willing obedience. In fact, believers cannot really claim to possess faith or love God if they are not seeking a life of obedience. Obedient actions are like a spiritual hormone indicating that new life is really kicking inside the believer's heart.

The Horrific End of Nadab and Abihu

Big Idea *We must respect the holiness of God.*

Understanding the Text

The Text in Context

In Leviticus 8–9 the priests have been ordained and sacrificial worship has been initiated with "Aaron and his sons [doing] everything the LORD commanded through Moses" (Lev. 8:36; see also 8:9, 13, 17, 21, 36; 9:10, 21). God shows his pleasure by sending fire to consume the offering on the altar while the people shout for joy (Lev. 9:24). Everything has gone beautifully. But in Leviticus 10 the opposite takes place. Nadab and Abihu worship "contrary to [God's] command" (Lev. 10:1), and God shows his displeasure by sending fire to consume Nadab and Abihu

(Lev. 10:2–3), causing Aaron to become silent and the people to mourn (Lev. 10:3, 6). Thus obedience has changed to disobedience; shouts of joy have turned into silence and mourning; the fire of God's pleasure has become the fire of God's wrath.

The death of Aaron's sons leaves the reader stunned. Something has gone wrong. This chapter explains why: they have failed to respect the holiness of God.

Historical and Cultural Background

An essential part of Israel's culture involved distinguishing between the holy and the common, the clean and the unclean (Lev. 10:10) in various realms.

In the animal realm were clean animals that could be sacrificed on an altar, and clean animals (wild game, fish) that could be eaten but not sacrificed on an altar. Animals sacrificed on the altar became

God communicates specific instructions about how incense is to be made, burned, or offered before the Lord. This painting from the tomb of Userhet (1298–1235 BC) shows two priests identified by their leopard-skin robes. One pours out a libation; the other holds a censer for offering incense.

The Clean/Unclean System

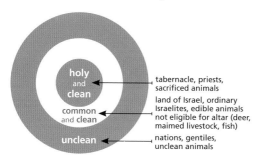

- holy and clean → tabernacle, priests, sacrificed animals
- common and clean → land of Israel, ordinary Israelites, edible animals not eligible for altar (deer, maimed livestock, fish)
- unclean → nations, gentiles, unclean animals

"holy." Other clean animals were merely "common." Unclean animals (Lev. 11) were not to be eaten or sacrificed. In the human realm priests were "holy" and separated from other Israelites for service in the sanctuary. Ordinary Israelites were both "clean" and "common." Non-Israelites, however, were "unclean." There was a similar system of separation of space: the tabernacle (associated with priests) was holy; the land (associated with the Israelites) was clean/common; and the rest of the world associated with gentiles was unclean.

This basic system is illustrated in the figure and in the table below:

	Holy/Clean	Common/Clean	Unclean
Places	Tabernacle/temple	Land of Israel	Nations
Persons	Priests	Ordinary Israelites	Gentiles
Animals	Sacrificed animals	Edible animals	Unclean animals

The details of this system will be expounded in Leviticus 11–15.

Interpretive Insights

10:1 *Nadab and Abihu . . . offered unauthorized fire.* Nadab and Abihu are Aaron's two oldest sons (Exod. 6:23). They have just been ordained with Aaron and their two

- Maintain the holiness of God in worship.
- We are obliged to worship God properly.

brothers as priests (Lev. 8; cf. Exod. 28:1). The "censers" (or "firepans" [NASB]) are used by priests to carry live coals and incense in tabernacle worship (Lev. 16:12; Num. 16:7, 17). "Incense" is not the term for frankincense (see Lev. 2:1), and its composition is uncertain, though it provides a similarly fragrant smoke. The "unauthorized fire" (*'esh zarah*) is literally "strange/different fire" (cf. NET, NLT). The term *zar* is used of non-Israelite foreigners (Exod. 29:33) and things inappropriate or illegitimate (strange gods, a strange woman). Nadab and Abihu's actions violate the command of Exodus 30:9: "Do not offer on this altar any other [strange] incense." What is wrong here? We can only speculate. Do they encroach upon the holy of holies, thus making the fire "unlawful"?[1] Leviticus 16:1–2 alludes to this incident in warning Aaron not to enter the most holy place behind the curtain except on the Day of Atonement, suggesting that this may have been the offense of Aaron's sons. Ordinary priests cannot enter it at all. But if the essential sin is encroachment of sacred space, it is odd that Leviticus 10 emphasizes the fire and does not mention the encroachment. Conceivably, this fire is "foreign" because it is from a pagan-derived ritual.[2] Richard Hess points to ritual texts from thirteenth-century BC Emar, where the installation of a priestess involved fire ("a torch") and intoxicating drink (cf. Lev. 10:9), to suggest that the sin in Leviticus 10, which follows chapters on the ordination of priests (Lev. 8–9), is the use of pagan (foreign) rites.[3] Or, more simply, the coals may be "strange" because they have been taken from a profane source outside the tabernacle rather than the altar.[4]

10:3 *I will be proved holy.* Or "be treated as holy" or "show myself holy." This verse provides the moral to the story. Priests must not take lightly the awesome presence of their holy God. It is thus indispensable for priests to maintain purity and follow ritual procedures exactly as God has directed.

Aaron remained silent. Is Aaron dumbfounded by grief for his sons? Does he fear that any complaint will bring God's wrath on him too? Does he not want to suggest any disagreement with God's holy punishment by publicly grieving? Is he shocked beyond words by the fierceness of God's holiness? Perhaps his silence results from a combination of these causes.

10:4–5 *Mishael and Elzaphan.* These men are Moses and Aaron's paternal first cousins, children of their father Amram's brother Uzziel, of the Korath clan of Levites (Exod. 6:16–22). If a priest has contact with a corpse, he becomes unclean and unfit for his duties. The high priest is forbidden to have any contact with the dead (Lev. 21:10–12). To avoid impurity, Aaron's cousins are called in to remove the bodies of Nadab and Abihu.

10:6 *Do not let your hair become unkempt and do not tear your clothes.* The command to Aaron and his sons Eleazar and Ithamar concerning unkempt hair possibly refers to removal of their head caps ("Do not uncover your heads" [NIVmg]; cf. Lev. 8:13), though the similar expression at Leviticus 13:45 seems more likely to refer to the hair hanging loose. The command against tearing their clothes has a stronger negative in the Hebrew, suggesting that it is never appropriate to tear their sacred vestments. Regular priests are usually allowed

to bury close family members (Lev. 21:1–4), but not on this occasion; here the rule for the high priest applies (Lev. 21:10–12). The threat of God punishing them and the whole community with death ("you will die") for disobedience is clearly not an idle one, given what has just happened.

10:7 *because the LORD's anointing oil is upon you.* Because of their special status as anointed priests (see Lev. 8:30), Eleazar and Ithamar are not to leave the sanctuary for the burial. Why are they not allowed to mourn? Would their mourning for those struck by God have suggested resentment against what God had done?[5] Is it because, unlike later ordinary priests, they have been anointed with oil as their father was (Exod. 40:15) and so must follow the stricter rules of the high priest?[6] Perhaps the best explanation for this command is practical: since only three priests remain alive, they cannot be relieved of their duties.

10:9 *You and your sons are not to drink wine or other fermented drink.* God normally speaks through Moses, but here he addresses Aaron directly. The context of this command suggests that Nadab and Abihu are drunk. "Fermented drink" (*shekar*) primarily refers to beer made from barley or wheat, as does the cognate in Akkadian, though it may include wines made from figs, dates, or pomegranates. Alcoholic beverage is as inappropriate for priests leading worship (Ezek. 44:21) as it is for kings acting as judges (Prov. 31:4–5).

10:10 *distinguish between the holy and the common, between the unclean and the clean.* See "Historical and Cultural Background" above.

10:11 *teach the Israelites.* Besides conducting rituals, priests are supposed to instruct the Israelites about the laws (Mal. 2:7), especially the rules of ritual purity (Ezek. 44:23; Hag. 2:11–13), though at times they fail to teach this properly (Ezek. 22:26).

10:12–15 *eat it . . . Eat them*. Despite what has just happened, Aaron and his remaining sons need to fulfill their duty of eating of the holy offerings: the grain offering that male family members are permitted to eat (Lev. 6:16–18), and the breast of the fellowship offering that has been waved (Lev. 7:28–34), which their daughters may also eat.

10:16–20 *the sin offering . . . had been burned up*. Priests are supposed to eat the sin offering (Lev. 6:24–30), though sin offerings on behalf of the priest or the nation are not eaten (Lev. 4:5–7, 16–18). The priest himself plays a role in atonement: his eating a sin offering helps to "take away [or "bear"] the guilt of the community by making atonement for them" (v. 17) (see "Theological Insights" below). Given what had happened earlier, Moses is furious that the rite has not been followed exactly. Aaron, however, engages in his teaching role as priest (v. 11) on behalf of his sons. He counters that eating the sin offering at this time, given "such things as this have happened to me" (the Nadab and Abihu incident), would not be pleasing to God (v. 19). Those in mourning generally are to avoid holy things (Deut. 26:14). Perhaps Aaron has reasoned either that it is inappropriate to enjoy the priestly privilege of eating meat at this sad time or that it is inappropriate because Nadab and Abihu's sin and nearby carcasses have desecrated this particular sin offering. Either way, in an ironic role reversal, Moses the "lawgiver" is instructed about the law by the high priest, whose interpretation he accepts (v. 20).

Theological Insights

The priest himself plays a role in atonement: his eating the sin offering helps to "take away [or "bear"] the guilt of the community by making atonement for them" (Lev. 10:17). How does this work? Evidently, impurity absorbed by the offering is symbolically transferred to and dissipated in the priest as God's representative when he eats of it. Compare the "scapegoat" on the Day of Atonement (Lev. 16:21). Symbolically the holy priest's eating the sin offering symbolizes holiness swallowing up impurity.[7]

This role of priests in bearing impurity illustrates the work of Christ. Christ is described in Hebrews as our great high priest (Heb. 8:1–4). As the priest in the Old Testament absorbed and dissipated the impurities from the sin offering in his own holy person through partaking of it, so Jesus Christ both as sacrifice and as priest absorbed, bore away, and dissipated our sins in his own person (1 Pet. 2:24).

Teaching the Text

This passage teaches us the need to respect the holiness of God. This affects how we worship him.

1. *Maintain the holiness of God in worship.* A key lesson of this passage is that "among those who approach me I will be proved holy" (Lev. 10:3). It is a great privilege to have God's glorious presence in our midst, and we must take this seriously and not trifle with it. God holds his ministers especially accountable for maintaining proper respect. They must show moral integrity, unlike Nadab and Abihu, who disobey God and who may have been intoxicated while on duty (cf. Lev. 10:9). But laypeople likewise are responsible for properly regarding God's holiness in worship.

Catholic and Orthodox Christians continue their traditions of maintaining a sense of sacred space in worship, whereas services at evangelical Christian churches typically lack a profound sense of the holy. Evangelical places of worship generally lack the feel of holiness that the tabernacle/temple had. Part of this may be justified: the sacred space of the tabernacle/temple has been abolished in Christ, replaced, arguably, by a "sacred heart" attitude. But do we really have such an attitude in our worship? Too often we do not. The lack of holiness in our worship may instead stem from a lack of respect for the holiness of God. Even today the admonition applies: "By those who come near me I will be treated as holy" (Lev. 10:3b NASB).

2. *We are obliged to worship God properly.* Not every expression of worship is acceptable to God. Nadab and Abihu's offering of "unauthorized fire" is clearly unacceptable.

This is not the only time that improper worship leads to God's wrath. The 250 followers of Korah use censers to present incense before God and, like Nadab and Abihu, are struck dead with fire from God (Num. 16:35). The Hebrew word rendered "unauthorized" (Lev. 10:1) is used in the Korah story of an unauthorized person ("stranger" [KJV] or "outsider" [ESV]; not translated by the NIV) who encroached on the role of the Aaronic priesthood (Num. 16:40). Worship led by persons not called by God to minister is improper.

The Bible mentions other acts of improper worship: worshiping images (Exod. 20:3–6) or angels (Rev. 22:8–9), wearing immodest or lewd attire in worship (Exod. 20:26; 1 Tim. 2:9), worshiping in a spirit of anger or in animosity (Matt. 5:23–24; 1 Tim. 2:8), and allowing the money changers in the temple (Matt. 21:12–13). The dishonest and deceptive "worship gift" of Ananias and Sapphira (Acts 5:1–11) has an outcome as severe as the case of Nadab and Abihu.

Some innovations in worship may be contrary to proper worship. Those who conduct Christian worship must make sure that the worship is consistent with the teachings of Scripture and that it respects the holiness of God.

Illustrating the Text

We are called to worship God on his terms.

History: In the 1990s there was a series of conferences called "Reimagining Conferences." These conferences were run by radical-feminist professing Christians who were seeking to combine their feminism with Christian traditions. In order to emphasize their feminist commitment, they worshiped God under the feminine name "Sophia" (Greek for "wisdom") and instead of the bread and wine of the Lord's Supper substituted milk (a product of females) and honey.

These conferences were rightly condemned by many as blatantly heretical. The worship of the goddess Sophia was essentially idolatry. The use of milk and honey in worship had no authorization in Scripture. Worse, replacing the bread and wine authorized by Jesus Christ constituted a repudiation of the centrality of the incarnation and atoning death of Christ. These practices are thus analogous to the case of Nadab and Abihu. Nadab and Abihu offered unauthorized fire to Yahweh, and the leaders of these conferences offered unauthorized milk and honey and worshiped God under an unauthorized label.

We cannot approach God casually.

Sports: Both gardening and hunting provide food for the table, but our approach to each is quite different. In gardening, the main safety concerns involve the use of insect repellents and sunscreen. Hunting, on the other hand, requires training, care, and constant vigilance. One moment of carelessness can lead to injury or even death. Handling a gun is a serious responsibility.

Our God welcomes us into his presence, but he demands that we approach him with reverence and respect. He is our loving Father. He is the King. We live in the new covenant, but still we are approaching the God who demanded great care of Israel.

In setting our standards for worship, we should strive for biblical fidelity much more than cultural acceptability.

Anecdote: Tell the tale of a medieval traveler who made a tasty batch of "nail stew." After a long day of walking, this pilgrim comes into a village, hoping for hospitality.

His first mistake is knocking on the door of the home of a woman who is the town's most notorious miser. When asked if she can spare room and board in exchange for labor, she refuses. Undeterred, the traveler asks if she can spare a pot of water instead. The woman wonders, "What for?" The traveler replies, "To make a pot of my famous nail stew." Interested in seeing the traveler eat nails for supper, the miserly woman acquiesces. Soon after the water comes to a boil, the traveler drops a nail into the pot, stirring frequently and making much of the aroma. "Ah," he sighs, "it's perfect. If only I had a pinch of salt." The woman, wanting to see the traveler eat a salty nail, acquiesces. After a while, the traveler sighs. "Ah, this will be my best stew ever. Perfect. It's missing only a bit of onion." She provides an onion. And so the story goes. Bit by bit, the traveler dupes the woman into providing all the ingredients he needs for a healthy batch of "nail stew." The meal just happens to have every ingredient common to beef stew—with the minor addition of a nail at the bottom.

In this story, the woman is the "villain" who is duped into sharing her ingredients, and it shows how easily seemingly insignificant things can accumulate. As Christians, we need to be careful in worship that we don't let seemingly insignificant concerns take over. If we are not, we can, bit by bit, allow our worship to be transformed from a God-centered event to a human-centered affair. Instead of stealthily crafting a rich soup, we will be steadily tainting God's good recipe. When the primary questions become "How will people enjoy this? What do we prefer? Will this offend anyone?" it's time to be careful.[8]

Unclean Animals

Big Idea *The food laws helped Israel to be a holy people.*

Understanding the Text

The Text in Context

Ritual purity must be maintained not only at the sanctuary but also in the whole camp. The death of Aaron's two sons in Leviticus 10 and the allusion to it in Leviticus 16:1–2 bracket Leviticus 11–15 on Israel's purity system. That system serves to maintain purity among all Israelites. Nadab and Abihu have failed to maintain purity in the sanctuary. Now the Israelites are taught various other ways that they can become impure and thus unfit to approach the sanctuary.

A person can become ceremonially unclean in many ways: eating unclean animals (Lev. 11); having bodily discharges (Lev. 12;

15); having skin diseases or contact with mildew (Lev. 13–14); touching corpses (Lev. 21:1–4,12; Num. 6:9–12; 19:1–20; 31:19–24; Ezek. 44:25–26); touching the carcass of an unclean animal (Lev. 11:24–28) or of a clean animal that has died on its own (Ezek. 44:31).

Leviticus 11 treats impurity through contact with unclean animals. Its purpose concerns respecting the holiness of God (Lev. 11:44–45). Deuteronomy 14:1–21 gives a parallel list of unclean animals.

Historical and Cultural Background

Israel's neighbors did not have food laws like Israel's. Pork (v. 7) was a staple meat among gentiles. It appears, based on archaeological evidence from bones, that pork was periodically eaten illicitly by Israelites.[1]

Interpretive Insights

11:1–47 Leviticus 11 divides creatures into land animals (vv. 2b–8), aquatic animals (vv. 9–12), flying birds and mammals (vv. 13–19), flying insects (vv. 20–23), and swarming creatures (vv. 41–45), with an excursus in the middle (vv. 24–40) on purification procedures for uncleanness due to forbidden land and swarming creatures.

The camel is considered ceremonially unclean and may not be eaten by the Israelites.

The species intended is often difficult to determine precisely. Some may have become extinct. See table 1, which lists animals whose precise identifications are problematic.[2]

11:1 *The Lord said to Moses and Aaron.* Aaron is addressed with Moses because the priests are responsible for teaching Israelites about purity (Lev. 10:10–11).

11:2–8 *animals that live on land.* The chapter concerns edible animals (v. 2b) or those whose carcasses they could touch (v. 8). The text provides a mnemonic device for categorizing land animals: animals that have a divided hoof and chew the cud (cattle, sheep, goats, deer) are clean (v. 3). Chewing the cud refers to regurgitating

Key Themes of Leviticus 11:1–47

- Be holy.
- The food laws associate God with life, not death.

material to chew it a second time. Other land animals are unclean. "Rabbit" should be translated "hare" (ESV, KJV, NRSV). Rabbits are not native to Syro-Palestine. Neither the hyrax nor the hare is a true ruminant, but both appear to be; they move their jaws from side to side as if chewing the cud. On pigs, see "Historical and Cultural Background" above. The camel is eaten in the Arab world.

11:9–12 *creatures living in the water.* Limiting edible sea creatures to those

Table 1. Animals in Leviticus 11 That Are Difficult to Identify

NIV	Alternatives	NIV	Alternatives	NIV	Alternatives
hyrax	rock badger, rock rabbit, and daman are alternative labels for the (Syrian) hyrax. Probably not a coney (NIV 1984)	gull	long-eared owl	heron	cormorant, hawk
rabbit	hare	hawk	vulture, sparrow hawk, kestrel	locust, katydid, cricket, grasshopper	may instead refer to stages of locust development (e.g., migratory locust, sedentary locust) or varieties of locust
eagle	griffon-vulture	little owl	tawny owl	weasel	rat, mole
vulture	bearded vulture, lamb vulture	cormorant	fisher owl, pelican	great lizard	thorn-tailed lizard, dab lizard
black vulture	falcon, bearded vulture	great owl	long-eared owl, screech owl	gecko	ferret, hedgehog
red kite	kite, hawk	white owl	barn owl, little owl, screech owl	monitor lizard	spotted lizard, chameleon
black kite	hawk, falcon	desert owl	scops owl, horned owl	wall lizard	common lizard, gecko, newt, salamander
horned owl	ostrich, eagle owl	osprey	carrion vulture	skink	sand lizard, newt, snail
screech owl	short-eared owl, barn owl, kestrel	stork	heron	chameleon	salamander

Leviticus 11:1–47

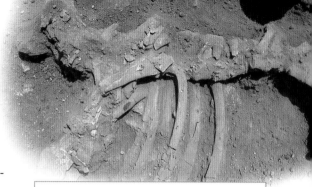

with fins and scales eliminates shell-fish, shrimp, and the like. The word "unclean" (*sheqets*) in verses 10–12 (also vv. 13, 20, 23, 40–41), whose root means "spurn, scorn,"[3] could be rendered stronger: "detestable" (NRSV, ESV), "abhorrent" (NASB), or "abomination" (KJV).

11:13–19 *birds.* The birds here are primarily predatory or carrion-eating. The bat, a mammal, is listed with birds as a flying creature.

11:20–23 *flying insects . . . that walk on all fours.* "Walk on all fours" is an idiom—insects obviously have six legs—in contrast with birds that stand on two legs (vv. 13–19). The "locust" (*'arbeh*) plagued Egypt (Exod. 10:4, 12–19) and Judah (Joel 1:4; 2:25). "Katydid" represents a Hebrew word (*sol'am*) that is cognate with an Aramaic root meaning "to swallow," so it may mean "devourer." It is uncertain whether the Hebrew terms rendered "katydid," "cricket," and "grasshopper" are actually species of the order Orthoptera, or whether they are terms for "locust" (stages of locust development, diverse species of locust). The Septuagint Greek renderings (*attakēs*, "a kind of locust"; *akrida*, diminutive of *akris*, "grasshopper, locust, cricket"; *ophiomachēs*, "a kind of locust")[4] suggest that all might be locusts. John the Baptist ate locusts/grasshoppers (Greek *akris*) in accord with this law (Matt. 3:4; Mark 1:6).

11:24–40 *You will make yourselves unclean by these.* Touching the carcass of an unclean animal (vv. 24, 28, 31) or touching or eating the carcass of a clean animal that has died of itself (v. 39) results in minor uncleanness: such persons are unclean only "till evening" (vv. 24–25, 27–28, 31, 39–40)

The Israelites' dietary laws helped them to remain a separated people, as fellowship with other inhabitants of the land, whose diet included the pig, would have been discouraged. Archaeologists have unearthed many pig bones and skeletons, like the one shown here from Tell es Safi (biblical Gath), which shed light on the dietary habits of those dwelling in the land.

and must "wash their clothes" (vv. 24, 28, 40) and, presumably, themselves. "Wood, cloth, hide or sackcloth" become temporarily unclean until evening (v. 32). Porous clay pots and (clay) ovens absorb impurity, and so when contaminated must be destroyed (vv. 33, 35). A spring or cistern, as well as dry seed (i.e., grain), is immune from impurity (vv. 36–37), but wet grain becomes permeable and so is not immune (v. 38).

11:41–43 *creature that moves along the ground.* Animals that move close to the ground are generally unclean.

11:44–45 *consecrate yourselves and be holy, because I am holy.* Here the purpose of these laws is stated. See "Additional Insights" following the unit on Leviticus 19:1–37.

11:46–47 *the regulations concerning animals . . . the unclean and the clean.* Just as priests have to distinguish between clean and unclean (Lev. 10:10), so Israel has to distinguish between clean and unclean animals.

Theological Insights

One clear purpose of the laws of purity is to separate Israel from the gentiles (see

Lev. 20:25–26). The purity system divides animals into three categories: animals to be sacrificed on an altar (holy), animals that can be eaten but not sacrificed (clean-common), and animals that cannot be eaten or sacrificed (unclean). This separation among animals parallels that of people: priests (holy), ordinary Israelites (clean), and non-Israelites (unclean).

The Clean/Unclean System

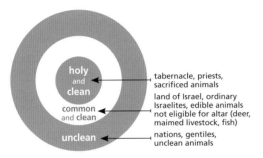

tabernacle, priests, sacrificed animals

land of Israel, ordinary Israelites, edible animals not eligible for altar (deer, maimed livestock, fish)

nations, gentiles, unclean animals

The abolition of the food laws in the New Testament (Mark 7:19; Acts 10:15; 11:9; Rom. 14:14) conveys deep theological symbolism. As the food laws symbolized the separation between Israelites and gentiles, their abolition symbolizes a breaking down of the barrier between Jews and gentiles. Thus God teaches Peter in Acts 10–11 that he now declares the gentiles "clean"; Peter must not think of them as unclean (Acts 11:9).

Under the new covenant God's people are still to be holy, but the lines drawn are no longer ethnic in character. Jews and gentiles alike can now be one in Christ, as is symbolized by the abolition of unclean food laws by Christ.

Teaching the Text

The distinction between clean and unclean animals predates this chapter (see Gen.

7:2). It is also mentioned elsewhere: As a Nazirite, Samson is supposed to avoid eating anything unclean (Judg. 13:4, 7, 14; cf. Num. 6:5–8). Daniel refuses to eat what may have been nonkosher foods (Dan. 1:8). Eating unclean swine and mice is condemned as an act of impiety (Isa. 65:4; 66:17). But what is the significance of these food laws?

1. *Be holy.* All purity laws teach the holiness of God and the need for his people to be set apart. That follows from the previous chapter: Nadab and Abihu die because of lack of holiness (Lev. 10:1–3). The food laws also teach holiness:

> I am the LORD your God; consecrate yourselves and be holy, because I am holy. Do not make yourselves unclean by any creature that moves along the ground. I am the LORD, who brought you up out of Egypt to be your God; *therefore be holy, because I am holy.* (Lev. 11:44–45)

Leviticus later says that the holiness of the food laws symbolizes separation from the nations:

> You must therefore make a distinction between the clean and the unclean animals and between unclean and clean birds. Do not defile yourself by any animal or bird or anything that moves along the ground—those that I have set apart as unclean for you. You are to be holy to me because I, the LORD, am holy, *and I have set you apart from the nations to be my own.* (Lev. 20:25–26)

Israel is to be a separated people. The food laws discourage table fellowship with Canaanites, whose diet includes the pig. These laws are thus a practical means of maintaining Israel as a holy people set apart from gentiles.

Leviticus 11:1–47

It is not inherently immoral to eat pork or lobster. However, these distinctive customs, even if arbitrary and without any inherent moral value, cultivated the virtue of self-control, an indispensable first step in the attainment of true holiness. Moreover, they created in Israel a sense of self-identity as a "separated" people.

Although Christians are no longer required to keep these food laws (see "Theological Insights" above), they still are required to be a holy people. Indeed, the words "Be holy, because I am holy" (Lev. 11:44–45) are quoted in the New Testament and applied to the church (1 Pet. 1:16).

2. *The food laws associate God with life, not death.* The purity system conveys in a symbolic way that Yahweh is the God of life (order) and is separated from that which has to do with death (disorder).[5] Many unclean animals in Leviticus 11 are associated with death as predators/scavengers. Some, like the hyrax, lived in tomb-like caves. In verse 13 the Hebrew word behind "vulture" (*peres*) may mean "breaking," referring to the bird breaking the bones of its prey. It was a creature of death.

Even clean animals, when dead, could convey uncleanness (Lev. 11:39). Death is inherently unclean. The pig, in addition to being a scavenger, was associated with the worship of chthonic or underworld deities or demons among the Hittites, the Egyptians, and the Mesopotamians. This association with death may have contributed to its being categorized as unclean. Some of the animals may have been categorized as unclean because they undermined Israel's life. Rodents (Lev. 11:29) infest and destroy life-giving stockpiles of grain. Vipers (Lev. 11:42) and certain predatory or slimy or creeping animals are dangerous to human life.

The food laws inculcated reverence for animal life by severely limiting the slaughtering of animals: only for food, only certain species, and only following certain procedures.[6] The practical effect of modern Jewish kosher laws has been that many observant Jews become vegetarians.

These laws contributed to Israel's health. The avoidance of carcasses or of eating animals that had died of natural causes plus the required washings to return to a state of cleanness contributed to hygiene. Certain unclean animals can transmit diseases: the pig bears trichinosis (tapeworm), and the hare tularemia; carrion-eating birds harbor disease; and fish without fins and scales attract disease because they are mud burrowers. However, health is at best a secondary reason for these laws. Not every animal was a health hazard: camels, for example, are a delicacy for Arabs to this day, and there is no evidence that they transmit disease to humans. Wild boars rarely have trichinosis, and the proper cooking of pork, in any case, makes its transmission to humans rare. Poisonous plants are not mentioned, which would be strange if health were the main purpose of these laws. Furthermore, some of the clean animals present health hazards: the ruminants of "clean" cud-chewing animals are host for a number of parasitic organisms. From a Christian perspective, it seems inconceivable that Christ would have abolished these laws (Mark 7:19) if health were their primary purpose. Nonetheless, these rules did contribute to Israel's life and health to some extent.

Like Israel, we are to associate God with life. Preoccupation with death moves one away from God. Rather, we are to associate God with the one who said, "I have come that they may have life, and have it to the full" (John 10:10), and who will overcome death itself (1 Cor. 15:24–26).

Illustrating the Text

The Jewish food laws have been a source of unity and disunity throughout history.

History: The food laws united the Jewish people and helped them maintain their identity as a people for centuries without a homeland. But those laws once served to divide them.

The vulture is considered an unclean animal because it is a scavenger, feeding off dead animal carcasses. This griffon vulture is one of the species common to the Middle East.

Isaac Mayer Wise was a leader of liberal Judaism in the nineteenth century. Liberal Judaism emphasizes the moral aspects of Judaism but downplays the importance of ceremonial laws. Wise was trying to unite Jews of various theological stripes around his theological seminary, Hebrew Union College, founded in 1875 in Cincinnati. Although some Jews were leery of Wise's version of Judaism, he succeeded in getting many of them to cooperate together—until he invited them to a dinner.

In 1883 Hebrew Union College put on elaborate ceremonies for its first graduating class. Wise's Plum Street Temple was filled to capacity with graduates, friends, and over one hundred rabbinic and lay leaders representing seventy-six congregations from around the country. Wise seemed close to his goal of uniting a diverse coalition of American Jews.

But after the graduation ceremony, everything Wise had striven for was undone. The graduation banquet was at Cincinnati's posh Highland House. Most of Wise's outside guests kept kosher. They were appalled to see set before them foods forbidden by Mosaic law: clams, crabs, shrimp, and frog's legs. The dinner also mixed meat and dairy products, something not forbidden in the Bible but proscribed by later rabbinic food laws. Deeply offended by this *trefa* ("unclean") banquet, many of the guests walked out. Others left determined to start a different Jewish seminary that would uphold kosher. They ultimately founded the Jewish Theological Seminary of America, dashing Wise's dream of a united Judaism. All of this occurred because of a nonkosher meal.[7]

Leviticus 11:1–47

Uncleanness Due to Childbirth

Big Idea *God provides for people's health, cleansing, and restoration regardless of social standing.*

Understanding the Text

The Text in Context

This chapter continues the laws of purity for all Israel that specify what can cause ceremonial uncleanness (Lev. 11–15). Uncleanness is caused by eating or touching unclean animals (Lev. 11), by childbirth (Lev. 12), by certain skin diseases and molds (Lev. 13–14), and by sexual emissions (Lev. 15). The discussion thus moves from external uncleanness (animals) to uncleanness related to one's own person (bodily emissions and diseases).

The present chapter, on uncleanness due to childbirth, has baffled many readers. The discussion here attempts to make sense of this strange law.

Historical and Cultural Background

There was a similar purification ritual after the birth of a child among the Hurro-Hittites.

As in the Bible, sacrifices were made, and there was a longer purification ritual for the birth of a female child than for a male. Yitzhaq Feder argues that the Hittite ritual was meant to appease the gods, the breaking of the birth apparatus (when the mother's amniotic sac of water breaks) being interpreted as an expression of divine anger.[1] That seems unlikely in the biblical ritual (see below). Unlike the biblical ritual, the Hittite ritual includes no mention of circumcision.

Interpretive Insights

12:1–5 *A woman who becomes pregnant and gives birth . . . will be ceremonially unclean.* Given the length of impurity, childbirth appears

A woman who becomes pregnant and gives birth to a son will be unclean for seven days. If she gives birth to a daughter, she will be unclean for two weeks. Shown here is a figurine of a pregnant woman (sixth to fourth century BC).

second only to "leprosy" (Lev. 13–14) in degree of seriousness. A woman at childbirth becomes unclean for forty days if she has borne a boy (see the sidebar for a discussion of the differing regulations at the birth of a girl). That period begins with seven days of maximum uncleanness as during a woman's "monthly period" (lit., "the days of her menstruation illness") (see Lev. 15:19–24). During this time she must avoid anything sacred, such as the meat from a fellowship offering (Lev. 7:19–20), a Passover lamb (cf. Num. 9:6), or the tithe of the crop dedicated to God (cf. Deut. 26:14). She must also avoid approaching the sanctuary. On the eighth day "the boy" (lit., "the flesh of his foreskin") is to be circumcised. Mary carried this out for the baby Jesus (Luke 2:21). The woman remains unclean to a somewhat lesser degree an additional thirty-three days. If she has borne a girl, the mother's uncleanness doubles to eighty days: two weeks of maximum uncleanness and sixty-six days of lesser uncleanness. The reason for the numbers "seven" and "forty" is not explained in the text, though a case can be made for their being numbers symbolizing wholeness/completeness. Seven days represent the completion of the period of greatest impurity, and forty days represent completion of all impurity.

12:6–7 *she is to bring . . . a burnt offering . . . a sin offering.* The bringing of a lamb for a burnt offering is an appeal to God for favor (see comments at Leviticus 1). A young pigeon or a dove is brought for a "sin offering," which here should be rendered "purification offering" (NIVmg). The rendering "sin offering" is problematic here. See comments on verse 8 and "Theological Insights" below.

Key Themes of Leviticus 12:1–8

- God is associated with life and purity, not death.
- God makes accommodations for the poor.

Uncleanness and Gender

Why was the time of uncleanness double for a woman when she gave birth to a girl? The reason for the distinction between the sexes in postpartum uncleanness is not stated. Some believe that it reflects bigotry against women on the part of the biblical writer. Older commentators sometimes relate this rule to Eve's role in the fall in Genesis 3, even though in the New Testament Adam gets the primary blame for the fall (Rom. 5:14; 1 Cor. 15:22).

It must be admitted that the exact reason for this difference is unclear. However, a good case can be made for a ritual rather than a sexist explanation for this difference. Physician D. I. Macht states that it is scientifically observed that a woman has a somewhat longer average discharge (though not double) after the birth of a girl as compared with the birth of a boy.[a] A longer discharge means greater uncleanness symbolically. Moreover, J. Magonet points out that the withdrawal of maternal hormones at birth causes roughly one in ten female babies to experience vaginal bleeding, a fact that is regularly communicated in modern times to beginning midwives so that they will not be overly concerned.[b] Arguably, that additional vaginal bleeding from the baby girl (whose impurity is reckoned to the mother) also increases the degree of uncleanness.

Conversely, a baby boy, unlike a baby girl, was circumcised on the eighth day (Lev. 12:3). That ritual act may provide a degree of ritual purification and thus reduce the degree of ceremonial uncleanness for the mother who bore the boy. The increase of bleeding and uncleanness when a girl is born and the reduction of uncleanness through the purifying ritual of circumcision might together account for the different periods of uncleanness required after the birth of a girl versus that of a boy. This ritual explanation is preferable to the view that the difference derives from bigotry against girls.

[a] Macht, "Scientific Appreciation."
[b] Magonet, "'But If It Is a Girl.'"

12:8 *if she cannot afford a lamb.* Accommodation is made for a poor woman, who can offer the cheaper pigeon or dove as a burnt offering instead. This is exactly what Mary did: Jesus was circumcised on the eighth day per Leviticus 12:3, and Mary presented the cheaper offerings for her purification per Leviticus 12:7b–8 (Luke 2:21–24).

she will be clean. This statement shows that this particular offering is not for sin but rather for ritual impurity. For sin, the language would be "she will be forgiven" (cf. Lev. 4:20, 26, 31, 35; 5:10).

Theological Insights

Why does childbirth produce impurity and require a purification ("sin") offering? Is it sinful to have a child?

Of course, God is not against people having children. Indeed, God blesses people's being fruitful and multiplying and having a "quiver full" of children (Gen. 1:28; Ps. 127:3–5). Nor is there any sin involved in childbirth. Feder attempts to associate this "sin offering" with sin. Based on the similar Hittite ritual, he suggests that originally the woman performed this rite to express penitence before God for prior offenses.[2] But the language used in Leviticus 12 is of purification from uncleanness ("will be clean" [v. 8]), not forgiveness of sin ("will be forgiven" [cf. Lev. 4:20, 26, 31, 35; 5:10]), because there is no sin to be forgiven. Thus the rendering "sin offering" is unfortunate. Many things make one unclean that involve no sin: giving birth (Lev. 12), burying the dead (Num. 19), having a skin disease (Lev. 13–14), and having an ejaculation or menstruation (Lev. 15). Thus, here "sin offering" is better rendered "purification offering" (NIVmg).

The purity laws do remind us that by nature we are contaminated. We are part of a sin-cursed world. The fact that according to the ritual laws everyone by nature becomes impure from time to time is arguably symbolic of the impurity of sin in the world, the sinful nature of humankind, and the need for people to be cleansed morally. But in this particular case, the mother committed no moral offense (sin) by bearing a child.

Teaching the Text

1. *God is associated with life and purity, not death.* Why does childbirth result in uncleanness? The answer goes back to blood. Childbirth involves the discharge of the bloody placenta from the vagina. Loss of blood speaks symbolically of a movement toward death. But God is associated with wholeness and life, not death. Movement toward death is symbolically a movement away from God. It is primarily for this symbolic reason that a woman was considered unclean after childbirth (Lev. 12:1–8) and needed to offer a purification offering. Forty days is about the period of time necessary for the womb to undergo the process of devolution and destruction followed by regeneration during which it goes from being uninhabitable/dysfunctional (for reproduction) to being once again restored to "wholeness" and full sexual function. With that return to wholeness and life comes a renewed state of cleanness.

It is not only childbirth but also other bodily emissions that symbolically represent movement toward death, which made both men and women unclean. Males' ejaculation (Lev. 15:1–18) and females' vaginal bleeding from menstruation (Lev. 15:19–30) also symbolize loss of life (sperm/blood) and vitality (the fatigue of men after ejaculation) and hence movement toward death in contrast with God and life. As mentioned in the commentary on Leviticus 11, many of the unclean animals were also associated with death. The general rule is the following: that which moves toward death is a movement away from God and is unclean, while that which moves toward life is clean.

A mother obeying the law of Leviticus 12 would actually enhance her life and health. The forty- to eighty-day period of uncleanness allows the woman to rest and recuperate before resuming her normal activities. Since she is unclean, her husband is not to seek to have sex with her (cf. Lev. 18:19). She cannot be asked to prepare a meal, since she would convey her uncleanness to the food by touch and thus make others in the family unclean. Thus uncleanness severely limits a woman's activities at the very time when she most needs reduced activity to recover from her childbearing.

God's people need purity and life. God here promoted health, cleansing, and restoration rather than death, impurity, and alienation. Similarly, we should associate with that which promotes life, health, and purity.

2. *God makes accommodations for the poor.* It is interesting that this law allows an exception for poor women, who would find the sacrifice of a lamb extremely burdensome. This is not the first time that the ceremonial laws have made accommodations for the poor. The law allows the poor to substitute a cheaper animal or even a grain offering for the lamb of a sin offering (Lev. 5:7, 11), and a case was made that the grain offering served as a poor person's burnt offering (see comments at Lev. 2). Accommodation is also made for poor lepers (Lev. 14:21–22, 30–32). In the case of a poor mother, a pigeon or dove can substitute for the more expensive lamb for her burnt offering (Lev. 12:7–8). She still is

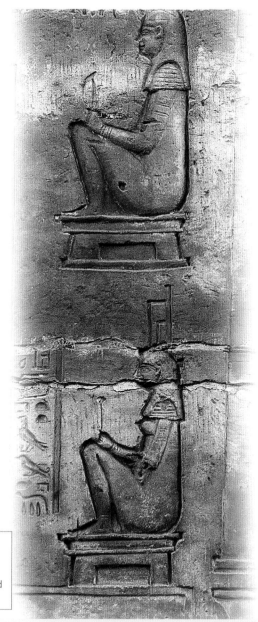

A woman is considered unclean after childbirth because the blood that is part of the birth process is symbolically associated with death. These female figures on a temple relief at Kom Ombo are seated on birthing stools (second to first century BC).

Leviticus 12:1–8

obligated to offer a sacrifice, even if she is poor, but God mercifully lets her offer something more affordable.

Use of this law is evidenced by a New Testament character: Mary the mother of Jesus. Mary undergoes the required purification ritual after the birth of Jesus (Luke 2:22–27). The fact that she offers a bird instead of a lamb indicates that she and Joseph are poor. And yet God accepts the small sacrifice of a poor person as much as the more expensive sacrifice of rich people (cf. Luke 21:1–3).

Both in our churches and in our society, we too are morally obligated to make accommodations for the limitations of poor people. In society there are many programs for the poor sponsored by both the church and the state. In the church sometimes scholarships are provided for youth of poor families to go to church camps or on mission trips along with the more affluent.

And yet a sacrifice that costs nothing is no sacrifice at all. Although allowed to present a lesser sacrifice, a poor woman was to sacrifice something after the birth of her child. So it is in keeping the dignity of the poor and for their spiritual well-being that they contribute something as a sacrifice to God as well, even if their contribution can only be small.

Illustrating the Text

God institutes a culture of life that opposes the culture of death.

Quote: In his encyclical *Evangelium Vitae*, Pope John Paul II contrasted the "culture of death," fostered by a secular age without God-consciousness, and the "culture of life," which is the God-intended overflow of his life in our world. He comments, in particular, on how God most clearly reveals life in the midst of death:

> We find ourselves in the midst of a dramatic conflict between the "culture of death" and the "culture of life." But the glory of the Cross is not overcome by this darkness; rather, it shines forth ever more radiantly and brightly, and is revealed as the centre, meaning and goal of all history and of every human life.
>
> Jesus is nailed to the Cross and is lifted up from the earth. He experiences the moment of his greatest "powerlessness," and his life seems completely delivered to the derision of his adversaries and into the hands of his executioners: he is mocked, jeered at, insulted (cf. Mark 15:24–36). And yet, precisely amid all this, having seen him breathe his last, the Roman centurion exclaims: "Truly this man was the Son of God!" (Mark 15:39). It is thus, at the moment of his greatest weakness, that the Son of God is revealed for who he is: on the Cross his glory is made manifest.[3]

While seemingly unfamiliar and strange, many of the Levitical laws promoted flourishing for women within their cultural context.

Missions: A missionary couple from America was sent to minister among a previously unreached people in a Central American jungle. They were faced with the challenge that all travelers confront: learning to understand a wholly different culture. One aspect of this tribe's social structure was particularly troubling to these missionaries. It seemed that the women of the tribe were not valued. Generally, the wives walked behind the husbands. Often, they carried loads while the husband did not. Initially, the missionary couple thought these practices to be the signs of a repressive culture, but soon they learned better. Very often, couples had to make their way through tall grasses and thick jungle. The husband would walk first, wielding a machete and clearing a path, an impossible task for someone with both hands full. The missionaries came to understand that certain initially off-putting "norms" were there for very good reasons.

Woven through the law is a clear concern for the poor.

Nature: The expression "pecking order," used to describe levels of social organization among humans, has its origins in nature. Farmers observe the ways that chickens relate to one another, beginning from the earliest age. Far from being harmonious animals, young chicks will exploit any weakness that they observe in other chicks, sometimes pecking them to death. It was based on these observations that the phrase "pecking order" came to be used.

In our world, we can establish pecking orders based on income and apparent financial status. But this is not how it should be with God's people. Far from devaluing or demoting the poor, we are called to recognize that all of us can contribute and be meaningfully engaged in God's work.

If a new mother cannot afford a lamb for her burnt offering, the law allows her to offer a dove instead. This fragment from some type of stone vessel dated to the first century AD has simple line drawings of two dead doves (see sketch below of vessel fragment) and the Hebrew word for "offering" on its surface.

Diagnosing "Leprosy"

Big Idea *God is associated with life and wholeness.*

Understanding the Text

The Text in Context

Leviticus 13–14 continues the section of Leviticus on ceremonial uncleanness (Lev. 11–15). Unclean animals (Lev. 11) and uncleanness due to childbirth (Lev. 12) have been discussed, and discussion of uncleanness due to sexual emissions follows (Lev. 15). The present chapter concentrates on the identification of skin conditions (loosely, "leprosy") that render a person unclean as well as the identification of similar-looking molds or mildews on garments that also convey uncleanness. The next chapter will speak of their cleansing.

Historical and Cultural Background

These rules about leprosy became embedded in Israel's culture. The rabbinic laws of the Mishnah devote a whole section, *Nega'im* (lit., "plagues," referring to "leprosy-signs"), to elaborating and attempting to explain these rules for actual practice.[1] Jewish homiletical-exegetical commentaries known as the midrashim (*Leviticus Rabbah* 17.3.1–3) identify ten causes of leprosy: idolatry, promiscuity, murder, profaning God's name, blaspheming God's name, robbing from the community, stealing, arrogance, gossiping, and grudging ("the evil eye").[2] It was widely assumed in rabbinic Judaism that leprosy was a punishment from God. Lepers were socially ostracized from the community and consequently often were impoverished. This backdrop shows how remarkable it was when Jesus touched lepers (Matt. 8:2–3; Mark 1:40–43; Luke 5:12–13). Ordinarily, Israelites were forbidden from physical contact with lepers in order to avoid contracting ceremonial uncleanness.

Interpretive Insights

13:1–59 The most serious case of uncleanness for Israelites is the skin disease described in this chapter (Lev. 13:1–46). Uncleanness is also conveyed by similar-looking molds or mildews in cloth or leather (Lev. 13:47–59). Afflicted items or at least the affected spot must be burned.

13:1–44 *When anyone has . . . a defiling skin disease.* The term "skin disease" translates the Hebrew word *tsara'at.* The traditional rendering "leprosy" (NIVmg) is derived from the early Greek translation, the Septuagint, which renders the Hebrew with *lepra,* which has to do with being "scaly, scabby, rough." A person with this disease remains permanently unclean and must live apart from others outside the camp unless healed (Lev. 13:46). Since the consequences of being identified with "leprosy" are severe, it is essential that the priest follow elaborate procedures to assure a correct diagnosis. The colors of the skin and hair and the depth of the affliction in the flesh had to be right. The affliction must persist or spread rather than fade. Only when all other diagnoses have been eliminated is a person declared unclean due to "leprosy."

But the rendering "leprosy" is misleading. The term "leprosy" in modern times has come to denote Hansen's disease, an illness characterized by skin lesions and destruction of the peripheral nerves, whereas *tsara'at* appears to include ailments other than Hansen's disease and is also used to indicate mildew (or mold) on fabrics and houses (Lev. 13:47–58; 14:34–45). The consensus of biblical scholars (e.g., Wenham, Harrison, Hartley, and Milgrom) is that the term is not limited to modern clinical leprosy (Hansen's disease) but instead encompasses a variety of skin diseases. There has even been some question about whether Hansen's disease existed in Old Testament times.[3]

According to some texts, *tsara'at* is "like snow" (Exod. 4:6; Num. 12:10; 2 Kings 5:27), traditionally understood to designate its color as

Key Themes of Leviticus 13:1–59

- God wants to protect people from disease.
- The law of the "leper" symbolizes that God is separate from sin.

"white." The comparison with snow may instead involve its texture: flakiness. Also *tsara'at* makes one look like a stillborn baby (Num. 12:12), and such babies often have skin that flakes off easily. Jacob Milgrom suggests "scale disease" as the most accurate rendering.

Leviticus's *tsara'at* in some ways resembles psoriasis, eczema, seborrhea, certain mycotic infections, or pityriasis rosea. Dermatologists increasingly reject that *tsara'at* has anything to do with Hansen's disease. For example, Leon Goldman, Richard Moraites, and Karl Kitzmiller presented the symptoms in Leviticus 13 as a "Case for Diagnosis" to a number of dermatologists and leprologists nationwide, not one of whom made a diagnosis of leprosy.[4] Others agree that this is not Hansen's disease.[5] However, dermatologists have had difficulty finding any disease that fits the description of biblical *tsara'at*. Goldman, Moraites, and Kitzmiller state, "This description does not fit any single disorder as we know it today."[6] David Kaplan argues that virtually no skin disease would be diagnosed as *tsara'at* if these criteria were strictly followed. He concludes that what priests in effect did was reassure and exonerate those with skin diseases that they did not have the kind that excluded them from the community and the sanctuary.[7] Dermatologist Marvin Engel has also concluded that no skin disease known to him fits the descriptions in Leviticus 13.[8]

The comparison with a stillborn child (Num. 12:12) does suggest rotting as in Hansen's disease, though Leviticus 13 does not mention rotting as a symptom. Any flaking skin would be associated with death because the flesh desiccates from a corpse. Complicating analysis is the uncertainty about how to translate some of the medical terminology used to describe the disease's colors and lesions, a fact that renders attempts to make an exact diagnosis more difficult. Diseases now unknown cannot be ruled out. Biblical "leprosy" in any case appears to be a rare disease, so the ostracizing would be correspondingly rare.

We must acknowledge that there are ambiguities in translating this passage that we cannot presently resolve, so lessons built on it must take them into consideration.

13:45–46 *Anyone with such a defiling disease.* Those diagnosed with this disease are required to wear torn clothes, leave their hair unkempt, cover the lower part of their face, and cry out, "Unclean!" By their appearance and their words they caution others to keep away, warning any who approach of the danger of contracting ceremonial impurity. They are further required to live in isolation, outside the camp, until they

Along with crying out "Unclean! Unclean!" those with defiling skin diseases also must wear torn clothes, cover their lower face, and keep their hair uncombed. This wooden comb is from Egypt (sixteenth to eleventh century BC).

are cured, to avoid transmitting their uncleanness to others. On whether this is also a quarantining of a contagion, see "Teaching the Text" below. The "hair" is literally "head." It may refer to an uncovered head without a turban (NIVmg; see comments at Lev. 10:6) or, more likely, connote having the hair hanging loose (ESV). "Unkempt" (root *para'*) is used of wild, unrestrained mobs (Exod. 32:25), suggesting hair that is wild—untrimmed and uncombed. The rule to cover "the lower part of the face" is literally to cover the "upper lip" (ESV) or "mustache" (ESVmg).

13:47–59 *any fabric that is spoiled with a defiling mold.* Here "mold" (v. 47) translates the same Hebrew word (*tsara'at*) heretofore rendered as "skin disease" (traditionally, "leprosy"). Hence the ESV renders verse 47 as "leprous disease in a garment." This mold (or mildew) here describes a fungal outbreak in clothes or leather, and in the next chapter it describes similar outbreaks in houses (see Lev. 14:33–57). A garment or leather object in a household that contracts mold or fungus that looks like biblical "leprosy" and that persists or keeps spreading for a week is deemed unclean and must be entirely burned (vv. 47–52). If the spot fails to fade after washing, the whole garment must be burned (vv. 53–55). But if the spot fades and does not break out elsewhere, only the contaminated spot needs to be cut out and burned, whereas the rest of the material, upon washing, is clean (vv. 56–59).

Theological Insights

Was it fair that those with this skin disease were ostracized from God's presence and God's people? In some cases the answer is yes. Most cases of "leprosy" in the Old Testament are said to be a result of sins such as envy/racism (Num. 12:1–16), usurping the role of Aaronic priests (2 Chron. 26:16–21), murder (2 Sam. 3:29), and greed/deception (2 Kings 5:15–27). Where leprosy was sent by God as a result of sin, it was not unfair for God to have people ostracized as part of the punishment. Scripture teaches that God sometimes used skin disease to discipline his people (see Deut. 28:27, 35; Isa. 3:16–17).

But was leprosy only a result of sin? The rabbinic view (see "Historical and Cultural Background" above) assumes that it was. Perhaps this was a supernatural affliction that only God could cause and cure. But the lack of any reference to sin, supplication, or forgiveness in Leviticus 13–14, and its placement between chapters on impurities for childbirth and sexual emissions over which one has no control (Lev. 12; 15), strongly imply that sin was not necessarily involved.[9]

If *tsara'at* was usually a natural disease not directly caused by sin—save that all death and diseases are a result of Adam's sin indirectly (Gen. 3; Rom. 5:12)—was it fair for people under those conditions to be excluded from the sanctuary and God's people? No. Neither was it fair for God to allow Satan to afflict the innocent Job with boils (Job 2:7–8). God can allow unfair illnesses for his own purposes. He used affliction to test Job's faith. Illnesses can lead us to pray and look to God, and so grow spiritually (Job 33:26). God used the innocent suffering of Jesus Christ and his being ostracized from the Father to save the world.

In the purity system God is associated with life and wholeness but is disassociated from death and defect. That which involved death or movement toward death is unclean. "Leprosy" involves movement toward death. This is behind the required separation from the sanctuary and the people of God. Neither should be defiled. Yet this is not the end of the story. As Leviticus 14 indicates, God can heal and restore.

Teaching the Text

Why did God give Israel these laws? The exact rationale is difficult to determine, though hygiene and symbolism may be involved.

1. *God wants to protect people from disease.* A popular explanation for these laws is that they concern health and hygiene. There is an incidental contribution to health in these rules. The exclusion from the camp of those with certain skin diseases in effect quarantined these persons and contributed to public health. Similarly

molds not only can mar fabric and leather but also can harm the health of people (see "Illustrating the Text" below). The burning of garments or leather infected with mold contributed to Israel's public health.

Yet protecting health is at best a secondary explanation for these laws. Hansen's disease, which some identify with biblical leprosy (see above), is not highly contagious.[10] Other diseases that are highly contagious and harmful to public health did not require exclusion from the camp. This would be odd if hygiene were the primary motive. Nonetheless, there is perhaps a component of health and hygiene behind these laws.

2. *The law of the "leper" symbolizes that God is separate from sin.* A better explanation for this law involves symbolism. There is a symbolic relationship between sin and uncleanness, including "leprosy." Many sins in the Pentateuch are described using the language of uncleanness. Rape (Gen. 34:5, 13, 27), adultery (Lev. 18:20; Num. 5:19), bestiality (Lev. 18:23), all the various "sins" that led God to remove the Canaanites (Lev. 18:24–26), remarriage to a first husband after divorce and marriage to a second husband (Deut. 24:4), consultation with mediums (Lev. 19:31), child sacrifice to Molek (Lev. 20:3), and murder (Num. 35:33–34) all employ the language of purity and impurity. The sin (or purification) offering served to cleanse both sin and ceremonial uncleanness (Lev. 5:1–5; 16:16–22). Both sin and uncleanness threatened God's continued presence in the midst of his people.

In Lamentations the language of leprosy is used of those taken into exile who are unclean because of sin (Lam. 4:15; cf. Lev. 13:45). Both "leprosy" and the impurity of sin represent a movement away from life/ God and toward death. David, in his confession of sin in Psalm 51, draws on this symbolic connection between sin and leprosy. As a result of his adultery with Bathsheba and his murder of her husband, Uriah (superscription of Ps. 51), David prays, "Purify me with hyssop, and I shall be clean; wash me, and I shall be whiter than snow" (Ps. 51:7 NASB). This language draws on the ritual of the cleansing of the leper in the next chapter (Lev. 14:5–8). In other words, David feels like a leper morally and spiritually. Just as leprosy separates a person from God and his presence in his sanctuary, so sin makes David feel estranged from God and in need of cleansing and reconciliation.

Leprosy serves as a symbol of the uncleanness of sin. Why other diseases are not similarly symbolic in the Bible I cannot explain. Leprosy separated a person from God's sanctuary and God's people

> If the priest determines that mold is present in any woolen or linen fabric or any leather article, it is burned. Sandals were typically made of leather. These were found in the Cave of the Letters in the Judean Desert (AD 132–35).

during this life. But sin threatens to separate persons from God and his people in this life and the next. Leprosy was a serious thing that required drastic actions. So is sin.

Illustrating the Text

The health risks addressed in the Levitical law are recognized by modern science.

Science: According to the Centers for Disease Control, molds represent a significant health risk to people:

> Mold exposure does not always present a health problem indoors. However some people are sensitive to molds. These people may experience symptoms such as nasal stuffiness, eye irritation, wheezing, or skin irritation when exposed to molds. Some people may have more severe reactions to molds. Severe reactions may occur among workers exposed to large amounts of molds in occupational settings, such as farmers working around moldy hay. Severe reactions may include fever and shortness of breath. Immuno-compromised persons and persons with chronic lung diseases like COPD are at increased risk for opportunistic infections and may develop fungal infections in their lungs.

In 2004 the Institute of Medicine (IOM) found there was sufficient evidence to link indoor exposure to mold with upper respiratory tract symptoms, cough, and wheeze in otherwise healthy people; with asthma symptoms in people with asthma; and with hypersensitivity pneumonitis in individuals susceptible to that immune-mediated condition. The IOM also found limited or suggestive evidence linking indoor mold exposure and respiratory illness in otherwise healthy children.[11]

We thus know today more about the dangers from the kind of molds that Israel was commanded to burn.

Like leprosy, sin leaves us estranged from God, in need of reconciliation.

Informational: The English word "reconcile" comes from two Latin words, *re* + *conciliare*. *Conciliare* means "to make friendly" or "to make friends." *Re* is a frequently used prefix that simply indicates "to be done again." When these words are taken together, "to be reconciled" literally means "to be made friends again." When we have been separated from God by our sin, our hearts long to be made friends with God again.

Purification from "Leprosy"

Big Idea *Impurities that separate people from God can be cleansed.*

Understanding the Text

The Text in Context

Leviticus 13–14 is in a larger unit dealing with ceremonial uncleanness generally (Lev. 11–15). Leviticus 13 identifies the problem of a skin condition (loosely termed "leprosy" in English) and similar-looking molds that produce ceremonial impurity. For persons struck with this condition, the consequences are serious, involving separation from God's sanctuary and separation from the people of God.

Leviticus 14 envisions a possible remedy or resolution to the uncleanness caused by "leprosy." If God graciously cures the person, there is a ritual by which the healing can be recognized and the person returned to the community and sanctuary. It also deals with cleansing from fungal "leprosy" on houses.

Interpretive Insights

14:2 *These are the regulations for any diseased person at the time of their ceremonial cleansing.* The "diseased person" (*m^etsora'*) is the "leprous person" (ESV, NRSV) as described in Leviticus 13 (*m^etsora'* is related to "skin disease, leprosy" [*tsara'at*] at Lev. 13:2). On the meaning of "leprosy," see comments at Leviticus 13.

14:3–32 The "leprous person" can be purified upon healing through the following process. First, a priest must meet the person "outside the camp" (v. 3), which is where the person was sent upon diagnosis (Lev. 13:46), confirm the healing, and conduct a cleansing ritual using two live birds (vv. 3–7). Further cleansing occurs over the course of a week with the washing of the leper's clothes and self and shaving all hair at the beginning of the week and again on the seventh day (vv. 8–9). On the eighth day guilt and sin offerings at the sanctuary finalize the cleansing (vv. 10–20),

The branches of the hyssop plant are used by the priest for sprinkling blood or water in prescribed rituals. This plant is most likely *Origanum syriacum*, shown here.

at which point the person is fully "clean" (v. 20). Allowance is made for the poor to offer less expensive birds rather than lambs for the sin and burnt offerings at the sanctuary, though otherwise the ritual is the same (vv. 21–32).

14:4–7 *live clean birds . . . fresh water . . . cedar wood . . . scarlet yarn . . . hyssop . . . blood.* All of these are symbols of life. A "live animal" (*hayyah*) can refer to "free-living, untamed animals as distinct from domesticated animals."[1] There is no point in specifying a bird as "living," since animals are assumed alive unless otherwise stated, so here it probably means "wild" (so ESVmg), though they are called "live" to underscore the life symbolism. "Fresh water" is literally "living water." "Living water" refers to water from a spring or river that seems alive and is sweet as opposed to stagnant or bitter water. Blood is a common symbol of life in Leviticus (see comments at Lev. 17:11). Cedar and scarlet yarn are reddish in color and further symbols of blood and life. All these references to symbols of life indicate that the leprous person has moved away from death and back toward life and the holy. Hyssop is a shrub-like plant whose hairy leaves and branches are used for sprinkling water or blood in priestly cleansing rituals (Exod. 12:22; Num. 19:6, 18). The sprinkling is done seven times, the number "seven" being a symbol of holiness, indicating movement toward the holy. Despite the command to "pronounce them clean," cleansed lepers at this stage are not fully clean. Further purification rituals follow. The bird is to be released "in the open fields," literally, "over the face of the field." The bird dipped in the water mixed with blood symbolically

Key Themes of Leviticus 14:1–57

- God can heal and purify the "leper."
- God can purify from sin.

absorbs impurity and is set free to represent impurity's removal. A similar symbolic removal of impurity occurs with the "scapegoat" (Lev. 16).

14:8–9 *wash . . . shave . . . bathe.* The next step for the leper is the washing of clothing, shaving of hair, and bathing of the body. All body hair, including eyebrows, must be shaved, symbolizing removal of any hair possibly contaminated by leprosy's impurity. Then, for a second time, the leper is pronounced clean, but, as before, not completely so. After the initial washings and shaving, the person is sufficiently clean to enter the camp, but not sufficiently clean to enter his or her own tent, for which a seven-day waiting period is required. "Seven" is again a symbol of holiness. Time also serves to dissipate ceremonial impurity. Over the week the leper becomes gradually less impure, moving in the direction of holiness. When on the seventh day the procedure is repeated again, the leper is for the third time declared "clean," this time sufficiently clean to offer sacrifice at the entrance of the sanctuary (see vv. 10–20). Since the sacred is more susceptible to defilement than the common, one more degree of cleansing ritual is required before the person can approach the sanctuary.[2]

14:10–20 *guilt offering . . . sin offering.* Two male lambs and one ewe lamb are offered (v. 10). The ewe is for the sin offering (cf. Lev. 4:32; 5:6), the males for the guilt and burnt offerings (Lev. 1:3; 5:18). The guilt offering (v. 12) deals with possible defilement of God's holy things while the person has been unclean (cf. Lev. 5:14–19). This offering involves putting blood and oil on various parts of the body (vv. 14–18). Compare a similar ritual for the ordination of priests (Lev. 8:23–24). This ritual symbolizes that the leper has been totally cleansed by the blood—head to toe—so as to be restored to the community and totally consecrated by the oil to live before God, whether by hearing/obeying (ear), doing (hand), or going (foot). The sin offering purifies the sanctuary from the person's defilements. Burnt and grain offerings appeal to God for favor and appeasement and complete the cleansing ritual (v. 20a). Note that every means available for making atonement is used. Having been declared clean for the fourth time, the leper is now actually fully clean (v. 20b).

14:21–32 *If . . . they are poor and cannot afford these.* Anyone who had been a leper for very long probably is destitute. Thus allowance is made for the poor to offer birds instead of lambs for their sin and burnt offerings (vv. 21–32). Similar accommodations for the poor have been made earlier (see Lev. 5:7; 12:8).

14:34 *a spreading mold in a house in that land.* The regulations about mold in houses given in verses 35–53 would apply only when the Israelites had entered the promised land ("When you enter the land of Canaan" [v. 34]), where they could build permanent houses. Living in tents in the desert gave no occasion to apply this law. "Mold" (v. 34) is the same Hebrew word as for "leprosy" in Leviticus 13–14 (tsara'at), though here the term refers to mold or mildew resembling "leprosy" in humans that could occur on garments or leather (Lev. 13:47–59) as well as the walls of a house.

14:35 *go and tell the priest.* Mold-leprosy must be diagnosed by a priest just as leprosy is in Leviticus 13. In both cases specific colors, penetration into the surface, and spreading are required to verify the identification (vv. 37–39; cf. Lev. 13:3–4, 7, 20–23). In both cases a suspected occurrence is confirmed or not confirmed after seven days (vv. 38–39; cf. Lev. 13:5–6, 21).

14:40 *unclean place outside the town.* With mold-leprosy, the plaster is scraped off and replaced, and the affected part of the wall is removed. Disposal in an "unclean place" contrasts with the handling of refuse from the sin and burnt offerings, which must be disposed of at a "clean place" (Lev. 4:12; 6:11; Num. 19:9). Mold never has any holiness, and putting it in an impure place will help people avoid contact with it and thus deter further spreading of it.

14:43 *If the defiling mold reappears.* Persistent cases, upon confirmation by a priest, require destruction of the whole house.

14:46 *unclean till evening.* Those who have come into contact with this mold-leprosy are unclean until evening and must undergo a simple purification rite of washing their clothes. Presumably, this also applied to the priest who has entered the house to make the diagnosis.

14:49 *two birds and some cedar wood, scarlet yarn and hyssop.* A house "cured" of mold-leprosy undergoes a ritual similar to that of a cured human "leper." On the symbolism of each element, see on verses 4–7 above. Since houses, unlike people, do not approach the sanctuary or have a relationship with God, there is no need for sacrifices at the sanctuary for the house (contrast Lev. 14:10–32).[3]

14:54–57 *These are the regulations for defiling skin diseases and defiling molds.* The last verses summarize the whole of Leviticus 13–14.

Theological Insights

This chapter hints at the power of God to heal even the most intractable diseases. It also directs human gratitude for divine grace.

In the New Testament, Jesus requires lepers whom he has cleansed to show themselves to the priest in accord with this Mosaic law (Matt. 8:4; Luke 17:14). In the Lukan episode (Luke 17:11–19), all ten lepers should be grateful to Jesus for cleansing them, but only one returns to thank him. In Leviticus 14 the purpose of having cleansed lepers come to the sanctuary and offer a sacrifice is, in part, to give them an opportunity to show gratitude to God for the miracle of healing and cleansing from disease. It allows them to testify to the power of God to heal. God is gracious, and in his mercy and grace he often heals our diseases (Ps. 103:3) or helps us to remove defilements from our homes (Lev. 14:33–57). For such things he deserves our thanks.

Teaching the Text

1. *God can heal and purify the "leper."* "Leprosy" in a person represents a movement toward decay and death. A house with mold-leprosy is in decay and likewise represents movement toward death. But the good news is that it is possible for God to cure leprosy and move things back toward wholeness and life. This is God's ultimate plan for his people.

If God heals a leper, the person can undergo a purification ritual over eight days to return to full cleanness (Lev. 14:1–32). That ritual involves two birds and various symbols of life: blood, cedar wood, crimson yarn, hyssop, and "living" water. By analogy with the Day of Atonement sacrifice and the "scapegoat" (Lev. 16), slaughter of the one bird represents purification by

The regulations regarding spreading mold in houses are for homes built as the Israelites settle in the promised land. The pillared style shown here from Tel Hazor was typical of Israelite home construction design.

blood atonement, and the release of the live bird symbolizes removal of uncleanness and restoration of the leper to a condition of life and wholeness. Subsequent rituals provide further cleansing. Thus, the leper has moved away from death and back toward life. A similar ritual accompanies a house's restoration from mold-uncleanness to a state of purity. All of this represents a movement back toward wholeness and life. The use of blood and other symbols of life represents symbolically a victory of life over death.[4] The ritual connects this victory with God and in effect expresses gratitude to God.

What do we do when God heals and cleanses us? The leper was to approach God with sacrifices that acknowledged God's role in the healing. Do we acknowledge God's grace and mercy when he heals us? Do we thank God and give witness to others of his power to heal?

2. *God can purify from sin.* As noted in the last chapter, ceremonial impurity serves as an analogy for ethical impurity. David, in Psalm 51, sees this connection. He compares his own alienation from God as a murderer and adulterer to the leper's exclusion from the community and the sanctuary. He cries out like a leper wanting to be cleansed and restored, "Purify me with hyssop, and I shall be clean; wash me, and I shall be whiter than snow" (Ps. 51:7 [alluding to Lev. 14:4–6]). But the good news is that just as God can cure and restore a person who has the most hideous of diseases, such as leprosy, so also God can cleanse and restore a person guilty of the most heinous sins, even murder.

What is necessary for the cleansing of the leper or a house infected with mold-leprosy is blood atonement. A bird must be sacrificed, and its blood must be applied to the person or thing that has been unclean so that it can be declared clean again. This restoration of cleanness is made more vivid by the live bird that takes the uncleanness

In Leviticus 14, the priest goes outside the camp to those who have been healed of their skin disease and conducts the rituals that will bring cleansing and officially pronounce them clean. During Jesus's ministry, after healing the leper, Jesus tells him to show himself to the priest (see, e.g., Mark 1:43–44). During the Second Temple period, part of the complicated ritual necessary to become ceremonially clean took place at the temple complex. In the northwest corner of the court of the women was the chamber of the lepers, where those who had been cured would come to bathe on the eighth day of their purification process and wait for their guilt, sin, and burnt offerings to be sacrificed by the priests. That location is labeled on this photo of the Second Temple model.

chamber of the lepers

court of the women

upon itself and symbolically flies away with it to the open field (Lev. 14:7, 53).

God still cleanses on the basis of blood atonement. Just as the live bird bore away the leper's uncleanness, so Jesus "bore [away] our sins on his body on the cross" (1 Pet. 2:24). Without the atoning work of Christ, we would be unfit to be part of God's community or in God's holy presence. And yet through the blood of Jesus Christ we can enter where God is: "Let us draw near to God with a sincere heart and with the full assurance that faith brings, having our hearts sprinkled to cleanse us from a guilty conscience and having our bodies washed with pure water" (Heb. 10:22).

Illustrating the Text

Jesus's blood brings healing.

Literature: *Ben-Hur: A Tale of the Christ*, by Lew Wallace. Wallace's renowned novel (1880) and its classic film version (1959) center on the story of Judah ben Hur, who lived at the time of Jesus Christ. Judah is forced to be a galley slave. While he is away, Judah's mother, Miriam, and his sister, Tirzah, are thrown into prison, where tragically they contract leprosy. The two are later expelled from the city to the Valley of Lepers. Wallace imagines the pitiful condition of Miriam and Tirzah:

> SHE AND TIRZAH WERE—LEPERS!
> Possibly the reader does not know all the word means. Let him be told it with reference to the Law of that time, only a little modified in this.
> "These four are accounted as dead—the blind, the leper, the poor, and the childless." Thus the Talmud.

That is, to be a leper was to be treated as dead—to be excluded from the city as a corpse; to be spoken to by the best beloved and most loving only at a distance; to dwell with none but lepers; to be utterly unprivileged; to be denied the rites of the Temple and the synagogue; to go about in rent garments and with covered mouth, except when crying, "Unclean, unclean!" to find home in the wilderness or in abandoned tombs; to become a materialized specter of Hinnom and Gehenna; to be at all times less a living offence to others than a breathing torment to self; afraid to die, yet without hope except in death.[5]

When Judah wins release from slavery and returns to find his mother and sister, they do not want Judah to know of their pitiful condition. So Judah is told the lie that they have died in prison. Yet this story has a happy ending. Judah eventually discovers that his mother and sister are alive but suffering from leprosy, and Tirzah is dying. He desperately tries to bring them for healing to Jesus, whom Judah has encountered earlier in the story. Jesus, however, is arrested before they can do so. In the film version, Judah and his sister and mother watch as Jesus is crucified and dies. But at his death a cleansing rainstorm begins. The water mixes with Jesus's precious blood, just as the blood of the bird slaughtered for the leper in Leviticus 14 is mixed with living water. When the water rinses them, Judah's mother and sister are healed of leprosy. Then, the viewer's eyes are directed to the sight of Christ's healing blood running out in wider and wider streams as the water spreads. Thus, the film brings out the typology between the slaughtered bird for the cleansing of the leper in Leviticus 14 and the healing, life-giving blood of Christ.

Sexual Discharges

Big Idea *God wants to promote life, virtue, and an awareness of his holiness among his people.*

Understanding the Text

The Text in Context

Leviticus 15 completes the section in Leviticus on uncleanness (Lev. 11–15). The preceding chapters have treated unclean animals (Lev. 11), uncleanness due to childbirth (Lev. 12), and uncleanness due to "leprosy" (Lev. 13–14). The present chapter (Lev. 15) treats uncleanness due to sexual emissions. All this prepares the way for Leviticus 16 on the Day of Atonement, a chapter that will provide a remedy for the problem of the holy God dwelling in the midst of Israel's uncleanness.

Leviticus 15 follows a chiastic structure:[1]

A Introduction (vv. 1–2a)
   B Abnormal male discharges (vv. 2b–15)
      C Normal male discharges (vv. 16–17)
         D Marital intercourse (v. 18)
      C′ Normal female discharges (vv. 19–24)
   B′ Abnormal female discharges (vv. 25–30)
A′ Motive and summary (vv. 31–33)

Historical and Cultural Background

Israel's neighbors also had some concerns about sexual impurity, though far less prominently than in Israel. In Egypt a Ptolemaic inscription states that people who became impure through sexual intercourse, birth, miscarriage, and so forth had to pay dues before being admitted to a temple. In Mesopotamia a text says, "If a man touches a *musukkatu* woman [menstruant] who is passing by, for six days he will not [be pure]."[2]

Times of sexual abstinence due to menstruation (Lev. 15:19–24) were more limited for ancient Israel than they would be today. Menstruation was then, and in poor countries still is, less frequent because women were more often pregnant, breastfed longer (until the child was about age three), and had a poorer diet, which delays the onset of menses to age fourteen and brings on menopause around age thirty-five to forty. A woman today typically menstruates from age twelve to fifty.

The required bathing for various forms of uncleanness (e.g., Lev. 15:5–8, 10–11, 13, 16, 18, 21–22, 27) led to the wide use of the public ritual bath (*mikveh*) for undergoing purification. A number of these baths dating to biblical times have been found by archaeologists around Jerusalem. This is probably why David is able to see Bathsheba "bathing" from the palace roof in 2 Samuel 11:2: she is undergoing ritual purification in a public bath. After adultery with David, Bathsheba again "purified herself from her uncleanness" (2 Sam. 11:4 [cf. Lev. 15:18]). If the bath mentioned in 2 Samuel 11:2 is for menstrual uncleanness, it shows that David, not Uriah, impregnates Bathsheba. Ironically, Bathsheba is strictly following the rules of ritual purity just before getting involved in moral impurity.

Interpretive Insights

15:1 *The LORD said to Moses and Aaron.* Typically, Moses as revelator is addressed in laws, but Aaron is addressed here as well because he would be involved in making rulings about uncleanness.

15:2 *When any man has an unusual bodily discharge.* The "unusual bodily discharge" is literally "a flow/discharge from his flesh" (cf. KJV). "Flesh" is euphemistic for the genitals (also v. 19). Disorders of the male genitals such as gonorrhea or urinary infections appear to be in mind.

is unclean. Unlike the leper (Lev. 13), unclean persons in this chapter are not banished from the community, but certain precautions are necessary. This man's uncleanness transfers by touch to objects such as beds and chairs (v. 4) or by his spitting up on someone (v. 8). Those touching the man or touching anything that he has touched contract minor uncleanness: they become unclean until evening and must bathe and launder their clothes (vv. 5–7, 9–11).

15:12 *A clay pot . . . must be broken . . . wooden article . . . rinsed with water.* Clay pots are porous and absorb impurity, making them impossible to wash clean. Wood is less porous than clay, so its ritual impurity can be removed by washing.

Key Themes of Leviticus 15:1–33

- The rules on discharges promote health and self-control.
- The rules on discharges disassociate God from sexuality.
- The rules on discharges associate God with life.
- The rules on discharges show human impurity before the holy God.

15:13 *When a man is cleansed from his discharge.* The man with an unusual genital flow, like the leper, remains unclean until cured.

seven days . . . wash his clothes . . . bathe himself. Once the flow ceases, the man undergoes ritual purification. That purification involves time (seven days) and washings of body and garments to dissipate impurity. Lepers also undergo ritual purification over the course of a week (Lev. 14:8–9), though their ritual is more rigorous, involving a second bathing and shaving all hair. Leprosy is a more serious kind of impurity, bringing the person closer to death, which explains why its ritual is more elaborate.

15:14–15 *eighth day . . . two doves or . . . pigeons . . . sin offering . . . burnt offering.* The ritual is completed on the eighth day with an offering of two inexpensive birds, reflecting the relatively minor nature of this impurity. The sin (or purification) offering purges the sanctuary of this man's ritual uncleanness (see comments at Lev. 4), and the burnt offering appeals to God for favor or appeasement or both (see comments at Lev. 1).

15:16–18 *When a man has an emission of semen.* The idiom *shikbat zaraʿ* means "a lying down [or "outpouring"] of seed." This could indicate semen deposited while one is "lying down," related to the verb *shakab* ("lie down") as a euphemism for sexual intercourse (see vv. 18, 24, 33), or it could refer to what is laid down, as in "a layer of dew" (Exod. 16:13–14). Perhaps it is a double entendre. A man who ejaculates apart from ordinary marital intercourse (e.g., after a nocturnal emission or masturbation) has minor uncleanness; he must bathe and launder affected clothes, and both he and his clothes are unclean until evening. Ordinary marital sexual intercourse also makes both the husband and the wife unclean; they must bathe ritually and remain unclean until evening. "Emission of semen" in verse 18 is again literally "a lying down of seed."

15:19–23 *When a woman has her regular flow of blood.* The "impurity" of her monthly period renders the Hebrew word *niddah*, which refers to a woman's menstrual bleeding (see "Historical and Cultural Background" above). It may be derived from a root meaning to "cast, hurl, throw," referring first to a woman's monthly "casting off, expulsion" of blood (menses). By association, this word came to refer to impurities and abominations (sins) in general (2 Chron. 29:5; Ezra 9:11; Ezek. 36:17; Zech. 13:1). Women undergoing menstruation are unclean seven days (v. 19). Anyone touching her or her bed contracts minor uncleanness.

15:24 *If a man has sexual relations with her.* Literally, it is euphemistic: "lies with her." He will be unclean for seven days. Sex with a menstruating woman conveys

a more serious form of ceremonial uncleanness than simply touching her. On this law's rationale, see "Teaching the Text" below.

15:25 *When a woman has a discharge of blood . . . other than her monthly period or . . . beyond her period.* Abnormally long vaginal bleeding is a medical condition known as hypermenorrhea. It can be caused by infections, hormonal problems, or tumors. A woman with this condition remains unclean indefinitely until cured. The Gospels record a woman who had been in this condition for twelve years (Matt. 9:20; Mark 5:25; Luke 8:43).

15:28 *When she is cleansed from her discharge.* "When" here translates the Hebrew word *'im*, whereas *kiy* is used in the parallel case with a man (v. 13 above). *Kiy* typically introduces new legal cases, whereas *'im* introduces subordinate cases. This suggests that this regulation builds off the earlier case with the man.[3]

15:28–29 *count off seven days . . . On the eighth day.* The ritual for purification of a woman healed of an abnormal genital discharge is identical with that of the man with an abnormal discharge (vv. 13–15), except that it does not specify that the woman must bathe in spring water and launder her clothes. However, this case, being subordinate to the earlier one (see comments above), assumes those details from verse 13.

15:31–33 *You must keep the Israelites separate from things that make them unclean.* The NIV rendering is problematic because most instances of uncleanness from discharges are a result of biology over which people have no control. Rather, the text means that Moses and Aaron are to "separate the children of Israel from their uncleanness" (NKJV); that is, they are to purge their uncleanness by ritual and sacrifice as described in this chapter. Failure to follow these regulations could defile God's dwelling, the tabernacle, in Israel's midst and could incite God to inflict sudden death on offenders (v. 31b), whether it be a man or a woman with genital discharges or one who has contracted impurity by sexual contact (vv. 32–33).

Theological Insights

Sexuality is regarded by the Bible as a blessing from God to be enjoyed (see the Song of Songs). Yet the Bible also teaches that sexuality has been marred by human sin and impurity. The ideal sexuality of the garden of Eden changes with the fall of Adam and Eve. In place of openness comes shame (Gen. 3:7). Joy and love are replaced by pain, lust, and domination (Gen. 3:16). Sex can be wonderful, beautiful, and wholesome, but it can also be an expression of denigration, sadism, and perversion. Those who engage in wanton sex, such as prostitution, are stigmatized as outcasts by these laws. Note that it is not just women who are regarded as unclean; men are equally unclean by their sexual emissions. The sinful nature of humankind finds expression in the sexuality of both genders. This warping of sexuality after the fall is perhaps one reason why the Pentateuch makes sexual expressions, both male and female, a source of ceremonial uncleanness. Being aware of this problem allows corrective action in the direction of wholesomeness.

The Gospels (Matt. 9:20–22; Mark 5:25–34; Luke 8:43–48) record a case of a woman with an abnormal discharge as described in Leviticus 15:25–30. For twelve years she has spent her money on doctors, futilely looking for a cure. She is thus stuck in a state of perpetual uncleanness, excluded from the temple. Even her family members would have been reluctant to touch her. But then she seeks out Jesus. She cannot approach Jesus openly, for to do so would reveal her indiscretion. Perhaps she touches the edge of Jesus's garment to avoid defiling the holy man by touch. But when she does touch it, Jesus is not defiled. Instead, she is healed. Her healing comes not by touching the cloak, as she superstitiously supposes, but by her faith. Her faith has "saved" her (Matt. 9:22 NASBmg). This incident shows the superiority of Christ over impurity.

Teaching the Text

Although laws about discharges no longer apply under the new covenant, they do teach some abiding lessons. They teach about health and self-control. They disassociate God from sexuality while associating him with life. And they illustrate the problem of human impurity before the holy God.

1. *The rules on discharges promote health and self-control.* Limiting contact with people with symptoms of gonorrhea, urinary infections, or vaginal infections (Lev. 15:2–3, 25) and encouraging people to bathe their bodies and launder their clothes frequently had positive health side effects. Jewish women who refrain from intercourse during menstruation have a significantly lower incidence of cervical cancer.[4]

These rules also promoted the virtue of self-control. Sexuality is a powerful human drive and very dangerous if not controlled.

The news media are constantly abuzz with cases where the sexuality of famous people has gone awry. The rules of ceremonial uncleanness prohibited sex during times of a woman's menstrual uncleanness. Ritually, men had to restrain from sex at this time to avoid uncleanness, which in turn helped Israelite men learn sexual self-control. Men do not have absolute ownership of their wives' sexuality; there are times when they must refrain from touching their wives sexually. For those women who experience discomfort with sex during their periods, this would be a welcome relief from unwanted advances.

2. *The rules on discharges disassociate God from sexuality.* Although the practice of "sacred prostitution" probably was not as widespread in biblical times as commentators once thought,[5] there is limited evidence for its existence in Greece and the ancient Near East. There was a brothel related to Aphrodite worship at Corinth. According to Herodotus, the Babylonians' "worst custom was this: Every woman must go once in her life to the temple and have sex with a stranger, whoever pays her first" (*Hist.* 1.199). In sharp contrast, the laws of Leviticus 15 associate sexual expressions with ceremonial uncleanness. An Israelite had to refrain from sex before entering the presence of God (Exod. 19:15; 20:26; 28:42–43). Even ordinary sexual intercourse between a husband and wife produced uncleanness (Lev. 15:18). Any notion of sacred prostitution would have been inconceivable for a devout Israelite. Thus, unlike certain ancient pagan cults, Israel totally separated sex from worship.

3. *The rules on discharges associate God with life.* Menstrual bleeding represents loss of life (blood) and movement toward death. A man's discharge of semen also represents loss of life (seed), loss of vitality (the fatigue of men after ejaculation), and movement toward death. Intercourse with a menstruating woman produces the wrong symbolism: it mixes potentially life-giving semen with a womb undergoing destruction and (temporary) death. Mixing symbols of life with symbols of death is incongruous. Abnormal discharges are even more symbolic of death, for they are not infrequently associated with disease and illness. All these discharges arguably symbolize loss of life and movement toward death. In contrast, God is to be associated with life. Movement toward death is symbolically a movement away from God.

4. *The rules on discharges show human impurity before the holy God.* These rules of purity arguably teach the concept of the holiness of God and the sinfulness of humans. Every Israelite by biology inevitably contracts uncleanness. It is unavoidable. Women cannot help but have periods, and men will intentionally or involuntarily ejaculate from time to time. But these mundane aspects of everyday life have no place in the vicinity of God's holy dwelling. They make people unclean. Uncleanness is simply part of everyday life for Israelites.

Symbolically, the lesson may be this: just as Israelites by nature are frequently unclean ceremonially, so people are by nature unclean morally and spiritually. In other words, the unclean system hints at the doctrine of the sinful nature of human beings.[6]

Sexual discharge is used metaphorically for moral uncleanness. Isaiah states that all his people have become "like one who is unclean" and that their righteous deeds are like "filthy rags," literally like "a menstrual cloth" (Isa. 64:6). Just as a spent tampon or sanitary napkin seems disgusting—at least to me as a man—so are human sin and hypocrisy to God.

But the analogy can be pressed further. When people become unclean, they are excluded from the tabernacle, the dwelling place of God. If they ignore these purity rules, they are subject to sudden death (Lev. 15:31). Returning to a state of cleanness so that one can approach God requires cleansing and atonement. Similarly, human sin separates people from God. Sin unaddressed leads to (eternal) death (John 3:16; Rom. 6:23; 2 Pet. 3:9), but the atoning work of Christ brings (eternal) life (2 Tim. 1:10; 1 John 5:13).

Illustrating the Text

In a culture obsessed with gratification, self-control is an often-ignored virtue.

Human Experience: Using a bag of marshmallows as a prop to illustrate, talk about the famous "Stanford marshmallow experiment" conducted in the 1960s and 1970s by psychologist Walter Mischel. Studying the power of delayed gratification in character formation, Mischel had testers present a child with one marshmallow and the promise of a second if the child would refrain from eating the first one until the tester returned. The tester would exit the room and come back to see whether the child had resisted the temptation to eat or had given in. The study tracked the lives of the children and found that those willing to practice delayed gratification were more successful in life.

Our culture is filled with powerful marketing and easy credit. The results can damage much more than our bank account. Our capacity for self-control, a fruit of the

In Mark 5:25–34 when a woman suffering from a bleeding disorder touches the cloak of Jesus, she is miraculously healed rather than making Jesus unclean. That encounter is depicted on this fourteenth-century AD mosaic.

Spirit and a virtue of the Christian life, will impact all our life before God.

If you have the capacity to show video, you might want to provide a taped example of this kind of test with children. Go online and search for videos with the words "marshmallow test." The video will seem light and humorous, but you can contrast this experiment with the serious consequences of giving in to temptation and not exercising self-control.

Like the Israelites, Christians should be aware of their constant need for cleansing and forgiveness.

Object Lesson: One of the most basic laws of vehicle maintenance is to change the oil regularly. Display used motor oil and new motor oil in two different glass jars. Talk about the reality that as the oil moves through the engine, lubricating the moving parts and reducing friction points, the oil picks up dirt. If left unchanged, the oil that originally protected the engine will actually promote breakdown.

It is impossible for us to live in this world of sin without being impacted by it. We are "saved sinners." Though we have forgiveness in Christ, we must seek forgiveness every day. Doing so is routine maintenance.

Leviticus 15:1–33

The Day of Atonement

Preparation

Big Idea *The high priest must be purified before conducting the Day of Atonement sacrifices.*

Understanding the Text

The Text in Context

Leviticus 16, on the Day of Atonement, is a transitional chapter, giving a general remedy for the problem of uncleanness described in Leviticus 11–15. It also prepares the way for the laws of holiness that follow (Lev. 17–27).

Leviticus 16 is arguably the most important chapter in Leviticus, introducing the Day of Atonement, the highest and most sacred day in the Israelite calendar. Its importance is seen in the elaborate preparation ritual that Aaron undergoes to be qualified to conduct the main sacrifice later. Leviticus 16:1–14 sets out that preparation ritual.

Interpretive Insights

16:1 *the death of the two sons of Aaron.* This refers to Nadab and Abihu, who had died after offering "unauthorized fire" before Yahweh (Lev. 10:1–5). This incident warns all priests that they must respect the sanctity of God and his dwelling place, the tabernacle.

16:2 *he is not to come whenever he chooses . . . or else he will die.* "Whenever he chooses" is literally "at any time" in Hebrew (cf. NRSV). "Or else he will die" is better rendered "lest he die" (NKJV) because the wording in Hebrew does not necessarily mean that he will die, but means only that he is liable to sudden death.

the Most Holy Place behind the curtain. More simply, it is "the holy place" (KJV, NASB, HCSB) or "the sanctuary" (NRSV). "Behind the curtain" can also be "inside the veil" (ESV, NASB). The curtain separates the holy place in the tent from the most holy place, where the ark of the covenant stands (see Exod. 26:31–34). Ordinary priests can never go "behind the curtain." Only the high priest can, once a year on the Day of Atonement as described in this chapter.

For I will appear in the cloud. During the exodus the glory of God had manifested itself in a "cloud" that would descend into the holy of holies wherever Israel camped. At that point access to the tent of meeting had been limited (Exod. 13:21; 40:34–38). The purpose of the curtain is to block any unveiled, close-up view of the presence of

God in the most holy place. Although it is permissible to view God's pillar of cloud from a distance, to do so unveiled and up close can be fatal.

the atonement cover. The "atonement cover" (*kapporet*) is the lid of the ark of the covenant. It is 2.5 by 1.5 cubits (roughly 3.75 feet by 2.25 feet) and made of pure gold. The rest of the ark is a wooden box covered with gold, and at the ends of the cover are two angelic cherubim made of hammered gold. See Exodus 25:17–22. The ark is kept in the most holy place and is the most sacred object in Israelite religion. "Atonement cover" has traditionally been rendered "mercy seat" (KJV, NRSV, ESV), though the Hebrew is only indirectly related to the concept of mercy and does not in itself convey the sense of seat. The

kapporet is understood to be the throne upon which God sits surrounded by cherubim as his royal entourage (1 Sam. 4:4; cf. Exod. 37:7; Pss. 80:1; 99:1; Isa. 37:16). That is one basis for the traditional rendering "mercy seat." Alternatively, the ark may be regarded as the earthly footstool for God's heavenly throne.

Some translators render *kapporet* simply "cover" or "lid" (NRSVmg) based on the meaning of *kapporet*'s root *kapar*, which in the Qal stem allegedly means "to cover." However, this rendering is problematic. First, *kapar* probably means not "to cover" but instead "to daub with pitch" (*koper*) (Gen. 6:14). Second, the doubling of the middle consonant "*p*" in *kipporet* indicates that the noun is related to *kipper*, the Piel form of the root, not the Qal meaning. In the Piel *kapar* means specifically "to make atonement" rather than "to cover, apply pitch" (see "Additional Insights" following the unit on Lev. 4:1–35). Third, the prominent place of the *kapporet* in the Day of Atonement (*yom kippurim*) ritual in Leviticus 16 makes the association of the word *kipporet* with the concept of atonement (*kippurim*) highly probable. Theologically, the *kipporet* is the place where the blood of the atoning sacrifice is applied on the Day of Atonement (Lev. 16:13–16). It is there where atonement

Access to the most holy place is limited to the high priest and only once a year. In the tabernacle, a curtain separates the most holy place from the holy place and hides the ark of the covenant from view. Shown here is the curtain protecting the holy of holies in the tabernacle model at Timna, Israel.

takes place. The Septuagint rendering of *kapporet* is *hilastērion*, rendered "mercy seat" (ESV, KJV) or "atonement cover" (NIV) in Hebrews 9:5, but the cognate verb *hilaskomi* (Heb. 2:17) is translated "make atonement" (NIV) or "make propitiation" (ESV), and the cognate noun *hilasmos* is rendered "atoning sacrifice" (NIV) or "propitiation" (ESV) (1 John 2:2; 4:10). These cognates suggest that the Septuagint considers the *hilastērion/kapporet* to be more than a mere "cover." Romans 3:25 may see a typology that relates the atonement cover (*hilastērion*) with Christ (cf. NIVmg): the blood of the atoning sacrifice that purges sin before God's throne is that of Christ on the cross.

16:3–10 These verses give a synopsis of the sacrifices: a bull, two rams, two goats.

16:3 *bull for a sin offering.* Sin offerings for a high priest are always bulls (Lev. 4:3). This provides purification for Aaron and his fellow priests (see v. 6), purging the sanctuary of Aaron's personal sins and impurities. Only after the sin offering has been offered is the high priest permitted to enter the most holy place on the Day of Atonement. Verses 11–14 below describe this offering in more detail.

ram for a burnt offering. This offering takes place at Leviticus 16:24. It seeks further appeasement for any priestly offenses and seeks God's goodwill for the Day of Atonement goat offering.

16:4 *the sacred linen tunic, with linen undergarments next to his body . . . linen sash . . . linen turban.* See Exodus 28:4, 39; Leviticus 8:7–9. These are "sacred" or "holy" because they are set apart for use in the sanctuary. "Linen" (*bad*) is a kind of simple white cloth made from relatively

rough flax.[1] Angels in the presence of God also are described as wearing linen (Ezek. 9:2–3, 11; 10:2; Dan. 10:5). "Body" is literally "flesh" and may also indicate "genitals." No mention is made of the robe, the ephod, or the breastplate (Lev. 8:7–8) until the end of the ritual (v. 24), when Aaron puts on his "regular garments." Aaron evidently had been attired like an ordinary priest (cf. Exod. 28:27–29), perhaps as an act of humility before God. This would also save the fancier vestments from getting stained with blood.

bathe himself with water. Ordinarily priests must wash their hands and feet before officiating (Exod. 30:19), but the high priest on this day needs more thorough purification and must bathe his whole body. He will do the same at the end of the ritual (Lev. 16:26).

16:5 *From the Israelite community.* These animals are offered on behalf of the Israelites.

two male goats for a sin offering and a ram for a burnt offering. The two goats constitute one sin offering even though one is slaughtered (Lev. 16:15–19) while the other is not (Lev. 16:20–22). The ram is probably the burnt offering for Aaron at the conclusion of the Day of Atonement ceremonies in Leviticus 16:24.

16:6 *offer the bull . . . to make atonement for him and his household.* This fulfills verse 3 above. "Household" means especially Aaron's priestly sons Eleazar and Ithamar.

16:8 *cast lots for the two goats.* To be chosen by lot indicates being chosen by God (cf. Prov. 16:33). One lot is cast for Yahweh, and this goat is slaughtered as a sin offering. The other lot is cast for the "scapegoat" (*'aza'zel*), and this goat is sent into the desert (v. 10).

16:10 *sending it into the wilderness as a scapegoat.* See "Additional Insights" following this unit.

16:12–13 *fragrant incense . . . will conceal the atonement cover.* Expanding on the directions in verse 6 regarding the bull as a burnt offering for Aaron, the text adds the need to offer burning incense along with the bull, which would both mask the putrid smell and conceal the atonement cover to prevent Aaron from a potentially fatal direct viewing of God's presence ("so that [Aaron] will not die" [v. 13]). Looking directly at the visible presence of God that shows itself above the atonement cover (see v. 2) unveiled and close up could be fatal, for no one can see God and live (Exod. 33:20). So when the high priest enters the holy of holies, God's appearance must be masked with the smoke of incense.

tablets of the covenant law. "Covenant law" (*'edut*) is also rendered "testimony" (KJV, NIV 1984), "pact" (NJPS), or "covenant" (NRSV). It is an abbreviated way to refer to the "ark of the *'edut*" (Exod. 16:34; 27:31; 30:6, 36; Num. 17:4, 10). Traditionally, *'edut* is derived from the Hebrew word *'ud* ("to bear witness") and taken to mean "testimony." It could instead be derived from the Akkadian word *adu* ("a type of formal agreement"), thereby making "ark of the *'edut* [= pact]" equivalent to "the ark of the covenant." Either way, *'edut* is related to the tablets of the covenant law that have been placed in the ark (Exod. 31:18; 40:20), referring either to the law's witness or to those tablets as a symbol of the pact between God and Israel.

16:14 *sprinkle some of it . . . seven times before the atonement cover.* The number "seven" is ubiquitous in the rituals, conveying an aura of holiness derived from the seventh day of creation (Gen. 2:3). On the "atonement cover," see verse 2. The tabernacle is purged by blood of priestly defilement as far as the high priest goes, to the throne of God itself.

Theological Insights

Rituals are a way of underscoring the importance of a society's or group's values. In the United States, saying the Pledge of Allegiance as the school day begins is a way of inculcating patriotism and loyalty to one's country, as are flag-raising ceremonies and fireworks on the Fourth of July. Graduation ceremonies underscore the value placed on academic achievement. The common ritual of serving turkey at Thanksgiving is a way of highlighting the importance of family gatherings.

The Bible's rituals similarly serve to underscore important core values. The more elaborate the ritual, the more important the values. The complexity of these rituals shows the theological importance of the Day of Atonement sacrifice. The Israelites did not just perform the sacrifice. There were many ritual preliminaries before they could even start.

The rituals of Leviticus 16 show the value of respecting the holiness of God and the need for atoning sacrifice before attempting to approach him. God's holiness is incompatible with human impurity. God wanted to be there in Israel's midst, but he could not compromise his holiness, so he provided rituals to be performed so that his presence could be maintained despite Israel's impurities (Lev. 16:16). God's presence in the holy of holies is important because it was the means through which his relationship with Israel functioned at that time.

The church too has its rituals to underscore its important values. Baptism shows the importance of initiation and entrance into God's church through the death and resurrection of Jesus Christ (Rom. 6:4; Col. 2:12). The Lord's Supper underscores the importance of the death of Christ—a death foreshadowed by the Day of Atonement ritual—and his awaited return (1 Cor. 11:23–26). It is called the "Lord's table" (1 Cor. 10:21), a reminder of his invisible presence serving as host. The rites of baptism and the Lord's Supper together underscore the importance of Christ's incarnation, death, resurrection, presence, and second coming, each cherished, foundational doctrines of the faith. There, as here, elaborate ritual underscores that something is theologically important.

Teaching the Text

Leviticus 16:1–14 shows the imperfection of human priests in contrast with the holiness of God.

1. *Human priests are imperfect.* The central focus of Leviticus 16 is the ritual involving the two goats, but Aaron has much to do first. He must bathe (v. 4b) and put on simple linen clothing (v. 4a), symbolically humbling himself, and he must offer a bull as a sin offering to purify the sanctuary of his personal impurities (vv. 6–14). Only then can he conduct the main ritual, involving the goats. All human beings, including the holy high priest, are subject to contamination by sin and impurity. He cannot offer purification rites for Israel until he does so for himself.

The writer of Hebrews uses this ritual to show the superiority of Christ's priesthood. Aaron, as a sinner, must sacrifice for himself before entering the most holy place, but Christ, being "unblemished," does not (Heb. 7:26–27; 9:7, 14).

There is an analogy with the Lord's Supper. Aaron had to deal with his own sin and impurity before the Day of Atonement sacrifice. Similarly, each one of us is to conduct self-examination before partaking of the Lord's Supper (1 Cor. 11:28). All of us need cleansing before approaching the presence of God.

2. *God is holy.* The text begins by recalling how Aaron's two sons died because they approached God improperly (v. 2; see

Aaron is required to bathe himself in preparation to enter the most holy place. Washing to make one ritually pure was an important practice in the ancient world. Here is a bath with interior seat that was found near the cultic site at Tel Dan, Israel. It may have been used for ritual immersion and purification (ninth century BC).

Lev. 10). It is dangerous for sinful priests to be so close to the holy God. That is why ritual purification is essential—the bull for a purification offering, and a ram for a burnt offering—to purge the sanctuary of a priest's defilements to make it safe for the priest to enter. No one can see God and live (Exod. 33:20). It is necessary to fill the room with incense to obscure the priest's vision of the Holy One enthroned above the ark (vv. 12–13) so that Aaron can safely apply the blood with his finger to the front of the atonement cover and dash blood seven times in front of it (v. 14) without dying. All this in turn expresses proper recognition of God's holiness so that God will find Aaron's sacrifices for the people of Israel acceptable and be pleased to continue to dwell among them.

It is easy for us today to forget the severe holiness of God. Modern worship is often too casual, viewing God as little more than the worshiper's "buddy." Rarely does one come away with a sense of the fearsome holiness of God in worship. But this is unfortunate. God is still a holy God. The preparation ritual of Aaron before performing the Day of Atonement sacrifice is a reminder of that which we ought not forget.

Illustrating the Text

The Aaronic priesthood pointed to Jesus Christ, the only perfect priest.

Scenario: There are a few basic elements of a groundbreaking ceremony: shiny shovels, hard hats, and soft ground. Those closest to the project, often including honored guests, the architect, and the contractor, push shovels down into the ground and turn over the earth. Everyone present understands that this act is symbolic of what will actually take place. For a building to be completed, the foundation must be dug out and poured. A frame must be erected. Electricity and plumbing must be installed. And much more must be done. The groundbreaking is just the first step, pointing toward a process that will be completed only with a ribbon-cutting ceremony, when the building is actually completed and ready for use.

God gave Israel the priesthood and sacrificial system to prepare it. The system provided a picture of the perfect priest who would come. The work that these priests did pointed to the perfect work that only Jesus could do.

We must prepare our hearts for fellowship with the holy God.

Economics: One of the critical steps in purchasing a home is determining that the title is in order. This is why it is essential to secure the services of a title company. Such an agency works to ensure that the person who purchases a home will, in fact, be the legal owner. The company guarantees the purchaser that the property really belongs to him or her—free from outstanding claims or unpaid debt. In the end, it is important for the person who purchases the property to know that all other parties have renounced any claim on the property.

Part of preparing our hearts for worship involves renouncing. We must renounce our interest in the things of the world. We must settle our debts with the Lord, ensuring that we are not still tied to things of this world.

The Scapegoat

A major crux of interpretation in Leviticus 16 is the meaning of the term *'aza'zel* (see NIVmg) in verses 8, 10, 26. This term has traditionally been taken to mean "scapegoat" (NIV, KJV, NASB, NKJV). Others take it as a proper name of a god/demon called "Azazel" (ESV, HCSB, CEV, NASBmg, NRSV). A third option is that this is a proper name of a geographic place, "wilderness of Azazel" (NLT).

The traditional view, translating the term as "scapegoat," understands *'aza'zel* as a compound word: *'az* ("goat") plus *'azal* ("to go"). Hence, the word would mean "the goat that goes [away], escapes" or the "(e)scape-goat." This fits the fact that the goat designated as the *'aza'zel* is the one driven into the desert, and it thus escapes being slaughtered. This view was taken by the Greek Septuagint (second century BC),

which renders it "one for *apopompaios*," meaning "one for sending-away." This view is reflected also in the Latin Vulgate, Tyndale's English translation (1530), and the KJV. Against this view, compound words in Hebrew (unlike Greek) are very rare except in proper names.

A second view takes *'aza'zel* as the proper name. "Azazel" is often taken as a name of a god or demon, perhaps a goat-demon (*'az* means "goat" in Hebrew) or some other demon unrelated to goats. This view is supported by the parallel formulation "one lot for the Lord [Yahweh] and the other lot for Azazel" (v. 8 ESV). That parallel formulation suggests that both *Yahweh* and *'aza'zel* are proper names. A version of this interpretation is found in the intertestamental pseudepigraphical work *1 Enoch* (e.g., 8:1; 9:16; 10:10),

On the Day of Atonement two male goats without defect are chosen from the herds to be the sin offering for the community of Israel. One is sacrificed, the other sent into the wilderness. The Israelites had brought all their flocks and herds from Egypt, and their goats probably looked similar to the ones on this Assyrian relief. See the three male goats at the front in the top and bottom rows. This herd was taken by the Assyrians after one of their conquests (744–727 BC).

which dates from roughly the second century BC, in which Azazel (spelled "Azael") appears as the leader of the fallen angels. The church theologian Origen, writing in the third century AD, took "Azazel" as a title for the devil (*Against Celsus* 6), a view compatible with his "ransom to the devil" theory of Christ's atonement. Against the goat-demon view, however, is the fact that no demon by the name Azazel is known from the ancient Near East outside the Bible, and no Bronze Age goat idols have been discovered archaeologically in ancient Syro-Palestine. Leviticus itself explicitly prohibits making sacrifice to goat-demons (Lev. 17:7) or gods other than Yahweh (Lev. 19:4). While Leviticus 17:7 suggests that belief in goat-demons existed, the idea of sending a Day of Atonement goat to one of them seems at odds with the prohibition against sacrificing to them.

A third view takes *'aza'zel* as a proper name not for a living demon but rather for an impersonal geographic location ("wilderness of Azazel" [NLT]) or some other feature in the wilderness. This could be combined with the demon interpretation: even if Azazel has no real existence, sending the goat to Azazel may mean sending it to the place associated with Azazel, namely, the hideous desert. Parallel language supports this line of interpretation: sending the goat away into the wilderness (Lev. 16:21) arguably means the same thing as sending it away to Azazel (Lev. 16:26). Compare 1 Corinthians 5:5, where turning a church member "over to Satan" means putting that person out of the church and into the world dominated by Satan. Unfortunately, *'aza'zel* as a geographic term is not attested elsewhere in the Bible or in other ancient writings.

In sum, a good case can be made for all three views. For me, the demon view, while not impossible, seems the most problematic of the three since the sending of a goat to any demon seems inconsistent with biblical teaching. "Azazel" as a geographic term is a plausible view, but it lacks any corroborating evidence. Perhaps the traditional view that *'aza'zel* is the one designated for "sending away" (LXX) as the "(e)scape-goat" remains the most likely among the three views unless and until new evidence from the ancient world comes to light supporting "Azazel" as a geographic term or as a term for a god/demon.

The Day of Atonement

The Two Goats

Big Idea *God forgives and forgets the sins of his people.*

Understanding the Text

The Text in Context

The Day of Atonement was and is the most solemn and sacred day in Judaism. It provides a general remedy for the problem of uncleanness described in Leviticus 11–15, as well as the problem of sin generally. This chapter is arguably the most important in the book of Leviticus.

The Day of Atonement ritual shows the incompatibility of the holy God dwelling with the people's impurities. The regular sin offering deals with this to a considerable degree. But for God to continue to dwell in their midst, an annual purging of all the people's sins and impurities from the sanctuary is required, one that covers offenses missed by the regular sacrifices.

Historical and Cultural Background

On the Day of Atonement, Israelites were supposed to fast (Lev. 16:29, 31). Fasting was often done ad hoc in conjunction with prayers for mercy (e.g., 2 Sam. 12:16–23; 1 Kings 21:27–29; Jon. 3:5–10). Jews in Elephantine, Egypt, prayed and fasted in 408 BC in conjunction with a request to build a temple of Ya'u (Yahweh) in Yeb, Egypt.[1] The Balaam Inscription from Tell Deir Alla, a pagan (perhaps Ammonite) text found in modern Jordan and dating to the Iron Age, describes Balaam as fasting and crying because of what the gods had decreed.[2] Fasting prepared worshipers to meet with God (Exod. 24:28; 1 Kings 19:8; Daniel 9:3; 10:3). However, the Day of Atonement is the only fast day prescribed in the Pentateuch. By denying themselves food, worshipers expressed humility. Four other fast days are mentioned in Zechariah (Zech. 8:19; 7:3, 5). According to talmudic tradition, these corresponded to stages in Babylon's capture of Jerusalem. By New Testament times, some Pharisees fasted twice a week (Luke 18:12).

Interpretive Insights

16:15 *the goat for the sin offering of the people.* See Leviticus 16:5. "Purification offering" (NIVmg) is better here than "sin offering." See comments at Leviticus 4:3.

as he did with the bull's blood. See Leviticus 16:12.

on the atonement cover. The sanctuary was cleansed as deeply as any Israelite, the high priest included, could go: the ark's "atonement cover" (see comments at Lev. 16:2). On "atonement," see "Additional Insights" following the unit on Leviticus 4:1–35.

16:16 *the Most Holy Place.* This is better rendered literally, "the Holy Place" (ESV, KJV), meaning the whole tabernacle, not just the holy of holies.

uncleanness . . . rebellion . . . sins. This purification offering cleanses the tent of both Israel's moral offenses (rebellion and sins) and nonmoral, ceremonial uncleanness. "Rebellion" (lit., "rebellions" or "transgressions" [KJV, ESV, NASB, NRSV]) expresses defiance against God. On "sins," see comments at Leviticus 4:2.

He is to do the same for the tent of meeting. This should be rendered instead, "And so he will do for the tent of meeting" (ESV, NRSV), summarizing what has just been, not introducing a new act.

among them in the midst of their uncleanness. Purification is necessary because God dwells in the tent surrounded by Israel's impurities. For God to remain in their midst without his wrath breaking out, his sanctuary must be "fumigated" of the people's sins and uncleanness. This in effect "reset the equilibrium of the entire sacred compass"—that is, the concentric circles of holiness (see illustration).³

16:17 *Aaron goes in . . . the Most Holy Place.* Only the high priest, and even he only on the Day of Atonement, can enter the most holy place to sprinkle purifying blood before the ark. This access is limited to the high priest because only he is in the same circle of holiness as the holy of holies

- God is holy.
- God's forgiveness is complete.

(see illustration). Other priests can provide purification of less-holy zones.

16:18 *come out to the altar.* This is the altar of incense that is "before the Lord" in the holy place outside the most holy place (Lev. 4:7, 18), not the altar of burnt offering east of the tent on which blood is applied with sin offerings for leaders or commoners (Lev. 4:25, 30).

16:19 *sprinkle some of the blood . . . seven times.* This is done for the priest or the people in front of the curtain of the sanctuary near the altar of incense (Lev. 4:6, 17).

16:20 *bring forward the live goat.* The "live goat" here is the "scapegoat" (Lev. 16:8–10, 26; see "Additional Insights" following the unit on Lev. 16:1–14).

16:21–22 *lay both hands on the head of the live goat.* One hand is leaned by the worshiper on the burnt offering (Lev. 1:4), the fellowship offering (Lev. 3:2, 8, 13), and the sin offering (Lev. 4:4, 24, 29, 33). Leaning with two hands by the priest

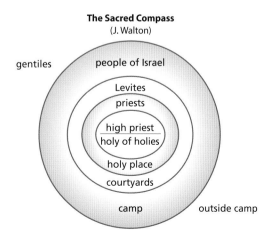

The Sacred Compass
(J. Walton)

gentiles

people of Israel

Levites

priests

high priest
holy of holies

holy place

courtyards

camp

outside camp

On the Day of Atonement, blood from the sin offerings is sprinkled on the atonement cover to make atonement for the high priest, his household, and the people of Israel. This illumination from an AD 1411 version of the Bible Historiale depicts Aaron inside the tabernacle.

symbolizes transference of sin onto the animal (v. 21b; cf. Lev. 24:14). Transfer rituals in which touching an animal was thought to cause sickness or impurity to pass from a person to the animal (e.g., a puppy) are also known among the ancient Hittites.[4] In the Mesopotamian *Asakki Marsuti* incantation ritual for fever, the goat that is the substitute for the sick person is sent out into the wilderness.[5]

confess. In confessing Israel's sins, the high priest on the nation's behalf is both acknowledging and repudiating Israel's sins. Various terms for "sin" show that offenses of every kind and degree are borne by this goat.

wickedness . . . rebellion . . . sins. "Wickedness" translates ‘*awon*, from a root meaning "to bend, twist, distort," and has to do with twisted, warped human behavior that distorts what God requires. On "rebellion" and "sin," see on verse 16 above.

send the goat away into the wilderness . . . to a remote place. This act symbolizes the removal of Israel's sins from the camp. The "remote place" is literally a land "cut off" (*gᵉzerah*) from people.

16:23 *take off the linen garments.* Having entered the most holy place, Aaron's linen garments are either contaminated with some of Israel's impurity or more likely supercharged with divine holiness.[6] Thus, after completing the sin offerings and sending forth the goat, he is to remove and leave behind his simple linen garments (cf. Lev. 16:4).

16:24 *bathe himself . . . in the sanctuary area.* "Sanctuary area" is better rendered literally, "holy place" (NRSV). Bathing cannot take place in the tent of meeting because exposing one's genitals during ritual worship is forbidden (Exod. 20:26). Indecent exposure can make the priest "incur guilt and die" (Exod. 28:42–43). Presumably, a changing screen in the courtyard is used.[7]

put on his regular garments. These literally are simply "his garments" (ESV, KJV), the formal "vestments" (NRSV). Until now, he has worn simpler garb (see comments at Lev. 16:4).

16:26 *The man who releases the goat as a scapegoat must wash his clothes and bathe himself.* Less likely, "goat for Azazel" (ESV, NRSV). See "Additional Insights" following the unit on Leviticus 16:1–14. The man touching the scapegoat (v. 26) and burning the sin-offering carcasses (v. 28) evidently becomes contaminated by the animals' absorbed impurities.

16:27 *The bull and the goat . . . taken outside the camp . . . burned up.* Ordinarily, the priests eat the flesh of the sin offerings (see Lev. 6:24–29), but since these sin offerings are on behalf of the priests and the nation of which they are part, everything must be burned, with nothing saved for the priests.

16:29–30 *lasting ordinance . . . tenth day of the seventh month.* Here the Day of Atonement is established as an annual holy day. The seventh month is Tishri, September–October on our calendars. This holy day occurs five days before the less-somber Festival of Tabernacles (Lev. 23:34).

deny yourselves. "Deny" could also be "humble, afflict" (NASB, ESV, KJV). This is a reference to fasting (NIVmg). Note Psalm 35:13: "I . . . humbled myself with fasting." Later this day is simply called "the Fast" (Acts 27:9 NRSV). Fasting here is an expression of repentance. Apart from repentance the sacrifices are not acceptable to God.

not do any work . . . because on this day atonement will be made . . . to cleanse you. All work is forbidden, whether by an Israelite or a foreigner, to emphasize the importance of this occasion when sacred space and the people are cleansed and the equilibrium between them that impurity disrupts is reestablished.[8]

16:31–34 *a lasting ordinance . . . make atonement . . . once a year for all the sins of the Israelites.* Provision is made for future priests to continue this ritual to cleanse the sanctuary and the people of Israel's impurities annually.

Theological Insights

What was purged on the Day of Atonement: the people or the sanctuary?

First and foremost, it cleansed the sanctuary. Whatever blood was applied to was cleansed. The blood of the goat was applied to the atonement cover and the altar of incense in the holy place to "made atonement for the Most Holy Place" and to "cleanse it [the altar] . . . from the uncleanness of the Israelites" (Lev. 16:15–20).

Nevertheless, the inclusion of the ritual using the live goat (scapegoat) implies the transfer and removal of Israel's impurities from the entire community: "The goat will carry on itself all their sins to a remote place" (Lev. 16:22a). The Day of Atonement is also said to cleanse the people from their sins (Lev. 16:30).

So the correct answer is both: the Day of Atonement symbolically cleansed the sanctuary through a blood ritual and symbolically removed sin from both the people and the sanctuary by a transfer ritual involving the live goat. Roy Gane explains the overall system as follows.[9] First, during the year various sacrificial rituals transferred impurity from the people to the sanctuary, at which times people received forgiveness. A second stage took place on the Day of Atonement, when rituals symbolically removed from the sanctuary the impurities that had accumulated there throughout the year.

Failure to remove the accumulated sins of the people from the sanctuary would have had dire consequences. Eventually, that sin would have reached "critical mass," resulting in a "nuclear blast" of God's wrath against the people.

Teaching the Text

Leviticus 16 describes the Day of Atonement (Yom Kippur), the most solemn and sacred of all of Israel's holy days, for it deals with purging the sanctuary of Israel's sins and its ceremonial impurities.

1. *God is holy.* The whole ritual of the Day of Atonement assumes the holiness of God, a holiness that cannot dwell indefinitely "in the midst of [Israel's] uncleanness" (Lev. 16:16) without it being addressed.

When Aaron entered the most holy place, his clothes seem to have contracted holiness, so they must be taken off and left in the sanctuary (Lev. 16:23). Compare the holiness that Moses contracts on Mount Sinai (Exod. 34:29–30). In Leviticus 16 the whole ritual is an acknowledgment of the holiness of God, from elaborate preparation sacrifices that Aaron conducts before approaching God's presence (vv. 3–14), to the blood manipulations in the sanctuary (vv. 16–19), to the ritual washings to remove impurities contracted from the goats (vv. 24, 26), to the changing to regular vestments as less holy activities occur (v. 24a), and the postlude burnt offerings (v. 24b). Everything underscores for Israel that the holy God dwells in its midst, a holiness that it must respect. We too need to be aware that God is holy and must be approached with the highest respect.

2. *God's forgiveness is complete.* The ritual centers on two goats. The one goat chosen by lot is sacrificed as a sin/purification offering; the other goat (or "scapegoat" [see "Additional Insights" following the unit on Lev. 16:1–14]) is driven into the desert, symbolically bearing away the sins of the people.

The purpose of the Day of Atonement ritual is to address the problem of sin and ceremonial uncleanness, which are incompatible with the holy God dwelling among people. Both the live goat and the sacrificed goat symbolize atonement or purging (Lev. 16:10, 15–16).

Apparently, the slaughtered goat's blood symbolically dislodges and transfers impurity from the inner sanctuary to the high priest, who in turn transfers it to the live goat that then carries it completely away (see "Theological Insights" above).

Walter Kaiser sees the following symbolism.[10] The first goat represents sins forgiven. Blood sacrifice is the means for forgiveness of sin (Lev. 17:11). Thus, the slaughtering of the first goat and the sprinkling of its blood in the most holy place illustrates how Israel's sin was atoned for and forgiven through blood sacrifice. The second goat represents sins forgotten. Israel's sins are confessed over and symbolically transferred to the second goat by laying two hands upon it; the animal is then driven into the desert. This ritual represents Israel's sins being completely removed and forgotten by God.

God has graciously provided the Israelites a means for their sins to be forgiven and forgotten while remaining holy himself. Or as the psalmist says, perhaps alluding to the Day of Atonement scapegoat, "As far as the east is from the west, so far has he removed our transgressions from us" (Ps. 103:12).

The book of Hebrews sees the atoning sacrifices as foreshadowing the atoning work of Christ on the cross. As the high priest purged God's earthly sanctuary on

The high priest symbolically transfers the sins of Israel to the live goat, which is then sent into the wilderness. Two Mesopotamian series of texts, the Asakki Marsuti and the Utukki Lemnuti, describe rituals where sickness or demons are transferred onto the body of a goat. This tablet, a section of Utukki Lemnuti, is dated to the third to second century BC.

the Day of Atonement, so Christ enters the heavenly sanctuary to purge it of our sins (Heb. 9:24). But unlike the Day of Atonement sacrifice, Christ's sacrifice must be offered only once, not annually (Heb. 9:25–26). As Day of Atonement sin offering carcasses were burned "outside the camp" (Lev. 16:27; cf. Lev. 8:17), so Jesus suffers "outside the city gate" (Heb. 13:11–12).

Christians meditating on the Day of Atonement will naturally end up examining themselves and how their sins offend God. But we will also consider what Christ has done for us in making atonement for our sins by bearing them away so that our sins can be completely forgiven and forgotten.

Illustrating the Text

The Jewish Day of Atonement points us to Jesus, the real sacrifice.

Informational: The Day of Atonement, or Yom Kippur, is to this day the most sacred and solemn day in Judaism. It is traditionally dedicated to prayer, complete fasting (with medical exceptions), and attending a synagogue service with an unusually long liturgy. Orthodox Jews may attend a service from 8:00 or 9:00 a.m. to 3:00 p.m., followed by an evening service at 5:00 or 6:00 p.m. that continues until sundown. Interspersed in the liturgy are confessions of sin ("We have been treasonable, we have been aggressive, and we have been slanderous") and petitions for forgiveness. There is also a catchall confession: "Forgive us the breach of positive commands and negative commands, whether or not they involve an act, whether or not they are known to us."[11]

Even among Reform Jews, this is a somber day on which sins are confessed. As a new student in the dorm at Hebrew Union College–Jewish Institute of Religion in Cincinnati, I made the mistake of saying to a rabbinical student on the morning of Yom Kippur, *hag sameah*, meaning "happy holiday." The rabbinical student looked at me sternly and responded, "Actually, this one is not supposed to be." It is not a happy holiday; it is a solemn one meant for self-examination and confession of sin.

Since the destruction of the temple in AD 70, Jews no longer sacrifice a goat on the Day of Atonement. Given the centrality of blood in the system of atonement in the Bible (cf. Lev. 17:11), how then can religious Jews suppose that they receive atonement and forgiveness without any bloody sacrifice? Jewish theology responds that repentance now serves as a substitute for blood sacrifice. In Christian theology, in contrast, Christ is the substitute for these sacrifices.

Unlike its usage in modern English, "scapegoating" is a good thing in Scripture.

Popular Culture: In modern English a scapegoat is an innocent person who is blamed for what someone else has done, as was the scapegoat in ancient Israel. An example of scapegoating is when a political leader fires a staff member in order to blame that person for failed or unpopular policies that the leader had in fact promoted. In such a case, just as the scapegoat bears the guilt for Israel's sins, so the member of the staff is blamed for the leader's mistakes.

Scapegoating in this sense is a bad thing. But the sort of scapegoating found in the Bible is a good thing. It was good and necessary that the scapegoat bore away Israel's sins in order for God to remain in Israel's midst. And it is good that Christ bore our sins (1 Pet. 2:24).

Leviticus 16:15–34

Blood

Right and Wrong Uses

Big Idea *Blood and sacrifice are important, though they can be abused.*

Understanding the Text

The Text in Context

Leviticus 17–27 forms a major unit in Leviticus in which "holiness" is emphasized, for which reason it has come to be labeled the "laws of holiness." Leviticus 17 introduces this unit by emphasizing the holiness of proper sacrifice, the prohibition of idolatry (sacrifice to goat-demons), and the proper use of blood. John Walton describes this chapter as "maintaining holiness from outside the camp" (see "Introduction to Leviticus").[1]

> Israel is warned not to offer sacrifices to goat idols. The Egyptians worshiped Khnum, a god depicted with a ram's head, as shown in this relief from Medinet Habu.

Historical and Cultural Background

In Leviticus 17:7 Israel is accused of worshiping male goats (see below). Israel learned idolatry in Egypt. I know of no specific goat-gods in Egypt, but many Egyptian gods had heads of animals. One of the Egyptian gods was the ram- or bull-headed god Khnum, the patron god of potters. Banebdjedet or Banebdjed was a ram god of Lower Egypt at Mendes. In Greece there was the goat-footed god Pan, whom the Greeks later identified with the Egyptian god Min.

Idolatry was a problem throughout Israelite history. Of all ancient people groups, only Israel affirmed monotheism. And it often lapsed.

Interpretive Insights

17:1–2 *Speak to Aaron and his sons.* The ones responsible for sacrifices are addressed first before the Israelites are instructed.

17:3 *Any Israelite who sacrifices.* The verb *shahat* ("sacrifices") is usually rendered "slaughters" (NASB, NRSV) or "kills" (ESV, KJV, NKJV). The NIV here takes it to mean "slaughter as a sacrifice," a view defended by Rabbi Akiba (see "Additional Insights" following this unit). Verse 5 calls what they had been doing in the open field "sacrifices." Verse 7 adds that these sacrifices were to demons or gods.

an ox, a lamb or a goat. These are precisely the animals eligible to be sacrificed as fellowship offerings (Lev. 3:1, 6, 12). If "slaughter as a sacrifice" is the meaning, this largely resolves the alleged contradiction between Leviticus 17:3–9 and Deuteronomy 12:20–25, where profane, nonsacrificial slaughter is allowed. Under Akiba's view, verses 3–4 mean only that the fellowship sacrifices must take place at an official altar and say nothing about profane slaughter. Alternatively, Rabbi Ishmael argues that *shahat* means "to slaughter, kill," not "to sacrifice." Thus, verses 3–4 preclude profane slaughter outside the sanctuary temporarily while Israel was in the wilderness, though the rule ceased upon Israel's entrance into the land. For more details, see "Additional Insights" following this unit.

17:4 *guilty of bloodshed.* In the Hebrew text "bloodshed" is simply "blood." This can refer to murder (Exod. 22:2–3; Num. 35:33), though here improper animal sacrifice is reckoned as a kind of bloodshed (also Gen. 9:3–5).

cut off from their people. See "Additional Insights" following the unit on Leviticus 6:8–7:38.

17:7 *goat idols.* The Hebrew word is *se'irim* (lit., "hairy ones"), ordinarily used in reference to male goats (e.g., Lev. 16:5–10). This probably refers to some sort of goat-gods or goat-demons, though the Aramaic

Key Themes of Leviticus 17:1–16

- God's people are in danger of falling into idolatry.
- Blood is of great importance in sacrificial theology.

Targum Onqelos renders *se'irim* simply "demons" (compare), while the Greek Old Testament renders it "empty/worthless things" without mentioning goats. Compare Azazel of the Day of Atonement (see "Additional Insights" following the unit on Lev. 16:1–14). Concrete archaeological evidence for goat idols in ancient Egypt and Bronze Age Syro-Palestine is lacking. On an ivory found at Megiddo is an image of a predatory eagle-winged creature with a human head falling upon an ibex. Otto Eissfeldt has identified that winged creature with the demon Azazel, who devoured goats.[2] In Mesopotamian art goats sometimes appear rearing on a sacred tree, and sometimes they symbolize sweet, underground water.[3] The relevance of any of these instances for the present passage is uncertain. Later in Israelite history, worship at the "high places" had similarly to be suppressed by Hezekiah and Josiah because it mixed Yahweh worship with idolatry (2 Kings 18:4; 23:5).

prostitute themselves. This could mean that Israel's worship constitutes spiritual adultery against Yahweh, with Israel being the prostitute (cf. Jer. 2:20; 3:1). But the metaphor may go the opposite direction: Israelites give a fee for the god's services, just as the people give a fee for a prostitute's services.

lasting ordinance for them and for the generations to come. This more naturally applies to the whole law, though it could be limited to the prohibition against goat idols in verse 7a.[4]

17:8–9 *Any Israelite or any foreigner.* "Foreigner" could also be translated "sojourner"; see verse 15 below. Even those of pagan heritage living with the Israelites must follow the same rule.

does not bring it . . . to the tent . . . to sacrifice it. Sacrifice outside the tent of meeting, whether a burnt offering or a fellowship offering, is tantamount to idolatry, a capital offense (Exod. 22:20).

cut off from the people of Israel. The Hebrew text lacks "of Israel" (cf. NRSV). This may rather refer to one's ancestors in the afterlife rather than the whole nation. A dead person is "gathered to his/your people" (Gen. 25:8; Num. 20:24; 27:13) in the sense of going to one's "ancestors." On "cut off," see "Additional Insights" following the unit on Leviticus 6:8–7:38.

17:10 *eats blood.* This means eating meat without first offering the blood to God (see "Teaching the Text" at Lev. 3:1–17). For fellowship offerings, that means pouring out the blood to God at the altar (v. 6 above), though with wild game it means pouring out the blood to God on the ground (vv. 13–14).

17:11 *For the life of a creature is in the blood . . . it is the blood that makes atonement for one's life.* "Creature" is literally "the flesh." Verse 11 is a crux of interpretation. Verse 11b can be rendered in three distinct ways: "It is the blood that makes atonement *by the life*" (cf. ESV), or "It is the blood that makes atonement *for the soul*" (NKJV; cf. NIV), or "It is the blood, *as life*, that expiates" (NJPS; similarly NRSV). The first rendering means that the blood ransoms by means of the animal's life (*nepesh*, "life, soul, self") being forfeit. The second means that the animal's shed blood ransoms the human's life. The notion of substitutionary sacrifice is involved

in both of these interpretations. The third view, first proposed by Jacob Milgrom but later abandoned by him, implies that it is the life force of blood that atones. Milgrom's former view limited the atonement here to cleansing from the offense of killing an animal and eating its flesh that would otherwise cause bloodguilt (cf. v. 4 above).

The interpretation of verse 11b hinges on the meaning of the Hebrew verb *kipper* ("to make atonement") in combination with the Hebrew preposition b^e. Although the preposition b^e can mean "for" (the *bet* of price/exchange), or "as" (the *bet* of identity [*bet essentiae*]), or "by [means of]" (*bet* of means/instrument), as the three renderings above indicate, in combination with "atone" the *bet* regularly has an instrumental sense and never means "for" or "as."[5] This observation led Milgrom[6] to abandon his interpretation: "It is the blood, *as life*, that expiates." The same observation undermines the NIV's interpretation as well because rendering "makes atonement for" requires an otherwise unattested meaning for *kipper* + b^e. Thus Leviticus 17:11b probably is saying that it is "by means of the [animal's] life that atonement is made" (cf. ESV).

Although the fellowship offering has been primarily discussed in this chapter (though see v. 8), and the fellowship offering is not an atoning sacrifice, even its blood is significant because of the importance of blood in the sacrificial system as a whole.

17:15 *anyone . . . who eats anything found dead or torn by wild animals.* Neither a native Israelite nor a "foreigner" (or "sojourner" [*ger*]) is allowed to eat carrion. The foreigner in mind is the sort who if circumcised can keep Passover (Exod.

12:48), whereas a foreigner who does not identify with Israel's exodus and covenant cannot (Exod. 12:43). Eating carrion is proscribed whether the animal has been killed by predators or has died on its own. Such food, besides being disgusting and unhealthy, cannot have had its blood properly poured out to God as required by verses 10, 13. It makes a person "ceremonially unclean," making it dangerous to approach that which is holy. It is inconsistent with the holiness of God's people: "You are to be my holy people. So do not eat the meat of an animal torn by wild beasts; throw it to the dogs" (Exod. 22:31). Nonetheless, one can use the fat of carrion for purposes other than eating (Lev. 7:24), and one can sell it to a different category of foreigner (Deut. 14:21) not closely identified with Israel and its covenant.

Theological Insights

John Stott, in a sermon titled "Why Was Blood So Important?,"[7] points out that there is a medical condition known as hemophobia, the inordinate or irrational fear of blood. A certain amount of fear of blood is normal. It is such fear that helps make vampire and slasher movies so scary. Some people grow faint at the sight of blood, including not a few brave husbands who have passed out while watching their wives give birth.

Stott goes on to observe that some people have hemophobia with regard to the mention of blood in the Bible. They find references to blood offensive and off-putting. They would like to explain the teachings of the Bible without reference to blood, whether the blood of sacrifices or the blood of Jesus Christ. But this is to adopt a view of blood that is at odds with what the Bible itself says. Blood was an essential element of the sacrificial system of the Old Testament through which atonement and forgiveness were made available. It is also essential to the New Testament's theology of the work of Jesus Christ.

Christian hymnody has correctly seen the connection between the blood of Christ, sacrifices in the Old Testament, and our cleansing and forgiveness.[8] Many contemporary Christian praise songs also refer to the blood of Christ.[9]

Theological hemophobia is also a pathological condition that must be overcome. Blood was central in the theological system of atonement in the Old Testament (Lev. 17:11); it is equally essential for understanding the cross in the New Testament.

Teaching the Text

Blood and sacrifice play an important role in Leviticus. Leviticus 17 teaches the error of offering sacrifice to idols and the importance of blood.

1. *God's people are in danger of falling into idolatry.* Although the first of the Ten Commandments forbids idolatry ("no other gods"), there is always a danger of God's people falling into idolatry. That certainly is the case for some Israelites in Leviticus 17, when certain people take it upon themselves to begin offering sacrifices to the goat idols. The exclusive claim to worship that Yahweh makes evidently seems intolerant and unreasonable to them. Surely it is acceptable to worship some other gods alongside Yahweh, is it not? The answer of this text is no. God will not share with other gods the worship that he alone deserves.

Some people today, including some raised in Christian homes, also question the exclusive claims of Christ and the Bible. Are there not truths in Hinduism, Islam, and Buddhism? Could we not dabble in New Age thought and still be good Christians? Masonic Lodges freely intermix images of Christian and non-Christian religious traditions. Is it really a rejection of Christ to intermix in our lives Christian and non-Christian religious ideas? Traditional Christianity seems so intolerant in its exclusivity.

But just as it was wrong for Israel to mix Yahweh with goat-gods, so is it improper for us to mix Christ and Belial (2 Cor. 6:15). The God of Jesus Christ makes an exclusive claim on our lives. He does not tolerate sharing his people's allegiance with other "gods."

2. *Blood is of great importance in sacrificial theology.* Leviticus 17:10–12 underscores the importance of blood in Leviticus's theology. Why is there this emphasis on blood?

First, not eating blood acknowledges the value of animal life and God's permission to take life. "Eating blood" is eating meat without first pouring out the blood to God (see "Teaching the Text" at Lev. 3:1–17). This requirement shows God's respect even for animal life. It is only by special divine permission that people are permitted to kill and eat animal flesh, something not permitted to humankind until after the flood (Gen. 9:3–4). Offering the blood back to God is a way of acknowledging that divine permission. Failure to do this brings bloodguilt (Lev. 17:4) for killing animals.

Second, blood is God's means of atonement. It is through blood that atonement is made. Atonement is regularly associated with the shedding of blood. According to Leviticus 17:11, blood either makes atonement for one's life (NIV) or, more likely, makes atonement by means of the life given up (ESV). Either way, behind this is the concept of substitutionary atonement. The animal dies for human offenses so that humans do not have to die.

Two things are related to this requirement of blood. First, God considers sin to be a very serious thing. He cannot simply ignore sin. His justice demands that some sort of punishment take place. But in his mercy God allows the Israelites, on the principle of "life for life," to provide animal substitutes. With but a few exceptions, atonement requires the death of a substitute involving the shedding of blood. That is why the writer of Hebrews can say, "The law requires that nearly everything be cleansed with blood, and without the shedding of blood there is no forgiveness" (Heb. 9:22). Only the shedding of blood can deal with the seriousness of human sin.

Second, atoning blood is not something that human beings merit; rather, it is a gift from God. The text states, "I have *given* [the blood] to you to make atonement for yourselves on the altar" (Lev. 17:11b). The blood of the atoning sacrifices is a gift from God. The sacrifices do not represent human-initiated efforts to appease God; rather, God initiates blood sacrifice as the means of satisfying his demand to punish and remove sin. The animal is offered on the person's behalf. Its blood is the divinely appointed means of making forgiveness available. People merely employ and acknowledge that gift by carrying out the sacrifice. If God had not given it, no human effort to appease God could have succeeded.

Leviticus's teaching about the importance of blood in atoning sacrifice forms the backdrop for the language of blood in the New Testament. A word search on "blood" quickly shows how often the New Testament echoes the sacrificial language of the Old Testament (e.g., Matt. 26:28; John 6:53–57; Rom. 3:25; Eph. 1:7; Heb. 9:14; 10:19; 1 Pet. 1:2; 1 John 1:7; Rev. 1:5; 5:9). The blood of Jesus Christ, like the blood of sacrificial animals in the Old Testament, is the divinely appointed gift that satisfies God and allows us to be forgiven.

Illustrating the Text

Christianity makes exclusive claims that will not be popular in our pluralistic culture.

History: Chemist Ascanio Sobrero synthesized nitroglycerin in 1864 and immediately destroyed his notes, for he realized how unstable the explosive is. A San Francisco tragedy emphasized that Sobrero was right to fear his invention. Workers, seeing that one of their unmarked crates had a leak, made the mistake of roughly prying open a container of nitroglycerin. The explosion that followed leveled the Wells Fargo office and killed fifteen people.

Certain topics are explosive and must be handled with care.

The fact is that Christianity does make exclusive truth claims. Christians should be prepared for explosive responses when they make those claims.

Many truth claims will ignite an indignant response from our secular culture, but that does not mean we should pack beliefs in straw and put them in storage. Just as the explosive components of nitroglycerin helped clear ground for the transcontinental railroad, the truth claims of Scripture can break down strongholds of deception in the minds of unbelievers (2 Cor. 10:4).

Only Jesus's blood can pay the penalty for our sin.

Quote: Charles Spurgeon. Speaking of Jesus's atoning sacrifice, Spurgeon remarked,

Dear hearer, Christ is mighty to save, because God did not turn away the sword, but He sheathed it in His own Son's heart! He did not remit the debt, for it was paid in drops of precious blood! And now the great receipt is nailed to the Cross and our sins with it so that we may go free if we are Believers in him! For this reason He is "mighty to save," in the true sense of the word.[10]

Because the Israelites have been making sacrifices in the open fields and to goat idols, God instructs them to offer sacrifices only at the entrance to the tent of meeting. These figurines of two goats and a sacred tree were found at Horvat Qitmit and may have been part of an Edomite shrine (seventh to sixth century BC).

Leviticus 17:1–16

Do the Altar Laws Contradict One Another?

Critical scholars often say that Leviticus 17 contradicts other passages of Scripture. For example, Leviticus 17:3–7 limits animal slaughter to the tabernacle's altar, but Exodus 20:24–26 envisions various altars of stone besides the tabernacle's altar (cf. Deut. 27:1–8; Josh. 8:30–31; Judg. 6:24; 1 Sam. 7:17; 14:35; 1 Kings 18:30). Could meat be slaughtered and eaten anywhere even by the ceremonially unclean (Deut. 12:15, 21–22), or was it limited to the sanctuary's altar (Lev. 17:3–7), to be eaten only by the ceremonially clean (Lev. 7:19–21)?

> An example of a stone sacrificial altar is this one found at Tel Beersheba, eighth century BC, and reconstructed.

The rabbis recognized the difficulty in harmonizing these laws. Baruch Levine points to an ancient debate between Rabbi Akiba and Rabbi Ishmael over this matter.[1] Yehezkel Kaufmann in modern times has also made a proposal. Here is a survey of these views.

1. *The Kaufmann view: Leviticus 17 allows sacrifice on Exodus 20–type altars.* Yehezkel Kaufmann argues that Leviticus 17 does not preclude the use of lesser but official earthen/stone altars of the sort described in Exodus 20:24–26. It merely limits slaughter to legitimate altars of Yahweh. The expression "the altar of the LORD at the entrance to the tent of meeting" (Lev. 17:6) could be synecdoche (a part representing a whole) in which the preeminent altar stands for all legitimate altars of Yahweh. Practical considerations make this interpretation attractive: there were simply too many Israelites (censuses in Num. 1–4 count more than six hundred thousand males) to be served by a single altar. Kaufmann states, "The only plausible interpretation of Leviticus 17:3ff. is that it presupposes the existence of many legitimate local sanctuaries, each of which is represented here by the tent."[2]

2. *The Akiba view: Leviticus 17 does not preclude profane slaughter.* Akiba's view argues that the word "slaughter" (*shahat* [Lev. 17:3]) may be in the limited

sense of slaughter as a sacrifice,[3] a view adopted by the NIV. The verb *shahat* occurs in Leviticus 22:27–28, where it says that an animal cannot be "slaughtered" in the sense of being "brought before the LORD" as a sacrifice until the eighth day. Similarly, Exodus 23:18 says that one is not to "offer [*zabah*] the blood of a [Passover] sacrifice with anything leavened"; but the repetition of the same command in Exodus 34:25 uses *shahat* ("to slaughter") rather than *zabah*, suggesting that *shahat* can mean "to sacrifice." Leviticus 17:5 calls what the Israelites had been doing in the open field "sacrifices," and 17:7 adds that these sacrifices were for goat-demons and were spiritually immoral idolatry. Profane slaughter need not be in view.

If "slaughter" in this context means "slaughter as a sacrifice," it resolves the tension between Leviticus 17:3–9 and Deuteronomy 12:20–25, where profane, non-sacrificial slaughter is allowed outside the sanctuary. Leviticus 17 merely means that "fellowship sacrifices" (*zebah sh^elamim*) must take place at an official altar. This does not prohibit profane slaughter of, say, blemished animals that were disqualified for Yahweh's altar (Lev. 22:22; Deut. 15:21). If the text only prohibits sacrificial slaughter, then animals unfit for the sanctuary's altar could still be used for profane slaughter. This view could also be combined with the Kaufmann view that the tabernacle's altar is synecdoche for any legitimate altar and thus harmonize the passage with Exodus 20 as well.

3. *The Ishmael view: Leviticus 17 was a temporary measure.* Martin Lockshin calls Rabbi Ishmael's interpretation "the standard understanding of most halakhic exegetes."[4] It limits Leviticus 17 to the context of the Israelites living close to the tabernacle while traveling through the Sinai wilderness toward the promised land. It was a temporary measure implemented to combat the immediate problem of goat-idol worship (Lev. 17:7). Perhaps some were concealing their idolatry by saying falsely that they were merely slaughtering the animal for food. To close this loophole, they must now slaughter all animals at the sanctuary.[5] But later, when Israel scattered throughout the promised land, other altars would again be allowed per the altar law of Exodus 20:24–26, as subsequent narratives indicate.

The main problem with Ishmael's view is Leviticus 17:7b: "This is to be a lasting ordinance for them and for the generations to come." The Ishmael view takes this statement to apply only to verse 7a. C. F. Keil took that view: "The expression 'a statute for ever' refers to the principle of the law, that sacrifices were to be offered to Jehovah alone, and not to the law that every animal was to be slain before the tabernacle, which was afterwards repealed by Moses, when they were about to enter Canaan, where it could no longer be carried out (Deut. xii. 15)."[6]

Each of these views is plausible, and elements of them can be combined. Any of them is preferable to the view that the biblical altar laws contradict one another.

Living by God's Sexual Standards

Big Idea *God's moral and sexual standards bring life.*

Understanding the Text

The Text in Context

Leviticus 18 within the laws of holiness (Lev. 17–27) teaches holiness to laypersons in the areas of incest and sexuality. It exhorts the Israelites to live differently than do the Egyptians or the Canaanites (vv. 1–5) in those areas (vv. 6–23) or else be expelled from the land (vv. 24–30). The present chapter overlaps in content with Leviticus 20. In terms of sacred space, Leviticus 18–20 arguably describes things that disqualify a person from the camp.[1] See the introduction to Leviticus.

Historical and Cultural Background

The ancient Egyptians practiced incest, especially among royalty. By Hellenistic times brother-sister marriages in the Egyptian royal families had become so commonplace that Egypt came to be known as the "cradle of incest."[2]

In Egyptian mythology the gods Shu and Tefnut were united in a brother-sister marriage, and Isis was both the wife and the sister of Osiris.

Human sacrifice, though unknown in Egypt and Mesopotamia, evidently was practiced by the Canaanites, the Ammonites, and the Moabites (Lev. 18:21 [cf. vv. 25–27]; 20:2–5; Deut. 12:31; 2 Kings 3:27). Archaeological evidence of Canaanite child sacrifice (Lev. 18:21) is lacking in Palestine but is found in Tunisia near the ancient site of Carthage.[3] Carthage was a Phoenician/Tyrian colony, and the Phoenicians were Canaanites who lived outside Israel. Cemeteries there have thousands of funerary urns containing the burned remains of children, and a stela from

Israel is commanded not to allow sexual relations between close relatives. This differed from the sexual practices in Egypt, which mirrored their mythology. This bronze statuette shows the Egyptian goddess Isis nursing the son she bore by her husband Osiris, who was also her brother (Egypt, 664–332 BC).

Carthage depicts a priest holding a child as part of a sacrificial ritual.[4] Diodorus (*Bib. hist*. 20.14.4–7) and Porphyry (*Abst*. 2.56) describe these child sacrifices. Diodorus says that in 310 BC the Carthaginians came to believe that they had seriously offended the gods by replacing the children of the best families with children acquired for the purpose of sacrifice. To make amends they sacrificed two hundred children picked from the best families.[5]

Interpretive Insights

18:1–5 *You must not do as they do in Egypt . . . in the land of Canaan.* On "I am the LORD your God" (vv. 2, 4) and "I am the LORD" (v. 5), see "Additional Insights" following the unit on Leviticus 19:1–37. The "practices" (v. 3) are literally "statutes" (ESV). Israel is to live neither like Egypt, from which it had come, nor like Canaan, where it is going (v. 3). Rather, it must follow God's laws and decrees (vv. 4–5).

18:5 *The person who obeys them will live by them.* See "Theological Insights" below.

18:6–18 These verses deal with incestuous sexual relations. The Hebrew words behind "to have sexual relations" are literally translated as "to uncover nakedness." This is a euphemism for sexual intercourse. The general statement about a "close relative" (v. 6) includes daughters (see Lev. 21:2–3), even though they are not listed explicitly. Lot's incest with his daughters is Sodom-like behavior (Gen. 19:31–38). The "father's wife" (v. 8) is a stepmother (Paul applies this to the church [1 Cor. 5:1]). "Father's daughter . . . mother's daughter" (v. 9) includes half sisters. The "daughter of your father's wife" (v. 11) is a stepsister. The

Key Themes of Leviticus 18:1–30

- God's people live differently than the world does.
- God sets sexual standards for his people.

"wife" of the "father's brother" (v. 14) is an aunt by marriage. Levirate marriage constitutes a permitted exception (Deut. 25:5–10) to "brother's wife" (v. 16). "A woman and her daughter" (v. 17) refers to a biologically unrelated stepdaughter. This restriction is possibly limited to while the mother is alive (cf. v. 18). "Wife's sister as a rival wife" (v. 18) refers to polygamy with two sisters. The aunt on the mother's side is omitted, though Leviticus 20:20 probably includes her. Whether an uncle could marry a niece was debated in Jewish tradition: the rabbis said yes, the sectarians at Qumran said no.

18:10 *that would dishonor you.* Literally, the Hebrew text says "for/though they are your nakedness"; another possible rendering is "even though you have jurisdiction over their nakedness" (cf. NRSV). The latter interpretation fits the cultural milieu in which the grandfather as paterfamilias has final say over whom granddaughters may marry.

18:11 *born to your father.* This should rather be rendered "kindred to your father" (via marriage) or paraphrased "adopted by your father" (HCSB) or something similar in order to keep this verse distinct from verse 9, which already covers half sisters.

18:19–23 These verses (except for v. 21 [see below]) deal with other types of sexual relations.

18:19 *the uncleanness of her monthly period.* See Leviticus 15:19–24; 20:18.

18:21 *Do not give any of your children to be sacrificed to Molek.* Literally, "Do

Child sacrifice is forbidden in Israel, although it may have been practiced by Israel's neighbors. Tophets like this one in ancient Carthage were cemeteries for the remains of infants who many archaeologists believe were sacrificed to the gods.

not allow your seed/semen to pass over to Molek." Molek (Molech) is a god worshiped by the Ammonites (1 Kings 11:5–7). The Israelites violate this law during the monarchy in the Hinnom Valley (2 Kings 23:10). Although some suggest that this injunction refers to mixed marriages with pagan women (Molek = women who worship Molek) or to some sort of bizarre ritual involving offering a man's semen to a god, the severe penalty for this offense (Lev. 20:2–3) seems most consistent with child sacrifice (see "Historical and Cultural Background" above).

18:22 *sexual relations with a man as . . . with a woman.* This refers to homosexual anal intercourse (cf. Lev. 20:13). Note that the Bible condemns the act (same-sex copulation) but does not condemn the homosexual condition or orientation.

18:24–30 *Do not defile yourselves in any of these ways.* These verses describe how pagan practices bring expulsion from the land. "Defile" is the language of ceremonial uncleanness (vv. 24–25, 27–28, 30; also vv. 20, 23) and is used for moral offenses ("sin" [v. 25]). "Detestable" (vv. 22, 26, 29–30) translates *to'ebah*, traditionally rendered

"abomination." In secular contexts it is used for the revulsion that Egyptians had for Hebrews and shepherds (Gen. 43:32; 46:34); for moral indignation for such things as arrogance, murder, false balances, lying, and injustice (Prov. 6:16–18; 11:1; 12:22; 17:15); and in religious contexts for the abhorrence God has for idols (Deut. 7:25–26; 32:16). "Abominations" are things God "hates" (Deut. 12:31; Prov. 6:16). Incest and child sacrifice are so loathsome that God will cast the Canaanites out before Israel (vv. 24–25). "Vomited" (in vv. 25, 28) is proleptic (a prophetic perfect), speaking of the decreed expulsion of the Canaanites as if already accomplished.

18:28 *if you defile the land, it will vomit you out.* Israel does come to behave like the Canaanites, and God expels Israel from the land too (Israel in 722 BC, Judah in 586 BC).

18:29 *cut off from their people.* See "Additional Insights" following the unit on Leviticus 6:8–7:38. Sexual sins committed in secret are not immune from divine punishment.

Theological Insights

The law promises, "The person who obeys [God's laws] will live by them" (Lev. 18:5). But what kind of life? Eternal life?[6] Romans 10:5–8 cites Leviticus 18:5.

Moses writes this about the righteousness that is by the law: *"The person who does these things will live by them."* [Lev. 18:5] But the righteousness that is by faith says: "Do not say in your heart, 'Who will ascend into heaven?'" [Deut. 30:12] (that is, to bring Christ down) "or 'Who will descend into the deep?'" [Deut. 30:13] (that is, to bring Christ up from the dead). But what does it say? "The word is near you; it is in your mouth and in your heart," [Deut. 30:14] that is, the message concerning faith that we proclaim.

Does Paul take Leviticus 18:5 to mean that the Old Testament saint was supposed to merit eternal life by keeping the law? In this view, Paul quotes Leviticus to prove that eternal life under the law was supposed to be obtained by works, while Deuteronomy is quoted to show that it was possible only by faith. But would Paul really think that Deuteronomy contradicts Leviticus?

The real contrast in Leviticus 18:5 is not between works and faith but between obeying God and the practices of the Egyptians/Canaanites (v. 3). Israel had been redeemed from Egypt before the law was given (Exod. 20:1–2). Its relationship with God is based on God's love and grace (Deut. 7:7–8), not merit (Deut. 9:4–6). Leviticus 18:5 follows laws on blood atonement (Lev. 1–7; 16; 17:11) that clearly presuppose that the Israelites will be unable to obey the law so as to maintain a right relationship through law-keeping alone. Rather, they need, as lawbreakers, humbly to seek God's mercy via atoning sacrifices offered in faith. Paul would not have read Leviticus 18:5 as contradicting all this.

Paul is probably addressing legalists here. Legalists could quote Leviticus 18:5 to claim that eternal life is earned by law-keeping. Paul alludes to this viewpoint by citing Leviticus 18:5, though he knows that the text does not actually teach it. He cites Deuteronomy 30:12–14 to show that the legalists' understanding of Leviticus 18:5 is defective, and that faith is key. Ultimately, says Paul, Christ is the law's end or goal (Rom. 10:4). If one uses the law aright, it should lead a person to faith in Christ, not legalism.

Teaching the Text

Leviticus 18 promotes living differently than the world does, especially in sexual matters, in order to have full life (v. 5).

1. *God's people live differently than the world does.* Israel is to be different from Egypt, from which it has come, and from Canaan, to which it is going (Lev. 18:3). There is always a danger that believers will cease to live distinctively as the people of God and will come more and more to resemble the world and its values. That is why the Israelites need to hear the words "I am Yahweh." The law comes from God. And given their special relationship with God, they are obligated to obey.

Conversely, if they fail to obey but live like the world, they will be treated like the world. Just as God is about to drive out the Canaanites for their abominations, so too if the Israelites live like Canaanites, God will drive them out (Lev. 18:24–28). It is essential that Israel remain morally distinct from the world.

The danger of believers conforming to the world is as strong as ever. The values of the secular media, of intellectual elites, and of Hollywood that bombard us daily are decidedly different from Christian values. There is a constant temptation to jettison those biblical standards that differ from our surrounding cultural norms. Yet it remains essential for Christians to stand firm, to obey God, and to stay distinct from the world (1 John 2:15–17).

2. *God sets sexual standards for his people.* In no area of life do God's standards conflict more with the world's than in the realm of sexual behavior (vv. 6–23).

The fact that inbreeding produces genetic deformities in children is a secondary reason for these laws, though that fails to account for the prohibitions against marrying biologically unrelated in-laws. The primary motivation is to define and protect the integrity of the family from socially destructive forces that promiscuousness unleashes. Children incestuously molested often exhibit depression, poor self-image, guilt, substance abuse, sleep disorders, sexual disorders (e.g., promiscuity or frigidity), and the like. These laws protected unattached females from being reduced to concubinage for male family members. Clear sexual boundaries provided safety and prevented anarchy.

Biblical characters did not always live up to these rules, though some were not fully culpable because they lived before God revealed them. Abraham is married to his half sister Sarah (Gen. 20:12). Jacob is married to two sisters at the same time, Rachel and Leah (Gen. 29:21–28). Judah unwittingly sleeps with his daughter-in-law Tamar (Gen. 38:11–19). Reuben sleeps with his father's wife/concubine Bilhah (Gen. 35:22; 49:4). Moses's father, Amram, marries his father's sister Jochebed (Exod. 6:20). In New Testament times Herod Antipas marries Herodias, his niece and sister-in-law (Matt. 14:4; Mark 6:18). John the Baptist condemns this marriage for its incest and violation of the law, and eventually he is executed for having done so.

The American church has been immune neither from the sexual revolution and hedonism that began in the 1960s nor from practices that deviate from biblical norms, such as adultery and incest.

The law that most strongly conflicts with modern mores is the condemnation of homosexual acts (Lev. 18:22).[7] Attempts to explain away this prohibition have proven unsuccessful. Is homosexual intercourse really that bad? Its condemnation as "detestable" (see comments on vv. 24–30 above) suggests a strong moral revulsion against it, as does its status as a capital offense (Lev. 20:13). Are the laws of Leviticus 18 limited to Israel? No, the "detestable" practices listed in this chapter are also used to condemn the Canaanite "nations" (Lev. 18:24–27). Does this law condemn only a particular kind of homosexual copulation, such as pedophilia? No, Leviticus 18:22 is a broadly worded, general prohibition of male-male sexual intercourse "as . . . with a woman." Are these laws no longer applicable under the new covenant? Laws against adultery and child sacrifice are clearly still applicable (Lev. 18:20–21), and Paul directly applies one of the incest laws (Lev. 18:8) to a church member (1 Cor. 5:1), which suggests that the incest laws of the broader context are still valid. Moreover, Paul specifically applies the condemnation of homosexual copulation to the church (Rom. 1:26–27; 1 Cor. 6:9–10; 1 Tim. 1:10) (see "Theological Insights" at Lev. 20:1–27).

God's sexual regulations provide a stable framework in which human sexuality may be appropriately expressed. That stability promotes life (Lev. 18:5). Increasingly, Christians are disregarding God's sexual standards. But ignoring them can bring chaos and judgment (Lev. 18:24–30). Christians ignore God's sexual standards at their own risk.

When, guided by the Levitical laws, John the Baptist tells Herod Antipas, "It is not lawful for you to have your brother's wife" (Mark 6:18), who was also Herod's niece, John is arrested. These ruins are what remain of the fortress palace of Herod Antipas at Machaerus, where John was imprisoned. The pillars in the background are part of a reconstruction and surround one of the courtyards.

Illustrating the Text

We must resist conforming to the world.

Science: Solomon Asch, a psychologist, conducted a series of famous experiments on the power of peer pressure. He discovered that an otherwise rational person could be induced to provide wrong answers to questions if all the other participants, at the instruction of the examiner, provided the wrong answer. His experiments showed that more than a third of people subjected to this experience would cave to peer pressure rather than providing the obviously correct response. We must beware of the powerful pull of the crowd.

We must be prepared to speak the truth in love.

Scenario: What if a doctor valued patients' feelings more than their healing? The results could be deadly. Suppose the doctor has a patient who enjoys an active lifestyle—hiking, running, cross-country skiing. The doctor learns that the patient has a terrible cancer, one that will kill in a matter of months. The only cure is to amputate a limb. The doctor reasons, "But such an action would make it so hard for this person to enjoy the things he loves most." So instead of a painful, life-altering treatment, the doctor prescribes a bottle of placebos. "Take these, and in six months that pain in your leg will be gone." As believers, we must be ready to speak words that might hurt feelings but are the only medicine that can begin healing.

God's good gift of sex is dangerous when enjoyed illicitly.

Metaphor: One of the best parts of autumn is the fun of gathering around a bonfire. There is nothing like watching the wood ignite and spread its heat as the evening coolness descends. Hot dogs, s'mores, stories, songs—they are all part of the experience. Yet it seems that every year we hear of a fire that has gotten out of control. A camper somewhere is less than careful about handling the fire. The camper lights it during a "no-burn" warning and leaves it unguarded. In no time at all, it spreads from the fire ring to the forest floor. The results are devastating. Sex is like fire. In the right place it is warm and delightful, but outside of God's ordained context it is destructive and uncontrollable.[8]

Leviticus 18:1–30

A Lifestyle of Holiness and Love

Big Idea *The basis of biblical ethics is God's holiness and love.*

Understanding the Text

The Text in Context

Leviticus 19:2 emphasizes the theme that gives the laws of holiness (Lev. 17–27) their name: "Be holy, because I, the LORD your God, am holy" (v. 2). Leviticus 19 marks a conceptual center of Leviticus. It is surrounded by chapters with similar themes (Lev. 18; 20) to highlight the centrality of this passage.[1]

It is hard to see an organizing principle in the disparate laws of this chapter, save that each encourages Israel to live a holy lifestyle ethically and religiously. This chapter covers a gamut of concerns, overlapping with the Ten Commandments, ritual laws, and concerns for the poor and helpless. Holiness applies in all these areas.

Historical and Cultural Background

Neither a loving God nor the idea of God as ethically holy was typical outside of Israel. E. Jan Wilson notes, "Although one might expect the gods to be called holy, that does not occur with any great frequency," and even where applied, as with the goddess Inanna, the goddess shows no attribute of ethical holiness.[2] In Mesopotamia Akkadian terms for "holy" were only rarely applied to humans.[3] Mesopotamian gods often were not even considered "pure," much less "holy."[4] Wilson concludes that the Hebrew concept of holiness and holiness in ancient Mesopotamian religions are markedly different. Holiness in the broad sense indicated in Leviticus 19 is not among the expectations for the pious in the ancient world.

Interpretive Insights

19:1–2 *Speak to the entire assembly of Israel . . . "Be holy."* All Israel, not just priests, is to be holy, that is, "separate," both ritually and morally. Holiness is the basis of all commands.

19:3–4 *respect your mother and father . . . observe my Sabbaths . . . Do not turn to idols . . . I am the LORD your God.* These commands echo the Decalogue (Exod. 20:12, 8, 4, respectively). "Respect" is literally "fear." Abraham shows "fear" of God by obedience (Gen. 22:12). Note that the mother is no less worthy of respect than the father. Abusing parents, denigrating parents, or repudiating them in their old age are capital offenses (Exod. 21:15, 17; Deut. 21:18–21). Sabbaths set aside time for rest and for God, to recognize him as the source of order and stability. "Images" both of Yahweh and pagan gods are forbidden by this command. "Pagan images functioned as mediators for revelation and divine presence in the ancient world, and the needs of the gods were met through the images."[5] On "I am the LORD," see "Additional Insights" following this unit.

19:5–8 *sacrifice a fellowship offering . . . in such a way that it will be accepted.* Fellowship offerings help deepen one's relationship with God. See comments at Leviticus 3. Sacrifices by themselves do the offerers no good; only if God has "accepted" them do they accomplish their purpose. Acceptable sacrifices require right attitudes and right rituals. For fellowship offerings to be eaten by the third day, the offerer probably must share the meat with others. On "cut off," see "Additional Insights" following the unit on Leviticus 6:8–7:38.

19:9–10 *gleanings . . . for the poor and the foreigner.* Israel's welfare system requires landowners to show compassion by allowing the poor, including transient "foreigners," to scratch out a living by gathering leftovers after a harvest. Grain is cut by a

The Lord commands the Israelites, "Do not turn to idols or make metal gods for yourselves" (19:4). This partially gold-plated bronze figurine represents Baal, one of the gods that the Israelites were tempted to worship as they lived among the Canaanites in the promised land. The statuette is from Ugarit (fourteenth to twelfth century BC).

Key Themes of Leviticus 19:1–37

- God expects holiness.
- God commands love.

sickle close to the ears of grain and left on the ground for others to tie and gather. "Gleanings" are ears of grain that are left behind. Some inevitably are missed, but landowners are exhorted to make sure that they leave something to be gleaned. Boaz allows Ruth to utilize this system (Ruth 2:2–18).

19:11–12 *Do not steal . . . lie . . . deceive . . . swear falsely by my name and so profane the name of your God.* These behaviors (see Exod. 20:7, 15, 16) are incompatible with holiness (v. 2 above). Oaths often use the name Yahweh (e.g., "as the LORD lives" [Ruth 3:13; 1 Sam. 19:6]) to put oneself under a curse if one does not speak truthfully or keep one's affirmation. To swear falsely "profanes" God's name, showing disrespect for God by treating his name as not holy.

19:13 *Do not defraud . . . rob.* Milgrom renders the Hebrew behind "defraud" as "confiscate" (ESV as "oppress"). This Hebrew word can refer to technically legal though heartless acts: not paying a "hired worker" promptly (Deut. 24:14–15; Mal. 3:5), seizing pledges after a loan default (Ezek. 18:7), or using the authorities to confiscate houses or land or to reduce a person to slavery (Mic. 2:2). "Rob" can indicate theft that involves use of force, but used with "defraud," it probably refers to "repossession" of property using (legal) force after a default.

19:14 *Do not curse . . . put a stumbling block.* "Curse" here is verbal disrespect including cursing, insulting, slandering, or mocking. The Hebrew means "treat lightly." The perverse find this amusing because the deaf person cannot hear it. The cruel joke of putting a stumbling block in front of the blind denies the dignity of another human being.

19:15 *do not show partiality to the poor or favoritism to the great.* Given the law's concern for the poor, it is surprising that here it warns against being partial in their favor (cf. Exod. 23:3). God's justice requires that application of the law in court be blind to social standing.

19:16 *Do not . . . slander.* Like lies (v. 11c), slander is corrosive to good human relations and perverts justice in courts (Exod. 20:16; 23:1).

Do not do anything that endangers your neighbor's life. Literally, "Do not stand by the blood of your neighbor." This could refer to profiting by someone's bloodshed (NRSV) or to murdering, but given the court context of verses 15–16, the best view is that it refers to endangering an innocent life by inaction, namely, by refusing to testify.

19:17 *Do not hate a fellow Israelite . . . Rebuke your neighbor frankly.* Rather than brood in anger about "a fellow Israelite" (lit., "a brother"), try instead to correct him (v. 17b). Hebrew *yakah*, "rebuke," is used of fathers correcting sons or of the wise rebuking the wicked (Prov. 3:12; 9:7; 24:25). The wise learn from and appreciate a loving reproof (Prov. 9:8; 19:25; 28:23).

19:18 *love your neighbor.* See "Teaching the Text" below.

19:19 *Do not mate . . . plant . . . wear.* Symbolism rather than the well-being of livestock, soil, or clothing is behind laws on forbidden mixtures (cf. Deut. 22:9–11).

Mating, for example, donkeys and horses to produce mules, or sowing together wheat and barley, or combining wool and flax-linen in a garment (see Deut. 22:11) are not inherently immoral. But forbidding these mixtures serves as an object lesson in holiness. These injunctions may symbolize the prohibition of mixing with Canaanites (Deut. 7:3–6). Milgrom argues that they forbid encroaching on holy practices allowed only at the sanctuary, where some items of flax-linen and colored (wool?) yarn were mixed (Exod. 26:1, 31; 28:6, 15; 39:29)[6] and cherubim appear as crossbreeds (Ezek. 1:10). Against Milgrom's view, there is no evidence that priests used mixed-seed planting.

19:20–22 *If a man sleeps with a female slave who is promised to another man.* This is the case of an inchoately married (betrothed) slave girl whose marriage is not yet consummated and who has sex with a different man. With a freeborn woman, this would be considered adultery (Deut. 22:23–27), but here the girl is not executed because the betrothal has not been fully established by money and/or contract. At that point she becomes "freed" from the master and under the jurisdiction of her husband.

guilt offering. The offending man offers a guilt offering to God less because of the sexual sin than because of the sacrilege involved: a verbal oath pledging her to another has been violated (cf. Lev. 6:1–8). A guilt offering also compensates the master for his economic loss, for the deflowered girl is now "damaged goods." This law protects the long-term interests of vulnerable slave girls by discouraging male sexual misadventures with them.

19:23–25 *regard its fruit as forbidden.* The Hebrew behind "forbidden" is literally translated as "uncircumcised" (NIVmg). To keep "uncircumcised" fruit from being eaten, it, like an uncircumcised penis, needs to be "cut"; hence, this text seems to imply that the fruit of young trees be cut off and not allowed to develop. Such customs mark Israel as distinct from the nations. Moreover, not allowing the fruit buds of young trees to develop enlarges and strengthens the health of trees so that in the long run they produce more fruit.

19:26 *Do not eat any meat with the blood.* See comments at Leviticus 3:16–17.

Do not practice divination. Israel is to consult prophets of Yahweh who relate their prognostications to God's relationship with Israel, not the occult practices of Mesopotamia and Canaan based on the alleged whims of the gods (cf. Deut. 18:10–14, 18–19).[7]

19:27–28 *Do not cut the hair . . . your beard . . . Do not cut your bodies . . . or put tattoo marks on yourselves.* Avoiding these practices sets Israel apart from the nations (Deut. 14:1–2). This distinction is especially important for priests (cf. Lev. 21:5–6). Ultraorthodox Jews use verse 27 to justify side curls, but here cutting hair, perhaps to produce bald spots, probably refers to a mourning rite (Deut. 14:1; Ezra 9:3) (see "Historical and Cultural Background" at Lev. 21:1–24), as does verse 28a. Self-cutting was used by the prophets of Baal to get their god to act (1 Kings 18:28). On tattoos, see "Additional Insights" following this unit.

19:29–30 *Do not degrade . . . have reverence.* Note the contrast: prostitution, which degrades both women and society in general, versus reverent worship of God, which uplifts all.

19:31 *Do not turn to mediums . . . spiritists.* Necromancy, consulting the dead to

The Lord commands the Israelites, "Do not practice divination or seek omens" (19:26). In the ancient Near East, when people needed to make an important decision or wanted to know the best action to take, they often turned to divination. A question would be posed, an animal sacrificed, and its entrails examined. This clay model of a liver was used to help diviners interpret what the gods were communicating when a liver was inspected (1900–1600 BC).

divine the future, relates to the cult of the dead, in which the living "sustained" and honored dead ancestors with food offerings. This is a worldview incompatible with the Bible's theology.[8]

19:32 *show respect for the elderly.* This respect goes along with reverence for God.

19:33–34 *When a foreigner resides among you . . . Love them as yourself.* Prohibition of pagan practices does not justify mistreating pagan foreigners among the Israelites. Israel is to treat foreigners decently. They glean fields beside Israel's poor (Lev. 19:10), rest on Sabbaths (Exod. 20:10), sacrifice to Yahweh (Num. 15:14), and keep Passover if circumcised (Exod. 12:48). The Israelites' experience as foreigners in Egypt has given them a basis for empathy. "Love them as yourself" echoes Leviticus 19:18b. The foreigner is the Israelites' neighbor too. Compare Jesus's parable of the good Samaritan (Luke 10:25–37).

19:35–36 *Do not use dishonest standards.* Scales were used to weigh grains of silver used as money before coins were invented.

19:37 *I am the* Lord. See "Additional Insights" following this unit.

Theological Insights

Holiness is a key theme in Leviticus 19 (vv. 2, 8, 24), as is love (vv. 19, 34). They are also key themes in the New Testament. Peter applies Leviticus 19:2 (= 11:44), "Be holy because I . . . am holy," to the church (1 Pet. 1:16). Jesus lists Leviticus 19:18, "Love your neighbor as yourself," as one of the two greatest commandments (Matt. 22:36–40). Paul and James reiterate the importance of Leviticus 19:18 for Christian ethics (Rom. 13:9; Gal. 5:14; James 2:8).

But are holiness and love compatible? Some people play the one against the other, emphasizing the love of God at the expense of his holiness, or emphasizing God's holiness to the neglect of his love. But God is both loving (Exod. 34:6–7; 1 John 4:8) and holy (Lev. 19:2; Isa. 6:3). Love and righteousness can embrace each other (Ps. 85:10). God's justice and forgiveness are made simultaneously possible through the cross (Rom. 3:25–26).

Teaching the Text

1. *God expects holiness.* Holiness is an attribute of God that he expects his people to reflect (Lev. 19:2) so that God can remain in their midst. Arguably, holiness is behind all the laws of this chapter.

Reformed theologians sometimes divide the attributes of God into communicable and incommunicable.[9] Incommunicable attributes are ones that only God has:

omnipotence, omniscience, omnipresence, eternality, and the like. Communicable attributes are those that at least in part can be found in his human creatures: justice, purity, goodness, and love. The Israelites were to show holiness in the ethical sphere by being like God in these communicable attributes. By following the laws, they would be "set apart" from the nations morally and ritually.

Although ethical and ceremonial laws overlap, ethical laws promoting Israel's holiness are the easiest to apply today. The laws echoing the Ten Commandments (Exod. 20:1–17) concerning idolatry, taking God's name in vain, adultery, theft, false testimony, and honoring parents can be applied today directly, since all of them are repeated in some form in the New Testament. So is the command to love our neighbors. The Sabbath law has a ceremonial element that requires adjustment (Saturday), but its principles of rest and setting aside time for God remain applicable (see commentary at Lev. 19:3–4). Laws on helping the poor, treating the disabled and hired workers decently, and applying laws equally to all social classes seem universally valid. Though slavery is not legally practiced today (and should not be), the goal of Leviticus 19:20–22, 29–30 to protect vulnerable girls from sexual abuse remains an ethical imperative.

Laws that have more elements of ritual holiness are harder to apply today, though we can look for moral or religious principles behind such laws that still apply. Laws on breeding, sowing, wearing clothes, and "circumcising" trees (vv. 19, 23–25) inculcated in Israel a sense of being a holy people. Such laws no longer apply today, though we should seek in our own ways to cultivate a sense of being a holy people. Fellowship offerings (vv. 5–6), atoning animal sacrifices (vv. 21–22), and purity with meat and blood (v. 26a) ceased to function when Jesus established the new covenant, but the principles of seeking to deepen one's relationship with God and imploring God's forgiveness through blood atonement (through Christ) remain valid. Laws telling the Israelites to avoid things associated with paganism, such as idolatry, magic, and necromancy (vv. 4, 26b, 31), helped them to maintain holiness, as New Testament injunctions about not being of the world (John 17:14–16) and rejecting false doctrines do for Christians today.

2. *God commands love.* Like holiness, "Love your neighbor as yourself" (v. 18) is a basis for other laws, as Jesus and Paul state (Matt. 22:37–40; Rom. 13:9). Love of neighbor motivates generosity (vv. 9–10) and honesty (vv. 11, 35–36). Love of neighbor motivates treating one's workers decently (v. 13b). Eating fellowship offerings by the third day (vv. 5–6) can be an occasion to express neighborly love by inviting over family and friends—neighbors—so that the feast does not go to waste. Love can motivate delaying foreclosure of property even if legal (v. 13a), because love trumps legal rights. Love of neighbor is expressed by respect for parents (v. 3), the handicapped, and the elderly (vv. 3, 14, 32). Foreigners are neighbors too: "Love them as yourself," the text says (v. 34; cf. Luke 10:25–37); help them, do not exploit them (vv. 10, 33). Animosity or taking revenge is incompatible with loving neighbors, but reproving them can be an act of loving correction (vv. 17–18). Sexual impropriety is incompatible with truly loving a neighbor (vv. 20–22, 29). Love of neighbor motivates making courts fair to everybody regardless of social standing (vv. 15–16).

Love of neighbor is central to God's law. It undergirds every command concerning how people are to treat one another. And love of neighbor remains central to Christian ethics.

Illustrating the Text

We are called to reflect God's holiness.

Metaphor: Many people can remember walking through a funhouse hall of mirrors, laughing at the ways their image was distorted. Short and squat. Tall and thin. Big head and tiny body. It is amazing what mirrors can do. The people of God are called to reflect his holiness in the world. What kind of image do we project?

We are called to love our neighbors.

Television: The legend of Big Foot, or Sasquatch, found its way into a series of television commercials under the general heading "Messin' with Sasquatch." Each commercial involves someone maliciously teasing this mythical creature. In one commercial, a person offers to shake hands but is holding a practical-joke hand buzzer that shocks the creature. In another, Sasquatch is tricked into opening a can of soda that has been shaken. In each case Sasquatch gets mad and in poetic justice takes revenge on his taunters.

These childish and mean-spirited pranks done to Sasquatch can remind us of what Leviticus 19:14 describes: "cursing the deaf," who cannot hear the nasty words, or putting "a stumbling block in front of the blind" for the sheer amusement of watching them fall. But such things are the opposite of the command to "love your neighbor as yourself" (v. 19).

"I Am the LORD" | Tattoos

"I Am the LORD"

The Pentateuch frequently adds to a statement the interjection "I am the LORD [= Yahweh]" (e.g., Lev. 11:44–45; 18:2, 4–6, 21, 30; 19:3–4, 10, 12, 18, 25, 28, 30–32, 34, 36–37). This expression sounds odd to readers today. For example, I cannot imagine saying to my college students, "Do your homework; I am Joe Sprinkle." But that is the sort of thing God often says in the Pentateuch. What does it mean?

Perhaps this formula can be illuminated by similar pronouncements of ancient Near Eastern kings seeking to publicize their accomplishments.[1] It can introduce a statement about God's power to heal and sanctify Israel (Exod. 15:26; 31:13; Lev. 20:24), but it especially introduces God's accomplishment of redeeming his people from Egypt (Exod. 20:2; 29:46; Lev. 11:45; 19:36), God's great act of salvation in the Old Testament. Mentioning God's

The forbidden tattoos may have been those that were part of a mourning rite. Evidence of body tattoos can be seen on the leg, arm, and shoulder of this figure painted on a plaque from a palace door at Medinet Habu in Egypt (1187–1156 BC).

deliverance of the Israelites serves to motivate them on the basis of gratitude to obey God's laws and be holy: "I am the LORD, who brought you up out of Egypt . . . ; therefore be holy" (Lev. 11:45).

The expression "I am Yahweh" without a statement of accomplishment hints at the longer one that adds "who brought you up out of Egypt" and has a similar motivational function. It means, "It is I, Yahweh your God, your redeemer, who has spoken this, so give heed!" It is a way of saying that God's promises are sure because of who he is (Gen. 28:13; Exod. 6:6, 8; 7:17; 12:12; Lev. 26:45). It is used to emphasize that the Bible's laws are divine, so Israel must be especially careful to obey them (e.g., Lev. 18:2–6, 21, 26). There is also an implicit warning of judgment if laws are ignored (cf. Lev. 22:3). See Leviticus 19:14, 32; 25:17, where "fear your God" precedes "I am the LORD."

Christians too can reflect on the fact that they owe God their full allegiance and obedience because of who God is and because he has redeemed them (Rom. 12:1; 1 Cor. 6:20; 1 Pet. 1:18–19).

Tattoos

Leviticus 19:28 forbids putting "tattoo marks" on one's body. Tattooing was known in Mesopotamia and Egypt and was sometimes used to mark slaves.[2] Verse 28b, besides being a prohibition of gouging oneself in mourning (v. 28a), suggests that this tattooing is a mourning rite, though archaeological evidence of tattooing as a mourning custom is lacking.

Given the popularity of tattoos nowadays, the application of Leviticus 19:28 is of special interest. This verse was taken by Jewish philosopher Maimonides as prohibiting "tattooing the body after the manner of idolaters" (negative command #41) and Judaism took it as a general prohibition against tattooing.[3] This verse was used by the church to suppress tattooing in early Christian Europe, though the church sometimes allowed exceptions for religious tattoos. Some argue that tattoos constitute self-mutilation, something incompatible with treating the body as the temple of the Holy Spirit (1 Cor. 6:19–20). On the other hand, if, as seems likely, this verse is primarily prohibiting certain pagan mourning rites, then this law is less applicable to decorative tattoos than to avoiding things associated with idolatry.

Punishments for Sin

Big Idea *God holds people accountable for their sins.*

Understanding the Text

The Text in Context

Leviticus 20 is another chapter in the laws of holiness (Lev. 17–27), making its own explicit call to holiness (vv. 7–8) and, near the end of the chapter, issuing a concluding call to holiness (v. 26).

Holiness in this chapter revolves around idolatry and sexuality. The chapter overlaps considerably in content with Leviticus 18 (sexual offenses, Molek worship) and to some degree with Leviticus 19 between the two. Leviticus 20 differs from Leviticus 18 by adding specific penalties for many of the offenses listed in Leviticus 18. Such penalties would drive the nation in the direction of separation toward God—that is, holiness.

The outline of Leviticus 20 is roughly chiastic:[1]

A Stoning case (re: Molek) and necromancy (vv. 1–6)
  B Call to holiness (vv. 7–8)
    C Punishment for offenses of the individuals/families (vv. 9–21)
    C′ Punishment for offenses of the whole nation (vv. 22–24a)
  B′ Call to holiness (vv. 24b–26)
A′ Necromancers receive stoning (v. 27)

Interpretive Insights

20:2–3 *sacrifices . . . to Molek.* On sacrifice to Molek, see comments at Leviticus 18:21.

stone him . . . cut him off. Child sacrifice (see "Historical and Cultural Background" at Lev. 18:1–30 and comments at Lev. 18:21) is subject to a double penalty: stoning to death by the human community (v. 2) and being cut off from one's people by God (v. 3). Cutting off (see "Additional Insights" following the unit on Lev. 6:8–7:38) involves something beyond stoning, such as termination of one's line of descendants or, more likely, separation from one's relatives in the afterlife.

20:4–5 *if they fail to put him to death, I . . . will cut them off.* Failure to execute those engaging in human sacrifice is subject to the same penalty as the offense itself.

prostituting themselves. Hebrew *zanah* is a broad term for sexual offenses of all sorts, not restricted to prostitution. The immorality here is metaphorical for infidelity to Israel's covenant with Yahweh by engaging in pagan religion. Child sacrifice combines murder with idolatry and thus receives the most severe punishment of any offense in the chapter.

20:6 *anyone who turns to mediums and spiritualists to prostitute themselves.* On the

There are dire consequences for mediums and spiritualists and for those who seek their services. This stele venerates Khonsu, who has received the title "excellent spirit of Ra," indicating her intermediary status between the living and the gods (Thebes, Nineteenth Dynasty, 1295–1186 BC).

- There are different penalties for different sins.
- There are also exceptions to the penalties.

20:9 *Anyone who curses their father or mother.* Contrast "respect" for parents (Lev. 19:3). "Curses" is too specific a rendering. Hebrew *qalal* can mean "treat with disrespect," "abuse," "derogate," "denigrate," "repudiate," but rarely "curse."[2] Formally, it means "to treat as light" and is the opposite of "to honor" (*kabbed*; lit., "to treat as heavy") (cf. Exod. 20:12). Leviticus 20:9 refers to a breach of duty toward a parent so flagrant as to deserve death. Physical abuse of parents is such an offense (Exod. 21:15), but it is distinguished from "cursing" (*qalal*) (Exod. 21:17). A son's incorrigibility, a capital offense if the parents choose to prosecute (Deut. 21:18–21), is probably a case of *qalal*. Sons are to care for parents in their old age (see Ruth 4:15). Repudiating aging parents would be another case of *qalal*. A rabbinic rule that gave people an excuse not to care for elderly parents leads Jesus to cite this verse or its parallel in Exodus 21:17 in rebuke (Matt. 15:4–6; Mark 7:10–13).

20:10 *If a man commits adultery.* Adultery is a capital offense (also Deut. 22:24), but only if proven by the testimony of two or three witnesses (Deut. 17:6–7). Sometimes ransom or divorce will be accepted instead (Prov. 6:32–35; Jer. 3:8).

20:11–12 *If a man has sexual relations with his father's wife . . . with his daughter-in-law.* Incest with a stepmother is a capital offense even if the father is dead. If he is alive, the case is covered under adultery. On Paul's use of this, see "Theological Insights" below. Incest includes biologically unrelated in-laws ("daughter-in-law"), so

religious aspect of necromancy, see comments at Leviticus 19:31. On "prostitute themselves," see verse 5 above. God threatens to punish those consulting spiritualists personally, though no punishment by the state is mentioned. Thus, "users" of necromancy are threatened with direct divine punishment, while the "pushers" of this activity, the mediums and spiritualists themselves, are subject to human execution (v. 27 below).

20:7–8 *be holy, because I am the LORD.* Holiness, related to obeying God's commands, is the key theme of Leviticus 17–27. On "I am the LORD," see "Additional Insights" following the unit on Leviticus 19:1–37.

it is not a matter of genetic consequences; a sense of propriety plays a more significant role.

20:13 *If a man has sexual relations with a man.* On Paul's use of this passage, see "Theological Insights" below.

20:14 *burned in the fire.* This penalty is specified only for incest with a woman and her mother. "Burned" could refer to cremation after stoning (cf. Gen. 38:24; Judg. 15:6),[3] though it is odd that this penalty is stronger than that for other incest cases. "Branded" is another possible interpretation. If so, a lesser penalty is specified, since marriage to either woman is permitted, just not to both at the same time. Though known in Egypt,[4] branding is not attested in the Bible as a judicial penalty, with the possible exception of Leviticus 21:9.

20:15–16 *sexual relations with an animal.* Bestiality violates the divine hierarchy that separates humans made in God's image from animals (cf. Gen. 1:26–28). Though the beast has no choice, it is objectively guilty, and the repugnance of the act is underscored by having the beast executed along with the man or the woman. Compare Exodus 21:28–29, 35–36, where an ox that kills a person is executed, whereas an ox that kills an ox is not.[5]

20:17 *If a man marries his sister . . . and they have sexual relations.* The punishment of being "publicly removed" is literally "cut off in the sight of their people." To be "cut off" implies a punishment from God (see "Additional Insights" following the unit on Lev. 6:8–7:38). This is appropriate because offenses like incest are difficult to prove in court due to lack of witnesses.

20:18 *If a man has sexual relations with a woman during her monthly period.* It is

surprising to find this ritual offense listed alongside bestiality, incest, and homosexuality, with violators threatened with divine punishment ("cut off"). Richard Davidson concludes from this that the law in principle remains applicable today, arguing that it promotes health and wellness (see commentary at Lev. 15:19–24).[6] On the other hand, other laws of cleanness/uncleanness (Lev. 11–15) do not seem to function under the new covenant.

20:20 *they will die childless.* Childlessness is not necessarily a penalty from God, though it is threatened as one here.

20:21 *If a man marries his brother's wife.* Marriage to a brother's wife can occur after a brother divorces her or he dies. Levirate marriage, in which the brother's widow is childless, constitutes a permitted exception to this rule (Deut. 25:5–7).

20:22–23 *vomit you out.* This metaphor is fulfilled by God's directing Israel to drive the Canaanites out of the land. He commands this because of abhorrent sins like those listed in this chapter. But in an echo of the warning of Leviticus 18:24–28, if Israel does these forbidden things, the land will expel them too. Eventually, the Israelites act like Canaanites, including making human sacrifices to Molek (2 Kings 23:10), and they are expelled from the land first by Assyria in 722 BC (2 Kings 17:7–23) and then by Babylon in 586 BC (2 Kings 25:21).

20:24 *a land flowing with milk and honey.* The land is good for livestock and sweet things such as date syrup and bee's honey. See further comments at Numbers 13:27.

20:26 *be holy.* The warning of verses 22–24a leads to a renewed call to holiness. Holiness is symbolized by the clean/unclean animals system (v. 25 [see Lev. 11]), which teaches Israel to be different from other people groups.

20:27 *A man or woman who is a medium or spiritist.* See comments at verse 6 above.

Theological Insights

Are the human penalties recorded in Old Testament law still binding under the new covenant?[7] My answer is that Christians are not obligated to follow the law's sanctions, but they should accept the law's ethical principles.

Paul derives from Leviticus 20:11 that incest with one's father's wife is morally wrong, but Paul's sanction is excommunication (1 Cor. 5:1–12), not execution. Paul indicates that the offender is in danger of a divine penalty from which he needs to be "saved," but he gives no hint that Leviticus's death penalty might still apply.

Paul mentions other offenses like those in Leviticus 20 in 1 Corinthians 6:9–10:

> Or do you not know that wrongdoers will not inherit the kingdom of God? Do not be deceived: Neither the *sexually immoral* nor *idolaters* nor *adulterers* nor *men who have sex with men* [note that two Greek terms translated by this phrase refer to the passive and active partners in homosexual acts] nor thieves nor the greedy nor drunkards nor slanderers nor swindlers will inherit the kingdom of God.

The italicized terms parallel offenses found in Leviticus 20, where death is the sanction. A Greek term used for homosexual behavior here is actually derived from Leviticus 20:13. The second of Paul's words referring to homosexuals in 1 Corinthians 6:9, *arsenokoitai*, combines elements of the word "male" (*arsēn*) and the word "bed/intercourse" (*koitē*). This compound word, not found in any extant Greek text earlier than 1 Corinthians, apparently is derived from the pre-Christian Septuagint translation of Leviticus 20:13.[8] Thus, Paul's use of the term presupposes and reaffirms Leviticus's condemnation of homosexual acts for the Christian. He warns that those engaging in such behaviors are in danger of exclusion from the kingdom of God, but he never implies that homosexuals should be executed. Again, Paul affirms the morality of the law, but in view of the changed historical and theological circumstances, he does not apply its sanction.

In the book of Revelation behaviors found in Leviticus 20 are also condemned, but the sanction, though severe, comes from God, not from humans: "But the cowardly, the unbelieving, the vile, the murderers, the *sexually immoral*, those *who practice magic arts*, the *idolaters* and all liars—they will be consigned to the fiery lake of burning sulfur. This is the second death" (Rev. 21:8). Revelation 22:15 reiterates: "Outside [the heavenly city] are the *dogs* [term used of male prostitutes in LXX Deut. 23:18], those *who practice magic arts*, the *sexually immoral*, the murderers, the *idolaters* and everyone who loves and practices falsehood."

Again, the italicized terms parallel offenses mentioned in Leviticus 20. Those who practice the sorts of things described in Leviticus 20 are in danger of hell. This is hinted at in Leviticus 20's threat that offenders can be "cut off from their people" (vv. 5–6, 17–18), a punishment probably related to the afterlife (see "Additional Insights" following the unit on Lev. 6:8–7:38).

So while the Old Testament human sanctions no longer apply under the new covenant, the New Testament threatens even more-severe divine sanctions for the same offenses. Canaanite-type behaviors are incompatible with being in the promised land or in heaven (cf. Lev. 20:22). Those who persist in doing dreadfully wicked things betray through their behaviors that they do not belong to God (cf. Matt. 7:16–23). But the New Testament adds that even these people can be changed, forgiven, and become part of God's church through Christ (1 Cor. 6:11).

Teaching the Text

1. *There are different penalties for different sins.* Punishments in this chapter vary according to the offense:

Punishment	Offense
Stoning to death and divine cutting off	Child sacrifice (vv. 2–3)
Stoning to death	Mediums/spiritualists (v. 27)
Execution	Cursing parents (v. 9), adultery (v. 10), incest with father's wife or daughter-in-law (vv. 11–12), homosexual copulation (v. 13), bestiality (vv. 15–16)
Burning	Incest with woman and her mother (v. 14)
Bearing their penalty	Incest with biologically related aunt (v. 19)
Bearing their penalty/iniquity with childlessness	Incest with biologically unrelated aunts (vv. 20–21)
Divine cutting off	Tolerating child sacrifice (vv. 4–5), consulting mediums (v. 6), incest with half sister (v. 17), sex with a menstruant (v. 18)
The nation being expelled from the land	Living like Canaanites (vv. 22–24)

Note that some of these cases involve human punishment, while others involve divine punishment (e.g., childlessness, cutting off, and expulsion from the land). Knowing that some offenses are punished is appropriate, for incest is typically done in secret and is not readily subject to human prosecution. But eventually secret sins will be made public by God (vv. 17–18), and God will hold people accountable whether or not they are ever brought before a human court. Those punishments will vary according to the crime.

Not all crimes today should be punished equally. Some sins are worse than others and deserve greater punishment. Justice demands that penalties vary according to the crime.

2. *There are also exceptions to the penalties.* Are the laws here like modern case laws without exceptions unless exceptions are specified? On the contrary, biblical civil laws, like ancient Near Eastern laws (compare Hammurabi's Code), provide illustrations of justice rather than a law code. Raymond Westbrook writes of Mesopotamian laws, "[The court] looked to the code, not for an exact, mechanical precedent, but for the principle that the code indirectly laid down through its examples."[9] It would be up to judges to apply these principles, taking into consideration any mitigating circumstances. Accordingly, the penalties given in Leviticus 20 probably are maximum penalties. Capital offenses required two or three witnesses (Deut. 17:6), but eyewitnesses are difficult to find for sexual sins done in secret. A person might be an unwilling participant in an illicit liaison, such as a young boy coerced into homosexual sex or a female family member raped by a male relative. Surely, such persons would not be executed. Was there no leniency for remorse? Or for

age? Would a six-year-old girl who in a fit of anger "cursed" her parents be summarily executed without warning or taking her age into consideration? Surely not!

Even in the case of adultery, execution was not always carried out. The husband might be the only witness. He might accept ransom in lieu of execution (cf. Prov. 6:32–35). Or in mercy the offended husband, like the righteous Joseph in the New Testament (Matt. 1:19), might choose divorce over execution. God metaphorically "divorced" Israel rather than executing it for adultery (Jer. 3:8).

Even if these penalties were not always carried out, the seriousness of these offenses is underscored by the fact that they were potentially capital offenses or otherwise subject to a divine "cutting off." Moreover, these laws served as covenant stipulations that defined moral standards expected of God's people.

Illustrating the Text

The law provided guidance in understanding the nature and severity of sin.

Science: One of the important tools psychiatrists use for their work is the *Diagnostic and Statistical Manual of Mental Disorders*. The manual outlines various abnormalities, describing and listing symptoms. It provides a common vocabulary for clinicians to discuss the issues that they address. Ultimately, it is meant to help make the process of treatment more effective. In one way, the law served (and serves) a similar function. It helped people recognize and understand the problem of sin. It helped those who lived under the law to grasp where and when it arose and how serious it really was.

We should not assume that "secret sins" will remain so forever.

Quote: In his *Poor Richard's Almanac*, Benjamin Franklin cynically quipped, "Three can keep a secret, if two of them are dead." We must remember that there is always a witness to our secret thoughts and deeds.

Object Lesson: Using an ultraviolet marker, write a message on a piece of white paper as you speak. The message can be something convicting, such as "God is not mocked," or simple, such as "No more secrets." As you write the message, say, "Our every action is another sentence in the story of our existence. There are things we feel comfortable revealing and things we want to hide." At this point, hold up the message on the apparently blank paper. "But in the light of God's presence, every secret is revealed." As you say this, hold the message under an ultraviolet light to reveal the message.

The Levitical civil laws and their penalties provide an illustration of what justice looks like and give guidance for Israelite judges as they hear legal cases. The Levitical laws functioned in much the same way as collections of legal sayings from other cultures such as the stele of Hammurabi shown here (eighteenth century BC).

Holiness of Priests

Big Idea *Those who lead God's people in worship must show a special degree of separation to God.*

Understanding the Text

The Text in Context

Leviticus 21 is the first of two chapters on the holiness of priests, teaching how, as servants of Yahweh's holy things, they must maintain a special degree of holiness or else be disqualified from serving the sanctuary. This is thus a continuation of the theme of holiness found in what is commonly referred to as the holiness code (Lev. 17–27).

Leviticus 21:1–22:31 is arranged in a chiastic structure, with avoiding desecration of sacrifices as the central point:[1]

  A Relation of a priest to his family for sacrifice (21:1–15)

    B Blemishes of priests who sacrifice (21:16–24)

      C How a priest should avoid desecration of sacrifices (22:1–16)

    B′ Blemishes of animals for sacrifice (22:17–25)

  A′ Relation of an animal and its family for sacrifice (22:26–31)

Historical and Cultural Background

Leviticus 21:5–6 alludes to mourning rites that priests were to avoid. Mourning for Joseph lasted seven days (Gen. 50:10), and for Moses and Aaron thirty days (Num. 20:29; Deut. 34:8). Sometimes professional mourners were hired to add poignancy (Jer. 9:17–19). Acts of mourning included weeping, tearing one's clothes, walking barefoot, covering one's head, and wearing sackcloth (Gen. 37:29, 34; 2 Sam. 15:30). It might also involve not washing one's feet or trimming one's mustache or washing one's clothes or wearing cosmetic lotions (2 Sam. 14:2; 19:24). Egyptian rites sometimes involved beating one's head while mourning or raking one's face with the fingernails to make the cheeks bleed, and mixing blood, tears, and dust and tossing on the head.[2] Pagan rites could involve other self-mutilations, though Israelites and especially priests were forbidden from doing such things (Lev. 19:27–28; 21:5–6).

Interpretive Insights

21:1–4 *A priest must not make himself ceremonially unclean for any of his people who die, except for a close relative.* Unlike ministers today, Old Testament priests cannot conduct funerals. Contact with the dead makes people unclean for seven days (Num. 19:11) and makes a priest unfit to serve the sanctuary for seven days beyond that (Ezek. 44:25–27). God is to be associated with life, not death (cf. Deut. 30:15–20). Things concerning death are inimical to God's vibrant presence. See further "Teaching the Text" at Numbers 19.

21:5–6 *Priests must not shave their heads . . . the edges of their beards or cut their bodies.* These pagan mourning rites (LXX adds "for the dead" [cf. Deut. 14:1]) are discouraged for all Israelites (see Lev. 19:27–28), but abstaining from them is especially important for priests in God's sanctuary. Joy, rather than mourning, is usually more appropriate to being in God's presence (cf. Deut. 12:12), and pagan-style rites are doubly inappropriate. Self-inflicted blemishes would make priests unfit to carry out priestly duties, just as blemished animals are unfit for the altar (Lev. 22:22).

21:7–8 *They must not marry women defiled by prostitution or divorced.* All sexual emissions bring some degree of ceremonial uncleanness (see Lev. 15). Priests are to reduce their exposure to such uncleanness and maintain their elevated holiness by marrying virgins, though only the high priest is prohibited from marrying a widow (v. 14). That the list for the high priest adds the morally innocent "widow" (v. 14) suggests that ceremonial uncleanness

from previous sexual activity is primarily in view, not morality. The NIV's rendering "women defiled by prostitution" (*zonah wahalalah*) is too specific because *zonah* can refer to prostitutes who exchange sex for money or to sexually immoral women generally. Moreover, *halalah* probably refers to another category of woman, the "defiled/deflowered [i.e., raped] woman" (cf. ESV; order reversed in v. 14 below). A raped woman is likely morally innocent, but she is still ineligible to marry a priest due to the elevated ceremonial impurity contracted from the rape. Similarly, a divorced woman can be morally innocent but is excluded from marrying a priest because her previous sexual activity would bring into the marriage an elevated degree of ceremonial uncleanness.

21:9 *If a priest's daughter defiles herself.* "By becoming a prostitute" is better rendered "by promiscuity" (HCSB; see v. 7 above). "Disgraces her father" is better rendered "profanes her father" (ESV). The word *halal* in the Piel stem is used in priestly contexts of "defiling" or "desecration" of that which is holy, whether defiling holy fellowship and grain offerings (Lev. 19:8; Num. 18:32), or holy Sabbaths (Ezek. 20:13), or the

To remain holy before the Lord, priests are forbidden to shave their heads. There was no such restriction in Egypt, as this statue of an Egyptian priest attests (588–534 BC).

sanctuary (Lev. 21:23), or God's holy name (Lev. 19:12; 22:2). The NIV's rendering, "disgraces," though true, misses the point about defilement of the holy priest through his daughter's behavior. Her promiscuity brings an elevated level of impurity into the priest's household that can contaminate him and make him subject to divine wrath when entering God's presence. Because this daughter's behavior defiles a priest, she is punished severely, unlike seduced common maidens (see Exod. 22:16–17). "Burned" typically is taken to indicate execution and cremation (cf. Gen. 38:24; Judg. 15:6), an ignoble punishment for putting her father into mortal danger in the sanctuary. Unlikely but conceivable is an alternative view that this refers to branding to stigmatize her and mar her beauty (Isa. 3:24; cf. comments at Lev. 20:14).

21:10–12 *The high priest . . . must not make himself unclean.* The high priest is to maintain even stricter holiness and avoid ritual impurity more than ordinary priests because he alone enters the most holy place (Lev. 16:3). Accordingly, unlike ordinary priests (vv. 1–4 above), the high priest cannot even participate in the burial of his parents. A similar rule applies to Nazirites (Num. 6:7). On "anointing oil" and "priestly garments" (vv. 10a, 12b), see Exodus 29:5–7; Leviticus 8:5–9, 12, 30. On "unkempt hair" (v. 10b), see Leviticus 10:6; 13:45. Tearing clothes (v. 10c) is an act of mourning (Gen. 37:34). On "I am the LORD" (v. 12c), see "Additional Insights" following the unit on Leviticus 19:1–37.

21:13–15 *The woman he marries must be . . . a virgin from his own people.* Also to maintain the stricter holiness of the high priesthood, the high priest can marry only a virgin from priestly (or possibly Levitical) lineage. In addition to the categories of women that ordinary priests are forbidden to marry (v. 7), this list includes the "widow" (v. 14), which other priests evidently can marry. A widow is morally innocent, but her sexual activity in her previous marriage creates enough ceremonial impurity (see comments at vv. 7–8 above) to disqualify her from marrying the most-holy high priest, though not enough to keep her from marrying an ordinary priest. "Defile his offspring" (on *halal* ["defile"], see v. 9) warns a high priest that if he disobeys this rule by marrying a nonvirgin, he will disqualify his children from priestly service or prerogatives.

21:16–23 *none of your descendants who has a defect may come near.* Physical handicaps preclude certain people today from certain jobs—for example, a blind person from being an airplane pilot. So certain physical conditions preclude a person from being a priest. In Israel holiness is related to wholeness: physical defects transfer a priest from the category of "holy" to that of "common," rendering him like lay Israelites, unqualified to serve at the altar. Not coincidentally, analogous defects in animals render them "common" and hence unfit to be a "holy" sacrifice offered on the altar (Lev. 22:21–25). On the significance of this injunction, see "Theological Insights" below.

Theological Insights

Priests are set apart from ordinary Israelites as holy (Lev. 21:6, 7, 8, 15, 23). As God's special servants, they are to reflect as much as possible the purity and perfections of the realm of the divine.[3] God is to be associated with life, not death, so priests—especially the high priest—must avoid that which has to do with death, including mourning rituals for the dead (Lev. 21:1–8, 10–12). God is completely pure, so priests even in their marriages must minimize ritual impurity by their choice of wives (Lev. 21:7, 13–14). God is perfect, so the priest must symbolize this perfection by being physically whole. Accordingly, physical defects disqualify persons from serving as priests (Lev. 21:16–23).

The New Testament sees in the holiness that priests were to display a reflection of the greater high priest, Jesus Christ (cf. Heb. 3:1; 4:14; 10:21). Christ as high priest really is what Aaronic priests were supposed to be: "holy, blameless, pure, and set apart from sinners" (Heb. 7:26). He is also completely unblemished morally (Heb. 9:14; 1 Pet. 1:19) and, to a degree, physically (John 19:36). As God's Son, he reflects in his person the purity and perfections of the divine realm as no other Israelite priest ever could (cf. Heb. 1:3).

Teaching the Text

God's ministers have a special sanctity. Leviticus 21, on the special holiness of priests, at first seems completely irrelevant to Christians because the Levitical priesthood has been abolished under the new covenant. And yet the passage does remind us of the special holiness that one should expect of Christian leaders. There are special requirements for church leaders as there were special requirements for Israel's priests. These requirements reflect similar principles.

In the New Testament, elders or overseers (these terms are interchangeable) must, like priests, be holy (Titus 1:8). Just as priests must have special purity in their marriages (Lev. 21:7–8, 13–14),

Being near a dead body renders one unclean, so there are special guidelines for the priests. The high priest is required to avoid a dead body, while other priests may help with the death of a close relative. However, all priests are to avoid certain mourning rituals to maintain their holiness before the Lord. This relief, which was part of the wall of a tomb at Saqqara in Egypt, shows mourners demonstrating their sorrow while participating in a funeral procession (1550–1292 BC).

Leviticus 21:1–24

so there are requirements for marital purity for church elders/overseers: if married, he must be "faithful to his wife" (lit., "of one woman a man" [1 Tim. 3:2; Titus 1:6]). Priests can be defiled by their daughter's bad behavior (Lev. 21:9), so elders/overseers can be disqualified from service by the bad behavior of their children: elders must manage their own households well and raise children who are believing and obedient (1 Tim. 3:4–5; Titus 1:6–7). Priests must have ritual purity and physical integrity—they cannot be blind or lame or otherwise deformed—whereas Paul says that Christian elders and deacons must have moral integrity and lack moral blemishes such as quick-temperedness or drunkenness (see 1 Tim. 3:1–13; Titus 1:5–9). Just as pagan mourning practices disqualify a priest from service, so non-Christian or pagan beliefs and practices disqualify a person from Christian leadership, for only those affirming "sound doctrine" can serve as elders (Titus 1:9).

Thus Christian leaders, like Israel's priests, are to maintain a special degree of holiness. Christian leaders are to do what all Christians are supposed to do, but they are expected to do so more consistently. Christian leaders should be held to Christian standards more strictly than laypeople, just as Israel's priests were held to stricter standards than common Israelites were. As Warren Wiersbe deduces from this passage, "If we want to have God's blessing

"No descendant of Aaron the priest who has any defect is to come near to present the food offerings to the Lord" (21:21). In contrast, this papyrus reconstruction of a stele relief shows an Egyptian priest with a deformed leg presenting offerings.

on our ministry, we must keep ourselves, our marriages, and our families pure and dedicated before God."[4]

Illustrating the Text

Church leaders must seek to live morally pure lives.

History: Before doctors knew about "germs," the Hungarian physician Ignaz Semmelweis made a medical observation that contributed to the progress of medicine. He became aware in the 1840s that mothers whose babies were delivered by physicians at his hospital had double the incidence of maternal mortality from puerperal fever than mothers whose babies were delivered by midwives. Having no idea about what might be causing this, he latched upon the theory that it had something to do with cleanliness. Medical students did autopsies on cadavers and would at times come from that activity to deliver a baby without carefully washing. Perhaps they were bringing "cadaverous particles" that were killing the mothers. In fact they were: they were bringing bacteria on their hands and scalpels. The midwives, in contrast, did not handle cadavers and so infected the mothers less often.

Semmelweis followed up his theory by insisting that medical students and doctors wash their hands in a solution of chlorinated lime before delivering babies. Many of them considered this an unnecessary burden and resisted. But after the practice was adopted, the mortality rate among mothers giving birth dropped 90 percent.

Those who lead God's people must be like good doctors. Doctors are to cleanse themselves of all bacteria and infection. Church leaders similarly are to be holy and uncontaminated morally. If they fail to live up to that standard, they may, like physicians before Semmelweis, end up contaminating and harming those whom they are supposed to help and serve.

Sin is insanity.

Story: A young pastor in his first ministry calling had the opportunity to spend regular time being mentored by the senior pastor, who happened to be his father. Periodically, they would head out of the office for a walk or a cup of coffee. They would talk about family, life, and ministry. The young pastor would ask questions. Often, his father would share stories. On one of these days, the older pastor shared a series of stories about pastors he had known, some personally and others professionally. One theme wove through each tale: gross moral failure. Each story began with a person who was "at the top of his game" and ended with broken lives and devastated churches. When the father finished telling these stories, he turned and said, "Son, sin is insanity. If you let it grip you, you lose all sense of perspective. You'll do anything." All people, especially leaders in the kingdom, must beware of the mind-breaking power of sin.

You might want to share this story, or one of your own stories about how you have seen sin lead people to insane behavior.

Holy God, Holy Priests, Holy Offerings

Big Idea *When God's people and their spiritual leaders show respect for God and his word, God molds them into a holy people.*

Understanding the Text

The Text in Context

Leviticus 22 is the second of two chapters on the holiness of priests, teaching how they as servants of Yahweh's holy things must maintain a special degree of holiness. This is thus a continuation of the theme of holiness found throughout in the holiness code (Lev. 17–27).

This chapter continues the chiasm from the last chapter:[1]

  A Relation of a priest to his family for sacrifice (21:1–15)
    B Blemishes of priests who sacrifice (21:16–24)
      C How a priest should avoid desecration of sacrifices (22:1–16)
    B′ Blemishes of animals for sacrifice (22:17–25)
  A′ Relation of an animal and its family for sacrifice (22:26–31)

Leviticus 22:32–33 follows this chiasm with a summarizing conclusion on holiness.

Interpretive Insights

22:2 *the sacred offerings.* The term includes votive offerings of silver and gold (1 Kings 15:15), but here edible offerings are in view: grain offerings (Lev. 2:3), sin and guilt offerings (Lev. 6:17), and probably fellowship offerings that require a person to be in a ceremonially clean state to eat them (Lev. 7:20–21).

not profane my holy name. On *halal* ("to profane"), see comments at Leviticus 21:9. On "name theology," see "Theological Insights" below. Inappropriate behavior by priests diminishes God's reputation for holiness.

22:3 *must be cut off.* See "Additional Insights" following the unit on Leviticus 6:8–7:38. Priests are threatened with sudden death from God (cf. v. 9 below) if they treat the sacred offerings with disrespect or handle them in a state of uncleanness. "Must be cut off" should instead be "shall be cut off" (ESV, KJV, NASB, NRSV) or "is subject to being cut off." This is an act of God with no human agency in view. On "I am the Lord," see "Additional

Insights" following the unit on Leviticus 19:1–37.

22:4–8 *If a descendant of Aaron has . . . become unclean.* If a priest contracts uncleanness, he becomes unfit for eating sacred food. The reasons why these things produce uncleanness are discussed elsewhere: skin disease (Lev. 13), bodily discharge / emission of semen (Lev. 15), corpse contamination (Lev. 21:1–4, 11; Num. 19, esp. v. 22), touching an unclean crawling thing (Lev. 11:29–31), or eating something that has died on its own or has been killed by predators (Lev. 7:24; 17:15).

22:9 *The priests are to . . . not become guilty.* "Become guilty," or more literally, "bear sin" (ESV), is perhaps a double entendre involving both culpability and liability to punishment, namely, death ("cut off" [v. 3]), if they ignore their rules of holiness.

22:10–13 *No one outside a priest's family may eat the sacred offering.* Only priests or their families can eat the sacred food. For more rules concerning family members eating sacred offerings, see Numbers 18:8–19.

22:14–16 *Anyone who eats a sacred offering by mistake.* A layperson who unintentionally eats something dedicated to the priests must follow the rules of the guilt

Key Themes of Leviticus 22:1–33

- God's ministers are to be holy.
- Gifts to God are to be holy.
- God's people are to be holy.

offering for profaning a holy thing (Lev. 5:14–16): making restitution for the item profaned and adding 20 percent value to it. "Guilt requiring payment" (v. 16) should instead be rendered similarly to the NRSV: "causing them to bear guilt requiring a *guilt offering*, by eating their sacred donations." The second word translated as "guilt" in the NRSV, *'ashmah*, can mean punishment ("payment") for guilt per the NIV, but given the clear allusion to the guilt offering of Leviticus 5:16, *'ashmah* probably means "guilt offering," the specific remedy (along with restitution plus 20 percent) for this kind of offense.

22:17–25 *Do not bring anything with a defect . . . They will not be accepted on your behalf.* Things that disqualify an animal from being a sacrifice are largely identical with the things that disqualify a person from priestly service (see Lev. 21:16–23). The purity system makes a broad, conceptual parallel between people and animals.

Contact with a corpse or anything a corpse has touched renders a priest ritually unclean, preventing him from partaking of the sacred offerings. As a result, priests do not participate in any ritual burial procedures like those practiced in Egypt. Here three priests stand in front of the mummy of the deceased to perform the Opening of the Mouth ritual, which they believed would reanimate the dead in the afterlife. This scene is from the papyrus of Ani (1295–1186 BC, Thebes).

Leviticus 22:1–33

Animals that can be eaten are "clean"; those that cannot are unclean. With people, Israelites are clean, while gentile nations are unclean (Amos 7:17 NRSV). Only certain clean animals can be offered on Yahweh's altar and become holy. Wild game, fish, and livestock with defects can be eaten but not sacrificed. Similarly, non-Aaronites cannot serve as priests, nor can Aaronites with physical defects. This conceptual system promotes separation from unclean gentiles (Lev. 20:25–26) and associates the concept of holiness with the ideas of wholeness, completeness, and healthiness. A sacrifice not accepted by God accrues no benefit to the offerer from God.

The exception for an animal with "deformed or stunted" limbs for a "freewill offering" but not for a "vow" (v. 23) is curious. Both the freewill and the vow offerings are subcategories of the fellowship offering (Lev. 7:11, 16). The freewill offering is completely voluntary, used to express love and gratitude to God for his blessings. A vow offering is a mandatory expression of gratitude to God at the completion of a vow, though choosing to make a vow is voluntary. The exception for a spontaneous freewill offering represents a "gracious condescension to one who had only that to offer,"[2] but the obligatory vow offering must be an animal of somewhat higher quality.

22:26–27 *remain with its mother for seven days. From the eighth day on.* The eighth day is when a boy is circumcised (Gen. 17:12) and is the first day an animal can be sacrificed. This wait assures that the animal is healthy.

22:28 *Do not slaughter a cow or a sheep and its young on the same day.* Just as it is incongruous to cook a kid goat in its mother's milk (Exod. 23:19), mixing death with a symbol of life,[3] and just as it is unseemly to mix a symbol of life with death by taking a mother bird with her chicks (Deut. 22:6–7), so also here it is inappropriate to sacrifice a calf, a lamb, or a goat (v. 27) with its mother on the same day (v. 28). A mother deprived of young probably can reproduce again later, and young deprived of their mother can reproduce later; however, killing a mother and its young simultaneously terminates the process of regeneration. Not killing the young with their mother on the same day is a way of showing respect for nature and nature's God, Yahweh, who has designed its pattern of procreation.

22:29–30 *a thank offering . . . must be eaten that same day.* The freewill offering and the vow offering may be eaten over two days (Lev. 7:16–18), but the third fellowship offering, the thank offering, expressing gratitude to God for answered prayer or deliverance, must be eaten the same day it is offered (Lev. 7:12–15; 19:5–7). The difference may be that the thank offering must be eaten within the sanctuary, whereas the freewill and vow offerings need not be (see more at Lev. 7:12–18).

22:31–33 *Keep my commands . . . I must be acknowledged as holy.* Obeying God's commands sanctifies God—sets him apart as holy and special—whereas disobedience profanes his name, treating him and his commands as common. God gives commands to his people to make them holy, just as he is holy (cf. Lev. 19:2). Having "brought you out of Egypt," God has the right to demand his people's holy obedience because he has first redeemed them.

Theological Insights

Respect for God's "name" is emphasized throughout the law. God instructs Israel to be careful not to "profane my holy name" (Lev. 22:2, 32). His name is "holy" because it is set apart from all other names, whether those of people or of other so-called gods.

In Exodus 3:12–15 God reveals his name to Moses. God's special name is "Yahweh," rendered by most versions as "Lord." There, God relates his name "Yahweh" to the expression "I am" and the fact that he will be with Moses as he confronts Pharaoh. This suggests that "Yahweh" may mean "He is" in the sense that he is present to help in time of need. The name "Yahweh," or at least its significance, had not been revealed to the patriarchs (Exod. 6:3).

The sanctuary is where God will "put his name" (Deut. 12:5–6). This indicates God's ownership and association with that place. Moreover, Israel is chosen to be God's holy people, called by his name (Deut. 28:9–10; 2 Chron. 7:14). That is, God owns Israel and associates himself with it.

Reverence for God's name is commanded in the Decalogue: "You shall not misuse the name of the Lord your God" (Exod. 20:7; Deut. 5:11). One misuses and profanes God's name by, for example, swearing the oath "As the Lord lives" and not keeping the oath-promise that one has sworn (Lev. 19:12). More generally, any disrespect that an Israelite shows for the person whom that name represents is in effect taking God's name in vain. An Israelite can profane God's name by bad behaviors such as idolatrous child sacrifice (Lev. 20:3), desecration of holy offerings (Lev. 22:2), or more generally by disregarding God's commandments (Lev. 22:31–32).

A cow or sheep and its young calf or lamb may not be sacrificed on the same day. An ivory carving of a cow suckling her calf is shown here (Arslan Tash, eighth century BC).

Those who blaspheme God's name can be executed (Lev. 24:16).

A similar name theology occurs in the New Testament with the name of Jesus. Christians welcome children in Jesus's name (Matt. 18:5), gather in his name (Matt. 18:20), pray in his name (John 14:13–14; 16:23), and are persecuted because of his name (John 15:20–21). The church baptizes in Jesus's name (Acts 2:38), performs miracles in his name (Acts 3:6), and preaches and teaches in his name (Acts 4:17; 5:28). The label "Christian" goes back to Jesus Christ, by whose name his followers are called (Acts 11:26). And invocation of that name demands worldwide homage and respect (Phil. 2:10–11).

Teaching the Text

1. *God's ministers are to be holy.* Leviticus 22 is addressed to the clergy, Aaron and his sons (v. 2), commanding them not to profane God's name by their behavior. Thus they must apply the rules of purity and holiness to their job. They cannot handle holy offerings in a state of uncleanness (v. 3–9). As holy priests, they and their family have the special privilege of eating the holy

offerings; they are not to allow ineligible people to eat the holy food, in accordance with strict rules (vv. 10–13).

Although ceremonial holiness is not required under the new covenant, it is still important that the religious leaders of the church be morally and spiritually holy. For when they fail to be, the name of our Lord becomes profaned.

2. *Gifts to God are to be holy.* The offerings given to God are holy, which is why priests alone can eat them. Except in the case of their own fellowship offerings, common people are not to eat the holy things dedicated to God. If somehow they do, they commit an act of sacrilege that requires a guilt offering (vv. 14–16). As holy offerings to God, only the best can be offered. Sacrifices must be unblemished animals: defects—blindness, injuries, being maimed, and so on—disqualify an animal from being given to God (vv. 21–25). Certain other factors of propriety disqualify a sacrifice, such as the animal being less than eight days old or being offered along with its mother (vv. 26–28).

The need to give one's best to God still applies today. Malachi remarks that just as Jews would not think of giving fifth-rate food offerings to their Persian governor, neither should they consider giving fifth-rate offerings to God (Mal. 1:7–8). And yet how many of us give God our leftovers rather than our best? Does God get the best of our material goods, or do we save the best for ourselves? Does God receive our best service and the full attention of our hearts, or do we offer him only token service and give our greatest attention to worldly things? When we do offer a significant gift to God's church, is it marred by some sort of impropriety? Are we truly sanctifying God

as holy through our gift, or are we in fact only seeking to glorify ourselves?

Many of us need to learn this lesson from Leviticus 22: God deserves our best. Our best should be excellent in quality and undiluted by any sin or impropriety. Less than that "will not be accepted on your behalf" (v. 25). That is, it will deserve no blessing from God.

3. *God's people are to be holy.* The goal of all these rules is to mold Israel into a holy people who acknowledge the holiness of the name of their God (v. 32a). The way they can grow in holiness is by keeping God's commandments (v. 31), including the rules for eating thank offerings (v. 30). Guiding his people by his word is God's means of sanctifying the Israelites (v. 32b). Indeed, he had redeemed them from Egypt for the very purpose of making them holy and to have a special relationship with them as their holy God (v. 33).

So it is with the church. God has given us his Word to mold us, to make us holy, and to teach us to glorify his name. He redeemed us from sin for that very purpose.

Illustrating the Text

Ministers are called to holiness.

Church History: A pertinent question that we find in church history is whether a wicked priest could consecrate the Eucharist (Lord's Supper). The question came to a head in the early centuries of the church in the Donatist controversy, and the church has consistently taught since then that the sinfulness of clergy does not affect the validity of the sacraments.

Thomas Aquinas takes up the question in his *Summa theologiae* (part 3, question 82, article 5).[4] Aquinas notes that the

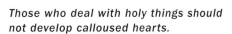

The priests must follow the rules of purity to serve before the Lord. One of the purity requirements is to wash hands and feet before entering the tent of meeting or presenting food offerings at the altar (Exod. 30:17–21). Purity rituals were practiced in other ancient Near Eastern cultures. At Hazor, the stone basin found near this sacred installation of standing stones may have held water for that purpose.

church father Jerome, in accord with the teaching about priests in Leviticus 21–22, said that such priests certainly may not serve it. Aquinas also notes that Pope Gelasius I questioned, "How shall the Holy Spirit, when invoked, come for the consecration of the Divine Mystery, if the priest invoking him be proved full of guilty deeds?"

Aquinas, speaking for Catholic tradition, agreed that such a priest was unworthy, and that his presiding over the Eucharist was an act of sin on the part of the priest. And yet it was also true that God could use the eucharistic service administered by a wicked priest to bless the congregant. Hence, it could be evil for the priest—done with a bad intention—and yet used by God for good.

It is always terribly disappointing to discover that a minister responsible for holy things has proven to be defiled in some sort of serious way. Such a minister should withdraw from the ministry. And yet in God's grace the Holy Spirit works even through unworthy vessels. When a minister who is morally or spiritually compromised preaches the Bible, God can still use the word to touch people's hearts, perhaps even help them to find Christ, even if that same word has not fully reached the preacher's heart.

If God can use an unworthy vessel, how much more is he able to use those who have kept themselves holy. Defiled ministers profane God's holy name and can lead others not to regard God as holy (Lev. 22:31–33).

Those who deal with holy things should not develop calloused hearts.

Quote: In 1951 Sheldon Vanauken asked the famous C. S. Lewis for advice: Should he continue in his postgraduate work in history or instead study theology? Lewis gave some practical wisdom. Would Sheldon enjoy this? Would it advance his career? But then he raised a surprising question: "Would it be better for your soul?" Studying theology and becoming a cleric, Lewis pointed out, is not always good for the soul. Lewis explains,

> Contrariwise, there is the danger that what is boring or repellent in the job may alienate one from the spiritual life. And finally someone has said, "None are so unholy as those whose hands are cauterised by holy things": sacred things may become profane by becoming matters of the job. You *now* want truth for her own sake: how will it be when the same truth is also needed for an effective footnote in your thesis? In fact, the change might do good or harm.[5]

Like the Old Testament priests, Christian ministers must be ever vigilant against reducing the sacred to the level of the common and mindful of God's demand that they themselves be holy.

Leviticus 22:1–33

Holy Days and Festivals

Big Idea *God uses religious occasions and holidays to teach his people to be holy.*

Understanding the Text

The Text in Context

Leviticus 23 continues the theme of holiness in the holiness code (Lev. 17–27) and the broader theme in Leviticus of maintaining an equilibrium between the human and the divine (see the introduction to Leviticus). Leviticus 21–22 deals with holy priests and holy offerings. Now the text moves on to holy days and festivals used by God to instill in Israel a sense of being a holy people in proper relationship with himself.

Interpretive Insights

23:2 *sacred assemblies.* This is perhaps better translated "holy occasions." The term *miqra'* ("assembly, convocation") could be from one of two homonym roots. The NIV takes it from the root *qara'* that means "call, summon," and hence *miqra'* would mean "assembly." But if *miqra'* is instead from the second *qara'*, which means "to encounter, happen," then *miqra'* would mean "occasion," not "assembly."

23:3 *sabbath.* The Hebrew word *shabbat* is from a root meaning "to cease, stop, rest." On the Sabbath work ceases, and one begins a period of rest. "Day of sabbath rest" should read instead, "a Sabbath of complete rest" (HCSB). As on the Day of Atonement (vv. 28, 31), no work whatsoever is allowed. Lesser holy days are less rigorous; on these days no regular or laborious work is permitted (vv. 8, 21, 25, 35–36). On "sacred assembly," see verse 2 above.

23:5–8 *Passover . . . Unleavened Bread.* See Exodus 12–13; 23:15; 34:18–20, 25; Numbers 28:16–25; Deuteronomy 16:1–8. Passover was and is celebrated on the fourteenth of Nisan (March/April). It commemorates God's deliverance of Israel from the plague of the firstborn and from Egyptian servitude, an event that marks Israel's birth as a nation. Seven days of eating unleavened bread (without yeast) follow Passover (Exod. 12:17–20). On "no regular work," see verse 3 above. Only the first and seventh days of Unleavened Bread are days of (intermediate) rest.

23:10 *bring . . . the first grain you harvest.* There is an offering of firstfruits of (barley) grain in conjunction with Passover and Unleavened Bread, accompanied by a burnt offering and a grain offering. Firstfruits express gratitude to God for the harvest.

23:11 *wave the sheaf . . . on the day after the Sabbath.* On "wave," see comments at

Leviticus 7:28–35. The Hebrew for "sheaf" is literally rendered as "omer." An omer is about one to two quarts of grain, but here it refers to a bundle of barley containing approximately that quantity of grain. In regard to the "day after the Sabbath," Jewish interpreters understood this "sabbath" as the Passover day, though it could originally have referred to the Sabbath occurring during the Festival of Unleavened Bread.

23:15–22 *count off seven full weeks.* This sacred occasion came to be called the "Festival of Weeks" (*shabu'ot* [Exod. 34:22; Deut. 16:10]) because it occurs seven weeks after the Sabbath (v. 15; cf. v. 11), traditionally understood as the Passover. It is also called the "Festival of Harvest" (Exod. 23:16), celebrating the early wheat harvest, and the "Day of Firstfruits" (Num. 28:26). In the New Testament it is called "Pentecost," based on the Greek word for "fifty," because it is celebrated fifty days (seven weeks plus one day) after Passover. Weeks is essentially a harvest festival celebrating God's giving of crops, though in later Jewish tradition it came to be associated with his giving the law at Sinai. The associated sacrifices appeal to God for favor (burnt offerings, grain offerings), seek to purge the sanctuary of inadvertent sin or impurity (sin offering), and express

joy in and gratitude for God's blessings and relationship (fellowship offering, bread of firstfruits). It is an intermediate-level rest day allowing "no regular/laborious work." Since Weeks is a grain harvest festival, the text uses it to remind Israelites to leave gleanings of grain for poor Israelites and foreigners (v. 22), just as they are to leave gleanings of grapes (Lev. 19:9–10).

23:23–25 *a day of sabbath rest . . . commemorated with trumpet blasts.* The Festival of Trumpets or Trumpet Blasts is a minor holiday on the first day of the seventh month (Tishri = September/October). The seventh month is especially important because the Day of Atonement (vv. 26–32) and the Festival of Tabernacles (vv. 33–43) occur that month. After Old Testament times, this minor holiday developed into the major Jewish holiday of Rosh Hashanah (the Jewish New Year). The number "seven," associated with God's rest on the seventh day of creation (Gen. 2:1–3), conveys an aura of holiness. Various holidays involve sevens: the Sabbath, the Festival of Weeks (seven weeks after the Passover Sabbath), the Festival of Trumpets (the seventh month), the Sabbath Year (Lev. 25:2–7), and the Year of the Jubilee (every

The Festival of Trumpets is commemorated with trumpet blasts as the Israelites gather in sacred assembly. The trumpets used were most likely made from ram's horns, like the one shown here from eighteenth century AD Germany.

7×7 years [Lev. 25:8–12]). On "no regular work," see comments at verse 3.

23:26–32 *the Day of Atonement . . . a day of sabbath rest.* Compare Leviticus 16. "Deny yourselves" ("humble" [NASB] or "afflict" [ESV, KJV] yourself) implies fasting (see comments at Lev. 16:29). This day and the Sabbath are strict days of rest (see v. 3), so no work is to be done. Violators can be "cut off," punished by God (v. 29). See "Additional Insights" following the unit on Leviticus 6:8–7:38.

23:32 *Sabbath . . . from evening . . . until the following evening.* This "sabbath" refers to the Day of Atonement. This is the only place in the Old Testament where a "sabbath" is said to run from evening to evening. Rabbinic interpreters generalized to conclude that all Sabbaths were from evening to evening, although it cannot be entirely ruled out that ordinary Sabbaths originally ran from dawn to dawn.

23:33–36 *Festival of Tabernacles.* See Exodus 23:16; 34:22; Numbers 29:12–32; Deuteronomy 16:13–16. Tabernacles or Booths (Sukkot) is observed on 15–22 of Tishri (September/October). As a harvest festival, it celebrates God's material blessings at the end of the agricultural season (v. 39). The Israelites are required to live in temporary shelters or "booths" for seven days (v. 42) as a reminder of their wilderness wanderings after the exodus and the blessings of permanent settlement in the land (v. 43).

23:37–38 *These are the LORD's appointed festivals.* Verses 37–38 make a summary statement about all the festivals, not just Tabernacles. These are days for food gifts to God, including burnt, grain, and drink offerings (appealing to God for favor), as well as fellowship sacrifices (expressing gratitude and joy). On sacrifices required for each holy occasion, see Numbers 28–29.

23:40 *branches from luxuriant trees.* The Hebrew word *peri* normally means "fruit" (ESV, NKJV, NRSV), but "luxuriant trees," unlike date "palms," bear no fruit during Tabernacles. Rendering something like "branches" goes back to the Jewish sect of the Karaites[1] (cf. "boughs" [KJV], "foliage" [NASB], "product" [HCSB, NJPS]). The Karaites revocalized *peri* ("fruit") to a variant spelling of *pora'h* or *pu'rah* ("branches"), a term used of magnificent trees (Ezek. 31:5, 6, 8, 12, 13) and "leafy branches of a tree, foliage" (Isa. 10:33). *Peri* might have a secondary meaning of "branches," as is suggested by the parallel terms "fronds" and "boughs." Elsewhere only branches, and not fruit, are mentioned in the celebration of Tabernacles (Neh. 8:15).

Theological Insights

Israel's Sabbaths and holy days parallel Christian-era special days.

The Sabbath led to the now ubiquitous seven-day week. Most Christians set aside a day, typically Sunday, as a day of worship and rest, just as Israel kept its Saturday Sabbath.

Passover and Unleavened Bread parallel the regular celebration of the Lord's Supper. The first Lord's Supper was a Passover meal (Luke 22:15), though elements of the meal (wine and bread) were reapplied to Christ's coming death. Christ is our "Passover lamb," and just as the Israelites had to throw out the old leaven before they could celebrate Passover, so Christians must throw out the "old leaven" of sin

The Feast of Tabernacles, also called Sukkot, is a harvest festival. The Israelites are required to live in temporary shelters, perhaps booths like this, as a reminder of how they lived when God brought them out of Egypt.

Like Tabernacles, it also reminds people of where God has brought them nationally, just as Israel remembered how God led them through the wilderness.

Special holy occasions still help remind Christians that they have been redeemed and blessed by God and should rejoice before him in worship.

(1 Cor. 5:7–8). The offering of firstfruits during Passover parallels Christ, who is the firstfruits from the dead that anticipates the eventual full harvest of resurrected believers (1 Cor. 15:20, 23). Thus the New Testament sees in the Passover, Unleavened Bread, and Firstfruits a foreshadowing of the even greater deliverance in Jesus Christ.

The manifestation of the Holy Spirit on Pentecost (= Weeks) in Acts 2 is a momentous event in the early church. On Pentecost Israel thanked God for his gift of agricultural blessings. The church on Pentecost thanks God for the gift of the Holy Spirit.

The Day of Atonement finds parallels with Good Friday, when Christians reflect on the somber truth of what God had to do through Christ to cleanse us from sin and impurity.

There is no church holiday parallel to Tabernacles, but Thanksgiving, a national holiday in the United States (November) and Canada (October), comes close. Thanksgiving is a fall harvest festival established to praise God for the blessing of bountiful harvests, as did Tabernacles.

Teaching the Text

1. *Learn holiness.* Each time Israel pauses from its normal activities for a Sabbath or a festival, it is reminded of God's grace and that it is God's special possession. Israel's gifts and offerings to God throughout the year (vv. 37–38) and Israel's holy days thus teach Israel how to be holy and worship its holy God. So Christian worship, offerings, and holy days—Christmas, Good Friday, Easter, and others—can do the same for Christians. The Christian calendar can be a tool in teaching holiness to Christians.

2. *Take time for God and rest.* The weekly Sabbath (vv. 3–4) reminds the Israelites to set aside time for God and for rest. Participating in weekly church services is one way that Christians set aside time for God. It is also important to set aside time for rest rather than being a "24/7" workaholic.

3. *Remember God's redemption.* Passover and Unleavened Bread (vv. 5–8) remind the Israelites that they are special because God had redeemed them from Egyptian bondage (Exod. 12–14). Analogous for Christians is the regular reminder at the

Leviticus 23:1–44

Lord's Supper of their redemption from the bondage of sin through Christ, the Passover lamb, and the need to purge the leaven of sin (cf. 1 Cor. 5:7).

4. *Acknowledge God as the source of blessings.* The offering of firstfruits (vv. 9–14) during Unleavened Bread reminds Israel that its agricultural blessings come ultimately from God. The Festival of Weeks, celebrating as it does the early wheat harvest, is similarly a day to acknowledge God as the source of agricultural blessings and to appeal to him for future blessings. In turn, the Israelites are to bless others by being generous: allowing poor Israelites and foreigners to glean their fields (v. 22). Christians too are to regularly thank God for all things, since all blessings, agricultural and otherwise, come from him (Eph. 5:20; James 1:17), and be generous in sharing their bounty with those in need (2 Cor. 9:11; 1 Tim. 6:18).

The seventh month, Tishri (September/October), is marked as special by trumpets (vv. 23–25). In Tishri is the solemn Day of Atonement (vv. 26–32; see Lev. 16), a day of fasting and confession of sin, reminding Israel that only through atoning sacrifice can God purge its impurities and remain in its midst. Analogous to this for Christians is the reminder that their atonement was possible only through the sacrifice of Christ. Tabernacles (vv. 33–43) was an agricultural festival celebrating the end of the harvest season (v. 39) and a remembrance of the wilderness wanderings when God let Israel live in temporary shelters (v. 42). So Christians should do no less than Israel did. They too should pause regularly to thank God for his blessings and for the hard times that God has seen them through.

Illustrating the Text

The Israelites' festivals helped them remember that they were a special people, called by God.

Cultural Institution: The national holidays of the United States have been created to inculcate a sense that America is a remarkably good country.

The Fourth of July celebrates America's unique liberties gained when it declared independence from England. Washington's and Lincoln's birthdays, now merged into the unhelpfully vague label "Presidents' Day," recognize the role of George Washington in founding this country and the role of Abraham Lincoln in abolishing slavery and preserving the Union. Memorial Day honors American soldiers who died in war, and Veterans Day honors all those who have served in the military; both remind us that our freedoms come at a cost of blood and sacrifice. Labor Day honors advances in workers' rights and status in this country. Martin Luther King Day celebrates both the abolition of state-enforced racism and advances in civil rights for black people and other minorities.

All these holidays reinforce the concept of American exceptionalism. Whether Americans really are as exceptionally good as these holidays suggest can be debated. But our expectation that the United States be exceptionally good can in fact contribute toward the country actually being good. These holidays provide ideals according to which Americans can strive to live. They also provide standards that may show where they fall short and need improvement.

Similarly, Israel's holidays reinforced the ideal that Israel was special, a holy people separated to God by their unique religious celebrations. Their holidays also provided ideals by which the Israelites were to live. And as they sought to do so, it made them into a better people as well.

Like Israel, Christians are called regularly to pause, rest, and remember.

Informational: The Hebrew word "Sabbath" can be translated "stop." God put a stop sign in the weekly rhythm of life. In a culture that is constantly emphasizing "the early bird gets the worm" and praising the "go-getter," we too are called to stop and remember that God is the true source of life and blessing. Consider the benefits:

1. Each time we stop, we are able to set aside our efforts to control outcomes. This will remind us that we are not really masters of our destiny and that the Lord is sovereign.

2. When we stop, we affirm that our identity is derived not solely from the work that we do but also, more importantly, from the people we love and the God we worship.

3. As we stop, the "enforced rest" that we receive allows the stress that can accumulate to bleed off, like a pressure valve on a boiler. If we regularly do this, the stress that can lead to sickness of body, mind, and heart will not have a chance to break us. This kind of self-care honors the God who crafted and cares for our whole being.

In Leviticus, the holy days and festivals that the Lord appoints for Israel to celebrate are the Sabbath, Passover, the Festival of the Unleavened Bread, Firstfruits, the Festival of Weeks, the Festival of Trumpets, the Day of Atonement, and the Festival of Tabernacles. Other ancient Near Eastern cultures had their own yearly festivals. Reliefs containing festival calendars have been found at many temple locations in Egypt. This relief from the temple at Kom Ombo records the dates and offerings for the special celebrations that occurred there.

Lamps, Cakes, and the Blasphemer

Big Idea *God, whose presence is in the midst of his covenant people, must be respected.*

Understanding the Text

The Text in Context

Leviticus 24 divides into two sections: Israel's requirement to supply oil and bread to the tabernacle in its daily worship (vv. 1–9) and the execution of a blasphemer (vv. 10–23). Verses 1–9 move from the obligations for Israelites to worship on holy days (Lev. 23) to obligations to maintain worship on a daily basis. The connection of the second section to the context is less clear.

The case of the blasphemer fits into the Pentateuch's pattern of intertwining laws and narratives. It is reminiscent of the narrative of Aaron's sons in Leviticus 10, in which "blasphemous" actions lead to death. It is also similar to the case of the Sabbath breaker (Num. 15:32–36). There, as here, Moses has no law but must consult Yahweh, who instructs Moses to execute the offender. But why put this story here? Perhaps it is simply because the incident occurred shortly after God revealed to Moses the laws of Leviticus 24:1–9.

Historical and Cultural Background

Examples of wood furnishings overlaid with gold (Lev. 24:6) were found in the Egyptian pharaoh Tutankhamen's tomb. Gold was befitting of royalty, in Israel's case their divine King.

Stoning (Lev. 24:14) was a special kind of punishment. Whereas simple homicide is subject to execution by the sword, stoning is sanctioned for cases of a different

A lampstand of seven lamps is made of pure gold according to God's instructions. It burns inside the holy place in front of the curtain that shields the ark of the covenant. The lampstand, or menorah, became an important motif in Jewish religious art. This mosaic found at Beth Shan is from the fifth century AD and depicts two lampstands on either side of the niche that housed the Torah scrolls in Jewish synagogues.

sort: worship of a foreign god, rebellious and disobedient sons, newly wed brides found not to be virgins, child sacrifice, sorcery, necromancy, blasphemy against Yahweh's name, violation of the Sabbath, an animal that takes the life of a human being, and taking something under the "ban."

J. J. Finkelstein notes,

Death by stoning, in biblical tradition and elsewhere in the ancient Near East, is reserved for crimes of a special character. In those cases there is no designated "executioner," for the community assembled is the common executioner of the sentence. Offenses which entail this mode of execution must therefore be of a character that, either in theory or in fact, "offend" the corporate community or are believed to compromise its most cherished values to the degree that the commission of the offense places the community itself in jeopardy. . . .

Most if not all of these offenses would, in modern juristic terms, be categorized as "victimless crimes." They are at the same time crimes of the most serious kind for they are revolts against God, or the world order which is ordained by the divine word.[1]

Stoning expresses the community's religious outrage. An ox that gored a human to death had usurped the position of human rule over nature, so it was not merely killed but stoned. But similarly outrageous in Israel were religious offenses such as idolatry, magic, and blasphemy. They too offended Israel's deepest values and required the whole community to act in concert against the offender through stoning.

Key Themes of Leviticus 24:1–23

- Take comfort that God is present.
- Remember God's covenant relationship with his people.
- Promote repect for God's name.

Interpretive Insights

24:2 *clear oil of pressed olives.* The clear (or "pure" [ESV]) olive oil was "pressed," better rendered as "beaten" (ESV, KJV, NASB, NRSV). Olive oil extracted by hand pounding with a mortar and pestle yields oil that is purer and burns more cleanly than that obtained by ordinary pressing.[2]

the lamps . . . kept burning continually. Compare Exodus 27:21–22. The seven lamps of the golden lampstand, the menorah (Exod. 25:31–40), are kept in the tent just outside the most holy place, where God's throne, the ark of the covenant, is kept.

24:3 *from evening till morning.* The menorah burns all night, though it is allowed to go out in the morning (see 1 Sam. 3:3).

24:5–9 *twelve loaves . . . two-tenths of an ephah . . . in two stacks . . . on the table of pure gold . . . incense.* The golden table, measuring two by one cubits (about 3 by 1.5 feet), is overlaid with pure gold and located in the holy place (Exod. 25:23–30). "Two-tenths of an ephah" is two quarts or about "7 pounds" (NIVmg). Elsewhere called "the bread of the Presence" (Exod. 25:30; 35:13; 39:36), the "twelve loaves" presumably symbolize the twelve tribes. Given the small table, they must have been flat cakes in two "stacks," not "rows" (contra KJV, NASB, NRSV). The loaves are not burned, but "incense" (or frankincense) placed beside the loaves is burned as a substitute to draw God's attention to the bread. The loaves are eaten by priests each Sabbath, at which times they are replaced with new ones. The priests of Nob allow David to eat the holy "bread of the Presence" (1 Sam. 21:4, 6). Rabbinic tradition states that the loaves were made without yeast/leaven, which seems probable, since only unleavened bread could last for a week without spoiling.

24:10–23 These verses narrate a specific incident of a man who commits blasphemy.

24:10 *Egyptian father.* Why no mention of the Egyptian father's name? Did the father remain in Egypt? Had he died? Mention of the man's checkered heritage indicates that he is of suspect character religiously.

24:11 *blasphemed the Name.* Compare Exodus 20:7. The offense is not that the man said the name "Yahweh," but that he slandered Yahweh.

a curse. Perhaps this "curse" involved saying something like, "May Re [or some other Egyptian god] curse Yahweh." In that case, the half Egyptian has shown a hidden loyalty to the Egyptian religion of his father over the religion of his mother. Alternatively, "curse" may be a mistranslation of the verb *qillel*.[3] The verb can mean "to repudiate, denigrate, belittle, revile, disrespect, dishonor" and the like. Perhaps the half Egyptian has verbally repudiated or denigrated Yahweh by saying, "Yahweh is evil" or something similar.

24:12 *until the will of the* LORD *should be made clear.* Moses is unsure what to do about the blasphemer. Does the offender's being half Israelite mitigate the punishment? God's answer is that even a person of pagan background who blasphemes in Israel is to be stoned.

24:14 *lay their hands on his head.* This gesture confirms they have heard the blasphemy from this specific man and he has brought punishment onto his own head. It may transfer guilt from the people to the offender, as laying hands on the scapegoat does (Lev. 16:21); for having witnessed this violation, the people are guilty until they mete out Yahweh's justice.

24:20 *eye for eye, tooth for tooth.* The formula in verses 19–21, known as the *lex talionis*, or "law of retaliation," gives the legal principle that the degree of punishment administered by courts must correspond with the crime. It is not intended to justify personal revenge (as Jesus's opponents wrongly think [Matt. 5:38–39]). Nor is this formula always applied literally: if the victim is willing, the offender can ransom his body part or even his life with money (see Exod. 21:18–19, 24–27, 29–30; 1 Kings 20:39), though never in cases of premeditated murder (Num. 35:31). The case of the blasphemer is a nonliteral application of the *lex talionis* principle: he has slandered/cursed God, but the community stones him. Nonetheless, the principle "as he has done it shall be done to him" (v. 19 ESV) applies figuratively in that he receives the punishment that he deserves.

24:22 *I am the* LORD. See "Additional Insights" following the unit on Leviticus 19:1–37.

Theological Insights

It is shocking to the modern person to read about the punishment of the blasphemer (Lev. 24:10–23). Taking God's name in vain is so commonplace today that often we do not even notice when it happens. But Israel was to show such

זה המערה ואהרן נתן שמן כנירות

One of Aaron's tasks is to "tend the lamps before the Lord from evening till morning, continually" (24:3). This illumination from a collection of texts known as the "Northern French Miscellany" (AD 1277–86), shows Aaron refilling the lamps with oil.

respect for God that anyone who cursed or maligned God could be executed (see also Exod. 22:28; 1 Kings 21:13).

The issue is not that this man is half Egyptian, half Israelite. If anything, his having an Egyptian father might be considered a mitigating factor against executing him. A half foreigner might know no better. But in the end, exactly the same sentence is carried out against him as would have been had he been a full Israelite. Those living in Israel's society, whether Israelite or foreign born, must live by Israel's laws. Specifically, they must be careful when invoking God's name, and certainly they should never curse or slander Israel's God.

The New Testament also speaks of blasphemy. Blasphemy against the Holy Spirit is identified as an unforgivable sin (Mark 3:29). Jesus is falsely accused of blasphemy. When Jesus claims to do what only God can do, forgive sin, he is thought to be blaspheming (Mark 2:7; Luke 5:21). When Jesus claims to be equal with God, some Jews want to stone him for blasphemy (John 10:33). And Caiaphas condemns Jesus to death when Jesus claims to be the "one like a son of man" of Daniel 7:13–14, a claim that Caiaphas considers blasphemous (Mark 14:62–64). But these claims are not blasphemous because each of them is true.

Although the New Testament does not command that blasphemy be a capital offense under the new covenant, it does condemn speaking ill against God as a sin (1 Tim. 1:13, 20; James 2:7; Rev. 13:6). God is worthy of utmost respect. Speaking ill of him, then and now, is to be condemned.

Teaching the Text

1. *Take comfort that God is present.* The golden lampstand is to be lit by the high priest (Aaron) at dusk and kept burning till dawn (vv. 1–4). Only the finest of olive oils are to be used for this purpose. What is the symbolism of this action? Probably the light stands for the presence of God. God often is portrayed as light or fire: a firepot (Gen. 15:17), a burning bush (Exod. 3:2), a pillar of fire (Exod. 13:21). God is described as a consuming fire (Deut. 4:24) and as speaking out of fire at Sinai (Deut. 4:33; 5:24). In the darkest hours of the night, when campfires had died out, Israelites who awoke could take comfort looking

toward the tent of meeting in the middle of the camp. There they would see not only light from the altar of burnt offering but also a flickering of light from within the tent itself, a continual reminder that God was in their midst. Just as the lamps that symbolized the presence of God had to be "kept burning continually," so we need to kindle and maintain our sense of God as the ever-present light of our lives.

2. *Remember God's covenant relationship with his people.* Three things are key to understanding the significance of the bread of the Presence: twelve loaves, the covenant, and the Sabbath. The loaves represent Israel's continual expression of gratitude for its blessings before the presence of God. Sharing a meal is an act of hospitality and friendship. This symbolic offering of food to God in his presence is a token of Israel's friendship and relationship with God. That is why it is related to the concept of covenant: God has established with Israel a "lasting covenant" (v. 8)—that is, a lasting relationship. The weekly offering of the bread of the Presence to God is thus a

reminder of that relationship. It is also connected with the Sabbath, itself a sign of Israel's lasting covenant with God (cf. Exod. 31:13–17). By analogy, the church is also in covenant relationship with God, to whom we should continually express gratitude and for whom we should set aside time.

3. *Promote respect for God's name.* Like Israel, the whole Christian community should be outraged when the name of our God is publicly slandered or treated with disrespect (vv. 11–12). When someone uses God's name in vain, it would not be inappropriate to tell that person that you found his or her words offensive. It is still more appropriate to say that when the offender is a professing Christian. A collective expression of Christian moral outrage can be fitting at times. We should

Twelve loaves of bread are placed before the Lord and refreshed weekly, serving as a reminder of the covenant relationship between God and Israel. This model of the table holding the bread of the Presence is part of the tabernacle replica at Timna, Israel.

still be jealous for the name and reputation of our God and defend it where appropriate.

Illustrating the Text

Stoning was and is a particularly gruesome punishment.

Informational: Stoning was a punishment for blasphemy in the Bible. It endured as a punishment in postbiblical times and has been revived as a form of execution by Islamic militant groups in Somalia and elsewhere.

The tractate *Sanhedrin* (6:1–4) in the Mishnah (second century AD) describes how Jewish stoning was to take place according to the rabbis. A herald went before the condemned, announcing that this person was to be stoned and for what offense, named the witnesses, and called for anyone who had exculpatory evidence to come forth before the sentence was carried out. Fifteen feet from the place of stoning, condemned persons were allowed to confess their sins so that they might have life in the world to come. Six feet from the execution place, the condemned were stripped (not completely, if a woman). One of the witnesses was to push the condemned person off a precipice twice the height of a human being—perhaps off the second story of a building or into a pit. Then a second witness was to drop a stone on the condemned person's chest. If the person was still alive, the others present continued to drop stones until death occurred.

One case of modern-day stoning was when Somalia's al-Qaeda-inspired group stoned a man to death in June 2011 after accusing him of committing rape.

Sharma'arke Abdullahi Mohamoud was killed in a square in the Mahas district of the Hiran region as hundreds of local inhabitants watched. An al Shabaab official said that an Islamic court had reached the decision after Mohammed [*sic*] confessed he had forcibly raped a young girl, Deqa Abdulle Nur. The official said the man was stoned because he committed the rape as a married man. An eyewitness said before the stoning was carried out, the convicted man was buried up to his head.

"He was screaming with blood flowing from his head as al Shabaab fighters hit his head with big stones. After several minutes his soul left and stopped moving," an eyewitness added in a translated interview.[4]

This was, and is, a gruesome form of execution.

Sometimes, jealousy is called for.

Literature: William Shakespeare is believed to have coined the phrase "green-eyed monster" to describe jealousy. In *The Merchant of Venice*, Portia proclaims, "How all the other passions fleet to air, as doubtful thoughts, and rash-embraced despair, and shuddering fear, and green-eyed jealousy! O love, be moderate." The "green eyes" of jealousy indicated sickness. Jealousy can be a vice, but it can be a high virtue when directed properly. Although envy is never a proper expression of jealousy, zeal for what rightly belongs to God is. We are called to be jealous for God's glory.

Leviticus 24:1–23

Sabbath Year and Year of Jubilee

Big Idea *God wants people to be free to serve him and not be trapped in permanent poverty.*

Understanding the Text

The Text in Context

Leviticus 23 describes special religious days during Israel's calendar year. Leviticus 25 describes special religious years: the Sabbath Year and the Year of Jubilee. These "consecrated" and "holy" years (25:10, 12) contribute to making Israel a holy people, the theme of Leviticus 17–27. This chapter's introduction (25:1) also serves to introduce the next chapter (see further comments there).

Historical and Cultural Background

Ancient Near Eastern kings sometimes released debts at the beginning of their reigns. The most famous example is the Edict of Ammi-saduqa, a seventeenth-century BC Babylonian king. Kings could declare *an-duraru* ("release") to establish *misharam* ("equity, justice"), in which debts were canceled, slaves were released, and seized lands were returned to original owners. The Sabbath Year and Jubilee Year regulations thus standardized a well-known custom in the ancient world.[1]

Interpretive Insights

25:1–7 These verses describe the Sabbath Year, first mentioned at Exodus 23:10–11. It is a year of suspending payment of debts (Deut. 15:1–11). Without a harvest, debts, of course, cannot be paid. Nehemiah later tries to reinstitute the Sabbath Year (Neh. 10:31).

25:2 *When you enter the land.* Clearly, these rules are inapplicable in the desert.

25:4 *a year of sabbath rest.* See Exodus 23:10–11.

25:6 *Whatever the land yields during the sabbath year will be*

Israelites working to pay off debt are to be released during the Year of Jubilee. Similar decrees, like the Reforms of Uruinimgina inscribed on this cuneiform cone (2350 BC), were made by rulers in the ancient Near East when they first came to power. One of Uruinimgina's reforms was the freeing of those imprisoned for debt.

food for you. While sowing and pruning are prohibited, some grain will germinate from seed dropped during the harvest previous to the Sabbath Year, and low-quality grapes will grow from unpruned vines. Some people eat grain previously stockpiled (vv. 21–22 below). Others "glean" the fields, like the poor.

25:8–55 These verses describe the Year of Jubilee. The word *yobel* ("jubilee") may relate to its homonym *yobel*, meaning "ram's horn" (Exod. 19:13), signifying the blowing of a horn or trumpet to mark the year as special (v. 9).

25:9 *trumpet.* A "trumpet" (*shopar*) was to be blown to proclaim Jubilee, beginning after the Day of Atonement's purging of sin from the people and God's sanctuary (Lev. 16).

the seventh month. This is September/October, after most harvesting has been done.

25:10 *the fiftieth year.* See the sidebar "Sabbath Year and Jubilee Calendars."

25:11 *do not sow and do not reap.* Jubilee follows the same rules of not sowing or harvesting as the Sabbath Year (vv. 11–12; see vv. 1–7 above).

25:12 *eat only what is taken directly from the fields.* This stands in contrast to harvesting and stockpiling.

25:13 *everyone is to return to their own property.* Canaan is to be distributed by lot to each of Israel's tribes in proportion with their populations after the conquest (Num. 33:54). On Jubilee Israelites can return to their ancestral allotments even if the property has been sold during the intervening forty-nine years.

25:14–17 *If you sell land.* Buying land is really only leasing it for harvesting crops (v. 15) until Jubilee. At Jubilee the land returns to its original owners without further

---

Key Themes of Leviticus 25:1–55

- God wants his people to be free.
- God wants his people to avoid the trap of permanent poverty.

---

financial transaction. Prices for land must be adjusted down when "sold," depending on how many harvests can be reaped before the next Jubilee (v. 16).

25:20–22 *What will we eat . . . if we do not plant or harvest . . . ?* Sabbath Year and Jubilee Year rules raise fears of famine. God promises to provide Israel with food security during these years (vv. 18–19). Not sowing might seem foolhardy (v. 20), but God encourages faith that he will provide crop yield in the sixth year "enough for three years"—that is, enough to cover years six and seven and until the harvest of the eighth year (vv. 21–22). The same principle applies to the Year of Jubilee in the fiftieth year.

25:23–24 *the land is mine . . . you must provide for the redemption of the land.* God is the real owner of the land; he merely allows his people to live there as "foreigners and strangers," not permanent owners (v. 23). Thus, the land is not a person's to sell permanently. If land has been sold, the original owner, if able to afford it, can buy it back before Jubilee (v. 24). Redemption and restoration of blessing are the will of the divine Owner.

25:25–28 *their nearest relative is to . . . redeem.* The word *ga'al* ("to redeem") is related to *go'el* ("relative" or "redeemer" [ESV]) in the same verse. *Ga'al* means "to act as a relative," which contextually means "to redeem." Near relatives are expected, if able, to help their kin by buying back their land if it has been hocked. If no relative is willing to buy it back, one can save up money to redeem it personally, with the price prorated downward according to the number of years left until Jubilee (vv. 26–27). If neither the original owner nor a relative can redeem the land earlier, the original owner (or his heirs) can nonetheless repossess it at Jubilee (v. 28).

25:29–31 *a house in a walled city . . . houses in villages without walls.* The rules of Jubilee are not practical for walled cities, whose economies are less agriculturally based. A person forced to sell a home in a walled city only has a year to buy it back before it belongs permanently to the buyer (vv. 29–30). But the rules of Jubilee apply to houses in unwalled villages. They can be bought back by the original owner at any time and return to the original owner (or his heirs) at Jubilee (v. 31).

25:32–34 *The Levites . . . houses . . . pastureland.* Levites are not given large agricultural allotments. Their houses are their primary possession. They retain the right to repurchase a sold house even if they live in walled cities, and they repossess sold houses at Jubilee. Levites are forbidden from hocking pastureland around Levitical cities.

25:35–37 *If any of your fellow Israelites become poor . . . Do not take interest or any profit from them.* After land foreclosure, a person might be unable to earn a living. Others, out of charity, should hire such a person as a day laborer as one would a foreigner (v. 35) or provide no-interest loans (vv. 36–37). "Interest" (*neshek*, lit., "bite") may refer to "interest in advance" (NRSV), such as points on a house loan, and "profit" (*tarbit/marbit*, lit., "increase") may refer to accrued interest at the end of the loan period.

25:39–54 *If any of your fellow Israelites become poor and sell themselves to you.* Israelites are never to become permanent

chattel slaves (v. 39), nor are they to be treated harshly like a slave (vv. 43, 53). Servitude for debt is restricted to six years (Exod. 21:2; Deut. 15:12), though one can choose to become a permanent slave (Exod. 21:5–6; Deut. 15:16–17). Jubilee is an additional occasion for release (v. 40). At Jubilee the debt bonds that have forced one into bondage and the bills of sale that have transferred one's land inheritance to others become legally null and void, allowing such a person to return free to ancestral land (v. 41). God had redeemed Israel from Egyptian bondage so that they can be his slaves exclusively (v. 42). Foreigners can be reduced to chattel slavery, but Israelites are not to be reduced to permanent slavery (vv. 44–46). On the other hand, a wealthy foreigner living among the Israelites can buy an Israelite as an indentured servant (v. 47), though the servant has the right, and kinsmen the duty, to redeem the servant if they can (vv. 48–49). The redemption price of an indentured servant is to be prorated according to the years until Jubilee (vv. 50–52), but if no one is able or willing to provide redemption, the servant is released at Jubilee (v. 54).

25:55 *the Israelites . . . are my servants.* See verse 42. God had released Israel from Egypt to be slaves to him, not slaves to human beings. Thus God has given these laws on redemption and Jubilee.

Theological Insights

A fundamental theological principle of the Sabbath Year and Jubilee laws is that God is the true owner of the land and of Israel: "The land must not be sold permanently, because the land is mine and you reside in my land as foreigners and strangers"

(Lev. 25:23). This is why God could mandate to Israel how the land is to be "sold," redeemed, and restored to original owners in the Year of Jubilee. Also God's people are his "servants" (v. 55) and ought not be made into anyone else's permanent slaves.

The rest of the Old Testament elaborates on the notion that God ultimately owns everything. This includes not just Israel but the whole world.

> The earth is the LORD's, and everything in it, the world, and all who live in it. (Ps. 24:1)

> For every animal of the forest is mine, and the cattle on a thousand hills. . . . The world is mine, and all that is in it. (Ps. 50:10, 12)

> "The silver is mine and the gold is mine," declares the LORD Almighty. (Hag. 2:8)

> Everything under heaven belongs to me. (Job 41:11)

The New Testament refers to both Christian leaders and common Christians as slaves/servants of God (Rom. 6:22). Not only does everything we own belong to God, but even we ourselves.

It changes the way we look at material possessions when we recognize that ultimately all that we are and have really belongs to God. He grants us life and allows us to be stewards of some of his possessions. But we must live and use our possessions in the light of who the real owner is.

Sabbath Year and Jubilee Calendars

There is some question whether these rules follow a spring religious calendar or the more agriculturally oriented fall calendar. The fall calendar is used in the tenth-century BC *Gezer Calendar* and is suggested by the statement that the Year of Jubilee began on the tenth day of the "seventh" month (v. 9). A fall calendar meshes together Sabbath Years and Jubilee better, and it also seems more logical with the sequence of "sow" followed by "reap" (vv. 4–5).

Table 1. Sabbath Year Agricultural Pattern

Assuming a Fall Calendar	Assuming a Spring Calendar
Year 6 Spring/Summer—Harvest	Year 6 Fall/Winter—Sow
Year 6 Fall/Winter—Sow	Year 6 Spring/Summer—Harvest
Sabbath: Year 7 Spring/Summer—Glean only	**Sabbath:** Year 7 Fall/Winter—No sowing
Sabbath: Year 7 Fall/Winter—No sowing	**Sabbath:** Year 7 Spring/Summer—Glean only
Year 8 Spring/Summer—Glean/harvest what grows by itself	Year 8 Fall/Winter—Sow
Year 8 Fall/Winter—Sow	Year 8 Spring/Summer—Harvest

Some interpreters have suggested that Jubilee's fiftieth year occurred during the seventh Sabbath Year, making the seventh Sabbath Year count as the forty-ninth and fiftieth simultaneously, though this understanding is based largely on a belief that it would be impossible to let the land lie fallow for two years. Gordon Wenham (following Hoenig) renders verse 8b "and the forty-nine days of the seven sabbatical years shall be for you a year," allowing the sabbatical "year" to be a forty-nine-day "leap year" within the forty-ninth year.[a] That would help to explain why Jubilee began in the seventh month.

On the other hand, the fact that both sowing and reaping are prohibited during Jubilee (v. 11) implies that it was a full year, though year fifty would be concurrent with year one of the next Jubilee cycle to keep Sabbath Years going in unbroken succession (vv. 3–4).

Table 2. The Seventh Sabbatical Year and the Fiftieth Jubilee Year

Assuming a Fall Calendar
Year 48 Fall/Winter—Sow
Year 48 Spring/Summer—Harvest
Sabbath: Year 49 Fall/Winter—No sowing
Sabbath: Year 49 Spring/Summer—Glean only
Jubilee: Year 50/1 Fall/Winter—No sowing
Jubilee: Year 50/1 Spring/Summer—Glean only
Year 2 Fall/Winter—Sow
Year 2 Spring/Summer—Harvest

Note: Table after Gane, Leviticus.

[a] Wenham, *Leviticus*, 319–20.

Teaching the Text

1. *God wants his people to be free.* The rules of Jubilee sought to improve the lot of Israelite bondservants. Such servants are not to be treated "ruthlessly" (vv. 43, 46, 53), for the Israelites have been redeemed from Egyptian bondage to be slaves only to God (v. 55), not permanent slaves to anyone else (vv. 39, 42).

Freedom is a biblical value. The Year of Jubilee begins with a proclamation of "liberty" (vv. 9–10). That liberty means freedom from bondage (vv. 41, 54) and freedom to return to families and land (vv. 10, 13, 28).

In Luke 4:16–19 Jesus quotes from Isaiah 61:1–2, which alludes to Jubilee. There Jesus says that he has come to "proclaim freedom" and "proclaim the year of the Lord's favor." This echoes the language of Jubilee. Indeed, "freedom" in Isaiah 61:1 represents the very same Hebrew word (*deror*) used for that in Leviticus 25:10. Jesus proclaims not a literal Jubilee but rather the era of salvation, the era of freedom that Jubilee has foreshadowed. This is a Jubilee that we can still enjoy.

Likewise, Paul calls upon Christians to treat slaves decently (Eph. 6:5–9). Paul and the Jubilee rules together planted a seed that eventually led many Christians to advocate for the abolition of slavery in Christian cultures, a goal they ultimately achieved.

2. *God wants his people to avoid the trap of permanent poverty.* Leviticus 25 notes three stages of destitution. First, an Israelite is forced to sell some ancestral property (v. 25). Second, after becoming more impoverished, the seller loses all the property and lives as a tenant farmer (v. 35). Finally, because he is unable to repay loans, the seller is reduced to servitude (v. 39). That process could easily trap a person in permanent poverty.

Jubilee regulations have been established to avoid that situation. For forty-nine years Israel is to operate with a market economy, with winners accumulating land and wealth while losers are reduced to poverty or slavery. But once in a lifetime, in the fiftieth year, slaves are supposed to be set free (vv. 40–41, 54) and all agricultural land returned to its ancestral owners (vv. 10, 13, 28, 31, 33).

This is not communism. Movable property—livestock and stockpiles of grain, silver, and gold—need not be redistributed at Jubilee. Such assets could have been used by rich Israelites to begin re-leasing lands forfeited at Jubilee. Moreover, cities are explicitly exempted (vv. 29–31), as are foreign slaves (vv. 44–46). Prices for land and redemption are to be adjusted downward depending on how many years until Jubilee (vv. 15–16, 50–51), so that those buying slaves and land will not be cheated. They pay only what the labor and land are worth until Jubilee. Hence, unlike communism, this process is not a thoroughgoing redistribution of wealth. Nonetheless, once in a lifetime it will allow impoverished Israelites a fresh start.

How practical were the Jubilee regulations? There is, in fact, no biblical evidence that the Year of Jubilee was ever put into effect. According to the book of Judges, it took centuries for Israel to control the land fully. Not until the time of King David was the promised land entirely controlled by Israel, but by then records of the original owners would have been fragmentary, and current owners would have vigorously resisted changing the rules. Though probably never enacted, Jubilee teaches the ideal that poverty should not become permanent in Israel.

Could Jubilee laws apply today? Not directly. Jubilee was to be based on a one-time event, the conquest. After the conquest Israel was to divide lands equally, with the land formally belonging to God, not people. Direct application of these rules, formulated for a rural society, to modern urban settings seems impractical. It became increasingly so for Israel itself. Nonetheless, the goal of Jubilee remains a good one. Having an underclass permanently trapped in poverty is unhealthy for any society. It is good to give those at the bottom of the economic ladder a path out of poverty. Exactly how to effect this change is a matter of economic and political prudence. Nevertheless, the laws of Jubilee remind us that it is a worthwhile goal.

Illustrating the Text

God did not want his people trapped in slavery.

History: An iconic symbol of freedom is the Liberty Bell. The bell is inscribed with the text of Leviticus 25:10:

> Proclaim LIBERTY throughout all the Land unto all the Inhabitants thereof Lev. xxv vs x.

The inscription celebrated the fact that the colony of Pennsylvania gave its citizens the right to choose whatever religion they wished to follow. It was thus cited to celebrate freedom of religion.

It is assumed that the Liberty Bell, hung in 1753, was among scores of bells rung on July 8, 1776, in conjunction with the reading of America's Declaration of Independence from England. Thus it was almost

certainly used at that time to "proclaim liberty" in that sense.

The bell was not called the "Liberty Bell" until the 1830s, when a group seeking to abolish slavery referred to it by that name as a symbol of the abolitionist movement. This was not inappropriate. The "liberty" of Leviticus 25:10 inscribed on the bell was liberty or release in conjunction with the Year of Jubilee, the year that slaves were to be set free (Lev. 25:39–41). This use of the bell's citation of Leviticus comes closer to the verse's original meaning than its use in 1753. One of the few times in living memory that the bell has been struck was on D-Day, June 6, 1944, when the mayor of Philadelphia struck the bell to proclaim liberty to those oppressed by tyranny in Europe. This sounding of the bell was broadcast nationwide, and a recording has been preserved.[2]

The text of Leviticus 25:10 is inscribed on the Liberty Bell.

The Choice

Obedience or Punishment

Big Idea *Obedience and disobedience have profound consequences.*

Understanding the Text

The Text in Context

Leviticus 26 is a continuation of Leviticus 25. The two chapters have a common introduction (25:1–2a) and conclusion (26:46), both emphasizing Mount Sinai. Leviticus 26 refers back to Leviticus 25's instructions to give the land its Sabbath rests (26:34–35, 43). Its command to keep the Sabbath (26:2) naturally follows Leviticus 25's Sabbath Year theme. But in a broader sense this chapter sums up the entire holiness code (Lev. 17–27) by spelling out the consequences of obeying its commands and the consequences of disobeying them. Four decades later, when Moses renews the covenant, the blessings/curses theme of Leviticus 26 is repeated for a new generation (Deut. 28). Yet despite disobedience, God will receive the people of Israel back when they repent (Lev. 26:40–45).

Leviticus 26 may be outlined as follows:

1. Rules about idols, Sabbaths, and the sanctuary (vv. 1–2)
2. Blessings for obedience to God's commands (vv. 3–13)
3. Curses for violation of God's covenant (vv. 14–39)
4. Promise of covenant renewal despite disobedience upon repentance (vv. 40–45)
5. Conclusion of Leviticus 25–26 (v. 46)

Historical and Cultural Background

George Mendenhall has observed that God's covenant with Israel is very much like treaties made between suzerains (monarchs) and their vassals among the Hittites.[1] A list of divine curses for noncompliance is a common element in second-millennium BC covenant treaties.

Interpretive Insights

26:1–2 *Do not make idols or set up an image or a sacred stone . . . Observe my Sabbaths.* Compare Exodus 20:4–5, 8–11; Leviticus 19:3–4, 30. A "sacred stone" refers to stelae/pillars, which symbolize a deity and can be worshiped as such.

I am the LORD. See "Additional Insights" following the unit on Leviticus 19:1–37.

26:3–13 These verses lay out the consequences of obedience to God's laws.

26:3–10 *If you follow my decrees and . . . obey my commands.* "Commands" are all-encompassing, not limited to Leviticus 25–26 (cf. Deut. 30:10, 16). If Israel obeys, God promises that it will be blessed in various ways: good crops (vv. 4–5a), safety (vv. 5b–6), military victories (vv. 7–8), population growth (v. 9), food (v. 10), and an intimate friendship with the God who has saved it from Egyptian bondage (vv. 11–13).

26:11 *I will put my dwelling place among you.* "Dwelling place" translates the Hebrew word for "tabernacle" (NIVmg, KJV), though here it emphasizes God's special presence promised in the future rather than a physical structure that is presently in Israel's midst, and so is better rendered "dwelling" (ESV, NASB, NRSV).

I will not abhor you. See verses 14–39.

26:12 *I will walk among you.* Compare Adam and Eve encountering God walking in the garden of Eden (Gen. 3:8).

I will . . . be your God, and you will be my people. This is a covenant formula (Exod. 6:7; Jer. 7:23; 30:22; Ezek. 36:28; Hos. 1:9).

26:14–39 These verses lay out the consequences of disobedience to God's laws.

The Israelites are warned not to set up sacred stones for themselves. Examples of standing stones discovered at Gezer are shown here. Erected during the Middle Bronze Age II (1800–1550 BC), their function is still uncertain.

Key Themes of Leviticus 26:1–46

- God blesses those who obey his word.
- Disobeying God can be disasterous.
- God shows mercy to repentant sinners.

26:14–15 *if you reject my decrees . . . and fail to carry out all my commands.* Conversely, if Israel disobeys, instead of blessings will come various punishments from God.

26:16 *wasting diseases.* Probably "consumption," a wasting of the body from tuberculosis.

26:18 *seven times over.* This phrase is figurative, indicating that more disobedience results in even more severe punishments.

26:19 *stubborn pride.* Literally, the Hebrew says "the pride of your strength." Pride is broken by removing that of which they are proud and that which makes them strong.

sky . . . like iron . . . ground . . . like bronze. The clouds will be impervious to letting the rain pass through, producing drought-hardened ground incapable of producing crops (cf. vv. 4–5a). Deuteronomy 28:23 reverses the iron/bronze similes.

26:21 *hostile.* Hebrew *qeri* appears to be derived from *qarah*, "to meet, encounter." Thus, *qeri* refers to Israel's combative, stubborn opposition toward God, which God promises to reciprocate (cf. vv. 23–24, 27–28).

26:22 *wild animals.* Contrast verse 6.

make you so few in number. Contrast verse 9 and the patriarchal seed promise of many descendants (e.g., Gen. 13:16; 15:5).

26:23–24 *If . . . you do not accept correction . . . I myself will be hostile.* The word *yasar* in the Piel can mean "to discipline through punishment" (vv. 18, 28), but here in the Niphal it means "to respond rightly to punishment/discipline" ("accept correction"). If they do not, they can expect hostility from God (see v. 21) and to receive even more severe ("seven times over" [cf. v. 18]) retributions (v. 24), including war, plague, and famine (vv. 25–26; contrast vv. 3–4, 6b).

26:26 *ten women . . . one oven.* There will not be enough dough or wood during the siege to use more ovens.

dole out the bread by weight. This refers to rationing food because of famine from besiegement.

26:27–28 *seven times over.* Again, even worse punishments will follow continued disobedience.

26:29 *You will eat . . . your sons and . . . daughters.* The famine will be so brutal that people will cannibalize their children (cf. 2 Kings 6:28–29; Lam. 4:10).

26:30 *high places.* These are shrines where Yahweh is often worshiped in idolatrous or polytheistic ways. Good kings, like Hezekiah and Josiah, suppressed the high places (2 Kings 18:4; 23:8, 13), while bad kings, like Jeroboam I, promoted them (1 Kings 12:31–32).

dead bodies on the lifeless forms of your idols. The same Hebrew word (*peger*) is used here for "dead bodies" and the "lifeless forms" of idols to mock idolatry.

I will abhor you. Contrast verse 11.

26:31 *I will take no delight in . . . your offerings.* See comments at Leviticus 1:9. Not even sacrifice will soothe God's anger.

26:33 *I will scatter you among the nations.* Compare Leviticus 18:28.

26:34–35 *the land will enjoy its sabbath years.* God foresees Israel's neglect of Sabbath Year and Jubilee laws (Lev. 25). Accordingly, he promises rest to the land by expelling Israel, leaving no one to cultivate the land. The Hebrew behind "enjoy" is uncertain. "Make up for" (HCSB, NRSVmg), "satisfy" (NASBmg), and "pay for" (ESVmg) are other guesses.

26:36 *those of you who are left.* This refers to those not killed by the catastrophes mentioned in verses 23–35. The paranoia and militarily incapacitation described (vv. 36b–37) represent a complete reversal of verse 7.

26:38 *You will perish among the nations.* See verse 33. Here *'abad* could be rendered "be lost, go astray" rather than "perish." This alternative fits the promise of restoration in verses 40–45 better than the traditional rendering.[2]

26:40–45 These verses lay out the consequences of confession and repentance.

26:40 *if they will confess their sins.* See comments at Leviticus 5:5–6. Confession is the first step of repentance. It "transforms an advertent act into an inadvertent one, rendering it eligible for expiation."[3] Despite disobedience, God will still receive the Israelites back upon their repentance (cf. Deut. 30:1–10).

and the sins of their ancestors. Daniel, Ezra, and Nehemiah each confess the sins of their ancestors (Dan. 9:7–14; Ezra 9:6–7; Neh. 1:6–7).

26:42 *I will remember the land.* That is, God will remember the patriarchal land promise (e.g., Gen. 12:7). Though the land will be deserted so as to enjoy its Sabbath Years and Israel will be exiled to enemy lands, God will preserve a remnant through whom he can keep his covenant promises made to the ancestors (vv. 43–45).

26:46 *These are the decrees, the laws and the regulations that the LORD established.* This conclusion corresponds with the introduction of the previous chapter (Lev. 25:1), showing the literary unity of the two chapters.

Theological Insights

The most basic blessing is God's presence and intimate relationship with his people (vv. 11–12). This fundamental blessing came when God saved Israel from Egyptian bondage and offered it a covenant relationship (v. 13; cf. Exod. 19). God, not Israel, initiated this relationship. God's act of salvation came before the law was given for Israel to obey. In other words, Israel was saved by grace, not obedience. Nonetheless, to receive the full benefits of its covenant relationship required obedience.

This is also true for Christians. Like Israel, we have been saved by grace, but for good works (Eph. 2:8–10). Jesus echoes themes found in Leviticus 26: "Now that you know these things, you will be blessed if you do them" (John 13:17); "If you love me, keep my commands" (John 14:15); "Blessed rather are those who hear the word of God and obey it" (Luke 11:28). Israel's obedience flowed from gratitude for God's having saved it from Egyptian bondage. Similarly,

the Christian's obedience flows from having been saved from bondage to sin (Rom. 6:6, 16–24). Like Israel, we can expect God to bless us as we obey (compare the Beatitudes pronounced by Jesus in Matt. 5:3–11).

Teaching the Text

Leviticus 26 lays before Israel a choice: obey God or pay the dreadful consequences.

1. *God blesses those who obey his word.* Our blessings, like Israel's, flow from our relationship with God (see Lev. 26:11–13). One's relationship with God is established by grace (see "Theological Insights" above), but the full blessings of that relationship are contingent upon obedience. If we want the fullness of God's blessings, we must consistently obey God's commands.

2. *Disobeying God can be disasterous.* Israel learns by unfortunate experience that blessings flowing out of our covenant relationship with God can be

In Leviticus 26:14–39, God details the consequences the Israelites will suffer if they fail to listen to God and obey his commands. This is set out similarly to the suzerain/vassal treaties recorded by the Hittites. This Hittite cuneiform text (thirteenth century BC) is part of the treaty between King Shuppiluliuma and Hukkana of Halasa. It includes a pronouncement of destruction for Hukkana by the deities who witnessed the treaty if the terms of the treaty are not upheld.

forfeited by disobedience. Indeed, the severity of God's threatened punishment on Israel seems appalling. With increasing severity, the text describes the most horrific catastrophes that can possibly overtake a nation.

Sadly, Israel does disobey. The Israelites worship Baal and other gods (1 Kings 16:31), set up sacred stones (1 Kings 14:23; 2 Kings 17:10), and even profane the sanctuary with articles for Baal and Asherah (2 Kings 23:4). They desecrate God's Sabbaths (Ezek. 20:12–16) and, as far as we can tell, completely ignore the Sabbath Year and Jubilee laws (see Lev. 25). As a result of disobedience, catastrophes of increasing severity come upon Israel. The northern kingdom becomes subservient to Assyria and loses much of its territory to Tiglath-pileser III in 732 BC (2 Kings 15:20, 29). In 722 BC Israel is defeated by Assyria, ending Israel as a political unit (2 Kings 17:5–6). Scripture states that the destruction and exile of the northern kingdom is a direct result of sin (2 Kings 17:7–23).

The same is true of the downfall of the southern kingdom. In 586 BC the curses of covenant violation come upon Judah much as described here in Leviticus. Nebuchadnezzar captures all but a few of Judah's fortified cities (Jer. 34:6–7) and brings Jerusalem under siege. Although food is rationed (Ezek. 4:16; cf. Lev. 26:26), it runs out (2 Kings 25:3). Some are starved into cannibalism (Lam. 2:20; Ezek. 5:10; cf. Lev. 26:29), as had previously happened in Israel (2 Kings 6:25–30). Jerusalem is eventually burned and plundered (2 Chron. 36:18), including the holy temple (2 Kings 25:9; cf. Lev. 26:31). Many are slaughtered; some die while defending or hiding in the temple precincts (2 Chron. 36:17; cf. Lev.

26:30b). Thousands are deported to Babylon (2 Kings 25:11–12; Jer. 52:27–31), where no doubt they cower in fear and suffer further atrocities (cf. Lev. 26:36–39). Those who remain in the land are so devastated by war, famine, and disease that the land becomes desolate (Jer. 44:22; cf. Lev. 26:32–33). God gives the land seventy years of involuntarily Sabbath rest (2 Chron. 36:21; cf. Lev. 26:34–35), making up for Israel's neglect for at least 490 years.

The unhappy fulfillment of the predictions of Leviticus 26 is a warning for us. Do not presume the mercy of God. Do not underestimate the severity of God's sanctions against those who disobey. If we cease to be faithful to God and instead disobey his word, if we fall into our own form of idolatry, unbelief, and disobedience, we can expect to forfeit some of God's blessings and possibly even bring disaster upon ourselves. We must learn from Israel's example.

3. God shows mercy to repentant sinners. Though God's wrath is severe, his mercy and grace are even greater. By rights God could have destroyed and abandoned Israel, but in his mercy he refuses to do so (Lev. 26:44). Likewise today, God is willing to welcome wayward people back if they repent.

Repentance means accepting God's correction when it comes (Lev. 26:23) and acknowledging our sin and guilt (Lev. 26:40). Repentance means humbling our pride by admitting that God is right and we are wrong (Lev. 26:41). Once this is done, God can restore blessings. He does so for the Jewish people. When they repent of their idolatry, God returns them from exile to the land that he had given their ancestors (Lev. 26:42) under the leadership of Zerubbabel (Ezra 2), Ezra (Ezra 7), and Nehemiah (Neh.

1–2). God forgave and restored even the most wayward of sinners. He still does so today.

Jesus says that there is rejoicing in heaven whenever a sinner repents (Luke 15:10). Even if we have turned away from God and his word and fallen into wanton sin, even if we have reaped horrible consequences for our disobedience, it is still not too late to repent. God will welcome us back, just as he welcomed Israel, if we turn back to him.

Illustrating the Text

Obedience opens the door to blessing.

Hymn: "Trust and Obey," by John Sammis. This older hymn (1887) catches a theme taught not just in Leviticus 26 but throughout the Bible: a happy and blessed Christian is an obedient Christian. It begins,

> When we walk with the Lord in the
>   light of His Word,
> What a glory He sheds on our way!
> While we do His good will, He abides
>   with us still,
> And with all who will trust and obey.
> Trust and obey, for there's no other way
> To be happy in Jesus, but to trust and
>   obey.

God's mercy is greater than our sin.

Object Lesson: Using a tape measure or a one-minute sand timer, illustrate the concept of finite distance or time. As humans, we think in terms of "this far and no farther" or "this long and time runs out." Those limitations often influence our understanding of God. We can come to believe that God can extend mercy only to someone who has gone "this far" from him. We mistakenly believe that God will be patient only for "this long," and then his patience runs out. But Scripture

One of the punishments for disobedience to the Lord is that Israelite cities will become rubble. Second Kings 15:29 records that Tiglath-pileser III, king of Assyria, took the cities of Ijon, Abel Beth Maakah, Janoah, Kedesh, and Hazor and deported the people to Assyria. The archaeological record shows that Hazor was totally destroyed. This relief of Tiglath-pileser III is from his palace at Nimrud (728 BC).

teaches us that as long as we are breathing, we can be reconciled to God.

If your setting allows, it might be effective to have a volunteer walk the tape measure down the aisle until it comes to the end and then take one step beyond the reach of the tape measure, illustrating that God's mercy is beyond measure.

Heaven celebrates when sinners are saved.

Human Experience: Any first-time parent probably can remember what it was like when his or her child first began walking. She's learned to pull herself up. She's learned to stand with her hands out in front of her. But suddenly, in a moment, she moves forward in what seems a barely controlled fall. The first, fumbling steps are celebrated with shouting, clapping, and cheering. Likewise, heaven rejoices over the first steps each Christian takes into new life.

Leviticus 26:1–46

Vows, Redemption, and Tithes

Big Idea *Give to God both what is expected and more.*

Understanding the Text

The Text in Context

This chapter logically follows after the Jubilee regulations (Lev. 25), which it assumes (see 27:16–24). Leviticus 26's grand theme of blessings for obedience and punishments for disobedience in some ways seems a more fitting conclusion to Leviticus than does Leviticus 27. Why does the content of Leviticus 27 follow Leviticus 26 rather than precede it? Did God reveal this material on vows and redemption subsequent to revealing the literary unit of Leviticus 25–26? Did the desire to follow the Sabbath Year regulations immediately with the warnings of an involuntary Sabbath rest for the land if Israel ignores the Sabbath Year law (26:34–35) lead to Leviticus 26 taking precedence over the material of Leviticus 27? Perhaps it was thought desirable to end Leviticus with something less emotionally charged than the curses of Leviticus 26 by concluding as it began with regulations about the sanctuary.

The theme of special vows will be taken up again in Numbers 30.

Historical and Cultural Background

Votive offerings (offerings done in fulfillment of a vow to a deity) were made among Israel's neighbors. In Sumer statues of worshipers were placed in temples as votive offerings. In Mesopotamia victorious kings could dedicate war captives as slaves for temples.[1] Mesha king of Moab "devoted" seven thousand Israelite men and women to Chemosh by slaughtering them and giving plunder to Chemosh (Moabite Stone, lines 14–18; cf. Lev. 27:28–29 below).

Interpretive Insights

27:1–8 *If anyone makes a special vow.* The rendering "special" is uncertain. Others translate as "makes a difficult vow" (NASB) or simply "utters a vow" (LXX). Vows can promise to give to God one's child, slave, or self. The vow maker is obligated to deliver by a certain time the person vowed to the sanctuary to become its property. However, persons vowed to Yahweh can be redeemed by a standardized monetary substitute. The values vary according to the age and gender

Table 1. Redemption Prices by Age and Sex (Lev. 27:2–7)

Age	Male	Female
1 month–5 years	5 shekels	3 shekels
5–20 years	20 shekels	10 shekels
20–60 years	50 shekels	30 shekels
60+ years	15 shekels	10 shekels

of the vowed person, probably correlating with—perhaps about a fifth higher than (cf. vv. 13, 15, 19, 27, 31)—the market value of slaves for those categories.[2] Allowance is made for the poor person who cannot afford to redeem a person at full price (v. 8).

27:9–13 *If what they vowed is an animal.* Most animals vowed to God cannot be redeemed (v. 9). For the animal to "become holy" (vv. 9–10) means that it belongs to the sanctuary. Someone who substitutes another animal for the one vowed forfeits both. Exception is made for unclean animals unsuitable for sacrifice, such as camels or donkeys. They can be redeemed for 20 percent above their valuation established on a case-by-case basis by the priest (vv. 12–13) or else sold with the proceeds given to the sanctuary (see v. 27 below). Presumably, the same principle applies to blemished animals.

27:14–25 *If anyone dedicates their house . . . field.* Houses vowed to God can also be redeemed at 20 percent above the appraised value as established by priests (vv. 14–15). The appraised value of fields depends on how much seed is required to cultivate the land, with the value set at "fifty shekels" per "homer" of grain (v. 16). A homer is roughly 3.3 bushels or 26 gallons. If part of the land is rocky, that reduces the seed requirement and hence its appraisal. The appraisal is also prorated according to when the next Jubilee will

occur (vv. 17–18), since the land reverts to the owner at Jubilee. To get vowed lands back earlier than Jubilee requires that one pay 20 percent above its appraisal (v. 19). If someone consecrates to God a field bought from someone else, the valuation for redemption again takes into consideration Jubilee's return of the land to the original owner (vv. 22–24). Money to redeem consecrated property is by weight of silver determined by a balance against a standard weight. The commercially used "shekel" (Gen. 23:16) varies from the official sanctuary weight, so it is necessary to specify sanctuary weight. The shekel is roughly 0.4 ounce, though exact weights vary over time and region. The "gerah" is the smallest measure of money, worth one-twentieth of a shekel (0.02 ounce).

27:20–21 *If . . . they do not redeem the field, or if they have sold it to someone else.* Verse 20 could instead be rendered "not redeem the field, *but* has sold

Worshipers in the ancient Near East would bring votive offerings, perhaps statues like these, to the temples of their gods. These figurines were found in temple excavations at Tel Asmar.

Leviticus 27:1–34

The monetary value of redemption set by the priest is based on the sanctuary shekel, which is twenty gerahs to the shekel. One shekel weighs out 11.4 grams of silver. Shown here are a series of weights. The weight at the top left is a shekel and then multiples continue to the right. The lower weights are fractions of a shekel, and the five in the lower right are gerah weights.

the field to another man" (NASB). On this rendering, the dedicated land continues to be worked by the owner, not the priests, who lack the time and skills to work fields. Instead, the crop of this dedicated land goes to the sanctuary. If working a field for which no personal benefit is derived proves onerous to the original owner, that owner can redeem the field as stated in verse 19. But the field can also be "sold" (in practice "leased") to someone else to end the original owner's requirement of paying the sanctuary. But if the original owner "sells" it without first redeeming it from the sanctuary, at Jubilee the land reverts not to the original owner but to the priests. This in effect makes a vow of land to God permanent at Jubilee. The priests in turn can sell it to a new permanent owner.

27:26–27 *No one . . . may dedicate the firstborn of an animal.* Firstborn animals cannot be vowed because Mosaic law has already mandated that firstborn animals be given to God (Exod. 13:2, 15; 34:19; cf. Num. 18:15). Just as unclean animals—such as donkeys, camels—vowed to God can be redeemed (see vv. 11–13 above), so unclean firstborn livestock can be redeemed by paying their value plus 20 percent, or else sold and the money given to the sanctuary instead.

27:28–29 *Nothing that a person owns and devotes to the LORD . . . may be sold or redeemed.* To "devote" (*haram*) (cf. v. 21) is to give something irrevocably to God or

his sanctuary. The verb and related noun are used in conjunction with "holy war" against the Canaanites in which persons, animals, and goods can be declared *herem*, that is, given over to God for destruction, or if unable to be destroyed (e.g., precious metals), given to the sanctuary treasury (Josh. 6:17–21; 1 Sam. 15:3). Leviticus 27:21, 28 refer to peacetime *herem* in which fields, people, and animals are devoted. Fields as *herem* become the property of the sanctuary priests (v. 21). Foreign slaves, animals, or fields declared *herem* by their owners become the irredeemable property of Yahweh (v. 28). Leviticus 27:29 probably references *herem* of a different sort: persons declared *herem* by the courts as a judicial penalty (see Exod. 22:20, where the verb *haram* is used) or an enemy vowed as *herem* to God (Num. 21:1–3; Deut. 13:15; 1 Sam. 15:3). Such persons are executed. Making something *herem* is the highest degree of consecration to Yahweh.

27:30–33 *tithe . . . from the land . . . of the herd and flock.* As firstborn livestock are to be given to God, so are the tithes.

One-tenth of one's crop is to be given to the sanctuary (v. 30), though one can substitute a 12 percent tithe in silver: the commodity's monetary value plus 20 percent (v. 31). The phrase "passes under the shepherd's rod" (v. 32) refers to a means of counting (Jer. 33:13) to assure that every tenth animal counted goes to God and that the herder does not tithe only the worst ones.

27:34 *These are the commands the* LORD *gave Moses.* This verse concludes both the chapter and Leviticus.

Theological Insights

Is God sexist? After all, the valuation of a boy child is higher than the valuation of a girl child, that of a boy youth more than that of a girl youth, that of a man more than that of a woman, and that of an elderly male more than that of an elderly female (Lev. 27:1–8). While it is true that an adult woman is worth more than a male child, youth, or senior citizen, females are always worth less than the male of the same age category in these regulations.

But the conclusion that God is sexist is unnecessary. As some scholars have noted, these valuations appear to be roughly the market value of slaves at that time. They reflect economic realities in which prime-aged, adult workers were generally of greater monetary value than children or the elderly, and males were of greater economic value as day laborers than females. These economic valuations have nothing to do with the person's inherent worth as a human being made in God's image. That is priceless.

Even today a person's economic value does not correlate with her or his value as a human being. If professional baseball were completely open to players regardless of gender or age, there would be no children and no senior citizens playing in the major leagues. The economic value of those age groups to Major League Baseball as players is zero. And there would be few if any women. By biology God has made the most elite men athletes stronger and faster and hence better in baseball (and most other sports) than the best women athletes. But women are not less valuable in inherent worth to God just because they cannot throw a hundred-mile-per-hour fastball!

Teaching the Text

This chapter on tithes, vows, and redemption seems an unpromising one for finding spiritual lessons, and yet they are there. The main overall lesson is that we are to keep our commitments to God.

1. *We must give what is expected.* God mandates that firstborn and tithes be given to him by Israel. When God redeems Israel from Egypt in the plague of the firstborn, he makes a special claim on firstborn animals (Exod. 13:2; 22:29–30). Thus the firstborn is not an Israelite's to vow. The firstborn already belongs to God (Lev. 27:26). Similarly, God expects Israel to give him a tithe of crops and herds (Lev. 27:30–33). God has given Israel the land. In gratitude for the blessings of the land, Israel is to give God tithes. It is assumed that the gift is the literal commodity or animal, though for a price one can substitute money (v. 31). Animals tithed must be a random sample of the herd/flock (v. 32), and not just the weaker animals (v. 33). Other things expected by God are things "devoted" according to the

rules of holy war. They belong to God and cannot be redeemed (Lev. 27:29).

God still expects us to express gratitude for material blessings by giving back to him a significant part of our income. The New Testament does not mandate a percentage, but the Old Testament tithe does seem to give an order of magnitude for our expected giving to God.

2. *We should give beyond what is expected.* Vows dedicate to God persons, animals, or things over and above the regular tithe. This vow can be a promise made on condition of answered prayer, as when Hannah vows Samuel (1 Sam. 1:11). Consequently, Hannah delivers the child Samuel to Eli the priest after the child is weaned (1 Sam. 1:24–28). Absalom vows to worship God in Hebron—presumably this includes votive offerings—if God allows him to return to Israel (2 Sam. 15:8). One can also simply vow something to God as an expression of gratitude.

Votive offerings are allowed and generally welcomed by God, but they are not obligatory. They represent gifts over and above the minimum expected. So today, a person may give to God gifts beyond a simple tithe. A person out of gratitude to God and a desire to further his kingdom might give money to build a chapel or church, land for a Christian camp, or something else to further the church and its ministry. And if done in the right spirit and for the right reasons, this is entirely praiseworthy.

3. *Failure to give what one promises to God is a sin.* Votive offerings can be imprudent. A woman could vow a child to God, as Hannah does (1 Sam. 1:11), but then decide that she cannot part with the child. The law allows that option. Hannah could

have redeemed the little boy Samuel for five shekels and brought him home (Lev. 27:6). The same is true of animals, houses, and fields vowed to God (vv. 13, 15, 19). Vows that seem noble and right at the time might, in retrospect, seem foolhardy. But God in his mercy allows vows to be "redeemed" with money, though the 20 percent penalty discourages rash vows.

It is not wrong to make promises to God, but such promises should be kept (cf. Num. 30:2). It is wrong to promise God something that we can neither physically nor emotionally deliver. And yet sometimes we think that we are capable of giving God more than we actually can supply. But as Leviticus 27 shows, God in his grace makes generous allowances for this kind of human excess caused by imprudent zeal. Such excesses are preferable to apathy that promises God nothing.

Illustrating the Text

We are to give freely to God, not only what is expected but beyond.

Literature: "Babette's Feast," by Isak Dinesen. This story by Danish writer Isak Dinesen (1885–1962) was first published in *Ladies Home Journal* in 1950. In 1987 Gabriel Axel made it into a film, which won the Oscar that year for best foreign-language film. It is a story of complete, extravagant giving. The main character, Babette, a famous European chef, escapes war in nineteenth-century France by going to a remote village in Jutland, where anonymously (she does not tell the villagers what her position has been) she begins to serve a disgruntled religious community lost in false and joyless piety. After a few years

"Every tithe of the herd and flock—every tenth animal that passes under the shepherd's rod—will be holy to the LORD" (27:32).

of observing them, and having won the lottery with a ticket purchased long before, Babette asks to make a meal for the people to celebrate their founding father's birthday. Though they are suspicious, she proceeds and presents the gathering with a sumptuous and exquisitely beautiful and delicious multicourse feast. Eventually softened by the sensuous delight of the food, the group forgets their petty disputes, and mercy and truth are restored to their spirits. It is discovered later that Babette has spent her entire winnings, holding back nothing,

on the food so that these people's spiritual lives might be refreshed.

We must keep the commitments that we make to God.

Personal Story: Years ago, when I was an elder on a church board, a generous, well-to-do couple decided to donate some land to the church and build a small retreat center on it for church use to promote discipleship. Everything was built to exacting standards of quality. Nothing was spared. The result was a simply beautiful facility. When it was completed, and after ownership was transferred to the church, a problem arose with zoning that did not allow the facility to be used right away. At that point, the couple had second thoughts. They wondered if they might have the property back for their grandchildren. This created a great dilemma among the elders. How should they respond?

It did not occur to me at that time, but Leviticus 27 would have been an appropriate passage to consider in dealing with the situation. The property was essentially a votive offering. In such a case in ancient Israel, a person who felt unable to part with a vowed gift to God could redeem it with a monetary gift of the item's value plus one-fifth. Something similar might well have been considered in this case.

Church Life: Consider reading the vows that new members make when received into your church. After this reading, the question could be asked about how seriously the members take their church membership vows to support God's church with gifts, talents, and service.

Introduction to Numbers

Numbers tells the unhappy story of how the generation of Israelites that departed from Egypt failed to enter Canaan because of unbelief. And yet the next generation of Israelites moved into position to begin the conquest of the land.

Title

The title "Numbers" is based on the Latin Vulgate's *Numeri*, which in turn is based on the Greek Septuagint's title, *Arithmoi*, in reference to the censuses taken in the book. Its Hebrew title is *Bemidbar*, meaning "in the desert," based on the opening words of this book. The Hebrew title is not inappropriate, since most of the events recounted in this book took place while Israel lived in the desert.

Setting

Numbers continues the story of Leviticus. At the beginning of Numbers, the Israelites remain at Mount Sinai, though they will leave Sinai and move eventually to the plains of Moab.

Chronologically, Numbers begins in the second month of the second year after the Israelites leave Egypt (1:1) and continues through the fortieth year after the exodus (33:38), thus covering all the years of wilderness wanderings.

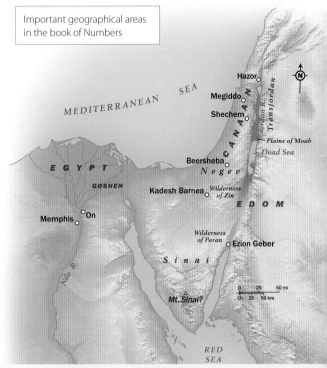

Important geographical areas in the book of Numbers

Table 1. Book of Numbers Analyzed Geographically

Location	Text	Actions
Sinai	Numbers 1:1–10:10	The Israelites are at Mount Sinai, where their population is counted and they receive further laws.
Kadesh Barnea and Desert	Numbers 10:11–20:13	The Israelites travel to Kadesh south of Canaan, but because of unbelief they are condemned to wander in the wilderness for forty years.
From Kadesh to Moab	Numbers 20:14–36:13	At the end of the forty years, the Israelites move from the desert to the land of Moab on their way to conquer Jericho.

Outline of Numbers

The chronological framework of Numbers and its geographic movement from Sinai to the plains of Moab are clear, but the organizing principles within the book are less clear. To many, the book's contents seem like a poorly organized junk room.

This impression is challenged by Dennis Olson, who argues that Numbers is reasonably well organized.[1] He proposes the following macrostructure:

Numbers 1–25	**The End of the Old Generation of Rebellion** The first, rebellious generation of God's people out of Egypt on the march in the wilderness
Numbers 26–36	**The Birth of the New Generation of Hope** The second generation of God's people out of Egypt as it prepares to enter the promised land

Numbers 1–25 describes the old, rebellious generation numbered by the censuses (Num. 1–4). This generation is organized for battle and begins the journey toward Canaan (Num. 5–10), but the people grow increasingly weary and rebel against God and Moses (Num. 11–12). The climax comes at Kadesh Barnea, where the people refuse to enter the land and are condemned to wilderness wanderings (Num. 13–14). Further episodes of rebellion by this first generation follow (Num. 16; 20–21; 25).

Numbers 26 counts the new generation at the end of the wilderness wanderings. Rather than rebellion and death, the book now emphasizes hope. Potential rebellions involving Moses's successor and inheriting the land are defused and resolved (Num. 27; 32; 36). The laws in this part of the book look forward to the impending inheritance in the land, and the book ends with Israel on the plains of Moab ready to begin the conquest.

Olson points out interconnections between the two halves of Numbers that show literary cohesion.

Alan Chan proposes a variation on Olson's schema that sees a first unit (Num. 1–26) bracketed by two censuses (Num. 1–4; 26), and a second unit (Num. 27–36) bracketed by the two accounts of the daughters of Zelophehad (Num. 27; 36).[2] See the illustration for a visual representation.

Authorship

The question of the authorship of Leviticus and Numbers was discussed in the

The Structure of Numbers
(A. Chan)

Num. 26:33

| Opening bracket | | Closing bracket | Opening bracket | | Closing bracket |

| Num. 1 | Num. 2–25 | Num. 26 | Num. 27 | Num. 28–35 | Num. 36 |

introduction to Leviticus. There I argue that Moses wrote down what God revealed to him (e.g., Num. 1:1; 2:1; 3:5; 4:1) and recorded events of his day (e.g., Num. 33:2), but this material from Moses has been edited and updated for a later audience. In addition to the Mosaic materials, the editor utilized an ancient hymnbook, called "the Book of the Wars of the LORD" (Num. 21:14), and an Amorite poem (Num. 21:27–30).

Theological Themes

1. *Danger of failing to live up to one's calling.* In Numbers God's people fall into a spirit of rebellion and ingratitude, and they lose the blessings of the land for forty years. Paul refers repeatedly to the book of Numbers in 1 Corinthians 10:6–12:

> Now these things happened as examples for us, that we should not crave evil things as they also craved [Num. 11:4, 34]. . . . Nor let us act immorally, as some of them did, and twenty-three thousand fell in one day [Num. 25:1–9]. Nor let us try the Lord, as some of them did, and were destroyed by the serpents [Num. 21:4–9]. Nor grumble, as some of them did [e.g., Num. 11:1; 14:2–4; 16:11, 41], and were destroyed by the destroyer [perhaps the "fire of Yahweh"] [Num. 11:1]. Now these things happened as an

Table 2. Interconnections between Numbers 1–25 and Numbers 26–36

Old Generation of Rebellion	New Generation of Hope
Census of tribes, Levites (Num. 1; 3)	Census of tribes, Levites (Num. 26)
Legal ruling on women (Num. 5)	Legal ruling on women (Num. 27)
Laws on vows (Num. 6)	Laws on vows (Num. 30)
Lists/laws on offerings (Num. 7; 15)	Lists/laws on offerings (Num. 28; 29)
Passover (Num. 9)	Passover (Num. 28:16–25)
Blowing trumpets (Num. 10:9–10)	Blowing trumpets (Num. 31:6)
Spies from twelve tribes (Num. 13)	Leaders from twelve tribes (Num. 34)
Spy story (Num. 13–14)	Spy story recalled (Num. 32:6–15)
Provision for Levites (Num. 18)	Levitical cities for Levites (Num. 35)
Sihon and Og defeated (Num. 21:21–35)	Sihon's and Og's lands assigned to Reuben, Gad, half of Manasseh (Num. 32)
Balaam and Midianites sin against Israel (Num. 22–25)	Balaam and Midianites punished (Num. 31)

Note: Table from Olson, *Numbers*, 5–6.

Introduction to Numbers

example, and they were written for our instruction, upon whom the ends of the ages have come. (NASB)

2. *Promise.* Numbers moves toward fulfillment of the promise to the patriarchs of land, seed (descendants), and blessing (Gen. 12:1–3). The censuses show fulfillment of the seed promise (about six hundred thousand males [Num. 1–4, 26]), Israel makes progress toward the land promise (Num. 21), and the book reasserts Israel's blessing (Num. 24:9–10). Balaam and Balak try to curse Israel and end up cursed themselves (Num. 24:17; 31:8).

3. *God's nature.* Numbers reveals much about God. It shows God to be unchangingly true to his promises and committed to blessing Israel (Num. 6:22–27; 23:19–20). Life itself is impossible unless God wills it (Num. 24:23). God organizes his people and prepares them both for worship and for warfare (Num. 1–10). He leads them through the fire cloud and provides them food, water, and victories (Num. 11:9, 31–32; 14:14; 20:1–13; 21:3, 33–35). He intervenes to protect Israel from Balaam's curses and plots (Num. 22–25). Numbers speaks of how to avert God's wrath through intercession (Num. 11:1–2; 12:13–15; 14:13–19; 15:22–28; 16:22, 42–48; 21:7–8).

4. *Worship.* Worship for Israel is active, expressed through giving gifts to God, listening to him speak, and purifying oneself before meeting with him (Num. 7–8). Worship involves special holy days and festivals (Num. 28–29). It can involve vows that dedicate things to God (Num. 30) or oneself to God as a Nazirite (Num. 6).

5. *Leadership.* Numbers conveys many lessons about spiritual leadership. True leaders are chosen by God (Num. 17; 27), while false leaders choose themselves (Num. 16 [Korah]). God's leaders have God as their essential inheritance and should be financially supported (Num. 18). There can be jealousy among God's leaders (Num. 12 [Aaron and Miriam]). Spiritual leaders delegate responsibilities (Num. 1; 11), guard that which is sacred and holy (Num. 3–5), are dedicated to God to bless

As the book of Numbers opens, the Israelites are camped in the Desert of Sinai. This dry, rocky region is shown here. Throughout their wilderness wanderings, God faithfully supplies the food and water they need.

others (Num. 6), assist God's people in worship (Num. 7–8), guide God's people into action and spiritual warfare (Num. 10), but also can fail to live up to God's calling (Num. 20).

6. *Sins condemned*. Various sins are condemned in Numbers, including sacrilege (Num. 5), jealousy (Num. 5), ingratitude (Num. 11), gluttony (Num. 11), envy (Num. 12; 16), racism (Num. 12), Sabbath breaking (Num. 15), rebellion against God (Num. 16; 21), false teaching (Num. 16), and idolatry and sexual immorality (Num. 25).

7. *Renewal*. Though the first generation in the wilderness falls short, hope and renewal come through the next generation (Num. 26–36). New leaders (Eleazar, Joshua) arise to replace old leaders (Aaron, Moses) (Num. 20; 27); they would bring Israel into the land, something that the old leaders are unable to do. The promise of a star and scepter from Israel that will crush Moab (Num. 24:17) renews Israel's hope that it will enter the land, a promise that anticipates both David and, ultimately, Jesus Christ.

The Census of the Twelve Tribes

Big Idea *God fulfills his promises.*

Understanding the Text

The Text in Context

Numbers begins with Israel still "in the Desert of Sinai," where it has received the Ten Commandments (Num. 1:1; cf. Exod. 19:1–2). Numbers continues the story of Exodus and Leviticus. At the end of the book of Exodus, Israel constructs the tabernacle, or "tent of meeting." The book of Leviticus gives rules for how Israel is to use the tabernacle. Now from that tent at Mount Sinai God gives further instructions.

Centuries earlier God had promised Abraham to make his descendants into a great nation as numerous as the stars in the sky and the sand upon the seashore, and to give them the land of Canaan (Gen. 12:1–3, 7; 15:7, 18–20; 17:8; 22:17–18). Subsequently, Israel had grown prolifically in Egypt (Exod.

1:7). It is now April or May, twelve and a half months since Israel had left Egypt in the exodus (Num. 1:1). At this point a census is taken that demonstrates empirically that God has fulfilled his seed promise to the patriarchs. This census also serves to organize the army in preparation for the military conquest of the promised land.

Interpretive Insights

1:1 *the tent of meeting in the Desert of Sinai.* "Tent of meeting" is another name for the tabernacle, so named because God has promised to meet with Moses there to communicate his commandments (Exod.

> The tabernacle is centrally located in the Israelite camp. The Levites pitch their tents immediately adjacent to it. Shown here is the tabernacle model at Timna, Israel.

25:22), as God does here. "In the Desert" translates *bemidbar*. This is the title of the book of Numbers in the Hebrew Bible. On the location of "Sinai," see comments at Numbers 33:15.

on the first day of the second month of the second year after the Israelites came out of Egypt. This is eleven months since they had arrived at Sinai (see Exod. 19:1) and twelve and a half months since departing from Egypt.

1:2 *clans and families.* Israel is a tribal society in which the tribes are subdivided into clans (*mishpahot*), which are further subdivided into families (*bet 'abot*; lit., "house of fathers") (cf. Josh. 7:14–18).

every man by name. Literally, "according to the number of names, every male" (ESV), which may or may not mean individual names are listed.

1:3 *twenty years old or more and able to serve in the army.* The census has a military purpose: organizing the army for the anticipated conquest. Conscription into the army begins at the age of twenty and has no specific upper limit. Contrast the census of the priests in Numbers 3–4, which has

Key Themes of Numbers 1:1–2:34

- God's place among his people must be protected.
- Spiritual leaders are needed to delegate and make preparations.

a different purpose and operates on a different principle.

1:4 *One man from each tribe . . . is to help you.* Only by Moses and Aaron delegating the responsibility of taking the census to representatives can it be accomplished efficiently and quickly.

1:5–16 *These are the names of the men who are to assist you.* This list of twelve tribes omits Levi because that tribe is exempt from military service.[1] It reaches twelve despite the omission of Levi by counting Joseph as two tribes through his sons Ephraim and Manasseh. The tribes are listed in the order of the mothers as listed in Genesis 35:22–26: Leah (Reuben, Simeon, Judah, Issachar, Zebulun), Rachel (Joseph, Benjamin), Rachel's maidservant Bilhah (Dan, Naphtali), and Leah's maidservant Zilpah (Gad, Asher).

The theophoric names in this list refer to the deity as "El" ("God") and "Shaddai" ("Almighty"). Like patriarchal names in

Table 1. "El" and "Shaddai" Names in Numbers 1:5–16

"El" Names		"Shaddai" Names	
Elizur	"[My?] God is a rock"	Zuri**shaddai**	"Shaddai is [my?] rock"
Shelumi**el**	"God is [my?] peace"	Ammi**shaddai**	"Shaddai is [my?] kinsman"
Nethan**el**	"God has given"	Shedeur if revocalized to **Shaddai**ur	"Shaddai is a flame"
Eliab	"God is [my?] father"		
Elishama	"[My] God has heard"		
Gamali**el**	"God is [my?] goodness/ reward(?)"		
Pagi**el**	"God is [my?] entreaty(?)"		
Eliasaph	"[My?] God has added [a child]"		
Deu**el**	"They sought [or "Seek!"] God"		

Table 2. The Census of Numbers 1:20–46

1. Reuben: 46,500	5. Issachar: 54,400	9. Benjamin: 35,400
2. Simeon: 59,300	6. Zebulun: 57,400	10. Dan: 62,700
3. Gad: 45,650	7. Ephraim: 40,500	11. Asher: 41,500
4. Judah: 74,600	8. Manasseh: 32,200	12. Naphtali: 53,400

Total: 603,550

Genesis, none of them employs forms of the divine name "Yahweh." This suggests that the list is authentically ancient, since after Moses theophoric names regularly use the element "Yahweh" (names in English beginning with "Jo-" or "Jeho-" or ending with "-iah").

1:17–46 *Moses and Aaron . . . called the whole community together . . . The people registered.* This census taken at the beginning of the wilderness totals 603,550 men (v. 46), not counting women and children. After forty years of wilderness wanderings the number goes down a little to 601,730 (Num. 26:51). The message in context is that every man is counted on to fight in the coming conquest of Canaan.[2]

1:18 *the whole community.* The "community" ('edah) can refer to Israel's entire population or to the adult male population (e.g., Num. 1:2), though when Moses meets with the whole community, it is almost certainly limited to tribal and clan representatives. The census takers are chosen from among this body (Num. 1:16). It would have been impossible for Moses to meet in the desert with a population of sixty thousand, much less six hundred thousand.

1:46 *603,550.* This number is used in Exodus 38:26 to estimate the total of the half shekel of silver temple tax levied on Israel. Such a tax is demanded whenever Israel takes a census (Exod. 30:12–16).

1:47–54 *The ancestral tribe of the Levites . . . was not counted along with the others.* Levites are to serve the tabernacle. Being a soldier is incompatible with the duties of Levites because killing will make Levites ceremonially unclean (see Num. 19) and therefore unfit for serving the tabernacle. Because this census is in preparation for the war against Canaan, there is no need to number the Levites at this point. The Levites' camping immediately adjacent to the tabernacle will keep the Israelites from encroachments on the tabernacle's sacred space (v. 53), something that can result in God's wrath breaking out. Compare Leviticus 10:1–3.

2:1–34 This unit, while repeating the census numbers and the names of each tribe's leader from the preceding chapter, is meant to describe Israel's deployment around the tabernacle, in which each tribe gathers to its tribal banner (v. 2). Then follow eastern (vv. 3–9), southern (vv. 10–16), central (v. 17), western (vv. 8–24), and northern (vv. 25–31) encampments. All but the central grouping are described in triads in which the most prominent of the triad is listed first. The tribes take these positions when they camp, and the order of their groupings determines when they "set out" to relocate the camp (vv. 9, 16, 24, 31). See the illustration.

2:3–9 *On the east . . . Judah . . . Issachar . . . Zebulun.* East of the tabernacle are Judah, Issachar, and Zebulun. Judah, the tribe destined to be the ruling tribe (Gen. 49:10), is given the most prominent position, immediately in front of the tent of meeting, which faces east. Although modern maps orient to the north, ancient Israelite directions oriented "toward the sunrise" (Num. 2:3). This orientation was once common. Compare the English geographic word "Orient," which means "East." Issachar and Zebulun follow Judah in the census of Numbers 1, thus representing the fourth, fifth, and sixth sons of Leah.

2:10–16 *On the south . . . Reuben . . . Simeon . . . Gad.* Reuben was the firstborn son of Leah. Reuben had forfeited his right of firstborn to Ephraim by virtue of committing incest with Jacob's maidservant Bilhah (1 Chron. 5:1–2; cf. Gen. 35:22; 49:3–4). Given that the Israelites orient toward the east, the tribe of Reuben's position at the "right hand" of the tabernacle is a sort of consolation prize for its patriarch's having forfeited his original position of prominence. Simeon was Leah's second child. Skipping Leah's third child, Levi, the text goes to Gad, the first son of Zilpah, Leah's maidservant.

2:17 *Levites . . . in the middle of the camps.* The tent of meeting is at the center of the camp with the priestly tribe of Levi immediately surrounding it. The Levites will be in the same position when the camp relocates and "set[s] out" (v. 17). For specifics about this encampment, see Numbers 3.

2:18–24 *On the west . . . Ephraim . . . Manasseh . . . Benjamin.* The western triad represents the descendants of Rachel: her grandchildren Ephraim and Manasseh through her son Joseph and her son Benjamin. Rachel died giving birth to Benjamin (Gen. 35:18). Ephraim, though younger than Manasseh, was given prominence in Jacob's special blessing (Gen. 48:14–20). Ephraim took Reuben's role as firstborn (1 Chron. 5:1–2) and thus is given prominence in this triad.

2:25–31 *On the north . . . Dan . . . Asher . . . Naphtali.* These are the descendants of the children of Jacob's slave-wives: Rachel's maidservant Bilhah (Dan, Naphtali) and the second born of Leah's maidservant Zilpah (Asher). Dan's prominence in this triad probably relates to his being born before the other two, though Naphtali seems to have been born before Asher (Gen. 30:4–13).

2:32–34 *These are the Israelites . . . the Israelites did everything the* LORD *commanded Moses.* These verses summarize the chapter, emphasizing Israel's total obedience.

Positions of the Encamped Tribes

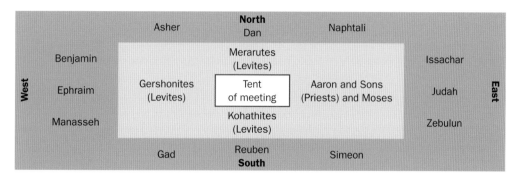

Theological Insights

One of the most important themes in the Pentateuch is the promise to the patriarchs (Gen. 12:1–3). That promise has three elements: land, seed, and blessing. God had promised to make Abraham's descendants (seed) as numerous as the stars of heaven and the sand on the seashore (Gen. 22:17). This census shows that God has kept the seed promise: Israel has multiplied prodigiously. It also anticipates the fulfillment of the land promise: the conquest of Canaan, for which the census was a prelude. With the census, the dream of returning to the promised land is becoming attainable, showing God to be faithful in keeping the promises that he makes to his people.

The promises to Christians are even better than those under the old covenant (Heb. 8:6). God's promised blessings include Christ's second coming for his people (2 Pet. 3:4), heavenly rest (Heb. 4:1), an eternal inheritance in the kingdom of God (Heb. 9:15; James 2:5), and eternal life (James 1:12; 1 John 2:25). The fact that God kept his promises to Israel gives us confidence that he will keep his promises to us.

Teaching the Text

1. *God's place among his people must be protected.* Israel literally camps around God. The tribes surround the tabernacle or tent of meeting to protect and cherish it. Clearly, it is the most valuable of all the Israelites' possessions because it symbolizes God's dwelling among them and the values that motivate them represented by the laws stored there. The central location of the tabernacle is a reminder of the central role that God plays in their lives. Similarly, we need to guard the centrality of God and his values in our lives.

2. *Spiritual leaders are needed to delegate and make preparations.* Although Numbers 1–2 gives no authoritative teaching on matters of church leadership today, the actions of Moses and Aaron at God's direction can be seen to illustrate wise and prudent principles of leadership.

For example, Moses and Aaron could never complete the census of Israel by themselves. They need assistants to accomplish this large task, just as Moses has previously needed help in judging Israel (see Exod. 18). For that reason, representatives from the tribes—their importance is emphasized by listing them by name in Numbers 1–2—are selected to help Moses by coordinating this activity for each tribe. These representatives will in turn have needed helpers among the clans and families to complete this great task. So too today, pastors and elders can accomplish only a little by themselves, and they should prepare others for additional works of service (Eph. 4:11–12). God's people can accomplish much more for the kingdom of God if they all share the responsibilities of doing God's work with their spiritual leaders.

One purpose of Israel's census is practical: it serves to prepare the nation for war in Canaan. The census indicates how many men would be in the army. This forms the first stage in organizing them into units for battle. Some Christians downplay the need for planning and preparation for spiritual tasks, but this is very shortsighted. Planning ahead for tasks that God has asked his people to accomplish is a matter of prudence. It is not incompatible with authentic spirituality.

"The Israelites are to set up their tents by divisions, each of them in their own camp under their standard" (1:52). A standard is carried by one of the soldiers in this painted wall relief fragment from the Hatshepsut Temple in Deir el-Bahri, Egypt (Eighteenth Dynasty, ca.1470 BC).

Illustrating the Text

Promises inspire hopeful perseverance.

History: General Douglas MacArthur was the commander in charge of the Philippines at the time it was overrun by imperial Japan in 1941. As the situation worsened, MacArthur was ordered by President Roosevelt to leave the Philippines and relocate to Australia. He reluctantly obeyed that order, even though it meant leaving his troops in the Bataan Peninsula without him. But while in Australia, he made a speech in which he vowed to win back the Philippines: "I came out of Bataan and I shall return." He subsequently repeated that promise many times, to the point that the phrase "I shall return" became MacArthur's famous motto. And ultimately he was able to keep that promise. Armies led by MacArthur landed on the Philippines in October 1944 to drive the Japanese out. When MacArthur made his vow, he had no way of knowing whether he would ever be able to fulfill it. But his promise to return inspired many Americans to fight on. So God's promises, which are infinitely more reliable than MacArthur's vow, inspire us to go on living for God.

The tabernacle, the place of God's presence, was protected above all things.

Object Lesson: In the game of chess every piece is expendable except one. Pawns are regularly given up for tactical reasons, and even the very valuable queen is expendable if one can gain advantage by sacrificing it. Only the king is indispensable. If one's king is lost—or, more precisely, is trapped in such a way that after the next move it would be lost—the game is over: checkmate. For that reason, chess players must make every effort to protect their kings. It is clear from the deployment of the camp of Israel that the indispensable piece in this "game" is the tabernacle. The armies of Israel surrounded the tent of meeting, where Israel went to meet with God. The tabernacle was the dwelling place of Israel's divine King and the site of his earthly throne (the ark). The various tribes protected it from external threats all around. The Levites served to protect it from internal threats: encroachments by other Israelites. Everything else was expendable. Protecting God's dwelling and throne was essential. Likewise for us, God and the spiritual values associated with him must be indispensable in our lives. We must guard against all encroachments on our place of meeting with God.

This illustration could be enhanced by having a chessboard in view. The speaker could give a brief introduction to the game of chess, explaining what some of the pieces do, finishing with the king and its essential place in the game.

On the Large Numbers in the Census

The large numbers in Israel's census lead some readers to question their accuracy. Since it would take a miracle for a large number of people to survive in the Sinai Desert, rationalists who do not believe in miracles naturally dismiss these numbers as impossible. Those who are theologically conservative cannot accept as an argument the denial of God's ability to perform miracles. Indeed, the Bible itself is well aware that for Israel to survive in the desert, it required various miracles involving manna, quail, and water. But many conservative scholars also have reservations about these large numbers.

Some who reject these large numbers think that they have been made up and lack any historical basis.[1] Others debate whether the numbers can be reduced by arguing that scribes garbled the meaning by taking the word *'elep* to mean "thousands" when what was intended was a secondary meaning of this term, "clans, groups, troops" or the like.[2]

Traditional conservatives point out that the Bible itself indicates that the Israelites had multiplied prodigiously to the point that Pharaoh found their numbers threatening (Exod. 1:7, 9). If Israelite couples averaged about four to five reproducing children each, starting with seventy individuals (Exod. 1:5), over 430 years (Exod. 12:40) they could grow to about two and a half million (six hundred thousand men plus women and children).[3] That is incredibly rapid growth, but not theoretically impossible.

On the other hand, taken literally, the numbers are difficult to reconcile with certain other Scriptures: Canaan is said to have seven nations "larger and stronger than you" (Deut. 7:1), and Israel is referred to as "the fewest of all peoples" (Deut. 7:7). This seems to imply seventeen million in Canaan, more than twice the modern population.[4] There is no archaeological evidence of a population of that size ever living in Palestine. Pharaoh addresses only two midwives as being the ones serving the Hebrews (Exod. 1:15), which would be impossible if there were millions of them. The Israelites were terrified by six hundred

To register every family and record the names of men twenty years of age and older would have taken the skills of a scribe like the one shown here (Saqqara, Egypt, date unknown). How to understand the final totals is a question that has yet to be answered satisfactorily.

chariots (Exod. 14:7), but surely six hundred thousand men by sheer numbers could overwhelm a few hundred chariots. Exodus 18 indicates that Moses sat from morning to evening judging the people, leading Jethro, his father-in-law, to advise him to appoint judges under him to reduce the task (Exod. 18:13–23). That Moses would have single-handedly attempted to settle all the disputes of two and a half million people seems unimaginable. The Israelites were emotionally devastated by the defeat at Ai in which thirty-six Israelite men died (Josh. 7:5), but what is a loss of thirty-six if there are six hundred thousand to start with? Problems of these sorts lead some conservative scholars also to question whether these numbers are meant to be taken at face value.

How to resolve the problem is not entirely clear. One suggestion is that the numbers were never meant to be taken literally. Assyrian texts appear to inflate numbers to give importance to the deeds narrated.[5] In some places in Indonesia, one's age is a statement not about how long a person has lived but about that person's status and respect in the community. Hence, someone who is thirty-five might be described as a "fifty-year-old" based on that person's status. This is not lying or deceiving, but rather a rhetorical device versus a strict quantifier. Perhaps the numbers in the census in the book of Numbers are following some convention of hyperbole now lost to us.[6] Some suggest reducing the numbers by a factor of ten to get the real number (note that all of them end in zero).[7] That would reduce the population to something more reasonable. A fully satisfactory solution to this problem remains to be found.

The Census and Duties of Levites

Big Idea *That which is holy must be guarded.*

Understanding the Text

The Text in Context

The census of Israel (Num. 1–2) is followed by the census of the Levites (Num. 3–4). The priests and Levites are not counted in the census of Numbers 1–2 because they are not to participate in the conquest in view of their sacred duties (see the sidebar). But in Numbers 3–4 they have their own census on different principles. In Numbers 3 they count every male from one month old and above who serves as a substitute for Israel's firstborn. Numbers 4 counts only those eligible for sacred service (males age thirty to fifty).

Numbers 3–4 can be outlined as follows:

1. The family of priests (3:1–4)
2. Guard duties of Levites (3:5–10)
3. Levites substitute for the firstborn (3:11–13)
4. Census and other duties of Levites (3:14–39)
5. Redemption of the firstborn (3:40–51)
6. Duties of active priests (4:1–49)

Interpretive Insights

3:1 *the family of Aaron and Moses.* All other Levites report to Aaron and Moses. Aaron is mentioned before Moses as firstborn and because the chapter emphasizes priests. Moses, like Aaron's family, camps in the privileged position east of the tabernacle (Num. 3:38).

3:3 *anointed priests.* Moses anoints priests with oil and blood (Lev. 8:30).

3:4 *Nadab and Abihu . . . died.* See Leviticus 10:1–7.

3:6–10 *the tribe of Levi . . . perform duties . . . take care of.* The Hebrew behind "perform duties" (*shamar mishmeret* [v. 7]) is better

> Numbers 3 opens with the genealogical record of Aaron. Aaron and his sons serve as priests before the Lord. Genealogies were important in the ancient world. This wall fragment records a genealogy of the high priests of Memphis (946–736 BC).

rendered "keep guard" (ESV) (cf. Num. 1:50–53), and "take care of" (v. 8) is better rendered "guard" (ESV). Guarding the tabernacle is the Levites' most regular duty. They collapse, move, and erect the tabernacle as needed, but they are always in charge of guarding it, even killing intruders (v. 10b). Thus they protect Israel from God's wrath, which could accompany encroachment on his sacred space (cf. Lev. 10). They also guard the sacred treasuries (1 Chron. 26:20), which constitute a considerable amount of wealth. They are also gatekeepers, not only protecting the sanctuary from intruders, but also regulating who is allowed to enter the sanctuary area for specific and legitimate purposes (1 Chron. 9:17–27).

3:12–13 *all the firstborn are mine.* God makes a special claim on all firstborn males, both human and livestock, when he redeems the firstborn through the Passover lambs (Exod. 12:11–13, 23; 13:1–2). Israel is subsequently to give the firstborn livestock to God and offer a lamb to redeem firstborn sons (Exod. 13:12–13; Num. 18:15). Firstborn sons, having been specially redeemed by God, in principle are dedicated to God for sacred service. Perhaps because many of these firstborn sons had fallen into worship of the golden calf while the Levites had supported Moses in opposition to it (so Rashi), God chooses to set apart the tribe of Levi instead of the firstborn sons for sacred duties (v. 12; cf. Exod. 32:29). See also comments at 3:40–51 below.

3:15–39 *Count the Levites.* This census is based on everyone one month old and up (v. 15) and is used to compare the number of Levites to the number of firstborn in the rest of Israel to determine how many firstborn need to be redeemed (see 3:40–51).

Key Themes of Numbers 3:1–4:49

- It is necessary to protect the sacred.
- Substitution and redemption are key theological concepts.

The Levites

The Levites were the descendants of Levi, the third son of Jacob and Leah (Gen. 29:34). Of Levites, only Aaron and his sons were designated and ordained as priests (Exod. 28:1; Lev. 8–9). Other Levites were set apart (Num. 8:5–23) to be in charge of the tabernacle, and they were gatekeepers guarding and caring for its furnishings, its sacred utensils, and its treasuries (Num. 1:47–53; 1 Chron. 26:20–28; see comments at Num. 3:6–10). Levites thus had an elevated degree of holiness compared with other Israelites, but most were less holy than priests. Levites were set apart from other tribes when they joined Moses in executing a thousand of the worst offenders in the incident of the golden calf (Exod. 32:26–29). They had a special role in the construction of the tabernacle (Exod. 38:21) and had special rights of redemption around their forty-eight Levitical cities (Lev. 25:32–34; Num. 35:7; Josh. 21:41), six of which served as cities of refuge where manslayers could flee and receive a trial (Num. 35:6, 10–15). In fulfillment of Jacob's curse on Levi for his shedding blood at Shechem (Gen. 49:5–7; cf. Gen. 34:25–30), the Levites did not inherit territory like the other tribes, but their cities were scattered among the other tribes. In compensation they were supported through the tithes of the other Israelites (Num. 18:21, 23). Levites reported to Aaron and his sons, who directed their activities (Num. 3:9–10a).

See the table for a summary of the clans, counts, leaders and duties of the clans of Gershon, Korath, Merari, and Aaron.

3:15 *Count every male a month old or more.* High infant mortality is probably behind not counting babies less than one month old.

3:21–35 *Gershon . . . Kohath . . . Merari.* The leaders of these three clans are "Eliasaph" ("[My?] God has added"), "Elizaphan" ("[My?] God protects"), and "Zuriel" ([My?] rock is God"). As with the tribal leaders in Numbers 1–2, so the names of the

The Clans of the Levites

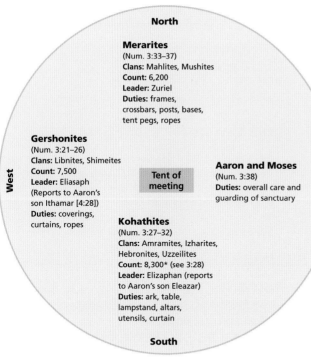

North

Merarites
(Num. 3:33–37)
Clans: Mahlites, Mushites
Count: 6,200
Leader: Zuriel
Duties: frames, crossbars, posts, bases, tent pegs, ropes

Gershonites
(Num. 3:21–26)
Clans: Libnites, Shimeites
Count: 7,500
Leader: Eliasaph
(Reports to Aaron's son Ithamar [4:28])
Duties: coverings, curtains, ropes

West

Tent of meeting

Aaron and Moses
(Num. 3:38)
Duties: overall care and guarding of sanctuary

East

Kohathites
(Num. 3:27–32)
Clans: Amramites, Izharites, Hebronites, Uzzeilites
Count: 8,300* (see 3:28)
Leader: Elizaphan (reports to Aaron's son Eleazar)
Duties: ark, table, lampstand, altars, utensils, curtain

South

leaders of Gershon, Kohath, and Merari use the term "El" ("God") rather than "Yahweh" as the theophoric element, an indication that this list is ancient.

3:27 *Amramites.* Amram son of Kohath is Moses and Aaron's father, possibly in the sense of ancestor (Exod. 6:18–20).

3:28 *8,600.* The numbers in verses 22, 28, 34 in the Hebrew text add up to 22,300 rather than 22,000 (see v. 39). The reading "8,600" probably should read instead "8,300" (NIVmg). The Septuagint preserves the correct reading, "8,300." The corruption involves an accidental loss of a single letter in the transmission of the Hebrew text, by which *shlsh* ("three") became *shsh* ("six") by the dropping of one letter.

3:38 *Moses and Aaron.* Moses and Aaron are descendants of Kohath (see 3:27 above), but their families are separate from

others Kohathites due to their priestly and leadership duties. Other Levites report to Aaron, and all the tribes report to Moses.

east of the tabernacle. This position is the most prominent, immediately in front of the sanctuary. Kohath, on the south (right-hand) side of the tabernacle (v. 29), has the second most prominent position.

3:39 *22,000.* This is the sum of verses 22, 28 (as corrected above), and 34.

3:40–51 As some firstborn animals can be redeemed with a lamb as a substitute (Exod. 13:12), so Levites substitute for the firstborn. But there is a problem: the count of Levites one month and older is less than the number of firstborn by 273. Thus, 273 still require redemption. The redemption price is five shekels of silver each (1,365 shekels total), the price of redemption for slaves dedicated to the sanctuary one month to five years in age (cf. Lev. 27:6). Also the cattle of the Levites substitute for the cattle of the firstborn that heretofore had belonged to Yahweh.

3:43 *22,273.* The census figures of Numbers 1–2 seem too large, while the number here seems too small for a population with 603,550 in its army. C. F. Keil speculates that only the firstborn after the exodus are being counted, but this explanation lacks supporting evidence. If the numbers of Numbers 1 are reduced by a factor of ten (see "Additional Insights" following the unit on Num. 1:1–2:34), 22,273 firstborn becomes a more reasonable figure.

4:2–49 Only male Levites thirty to fifty years of age can actually do the sacred service. The census of this chapter counts them. There are 8,580 active Levites (v. 48), as compared with 22,000 total Levites (3:39).

4:2–20 *Take a census of the Kohathite branch.* This tribe deals with the most holy objects (cf. Exod. 25:10–26:14; 27:1–8; 30:1–6) and is to treat them with utmost sanctity. Only the priests, not the Kohathites, can touch these objects. The ark, God's throne, is especially holy. It is to be covered by the sons of Aaron with the curtain, hides, and a blue cloth. While Israel is on the march, the ark will stand out as the only blue item, with other items covered with leather outer wrappings.[1] Aaron's sons will also put the poles through the carrying rings (vv. 4–6). The other objects are prepared by Aaron's sons in decreasing degrees of holiness: the table of Presence (vv. 7–8), the lampstand (vv. 9–10), the gold altar (vv. 11–12), and the bronze altar (vv. 13–14). Only after these are covered by the sons of Aaron can the Kohathites safely carry them on poles or frames (v. 15a). Touching or even looking on these holy objects can result in a Kohathite's death (vv. 15b, 19–20). Compare the incident involving Uzzah (2 Sam. 6:6–8). Aaron's son Eleazar is in charge of the oils, incense, and grain offering, and he oversees the overall activity of preparing the holy objects for the Kohathites (v. 16).

4:22–28 *Take a census . . . of the Gershonites.* They are in charge of transporting the tent proper and the screen at the east entrance of the fence around the tabernacle enclosure (see Exod. 26:1–14, 31–37; 27:16). These items are less holy than the items for which the Kohathites are responsible, so there is no warning about death for touching or looking at these things. Once the most sacred objects are removed by Aaron's sons and the Kohathites, the Gershonites can directly dismantle the rest of the tent themselves. This section adds to Numbers 3:21–26 that the Gershonites report to Aaron's son Ithamar.

4:29–33 *Count the Merarites.* They are in charge of the poles and crossbars of the tabernacle (see Exod. 26:15–30) and its precinct fence (see Exod. 27:9–19). Again, these things are less holy than the items carried by the Kohathites, so there is no danger of death. Like the Gershonites, the Merarites report to Ithamar.

4:34–49 *Moses, Aaron and the leaders counted all the Levites . . . Thus they were counted, as the* LORD *commanded Moses.* The summary of the census of active Levites (8,580 in total) emphasizes obedience to God's command.

Theological Insights

The Levites have the function of guarding the sanctuary. They are to protect it against intruders who might profane it or attempt to steal its gold-covered sacred objects. The task is important because of what the tabernacle symbolizes: the presence of God in the Israelites' midst, the law, the covenant, and the blood-atoning sacrificial system that allows God to purge the people's sin and uncleanness and maintain his presence among them. The tabernacle represents all that is sacred for Israel, and therefore it must be jealously guarded.

Today, the sense of the holiness of space and objects is widely lacking among evangelical Christians. That sense is much greater in Catholic and Orthodox circles. Orthodox Christians maintain their churches as sacred spaces with different degrees of holiness. By comparison, most Protestant churches seem lacking in holiness.

I once visited an Orthodox Church to learn more about that tradition. It was 5:15 in the afternoon, and there was to be a service at 6:00. An assistant had come to prepare the church for the service. The priest put on his vestments, repeating appropriate recitations as he did so, and he asked me to go around to the other side, where he would prepare the bread of the Eucharist for the service. Although I thought that I was doing what I was asked to do, when I began to walk in front of the altar, a space where only priests could go, the assistant looked at me aghast, stopping me in my tracks. I had nearly committed a social blunder. Fortunately, I was in no danger of being killed, as those who encroached on the ancient Israelite tabernacle were.

Under the new covenant, the geographic sacred space of the tabernacle, whose existence derived from the tangible presence of God in its midst, has been replaced by the anthropological sacred people of God, who individually and collectively are indwelt with God's Spirit and who now constitute God's temple (1 Cor. 3:16–17; 6:19; Eph. 2:19–22). Nonetheless, Protestants can learn from the Old Testament and from the Catholic and Orthodox traditions that symbolize the holiness of God by maintaining the holiness of spaces of worship in a way close to the spirit and practice of the Old Testament. Protestants, too, could invest into their places of worship a greater sense of holiness.

Teaching the Text

Although this passage contains no direct mandates for Christians, there are analogies here to New Testament teachings.

1. *It is necessary to protect the sacred.* Levites kept guard over the sanctuary, moved its objects, and maintained it. As the Levites guarded and maintained Israel's most holy things, so we should protect and maintain that which is holy for us. Beyond locking up the church to protect it from thieves, this involves preserving sound doctrine (Titus 1:9; 2:2), suppressing false teachers (1 Tim. 1:3), and correcting the wayward (Gal. 6:1; 1 Thess. 5:12–14). It involves guarding God's presence among us. Whatever encroaches upon God's rightful place in our lives must be mortified, just as those who encroached on the tabernacle were to be killed (Num. 3:38). Guarding the sacred in our lives individually and corporately is still an important activity.

2. *Substitution and redemption are key theological concepts.* The firstborn sons belong to God in a special sort of way because they have been purchased by God by his provision of the Passover sacrifice in the exodus narrative. Since they have been redeemed by God, they in principle owe him their service. To keep from being given over to servitude to God, they in turn must be redeemed by the substitutionary sacrifice of a lamb to God (Exod. 13:13, 15). In Numbers 3–4 the firstborn are redeemed by the substitution of the Levites, who serve God in their place.

Redemption and substitution are important biblical concepts. Because Christ has redeemed us through his death, we owe him our service (1 Cor. 6:19b–20). The meaning of Christ's death is clarified by the concept of substitution seen both in the sacrifices (see comments at Lev. 1; 4; 17) and, here, in the Levites taking the place of the firstborn. Christ died instead of people (John 11:50). He took the curse we deserved (Gal. 3:13) and died as a ransom for (or instead of) many (Matt. 20:28). Thus the substitution of the Levites for the firstborn provides a conceptual framework for understanding how Christ serves as a substitute for us.

Illustrating the Text

Every person in the church has a part to play.

Music: The first violin takes the prominent position in the orchestra. It usually plays the more technically challenging melody parts that draw more of the audience's attention. The second violin plays the less difficult harmony parts. There is an old saying, "It takes more grace than I can tell to play second fiddle well." The Levites from other families played second fiddle to the Aaronic priests. They did the arduous labor of transporting the tabernacle. The priests had the prominent public role of conducting the worship. But just as an orchestra needs second violins and not just first violins to play its best, so the church needs more than pastors. It needs the less prominent persons to contribute their part to making the church function well.

We must guard the sacred in our lives and churches.

Theological Reference: Some theological terms come into and go out of fashion. One phrase that might not be familiar to many is "fencing the table." It refers to the call of church leaders, and each individual Christian, to protect the sanctity of the Lord's Supper. Only someone who has believed the gospel, confessed sin, and seeks to live in obedience can come to the table for Communion. The only way through the "fence" that (metaphorically) guards the table is the gateway of faith in the gospel. Anyone who approaches without this faith stomps on something sacred. That is why the church, through careful teaching and preparation, should "set a fence" around this sacred act.

We cannot understand Jesus unless we understand the concept of substitution.

Education: A substitute teacher is called to do something very specific: fulfill the duties of the teacher who normally leads the class. The regular teacher, for whatever reason, is unable to fulfill the required workload, so the substitute steps in and completes the task. The miracle of redemption is that the Son of God did what we cannot do. And far from being just a temporary replacement, Jesus's substitution has eternal benefits we could never gain on our own. Every person owes a debt of obedience, love, and worship to the God of the universe. Left to ourselves, we would perish with this job unfulfilled. The punishment would be eternal. But Jesus substituted himself for us. He was obedient where we could not be and suffered the punishment that we deserved.

The Levite clans are given different responsibilities to pack and transport the tabernacle. The ark of the covenant, the table of Presence, the gold incense altar, and the bronze altar are conveyed using poles. Egyptian priests also used poles to transport the sacred bark as shown in this relief from the Ramesseum in Thebes (thirteenth century BC).

Impurity, Repentance, and Jealousy

Big Idea *God's people must deal with ritual and moral impurities.*

Understanding the Text

The Text in Context

Following the census of priests and Levites in Numbers 3–4, Numbers 5 introduces laws that involve priests:

1. Cases of ceremonial impurity (vv. 1–4) (cf. Ezek. 44:33)
2. Restitution given to priests for false oaths (vv. 5–10)
3. A priestly ritual regarding a jealous husband (vv. 11–31)

In each of these cases the issue involves the need for Israel to be pure.

Historical and Cultural Background

Requiring those accused of crimes to take oaths was also a practice among non-Israelites in Old Testament times. In Babylon there was a law about a jealous husband that, like Numbers 5:11–31, required a suspected adulteress to take an oath: "If her husband accuses his own wife [of adultery], although she has not been seized lying with another male, she shall swear (to her innocence by) an oath by the god, and return to her house" (Laws of Hammurabi ¶131).[1] If the person taking the oath swore falsely, he or she was under a self-curse and subject to punishment from the deity.

Interpretive Insights

5:2 *send away from the camp.* Anyone contracting serious ceremonial uncleanness is to move away from the sanctuary (see v. 3).

defiling skin disease. Traditionally, "leprosy." See Leviticus 13–14.

discharge of any kind. Discharges include genital discharges (Lev. 12; 15) and possibly defecation (Deut. 23:12–14; Ezek. 4:12–13).

dead body. Since corpses ceremonially defile, priests generally avoid them (Lev. 21:1–4, 11; 22:4). On corpse impurity, see Numbers 19. This list omits another major source of impurity: taboo foods/animals (Lev. 11; Deut. 14).

5:3 *so they will not defile their camp, where I dwell among them.* Leviticus 15:31 explains further: "You must keep the

Israelites separate from things that make them unclean, so they will not die in their uncleanness for defiling my dwelling place, which is among them."
To approach the sanctuary at the center of the camp (Num. 2:17) while unclean is to endanger oneself and the whole community. Everyone contracts uncleanness periodically. Perhaps the distance a person is required to move away from the camp varies with the degree of uncleanness (so Rashi).

5:6 *is unfaithful . . . is guilty*. The law in verses 6–10 about sacrilege overlaps with Leviticus 5:14–6:7 (see comments there). The word *ma'al* ("is unfaithful") is better rendered "commits sacrilege" (see comments at Lev. 5:15). Leviticus 6:1–7 indicates that the offense is twofold: defrauding another person and committing sacrilege against God by swearing a false oath about it. "Is guilty" should be rendered "and that person *feels* guilty" (see comments at Lev. 6:4–7). It is the guilt that leads to the confession, restitution, and sacrifice that follow.

5:8 *if that person has no close relative*. This case differs from Leviticus 5:14–6:7 in that here the wronged person has died before the offender has repented, leaving "no close relative" (lit., "kinsman redeemer" [*go'el*]) to whom restitution can be made. In that case, the restitution goes

- God's holiness is in conflict with uncleanness.
- Repentance is a remedy for guilt.
- Irrational jealousy must be addressed.

Leviticus 5 details the procedure that a married couple and the priest are to follow if the husband suspects the wife of unfaithfulness. This plaque shows a man and a woman with their arms entwined, a pose that in the ancient world would have been appropriate only for married couples (Ur, 2000–1750 BC).

to God by his proxy, the priest. The priest also keeps the meat offered to God as a guilt offering, as is the case with the sin offering (vv. 9–10; cf. Lev. 7:7). This is in contrast with the fellowship offering, in which most of the meat goes back to the worshiper (a thigh and breast go to the priest [Lev. 7:32–34]), and the burnt offering, for which the whole animal is burned (though the priest keeps the hide [Lev. 7:8]).

5:11–31 These verses are about a husband's jealousy concerning his wife's suspected adultery, charges that she denies and that he is unable to prove with two or three witnesses. Adultery is potentially a capital offense (Lev. 20:10; Deut. 22:24). This regulation seeks to resolve the impasse by a ritual oath.

5:12 *If a man's wife . . . is unfaithful to him*. The same Hebrew verb behind "is unfaithful" (*ma'al*) is used in verse 6, where the offense is oath violation. This violation of the marriage covenant may also involve oath violation (i.e., marriage vows).

5:13 *another man has sexual relations with her.* Literally, "A man lay with her with outpouring [laying] of semen" (see comments at Lev. 15:16–18). Improprieties not involving "outpouring of semen" do not constitute adultery.

this is hidden from her husband . . . her impurity is undetected . . . there is no witness . . . she has not been caught in the act. The husband has no legal case against his wife because he lacks any proof. If there had been witnesses, the case would have gone to a court, not the sanctuary.

5:14 *if feelings of jealousy come over her husband.* The purpose of the ritual described is to address the husband's jealousy (cf. v. 30). The same ritual applies whether his wife is guilty of adultery or innocent. The oath ritual can vindicate either the husband or the wife.

5:15 *he is to take his wife to the priest.* Possibly better, "he *may* take his wife to the priest," as an option rather than a mandate.[2]

He must not pour olive oil on it or put incense on it . . . it is a grain offering. On grain offerings, see Leviticus 2. Oil and incense are omitted because their beautiful aroma and symbolism of joy (Ps. 104:15; Prov. 27:9) are inappropriate for this somber occasion.[3] Incense is also omitted with the grain offering used as a sin offering (Lev. 5:11).

5:16 *have her stand before the LORD.* The suspected adulteress stands before the presence of God at the entrance to the tabernacle.

5:17 *holy water . . . clay jar . . . dust from the tabernacle floor.* Presumably, this water is taken from the laver (so Rashi). The clay jar, being a simple container rather than a beautiful cup, emphasizes the somberness of the ritual. The dust is holy, being from the immediate presence of God.

5:18 *he shall loosen her hair.* Loosed rather than ornately styled hair shows her humbled before God.

curse. She swears on pain of divine punishment that she has not committed adultery.

5:19 *the priest shall put the woman under oath.* The oath is a self-curse.

5:19–20 *If . . . you have not gone astray . . . But if you have gone astray.* The curse is conditional: harmless if she is innocent (cf. v. 28), but effective if she is guilty.

5:21 *your womb miscarry and your abdomen swell.* More literally, "your thigh waste away and your abdomen swell" (NASB). The thigh and abdomen probably refer to the woman's external and internal sexual organs. The word *beten* ("abdomen, belly") is rendered "womb" in Genesis 25:23–24 (NIV). "Thigh" (*yarek*) is used for the genitals/loins in Genesis 24:2; 46:26; Exodus 1:5 (see KJV). The curse may be sterility[4] (NIV: "her womb will miscarry"; contrast v. 28) or possibly the appearance of a false pregnancy.[5] There is a poetic justice in either case: the woman's sexual organs misused in adultery are cursed.

5:22 *Amen. So be it.* "So be it" in the Hebrew paraphrases the repeated "amen" (see, e.g., KJV, NASB, ESV). These words denote agreement to the terms of the curse.

5:23–24 *write these curses on a scroll and wash them off into the bitter water . . . make the woman drink the bitter water.* The curse is dramatized by a ritual symbolizing that the woman internalizes the curse pronounced by the priest, bringing it into the vicinity of her sexual organs.

5:28 *she will be cleared of guilt and will be able to have children.* An innocent woman will suffer no ill effects from the curse. Her sexual organs, rather than being cursed, will function normally. Exoneration of innocent women appears to be a major purpose of this ritual.

Theological Insights

God in his holiness calls Israel to purity: ceremonial, moral/religious, and sexual purity. Ceremonial defilement forces a person to move away from God (Num. 5:1–4). So also moral defilements separate a person from God, for only those with "clean hands and a pure heart" can approach him (Ps. 24:3–5). Sexual impurity can bring a person under God's curse (Num. 5:11–31). Where purity has been lost, God requires corrective actions. Ceremonial uncleanness requires avoiding the holy (Num. 5:3) and ritual cleansing (see Lev. 11–15). Confession, restitution, and sacrifice can provide cleansing from wrongdoing and/or sacrilege (Num. 5:5–9). Though God is holy, he provides for the cleansing from impurities of various sorts so that God's people can remain in his presence.

God himself is so pure that he cannot look tolerantly upon evil (Hab. 1:13). He demands pure offerings (Mal. 1:11). What could help keep Israelites pure? It requires fear of God and heeding God's word (Pss. 19:9; 119:9). God can himself act so as to purify peoples (Zeph. 3:9).

A woman suspected of unfaithfulness must undergo a trial by ordeal. The priest takes a clay pot into which holy water and the dust of the tabernacle floor are mixed. He recites and then records the words of a curse on the scroll. After washing the writing into the mixture, it is then given to the woman to drink. These clay cooking pots were excavated from Jokneam and Izbet Sartah in Israel (eleventh century BC).

The New Testament also speaks of moral, religious, and sexual purity. Disciples are to be pure in heart (Matt. 5:8; 1 Tim. 1:5) and in their devotion to Christ (2 Cor. 11:3). Morally we are to be blameless and pure from sin (Phil. 2:15; 1 Tim. 5:22). The marriage bed is to be pure from immorality (Heb. 13:4). Our hope in the second coming of Christ helps to purify us, just as Christ himself is pure (1 John 3:2–3).

Teaching the Text

Numbers 5 teaches about God's holiness, instructs us how to repent, and deals with the problem of sexual sin and irrational jealousy.

1. God's holiness is in conflict with uncleanness. The most important explanation of the rules of purity (see Lev. 11–15) is that they teach the concept of the holiness of

God in contrast with the contamination of people. The unclean are excluded from God's dwelling, the tabernacle (Num. 5:3; Lev. 15:31), precisely because uncleanness is a symbol of human sinfulness: human beings, as part of this sin-cursed, fallen world, are "contaminated" and are not automatically eligible to approach God. The purity system, by emphasizing the holiness of God and the impurity of humanity, teaches that humans must prepare themselves both ritually and morally before approaching the holy God.[6] See further discussions at Leviticus 11–15.

Although the laws of ceremonial purity have been abolished in Christ, some principles of the clean/unclean laws are still applicable. Christians should still disassociate themselves from anything morally defiling that hinders our ability to approach God.

2. *Repentance is a remedy for guilt.* What are we to do when we profane that which is holy? The text gives us good general guidance (5:5–10). The process involves (1) confession, (2) restitution, and (3) an appeal to God. Repentance begins with acknowledging one's guilt (v. 6c), for there can be no repentance if one senses no wrongdoing. Confession of the offense (v. 7a) follows naturally, acknowledging to others one's bad behavior. True repentance continues by trying to make amends to any person one has wronged (v. 7b). In some cases that will prove impossible (v. 8a). Perhaps the person wronged has died, or we have lost contact with the person we have wronged. In that case, one only needs to make amends to God (v. 8). But repentance is not complete until we not only acknowledge our offense against other humans but also admit our sin against God.

We must therefore go on to acknowledge our sin by appealing to God for restoration (symbolized by the guilt offering). Although Christians under the new covenant no longer offer animal sacrifices, the law about the guilt offering does illustrate a practical pattern of repentance that can be followed today. See more at Leviticus 5:14–6:7.

3. *Irrational jealousy must be addressed.* Numbers 5:15–31 censures adultery. Infidelity is not always detected. It can be hidden from a spouse for years. But this ritual reminds us that our sins cannot be hidden from God, who knows our secrets and can bring a "curse" on our misbehaviors, whether or not they can ever be proven in a court of law.

But another purpose of Numbers 5:15–31 is to protect a woman against her husband's frivolous accusations. If the woman is innocent, the ritual conveys no ill effects. Moreover, it obligates the husband to desist and accept her innocence. It thus serves to promote greater harmony within the marital relationship and protect a woman against an irrationally jealous husband.

The problem of irrational jealousy still exists today. Proverbs 27:4 says, "Anger is cruel and fury overwhelming, but who can stand before jealousy?" Jealousy is a powerful emotion. It can lead to anger and vengeance (Prov. 6:34). It can also lead to the breakdown of a marital relationship and divorce. Although the ritual of Numbers 5:15–31 at the tabernacle conducted by Levitical priests no longer applies under the new covenant, it does encourage us, with the Lord's help, to address and allay inappropriate feelings of jealousy toward a spouse. Addressing such feelings may mean the difference between a healthy marriage and a divorce.

Illustrating the Text

Humanity is infected with sin.

Literature: *The Strange Case of Dr. Jekyll and Mr. Hyde,* by Robert Louis Stevenson. The clean/unclean system implies the impure nature of humankind. All humans are somewhat like the main character in Stevenson's novella *The Strange Case of Dr. Jekyll and Mr. Hyde.* Dr. Henry Jekyll, disturbed by his past acts of evil and cruelty, performs an experiment to try to separate his good side from his bad side. He concocts a drug to accomplish this and drinks it. But the result is that he ends up with a split personality. At times he appears as the decent and friendly Dr. Jekyll, but the potion turns him into his evil side, the hideous and murderous Mr. Hyde. There is a bit of Mr. Hyde in all of us. It is that unclean side of our nature that makes us unfit for the presence of God and in need of purification to be accepted into his presence.

Perjury is a serious offense against God.

Cultural Institution: The biblical case of sacrilege in Numbers 5 is one of false oaths. We still take oaths today in court. A Christian who takes an oath in court to tell the truth but then lies is committing an act of sacrilege. And there is considerable evidence that this sacrilege is commonplace in our legal system. Well-known Harvard law professor Alan M. Dershowitz notes the epidemic of perjury in our legal system.

> On the basis of my academic and professional experience, I believe that no felony is committed more frequently in this country than the genre of perjury and false statements. Perjury during civil depositions and trials is so endemic that a respected appellate judge once observed that "experienced lawyers say that, in large cities, scarcely a trial occurs in which some witness does not lie." He quoted a wag to the effect that cases often are decided "according to the preponderance of perjury." . . . [And yet] the overwhelming majority of individuals who make false statements under oath are not prosecuted.[7]

Some who commit acts of perjury are professing Christians. It may be a woman accusing her husband of abuse to try to gain a better divorce settlement in court, or a man exaggerating the facts to win a lawsuit. Either way, it is an offense against humankind and God that should lead to restitution on the human level and an appeal to God for forgiveness.

Jealousy is not a joke.

Humor: People joke about jealousy: "There was a wife so jealous that when her husband came home one night and she couldn't find any hairs on his jacket, she yelled at him, 'So now you're cheating on me with a bald woman!'" But irrational jealousy is no joke, and Numbers 5:11–31 seeks to neutralize its poisonous effects.

The Nazirite Vow

Big Idea *Willingly dedicate oneself to God.*

Understanding the Text

The Text in Context

The Nazirite regulations continue the theme of purity from Numbers 5. The Nazirites are laymen and laywomen who in a special way have dedicated themselves to God. Amos lists the Nazirite with the prophet as a special kind of holy person (Amos 2:11–12). These regulations also continue the theme of oaths, for both the woman suspected of adultery and the Nazirite make oaths (Num. 5:15–31; 6:2).

Historical and Cultural Background

Nazirite vows in later Jewish tradition may illuminate the nature of Nazirite vows earlier in Israelite history. In mishnaic times Nazirite vows were typically conditional: "If God does [such and such], I will become a Nazirite for [x] period of time." A person might vow to become a Nazirite "if a son is born to me" (Mishnah *Nazir* 2:7–10). Queen Helena vowed, "If my son returns safely from the war, I will be a Nazirite for seven years" (Mishnah *Nazir* 3:6). Bernice, sister of King Agrippa II, did something that Josephus (*J.W.* 2.313–14) called "customary": she made a thirty-day Nazirite

vow during an illness, probably on condition of healing. There is also evidence in later periods of unconditional Nazirite vows made out of piety or gratitude.[1] According to the Mishnah, any length of time could be vowed, but the default length of a Nazirite vow was thirty days (Mishnah *Nazir* 1:3). Queen Helena's Nazirite vow was violated near the end of the vowed seven years, so it was reset. But then it was again violated toward the end of the second seven years, so she ended up being a Nazirite for twenty-one years.

Although Nazirite vows continued to be made into the Christian era, neither Christians nor modern Jews make them today.

Interpretive Insights

6:2 *If a man or a woman wants to make a special vow . . . as a Nazirite.* Unlike the priesthood, which is limited to male descendants of Aaron, anyone, regardless of gender, can become a Nazirite, though a woman's male authority, father or husband, can veto her vows (Num. 30:3–5). The NIV 2011 has changed "he" to "they" throughout this passage to clarify that these requirements are not gender specific. "Make a special vow" represents the

Hiphil of *pala'*. There may be two homonym roots for *pala', pala'* I and *pala'* II. *Pala'* I in the Hiphil normally means "to do something wonderful"[2] and is used to characterize acts of God as something that invoke human astonishment. Some scholars believe that *pala'* here must be a rare homonym (*pala'* II) with an entirely different meaning such as "pledge a vow" (cf. NKJV, CEV, NJPS).[3] If it does relate to wonder or astonishment, it characterizes the vow as remarkable, extraordinary, and/or difficult. A "vow" (*neder*) is normally a promise made conditionally, such as, "If God will be with me and will watch over me . . . , then the Lord will be my God" (Gen. 28:20–21), or "If the Lord takes me back to Jerusalem, I will worship the Lord in Hebron" (2 Sam. 15:8). Hannah's dedication of Samuel to God, evidently as a Nazirite, is part of a vow: "Lord Almighty, if you will . . . give [your servant] a son, then I will give him to the Lord . . . , and no razor will ever be used on his head" (1 Sam. 1:11). The term "Nazirite" (*nazir*) means "separated one."

During the entire period of their vow, Nazirites are permitted no visits to the barber like the Egyptian ones depicted in this painting from the tomb of Userhat. "No razor may be used on their head" (6:5). The lower left register depicts barbers at work under sycamore trees (1438–1312 BC, Luxor).

Key Themes of Numbers 6:1–21

- Special dedication to God is available to all.
- Special dedication to God is voluntary.
- Special dedication to God can involve public commitment and sacrifice.
- We must deal with failed commitments to God.

6:3 *fermented drink . . . vinegar.* The word *shekar*, here rendered "fermented drink," is cognate with the Akkadian word for "beer, ale," so it probably denotes beer made from barley or wheat. It may also include wines made from figs, dates, or pomegranates. "Vinegar" is sour wine or beer in which the alcohol has fermented into acetic acid.

grape juice . . . grapes . . . raisins. None of these are ordinarily wrong to consume, but they are prohibited during the vow.

6:5 *no razor may be used on their head.* Long, unkempt hair is the most distinctive symbol of the Nazirite (cf. vv. 9, 18–19) and is a visible sign that a person is under Nazirite vow. Delilah famously causes the lifelong Nazirite Samson to break this requirement (Judg. 16:17–19).

They must be holy. "Must be holy" should instead be translated "shall be holy" (ESV). By virtue of their vows Nazirites are holy—that is, consecrated to God (cf. v. 8).

dedication. This term has the same root in Hebrew (*nzr*) as the word "Nazirite." There is no connection between "Nazirite" and Jesus being a "Nazarene" (Matt. 2:23), a term based on a similar sounding but unrelated root in Hebrew. A Nazarene is a person from Nazareth, not a Nazirite.

6:6 *The Nazirite must not go near a dead body.* The Nazirite's heightened holiness demands strict ceremonial purity and hence the avoidance of corpses (cf. Num. 19). The requirement that Nazirites avoid deceased immediate family members (v. 7) makes the Nazirite regulation stricter than the similar requirement for ordinary priests (Lev. 21:1–4), though identical with that of the high priest (Lev. 21:10–11). Samson egregiously violates this aspect of the Nazirite vow (Judg. 14:19).

6:9 *If someone dies suddenly in the Nazirite's presence.* The example that follows shows what a Nazirite must do if his or her vow is violated. Corpse contamination defiles for seven days, at the end of which there is purification even for non-Nazirites (see Num. 19:11–12). Also, the Nazirite shaves off defiled hair, a symbol of the vow, and offers three varieties of sacrifice—a sin offering, a burnt offering, a guilt offering—that serve, respectively, to cleanse the sanctuary, appeal to God for favor, and atone for the sacrilege of vow violation. The guilt offering is to be offered whenever holy things have been defiled or vows have been violated (cf. Lev. 5:14–19; 6:1–7; Num. 5:5–8). The Nazirite vow resets back to day one once violated, and it begins again for the same time period as the original vow.

6:13 *the law of the Nazirite when the period of their dedication is over.* The priestly ritual at the completion of a Nazirite vow takes place at the tabernacle.

6:14 *a burnt offering . . . a sin offering . . . a fellowship offering.* These perhaps cover any minor defilements accrued unbeknown to the Nazirite or atone for the offense of desanctification of someone previously dedicated to God.[4] Instead of a guilt offering for vow violation (see v. 12), the Nazirite presents a fellowship offering (vv. 14, 17–18). A fellowship offering is brought at the successful completion of a vow (Prov. 7:14) or in fulfillment of a vow to worship God if he answers prayer (Gen. 28:20–22; 2 Sam. 15:7–8; Jon. 2:9; cf. Judg. 11:30–31). The fellowship offering, along with the other food items, constitutes a sacred meal (vv. 15, 17, 19) expressing joy and gratitude for God's help in keeping the vow.[5] As with other fellowship offerings, only a portion of this sacrifice is burned or given to the priest. Most of the meat is given to the worshiper, who in turn eats it in joyful celebration "before the LORD" (Deut. 12:7–8; 27:7) at the sanctuary. The ritual cutting and burning on the altar of the Nazirite's hair (v. 18) along with the completion of the sacrifices by the priest (vv. 19–20) symbolize that the person is no longer a holy Nazirite and therefore is free to drink wine (v. 20).

Theological Insights

What does God think about long hair and alcohol? It is easy to jump to conclusions.

Paul seems to say that long hair dishonors a male (1 Cor. 11:14), whereas in Numbers 6 long hair is a symbol of the Nazirite's consecration to God. Interestingly, even the apostle Paul undertook a

Nazirite vow, cutting his hair at the end of the vow and presenting it to God in the temple to show to fellow Jews that he still respected the law (Acts 18:18; 21:17–26). Did Paul contradict his own teaching? Surely this means there are circumstances where longer hair on men is acceptable and other circumstances where it is not.

Likewise, one might deduce from the Nazirite vow that spiritual people abstain from alcoholic drinks (Num. 6:3a). However, by this reasoning spiritual people would abstain from plain grapes, raisins, and unfermented grape juice as well (Num. 6:3b). It is true that the Bible condemns drunkenness (Prov. 23:29–35; Eph. 5:18), yet it speaks positively of wine as a blessing from God (Ps. 104:15; Eccles. 10:19). Woman Wisdom serves wine at her table (Prov. 9:2), and Jesus both drank and served wine (Matt. 11:19; John 2:1–12).

All this is a reminder that we must allow all of Scripture to contribute to our theology on a given subject, and not just latch on to ideas that support our predilections.

Teaching the Text

Nazirite vows are no longer taken, but still, like Nazirites, we can dedicate ourselves to God in special ways. And if we do that because of some act of grace in our lives by God, then we will be acting in the spirit of the Nazirite vow.

1. *Special dedication to God is available to all.* Nazirites are not priests. Only male descendants of Aaron can be priests. Instead, these are laymen and laywomen. Yet during the period of their vows Nazirites are, like priests, "holy to the LORD." In some ways Nazirites keep rules more stringent than those of priests. One does not have to be a cleric to be dedicated to God. Indeed, laypeople are sometimes more devoted to God than clergy are. Even today laypeople can dedicate themselves to God in a special way for a limited period of time, such as undertaking a short-term mission trip, or volunteering to work at a church camp during a summer, or taking time off to help renovate a church. Like the Nazirite, anyone can make a commitment to special service to God for a finite period of time.

2. *Special dedication to God is voluntary.* The Mosaic law does not demand that anyone take a vow to become a Nazirite. Making that vow is completely voluntary, even though the person is obligated to keep that vow once made. Similarly, making an extraordinary commitment to serving God is something that Christians can choose to do. It is not a condition to having a relationship with God. Many never choose to make such special commitments. But times of special dedication can lead to a much deeper relationship with God and to spiritual growth.

3. *Special dedication to God can involve public commitment and sacrifice.* The Nazirite is a public figure. The vow is made in public at the courtyard of the tabernacle. The uncut hair of a Nazirite man is recognized by onlookers as a sign of someone who has committed himself to God by a vow. Nazirites make sacrifices in public—burnt, sin, and fellowship offerings—and they "sacrifice" things that ordinary Israelites can do. They cannot eat grapes. There is nothing inherently wrong with eating grapes. But while one is a Nazirite, grapes must be given up. Similarly, special dedication to God today may involve giving up

some good things in order to keep one's commitment to God.

Since Nazirite commitments often are made as the result of answered prayers, the public display that one is a Nazirite is in turn a public testimony to what God has done. Those making special commitments to God today can also choose to make those commitments public, both to fortify their commitment and to encourage others.

Not everybody liked Nazirites. In Amos's day some, out of resentment of their special dedication to God, forced Nazirites to drink wine in violation of their vow (Amos 2:11–12). Similarly, those today who are deeply dedicated to God may be resented by others who are not so committed.

4. *We must deal with failed commitments to God.* A Nazirite must maintain purity. But Nazirites violate their vow by becoming defiled by a corpse. Any serious violation of a Nazirite vow requires the Nazirite to start the vow all over again. So those who commit themselves to a deeper,

more dedicated discipleship may end up failing. When that happens, we, like the Nazirite, should repent, confess to the Lord our sin or impurity, and rededicate ourselves to being more faithful in the future.

Illustrating the Text

Christians throughout the ages have taken vows like the Nazirites.

History: Analogous to the Israelite Nazirites are monks and nuns.[6] Entrance to religious orders is available to both genders, just as both men and women could become Nazirites. Many monks and all nuns are laypeople rather than clergy, just as Nazirites were primarily laypeople rather than priests. The "lay brothers" perform manual labor or administration for the monastic community. Monks are men who have taken vows of poverty, chastity, and obedience in order to pursue a contemplative life apart from the world. Nuns also take vows to dedicate themselves to the service of God. Similarly, Nazirites took a vow to avoid wine/beer and the dead in their period of separation to God. Some orders of monks have adopted the distinctive hairstyle of tonsure, in which the back of the skull is shaved leaving a circle of hair. This was a style used on Greek and Roman slaves, and indicates that the monks are slaves of Christ. Similarly, Nazirites adopted a distinctive hairstyle of uncut hair. Most Nazirite vows were temporary, though one could become a permanent Nazirite. Most monks and nuns intend to be

A Nazirite must abstain from wine and other fermented drink as well as grape juice. Shown here is an ancient winepress with its upper rock depression, where grapes were crushed, and its lower basin into which the juice would flow.

permanently so, though there is a process of trying out the monastic life as a novice before it becomes permanent, so for some it can be a temporary thing. The analogy here is not perfect. There were no orders of Nazirites, and their vows usually took effect after an answer to prayer rather than being a pure, unconditional commitment to serve God,[7] while people only sometimes vow to become monks or nuns if God answered a prayer. Nevertheless, the monastic orders illustrate how laymen and laywomen have formally expressed a special dedication to God as did the Nazirites.

A disciple who falls should not despair, but rather rise, repent, and recommit.

Scripture: Perhaps the most poignant example of repentance in Scripture is the story of Peter. This courageous, sometimes loudmouthed fisherman had a knack for leaping first and looking later. He jumped out of a boat and began walking on water (Matt. 14:29). He suggested building tabernacles to camp out with Jesus, Moses, and Elijah (Matt. 17:4). And he promised never to betray Jesus (Matt. 26:33). Each of those stories ends with Peter looking a little foolish. His betrayal of the Lord, however, broke Peter. Scripture says that after denying Jesus, Peter wept bitterly (Matt. 26:75). Unlike Judas, whose despair led him to self-destruction, Peter's failure led him to a deeper understanding of the Lord's grace. In John 21 we read about the resurrected Lord restoring Peter to discipleship, leadership, and purpose. No matter how far we have fallen, the Lord can restore us when we turn back to him.

The Aaronic Blessing

Big Idea *God is the source of his people's blessing.*

Understanding the Text

The Text in Context

Why the Aaronic blessing occurs after the section on the Nazirite is not clear. Was it pronounced over the Nazirites at the beginning or the end of their vows? That is uncertain, though such blessings could occur after offering sacrifice (2 Sam. 6:18). In any event, the purpose of the blessings here is more general. Aaron's blessing sums up God's overall wish to bless his people, especially as they in turn strive for purity and dedication to him.

Historical and Cultural Background

In 1979 archaeologist Gabriel Barkay was leading an excavation of Iron Age tombs in the Hinnom Valley outside Jerusalem. These tombs dated from around the seventh century to early sixth century BC, about the time of King Josiah and Jeremiah the prophet. Barkay discovered in one of

Shown here are the remains of the seventh- to sixth-century BC tombs at Ketef Hinnom in Jerusalem, where silver scroll amulets were found inscribed with the words of Aaron's blessing found in Numbers 6:24–26.

these tombs two tiny silver plates that had been rolled into cylinders and buried with the dead as amulets. When the cylinders were unwound, he discovered an inscription containing familiar words. Though the text was broken and had folds and cracks that made the translation of the first lines tentative, the familiar words were clearer:

> [for ??? son/daughter of ???]
> May h[e]/sh[e] be blessed by Yahweh,
> the Warrior [or Helper] and the re-
>   buker of [E]vil.
> May Yahweh bless you, may he keep
>   you;
> May Yahweh make his face shine
> upon you and grant you p[ea]ce.[1]

Barkay had discovered on both scrolls a slightly abbreviated version of the Aaronic blessing in Numbers 6:24–26. This is the oldest citation of a biblical text ever discovered, centuries older than the Dead Sea Scrolls. Some scholars hypothesize that all ritual texts in Leviticus and Numbers are from a so-called priestly (P) source that they date to 550–400 BC, after Israel went into exile. But this blessing was buried in Iron Age tombs that predate the exile, raising questions about this whole hypothesis. That the blessing came to be buried in tombs of the late seventh century may reflect the positive influence of Josiah's reforms that suppressed idolatry and promoted biblical religion (2 Kings 23:1–7). Its burial in tombs shows a belief in the afterlife: the Aaronic blessing had become a prayer for the deceased to have felicity in the afterlife. It is thus an example of how a biblical text can be adapted to a different usage, just as Christian ministers have

Key Themes of Numbers 6:22–27

- God blesses.
- God protects.
- God shows favor.
- God shows grace.
- God grants peace.

adapted the Aaronic blessing to worship services today.

Interpretive Insights

6:23 *This is how you are to bless the Israelites.* The Aaronic blessing begins and ends with the idea of blessing (see v. 27). "Bless" (*barak*) means different things depending on who does the blessing and who receives it. Generally, it involves a pronouncement or bestowal of good. When we bless God, as in "Bless [*barak*] the LORD, O my soul" (Ps. 103:1 NASB), it means that we "praise [*barak*] the LORD" (Ps. 103:1 NIV), ascribing goodness to him.

6:24 *The LORD bless . . . and keep.* When the priests "bless the Israelites" (v. 23), it means, as the verses that follow show, that they pray for God to bless the Israelites. When God blesses people, he does not merely pronounce goodness on them; rather, being God, he is able to bestow the good that he wishes. Thus, when God blesses us, we actually get the "goods." That includes material blessings or wealth (Gen. 24:35). Aaron and his sons bless the Israelites by expressing a prayer that God bless them. "Keep" (*shamar*) concerns watching over to protect, as a shepherd does sheep. Compare Psalm 121:7: "The LORD will keep [*shamar*] you from all harm—he will watch over [*shamar*] your life."

6:25 *make his face shine . . . and be gracious.* This first phrase is an anthropomorphism, since God has no physical face. When someone's face "lights up" to see you, it means that he or she is favorably disposed toward you, is happy to help you. The result of God's shining face can be deliverance/salvation (Pss. 31:16; 80:3, 7, 19). God's grace can show itself in forgiveness of sin (Ps. 41:4), in answer to a prayer of distress (Ps. 4:1), or in deliverance from enemies (Ps. 9:13).

6:26 *turn his face.* Literally, "lift his face." This seems to mean much the same as "make his face shine" (v. 25), for here it is an indication of God's attentiveness: looking upon his people (favorably). The opposite is to hide the face as a sign of divine displeasure or ignoring (cf. Pss. 30:7; 44:24; 104:29).[2]

give you peace. "Peace" (*shalom*) has a wide variety of senses. Among the many ways that the NIV translates *shalom* are "well" or "well-being" (Gen. 29:6; Ps. 35:27), "welfare" (Esther 10:3), "good health" (1 Sam. 25:6), "goodwill" (Esther 9:30), "soundness" (Ps. 38:3), "prosperity" (Ps. 72:3, 7), "success" (1 Chron. 12:18), and "contentment" (Song 8:10), as well as "peace" in the sense of absence from war or dangers (Lev. 26:6). There is little reason to limit this verse to only one of these various meanings; *shalom* in all these senses is in mind.

6:27 *they will put my name on the Israelites.* A name on something is an indication of ownership. The priests associate Yahweh with Israel by offering a prayer of blessing to Yahweh by name, thus reminding Israel that it belongs to him by covenant. Invoking his name is the source of its blessings.

Priests have no magical powers to bless; power to bless is associated with God's name.

Theological Insights

The Aaronic blessing comprises some of the best-known words in the book of Numbers. It is often recited by Christian ministers as a benediction at the end of services. It was used in the early church, where its threefold invocation of "the Lord" ("Yahweh") was associated with the members of the Trinity. For the Israelites, the threefold repetition of the name Yahweh emphasizes that he alone is their source of blessing, and it is a reminder that his name is associated with them (v. 27).

The priestly blessing, "The Lord bless you," is a kind of prayer that addresses the worshiper but also God. It is a direct statement to people and an indirect prayer to Yahweh. Such blessings might be conveyed upon entering or worshiping in the sanctuary (Pss. 118:26; 134:2–3) or after sacrifice has been offered (2 Sam. 6:18). The prayer is poetic, with each of the three lines conveying two wishes:

> bless you . . . keep you
> make his face shine on you . . . be gracious to you
> turn his face toward you . . . give you peace

This blessing assumes that God is the source of Israel's blessing, protection, and peace. When the priests pronounce this blessing, it reminds Israel to look to God to provide these things for it. It also assumes that this blessing can somehow influence what God does. The poetic nature of the lines makes the blessing more memorable. It is often noted that the second element of each line is a result of the first: a result of God's blessing is that he protects us. A result of God's favorable shining or attentive face is his bestowal of grace and peace.

Teaching the Text

1. *God blesses ("May the* Lord *bless you").* Blessing encompasses all the other elements in this prayer. It has been God's purpose from the beginning to bless human beings. He "blessed" them at creation with ability to be fruitful and multiply (Gen. 1:28). God blessed his people with wealth (Gen. 24:35; Prov. 10:22), with the land (Ps. 37:22), with a good harvest (Pss. 65:10; 67:6), with food (Ps. 132:15), with deliverance from danger (Ps. 3:8), with successful children (Ps. 112:2), with peace (Ps. 29:11), with vindication (Ps. 24:5), with the joy of God's presence (Ps. 21:6), and with (eternal) life (Ps. 133:3). Deuteronomy 28:2–14 describes the breadth of how God can bless (children, crops, livestock, food, defeat of enemies, full barns, and prosperity). These blessings depend upon the obedience of God's people to his commandments. For us to receive God's blessings, we must live in the light of God's name being upon us and obey him.

2. *God protects ("keep you").* One of God's blessings is protection. God is the good shepherd who keeps us as his sheep (Pss. 23:1; 100:3). As our shepherd, God keeps us safe (Ps. 12:7). Psalm 121 uses the root rendered "keep" (also rendered "watch" [*shamar*]) in a way that illustrates God's protection: God is our constantly alert "keeper" who always "watches over" us (vv. 3–4). He "keeps" his people from accidents and other harm (v. 7) and "watches over" (or "keeps") them as they leave and return to his sanctuary (v. 8). The fact that God keeps us allows us to face the dangers of life with confidence that nothing can befall us unless God wills or allows it. As a rule, God protects us from harm, but if he does not, he has a good reason for it. If we believe this is so, it changes our whole perspective on suffering, and it also gives us the courage to face each day and its perils, trusting in God's protection.

3. *God shows favor ("make his face shine on you . . . turn his face toward you").* The expressions "make his face shine on you" and "turn his face toward you" seem to be indications of God's favor. These signify God's general readiness to bless, though again, God's favor can be forfeited by disobedience. Israel's sins lead to God's allowing disaster to befall Ephraim, Benjamin, and Manasseh. In response, Psalm 80, a national prayer of lament, prays three times, "Restore us, O Lord God Almighty; let your face shine upon us, that we may be saved" (Ps. 80:3, 7, 19). God's shining face is a sign

Aaron's blessing to the Israelites was part of the text that was discovered when this tiny silver scroll was unwound. Dated to the seventh to sixth century BC, it is our oldest copy of an Old Testament biblical passage.

that he is favorably disposed to save and restore. Since sin requires a constant battle in the lives of God's people, we must regularly pray for God's favor despite our sins.

4. *God shows grace ("be gracious to you")*. Moses teaches Israel that God is a God of grace and holiness at the same time: "The LORD, the LORD, the compassionate and gracious God, slow to anger, abounding in love and faithfulness, maintaining love to thousands, and forgiving wickedness, rebellion and sin. Yet he does not leave the guilty unpunished; he punishes the children and their children for the sin of the fathers to the third and fourth generation" (Exod. 34:6–7). On the gracious side, he is slow to get angry and forgives sins of all kinds and degrees. And yet he remains holy: "He does not leave the guilty unpunished." The strict requirements of the law show God's holiness. But there is a tension between God's holiness and God's grace. It is God's gracious character that allows him to forgive and forgo sending calamity when people repent (2 Chron. 30:9; Joel 2:13), even though strict holiness and justice would not allow that. It is only by God's grace that sinful human beings can have any hope of a relationship with the holy God. It is God's grace that led Christ to die in our stead (Heb. 2:9) and so allows us to be saved through faith (Eph. 2:8).

5. *God grants peace ("give you peace")*. As stated in the "Interpretive Insights" above, "peace" (*shalom*) has a broad range of associated connotations that go beyond mere absence of war or strife: tranquility, harmony, prosperity, welfare, wholeness, health, and well-being. It is God's desire for his people to experience all these sorts of peace. Eventually the messianic Prince

The descendants of Aaron (Kohanim) still pronounce the priestly blessing today. Known as the "Birkat Kohanim," it is recited during Jewish prayer services and on special Jewish holidays. This photo was taken during one of the Sukkot services at the Western Wall in Jerusalem. The Kohanim face the people with their heads and faces covered and hands raised under their prayer shawls as seen in this photo. A cantor leads the blessing with the priests repeating each of the words after him. (There are many recordings of this blessing on YouTube.)

of Peace will establish ever-increasing peace (Isa. 9:6–7) and a world without war (Isa. 2:4). For Christians, Christ himself is our peace, the one who has broken down the hostility between people (Eph. 2:14) and, more significantly, brought us peace with God (Rom. 5:1).

All these blessings are possible because God's name is associated with his people

(Num. 6:27). God's blessing, protection, favor, grace, and peace are poured out on his people precisely because they bear his name.

Illustrating the Text

If we want God's blessings, we must live under his authority.

News: Sean and Elizabeth Canning were thrust into the international spotlight in 2014 when their daughter, Tanya, secured a lawyer and sued them. Her contention: her parents should continue to provide financial support to their eighteen-year-old daughter even though she had left their home. According to reports, the young woman had been unwilling to live under her parents' rules, yet she expected them to provide the continued rewards of being their child: $664 in weekly child support and college tuition. How very sad!

When God allows suffering in our lives, it is for our salvation.

Theological Reference: Question 26 in the Heidelberg Catechism, in commenting on what it means to say that God is our Father, states,

> Q. What do you believe when you say, "I believe in God, the Father almighty, creator of heaven and earth"?

> A. That the eternal Father of our Lord Jesus Christ, who out of nothing created heaven and earth and everything in them, who still upholds and rules them by his eternal counsel and providence, is my God and Father because of Christ the Son. I trust God so much that I do not doubt he will provide whatever I need for body and soul, and will turn to my good whatever adversity he sends upon me in this sad world. God is able to do this because he is almighty God and desires to do this because he is a faithful Father.

In spite of the temptation to run and hide, we must turn to God when we sin, allowing him to forgive and restore.

Human Experience: Many people have witnessed the following cute behavior in a young child. Often, in an effort to hide from an adult, a toddler will cover his or her face and say, "You can't see me!" The child thinks that in covering his or her own eyes, the eyes of the grownup are blinded as well. In our own walk with God, we sometimes are tempted to take the route of shame walked by Adam and Eve after the fall: hiding from God. But our efforts are as immature as the child who, eyes covered, says, "You can't see me!" God invites us back to him for true forgiveness and restoration.

Preparations for Worship (Part 1)

Big Idea *Worship involves giving gifts to God and receiving revelation from God.*

Understanding the Text

The Text in Context

Israel's tabernacle is almost ready for use. The tent of meeting had been erected eleven and a half months after the exodus (Exod. 40:17). The Aaronic priests have been ordained (Lev. 8–9), and priestly rituals for using the tabernacle have been formulated (Lev. 1–7). The censuses (Num. 1–4) for organizing the army for conquest and for stationing the Levites for protecting and serving the tent of meeting have been described. Laws have been provided for the elimination of impurities that can defile the tabernacle: uncleanness (Num. 5:1–4; cf. Lev. 11–15), oath violations (Num. 5:5–14), adultery (5:11–31), and violations of Nazirite vows (6:1–21). And the sons of Aaron have been taught a formulation by which they can seek God's blessing on the people (Num. 6:22–27).

Thus in this context Israel is almost set to use the tabernacle fully for worship. However, Numbers 7 covers some things that remain before that can happen. Specifically, gifts must be received from the tribal leaders for the worship (Num. 7), and the Levites (as opposed to the

The leaders of the twelve tribes bring twelve oxen and six covered carts as offerings to the Lord. They are to be used by the Levites to transport the tabernacle. Shown here is a clay model of a covered wagon from Syria (2000–1800 BC).

priests) must be consecrated (Num. 8). Only then will the tabernacle worship be fully operational.

In the midst of Israel's completing these things, God begins to speak (Num. 7:89).

Interpretive Insights

7:1–88 The Aaronic blessing (Num. 6:22–27) is used by priests to seek God's blessings for Israel. Now comes a response of the twelve tribes, returning some of their material blessings as a lavish gift to God.

7:1 *When Moses finished setting up the tabernacle.* This may be a flashback to Exodus 40, which describes the construction of the tabernacle,[1] completed eleven and a half months after the exodus (Exod. 40:17). Thus Numbers 7–8 may date to the time of Numbers 9 (see Num. 9:1).

he anointed it and consecrated it. Preparation is made for using the sanctuary fully by applying fragrant oil as part of a celebratory occasion of receiving gifts for the sanctuary.

7:2 *the tribal leaders.* See Numbers 1:4–16.

7:7–9 *Gershonites . . . Merarites . . . Kohathites.* These are the three subtribes of the tribe of Levi. On their duties, see Numbers 4. Only two of these tribes receive the six carts with twelve oxen to pull them for the service of moving the tabernacle items when the camp moves. The Kohathites do not need this gift, since the most sacred objects—the ark, table, lampstand, altars, utensils, and curtain—are to be transported on their shoulders (v. 9) on poles (Num. 4:1–20), not on carts. Neglect of this rule led to the tragic death of Uzzah in David's day when the ark was being unlawfully transported on a cart. When the ark teetered because the oxen stumbled, Uzzah touched the ark to steady it and was struck dead as a result (1 Chron. 13:7–10; 2 Sam. 6:3–8). The Merarites, whose duties involve transport of the frames, crossbars, posts, bases, tent pegs, and ropes (Num. 3:33–37; 4:29–33), require more carts than the

Key Theme of Numbers 7:1–89

- Giving things to God is commendable.

Gershonites, who move the coverings, curtains, and ropes (Num. 3:21–26; 4:21–28).

7:10–83 The gifts of the twelve tribal leaders follow the same order as the arrangement of the tribal camps, and the names of the leaders are the same as in Numbers 2. The order there emphasizes Judah, Reuben, Ephraim, and Dan. For more on the significance of the order, see the comments there.

7:10 *dedication.* "Dedication" (*hanukkah*) is the term for the dedication of walls and temples (Neh. 12:27; Ps. 30 title; 2 Chron. 7:9). The Jewish holiday Hanukkah (same word in Hebrew) is named after the rededication of the temple in 164 BC, after it had been desecrated by the Greeks under Antiochus IV. Here, *hanukkah* is best understood as an "initiation"[2] or "inauguration"[3] of the tabernacle for its first use, in which initiatory gifts are brought over the course of twelve days by each tribal leader, starting with Nahshon of Judah (vv. 11–13).

The gifts of each tribe are identical, though the biblical text meticulously—and to Western eyes tediously—repeats the exact same list, item by item, for each of the twelve tribes. Thus, only Nahshon's list needs to be discussed, since the others are the same.

7:13 *one silver plate weighing a hundred and thirty shekels.* The "plate" is perhaps

Table 1. Tribal Camps and Leaders

East Camp	South Camp	West Camp	North Camp
1. Judah (Nahshon)	4. Reuben (Elizur)	7. Ephraim (Elishama)	10. Dan (Ahiezer)
2. Issachar (Nethanel)	5. Simeon (Shelumiel)	8. Manasseh (Gamaliel)	11. Asher (Pagiel)
3. Zebulun (Eliab)	6. Gad (Eliasaph)	9. Benjamin (Abidan)	12. Naphtali (Ahira)

a "bowl."[4] The weight of a shekel varies from place to place (note that the "sanctuary shekel" is specified), but the common shekel weights found archaeologically vary from 11.08 to 12.25 grams, averaging about 11.4 grams.[5] The silver plate is thus about 1.5 kilograms (3.25 pounds). For comparison, that means that each plate is worth the value of two adult male slaves and one adult female slave (see Lev. 27:1–8 and comments there). The monthly wage of an unskilled worker was only between a half and one shekel per month in Old Babylonian times[6] and between one-fourth to one shekel per month in late Babylonian times.[7]

one silver sprinkling bowl weighing seventy shekels. The "bowl" is perhaps a "basin" (ESV). The seventy shekels equal 0.8 kilograms (1.75 pounds).

each filled with the finest flour mixed with olive oil as a grain offering. For the grain offering, see Leviticus 2. Oil adds to the joy of this gift.

7:14 *one gold dish weighing ten shekels, filled with incense.* This is about four ounces. In later Persian times gold, according to Herodotus (*Hist.* 3.95.2), was about thirteen times more valuable than silver.[8] "Dish" (*kap*) is the same word used to refer to the hollow of the hand. This item, like the cup of the hand, can hold a small amount of incense, which adds an olfactory, sensual experience to the offering.

7:15–17 *to be sacrificed.* The various animals listed here probably are not offered immediately, but rather join flocks, herds, and supplies dedicated to eventual sacrifice for the public as either a burnt, sin, or fellowship offering.[9] One reason for this conclusion is that the sin offering is made by an individual only after he or she becomes aware of a sin or uncleanness, whereas no offense is listed here. Another reason is the lack of a guilt offering. The guilt offering is a sacrifice offered only by individuals, not for the public. Finally, the total of animals in Numbers 7:87–88 suggests that they have been collected rather than immediately sacrificed. The same is true for the incense and flour (grain offering) in verses 13–14.

7:18–88 These verses indicate that each of the other eleven tribal leaders offers gifts for the sanctuary identical with the ones that Nahshon of

Moses hears God's voice coming from between the two cherubim on the atonement cover of the ark of the covenant. The tabernacle replica at Timna, Israel, includes a model of the ark of the covenant, shown here.

Judah has brought, and the totals are added up at the end.

7:89 *When Moses entered the tent of meeting . . . he heard the voice speaking.* A revelation from God takes place in the tabernacle.

from between the two cherubim above the atonement cover on the ark. The ark is a box of wood covered with gold with angelic cherubim statues on top (Exod. 25:10–22). It symbolizes the throne of God or his footstool on earth (see 1 Sam. 4:4; Pss. 80:1; 99:1). The ark is the only piece of furniture in the holy of holies and is the most sacred object in Israel's religion. The "atonement cover" is traditionally referred to as the "mercy seat." This is the lid to the ark of the covenant. See comments at Leviticus 16:2. God's speaking fulfills a promise made to Moses in Exodus 25:22 indicating that God will speak from the tabernacle. Moses goes in to speak to God, but instead he finds God speaking to him.[10]

covenant law. It is disputed among Hebraists whether the word rendered "covenant law" (*'edut*) in Numbers 7:89 (and Lev. 16:13; 24:3; Num. 1:50, 53; 4:5; and six other times in Numbers related to the ark or tent) is from a root meaning to "witness" and hence means "testimony" in reference to the law stored in the ark (Exod. 25:16, 21; 40:20), as it traditionally has been rendered, or whether it is from a different root meaning "pact" or "covenant law" or something similar (see NRSV, NJPS, NLT, TEV). The latter view takes *'edut* to be related to the Akkadian cognate *adu*, which refers to a type of formal agreement.[11] In that case, the "ark of the *'edut*" is a synonym for "ark of the covenant [*berit*]." This alternative view seems more likely than the traditional view.

Either way, the expression alludes to the copy of the Decalogue that is in the ark (Deut. 10:5; 1 Kings 8:9), which symbolizes or testifies to the covenant God made with Israel at Horeb/Sinai. It is because of God's covenant relationship with Israel that he has given them the revelation of his commandments.

Theological Insights

God spoke to Moses "from between the two cherubim above the atonement cover" (Num. 7:89). Part of the purpose of the tabernacle was that it be a place where God would speak to his people. God had earlier said to Moses, "There, above the cover between the two cherubim that are over the ark of the covenant law, I will meet with you and give you all my commands for the Israelites" (Exod. 25:22). There were two forms of revelation here: one was God's miraculous voice speaking to Moses, and the other was his "covenant law" (or "testimony") in reference to the law stored in the ark. Thus, the tabernacle served as a place to store God's revelation revealed in the past and as a vehicle for God's revelation of his will to his people in the present.

God's word remains important in Christian worship. The earliest Christian worship included not only hymns but also direct prophetic revelation and words of instruction, presumably from the Old Testament or the apostolic tradition that came to be embodied in the New Testament (1 Cor. 14:26). In Protestant worship in particular, the word of God through Scripture is central. This is why the Bible-based sermon is at the center of its worship. Just as God's word was stored in the ark and God spoke his word from above the

cherubim of the ark, so God speaks his word in Christian worship as Scripture is read and proclaimed. Worship even in the time of Moses was more than ritual and symbols. It included God's revelation. And it should continue to do so today.

Teaching the Text

Giving things to God is commendable. Numbers 7, in its uniquely redundant way, is an example of giving one's resources to support the worship of God.

Gordon Wenham points out the purpose of Numbers 7: "It seems likely that a theological purpose underlies this wordiness: to emphasize as strongly as possible that every tribe had an equal stake in the worship of God, and that each was fully committed to the support of the tabernacle and its priesthood."[12] Christians too should realize

that they each have a stake in the worship of God and should fully support their church facilities and their ministers.

Believers can give of their resources to build and beautify sanctuaries. People out of love of Christ have built churches, sometimes ornate and beautiful churches, for divine service. They have also supplied for such buildings Communion cups, Communion tables, Communion bread and wine, banners, stained-glass windows, crosses, organs, artwork, and many other things intended to enable or to enhance Christian worship, just as the tribal leaders supplied carts, work animals, sacrificial animals, golden dishes, and silver plates for similar reasons. Numbers 7 reminds us that such gifts to God should not be despised. If given out of genuine devotion, they are welcomed by the Lord as an act of worship, just as the gifts of the tribal leaders were well received.

Illustrating the Text

Our gifts can enhance worship.

Art: One of the treasures of church art is the Ghent Altarpiece. It was commissioned by Jodocus Vijd and his wife, Elizabeth Vorluut, for a chapel that the couple had financed for the parish church of St. John.[13] Produced in the 1400s by Flemish artists Hubert and Jan van Eyck, it contains some twenty-four panels. One of the most striking of these is the lower center panel, *The Adoration of the Lamb*. That panel shows Christ as a pierced lamb, his blood flowing into a chalice, being worshiped by angels, apostles, prophets, bishops, men, and women. This altarpiece has, over the centuries, enhanced the worship of Christ, helping people to reflect on the "Lamb who was slain," just as the gift of the tribal leaders in Numbers 7 facilitated worship in the tabernacle, including the gift of lambs whose sacrifices foreshadow the sacrifice of Jesus as the Lamb of God.

Object Lesson: If it is appropriate in your context, consider highlighting some of the gifts that have been given to your church and the reasons for those gifts. Often, our church buildings are filled with objects given for deeply meaningful reasons that have been totally forgotten. Highlighting these original reasons can remind church members that what matters most is not the gift but rather the heart of the giver.

Preparations for Worship (Part 2)

Big Idea *Worship involves a sense of God's presence and a need for personal purity.*

Understanding the Text

The Text in Context

Numbers 7 ends with God's revelation to Moses from above the ark of the covenant (Num. 7:39); it continues in Numbers 8 with a specific message from God about the golden lampstand and about the consecration of the Levites in preparation for tabernacle service.

More generally, both Numbers 7 and Numbers 8 are part of the final preparations necessary to make the tabernacle and its maintenance staff ready for regular service.

Interpretive Insights

8:2 *set up the lamps.* God's revelation at this time relates to Aaron's care of the seven lamps of the "lampstand," the menorah (v. 2). Instructions about the lampstand had been given earlier (Exod. 25:31–40; 37:17–24; 40:4, 24), when it was specified that the menorah was to be shaped like a budding almond tree and placed in the part of the tent of meeting just outside the holy of holies on the south side of the tabernacle. Numbers 8:1–4 shows that these earlier commands have in fact been fully carried out by Aaron

at Moses's command "just as the LORD had commanded Moses" (v. 3) and "exactly like the pattern the LORD had shown Moses" (v. 4). In particular it is important that the menorah's lamps shine in the proper direction (v. 3).

8:5–26 These verses describe the consecration of the Levites. The Levites are not fit to serve the holy place until they have been thoroughly cleansed of both moral and ceremonial impurities. The first stage of cleansing involves washing and shaving their bodies and washing their clothes. The second stage involves the sacrifice of two bulls.

8:7 *cleansing.* This represents the same Hebrew word, *hatta't*, rendered "sin offering" in verse 8.

8:8 *sin offering.* Or "purification offering" (NIVmg). This offering serves to cleanse both from sin and ceremonial uncleanness (for more details, see comments on Lev. 4; 16).

8:10 *the Israelites are to lay their hands on them.* This gesture is likely carried out by the tribal leaders mentioned in Numbers 7. The laying of hands on the Levites parallels the laying of hands on sacrifices (v. 12; see Lev. 4:15; 8:14, 18, 22), indicating that the Levites are set apart as Israel's offering to God (v. 14) and serve as substitutes for their firstborn (see vv. 16–19).

8:11 *wave offering.* See Leviticus 7:30, 34. The precise meaning of *t^enupah* is debated. This noun is derived from the verb of motion *nup*, rendered by the NIV in verses 11, 13, 15, 21 as "present." At question is whether the motion is simply a lifting up of the gifts to God ("presentation offering" [HCSB] or "elevation offering" [NJPS, NRSV]), or whether a back-and-forth motion is implied ("wave offering" [NIV]). Whatever the precise gesture, *t^enupah* becomes a general term for offering and consecration. When Aaron here presents the Levites before Yahweh as a *t^enupah* (Num. 8:11, 13, 15, 21), this cannot mean that they are literally "waved" or "lifted up." Here the idea is metaphorical, with no specific literal motion implied. It means that they are consecrated before Yahweh as his special gift.

8:12 *sin offering . . . burnt offering.* The second degree of cleansing from more serious defilements

comes from sacrificing two bulls (v. 12). The sin (or "purification") offering covers various sins and ceremonial impurities (see Lev. 4). The burnt offering generally appeals to God for favor and appeasement (see Lev. 1).

8:16 *in place of the firstborn.* For discussion, see comments at Numbers 3:12–13, 40–51.

8:19 *make atonement for them so that no plague will strike the Israelites when*

God provides specific instructions for the design and placement of the lampstand that is to be placed inside the tent of meeting. Found etched into a plaster wall during excavations of a first-century BC house in Jerusalem, this drawing of the temple menorah, incense altar, and table of showbread, partially reconstructed here, is the earliest depiction of the temple furnishings that has been discovered.

they go near the sanctuary. It is the atoning sacrifices performed at the tabernacle by the priests with the assistance of the Levites that avert God's wrath and allow a sinful people to dwell with the holy God. Numbers 16:41–50 narrates a specific case where atonement by Aaron averts a plague caused by God's wrath against the people.

8:22 *just as the* LORD *commanded Moses.* An emphasis on exact obedience is underscored by this phrase near the beginning (v. 3) and the end of this section.

8:23–26 *This, then, is how you are to assign the responsibilities of the Levites.* Levites begin their formal service at age twenty-five but must retire from duty at age fifty (vv. 23–25), except for providing minor assistance (v. 26). Earlier, the time of service is said to begin at age thirty and end at age fifty (Num. 4:3, 23, 30), with no mention of limited duties after fifty. The rule for counting Levites was lowered to

age twenty during David's day, when their actual duties of carrying the tabernacle were being reduced (1 Chron. 23:24–27; cf. Ezra 3:8). How to resolve the conflict between Numbers 4 and Numbers 8 concerning when Levites began and ended their duties is a matter of speculation. The limited service after age fifty can be understood as giving additional details rather than being a genuine contradiction. What is more difficult to harmonize is the conflict with beginning Levitical service at age thirty versus age twenty-five. Source critics posit contradictory sources behind the two chapters. The Septuagint may suggest a text-critical error: it reads "twenty-five" instead of "thirty" in all cases in Numbers 4. But that may well be a harmonization by a scribe rather than the true variant reading. The rabbis suggested that there was a five-year period of apprenticeship for the Levites, so that they did not count

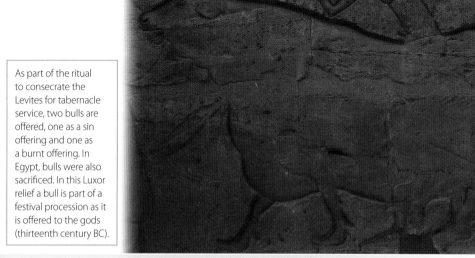

As part of the ritual to consecrate the Levites for tabernacle service, two bulls are offered, one as a sin offering and one as a burnt offering. In Egypt, bulls were also sacrificed. In this Luxor relief a bull is part of a festival procession as it is offered to the gods (thirteenth century BC).

for census purposes until age thirty (Num. 4), though they did count as doing some of the work at twenty-five (Num. 8:23–25). Another suggestion is that this chapter is a flashback to the time when the tabernacle was erected (cf. Num. 7:1, concurrent with Exod. 40), and that the subsequent census (Num. 4) indicated that there were too many Levites, so the age of service was raised to thirty.[1] The immaturity of Nadab and Abihu, which led to their tragic deaths (Lev. 10), might also be a factor in raising the age level to thirty.[2]

Theological Insights

The fire of the golden lampstand, the menorah, in the tabernacle (Num. 8:3–4) arguably symbolizes the presence of God. God appears elsewhere in the fire of the burning bush and in the pillar of fire at the exodus from Egypt (Exod. 3:2–3; 13:21–22). As a symbol of God's presence, the lampstand is made of pure gold. It requires carefully extracted, pure olive oil (Exod. 27:20), since only the best of oils is appropriate for the holy place.

It is important for Aaron to arrange the lamps on the lampstand so that they illuminate in the right direction (Num. 8:3). Part of this arrangement is to illuminate the other items in the holy place, especially the table of the bread of the Presence, which contains twelve loaves, symbolizing God's blessing and provision for all his people. But the fire of the lampstand serves as a visible reminder of God's presence among his people. The menorah is lit at evening and burns until morning (Exod. 27:21) so that an Israelite at night will from time to time see it flickering through the cracks of the curtain within the holy place. This flickering is a continual reminder throughout the night that the glow of God's presence is in the midst of his people.

Christian worship also includes a sense of the presence of God. This is not manifested with a lampstand or the bread of the Presence, but rather at Communion with the bread and cup of the Lord's table. It is the Lord's table because the invisible Lord presides over it. Some Christian traditions understand the elements of Communion to represent the "real presence" of Christ in worship. In any case, Christians are given the general promise that wherever two or three gather in Christ's name, he himself will be in their midst (Matt. 18:20), just as God in the tabernacle was present in the midst of Israel.

Teaching the Text

Purify yourself in preparation for worship. Before the Levites are fit to serve in the tabernacle, they must be cleansed completely from all forms of impurity. Thus there are washings and atoning sacrifices—bulls for sin and burnt offerings—symbolically to remove both moral and ceremonial uncleanness from them (vv. 8–11). Only then can they be presented to God as a "wave offering" (vv. 12–14)—that is, as a special gift to God, serving as substitutes for the firstborn (vv. 15–19). Having complied with these requirements (vv. 20–22), the Levites age twenty-five to fifty can begin their service (vv. 23–26).

Like the Levites, Christian believers also need to make sure that they are pure before engaging in worship. The 144,000 in the book of Revelation are commended for a purity that made them fit to be offered to God: "These are those who did not defile themselves with women, for they kept themselves pure. They follow the Lamb wherever he goes. They were purchased from among men and offered as firstfruits to God and the Lamb" (Rev. 14:4 NIV 1984). Just as the Levites were purified before being offered to God as a "wave offering," so all of us need personal purity so that we can be a fitting offering to God. The writer of Hebrews uses words that are reminiscent of the cleansing of the Levites when he says, "Let us draw near to God with a sincere heart in full assurance of faith, having our hearts sprinkled to cleanse us from a guilty conscience and having our bodies washed with pure water" (Heb. 10:22). Similarly, Paul warns the Corinthians, "So then, whoever eats the bread or drinks the cup of the Lord in an unworthy manner will be guilty of sinning against the body and blood of the Lord. Everyone ought to examine themselves before they eat of the bread and drink from the cup" (1 Cor. 11:27–28). Establishing personal purity before worship and serving God remains a Christian value.

> To purify themselves, the Levites are required to shave their whole bodies and wash their clothes. This photo shows a bronze razor from New Kingdom Egypt (1550–1070 BC).

Illustrating the Text

Being in the presence of our holy God is a powerful experience.

Human Experience: You are in the backyard with your family, standing at the grill. It is a beautiful, sunny summer day, muggy and warm. Suddenly, it is as if someone has turned off the sound or sucked it up with a silent vacuum cleaner. The birds stop singing. The breeze disappears. The air seems to drop several degrees in just a moment. What is it? It is "the silence before the storm." When weather conditions are right, a massive storm can move across the surface of the earth, eating up warm, moist air around it. Sometimes, such a storm system can actually be felt and sensed before it can be seen. It reaches out ahead of itself and changes the atmosphere in its path. This is what creates that "silence before the storm" effect. If you are fortunate, you read the signs and make it inside before the skies open up and the storm comes.

Psalm 29 describes the coming of the Lord to meet with his people. There, David likens the Lord's coming to that of a storm descending from the mountains. All the imagery points to one thing: the Lord is mighty! His presence is nothing with which to trifle.

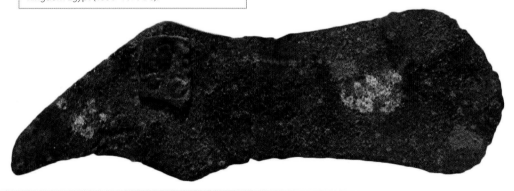

We should seek to purify ourselves before worshiping the Lord.

Object Lesson: Show a magnifying glass and talk about how it can enhance inspection. The lens helps us see things more clearly. It shows what we might miss if we simply glance at an object.

Scripture provides us with a clear lens for self-examination: the Ten Commandments. Throughout church history believers have used the Ten Commandments as a way of carefully inspecting their hearts and lives. When understood in light of the gospel, biblical law becomes a tool from the Lord to focus our eyes, using God's standard to examine ourselves.

Jesus summarized this law in two great commandments: love God with all your heart, soul, mind, and strength, and love your neighbor as yourself (Matt. 22:37–40; Mark 12:30–31). When we hold the lens of the law up to our lives, what do we see? By allowing the Holy Spirit to work in our hearts before we come to worship on Sunday, our songs will ring with greater joy, our ears will listen with increasing eagerness, and our hearts will burn with deeper gratitude for God's amazing grace.

Israel Celebrates the Passover

Big Idea *We need to recall how God saved us.*

Understanding the Text

The Text in Context

The book of Numbers begins with the census initiated twelve and a half months after the exodus (Num. 1:1, 18). But in Numbers 9 (and probably Num. 7–8 as well; see comments as Num. 7:1), the book flashes back to the previous month (Num. 9:1)—that is, to the very month when the tabernacle had been completed (Exod. 40:17).

Precisely one year after the initial Passover, the Israelites begin the first annual Passover commemoration around their newly completed

tent of meeting in remembrance of those events that had led to their departure from Egypt (Num. 9:1–14). This is part of their preparation for departing from Sinai toward the promised land.

Historical and Cultural Background

On the Passover, see Exodus 12 and Leviticus 23:4–8. The first Passover is associated with the tenth plague on Egypt, the plague of the firstborn, and the exodus itself that followed. The firstborn of Egypt died, while the Israelite firstborn were spared. Pharaoh relented—for the moment—and allowed Israel to leave Egypt (Exod. 12:29–31). Thus the first Passover marked Israel's great event of salvation when God redeemed the Israelites with an outstretched arm (Deut. 4:34). It was then that they

Only bread without yeast (shown here) is eaten during the Festival of Unleavened Bread, which is celebrated for the seven days that follow Passover.

gained their freedom from Egyptian bondage and oppression.

That plague did not affect homes of Israelites who offered the Passover lamb and marked the doors of their homes with its blood. Passover is followed by the seven days of the Festival of Unleavened Bread, when only bread made without yeast is eaten. In effect, the Passover marked Israel's national birthday because it initiated the exodus from Egypt and marked the beginning of Israel as a nation rather than just a people group. The celebration of Passover in Numbers 9 begins the annual commemoration for "generations to come" (Exod. 12:14) that continues among Jews to this day. It arguably marks the greatest act of salvation in the Old Testament.

Interpretive Insights

9:1 *the first month of the second year.* This month marks the one-year anniversary

Table 1. A Chronology of Events in Numbers 1:1–10:11

Month/Day (of Year 2)	Event
1/1	Tabernacle set up (Num. 7:1; cf. Exod. 40:17)
1/1–12	Gifts of the tribal leaders for tabernacle received (Num. 7:1–88)
1/13 (?)	Menorah lit and Levites dedicated (Num. 8:1–22)
1/14	Passover celebrated (Num. 9:1–5)
1/15–21	[Festival of Unleavened Bread celebrated? (see Exod. 13:7)]
2/1	Census taking initiated (Num. 1:1)
2/14	Passover celebrated for those unclean on 1/14 (Num. 9:6–13)
2/20	Israel departs from Sinai (Num. 10:11)

since Israel had left Egypt. In the Israelite calendar a new month begins with each new moon. Exodus 13:4 labels the first month "Abib," though later the first month is named "Nisan" (Esther 3:7), which is its Babylonian name.

9:2 *celebrate the Passover.* The Passover is now celebrated for the second time. The Passover was first celebrated "at twilight on the fourteenth day" of what became Israel's first month (Exod. 12:1, 6) in conjunction with the plague of the firstborn in Egypt (Exod. 11).

9:6 *ceremonially unclean.* Because the Passover sacrifice is quasi holy (cf. 2 Chron. 35:13), only those who are ceremonially clean can celebrate it. To eat while unclean is an offense, like eating a fellowship offering while unclean (Lev. 7:20–21). To offer the Passover while unclean requires intercession to avoid divine punishment (2 Chron. 30:17–19).

dead body. See Numbers 19. One might become ceremonially unclean by, for example, having to bury a relative who had died. Corpse contamination is only an illustrative example of what could make one ineligible to eat the Passover, as the rabbis rightly surmised (Mishnah *Pesahim* 9:4). Other forms of uncleanness would no doubt also make one ineligible.

9:8 *find out what the LORD commands.* When confronted with new legal issues,

Moses regularly inquires of God for direction, as in the cases of the blasphemer, the Sabbath breaker, and the daughters of Zelophehad (Lev. 24:10–22; Num. 15:32–36; 27:5–7).

9:10 *away on a journey.* God's response expands the case to cover reasons besides uncleanness for not keeping the Passover. A journey would separate a person from the tabernacle's altar, where presumably the Passover lamb is to be offered, and from the family gatherings, where it is to be eaten. The requirements are identical except for the date.

9:11 *fourteenth day of the second month at twilight.* This is one month after the regular Passover.

unleavened bread and bitter herbs. See Exodus 12:8. Unleavened bread is a reminder of the haste at the very first Passover, in which there was no time to wait for the yeast to make the bread dough rise before the Israelites fled Egypt (Exod. 12:39). The bitter herbs are a symbol of how Pharaoh's oppression had made their lives bitter in Egypt.

9:12 *They must not leave any of it till morning or break any of its bones.* The first part of this directive repeats Exodus 12:10, and the second part repeats Exodus 12:46. Jesus as the Christian's paschal lamb fulfilled this requirement (John 19:36; cf. John 1:29; 1 Cor. 5:7).

9:13 *cut off from their people.* Whether that expression indicates excommunication, execution, or divine punishment of separation from descendants in this life or the afterlife has been discussed earlier (see "Additional Insights" following the unit on Lev. 6:8–7:38).

9:14 *A foreigner.* A foreigner or "sojourner" (*ger*) is a person of non-Israelite descent who comes to live among the Israelites. There were such persons among the Israelites even during the exodus, labeled the "mixed multitude" in Exodus 12:38 (NASB, ESV). The Cushite woman whom Moses married (Num. 12:1) was one such foreigner. Ordinarily, foreigners were excluded from celebrating Passover with Israel (Exod. 12:43), but those who identified with Israel's covenant by having their males undergo circumcision, the symbol of the Abrahamic covenant (Gen. 17:10–14), could celebrate the Passover (Exod. 12:48–49). Such converts to Israelite religion, but not the uncircumcised, were welcome to celebrate the Passover.

Theological Insights

The one-year anniversary of the first Passover has come. The Israelites need to celebrate Passover before resuming their journey. Indeed, they are not ready to go forth with God toward the promised land until they pause to look back and remember God's great act of salvation in delivering them from Egyptian bondage.

As Israelites were called upon to remember God's great act of salvation through the Passover, so Christians are called to remember God's great act of salvation in Christ through the Lord's Supper. The first Lord's Supper was a Passover celebration (Matt. 26:17–30; Mark 14:16–26; Luke 22:13–20), including certain first-century Jewish Passover customs. But Jesus changed Passover's symbolism. The centrality of the Passover lamb is replaced by Christ himself, whose body would be given and whose blood would be shed for sin. Christ thus identified himself as the new Passover lamb.

Paul sees typology between Christ and the Passover. He refers to Christ as our Passover sacrifice offered for us (1 Cor. 5:7). Christ, like the Passover lamb, allows us to escape the judgment of God, if we are "marked by the blood." Just as the Israelites had to throw out the old leaven before they could celebrate Passover (Num. 9:11), so Christians, says Paul, must throw out the "old leaven" of sin. John too sees typology. Just as no bone of the Passover lamb was to be broken (Exod. 12:46; Num. 9:12), so no bone of Jesus as the unblemished Passover lamb was broken when he was crucified, though the soldiers had intended to do so (John 19:31–36). Thus, for the Christian, the Passover is a reminder of the work of Christ.

Teaching the Text

1. *Remembering God's salvation was mandated.* The events surrounding the first Passover mark God's greatest act of salvation in the Old Testament, Israel's

Passover is a reminder of God's deliverance of the Israelites from Egyptian slavery. For Christians, the celebration of the Lord's Supper is a time to remember God's provision of salvation through Christ. Leonardo da Vinci's depiction of the Last Supper has been designed to draw our eyes to the central figure of Christ, who is our Passover Lamb. It was painted in the late fifteenth century AD as a wall mural for the dining area at the Convent of Santa Maria delle Grazie, Milan.

deliverance from Egypt. For that reason, Israel is commanded to commemorate that event annually by celebrating Passover on the fourteen day of its first month. Numbers 9:1–14 marks the first commemoration of Passover since that original event. Israel's observance of Passover is not optional but mandatory.

The regular celebration of the Lord's Supper that Christians are commanded to keep is likewise a reminder to Christians of God's great act of salvation through Jesus Christ. But the deliverance celebrated by Christians at the Lord's Supper is not from physical oppression but rather from sin. In a sense, Passover is celebrated at every Communion service.

Numbers 9:1–14

thus makes accommodations for people so that as many as possible can eventually join in the Passover commemoration.

By analogy, Christian ministers regularly accommodate people who are unable to celebrate the Lord's Supper at the regular time. Sometimes Christians, due to infirmity or illness, are unable to come to church to celebrate it. Ministers often serve these people Communion in their homes or hospital beds. Remembering God's salvation in Christ through Communion is as indispensable for Christians as Passover was for Israel.

4. *Failing to remember God's salvation properly was punishable.* For Israelites, deliberately failing to keep Passover is a serious offense. It is so serious that it can result in being "cut off from their people" by God (Num. 9:13). Failure to remember God's salvation properly is a very bad thing.

There is again a parallel with the Lord's Supper. Just as one who refused to celebrate Passover was threatened with being divinely "cut off" (Num. 9:13), so Christians are warned that they may receive divine punishment, perhaps even death, if the Lord's Supper is wrongly celebrated. Someone celebrating the Lord's Supper improperly

2. *Remembering God's salvation prepared Israel to go forth for God.* Before the Israelites journey on to the future events of taking the promised land, they must prepare themselves by reflecting on what God has already done for them in the past. Subsequently, every generation of Israelites is to continue remembering that event annually. We too need a reminder of what God has done for us in the past before we are ready to march forth on the journey of life that God has in store for us.

3. *Remembering God's salvation was indispensable.* There are circumstances beyond a person's control that can result in him or her not being able to keep Passover at the regular time, as when that person contracts uncleanness or is away on a journey. Allowance is made for such people to celebrate a month late. God

"eats and drinks judgment on himself" (1 Cor. 11:29 NIV 1984) and can even die (1 Cor. 11:30).

Illustrating the Text

Like the Passover Seder for the Jews, the Eucharist brings Christians face-to-face with the story of our salvation from slavery.

Theological Reference: Observant Jews to this day continue to celebrate Passover following a ritual conducted in homes. That ritual is called the Haggadah or Passover Seder (*seder* in Hebrew means "order" of liturgy). At several points the Haggadah emphasizes the reason why celebrating this day is important. The youngest child at the gathering who is capable of doing so is to ask, "Why is this night different from all other nights?" The answer is then given:

> We were slaves to Pharaoh in Egypt. But the Lord our God took us out of there with a strong hand and a stretched out arm. And if God had not taken our fathers out of Egypt, then even we, and our children, and our children's children, might still be slaves to Pharaoh in Egypt.[1]

This is not just an old story but rather something with which each generation of Jews is to identify. Thus, the Haggadah emphasizes "us" when referring to the exodus story:

> In every generation one should feel as if it was he himself who went out of Egypt. . . . Not only did God save our fathers from Egypt, but He also saved

us with them. We find this in the answer that we give our children on Passover, "It was *us* that He brought out of there, so that He might lead *us*, and give *us* the land that he swore to our fathers" (Deut. 6:23).[2]

The rehearsing of the old story of the Passover thus helps Jews identify with God and the covenant that he made with his people at that time when he brought Israel out of Egypt.

Similarly, the Lord's Supper rehearses the old story of the death of Christ. The Lord's Supper helps us to identify with Christ and the covenant that he established for us through his death. And Christ died not just for the sins of the people of his day but also for us, who are alive today. And if Christ had not so died, we, and our children, and our children's children would still be slaves to sin.

If we forget the story of our salvation, we will never understand who we are.

Children's Book: *Harry Potter and the Philosopher's Stone*, by J. K. Rowling. In the opening volume of her deservedly famous heptalogy, J. K. Rowling tells how Harry Potter had been raised for the first years of his life without any knowledge of how he has come to be an orphan. His devious aunt and uncle, Petunia and Vernon Dursley, have convinced Harry that his parents perished in an automobile accident. In fact, they had been killed in a war against a terrible dark wizard, "He-Who-Must-Not-Be-Named." Discovering the true story transforms the hero's sense of self and sets him on a path of amazing adventure.

Following God's Leading

Big Idea *God leads his people both supernaturally and through his ministers.*

Understanding the Text

The Text in Context

In this unit the narrative flashes back to the first day of the first month of year two of the exodus (Exod. 40:17), when the pillar of fire had entered the tabernacle (Num. 9:15–23; cf. Exod. 40:34–38). This reminds the people that it is God himself who has led them in the wilderness. Jumping past the censuses taken in the first month (Num. 1–4), the text goes on to describe the silver trumpets made to direct the Israelites to their formations during the march, or to worship at the tent of meeting, or to defend themselves against enemies in war (Num. 10:1–10).

At that point, everything has been prepared for the journey, and six days after celebrating the Passover to commemorate the event that had led to their deliverance from Egypt, the Israelites depart from Mount Sinai and resume their trek toward the promised land (Num. 10:11).

Historical and Cultural Background

Archaeology has contributed to our understanding of the trumpets in Numbers 10:1–10. The trumpet came to be used regularly in tabernacle and temple worship.

A stone with a broken inscription that reads in part "To the place [lit., 'house'] of the trumpeting to . . ." (*leBeth haTeqi'ah le . . .*) was discovered in 1969 at Haram esh-Sharif near the Temple Mount in Jerusalem. Dating to the time of Herod's temple in New Testament times, this inscription is a reminder of how the silver trumpets of the sanctuary continued to be used in calling Jewish people to worship in

Found in the debris from the destruction of the temple near the southwest corner of the Temple Mount, this block of stone with its inscription most likely marked the location where the priest would stand announcing the beginning and the end of the Sabbath by trumpet blast.

the temple. Josephus (*Ant.* 3.12.6) indicates that in his day these trumpets were a bit shorter than a cubit (18 inches).

What a silver trumpet might have looked like is illustrated by a silver trumpet (with its wood insert) and a bronze trumpet discovered in Tutankhamen's tomb in Egypt in 1922. These trumpets date to mid-fourteenth-century BC Egypt, within a century or so of the time of Moses. The silver one is 58.2 cm in length (23 inches), and its bell is 8.2 cm (3.5 inches) wide and the tube between 1.7 cm near the mouthpiece and 2.6 cm at the bell joint (.66 inches and 1 inch, respectively). It is made of beaten silver with a thin gold band of decoration around the edge of the bell and a mouthpiece of plain thin gold, both beaten onto the silver. The conical tube and the bell were made in two separate pieces and then soldered together with silver.[1] In the spring of 1939, the silver trumpet was actually played twice using a modern mouthpiece. The first attempt shattered the fragile artifact,

Key Themes of Numbers 9:15–10:10

- Follow God's cloud.
- Heed God's clarion call to action.

but after repairs the second attempt was successful. The wooden insert kept Tutankhamen's silver trumpet from being dented when not in use.

The silver trumpets appear to be portrayed on the Arch of Titus. When Titus destroyed Jerusalem in AD 70, he plundered the temple. The arch portrays that plundering, including the lampstand (menorah) and two trumpets, presumably the silver trumpets as described in Numbers 10.

Interpretive Insights

9:15–23 These verses narrate the Israelites following God's pillar of cloud by day and fire by night.

9:15 *the day the tabernacle . . . was set up.* The tabernacle was completed on the first day of the first month, eleven and a half months after Israel left Egypt (Exod.

Table 1. The Tabernacle and the Cloud in Numbers 9:15–19 and Exodus 40:34–38

Numbers 9:15–19	Exodus 40:34–38
[15]On the day that the tabernacle was set up, the cloud covered the tabernacle, the tent of the testimony. And at evening it was over the tabernacle like the appearance of fire until morning. [16]So it was always: the cloud covered it by day and the appearance of fire by night. [17]And whenever the cloud lifted from over the tent, after that the people of Israel set out, and in the place where the cloud settled down, there the people of Israel camped. [18]At the command of the LORD the people of Israel set out, and at the command of the LORD they camped. As long as the cloud rested over the tabernacle, they remained in camp. [19]Even when the cloud continued over the tabernacle many days, the people of Israel kept the charge of the LORD and did not set out. (ESV)	[34]Then the cloud covered the tent of meeting, and the glory of the LORD filled the tabernacle. [35]And Moses was not able to enter the tent of meeting because the cloud settled on it, and the glory of the LORD filled the tabernacle. [36]Throughout all their journeys, whenever the cloud was taken up from over the tabernacle, the people of Israel would set out. [37]But if the cloud was not taken up, then they did not set out till the day that it was taken up. [38]For the cloud of the LORD was on the tabernacle by day, and fire was in it by night, in the sight of all the house of Israel throughout all their journeys. (ESV)

40:17). Verses 15–19 largely review the account given in Exodus 40:34–38 (see table 1).

looked like fire. God has previously manifested his presence in fire (Gen. 15:17; Exod. 3:2; 19:18; Deut. 5:24–26).

9:17–18 *settled . . . stayed.* Both words mean literally "tabernacled," using the verb (*shakan*) also used to form the noun "tabernacle" (*mishkan* [vv. 18–19]).

The LORD's command. God's command is not expressed verbally but rather is signaled by the movement of the cloud. When the cloud moves, the Israelites follow. When the cloud settles over the tabernacle, the Israelites camp. Thus, the movement and encampment of the Israelites, whether for a night, a month, or a year, is directed by the moving or settling ("tabernacling") of the divine fire cloud (vv. 20–23).

10:1–10 These verses describe the making and use of the two silver trumpets. The sounding of the trumpets can convey different messages, depending on how they are sounded. One kind of sound, perhaps a long, steady blast (NJPS), is meant to gather people to the tent of meeting.

1. **Sound two trumpets**: The "whole community" (v. 3) (perhaps a larger governing body of male Israelites) assembles at the tent of meeting.
2. **Sound one trumpet**: The "heads of the clans" (v. 4) assemble at the tent of meeting.

Another kind of sound, with a different quality of tone or rhythm (v. 7), is meant

Moses is commanded to "make two trumpets of hammered silver, and use them for calling the community together and for having the camps set out" (10:2). They may have been similar to this bronze trumpet with gold overlay that was discovered in Tutankhamen's tomb (ca. 1370–1352 BC).

to send camps on the march. These sounds may refer to short blasts (NJPS).

First (short) blast: Eastern camp sets out (v. 5).
Second (short) blast: Southern camp sets out (v. 6).

Presumably, a third and a fourth blast would set the western and northern camps in motion.

10:2 *two trumpets of hammered silver.* Like Tutankhamen's silver trumpet (see "Historical and Cultural Background" above), the metal of these trumpets was skillfully formed by an artisan hammering the metal to shape. This is also true of the golden lampstand in the tabernacle (Num. 8:4). These trumpets are used in worship and civil assemblies for calling the community together, and for military and travel purposes for having the camps set out.

10:8 *The sons of Aaron, the priests, are to blow the trumpets.* Priests are responsible for blowing these trumpets.

10:9 *you will be remembered by the LORD.* A trumpet blast not only can call for help from fellow Israelites during a battle but also can serve as a prayer to God. This happened when the priests in Abijah's day blew their trumpets. The army of Judah was fighting Jeroboam II and, finding itself surrounded, "they cried out to the LORD. The priests blew their trumpets. . . . At the sound of their battle cry, God routed Jeroboam" (2 Chron. 13:14–15).

10:10 *times of rejoicing . . . memorial for you before your God.* These trumpets presumably call people to come to the sanctuary for worship during holy days, but here their role as "memorial" is emphasized. "Memorial" (*zikkaron*) is more simply rendered "reminder" (ESV). The same Hebrew root is rendered "remembered" in verse 9. The trumpet blasts symbolically remind God—draw his attention to the fact—that they are obeying the commands concerning keeping the festivals and new moons (cf. Lev. 23:4–38).

Theological Insights

For God's people to reach the promised land, it is essential that God guide them. God guides them in various ways. He certainly instructs them through the laws. But he also personally guides them through the supernatural movements of the pillar of cloud/fire (Num. 9:18–22) and through specific directions using trumpets blown by his ministers, Aaron and the priests (Num. 10:3–8).

In a similar way, God's people today need guidance. That comes first through God's word, which is a lamp to our feet and a guide to our paths (Ps. 119:105). But guidance can come also through the proclamations of God's ministers and through the supernatural leading of God's Spirit (Rom. 8:14), just as God guided Jesus, Philip, and Paul through the Spirit (Luke 4:1; Acts 8:29; 16:7).

Teaching the Text

In this passage final preparations are made for the Israelites to resume their journey toward the promised land, carrying with them a little bit of the Mount Sinai experience through the tabernacle. Several final preparations were necessary for Israel to go forth effectively for God.

1. *Follow God's cloud.* One remarkable feature of the wilderness wanderings is the way that God's presence led them by a visible manifestation of himself in the pillar of cloud by day and the pillar of fire by night. The text becomes more poetic as this is described: "The elevated prose reflects the excitement of the impending march."[2] Their march will not be aimless but overtly directed by God. When the cloud lifts up, the Israelites will pull up stakes and follow; when the cloud settles in a spot, the Israelites will stop and set up camp.

Christians have no visible cloud that directs their journeys through life. Nonetheless, God still leads through his Spirit (John 14:26), as Jesus himself was led (Luke 4:1). The Holy Spirit indwells and leads the believer to avoid deeds of the flesh (John 14:17; Rom. 8:5–6, 9, 14) and guides the church into all the truth (John 16:13). The Spirit opens doors of opportunities for service (1 Cor. 16:9) where we may stay until the Spirit leads us to pull up stakes and serve elsewhere. Like Israel, Christians should "follow the cloud" where it leads.

2. *Heed God's clarion call to action.* Israel needs more than the cloud of God to guide it on the journey. For it to function in a coordinated fashion, it also needs the practical help of the silver trumpets (Num. 10:1–10). The trumpets sounded by the priests call tribal leaders or larger groups

to the tabernacle for prayer, revelation, and worship at the festivals (vv. 3–4, 7, 10). Or, with a different quality of sound, the trumpets set the Israelite camps into formations to travel on the journey (vv. 5–6). In war the trumpet blasts serve as a prayer appealing to God for help in the battle (v. 9).

So it is that Christian ministers, like the priests, provide a similar role. They gather people for prayer, the preaching of God's revelation, and worship. Ministers try to organize God's people for service and going forth for God in a coordinated, more-effective fashion. They trumpet God's word in preaching, and they pray on behalf of God's people who fight for God. It is important that God's message be expressed clearly and explicitly in church. As Paul says, "If the trumpet does not sound a clear call, who will get ready for battle?" for which reason he discourages the use of uninterpreted speaking in tongues (1 Cor. 14:8–9). At the sound of the archangel's trumpet, both the living and the dead in Christ will rise to meet the Lord in the air at his coming (1 Thess. 4:16–17). At the last trumpet, the dead will receive their resurrection bodies (1 Cor. 15:52), and the kingdoms of the world will become the kingdom of our Lord and of Christ (Rev. 11:15).

In the wilderness, hammered silver trumpets are used to call the Israelite community together and to announce when the camps are to set out. Once the Israelites settle in the promised land, trumpets continue to be used by the priests in the temple that was built in Jerusalem. Trumpets used during the Second Temple period are depicted on this portion of the Arch of Titus relief in the Roman forum, which shows the spoils brought back in triumph to Rome after the temple was destroyed by Titus in AD 70.

Illustrating the Text

Like Israel's silver trumpets, modern culture has its own ways to call people's attention.

Cultural Institution: Traditionally, churches had bells that functioned something like Israel's silver trumpets. Church bells, like the silver trumpets, could ring out to gather people for church services, whether a regular service, a wedding, or a funeral. They could also serve secular purposes such as chiming the hour or times of general celebration. Additionally, they could toll as an indication that someone had died. They sometimes were used to warn that the land was being invaded, and thus they were a call to battle stations. How can we in our culture call people to action for God?

Our prayers are like a trumpet call.

Literature: **The Chronicles of Narnia, by C. S. Lewis.** This series of books involves a horn that mimics one aspect of the silver trumpets of Israel. One of the functions of the trumpets was to bellow a prayer up to heaven to God for help (Num. 10:9). In Lewis's Chronicles of Narnia a horn is a gift given to the children by Father Christmas in the book *The Lion, the Witch and the Wardrobe.* Four children miraculously enter Narnia through a wardrobe. Father Christmas gives them gifts that are not toys but practical tools. He presents the horn to Susan with the promise that it should be blown when help is needed, and that help will then be forthcoming. The horn is not actually blown until the next book, *Prince Caspian.* In that story the rightful heir to the throne, Prince Caspian, centuries later by Narnian time, is in dire straits, surrounded by the forces of his uncle King Miraz, who is intent on killing him. Caspian has been given Susan's horn by his schoolmaster, who had kept the long-suppressed, old Narnian traditions. Seeing no other hope, Caspian blows the trumpet, at which point the Christ figure, Aslan the lion, calls the children (Peter, Susan, Edmund, and Lucy) back to Narnia for the purpose of helping to save Caspian. It is thus a prayer to God (Aslan) for help, as the blowing of the silver trumpets sometimes was.

Setting Forth with God

Big Idea *God leads and protects his people.*

Understanding the Text

The Text in Context

Numbers 10:11–22:1 forms a new major unit in the book of Numbers that describes the journey from Sinai to the plains of Jordan.

In Numbers 1:1–10:10 Israel had prepared for resuming its march toward the promised land. The tribal camps have been counted, and their positions around the tabernacle designated. The duties of the priests and Levites have been delineated. Gifts for the dedication of the tabernacle have been received, and silver trumpets to direct tribal movements fabricated. The Passover festival, recalling the foundational events of Israel's history, has recently been celebrated (Num. 9:1–14), and God himself in the pillar of cloud has appeared to direct Israel's journey. Thus, Israel now begins its march toward the promised land, following the cloud (Num. 10:11).

Interpretive Insights

10:11–28 These verses narrate the departure of the tribes.

10:11 *the twentieth day of the second month of the second year.* The second month is in April/May. The twentieth day

follows the makeup celebration of Passover on the fourteenth of the second month (see Num. 9:6–13). Having arrived at Mount Sinai on the third month of the first year (Exod. 19:1), Israel has been there for nearly a year.

The Israelites travel from the Desert of Sinai into the Desert of Paran. Moses persuades his close relative Hobab to travel with them rather than return to his homeland of Midian.

the cloud. That is, the visible presence of God that guides them in the wilderness (Num. 9:15–23).

10:11–12 *lifted . . . came to rest.* These are signs that Israel is, respectively, to depart and to camp (Num. 9:17).

Desert of Paran. This seems to be the east central region of the Sinai Peninsula, north and east of the traditional site of Mount Sinai (see map). On the location of Sinai, see comments at Numbers 33:15.

10:13 *The LORD's command through Moses.* This command is presumably conveyed to Israel by the blowing of the silver trumpets (Num. 10:1–10).

10:14–28 *The divisions.* The tribes set out exactly as described in Numbers 10:5–6 and in the description of the camps in Numbers 1–4. The names of the tribal leaders are identical with the names given in these earlier chapters (see comments at Num. 1:1–2:34). The "standard" (v. 14) is a banner on a pole that shows members of a tribe from a distance where they are going and assists their staying together as a group. The order is as follows:

1. Eastern tribes (Judah, Issachar, Zebulun) (vv. 14–16)
2. "Tabernacle" Levites (Gershonites, Merarites) (v. 17)
3. Southern tribes (Reuben, Simeon, Gad) (vv. 18–20)
4. "Holy things" Levites (Kohathites) (v. 21)

5. Western tribes (Ephraim, Manasseh, Benjamin) (vv. 22–24)
6. Northern tribes (Dan, Asher, Naphtali) (vv. 25–27)

Judah, as the tribe destined to have the Davidic kingship (Gen. 49:10; cf. Num. 24:17), leads the way. Special place is also given to the Levites. The Gershonites and the Merarites responsible for dismantling the tabernacle are first after the eastern group of tribes (v. 17). The Gershonites carry coverings, curtains, and ropes associated with the tabernacle (Num. 3:21–26), while the Merarites carry the tabernacle frames, crossbars, posts, bases, tent pegs, and ropes (Num. 3:33–37). The Gershonites are given two carts with four oxen, and the Merarites are given four carts with eight oxen to assist them in carrying all these things (Num. 7:6–8). The Kohathites (v. 21) come later. They carry the holiest things: the ark, the table of showbread, the lampstand, the altars, utensils, and curtains (Num. 3:27–32). They have no carts and instead carry these things by means of poles on their shoulders (Num. 7:9). When Israel makes camp again, the Gershonites and Merarites are

Order of the Tribes When Traveling

	6 Northern tribes (Dan, Asher, Naphtali) (vv. 25–27)	5 Western tribes (Ephraim, Manasseh, Benjamin) (vv. 22–24)	4 "Holy things" Levites (Kohathites) (v. 21)	3 Southern tribes (Reuben, Simeon, Gad) (vv. 18–20)	2 "Tabernacle" Levites (Gershonites, Merarites) (v. 17)	1 Eastern tribes (Judah, Issachar, Zebulun) (vv. 14–16)	
Rear							Front

responsible for setting up the tabernacle before the Kohathites arrive with its holy furnishings (v. 21).

10:29–32 These verses narrate the invitation to Hobab son of Reuel to join Israel.

10:29 *Hobab son of Reuel the Midianite, Moses' father-in-law.* The relationship of Moses to Hobab, Reuel, and Jethro is difficult to ascertain. Which one is Moses's father-in-law: Reuel (Exod. 2:16–18), Jethro (Exod. 3:1), or Hobab (Judg. 4:11 ESV, NASB)? Also, is Hobab a Midianite (Num. 10:29) or a Kenite (Judg. 4:11)?

Source critics typically attribute the problem to contradictory sources used by the biblical authors, though harmonization is possible. The Kenites were a Midianite tribe, so Hobab was both a Kenite and a Midianite.[1] As for the relationship between Hobab, Reuel, and Jethro, two harmonizations exist. One possibility is that "Jethro" and "Reuel" are differing designations for the same person. "Jethro" is his priestly title, meaning "his excellency" (cf. Akkadian *watru* ["preeminent, foremost"]),[2] making "Reuel" ("friend of God") his name. Reuel/Jethro's son Hobab would then be Moses's brother-in-law. This solution requires the word *hoten*, usually rendered "father-in-law," to mean more broadly "relation by marriage." If so, it should be rendered "brother-in-law" at Judges 4:11 (so the NIV). The other possibility, adopted by ancient rabbinic exegetes, is that Jethro and Hobab are the same person and Reuel is his father. If so, Reuel is Zipporah's "father" in the sense of her "grandfather" (Exod. 4:18), while Jethro/Hobab is her father and Moses's father-in-law.

the place. That is, the promised land. Hobab initially refuses the offer to share in Israel's land blessings, only agreeing to travel with Israel until he returns to his land and family (v. 30). Midianites lived in the vicinity of the Gulf of Aqaba along the eastern coast of the Sinai. But Moses implored him, as someone intimately familiar with this territory, to stay on and guide Israel through the wilderness and eventually share in the land's blessings (vv. 31–32). Judges 1:16 indicates that Hobab accepted Moses's offer. His descendants settled in the southern desert of Judah near Arad (east of Beersheba) within the borders of Israel, though relatively close to Hobab's original territory to the south.

10:33–36 These verses describe God's guidance and protection of the Israelites.

10:33 *three days.* The stages of Israel's journey can be short or long (Num. 9:22), but the first stage is only three days, which brings the Israelites to the vicinity of Taberah and Kibroth Hattaavah (Num. 11:3, 34).

the ark . . . went before them. Numbers 10:21 indicates that the Kohathites carry "holy things" in the middle of the procession, not at the front. Was an exception made for this first stage from the usual pattern to encourage the people to begin the journey? Or was there an unstated exception to Numbers 10:21 that the Kohathite carriers of the ark (though not the other Kohathites) regularly went first when Israel traveled? In Joshua 3:3–4 the carriers of the ark lead Israel to the banks of the Jordan.

10:34 *The cloud . . . was over them.* Both God's throne (ark) and his visible presence in the fire cloud are intimately interconnected in leading the people.

10:35 *May your enemies be scattered.* The so-called Song of the Ark (vv. 35–36) is a poetic prayer that Moses chants when the ark sets out and returns to the tabernacle. It addresses Yahweh by addressing the ark that represents his throne. The prayer that Yahweh's enemies be scattered (cf. Ps. 68:1) is an appropriate one for Israel organized as an army for conquest.

Theological Insights

This passage teaches that God guides and protects his people. He guides the Israelites through symbols of his presence, the cloud and the ark (vv. 11–12, 33). He guides them through men such as Moses and Hobab (vv. 13, 29–32). And he is the source of their protection who can be called upon to scatter their enemies (v. 35). These matters are elaborated upon in "Teaching the Text" below.

Teaching the Text

1. *God leads his people.* After nearly a year at Mount Sinai, at last the cloud, the visible presence of God, lifts from the tabernacle, signaling Israel to resume its journey toward the promised land. Each tribe, under its tribal leader, falls into position exactly as commanded, starting with Judah and ending with the tribes around Dan. Protected in the midst of the tribes are the clans of the Levites, who transport the sacred objects, though the ark actually leads the procession (v. 33). Thus the Israelites set out.

Several comments can be made:

1. **God leads Israel.** God does not expect Israel to find its own way. He guides it by his cloud and by Moses (vv. 11–13) and by Hobab (v. 31).
2. **Israel's journey is not easy.** In the initial march, the Israelites do not reach the promised land. Far from it. Rather, they start in the Desert of Sinai and stop in the Desert of Paran (v. 12). They go from one desert to another desert. Their journey does not get easier right away. God's people should not expect their journey through life to be easy, even though God is leading them.
3. **Israel starts well but does not finish well.** Israel has an auspicious resumption of its journey. Israel is obeying.

Under God's command and direction, the Israelites leave the Desert of Sinai and travel into the Desert of Paran, shown here.

God himself is leading. Every tribe does what it is supposed to do. But this good beginning will soon be undermined by Israel's complaints and unbelief. Good starts do not guarantee good finishes, then or now.

These are lessons for us. We too can expect God to lead us, though the journey probably will not be easy, and starting it well does not necessarily mean that we will finish well.

2. *Others are invited to join in.* Moses gives his in-law Hobab a special invitation to join with the people of God. This invitation requires several things that are similar to what God offers us when we become Christians.

1. **A new family.** Hobab has his own family (v. 30), but Moses in effect is inviting Hobab, though a non-Israelite, to identify with the larger family of God.
2. **A new inheritance.** Acceptance into the Israelite family means that Hobab will follow Moses to the land that God has promised Israel (v. 29). This means abandoning his original land (v. 30) and sharing in Israel's trials and difficulties as Israel makes its pilgrimage to the land. But Hobab will be treated well by Israel (v. 29), and he will receive a share in the blessings of the land of Canaan (v. 32). Judges 1:16 records the fulfillment of this: Hobab's descendants settle in the southern desert of Judah near Arad.
3. **A new mission.** Moses's offer to join Israel involves a mission for Hobab. The Israelites are essentially traveling blind, not knowing the land through which they are traveling. It is true that they have the guidance of God in the pillar of cloud. Nonetheless, this is not considered a substitute for human intelligence. They also need Hobab's "eyes" (v. 31) to direct them through the great and terrible Sinai Desert. Hobab, as a native of that area, can serve as an expert guide, bringing the people to the watering holes and helping them avoid pitfalls and enemies along the way.

Like the non-Israelite Hobab, non-Christians are given the opportunity to become part of the family of God, to share in that family's inheritance, hardships, and mission.

3. *God protects his people.* Israel is led by God though the cloud and by God's throne, the ark of the covenant (vv. 33–34). When the cloud arises and the ark goes forth from the tabernacle to lead the people or when the ark is brought back into the tabernacle, Moses chants a prayer to those visible signs of God's presence. Those words come to be part of Israel's priestly liturgy and later, under David, part of its hymnology (see Ps. 68:1–2).

The Song of the Ark reminds Israel that it is not alone in its struggles and trials in the wilderness journey from Sinai to Canaan. It reminds Israel that God is its protector. The Israelites have enemies, to be sure, but Yahweh in their midst is available to help them scatter their enemies. The second part of the song emphasizes God's presence among them. The ark is a symbol of God's throne and presence in the tabernacle in the middle of the Israelite camps. We too need to be reminded of God's presence and protection to give us courage to face the dangers that life presents.

Illustrating the Text

God invites others into his family.

Personal Testimony: Hobab was invited by Moses to be part of the family of God. For some people, an invitation to join a family can be very appealing. It certainly appealed to me. As an adolescent, I was very shy and had become socially isolated; I had very few friends, none close. But I got to know a kid at school, Paul. He and I were both brainy types, good students. For a while, Paul and I played chess during lunch hours, a game that appealed to egghead types like us.

Paul invited me to church youth group activities, and eventually I came to visit him at his home. Before I heard any gospel presentation, I found his family very appealing. It was a large family with five children, all of whom seemed to be committed Christians. A sense of love, joy, and faith pervaded that home. My own home was not a bad one, but it was almost purely secular in outlook. Somehow, my own home and family seemed to lack something in comparison.

Eventually, Paul invited me to a Bible camp in Ponca City, Oklahoma, that his family was heavily involved in. At that camp I heard for the very first time the gospel of how Christ died for my sins and how by faith in him I could be saved. By the end of that week of camp, I had made a commitment to Christ. But a factor in that decision was the attractiveness of becoming part of God's family, a family represented by the sponsors of that camp and particularly by Paul's wonderful family. Becoming part of this family of God was not my motive in accepting Christ and becoming a Christian, but it was subconsciously part of its appeal.

And having become a Christian, I found myself part of a new family, and I adopted as my own the mission God had given that family. Thus, like Hobab, I was not brought up as part of the family of God, but I was invited to become a member of that family. Accepting that invitation was the best decision I ever made.

Personal Testimony: You might want to have someone in your congregation share a testimony about how he or she became a follower of Jesus and how being part of God's family was a key part of that journey. This could be done live or on video.

God protects his people.

History: Charles Spurgeon, a great preacher in the nineteenth century, points out that Psalm 68:1–2, a text based on Numbers 10:35, was used by Oliver Cromwell, the Puritan leader who later became Lord Protector of England. He describes Cromwell preparing for the battle of Dunbar.

> Before the battle they, all of them, knelt on the heather and asked the Lord their God to be with them and then springing up they chanted this old Psalm—
>
> "Let God arise, and scattered let all His enemies be,
> And let all those who hate Him, before His presence flee.
> As the smoke is driven, so drive You them. As fire melts wax away,
> Before God's face let wicked men, so perish and decay."
>
> And then, home went their swords, and their enemies fled down the hill, and a speedy victory was given.[3]

Ingratitude and Judgment

Big Idea *Ingratitude toward God can lead to forfeiture of blessings.*

Understanding the Text

The Text in Context

After nearly a year at Mount Sinai, Israel resumes its march toward the promised land (Num. 10:11; cf. Exod. 19:1–2). It is an auspicious start. Everyone lines up as God has commanded through Moses (Num. 10:13–28) and as directed by the blasts of silver trumpets (Num. 10:1–10). God himself guides the Israelites in the fire cloud and with the ark (Num. 10:34–36). But after three days' journey from Sinai (Num. 10:33), this good start deteriorates into grumbling.

Numbers 11 sets the pattern for the remainder of the book of Numbers, where grumbling and complaining are ubiquitous. Numbers 11 shows how God and Moses deal with these complaints.

Historical and Cultural Background

Fish (see Num. 11:5) were abundant in the delta region of Egypt. Herodotus (*Hist.* 2.92–93) mentions that some inhabitants there lived on fish alone.

God provided quail for Israel in phenomenal numbers (Num. 11:31–32). Migratory quail breed in Europe and western Asia and fly mostly along the Mediterranean to winter in Africa. These were formerly seen in large numbers in the Middle East, where hunters used to knock them down using sticks, though unfortunately over-exploitation in the 1920s decimated these populations.[1] In this case an especially huge flock was blown off course and became accessible for miles ("a day's walk") around Israel's camp.

Interpretive Insights

11:1 *the people complained about their hardships.* This is better rendered that they complained "bitterly/openly" (NJPS, HCSB) or "in a wicked way" (LXX). The Hebrew word is *ra'* ("bad, evil").

Fire from the LORD burned among them. Perhaps lightning has ignited grasses into a wildfire.[2]

consumed some of the outskirts of the camp. The tabernacle, in the center of the camp, is not threatened.

11:2 *Moses . . . prayed . . . and the fire died down.* Moses often mediates to shield the people from God's wrath (Exod. 32:11–12; Num. 12:13; 14:13–19; 16:46–47; 21:7).

11:3 *Taberah.* Taberah ("burning"), named after this incident, is three days' journey from Sinai (Num. 10:33), though its exact location is unknown. Deuteronomy 9:22 indicates that Taberah is distinct from Kibroth Hattaavah. It might be the region around Kibroth Hattaavah,[3] or a resting place without full encampment. Israel's first camp is at Kibroth Hattaavah (Num. 33:16).

11:4–35 These verses narrate the people's complaints at Kibroth Hattaavah. Compare this incident with Exodus 16, when manna and quail are first provided.

11:4 *rabble.* The word *'asapsup* occurs only here in the Bible. Its root means "to gather." The rabble is distinguishable from "them." It may refer to "worthless foreigners" (CEV), the non-Israelite "mixed multitude" (Exod. 12:38 NASB, ESV).

crave other food. Literally, they "desired a desire," meaning they "craved strongly" (NRSV)—that is, for meat.

11:5 *fish . . . at no cost.* This hyperbole means that fish was cheap.

cucumbers, melons, leeks, onions and garlic. Vegetables are unavailable in the desert.

11:6 *manna.* Manna (*man*) relates to *man hu,* meaning "What is it?" (Exod. 16:15). The Israelites do not know what it is. God has provided manna six nights a week to sustain Israel (v. 9; cf. Exod. 16:4–5),

but a steady diet of it has grown monotonous (v. 6).

11:7 *coriander seed.* This is a gray seed/fruit the size of a small pea that is used as a spice in cooking.[4]

resin. The meaning of the word *bedolah* is uncertain. It might denote bdellium, a yellowish, transparent, fragrant gum of a South Arabian tree. The Septuagint took *bedolah* to refer to a pearl, crystal, or some other kind of precious stone.[5] Naturalistic explanations of manna (honeydew; excretions of insects; lichen growing on rocks; sap of tamarisk trees) do not fit this description of manna in the Bible.

11:10 *Moses was troubled.* Literally, "In the eyes of Moses it was bad [*ra'a'*]." Moses is troubled with God and filled with self-pity, as seen in the lament in verses 11–15.

11:12 *as a nurse carries an infant.* The participle *'omen* ("attendant, guardian"),

God provides quail in abundance so that the Israelites will have meat to eat. This fragment from Nebamun's tomb in Dra Abu el-Naga, Egypt, shows men using a net to catch quail (1350 BC).

here rendered "nurse," is masculine, suggesting a male child-care provider rather than a wet nurse. The masculine form was used of the attendants of Ahab's children (2 Kings 10:1) and of kings as surrogate fathers (Isa. 49:23). The feminine form denotes women (2 Sam. 4:4; Ruth 4:16). This metaphor bemoans Israel's infantile behavior.

11:15 *kill me.* Elijah and Jonah similarly ask to die (1 Kings 19:4; Jon. 4:3).

11:16 *seventy of Israel's elders.* These may be the seventy who had partially ascended Mount Sinai with Moses (Exod. 24:9–15). Compare Jethro's advice when Moses was overwhelmed judging disputes (Exod. 18). Though these seventy are, like Moses, endowed with God's Spirit, Moses's prominence remains: God speaks to Moses at the tent (v. 17), not to the seventy.[6]

11:18 *Consecrate yourselves.* This anticipates God's manifesting himself by a miracle.

11:18–20 *you will eat it . . . until . . . you loathe it.* In poetic justice they will come to loathe this coveted meat more than they have loathed manna (cf. v. 6).

11:21 *six hundred thousand men.* This rounds to the nearest hundred thousand the census number of 603,550 (Num. 1:46) plus 22,000 Levites (Num. 3:39). On the large numbers, see "Additional Insights" following the unit on Numbers 1:1–2:34.

11:22 *all the fish in the sea.* The hyperbole indicates that huge quantities are required.

11:23 *Is the LORD's arm too short?* This is a rhetorical question affirming God's ability to fulfill any promise. The plagues on Egypt had previously demonstrated God's immense power.

11:24 *seventy of their elders . . . around the tent.* This probably indicates a semicircle before the tent's entrance.

11:25 *the cloud.* See Leviticus 16:2; Numbers 9:15–22; 10:11–12.

the power of the Spirit. This fulfills the promise in verse 17 above.

they prophesied. The seventy behave like prophets to manifest evidence of God's Spirit. Normally, prophets are spokespersons for God (Deut. 18:18), though nothing is said here of any revelations. Perhaps, as when Saul "prophesied" (1 Sam. 19:20–21, 24), these elders are possessed by the Spirit of God and spontaneously go into an ecstatic state of worship (cf. 1 Chron. 25:2–3, where "prophesy" refers to praise-worship).

but did not do so again. The seventy have prophesied to validate their selection by God, but they have no mission to prophesy thereafter.

11:26 *Eldad and Medad.* Although, for some unknown reason, these two have not come to the tent, they too receive an endowment of God's Spirit and prophesy.

11:27 *young man.* This could mean "servant" (na'ar [cf. Gen. 22:3]).

11:28 *Joshua son of Nun.* Joshua is Moses's right-hand man.

11:29 *Are you jealous for my sake?* Joshua is jealous for Moses's prerogatives and authority, for Eldad and Medad have received the Spirit directly without mediation through Moses.[7]

I wish that all the LORD's people were prophets. Not only is Moses unconcerned, but he also approves of these "prophets."

11:30 *the elders . . . returned to the camp.* This is where they can begin exercising leadership responsibilities.

11:31 *a wind . . . drove quail.* The Hebrew word behind "wind" (*ruah*) is the same word for "spirit." The elders receive the ability to prophesy from God's *ruah* ("spirit" [see vv. 17, 25–26 above]), while Israel receives quail from a *ruah* ("wind") from God.

two cubits deep. About three feet. Harvesting so many constitutes gluttony.

11:32 *ten homers.* This is over sixty bushels (2,200 liters) each.

spread them out. Because the killed quail are too numerous to eat fresh, they are preserved by drying (v. 32b).

11:33 *while the meat was still between their teeth.* That is, while they are still chewing.

severe plague. The "plague" (*makkah*) is literally a "smiting." Jacob Milgrom (after Ibn Ezra) suggests that this plague could refer to overeating and choking to death on the meat, though Psalm 106:15 probably calls this a "wasting disease,"[8] perhaps transmitted by sick birds.

11:34 *Kibroth Hattaavah.* This means "graves of craving."

they buried the people who had craved other food. The plague has struck the guilty rabble, not the innocent. For the innocent, the quail are a blessing (cf. Ps. 105:40).

Theological Insights

Numbers 11 shows God's power over nature. God can send fire and divert flocks of birds (v. 31) or strike with a plague (v. 33). God's Spirit also empowers people for service (vv. 17, 25–26). God provides people with food: manna and quail (vv. 7–8, 31–33). Indeed his "arm" is not "too short" to provide for a huge horde (v. 23). God is merciful: he supplies coworkers for his overwhelmed servant Moses (vv. 16–17, 24–30). But he is also holy: he is angry with Israel's ingratitude (vv. 1, 10, 33) and dispenses punishment as a result. And yet his anger can be quelled by prayer (v. 2), and he mercifully continues to sustain Israel despite its unbelief.

Teaching the Text

1. *Avoid ingratitude.* Within days of leaving Sinai, the Israelites fall into an attitude of ingratitude toward God. This passage shows something of the nature of ingratitude, a sin to which we as Christians are also prone.

First, ingratitude involves forgetting God's blessings (vv. 1–9). Israel leaves the Desert of Sinai only to come to the Desert of Paran (Num. 10:12), going from one desert to another. Nothing has improved. The journey is hot and exhausting. And there is no end in sight. The rabble (v. 4) selectively remember what Egypt was like: the fish, the cucumbers, the melons, the leeks, the onions, and the garlic. They forget the harsh servitude.

Conversely, they forget how good the manna is. Manna (vv. 7–9) can be eaten as a seed or crushed. It can be baked or boiled. It has the rich taste of olive oil and is fresh with the dew. Though they are understandably tired of a steady diet of manna, Israel has "flocks and herds" (see v. 22) that allow them the luxury of occasional meals with meat. They are exaggerating how bad their current deprivation is. Moreover, they are forgetting that without the miraculous gift of manna they would have starved long ago. We must not forget God's blessings.

Second, ingratitude is an expression of unbelief (vv. 18–23). Desiring good food is not a sin. But Israel's complaints are not innocent. Their cravings lead them to reject God's plan for their lives. They complain, God tells them, "because you have rejected the LORD, who is among you" (v. 20). Many Israelites no longer believe that God has a better life in store for them in Canaan. Therefore, they wail, "Why did we ever leave Egypt?" (v. 20). It is their doubts about God that fuel their complaints. Even the great Moses is subject to doubts (vv. 21–23), as are we.

Third, ingratitude can lead to forfeiture of blessings (vv. 1–2, 20, 33–34). Israel's unbelief brings down God's judgment. At Taberah "fire from the LORD . . . consumed some of the outskirts of the camp" (v. 1). At Kibroth Hattaavah God rebukes the rabble's rejection of God (v. 20) and brings with the quail a deadly plague on the rabble "who had craved other food," many of whom die and are buried there (v. 33–34). Ironically, this "wasting disease" (Ps. 106:15) emaciates the gluttons and causes vomiting of the flesh out their "nostrils" (cf. v. 20). The rabble has received meat, but deadly judgment comes with it. We should take heed lest our ingratitude lead us to forfeit our blessings.

2. *Share leadership responsibilities.* In Numbers 11 Moses shows us the need for shared spiritual leadership over God's people. Several lessons for today about spiritual leadership can be derived from this passage.

The task of spiritual leadership can be overwhelming (vv. 10–16). Moses

The Israelites forget that manna was God's gracious provision for food. Gathered daily, it could be ground by a hand mill, crushed in a mortar (shown here), and cooked in a pot or baked into loaves.

complains, "Why have you brought this trouble on your servant?" (v. 11). Moses feels like a foster father to infantile people (v. 12). Dealing with them is too much to bear (v. 14), so Moses is ready to quit or even die (v. 15). The task of spiritual leadership is too much for any one person. God mercifully provides seventy elders to take some of the burden of leadership from Moses (v. 16).

Spiritual leaders need divine empowerment (vv. 17, 24–25). The elders receive a measure of the Spirit that has empowered Moses (v. 17), dispensed in a ceremony at the tabernacle (vv. 24–25). The ceremony at the tabernacle and the prophesying by the elders upon receiving the Spirit confirm that these leaders have been empowered and authorized by God.

Spiritual leaders must resist jealousy (vv. 26–30). When Eldad and Medad obtain God's Spirit without coming to the tent, this upsets Joshua, who is jealous for his master (vv. 28–29). Could this unauthorized ministry not undermine Moses's authority? But Moses is not concerned. He responds, "I wish that all the LORD's people were prophets and that the LORD would put his Spirit on them!" (v. 29). Even apart from a ceremony, God himself has confirmed that these leaders have been chosen along with the others to guide God's people. Good leaders welcome co-workers in ministry and do not jealously guard their prerogatives.

Illustrating the Text

Concentrating on the negative undermines happiness.

News: The national news media have a tendency to concentrate on the negative. Speechwriter William Safire caught this tendency in a speech that he wrote for Vice President Spiro Agnew: the national media are "nattering nabobs of negativity."

Quote: Ungrateful people who concentrate on the negative are simultaneously unhappy people. Dennis Prager, in his book *Happiness Is a Serious Problem*, puts it this way:

> Yes, there is a "secret to happiness"—and it is gratitude. All happy people are grateful, and ungrateful people *cannot* be happy. We tend to think that it is being unhappy that leads people to complain, but it is truer to say that it is complaining that leads people to becoming unhappy. Become grateful and you will become a much happier person.[9]

If we cultivate gratitude toward God and others, we will not only be more pleasant people, but we will be personally happier as a result.

Leadership can be a profound challenge.

Biography: John Perkins, a black minister in Mississippi, sought to break down barriers between black and white Christians in the days of strict segregation. He reached out to two white pastors in an attempt to find ways for white and black Christians to cooperate. One was a Reverend Odenwald, who, persuaded by Perkins, preached for two Sundays in a row to his white, middle-class congregation concerning the plight of the black community and the need to reach out to it. He received a profoundly negative reaction from his people, and under tremendous stress, Reverend Odenwald ended up committing suicide. Perkins also reached out to another white pastor of a Presbyterian church. He too was sympathetic to Perkins's ideas, and he even convinced his congregation to set aside three thousand dollars per year to assist a black ministry. But this pastor too came under pressure and turmoil because of this stand, and he too ended up committing suicide.[10] White prejudice against blacks was rampant in those days even among professing Christians. White pastors who tried to reach out to blacks were in danger of a backlash from their congregations.

Leading God's people can be very stressful. Even Moses at one point found things so difficult that he thought it might be better if he died (Num. 11:15). But Christian leaders need to follow God's will, even when their congregations make things difficult.

Racism and Envy

Big Idea *Racism and envy can bring about God's judgment.*

Understanding the Text

The Text in Context

When Israel leaves Mount Sinai, things quickly turn sour. Numbers 11 begins a series of three locations where the people grumble and complain. At Taberah they complain because of the hardships of the journey (Num. 11:1–3), and at Kibroth Hattaavah they complain because they are tired of manna and want the meat and vegetables that they had enjoyed in Egypt (Num. 11:4–35). Now at Hazeroth (Num. 11:35) two members of Moses's own family, his sister and brother, complain against him and challenge his authority.

Historical and Cultural Background

Moses has married a Cushite (Num. 12:1). Cushites were from Nubia south of ancient Egypt (Isa. 18:1 places Cush on the Nile) in what is now southern Egypt and northern Sudan. Cushites sometimes were captured in war and brought to Egypt (see illustration). Some suggest that this wife was from the Mesopotamian people called "Kassites,"[1] though Kassites are not otherwise mentioned in the Bible. More likely Moses's new wife is one of the foreigners who had left Egypt with the Israelites. Moses "sent away" his first wife, Zipporah, with Jethro (Exod. 18:2), and she then disappears from the biblical story. We do not know what happened to her, whether she died or whether separation turned into de facto divorce, or if she had quietly returned. Zipporah had come into conflict with Moses over the circumcision of their second son, Gershom (Exod. 4:22–24), which might have led to a permanent rift and divorce. In any case, Zipporah was a Midianite, not a Cushite (Exod. 2:15–21). The Aramaic targumim identify this Cushite as Zipporah, taking "Cushite" to mean "beautiful" rather than being an ethnic term.[2] But an older wife probably would not be labeled "beautiful," and there would be little reason for Moses's siblings to fuss over a decades-old marriage. The "rabble" that had instigated Israel's grumblings probably are foreigners (see comments at Num. 11:4), and that could be a factor in Miriam and Aaron's offense at this marriage. The medieval Jewish commentator Rashi asserts that black Cushites were proverbial for their beauty.

Interpretive Insights

12:1 *Miriam and Aaron.* Miriam is the daughter of Amram and Jochebed, and the sister of Aaron and Moses (Num. 26:59). Her name, the Hebrew form of "Mary," may be derived from Egyptian *Maryē*, meaning "beloved." Miriam is mentioned first, and the punishment falls mostly on her, evidently because she has instigated this challenge to Moses's authority.

talk against Moses because of his Cushite wife. Miriam and Aaron object to Moses's marriage to a non-Israelite. On "Cushite," see "Historical and Cultural Background" above.

12:2 *Hasn't he also spoken through us?* Objection to Moses's Cushite wife is a pretext for expressing an objection about Moses's preeminent authority. Are Miriam and Aaron not spiritual leaders too (cf. Mic. 6:4)? Miriam is a prophet (Exod. 15:20), and Aaron is sometimes directly addressed by God without mediation by Moses (Exod. 4:27; Lev. 10:8; Num. 18:1, 8, 20). The audience for this complaint is not Moses himself, but rather fellow Israelites to whom Miriam and Aaron are commending themselves at Moses's expense.

The LORD heard this. This is an ominous prelude to judgment.

12:3 *Moses was . . . more humble than anyone else on the face of the earth.* For Moses to have called himself "more humble than anyone else" would seem

Key Themes of Numbers 12:1–16

- Racism is a sin.
- Envy is destructive of unity.

a contradiction of his own statement, so the NIV interprets it as an editorial, parenthetical addition. It may mean that Moses out of humility would have let this challenge to his authority by his siblings pass without reaction,[3] showing Miriam's and Aaron's implied charge of arrogance to be the opposite of the truth.[4] But the word rendered "humble" (*'anaw*) can instead be translated here "afflicted" or "miserable." The people's complaints have already made Moses so miserable that he has wished he were dead (Num. 11:15). Now that his own sister and brother are speaking against him, he might well have said of himself—with only a little hyperbole—that he is "the most miserable man on earth."[5]

12:4 *Come out to the tent of meeting.* Moses, Aaron, and Miriam are litigants in a dispute called before God as judge.

12:5 *pillar of cloud.* See comments at Leviticus 16:2; Numbers 9:15–23.

he . . . summoned Aaron and Miriam. This can be rendered as direct speech: "He

The wife of Moses is not an Israelite. The text calls her a Cushite. Perhaps she was from the region south of Egypt known as Nubia or Cush. Tomb paintings show that Egypt used both Semitic and Nubian peoples, perhaps prisoners of war, as slaves. This painting from the Tomb of Rekhmire (fifteenth-century BC Thebes) shows Nubians and Semites making bricks.

called, 'Aaron and Miriam!'" (NASBmg, NJPS). If so, it provides the irony of God speaking to Aaron and Miriam to tell them directly that ordinarily he only speaks directly to Moses (v. 8).[6]

12:6–8 *Listen to my words.* Verses 6–8 break into poetry (so NIV, NRSV, HCSB, REB) to underscore the importance of Moses in God's program. Moses is unlike other prophets, including Miriam (Exod. 15:20), to whom God has revealed himself indirectly, through visions, dreams, and riddles. God dialogues with Moses directly, "face to face" (lit., "mouth to mouth" [cf. Exod. 33:11; Deut. 34:10]), and reveals himself in a visible form. Miriam and Aaron should have recognized Moses's special relationship with God and not dared to challenge his authority.

12:10 *Miriam's skin was leprous.* In color and/or texture the disease is like "snow," perhaps specifically a psoriasis that has red patches covered with white scales.[7] On the exact nature of biblical "leprosy," see comments at Leviticus 13:1–59. There is poetic justice here: Miriam's penalty for speaking against Moses's marrying a (presumably) black Cushite woman is that she becomes "white" with skin disease.[8]

Aaron . . . saw that she had a defiling skin disease. Aaron as priest is responsible for confirming the diagnosis of leprosy and declaring Miriam unclean (Lev. 13:2–3).

12:11 *Please, my lord.* Aaron reacts by begging Moses's forgiveness of their sin and foolishness. Aaron acknowledges Moses's authority and unique relationship with God by referring to his brother as "my lord."

12:12 *like a stillborn infant . . . with its flesh half eaten away.* "Leprosy" makes the appearance of the skin reminiscent to what happens to a dead body.

12:13 *Moses cried out to the* Lord. Moses tries to avert God's wrath, just as a crime victim might influence a judge to be lenient on the criminal who has wronged the victim. Although Miriam is guilty, Moses prays for her out of compassion and at the urging of his brother.

12:14 *spit in her face.* To spit in a person's face is a sign of contempt and humiliation (cf. Deut. 25:9), something from which the Suffering Servant does not turn his face (Isa. 50:6).

12:15 *confined outside the camp for seven days.* Apparently, if a father spits in his daughter's face, it puts the daughter in a state of disgrace for seven days. By analogy, Miriam's disrespect toward her brother leads to her humiliation and being unclean outside the camp (Num. 5:4) for seven days in accordance with the custom of shaming. Seven days of humiliation contrast with uncleanness for the rest of her life had the leprosy not been healed. Seven days also relates to the seven-day ritual described in Leviticus 14:1–20, which Miriam undoubtedly undergoes. Again there is poetic justice: having made the claim that she is close to God, Miriam's punishment is to go away from God's presence.

12:16 *Hazeroth.* This is tentatively identified with 'Ain Khodara northeast of traditional Mount Sinai (Jebel Musa) on the way to 'Aqabah.[9] Thus, along with Taberah (Num. 11:1–3) and Kibroth Hattaavah (Num. 11:4–35), it became associated with acts of rebellion and complaints against God and Moses.

Desert of Paran. Numbers 10:12 describes the trip from the Desert of Sinai to the Desert of Paran in a mere sentence, but it takes the rest of Numbers 10–12 to flesh out all that happens along the way.

Theological Insights

God appears in this passage as judge in a dispute between Moses and his siblings. The New Testament also portrays God as humanity's judge (Heb. 10:30; 12:23; 1 Pet. 1:17; Rev. 20:12–13). As judge, God decides in favor of Moses and metes out punishment to Miriam and Aaron.

But is God's judgment fair to Miriam? Is not the punishment excessive compared with the offense? Moreover, why is she punished severely while Aaron, apparently, gets off scot-free? Is there some sort of sexism that punishes an uppity female more severely?

In response to these questions, it must be said that Miriam is not punished more than Aaron because of sexism. It is instead because Miriam has been the chief instigator of this rebellion against Moses. This is why her name occurs first (Num. 12:1). Moreover, the punishment is not inappropriate given the context. Rebellions like this in Numbers culminate in the disaster of Israel's forty-year exclusion from the land (see Num. 14). The punishment of seven days of leprosy is not out of proportion for the sort of offenses that lead to catastrophe.

Also, it is not true that Aaron goes unpunished, though his punishment is no doubt mitigated because he immediately repents (Num. 12:11). He is shamed by God and frightened by God's threatened punishment (Num. 12:5–9). Moreover, Aaron is distressed by his sister's punishment (Num. 12:12), so that her punishment indirectly also punishes him. God can be trusted to judge everyone fairly, and he may in response to prayer and repentance show mercy and commute punishments that we deserve.

Teaching the Text

Miriam and Aaron seem to have fallen into two sins that are all too common among humans: racism and envy.

1. *Racism is a sin.* Moses marries a Cushite woman. Cushites were a people from Nubia south of Egypt in the direction of Sudan and Ethiopia. They were known as being "tall and smooth-skinned" (Isa. 18:7). Moses's wife certainly was darker in complexion than the Israelites (who themselves were darker than northern Europeans). She may well have been black.

This objection by Miriam and Aaron has racist overtones. This woman is not "one of us." She is obviously a foreigner, to be associated with the "mixed multitude" and the "rabble" that had proven themselves to be worthless troublemakers (see Exod. 12:38; Num. 11:4). Why would Moses marry one of *them*?

But God is not a racist, and neither should we be. A foreigner such as Ruth the Moabite, who converts to Israelite religion (Ruth 1:16), is welcomed into Israel. Ruth even becomes an ancestor of King David (Ruth 4:16–22) and Jesus Christ (Matt. 1:5). The foreigner Rahab the harlot, who helps the Israelite scouts, also converts and is welcomed into Israel (Josh. 6:25). She too becomes an ancestor of David and Jesus Christ (Matt. 1:5). Evidently, a Cushite woman marries into the royal family of Hezekiah and bears a son named "Cushi" ("Cushite"), from whom the prophet Zephaniah is descended (Zeph. 1:1). God predicts through Isaiah that in the future the Cushites will come to worship God in Zion (Isa. 18:7), a prophecy that Zephaniah repeats (Zeph. 3:10). Like God, we should welcome into God's family those of every nation, tribe, people, and language (Rev. 7:9).

2. *Envy is destructive of unity.* Miriam and Aaron are also guilty of envy. Their words addressed more to fellow Israelites than to Moses show their envy: "Has the LORD spoken only through Moses? Hasn't he also spoken through us?" (v. 2).

Miriam and Aaron have leadership roles already. Micah 6:4 lists Aaron and Miriam as the leaders who along with Moses lead Israel from Egypt. Miriam becomes a prophet and uses her musical abilities to lead women in singing and dancing to celebrate God's deliverance of Israel from Pharaoh's army (Exod. 15:19–21). Miriam is the most important female spiritual leader among all the Israelites of her day. Aaron also has a key leadership role as high priest. Apart from Moses, Aaron is the most prominent spiritual leader of Israel. Yet Miriam and Aaron are not content with their roles. Rather, they become envious of the special leadership role that God has given their brother, Moses.

Envy can destroy the unity of God's people. In tearing Moses down in order to build themselves up, Miriam and Aaron contribute to the grumbling and complaining that already threaten to tear Israel apart (Num. 11).

Even though Moses may have been too humble to protest Miriam's and Aaron's undermining of his authority (cf. Num. 12:3), God confronts their envy and vindicates Moses. Moses does indeed have a place of preeminence among the leaders of God's people and a special relationship with God. Miriam is a prophet, but only with Moses does God speak "face to face" rather than in visions, dreams, or riddles.

We today are not immune from the kind of envy that can destroy families and ministries. Here we can learn from Miriam's and Aaron's bad example.

Illustrating the Text

Sometimes, we are shaped by the fallen values of this world rather than the truth of Scripture.

Christian Organization: Racism has at times affected Christians. Up until 2000, the fundamentalist Christian Bob Jones University prohibited interracial dating among its students on the grounds that the Bible taught the strict separation of the races and therefore prohibited marriage between the races. This position was argued on the basis of the Bible's language that Israel was to be separate from the nations, and that God had given each nation its own lands and boundaries (e.g., Acts 17:26). But this ignores the fact that nations (a political designation) were often ethnically diverse. For example, the Assyrian Empire consisted of a plethora of races. More importantly, this view ignores or tries to explain away those places where the Bible approves of interracial marriages under the Mosaic covenant (Moses's Cushite wife; Rahab; Ruth), and that under the new covenant God has broken down the barrier between the races so that in Christ gentiles and Jews constitute "one new man" of the church (Col. 3:11). To most Christians, Bob Jones

When Aaron and Miriam challenge the authority of Moses, God's rebuke includes the statement that "with him I speak face to face" (12:8), indicating the unique and special relationship that God and Moses share. This illumination from La Bible Historiale, part 1, by Guyart des Moulins (ca. AD 1291–95), depicts Moses and a human figure representing God the Father in conversation in the tabernacle.

in place that were racially hurtful."[10] It took a while, but finally biblical teaching on this matter had prevailed, even at this once segregationist institution.

Envy destroys joy.

Economics: In his essay "The Downside of Inciting Envy," Arthur C. Brooks notes that, historically, the United States has been a culture motivated more by aspiration than envy. This has been noted throughout history by visitors from Alexis de Tocqueville to Bono, the lead singer of the rock band U2. Brooks comments,

> My own data analysis confirms a strong link between economic envy and unhappiness. In 2008, Gallup asked a large sample of Americans whether they were "angry that others have more than they deserve." People who strongly disagreed with that statement—who were not envious, in other words—were almost five times more likely to say they were "very happy" about their lives than people who strongly agreed. Even after I controlled for income, education, age, family status, religion and politics, this pattern persisted.[11]

University's arguments against interracial marriage were simply reading white Southern cultural mores into the Bible rather than finding this prohibition through exegesis of the Bible.

As a result of its stand on interracial marriage, Bob Jones University lost its tax-exempt status. Happily, however, in 2000 the school reversed itself on this issue and began to allow interracial dating among its students. In 2008 it issued an apology, saying it was "profoundly sorry" for having allowed "institutional policies to remain

Not only are the dangers of envy warned against in Scripture, but they are also evidently manifest in society.

Numbers 12:1–16

Failure to Enter the Land

Big Idea *Trust that God can overcome great difficulties.*

Understanding the Text

The Text in Context

The people had begun complaining at Taberah and Kibroth Hattaavah (Num. 11). At Hazeroth Moses's own sister and brother had expressed resentment against Moses and undermined his spiritual authority (Num. 12). In each of these cases God had intervened with a mixture of punishment and grace. Now they come to Kadesh (or Kadesh Barnea) in the Desert of Paran (Num. 13:26) just south of the land of Canaan.

Israel has not learned its lesson from the events of Numbers 11–12. After sending scouts on a reconnaissance mission into the land of Canaan and hearing the majority opinion that the land would be impossible to conquer, the Israelites again rebel against God and Moses. This rebellion will prove pivotal in Israel's failure to live up to its calling and achieve its goal of entering the land.

Interpretive Insights

13:2 *Send some men to explore the land of Canaan.* Deuteronomy 1:22–23 indicates that the Israelites had asked Moses to send scouts to spy out the land. God's command here is thus a response to the people's request.

13:4 *These are their names.* The tribal leaders listed in Numbers 13:4–15 are different from the ones specified in Numbers 1:5–15.

13:16 *Moses gave Hoshea son of Nun the name Joshua.* Joshua's original name was Hoshea (vv. 8, 16), meaning "He [God?] saves." Joshua (*Yehoshua*) means "Yahweh is salvation." Both are similar in meaning, but only "Joshua" refers explicitly to Yahweh. Joshua probably had not been renamed yet when he was a spy.[1] Perhaps Joshua was renamed when he was designated as Moses's heir apparent (Num. 27:12–23), akin to the throne names of kings.

13:17 *Negev.* The Negev is an arid desert and semidesert region from Beersheba south that is not quite as desolate as the Desert of Paran. Negev in Hebrew means "dry." This area later became southern Judah.

hill country. This is the mountainous backbone of the land of Canaan that goes north through what would become the territories of Judah, Benjamin, and Ephraim.

13:21 *Desert of Zin.* Zin is north of the Desert of Paran and Kadesh, from which the scouts are sent.

Rehob, toward Lebo Hamath. Rehob is a city in the vicinity of Lebo Hamath that can be identified with Laboue or Al Labweh in modern Lebanon. This is some 270 miles north of Kadesh, where the scouts begin. Lebo Hamath marks the northern border of Canaan (Num. 34:8) and was the northernmost city of David and Solomon's empire (1 Chron. 13:5; 1 Kings 8:65).

13:22 *Hebron.* This is the first major fortified city that Israelite invaders would have encountered. The text emphasizes its antiquity. Hebron was seven years older than the sometimes Egyptian capital city of Zoan (also known as Tanis) in the region where the ten plagues had occurred (Ps. 78:12; Isa. 19:11, 13).

Ahiman, Sheshai and Talmai. These individuals or subtribes are members of the Anakites (discussed in v. 33 below). Four

Key Themes of Numbers 13:1–14:9

- Don't be paralyzed by great obstacles to God's plan.
- Focus on the greatness of God.

decades later Sheshai, Ahiman, and Talmai are driven out of Hebron by the spy Caleb (Josh. 15:14; Judg. 1:10, 20), whose descendants then occupy Hebron.

13:23 *Valley of Eshkol.* In Hebrew this means the "Valley of [Grape] Cluster." It is located near Hebron in the central hill country of what became Judah.

grapes . . . pomegranates and figs. The scouts determine the number, location, and fortifications of the enemy, but they also show that the land is worth the fight by bringing back some of its abundant produce.

13:25–26 *they returned . . . they reported.* That the scouts' report is delivered also to "the whole Israelite community" does not indicate every Israelite, since it would have been impossible for six hundred thousand men to gather for such a meeting;

rather, it indicates a body of representative tribal leaders (see comments at Num. 1:18).

13:27 *the land . . . does flow with milk and honey!* This is not so much an idyllic description, except in comparison to the desert, as a categorization of what kind of land this is. This land is good for herds of cattle and goats that produce milk and is good for producing sweet things. It is not necessarily good for other kinds of agriculture. "Honey" (*debash*) is not limited to bee's honey but includes other sweets such as date or grape syrup. Honey in Deuteronomy 8:8 probably refers to date syrup. Nonetheless, direct archaeological evidence of bee domestication and bee honey harvesting in ancient Israel was found in 2005 at Tel Rehov dating to the tenth or early ninth century BC.[2]

13:28 *The people . . . are powerful . . . the cities are fortified and very large.* This is the negative side of their report.

descendants of Anak. This foe around Hebron (v. 22) is likely the first that Israel would face when invading from Kadesh.

13:29 *Amalekites . . . Hittites . . . Jebusites . . . Amorites . . . Canaanites.* The entire area is swarming with enemies from south (Negev) to north (the hill country), from west (near the Mediterranean Sea) to east (along the Jordan). Israel had already fought with the desert-dwelling "Amalekites" (Exod. 17:8–16). In Abraham's day "Hittites" occupied the area around Hebron (Gen. 23), though they appear to have been supplanted there by Anakites. The Canaanite-speaking Hittites of the Bible probably are not related to the non-Semitic Hittites based in what is now Turkey who in the thirteenth century fought with Egypt for control of the Levant. Rather, they are a

Canaanite tribe (Gen. 10:15) with a similar-sounding name. The "Jebusites" occupied Jerusalem (Judg. 1:21), which they called "Jebus" (Judg. 19:10; 1 Chron. 11:4), eighteen miles north of Hebron, until David defeated them (2 Sam. 5:6–8). The term "Amorites" is used in Akkadian in Mesopotamia for "westerners" (in the direction of Syria), some of whom apparently migrated south into the Transjordan (Deut. 1:44) and the hill country of central Canaan (Gen. 48:22), though "Amorite" is sometimes used of the entire population of Canaan (Gen. 15:16). The "Canaanites" are descendants of the son of Ham, whose sexual sin concerning Noah condemned Canaan's descendants to subservience to Shem (fulfilled through Israel) (Gen. 9:18–27). "Canaanite," like "Amorite," can be used of the entire population of the land of Canaan. Canaan was the father of the Hittites, the Jebusites, and the Amorites just mentioned (Gen. 10:15–19), though here "Canaanites" refers to a subtribe that lived along the Jordan River valley and the Mediterranean Sea (Num. 13:29).

13:30 *Caleb silenced the people.* The sole voice initially against the majority is Caleb, though Joshua later supports him (Num. 14:6–9). Why Joshua is silent here is not stated. Is he still making up his mind? Or does Caleb simply take the lead in the debate with Joshua silently supportive?

13:32 *The land . . . devours those living in it.* This reference to constant warfare among the Canaanite peoples finds extrabiblical support from the fourteenth-century BC letters from Canaanite vassals to Egyptian pharaohs in the Amarna tablets.

13:33 *Nephilim.* The Nephilim of Genesis 6:4 are the "heroes / mighty men of old"

during the days when the "sons of God" had married the "daughters of men" (Gen. 6:1–4). Some take the Nephilim there to be the offspring of angels ("sons of God") and humans ("daughters of men"), so that these Nephilim are superhuman figures. Perhaps the scouts view the Anakites, who are especially tall as a race (v. 32; cf. Deut. 2:10, 21), as demigods descended from the Nephilim of Genesis, invincible to Israelite attacks. How under this view the Nephilim could have survived the flood of Noah is not explained. Alternatively, $n^e pilim$ may mean "marauders, attackers, violent men," a class of warriors whose brutal activities help bring on the judgment of the flood.[3] To the scouts, the Anakite warriors seem of the same powerful and violent character as the legendary Nephilim of Genesis.

We seemed like grasshoppers in our own eyes. In comparison with these tall and mighty warriors, the scouts feel puny and subject to being squashed.

14:1–4 *the community . . . wept . . . grumbled.* The majority report brings despair and discontent, and it results in a call to return to Egypt. Grumbling against Moses is a recurring theme (Exod. 15:24; 16:2; 17:3; Num. 16:2, 41; 21:5; 26:9).

14:5 *Moses and Aaron.* As Israel's top spiritual leaders, Moses and Aaron, along with Joshua and Caleb (v. 6), try to calm the people.

fell facedown. This is often the posture of prayer or worship (see Lev. 9:24), but here it represents begging the people to reconsider.

14:6 *Joshua . . . Caleb.* These two have been among the scouts (Num. 13:6, 8). Caleb gives the minority report encouraging Israel to begin the conquest (Num. 13:30).

tore their clothes. This gesture of distress shows their seriousness (cf. Gen. 37:29, 34; 44:13; Josh. 7:6).

14:8 *If the LORD is pleased with us.* Success in the conquest is conditional. Rebellion against God can forfeit his favor (v. 9a).

a land flowing with milk and honey. See comments at Numbers 13:27 above.

Theological Insights

Only by faith could God's people actually be guided by God. God directs Moses to send the scouts into the land (Num. 13:1–3), and Joshua and Caleb correctly understand that

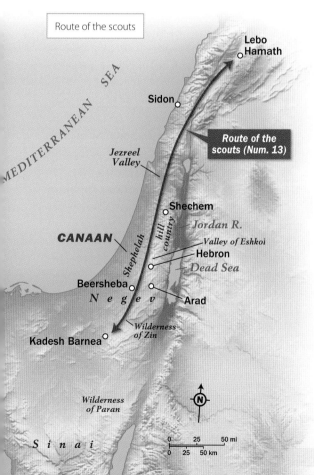

Route of the scouts

God would bring them victory over mighty enemies (Num. 14:8–9). But God's actions can seem mysterious or even malevolent. To the people, God seems intent on killing them (Num. 14:3). The difference in perspective is faith: Joshua and Caleb view God positively through the lens of faith, the people negatively through the lens of unbelief.

The importance of faith in God is also prominent in the New Testament. Indeed, a whole chapter, Hebrews 11, is devoted to it. Faith allows believers to "move mountains" (Matt. 17:20), resist the devil (1 Pet. 5:8–9), and overcome the world (1 John 5:4), whereas unbelief produces the opposite effects, then and now.

Teaching the Text

1. *Don't be paralyzed by great obstacles to God's plan.* The twelve scouts have much in common. Each of them is a leader of his tribe (Num. 13:1–16). Each is given the same forty-day reconnaissance mission to explore the land and determine the strength, position, and fortifications of the enemy (13:17–19). They have seen the same land and its fruitfulness (13:20). But two of the twelve scouts, Joshua and Caleb, stand apart from the others.

Everyone agrees that the land is a land that "does flow with milk and honey" (13:27). But ten of the twelve scouts focus on a more disturbing aspect of the land: the powerful enemies. Every part of the country is chock-full of formidable foes. Hebron, the first city that Israel will face, is occupied by the descendants of Anak (13:28). The Anakites are an intimidating, tall race (Deut. 2:10, 21) that the scouts associate with the powerful Nephilim of Genesis 6:1–4. In comparison with them, the scouts feel puny and impotent (Num. 13:31, 33).

Fear is a common emotion to which we are all too prone. That is why the Bible must reassure us so often. One of the most frequent exhortations in the Bible is "Do not be afraid." We are by nature fearful creatures. When we focus on great obstacles in life, we are likely to be overcome with fear and paralyzed into inaction. However, God's people should be characterized not by debilitating fear but rather by courage based on their faith in God. That is what Caleb and Joshua show us.

2. *Focus on the greatness of God.* Caleb and Joshua concentrate on the greatness of God, not the enemies. The conquest is not impossible. Caleb affirms, "We should go up and take possession of the land, for we can certainly do it" (13:30). Joshua may have taken a little longer to make up his mind or have kept silent at first because "his close affiliation with Moses would have discredited his opinion,"[4] but ultimately he affirms Caleb's viewpoint in support of Moses and Aaron. To both Caleb and Joshua, the issue is not the greatness of the enemies but rather the greatness of God.

The name Joshua (*Yehoshua*, "Yahweh saves") given him by Moses (13:16) reflects faith in God's ability to save. Joshua and Caleb affirm, "If the LORD is pleased with us, he will lead us into that land . . . and will give it to us" (Num. 14:8–9). God has promised Israel the land. God will carry through with his promises unless the people rebel (14:9).

A remedy for fear is faith in God. Through faith in God we can move mountains (Matt. 17:20; 1 Cor. 13:2). Through

When the scouts return, they report that the land of Canaan flows with milk and honey. This oil painting by Giovanni Lanfranco (AD 1582–1647) titled *Moses and the Messengers from Canaan* depicts the large cluster of grapes that was carried from the Valley of Eshkol as evidence of the fruitfulness of the land.

faith we can have the courage to act, to confront obstacles, and to accomplish much for God. But fear cannot solve a problem or overcome a difficulty. Fear leads to indecisiveness, confusion, and reluctance to attempt to do things for God. If we are to overcome life's difficulties and fulfill God's will for our lives, we must rely on God to enable us to carry out the tasks he has given us. God is sufficient and trustworthy, and we are in his hands. We must in faith concentrate on the greatness of God, not the greatness of our problems.

Illustrating the Text

Fear is the enemy of faith.

Nature: On February 12, 2014, car lovers everywhere gasped in horror when they woke to their morning news: an enormous sinkhole had opened up beneath the floor of a museum devoted to classic Corvettes. Eight of the cars had disappeared into the hole!

Sinkholes are formed as groundwater slowly erodes bedrock. Everything on the surface can look safe and stable, but underneath a great hole is being formed. At the right (or wrong!) moment, the hole can open up, swallowing homes, streets, even Corvettes.

Fear is like an acid to faith. When we fear, we are looking toward a future we cannot control. We are anticipating terrible outcomes. Ultimately, we are taking our lives out of God's hands and placing the responsibility for our protection into our own. Faith, on the other hand, trusts in the God who has called us his own and promises to work all things together for our good (Rom. 8:28).

When left unchecked, fear works beneath the surface of our lives. On the surface, the "ground level," we seem to believe the same things, sing the same songs, do the same deeds. But underneath, fear slowly erodes the bedrock of confident faith. When circumstances arise that challenge us to exercise faith, a life lived in fear will collapse. That is why we must identify areas in our lives that are infected with it. Do we fear people more than God? Do we fear the future rather than faithfully trusting the sovereign Lord? If so, beware: a sinkhole might be forming.

Numbers 13:1–14:9

Condemned to Wilderness Wandering

Big Idea *Disobedience can bring about forfeiture of God's blessings.*

Understanding the Text

The Text in Context

Numbers 14 constitutes the tragic climax of the Israelites' grumbling and rebelliousness. They send scouts into the land (Num. 13), but the majority have concluded that the enemy is too powerful to conquer. The people are again in revolt and ready to go back to Egypt (Num. 14:1–9). This rebellion will come to be listed as pivotal in Israel's failure to live up to its calling and achieve its goal of entering the land (Deut. 1:26–45). God threatens to annihilate Israel as he threatened previously during the incident of the golden calf (Exod. 32:10; Num. 14:12), for these two events represent the most egregious moral failures of Israel in the desert.

Interpretive Insights

14:10 *the whole assembly talked about stoning them.* "Talked about" could mean "thought about" or "threatened to" (NRSV).

the glory of the LORD appeared. God ominously manifests himself as a fire cloud (Exod. 16:10; 40:34–35; Num. 16:42) in the midst of this crisis.

14:11 *they refuse to believe . . . in spite of all the signs.* Israel has experienced the ten plagues, the parting of the Red Sea, and the miraculous provision of manna and quail, yet it lacks faith.

14:12 *I will strike them down . . . and destroy them.* This could be rendered "Let me strike them down . . . and let me destroy them,"[1] or as an expression of wish or intention: "I wish to" or "I am about to" instead of "I will." God asks for Moses's approval to destroy Israel—as at the golden calf incident (Exod. 32:10)—to get him to intercede in prayer.

I will make you into a nation greater and stronger than they. God can keep the patriarchal promises (Gen. 12:2) through Moses.

14:13–14 *the Egyptians will hear . . . they will tell the inhabitants of this land.* Moses responds by interceding for Israel. Destroying Israel would ruin God's reputation among the Egyptians and the Canaanites.

14:16 *The LORD was not able . . . he promised them on oath.* Non-Israelites would conclude that Israel's God is lacking in power or in integrity or both: God cannot keep his solemn oath giving Israel the land or lacks the integrity to do so or both.

14:19 *forgive the sin of these people.* Moses begs God not to destroy Israel because of its sins, but instead to act in accord with God's gracious and loving character as described in Exodus 34:6–7. For more, see "Theological Insights" below.

14:20 *I have forgiven them.* God's response, like God's character itself, is a mixture of holiness and mercy. On the merciful side, God agrees not to destroy Israel (cf. v. 12).

14:21 *Nevertheless.* God's holiness limits forgiveness to commuting the sentence rather than eliminating all punishment of this "wicked community" (vv. 27, 35).

as surely as I live. Having no other god to swear to, Yahweh swears on his own life and glory, symbolically raising his hand in oath (v. 30).

14:22 *tested me ten times.* "Ten times" probably is idiomatic for "repeatedly, over and over again," though the rabbis did come up with a list of ten specific occasions of rebellion in the previous narratives of Exodus and Numbers: (1) at the

Key Themes of Numbers 14:10–45

- Intercessory prayer is powerful.
- Some consequences of sin are potentially irrevocable.

Red Sea (Exod. 14:11–12), (2) at Marah (Exod. 15:23), (3) at the wilderness of Sin (Exod. 16:2), (4) at Rephidim (Exod. 17:1), (5) at Horeb with the golden calf (Exod. 32), (6) at Taberah (Num. 11:1), (7) at the "graves of craving" (Num. 11:4), (8) at Kadesh (Num. 14), and twice of some individuals at the giving of manna (9) who save it overnight (Exod. 16:20) and (10) who look for it on the Sabbath (Exod. 16:27).[2]

14:25 *Amalekites . . . Canaanites.* These are the first enemies that Israel will face invading from the south. They have already fought with Amalek in the desert (Exod. 17:8–16).

route to the Red Sea. That is, the way from which they came.

14:30 *Not one of you will enter the land . . . except Caleb . . . and Joshua.*

God had performed many miraculous signs, such as the parting of the Red Sea, yet the Israelites refuse to believe that the Lord can help them conquer the promised land. The carving on this fourth-century AD sarcophagus shows Pharaoh and his army at the Red Sea. Some of the Egyptians are being engulfed by the waters, while Moses and the Israelites are safe on the other side.

Because Caleb is the spy who has encouraged Israel to go ahead and begin the conquest (vv. 24, 38; cf. Num. 13:30; 14:6) and Joshua is the only spy to have agreed with Caleb (vv. 30, 38; cf. Num. 14:6), they are spared Israel's fate and will live to enter the land. In an act of poetic justice, Caleb will even be given possession of that fortified city of Hebron, whose inhabitants, the Anakites, the ten scouts had so feared (cf. Josh. 14:6–15). Moses and Aaron (v. 26), along with Aaron's sons, are also (for now) exempt from this exclusion from entering the land, for no Levite had been among the unfaithful scouts, and Aaron has supported Moses, Joshua, and Caleb against the mob (14:5–6). Moses and Aaron are later excluded from entering the land (see Num. 20:12, 24). Aaron's son Eleazar, presumably over the age of twenty at this time, is allowed to enter the land (Josh. 24:33).

14:31 *your children . . . enjoy the land.* Literally, they will "know, experience" the land.

14:33 *forty years.* This forty-year condemnation to living seminomadically in the desert corresponds symbolically to the time (forty days) that the scouts had investigated the land (v. 34; cf. 13:25). Forty years ensured that all the adults twenty or more years old would die before Israel entered Canaan (see vv. 29, 32–33). Ironically, the Israelites will get what they wished for: they had exclaimed, "If only we had died . . . in this wilderness" (Num. 14:2) and are afraid that they will "fall by the sword" (14:3), so in this wilderness they will fall dead (vv. 28–29). The ten scouts who spread the bad report die more immediately of a divine plague (vv. 36–37).

unfaithfulness. This is literally "harlotry," referring to the spiritual harlotry of unbelief and disobedience.

14:35 *I, the LORD, have spoken.* God's decision is final: Moses should not bother to intercede further.

14:40 *we are ready to go up to the land.* Having mourned bitterly (v. 39) and confessed their sin, the people now agree to go and take the land, but by doing so they now are in violation of God's new command to turn back toward the desert (v. 25; cf. Deut. 1:42). The attack will fail because Yahweh is not with them (vv. 42–43). God's sentence against them is final (cf. v. 35).

14:44 *neither Moses nor the ark . . . moved from the camp.* Invading without God's appointed leader, Moses, and God's presence, symbolized by his throne the ark (see comments at Lev. 16:2), proves futile.

14:45 *Hormah.* Hormah's location is unknown, but fittingly its Hebrew name means "destruction." Thus begin the forty years of wilderness wanderings.

Theological Insights

Moses's prayer in Numbers 14 conveys these theological truths about God's grace and God's holiness, truths that are, as it turns out, somewhat in tension with one another. On the one hand, "The LORD is slow to anger, abounding in love and forgiving sin and rebellion" (14:18a), but on the other hand, God "does not leave the guilty unpunished; he punishes the children for the sin of the parents to the third and fourth generation" (14:18b).

"Love" (*hesed*) encompasses the love, grace, mercy, loyalty, faithfulness, and the like that one shows to someone with whom one has a relationship. In pointing out that

God abounds in *hesed*, or "covenant love," Moses is beseeching God to act in love and mercy in view of his covenant relationship with Israel despite its sin. In Exodus 34:6, after Israel has made the golden calf, "God's love takes the shape of mercy and grace, of abstaining from anger and of being ready to forgive the thousands (i.e., numerous) of generations without any limit, although the punishment restricted to four generations would not fail to come."[3] In the incident of the golden calf, God had forgiven Israel's sin—that is, a veering from God's norms, specifically the commandment about images in the Decalogue. At Kadesh Israel had shown something else: rebellion against God's command (Num. 14:9). But Exodus 34:7 says that God forgives that too.

However, God's grace is in tension with his holiness, which "does not leave the guilty unpunished" (v. 18b). How can God be simultaneously gracious and holy with sinful people?

Moses does not resolve the theological tension between God's holiness and God's grace, a tension that is resolved in Christ (cf. Rom. 3:26). Moses merely prays that God choose to act on the basis of his gracious side (v. 19). And God answers that prayer: he does not destroy Israel (14:20), though in holiness he condemns that generation to the wilderness (vv. 21–35).

God, while holy, is inclined to forgiveness and grace. We, like Moses, can pray that God act on the basis of his grace.

Teaching the Text

1. *Intercessory prayer is powerful.* Although this passage is not intended to teach us how to pray, it shows several features of how Moses prayed for Israel that are suggestive for how we might pray.

We should pray out of love. God's people are not always very lovable. Moses's people had grumbled and complained and at times challenged his leadership. But despite all the people's faults and failings, Moses loves them, and he expresses that love through fervent prayer that God have mercy on them (14:19). We can do the same.

We should pray on the basis of God's honor. Moses does not pray selfishly. He prays on the basis of God's honor and

Moses intercedes on behalf of the rebellious and unbelieving people of Israel, just as he did when he heard that the Israelites were worshiping a golden calf. Shown here is a silver-plated calf figurine from the sixteenth century BC found housed in a small shrine in the excavations at Ashkelon, Israel.

glory. God's honor is intimately tied to his people, with whom he has made a covenant. In a sense, if God's people fail, God's great investment in them will fail also. That failure would ruin God's reputation among the gentiles (14:13–14).

Destroying Israel would bring into question God's power. Is God really "able to bring these people into the land he promised them on oath" (14:16a)? If not, it would raise doubts about God's faithfulness to his word. Moses wants to protect God's reputation. So should we.

We should also pray on the basis of God's grace. Some might suppose that God here is unreasonably harsh, and it took a compassionate human (Moses) to rein him in, but that is not accurate. This is the second time that Moses has prayed for God not to destroy Israel. The other time is in Exodus 32:9–14, at the making of the golden calf. Shortly after that incident God revealed something of his character as a compassionate and gracious God, slow to anger, abounding in love and faithfulness and yet holy (Exod. 34:6–7). Moses prays with the assurance of God's self-revelation that God is more inclined to forgive than to condemn. Arguably, God, who is omniscient, reveals his plans to Moses specifically to provoke Moses to pray for his people so that God can show mercy in response. In any case, God answers Moses's prayer by sparing Israel (v. 20), showing both the power of intercessory prayer and the extent of God's grace.

2. *Some consequences of sin are potentially irrevocable.* The people have provoked God repeatedly since departing from Egypt (v. 22). God in his mercy has limited the punishment, but God's patience has now run out. This is the last straw. God forgives them (v. 20) in that he will not annihilate them. But since God "does not leave the guilty unpunished" (v. 18), the Israelites will not enter the promised land until after they have wandered in the wilderness for forty years. God's promises are delayed and forfeited by a whole generation of Israelites. Even when some in part repent and agree to enter the land (v. 40), the damage has been done. It is too late.

Sin can have irrevocable consequences for us too. If you commit murder, repentance can bring God's forgiveness, as it does for David, who has Uriah killed so that he can take his wife (2 Sam. 12:13). But it cannot bring back from death the person killed. Nor will it necessarily keep you from being punished. David himself suffers loss, despite God's forgiveness (2 Sam. 12:11, 14). If you commit adultery and repent, God will forgive you, but your reputation may be sullied for years, and you may have so damaged your relationship with your spouse that you end up divorced. Lying or theft can get you fired at work and ruin your career. Sin can result in forfeiting some of God's blessings, even if we later repent and God forgives us.

Illustrating the Text

We should always hold God's holiness and grace in tension.

Informational: The rabbis recognized the tension between God's holiness and God's grace, as did Moses. Rosh Hashanah occurs on the first day of the month of Tishri. According to the rabbis of the *Leviticus Rabbah*, on Rosh Hashanah God sits on his "throne of judgment" and condemns people for their sins and failings. But upon the sounding of the trumpet marking the beginning of the year (Lev. 23:24), God rises up from his throne of judgment and sits on his throne of mercy, from which he reverses his judgments pronounced from the throne of judgment and forgives the world.[4] Thus the rabbis taught that God's mercy and grace are greater than God's judgment. Moses's prayer in Numbers 14:10–19 also assumes that God's mercy is greater than his judgment. And thus, despite God's characteristic of holiness, Moses can pray for God to graciously forgive Israel.

Sometimes the consequences of sin are irrevocable.

True Story: In 2009 Donté Stallworth, a wide receiver for the Cleveland Browns football team, unintentionally killed Mario Reyes, a fifty-nine-year-old construction crane operator. Stallworth, driving while intoxicated, hit Reyes with his car when Reyes was walking across a street in Miami. Afterward, Stallworth was burdened with the guilt of having done "irreparable harm" to the family of the man he killed, and he apologized for his "poor judgment."[5] But even if Stallworth were ever forgiven by the man's family, or forgiven by the NFL after a year's suspension from the league, or even forgiven by God, Mario Reyes remains dead because of Stallworth's foolish behavior. Stallworth has to live with the guilt of that choice. His sin has an irrevocable consequence.

Sin has consequences, sometimes permanent consequences. For that reason, we should never allow God's willingness to forgive to be a license for going ahead and sinning. We may be forgiven our sin, but, as Israel learned, some blessings from God may be permanently forfeited nevertheless.

Gratitude, Forgiveness, and Obedience

Big Idea *Fellowship with God and defiant sinning are incompatible.*

Understanding the Text

The Text in Context

Numbers goes from a narrative about scouts (Num. 13–14) to a seemingly unrelated chapter of laws concerning sacrifices, unintentional sins, Sabbath breaking, and tassels. Why this material is placed here rather than with similar material in Leviticus has mystified interpreters.

Numbers 15 does contribute one thing to the previous story. In Numbers 14 Israel is told that the adults will not enter the land (Num. 14:20–38), but Numbers 15 gives laws for "after/when you enter the land" (Num. 15:2, 18). These laws thus reassure Israelites who in the previous narrative have just been condemned not to enter the land that at least their children will enter.

Historical and Cultural Background

Observant Jews still follow the law concerning tassels, the *tsitsit*. These are intertwined with a blue thread and attached to the four corners of the prayer shawl, the *tallit*, in compliance with the law of Numbers 15:38. Traditionally, they also have 613 knots to symbolize the 613 commandments

God tells the Israelites to "make tassels on the corners of your garments, with a blue cord on each tassel" (15:38). The requirement for a blue cord was changed during the rabbinic period, when blue dye became expensive and scarce. Here men pray at the Western Wall wearing prayer shawls with tassels, or *tsitsits* (*tzitzits*), attached.

in the Pentateuch by rabbinic reckoning. These thus continue to serve as reminders of God's commandments for many Jews.

Interpretive Insights

15:1–21 These verses describe grain, oil, and wine offerings that accompany animal sacrifices, and dough offerings. Larger animals require larger portions of grain and wine.

15:2 *After you enter the land.* "After" might also be rendered "when" (KJV, ESV). Unbelief has delayed entrance into the land (Num. 14:20–38), but God's promise to give Israel the land remains sure.

home. "Home" (lit., "dwelling places" [KJV]) refers to permanent houses in contrast with tents in the desert.[1]

15:3 *food offerings.* See comments at Leviticus 1:9.

burnt offerings. See Leviticus 1.

sacrifices. This refers to "fellowship offerings" (Lev. 3) as in verse 8.

special vows . . . freewill offerings . . . festival offerings. These are fellowship offerings. Special vow offerings celebrate the successful completion of a vow or fulfill a promise made if God answers one's prayer (Gen. 28:20; Num. 6:14, 21; 2 Sam. 15:7–8; Prov. 7:14; Jon. 2:9). Freewill offerings express gratitude to God (Deut. 16:10; Ps. 54:6). Festival offerings are required at various feasts (Exod. 23:15; Lev. 23:8, 19, 37).

15:20 *a loaf from the first of your ground meal.* This probably refers to offering to God through a priest (Ezek. 44:30) dough from the kneading trough before cooking, presumably by women who do the kneading (Matt. 13:33). Hebrew *'arisah* ("ground meal") is better rendered "dough"

Key Themes of Numbers 15:1–41

- Show gratitude toward God.
- Sins that remain defiant are not forgivable.
- Set aside time for God (the Sabbath).

(LXX, ESV, NASB, NRSV). Unlike firstfruits, this offering applies to every home, not just farmers.[2] Like firstfruits, this offering may have occurred annually. Paul alludes to this offering (Rom. 11:16).

15:22–31 These verses list the reparations required for inadvertent sinning and the consequences for defiant sinning.

15:22 *unintentionally.* The triform root *shagah/shaga'/shagag* (the verb *shagah* [v. 22], the verb *shagag* [v. 28], the noun *sh^egagah* [vv. 24, 25, 26, 27, 29]) pertains to "going astray, wandering," like sheep without a shepherd (Ezek. 34:6) or a drunk staggering (Isa. 28:7), but it is used metaphorically for inadvertent sins[3] in contrast with sinning "defiantly" (v. 30). Inadvertent sins of the community are forgivable through two atoning sacrifices (burnt offering, sin offering), while an individual finds atonement through one (sin offering).

15:30 *defiantly.* Literally, this is sinning "with a high hand" (ESV)—that is, "boldly" (cf. Exod. 14:8).

cut off from the people. See "Additional Insights" following the unit on Leviticus 6:8–7:38.

15:32–36 These verses narrate the execution of a man who has broken the Sabbath.

15:32 *While the Israelites were in the wilderness.* This passage is not in chronological sequence with previous narratives.

a man . . . gathering wood on the Sabbath day. See Exodus 20:8–11.

15:34 *it was not clear what should be done to him.* Exodus 31:14–15 prescribes execution for violations of the Sabbath. Is the problem here to determine what method of execution should be used (so Rashi), or is it unclear whether this action actually constitutes "work"? Earlier, lighting a fire had been determined to be a violation of the Sabbath deserving execution (Exod. 35:2–3).

15:35–36 *the whole assembly . . . outside the camp.* Since this act has offended the corporate community's most cherished values, threatening to bring that community under divine wrath, the whole community participates in the stoning.[4] Execution is carried out outside the camp to avoid defiling the camp.

15:37–41 These verses discuss tassels attached to garments as signs of remembrance.

15:38 *tassels.* The Hebrew word behind "tassels" (*tsitsit*) is rendered "lock" (of hair) in Ezekiel 8:3, which a tassel of cords resembles.

corners. The word *kanap* is used of bird wings (Exod. 19:4), but here it refers to extensions of garments at the end of shawls or dresses.

blue cord on each tassel. The word *tᵉkelet* is "a rather vague colour marker" that runs the gamut from "deep-sea blue to violet to even green."[5] The requirement of only a single blue cord symbolizing the beauty and importance of God's commands perhaps indicates that the dye is too expensive for more. This color is used in tabernacle curtains and on priestly robes to give beauty and dignity appropriate for serving the divine King (Exod. 26:1; 28:6–8).

15:39 *not prostitute yourselves.* Imagery of deviant sexual behavior is a metaphor for ethical and especially religious violations (1 Chron. 5:25; 2 Chron. 21:11; Ps. 106:39; Isa. 1:21).

15:40 *be consecrated.* Obeying God's commands shows Israel to be set apart (holy). The emotionally charged reference to who and what God has shown himself to be in the exodus narratives serves to motivate the Israelites continually to remind themselves of the need to obey his commandments.

Theological Insights

Where people violate his decrees, God as judge metes out punishment (e.g., the Sabbath breaker [Num. 15:35–36]). Yet God also forgives on the basis of atoning sacrifice (Num. 15:22–29). Moses often prays on Israel's behalf that God will forgive them (Exod. 32:32; 34:9; Num. 14:19), and the sacrificial system facilitates God's doing so (Lev. 4:20, 26, 31, 35; 5:10, 16, 18). Forgiving sins of all sorts and degrees is part of the glory of the nature of God (Exod. 34:7). Various Scriptures celebrate how God forgives Israel (Ps. 103:3, 12; Dan. 9:9; Mic. 7:18).

Forgiveness remains central to the new covenant (Jer. 31:34; Heb. 8:12). Christians are taught to forgive as God forgives (Matt. 6:12; Luke 11:4) and to pray for the forgiveness of others (Luke 23:34). Jesus's sacrificial death allows God to forgive (Matt. 26:28). Yet as in the Old Testament, there is no forgiveness for "high-handed" sinning (Num. 15:29–31). When people say that Jesus cast out demons by the power of Beelzebub, Jesus calls this an "unforgivable sin" against the Holy Spirit (Mark 3:20–30). By insisting—contrary to all the external evidence as well as the internal witness of the Spirit—that Jesus is an evil man, they had cut themselves off from the only true source of forgiveness. Those who stubbornly refuse to respond to God's calling will eventually find themselves abandoned to their fate. God is willing to forgive everyone (2 Pet. 3:9), but not everyone is willing to be forgiven.

Teaching the Text

1. *Show gratitude toward God.* Numbers 15:1–21, on grain, oil, wine, and dough offerings, illustrates the principle that God's people need to show gratitude toward God. Their fellowship offerings express appreciation to God for various blessings (v. 3). Their grain offerings incorporate the fruit of the land into their worship. Women, perhaps at the beginning of the grain harvest, offer token offerings of dough/meal from the kneading trough (vv. 17–21) to thank God for the land's blessings. Foreigners participate as well (vv. 11–16). Everyone can enjoy fellowship with God and thank him for their blessings.

Under the new covenant, we no longer show gratitude to God through these particular offerings. Nonetheless, it remains important to express gratitude regularly in our own ways. We can daily pause to thank God for our blessings of food. We can give portions of our material blessings back to him as an offering of gratitude. We can pause to give thanks after God has answered our prayers or helped us through difficulties. In doing so, we will fulfill the spirit of Numbers 15:1–21.

2. *Sins that remain defiant are not forgivable.* When God gives Israel the law, he knows that Israel will fall short. For that reason, in his grace he provides the Old Testament sacrificial system to deal with the problem of failing "to keep any of these commands the LORD gave Moses" (Num. 15:22). But the kind of sin that God forgives is "unintentional" or, better, "inadvertent" sin. The sins that are forgivable are ones that do not genuinely represent what the sinner wants and insists on doing. This is illustrated by the use of the root *shagah/ shaga'/shagag* elsewhere (see comments on v. 22). A sheep does not want to go astray (Ezek. 34:6), though it deliberately acts in a way that leads it to do so. A drunk does not want to stagger (Isa. 28:7), but, because of the choice to drink in excess, ends up doing so. Similarly, one who sins "inadvertently" does not truly want to be in rebellion against God and his word, but he or she, at least for the moment, has nonetheless violated God's word.

Sins of "inadvertence" are forgivable through sacrifice, whereas "defiant" sins "with a high/raised hand" are not (Num. 15:30). But how can this be reconciled with the fact that God forgives (see "Theological Insights" above)?

Sinning with a "high hand" is the equivalent of shaking one's fist at God. Unlike an inadvertent sinner, who at heart really wants to do the right thing, high-handed sinners are in unrepentant rebellion. They cannot be forgiven because their heart attitude is one of blasphemy against God and contempt for his word (Num. 15:30–31). Conversely, if a sinner repents of sin, that sin ceases to be a defiant sin and becomes an inadvertent one, and hence forgivable. This is true in both Testaments: God does not forgive impenitent rebels, but on the basis of sacrifice, ultimately Christ's sacrifice, gladly forgives sinners who repent (Luke 13:3, 5; 15:7, 10; 24:47; Acts 2:38; 3:19; 11:18).

3. *Set aside time to God (the Sabbath).* The relevance of this passage for the Christian depends on how closely one connects the Jewish Sabbath theologically to the day of Christian worship.

Seventh-Day Adventists say that Christians, like Jews, must worship on Saturdays, the seventh day. Christian Sabbatarians see Sunday (the Lord's Day) as the substitute for the Jewish Sabbath and greatly restrict what activities can be done on their "Sabbath." Other Christians see the connection as less direct and allow more freedom. The Sabbath commandment is the only one of the Ten Commandments that is nowhere explicitly repeated in the New Testament. Thus, some argue that Christians are no longer obligated to maintain a "Sabbath" day.

Paul seems to have allowed Christians to follow their consciences on this matter. He writes, "One person considers one day more sacred than another; another considers every day alike. Each of them should be fully convinced in their own mind" (Rom. 14:5). For Paul, there is nothing wrong with Jewish Christians continuing to keep the Sabbath on Saturday or with gentile Christians making Sunday special in honor of the Lord's resurrection on the first day of the week. But *when* one sets aside time for God is less important than *that* one sets aside time for him. The basic purposes of the Sabbath were to set aside time for God and to rest from labor. Christians can keep the spirit of the Sabbath by doing these two things.

Whatever view one takes, there is no justification under the new covenant for the church making Sabbath violations capital offenses. Israel's death penalties for religious offenses were based on the special holiness of Israel, with God dwelling among them in the tabernacle/temple. Old Testament capital offenses such as adultery and incest are, under the new covenant, punished with divorce or excommunication, not death (Matt. 5:31–32; 1 Cor. 5:1–5). Nonetheless, the case of the wood gatherer in Numbers 15 still serves as a warning. God here condemns the person who has failed to set aside time for him and for rest. Would he also condemn us? Do we grant him minimal time, say an hour on Sunday morning, or perhaps even less time than that? Are we workaholics who do not regularly take time to rest and recuperate? The seriousness with which Israel kept its Sabbath is in sharp contrast to the lackadaisical attitude of many modern Christians in either making Sunday special or otherwise setting aside time for God. The liberty that Paul gives us should not be a license for robbing time's creator of the time he deserves from us.

Illustrating the Text

God cannot forgive a rebel who will not repent.

Quote: C. S. Lewis, in his chapter titled "Hell" in *The Problem of Pain*, describes the damned as successful rebels. He thus illustrates the nature of "defiant" or "highhanded" sinning.

> [The doctrine of hell, although barbarous to many,] has the full support of Scripture and, specially, of Our Lord's own words; it has always been held by Christendom; and it has the support of reason. If a game is played, it must be possible to lose it. If the happiness of a creature lies in self-surrender, no one can make

that surrender but himself . . . and he may refuse. I would pay any price to be able to say truthfully "All will be saved." But my reason retorts, "Without their will, or with it?" If I say "Without their will" I at once perceive a contradiction; how can the supreme voluntary act of self-surrender be involuntary? If I say "With their will," my reason replies, "How if they *will not* give in? . . .

. . . [Should God increase our chances to repent?] I believe that if a million opportunities were likely to do good, they would be given. But a master often knows, when boys and parents do not, that it is really useless to send a boy to a certain examination again. Finality must come sometime, and it does not require a very robust faith to believe that omniscience knows when.[6]

The tassels that the Israelites are commanded to include on their clothing are to remind them to obey God's commands. Tassels on clothing were not unique to Israel, however. Many examples can be found in the art of the ancient Near East. The tassels worn by captive sea peoples are shown here on the reliefs at Medinet Habu, Egypt (twelfth century BC).

Christians have had different understandings of what it means to honor the Sabbath throughout church history.

Church History: The Westminster Confession of Faith (1646) has greatly influenced Christians of the Reformed tradition to connect the Sabbath with Sunday. See chapter 21, "Of Religious Worship and the Sabbath Day," VII and VIII.

In this tradition not only "work" is prohibited but also "recreations." Playing cards and other games on Sunday was a practice that became common in the English court of the seventeenth century, though Puritans for this reason found that offensive.[7] Other Christians, especially in modern times, see "recreation" as relaxing and the opposite of "work." They thus consider recreational activities as not in violation of the spirit of the Sabbath law, even if they see Sunday as its Christian equivalent in some sense.

Christianity too has its useful symbols.

Object Lesson: For this illustration, gather some examples of tassels and also some pieces of jewelry that are made in the shape of or display the Christian cross, such as a pendant, brooch, earrings, or tie clip. Explain that the Israelites were to wear tassels, and many Christians choose to wear crosses. Wearing the tassel was a reminder of the need to obey God's commandments. Wearing a cross—in principle though not always in practice—serves to remind the wearer that he or she belongs to the Crucified One and is obligated to take up the cross and follow him (Luke 14:27). No Scripture commands anyone to wear such a symbol. However, to the degree that wearing a cross serves as a reminder of the need to follow Christ, it can be useful, just as the tassels served as a useful symbol reminding Israel to obey God's commandments.

Numbers 15:1–41

Korah's Rebellion

Big Idea *Envy and pride lead to rebellion and destruction.*

Understanding the Text

The Text in Context

Israel's record in the desert since leaving Sinai had been abysmal. The people had complained about hardships, the lack of meat, and the monotony of manna (Num. 11:1–6). Moses's own sister and brother had challenged his leadership role (Num. 12:1–2). And worst of all, Israel had been condemned by its unbelief to wander in the wilderness for forty years (Num. 14:1–10, 33).

This chapter introduces a new problem: the Levite Korah rebels. Korah's rebellious spirit also infects others to claim the priesthood for themselves. But God fulfills his promise to show who is truly holy (Num. 16:5) by bringing judgment on these rebels.

Korah and his followers present themselves before the Lord at the entrance to the tent of meeting. Each carries a censer filled with burning coals and incense. This incense altar and censer were found near a Philistine temple in Yavneh, Israel (ninth century BC).

Interpretive Insights

16:1 *Izhar.* Izhar is the brother of Moses's father, Amram (Exod. 6:18–21, 24; Num. 3:19).

Kohath. Kohathites include Korah's clan of Izhar. Kohathites, who camp south of the tabernacle, are responsible for carrying on their shoulders the ark, the table of showbread, the lampstand, the altars, the curtain, and related items when Israel is on the move (Num. 3:27–32). As a Kohathite, Korah already possesses a more sacred vocation than most Levites.

Reubenites. Reuben, Jacob's firstborn, had forfeited his rights as such because of incest with his father's concubine Bilhah (Gen. 25:22; 49:3–4). Firstborn sons had sometimes played a priestly role in the family. That role falls to the Levites as a substitute (Num. 3:12–13). Dathan and Abiram may have felt that their tribe had been cheated out of its leadership and priestly privileges as Jacob's firstborn.

became insolent. This could also be rendered "took men" (NIVmg). At issue is whether the verb is from *yaqah*, which in Arabic means "to be shameless," or from the very common root *laqah*, meaning "to take." The Masoretes, Jewish scribes who preserved the Hebrew Bible and added its vowels, vocalized the verb as if from the latter, resulting in renderings such as "took men" [NIVmg, KJV, ESV] and "took action" (NASB). This seems preferable to "became insolent," which postulates the existence of a root not otherwise attested in Hebrew.

16:3 *You have gone too far!* Literally, "[Too] much for you." These rebels think that Moses and Aaron have "too much"— too much power and too much prestige.[1]

The whole community is holy. Israel is "a kingdom of priests and a holy nation" (Exod. 19:6). Does this not imply a wider priesthood than Aaronites? Korah does not want everyone to be priests, but he does want priestly privileges for his own clan.

16:4 *Moses . . . fell facedown.* This posture of prayer and homage shows that Moses immediately brings this matter to God. God indicates that Korah and all his followers are to be publicly tested.

16:6 *censers.* Or "firepans." These are used by priests to carry live coals and incense in tabernacle worship (v. 7a; see Lev. 16:12).

16:7 *You Levites have gone too far!* Moses applies to Korah the charge that

Key Themes of Numbers 16:1–50

- We must resist the danger of rebelling against God.
- Intercession and atonement mitigate God's anger.

Korah has previously made against him (see v. 3): it is in fact Korah and his followers who have claimed too much power and prestige.

16:9 *Isn't it enough for you . . . ?* Rather than envying the Aaronites, Korah and the other Levites should consider their high privilege of caring for the holy things of the tabernacle. God had specifically designated Aaron and his sons alone to be the priests (Exod. 28:1; Lev. 8:1–3). Thus, rejecting the Aaronic priesthood constitutes defying the revealed will of God, and not Aaron.

16:12 *Dathan and Abiram.* These are Reubenites mentioned in verse 1. On is strangely omitted here. Had On dropped out of the rebellion?

We will not come! Dathan and Abiram twice refuse to obey (vv. 12, 14). They may have suspected that Korah would have the fate of Nadab and Abihu (Lev. 10), so they play it safe and support Korah from a distance.[2]

16:13 *Isn't it enough that you have brought us up out . . . to kill us in the wilderness?* Moses says to the Korahites, "Isn't it enough for you" to serve as Levites (v. 9)? Dathan and Abiram echo these words to mock Moses, whose promise of land in Canaan seems hollow (vv. 13–14a).

16:14 *treat these men like slaves?* Literally, "gouge out the eyes of these men." Since the eyes of slaves were not typically gouged, this is more likely an idiom for "deceive these men" (NIVmg)—that is, blind them to Moses's own failings.

16:15 *Do not accept their offering.* "Offering" (*minhah*) usually refers to the grain offering, though sometimes it is used more broadly of various offerings seeking God's favor (e.g., Gen. 4:3–5). Moses's prayer is a curse. It means "Do not accept the incense offering about to be made on their behalf by Korah," or "Do not accept their recent grain offerings," or "Do not accept any offerings from them." Moses does not think that they deserve any merit by virtue of offering.

16:16 *appear before the* LORD *tomorrow.* Compare the contest between Elijah and the prophets of Baal on Mount Carmel (1 Kings 18:16–46).

16:19 *the entire assembly.* This probably refers to Korah's supporters. The Septuagint reads "his assembly."

16:22 *But Moses and Aaron . . . cried out.* Though God tells Moses and Aaron to separate from the assembly because God is about to destroy them (vv. 20–21), out of compassion for their wayward opponents they make intercession on behalf of the assembly.

God who gives breath to all living things. God as creator has the right to give life to or take life from his creatures (cf. Ps. 104:29–30), and he can discern which human spirits are guilty or innocent, though in this case Moses and Aaron beseech him to spare the assembly.

only one man. This is a hyperbole to indicate that it is Korah who is especially responsible for this rebellion. This intercession does not stop God's judgment from spreading beyond Korah, but it does mitigate the punishment so that some of the line of Korah are spared (Num. 26:11).

16:26 *Move back from the tents of these wicked men!* That is, from the tents of Korah, Dathan, and Abiram. Korah may well have left the 250 and returned to his tents at this time,[3] for Numbers 26:9–10 indicates that Korah is swallowed up by the earth along with Dathan and Abiram.

16:28 *This is how you will know.* Prediction fulfillment is one test of a true prophet (Deut. 18:22). The fulfillment of Moses's predictions confirms his prophetic office (vv. 28–30).

16:30 *realm of the dead.* This translates *she'ol.* "Sheol" (cf. NASB, NRSV) can refer to the underworld, where the dead experience some sort of shadowy existence in the afterlife (Isa. 14:9–11), though here it merely refers to these people meeting their deaths by being buried alive. Hence, "grave" seems to be an appropriate translation here.

16:37 *Eleazar son of Aaron.* Aaron's son collects the censers from among the corpses of the 250 instead of Aaron because Aaron as high priest must take special care to avoid ceremonial corpse contamination (see Lev. 21:10–12).

the censers are holy. Despite the sinful motives of the 250 who have died, the censers are not defiled beyond use and remain dedicated to God.

16:38 *overlay the altar.* This overlay on the bronze altar reinforces its initial overlay (see Exod. 38:2). This serves to teach Israel that only a descendant of Aaron has permission to burn incense before Yahweh (v. 40). This command is violated by King Uzziah, who consequently is struck with leprosy (2 Chron. 26:16–20).

16:41 *You have killed the* LORD'S *people.* This is, of course, untrue. It is not Moses or Aaron but rather God who has killed them by overt miracles.

16:42 *The glory of the LORD appeared.* The appearance of God's fire cloud at the tent here portends punishment (cf. Num. 12:5; 14:10), the destruction of these people (vv. 44–45a).

16:45 *they fell facedown.* See verse 4.

16:46 *make atonement for them.* Here atonement involves appeasing God's wrath, which has already appeared in the form of a plague. This is a case where incense rather than blood sacrifice achieves this end. On atonement, see "Additional Insights" following the unit on Leviticus 4:1–35.

16:49 *14,700 people died.* Aaron's and Moses's intercessions stop the plague (v. 48), though nonetheless a large number have died.

Theological Insights

God calls different people to different vocations. Contrary to Korah (Num. 16:3), God had called only some, not all, Israelites to the priesthood. The priesthood was meant to help Israel, not harm it. When Korah selfishly demands an office to which God has not called him, Korah ends up harming Israel and undermining the purpose of the priesthood.

This is also true in the church. Paul compares the church to the body in which different members have different functions. Each member, though different in function, has a place in contributing to the whole (1 Cor. 12:12–26). God calls some, not all, Christians to be apostles, prophets, or teachers (1 Cor. 12:27–29). Korah as a Levite already had a high calling to minister in the tabernacle (Num. 16:9–10). But to rebel against those whom God has called to leadership is to rebel against God himself (Num. 16:11). It is important to do what God has called one to do rather than be envious of others whom God has called to lead his people.

Teaching the Text

1. *We must resist the danger of rebelling against God.* Korah is not satisfied with his station as a Levite. Rather, he is jealous of the Aaronites. Moreover, he influences others to join him in rebellion. Korah and his

The Lord directs Moses to warn the assembly to "move away from the tents of Korah, Dathan and Abiram" (16:24). The tents used by the Israelites while they wandered in the wilderness were probably much like the tent shown here, used by bedouin today.

New Testament Allusions to Korah

In discussing Hymenaeus and Philetus, Paul reminds Timothy, "The Lord knows those who are his" (2 Tim. 2:19a). This expression is a direct quotation of the Septuagint translation of Numbers 16:5. Paul is comparing Timothy to Moses and Aaron, and Hymenaeus and Philetus to Korah. Although some may be led astray by false teachers like Korah (2 Tim. 2:17–18), Timothy can be assured that God knows him—and not these false teachers—to be God's true servant, just as God knew that Moses and Aaron, rather than Korah and his followers, truly belonged to God. Moreover, as Moses had confronted Korah and his followers, so Timothy must separate from these two heretics (2 Tim. 2:19b).

Jude also cites the Korah incident: "Woe to them! They have taken the way of Cain; they have rushed for profit into Balaam's error; they have been destroyed in Korah's rebellion" (Jude 1:11). Just as Korah had been destroyed by God, so Jude warns that false teachers of his day will suffer an even worse fate: "the punishment of eternal fire" (Jude 1:7). Those who teach damnable heresies today are likewise subject to the judgment of God.

followers voice three complaints: (1) Moses and Aaron have set themselves above the rest of Israel (vv. 3, 13); (2) Moses has failed to bring Israel to the promised land (v. 14); (3) Moses and Aaron have arrogated the priesthood to themselves alone (vv. 7–11).[4] Each of these charges is untrue. God had called Moses to be Israel's leader (Exod. 3:7–10). Moses had been reluctant to accept this role (Exod. 3:11–4:17). It is the people's unbelief, not Moses's, that has kept Israel from entering the promised land (Num. 13–14). It is God, not Moses or Aaron, who has selected the priesthood (Exod. 28:1).

One of the ways the Bible describes sin is as rebellion against God. All of us are tempted from time to time to rebel. In our arrogance we may come to believe that our ways are somehow better than God's. Like Korah, we may be motivated by envy or selfish ambition. We may twist God's word to justify our actions, as Korah does with

Exodus 19:6 (see comments at Num. 16:3). We may out of ignorance or a desire to conform to the world follow people teaching rebellion against God. Christians, in contrast, must submit to the lordship of Christ and obey God's word. They must resist the temptation to rebel against God.

2. Intercession and atonement mitigate God's anger. The Korah incident teaches us important theological truths about God that remain true today.

First, God punishes sin. When God swallows up and sends fire on the rebels and their camps (vv. 31–35) and a plague on those who continue to grumble (vv. 41, 46), this reminds us that God's holiness is incompatible with human sin.

Second, God warns sinners to flee the judgment. God has allowed people time to repent and separate from the wicked so that they could escape their judgment (vv. 20–23). He calls on sinners today to do the same.

Third, God is willing to forgive on the basis of intercession and atoning sacrifice. Although the whole assembly is guilty (vv. 21, 45), God accepts the prayers and the incense that Moses and Aaron have offered to limit his punishment (vv. 22–23, 46–48). The fact that God is willing to be placated shows God's forgiving nature. We too have hope of salvation on the basis of Christ's intercession and sacrifice for us (Heb. 7:25; 9:26)

Illustrating the Text

False teachers twist Scripture to suit their own needs.

Cults: As James Sire points out in his book *Scripture Twisting*,[5] religious cults often defend their heretical views by distorting the teaching of Scripture. Such twisting of the Bible can take the form of misquotation or quoting words out of context. Sometimes it takes figuratively a text that is meant to be taken literally, or vice versa. But another way to twist Scripture is to cite one part of Scripture while ignoring other parts that contradict the interpretation of the text cited.

For example, Jehovah's Witnesses deny the deity of Jesus Christ. They take John 1:1 to mean that "the Word [Jesus] was a god" rather than "the Word was God." But they ignore the passages, even in John's Gospel, that indicate that Jesus was God: Jesus claimed equality with God (John 10:30, 33). John 12:37–41 says that Isaiah saw Jesus's glory when Isaiah saw God (Isa. 6:1–10). Thomas, upon seeing the resurrected Jesus, cries out, "My Lord and my God!" (John 20:28), indicating that Jesus is in fact God. John 1:1 can be read correctly only in the light of these other passages, not by ignoring them.

Korah and his followers were also guilty of twisting God's word. They recognized correctly that God by his word had made Israel "a kingdom of priests and a holy nation" (Exod. 19:6). Korah took this statement to mean that the priesthood was much broader than Aaron and his sons. But in order to maintain that view, he had to ignore the subsequent statements by God where he called Aaron and his sons to their special role as priests (e.g., Exod. 27:21; 28:41). Exodus 19:6 must not be understood in contradiction to these subsequent passages. It means that Israel as a nation had a priestly role in ministering to the other nations; it does not mean that every individual Israelite was a priest, for that would make Scripture contradict itself. Like false teachers today, Korah emphasized one part of the Bible at the expense of other parts.

Priesthood Confirmed and Its Mediation Duties Specified

Big Idea *God confirms his ministers and directs them to protect that which is sacred.*

Understanding the Text

The Text in Context

In Numbers 16 Korah challenges the exclusive privilege of priesthood by Aaron and his sons. But in the contest between Aaron and the followers of Korah, God shows Korah to be wrong by sending fire to consume the 250 non-Aaronites who have come to offer incense to God. A challenge also comes from Reubenites, who in sympathy with Korah claim that "the whole community is holy" (Num. 16:3b), not just Levites. They do not believe that God has appointed Moses and Aaron to their leadership and priestly positions (Num. 16:3c). These Reubenites maintain that the priesthood ought to be available to tribes other than Levi.

Numbers 17 answers this objection by the Reubenites. This is another contest between Aaron and those who want a wider priesthood. Aaron's staff blossoms when placed in the presence of God in the tabernacle, thus showing the special place of the Levites—Aaron in particular—in the tabernacle service. Numbers 18 goes on to specify how Aaron's service allows God to be worshiped without profaning him and bringing upon the people or the priests themselves God's terrifying and deadly wrath.

Interpretive Insights

17:1–18:7 The ordination of Aaronic priests is described in Leviticus 8–10, and the function of the Levites is given in Numbers 3–4. Numbers 17:1–18:7 reemphasizes the special calling of the tribe of Levi, both the Aaronites and other Levites, as taught in such passages. This section narrates the incident of the blossoming of Aaron's staff (17:1–11) and how the Aaronites serve to avert God's wrath (17:12–18:7).

17:2 *twelve staffs.* The Hebrew word behind "staff" (*matteh*) is translated "tribe" when the leader of each tribe has been chosen (Num. 1:4). Tribal leaders each have a stick or staff that symbolizes their leadership position, as a scepter does for a king (*matteh* is rendered "scepter" in Ps. 110:2). Since that staff in turn symbolizes the tribe, *matteh* came also to mean "tribe."

ancestral tribes. Literally, "fathers' houses" (ESV).

Write the name of each man. Having the leader's name on each of the thirteen staffs (twelve tribes plus "Levi"), specifically Aaron's name on Levi's staff, will remove any ambiguity about whose staff has miraculously blossomed (vv. 2c–3).

17:4 *the ark of the covenant law.* "Covenant law" translates *ʿedut*, traditionally rendered "testimony," and alludes to the law stored in the ark (Exod. 25:16, 21; 40:20). See Numbers 7:89. The text literally reads, "In front of the *ʿedut*," but it means "in front of the ark of the *ʿedut*." All staffs are placed in front of the throne of God in the most holy place, where God especially manifests his presence (Exod. 26:34), so the miraculous sprouting will indicate the tribe God has chosen to serve as priests, putting an end to Israel's grumbling against the Aaronic priesthood (v. 5).

17:8 *budded, blossomed and produced almonds.* The lampstand in the tabernacle is designed after the almond as symbol of life and blessing (Exod. 25:34; 37:19–20). This is not the first miracle associated with Aaron's staff: it had turned into a snake (Exod. 7:7–12) and had been used in turning the Nile into blood (Exod. 7:19–20) and in the plagues of frogs (Exod. 8:5) and of gnats (Exod. 8:16–17). It has also been used to draw water from rocks (see comments at Num. 20:1–13).

17:9 *all the Israelites . . . looked at them . . . each of the leaders took his own staff.* This exercise is meant to prove to all non-Levites that their staff (tribe) has not been chosen by God to serve the tabernacle as priests.

- God confirms the call of his servants.
- Ministers serve as protectors.

17:10 *as a sign to the rebellious.* Aaron's rod in the tabernacle, like the censers of the 250 used to overlay the altar (Num. 16:38), symbolizes that only Aaronites of the tribe of Levi can serve as priests.

17:12 *We will die! . . . we are all lost!* The destruction of the 250 and the camps of Dathan and Abiram lead the Israelites to realize that they lack sufficient holiness to serve in the tabernacle, so they panic and swing to the opposite extreme. If they cannot enter the tabernacle, perhaps they are also not holy enough to be camped anywhere near it. Even coming near Yahweh's tabernacle can result in death. So

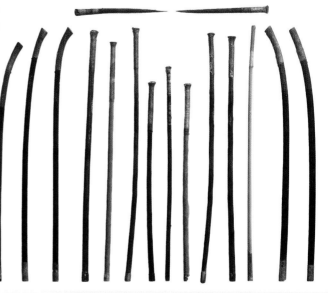

A staff from the leader of each tribe is presented to Moses to place in front of the ark of the covenant. God will reveal the man he has chosen as priest by causing his staff to sprout. This array of staffs from ancient Egypt is on display at the Egyptian Museum, Cairo.

they wonder if their proximity to the tabernacle might not cause them all to perish (v. 13).

18:1 *The Lord said to Aaron.* Revelations usually are mediated through Moses, but to underscore the importance of the Aaronites, here the message comes directly to the high priest. The remedy for the Israelites' fear of being near the sanctuary is the reminder of regulations already given in Numbers 3–4.

your family. This is literally "your fathers' house" (ESV), probably in reference to the Kohathite clan, from whom Aaron is descended (Exod. 6:16–20) and who were in charge of the most holy items in the tabernacle (Num. 4:2–20).

bear the responsibility for offenses connected with the sanctuary . . . for offenses connected with the priesthood. In other words, the Kohathites and the Aaronites come between God and the people to do the precarious work around the sanctuary. The Kohathites are in charge of transporting the most holy and therefore the most dangerous objects (furnishings, altar), but only Aaronites can actually touch them (vv. 3, 7;

cf. Num. 4:15). The Kohathites are to assist the Aaronites with the most holy objects (v. 6), but all non-Aaronite Levites are forbidden from encroaching upon the place of the priests, or else both the Aaronites and their Levite helpers can be struck down by God (vv. 2–3). All other Israelites must keep completely away (v. 4).

18:7 *be put to death.* Levites are responsible for guarding the sanctuary and killing intruders. Such killings will be regarded as acts of self-defense[1] to keep God's wrath from breaking out against the priests and Kohathites (v. 3) or spreading to the whole community (v. 5), as occurred when the 250 followers of Korah (himself a Kohathite; Num. 16:1) encroached on the sanctuary (Num. 16:28–35).

Theological Insights

Up until Korah's rebellion, many Israelites had not realized the danger of working in the sanctuary in the presence of the holy God. Now with the destruction of the 250, the swallowing up of the camps of Korah, Dathan, and Abiram (Num. 16), and the confirmation that only Aaron's tribe (symbolized by the rod that has blossomed) can thrive in

To maintain the holiness of sacred space and prevent God's wrath, the priests are responsible for the care of the sanctuary and the altar, while the Levites are given the job of caring for the tent and for carrying out the sentence of death for anyone who comes near the sanctuary. Also protecting God's presence are two cherubim, which are part of the atonement cover for the ark of the covenant. They may have been similar to the winged composite creature, shown here, which guarded the entrance to the temple at Ain Dara, Syria.

God's presence (Num. 17:1–11), the risks become clear. The Israelites now see how dangerous it is to dwell in the presence of the holy God. So they go from coveting the Aaronites' exclusive access to God to the opposite extreme of being afraid of God's presence and crying, "We will die! We are lost, we are all lost!" (Num. 17:12).

The holiness of God elsewhere in the Bible evokes, if not terror, at least reverential fear (Pss. 34:9; 89:7; Rev. 15:4). Holy ground created by God's holy presence leads Moses to show homage and respect by removing his sandals (Exod. 3:5). The one called "holy, holy, holy" causes even the temple to tremble and sinful people, including prophets, to cower (Isa. 6:3–5).

Christians often emphasize the love of God and the intimacy that we can have with God at the expense of his sometimes alarming holiness. But God paradoxically is both love and holiness at the same time. Christians too should show him the respect that he deserves as the holy God.

Teaching the Text

1. *God confirms the call of his servants.* God's reaffirmation of the ministry of the Levites illustrates several truths about ministry.

First, ministry comes from God. God has called everyone to serve him in a general way, but he has not called everyone to serve him in exactly the same way. Israel is "a kingdom of priests" and a "holy nation" (Exod. 19:6). The nation functions as a priest in the sense that Israel is to mediate God to the other nations. But only Aaron and his descendants have been chosen to serve individually as priests. Thus, the Reubenites have it wrong when they claim, "The whole community is holy, every one of them" (Num. 16:3). Not every Israelite is a holy priest.

A call to ministry is something that comes from God. There are many examples of such calls to ministry in Scripture: Moses (Exod. 3–4), Isaiah (Isa. 6), Ezekiel (Ezek. 1–3), and the apostle Paul (Acts 9:1–16; 26:13–19). But no one is to enter ministry by self-appointment. The ministry of anyone who does so will not be blessed by God.

Second, the ministry of the Levites illustrates that ministry is confirmed by God. Aaron may well have been discouraged by the events that he had faced. Trying to lead this grumbling and complaining people is in many ways a thankless task. When things are going badly, Aaron may well question whether he has really been called to serve Israel as a priest.

Whatever Aaron's feelings, God chooses to confirm Aaron's call to the priesthood by the miracle of the blossoming staff. The lampstand in the tabernacle is fashioned after an almond design (Exod. 25:34; 37:19–20), and the blossoming of Aaron's staff shows that he has been called to serve in that setting.

Although it is rare for God to confirm someone's call to ministry through such an overt miracle, he can do so in other ways: affirmation by others that one has the gifts and abilities to serve God in ministry, an inward conviction that one is being led by God's Spirit into ministry, and/or ministry opportunities that God puts in one's path. The story of Korah shows that one can easily be self-deceived in thinking that one is called to minister. But if one is really called, God over time will confirm that calling.

Finally, ministry by those called by God brings life. Not only does the blossoming of Aaron's rod signify divine choice, but also the nature of the sign expresses an abundance of life. The message is this: "Through my chosen servant you will find life."[2] This has already been seen when Aaron stands between the living and the dead (Num. 16:48). Those genuinely called by God to ministry will transmit to those to whom they minister abundance of life. If one's attempts to engage in ministry do not eventually produce life-enhancing fruit, then one is likely to have misread God's call.

2. *Ministers serve as protectors* (*Num. 17:12–18:7*). Both the sons of Aaron and the Levites stand between the holy items in the tabernacle and the people to protect the sanctuary from intrusion and to protect the people from God's wrath (18:1–7). Just as the Levites are God's gift to the priests (18:6), so the priests and Levites are by implication God's gift to Israel, serving to minister to and for the people.

While there is no direct application of this organization to the church, which lacks Levitical priests, there is an analogy to New Testament teachings about ministers. Ephesians 4:8 teaches that today ministers are God's gift to the church: "When he ascended on high, he took many captives and gave gifts to his people." Paul uses this paraphrased quotation of Psalm 68:17–18 to emphasize God's gift of apostles, prophets, evangelists, and pastor-teachers to the church (Eph. 4:11). Psalm 68:18 is

It is Aaron's staff that buds, confirming him as God's choice as priest. This illumination from the Northern French Miscellany (AD 1277–86) depicts one of the twelve staffs in full blossom.

possibly an echo of Numbers 8:6, 14; 18:6, "in which Yahweh takes the Levites from among the people and then gives the Levites back to the people as a gift."[3] Thus the teaching of Numbers about priests and Levites being God's gift reminds us to rejoice in God's calling people to guide and protect his church.

Illustrating the Text

God confirms his call through external and internal means.

Spiritual Autobiography: Billy Graham was perhaps the greatest evangelist of the twentieth century. But when he was young, he struggled over whether he was actually called to ministry.

Graham had been encouraged by others to preach the gospel. He had experienced visible success with a number of people being converted to Christ through his preaching. Both teachers and classmates urged Graham to commit himself to gospel ministry. But Graham still was not sure that he wanted to commit his whole life to preaching. Finally, he became emotionally distraught and walked around a golf course, questioning his call to ministry. One night he got down on his knees on the edge of one of the golf greens and poured out his heart to God in prayer. "Oh, God," he sobbed, "if you want me to serve you, I will." He received no sign from heaven, no voice from the sky. "But in my spirit I knew that I had been called to the ministry. And I knew my answer was yes."[4] In Graham's case, his ministry was not confirmed by an overt miracle like the blossoming of Aaron's rod. It was, nonetheless, confirmed.

Church leaders are called, like shepherds, to protect the flock.

News: On Monday, January 10, 2014, an average student from a small town in Pakistan performed an extraordinary act of valor. Fourteen-year-old Aitzaz Hasan saw a suicide bomber headed toward his school, aiming at a morning assembly of 450 children. Aitzaz ran and wrestled with the suicide bomber, causing the bomb to detonate and kill them both. Though he lost his own life, Aitzaz saved many more. He was awarded Pakistan's highest civil award for bravery. One of his teachers commented, "He has left his family grieving, but has prevented many others from that fate."[5]

Within the life of the church, God calls pastors to stand guard. They are called to protect the flock from dangers. In most of our churches those dangers will be spiritual, or doctrinal, or ideological. But the call is no less important, and the demand for courage no less urgent.

Portions for the Priests and the Levites

Big Idea *God provides for those whom he calls to ministry.*

Understanding the Text

The Text in Context

Numbers 16 deals with the question of who is holy and may thus serve as priests in the tabernacle (Num. 16:3). The followers of Korah discover to their shock that only the sons of Aaron can do this. In Numbers 17 the miracle of the staff that blossomed underscores that the tribe of Levi and especially the sons of Aaron have been set apart for divine service. Numbers 18:1–7 describes the role of priests and Levites as intermediaries and protectors between God and the people.

Although previously neither Moses nor Aaron has taken anything from the Israelites (Num. 16:15), God reiterates to Aaron (see Num. 18:1) the command that the Israelites support the priests and Levites through tithes and offerings in compensation for their service in the tabernacle and because they have no inheritance in the land except God (Num. 18:20, 24).

Numbers 18:8–32 specifies the rewards given to the Levites and priests for their services. God provides for his ministers through the tithe.

"I give you all the finest olive oil and all the finest new wine and grain they give the LORD as the firstfruits of their harvest" (18:12). The finest olive oil is extracted after the olives are first crushed. Shown here is one type of ancient olive crusher found throughout the land of Israel.

Historical and Cultural Background

Tithes (see Lev. 6:14–7:36; 27:30–32) were intended to support the priests and Levites. Israel did not always obey God in this matter. During Nehemiah's day the tithes were being withheld from the Levites, evidently by the priests who were hoarding it all for themselves. As a result,

Levite singers were forced to go to the fields rather than serving God in the temple (Neh. 13:10). Malachi 3:8–10, in approximately the same period as Nehemiah, reports a similar problem of the people failing to give the required tithe, describing this as "robbing God."

Interpretive Insights

18:8–24 For these Levitical regulations, God continues to address Aaron (see v. 1).

18:9 *the most holy offerings.* The portion of the offerings given to God on the altar from the grain, sin, or guilt offerings is regarded as most holy, meaning that it can be eaten only by a male in the priestly household: the high priest (Aaron) or his sons.

18:10 *Eat it as something most holy.* This translation (similarly, NASB, NRSV, NLT, NJPS) probably is better rendered, "In a most holy place shall you eat it" (ESV; cf. KJV, NKJV, CEV). In other words, it must be eaten in the tabernacle precincts, whereas the other offering of lesser holiness need only be eaten in a ceremonially clean place, as stated in Leviticus 10:12–18. Compare Leviticus 6:17–18; 8:31; 10:12–13; 22:14–15; 24:9.

18:11 *wave offerings.* These are fellowship offerings (see Lev. 7:28–36). These offerings and firstfruits (vv. 12–13) are less holy. The wave offering can be eaten by the whole household, including daughters of priests as well as their sons, as previously stated in Leviticus 10:14, a text that further specifies that it must be eaten in a ceremonially clean place.

18:13 *firstfruits.* "Firstfruits" (*bikkurim*) denotes a token portion of produce given to God as an expression of gratitude at the beginning of the harvest season. Firstfruits are not highly holy. They can be eaten by any member of the priestly household, male or female, slave or free, as long as the person is ceremonially clean.

18:14 *devoted.* Something "devoted" (*herem*) is dedicated to God. In Israelite holy war things devoted are dedicated to God for destruction in the case of livestock and goods, while precious metals that are devoted in holy war go to the sanctuary (see Josh. 6:17–19). Peacetime *herem* as a penalty declared by courts requires execution of the person devoted (see Lev. 27:29), but here the firstborn are devoted in a less destructive way, not as a judicial penalty. God demands that the firstborn males be presented to him when they are a month old by virtue of the fact that he had redeemed the firstborn when Israel was in Egypt (Exod. 13:2, 12–15). Since human sacrifice is forbidden to Israel and unclean animals (such as a donkey) cannot be offered on the altar, provision is made to pay five shekels as a ransom substitute for sacrificing them. Exodus 13:13 also gives the option of breaking the firstborn donkey's neck. Redemption money would have provided hard cash for the sanctuary operations. But the firstborn male of an ox, sheep, or goat would actually be sacrificed, with the meat given over to the priests like the wave offering (see v. 11).

18:19 *everlasting covenant of salt.* Salt is a symbol of perpetuity. See comments at Leviticus 2:11–13.

- Tithes and offerings are to be treated as holy.
- God is his servant's inheritance.
- Ministers should also "tithe."

18:20–24 Aaron is now told the theological basis for Israel's system of supporting the priests (see "Theological Insights" below). In verses 21–24 God continues his address to Aaron as leader of the Levites.

18:21 *tithes*. A "tithe" (*ma'aser*), literally a "tenth part," refers to a tenth part of the harvest or other earnings or its monetary equivalent given to God (see Lev. 27:30–34). Priests live on Israel's gifts and offerings, but Levites, who as a gift to the priests (Num. 18:6) do the maintenance work of dismantling, transporting, and assembling the tabernacle, live on Israel's tithes (vv. 21, 24). Levites, like the priests, receive no inheritance in the land (v. 23c; see v. 20), but they can go near the tent of meeting without threat of instant death (vv. 21–22).

18:23 *bear the responsibility*. Literally "bear their iniquity" (ESV, NASB). Levites do not bear iniquity for their own offenses (contra NRSV), but they bear Israel's iniquity should the Levites be negligent and allow any encroachments against the sanctuary. In that case, they can be the objects of divine wrath. The tithe is compensation for the danger of divine wrath to which Levites regularly expose themselves by working around the tabernacle.

18:25–32 God now addresses Moses instead of Aaron (cf. vv. 1, 8, 20).

18:29 *the best and holiest part*. The Levites are to tithe to the priests the best and

> The tithe the Levites receive from the Israelites includes grain from the threshing floor or juice from the winepress. The Levites then give the best tenth to the priests. The Egyptian harvesting scene shown here depicts workers bringing grain to the threshing floor. The hooves of oxen or a threshing sledge they pulled would release the grain from its stalk. This tomb painting is from Thebes (ca. 1550–1069 BC).

holiest part of the tithe they receive from the Israelites. Thus the lesser "clergy" (Levites) tithe to the more important clergy (priests). By giving the best and the holiest parts to the priests, the Levites are excused from eating these tithes in the sanctuary. They can eat them at home or anywhere else without fear of divine punishment (v. 31).

18:32 *you will not defile the holy offerings*. On "defile" (*halal*), see comments at Leviticus 21:9. If Levites desecrate holy tithes by allowing an unclean or unauthorized person to touch them, the Levites themselves come into mortal danger.

Theological Insights

A key theological concept behind Israel's tithe to the Levites is found in Numbers 18:20: "You will have no inheritance in their land, nor will you have any share among them; I am your share and your inheritance among the Israelites."

The priests and Levites have no inheritance of land of their own. But the priests have the best inheritance of all: God himself.

In compensation for not receiving a portion in the promised land, priests have as their special inheritance Yahweh, who in turn supports them through commanding the tithes and offerings. The priests thus must learn to depend on God rather than the land.[1]

In a sense, what was true of the Levites is true of Christians. Ultimately, we have no permanent inheritance in this world but rather are like foreigners and strangers here (Heb. 11:13). Our ultimate inheritance is Christ himself.

Teaching the Text

The Levites lived on the tithes of the other tribes, and the Aaronites lived on the tithes of the Levites. The following table shows how the system of tithing worked.

Portions Received by Priests	Portion Received by the Levites
1. Portions of "most holy" grain, sin, and guilt offerings (Num. 18:8–10)	1. The tithe of the Israelites (Num. 18:21, 24, 26, 28)
2. Breast and thigh of somewhat "holy" wave (fellowship) offerings (Num. 18:11, 18)	
3. Somewhat "holy" firstfruits of olive oil, wine, and grain (Num. 18:12–13)	
4. Five shekels of cash (redemption) for each firstborn son and firstborn unclean animal (Num. 18:14–16)	
5. Meat from somewhat "holy" firstborn oxen, sheep, and goats (Num. 18:17–19)	
6. A tithe of the best and holiest part of Israel's tithe to the Levites (Num. 18:25–32)	

There are several lessons in Numbers 18:8–32 about giving for God.

1. *Tithes and offerings are to be treated as holy.* Things given over to the priests and Levites are to varying degrees regarded as holy: some offerings are "most holy" (vv. 8–10), while others are less so but still require ceremonial cleanness to partake of them (vv. 11–13). The Levites' tithe is no doubt itself somewhat holy, but they are to tithe to the priests the "best and holiest" part of their tithe (v. 29).

It remains true today that what we give over to God is by definition "holy." Anything given to God today should therefore be treated with the respect becoming holiness. To embezzle the contributions to the church is an especially impious sacrilege against what is holy. But if we withhold that which should be given to God, that too is an offense against holiness. On the other hand, gifts to God treated and used appropriately to support the ministry of the gospel are a "fragrant offering, an acceptable sacrifice, pleasing to God" (Phil. 4:18).

2. *God is his servant's inheritance.* The priests and the Levites do not receive an inheritance of land in the promised land. Rather, God himself—including the ability to serve God in the tabernacle in the presence of God—is to be the priests' inheritance (v. 20). The Levites share in the Aaronites' inheritance in God (v. 24), and the offerings provide rations for both Aaronites and other Levites to eat (vv. 8, 11, 14, 19, 21–23). Both the Levites and the Aaronic priests lack a means of self-support, so they are dependent on God through his people providing the tithe for them (vv. 21–23).

Ministers today should see their primary inheritance as the deposit of the gospel that has been entrusted into their care (1 Tim. 6:20; 2 Tim. 1:14). The New Testament does not specifically command Christians to "tithe," but it does indicate that ministers of the gospel should look to God for financial support through the people of God (1 Cor. 9:3–14). Ministers who preach and teach ought to receive "double honor": the honor of respect and the honor of a financial honorarium (1 Tim. 5:17–18). Sometimes this is not possible, so ministers may, like Paul, have to resort to "tentmaking" (Acts 18:3) to support themselves while still engaged in ministry. But when freed from the need to earn a living, ministers, like the priests and Levites of old, can concentrate on God's work. That is why lay leaders of the church have the responsibility of trying to provide their ministers with adequate compensation. But the ministers for their part should not see their salaries as their true treasure. They could see financial support as the practical means of facilitating their ministries. Their real treasure is the word of God that they preach and the work of the kingdom of God that they advance.

3. *Ministers should also "tithe."* The Levites, who are "clergy," also tithe. They tithe to the priests a tenth of the tithe that they themselves have received (v. 25). Indeed, they are to give the "best and holiest" part of their holy tithe to the priests (vv. 29–30). Interestingly, the Levites are threatened with death if they fail to do this. Laypersons are subject to death if they encroach on the holy things (v. 22), but Levites are threatened with death if they refuse to give the best of the tithes to Yahweh (v. 32).

Are ministers today obligated to tithe? Although the analogy is imperfect—ministers are neither priests nor Levites—Numbers 18:25–32 suggests that ministers are not exempt from tithing. Those gifts need not necessarily go back to their own church. The congregation of Israel gave to the Levites, who then gave to the priests; similarly, a minister's offering might go to missionaries, ministries to the poor, or other Christian organizations. By doing this, ministers set a good example for their congregations. It is also an act of worship, showing gratitude to God for his provisions. On the other hand, there is no evidence that the Old Testament priests tithed.

Illustrating the Text

Whatever our convictions about laws concerning tithing, Christians should be more generous.

Informational: According to the Barna Group, few American Christians "tithe" in the sense of actually giving 10 percent or more of their income to their church or other charities. In the years 2000–2007, the number of adults who tithed varied from 5 to 7 percent. Those least likely to tithe are "people under the age of 25, atheists and agnostics, single adults who have never been married, liberals, and downscale adults," less than 1 percent of whom tithe.[2] Conservative, churchgoing Christians do relatively better, with some 12 percent who tithe, but this is nothing to brag about.

One reason why Christians might not tithe is theological: tithing is an Old Testament command rather than a New Testament command. Nevertheless, the principle of generosity to the needy and supporting God's workers in the world is not limited by the covenants. Even if we are not under a tithing "law," the law of love should move us in that direction. The Barna Group's statistics suggest that many of us should be more generous than we currently are.

The gifts we give to God are holy.

News Story: In 2008 Donald Ray Robinson was sentenced to three years in prison for stealing three hundred thousand dollars from Lane Metropolitan Christian Methodist Episcopal Church in Cleveland, Ohio.[3] He illegally mortgaged the parsonage and also drained the money from the church's benevolence funds. It turns out that he had done something similar to a group in Mississippi.

The image of the huckster preacher is embedded in the American psyche by news accounts like this one, and through literary characters such as Sinclair Lewis's fictional evangelist, Elmer Gantry.

The Bible is aware that not every minister is virtuous. Eli's two worthless sons "were treating the LORD's offering with contempt" (1 Sam. 2:17) rather than with the holiness that it deserved. Judas Iscariot stole from Jesus, taking money from the disciples' common purse (John 12:6).

Whatever is given by people to God should be regarded as holy. When it is not treated as such, it brings disgrace not only on the offender but also on the church and on God, in whose name the gift was given. That is why stealing from the tithes of God's people is especially reprehensible.

The Red Heifer

Big Idea *God wants his people to associate with life and disassociate from death.*

Understanding the Text

The Text in Context

Numbers 19 describes a purification ritual initiated by Aaron's son Eleazar, though carried out by laypeople, that involves the ashes of a red cow. This ritual is performed to purify persons ceremonially unclean because of a corpse. This ritual allows a corpse-contaminated layperson to be brought back to a state of purity and so restored to full participation in the religious life of the community.

This passage connects with what has come before in two ways. First, Numbers 19 continues the discussion of the role of priests found in Numbers 17–18. Second, Numbers 19's ritual regarding corpse contamination relates to the earlier narratives involving death. Most immediately, there is the death of the 250 followers of Korah and the death of 14,700 others in the plague that follows (Num. 16:35, 49). The same Eleazar responsible for the first red heifer ritual had been designated to go among the corpses to retrieve the censers of the 250 (Num. 16:39). Many would have been ceremonially contaminated by the corpses of that plague.

This regulation fits into the larger complex of laws of clean and unclean that required anyone contracting uncleanness to avoid that which was holy and to take steps to return to a state of purity lest the sanctuary be defiled (Num. 19:13, 20; cf. Num. 5:2–4; 31:19; Lev. 11–15). Such laws taken together emphasize the holiness of God in contrast with the defilement of human beings. It also parallels Deuteronomy 21:1–10, where the land is defiled by an unsolved murder, and a heifer is also sacrificed to purify the land from the defilement of death. It will later be applied in a case of soldiers and captives returning from war (Num. 31:19–24). Nazirites and priests require separate purification offerings for corpse contamination (see Num. 6:9–12; Ezek. 44:25–27).

Historical and Cultural Background

This law may be related to pagan cults of the dead.[1] The Canaanites and Egyptians felt that the felicity of the dead, and their own blessings from an ongoing relationship with the dead, depended on conducting rituals, such as food offerings, for the deceased. Palestinian archaeology shows evidence of offerings to "feed" the dead and of lamps to "guide" them in tombs of Canaan. Numbers 19, by associating contact with the dead with uncleanness, discourages such practices.

Interpretive Insights

19:2 *Tell the Israelites.* God speaks in the hearing of both Moses and Aaron (v. 1), but the command "tell" in verse 2 is singular for Moses, the prophet and mediator of the laws.

red heifer. Why is a cow rather than a bull specified? Jacob Milgrom speculates that a bull could not be used because that was the purification offering for the high priests (Lev. 4:1–12; 16:11) or the community (Lev. 4:13–21) rather than individual

The ashes from the sacrifice of a red heifer are required to make the water of purification used to cleanse both people and possessions made unclean by a human death. A heifer is a young cow that has not yet borne a calf. This painting from the Tomb of Nebamun (fourteenth century BC) shows that cattle came in many different colors, so a reddish brown cow could be obtained easily from the herd.

Key Themes of Numbers 19:1–22

- God is associated with life, not death.
- God's people must avoid the cult of the dead.
- War is inherently unclean.

Israelites. Red is the color of blood. The Hebrew word *dam* ("blood") probably is cognate to *adamah* ("red"). Perhaps the color anticipates use of blood later (Num. 19:4), symbolically adding more "blood" to the mix.[2] Alternatively, red could anticipate the animal being burned in the reddish fire (Num. 19:5–6).[3]

without defect or blemish and . . . never been under a yoke. This implies a young, healthy animal. The rabbis emphasized the rareness of a totally red cow: "If it had two black or white hairs [growing] from within a single hole, it is invalid" (Mishnah *Parah* 2:5). Certain modern Jews interested in restoring sacrificial worship have attempted to breed pure red cows.[4] However, the text more likely simply requires a common bay or reddish

brown cow in which an occasional black or white hair would make no difference.[5]

19:3 *Eleazar the priest.* Aaron's son rather than Aaron oversees the preparation of the ashes in order to prevent the high priest from contracting uncleanness (see v. 7; Lev. 21:11–12; similarly, Num. 16:39).

outside the camp. This is an area associated with lepers and excrement (Lev. 13:45–46; Deut. 23:12–14).

19:4 *sprinkle it seven times toward . . . the tent of meeting.* Despite the location outside the camp, this sacrifice is a purification offering (see v. 9) made before God, whose presence is at the tabernacle.

19:5 *While he watches.* An assistant completes the cremation of the cow's hide, flesh, blood, and intestines under Eleazar's supervision. Compare Leviticus 4:11–12, 21.

19:6 *cedar wood, hyssop and scarlet wool.* Each of these is used in the ritual purification of the leper (Lev. 14:4). Cedar and scarlet wool are red in color and symbolically add more "blood" to the mix.[6] Hyssop probably is *Origanum syriacum* or marjoram,[7] a small, aromatic bushy plant. Hyssop is used to sprinkle water or blood in other rituals (Exod. 12:22; Lev. 14:6–7). It is included symbolically as an additional purifying agent (cf. Ps. 51:7).

19:7 *wash his clothes and bathe himself . . . but he will be ceremonially unclean till evening.* Both Eleazar and the assistant become ceremonially unclean by preparing the ashes and thus require ritual purification. The carcass of the Day of Atonement sin/purification offering similarly must be burned, and its handler also requires purification before returning to the camp (Lev. 16:27–28). Too much contact with

that which absorbs impurity symbolically transmits impurity.

19:9 *A man who is clean.* The ashes are guarded by laypersons outside the camp, not by priests at the center of the camp. The ashes, being holy, can be handled and stored only by someone ceremonially clean (v. 9a), though, ironically, the handler contracts uncleanness (v. 10a; see vv. 7–8). The ashes can be rendered unusable if touched by a handler in an unclean state, so a ceremonially clean layman administers the ashes (see v. 18). Ashes mixed with water are sprinkled to cleanse both Israelites and foreign sojourners (vv. 9b, 10b), the latter being essentially converts to the Israelite religion who can also celebrate Passover and offer sacrifices (Num. 9:14; 15:14–16, 24–26).

it is for purification from sin. This appears to be a mistranslation (similarly RSV, NASB). Milgrom argues persuasively that it should be rendered "it is a purification offering" (cf. NRSV, REB).[8] The word *hatta't* means both "sin" and "purification offering" (traditionally, "sin offering"). The regular purification offering is described in Leviticus 4. The red heifer can be considered a special type of purification offering used only for corpse impurity. The regular *hatta't* offering is used for purification from sin; it also is used for cleansing from ceremonial uncleanness (see Lev. 12:6–8; 16:15–16). In Numbers 19 no sin is involved; removing a corpse from a tent (Num. 19:14) is not sinful, but it requires "purification."

19:11–13 *seven days.* Uncleanness from a corpse lasts seven days. Purification using the ashes (mixed with water) takes place on the third and seventh days (v. 12). Failure to do this invalidates the process, defiles the tabercle, and makes the person subject to being cut off from Israel (v. 13). On "cut off," see "Additional Insights" following the unit on Leviticus 6:8–7:38.

19:14–16 *in a tent . . . out in the open.* Not only is a person who touches a corpse unclean, but also anyone in the same room with a corpse becomes unclean for seven days (v. 14), and food left in open containers in a corpse's presence is unclean as well (v. 15). It is as if the "vapors" from the corpse contaminate the whole room,[9] though if a container is sealed from the vapors, the food remains clean. Outdoors, where vapors are dispersed, impurity is contracted only by touch, whether the person has been slain in battle or has died of natural causes (v. 16a). Touching bones in a grave or touching a grave itself also conveys uncleanness (v. 16b).

19:17–19 *ashes . . . hyssop . . . wash their clothes and bathe.* Purification requires three stages. First, someone must mix the red heifer's "ashes" (lit., "dust") with "fresh water" (v. 17). Fresh water is literally "living water"—that is, water taken from a flowing spring or stream. Second, a layman who is "clean" must use a branch of "hyssop" (see v. 6) to sprinkle some of the water-and-ash mix on the corpse-contaminated items and persons (v. 18). This is done on the third day and repeated for the people on the seventh day (v. 19a). The purification process ends on the seventh day with the contaminated person bathing and washing his or her clothes, becoming fully clean by that evening (v. 19b).

19:20–22 *those who are unclean . . . The man who sprinkles.* The warning in verse 13

Anyone in contact with a dead body, like the bodies shown here lying in front of their tents after a battle, is unclean for seven days. If someone dies in his or her tent, the tent and any open containers inside it are also unclean for seven days. Ritual cleansing is required using water mixed with the ashes from the red heifer sacrifice. This Assyrian relief is from the North Palace at Nineveh (645–635 BC).

is repeated: failure to follow this ritual defiles the sanctuary, and the offender merits being cut off (v. 20). The man who sprinkles the waters becomes mildly unclean, as if the impurity absorbed by the water and ashes rubs off onto the handler. Thus, he must wash and wait until evening (v. 21). A corpse-contaminated person conveys a mild form of corpse impurity by touch, though only until evening.

Theological Insights

According to the book of Hebrews, purging "uncleanness" through the ashes of the red heifer illustrates the spiritual cleansing of Christian consciences from dead works through the high priestly work of Christ (Heb. 9:13–14). The sacrifice of

Numbers 19:1–22

the heifer and the sacrifice of Christ have several similarities: the heifer is "without blemish" (Num. 19:2), and Christ is also "unblemished" (Heb. 9:14), though Christ is without blemish in the more profound sense of being sinless. Both Christ and the heifer shed their blood: the heifer's blood is sprinkled seven times toward the presence of God at the tent of meeting (Num. 19:4), and the blood of Christ is also offered to God (Heb. 9:14). The sacrifice of the heifer took place "outside the camp" (Num. 19:3), and the sacrifice of Christ is also "outside the camp," specifically outside the gate of Jerusalem (Heb. 13:11–13). Finally, both provide purification of the flesh: the heifer purifies the body of a person defiled by death, and Christ purifies in the more profound sense of cleansing the sinful nature and conscience (Heb. 9:13–14).

Thomas Dozeman suggests a further eschatological symbolism: the purging of death from the camp arguably anticipates the purging of death itself from the coming messianic kingdom.[10] Through Christ's death, death itself has been conquered (1 Cor. 15:54–56), and in the new heaven and earth death and things associated with it will be eliminated (Rev. 21:4).

Teaching the Text

1. *God is associated with life, not death.* One lesson that the purity system conveys symbolically is that Yahweh is the God of life (order) and is separated from that which has to do with death (disorder). Mary Douglas has shown the connection between cleanness/holiness and concepts such as "wholeness," "physical perfection," and "completeness."[11] Physical imperfections (Lev. 21:17–21; 22:20–24), representing a movement from "life" toward "death," move a person ritually away from God, who is to be associated with life. Corpses and carcasses render a person unclean because they have to do with death. Purification rituals symbolize movement from death toward life and accordingly involve blood, the color red, and spring (lit., "living") water, all of which are symbols of life (e.g., Lev. 14:5, 50; 17:11; Num. 19:2, 17). Since God is associated with life, Christians should emphasize that which affirms life, not morbid things.

2. *God's people must avoid the cult of the dead.* Baruch Levine states, "The hidden agenda behind Numbers 19 is the cult of the dead."[12] Israelite popular culture had been influenced by this cult (see "Historical and Cultural Background" above). The Bible, however, condemns making food offerings for the dead (Deut. 26:14) and even sitting among the graves (Isa. 65:4). Ancestor worship, including food offerings to the deceased, is still practiced in some parts of Africa, China, India, and Southeast Asia. Some Christians in those places are tempted to combine their Christianity with their ancestor worship traditions, but this practice goes against biblical teaching.

3. *War is inherently unclean.* Another lesson here is that war, even under Yahweh's command, brings uncleanness. War involves death. Killing defiles the killer and requires God's cleansing. A warrior culture of conquest seems incompatible with the symbolism of God being associated with life, not death. Christians are not to be warmongers.

Illustrating the Text

We are called to cultivate life, not death.

Nature: We learn from the time we are in elementary school that plants love light. The phenomenon of a plant actually growing toward the light is called "phototropism." It is caused when, in response to light, growth-inducing molecules within the stem of a plant actually migrate away from the side of the plant that is facing the light, causing an elongation of those cells, bending the plant toward the light. As Christians, in our own lives and in the things we support with our energy and resources, we should bend toward life. If your context allows, display photographs of plants shaped by phototropism or bring a plant that has grown toward the light, giving it an unusual shape.

God wants people to have abundant life.

Current Issue: Islamic extremists in the twenty-first century have developed their own cult of the dead in their glorification of martyrdom and suicide bombers. This ideology has developed into a slogan: "We love death more than you love life." This slogan undergirds an ideology that, in the name of Islam and God, has slaughtered thousands of innocent men, women, and children, most of whom, ironically, were Muslims. As journalist David Brooks notes, this "death cult is not really about the cause it purports to serve. It's about the sheer pleasure of killing and dying. It's about massacring people while in a state of spiritual loftiness. It's about experiencing the total freedom of barbarism—freedom even from human nature, which says, Love children, and Love life. It's about the joy of sadism and suicide."[13]

Such an attitude is completely alien from the God of the Bible as seen in Numbers 19 and elsewhere. God is to be associated with life, not death. Death defiles. It is not something to be glorified. Even killing for justifiable reasons makes a person unclean, according to the Bible. Unlike the view of these fanatics, the real God never revels in killing and death. He is the God of life who wants people to have abundant life.

Hymn: "All Creatures of Our God and King," by Francis of Assisi. The text of this classic hymn is based on a poem written by Francis of Assisi, a man who demonstrated a great love for God's creation. The words to his song reflect that love. More importantly, they affirm the God-glorifying purpose for which all things have been made.

Those associating with corpses are considered unclean, a practice that discourages the development of a cult of the dead in Israel. This photo shows a typical Egyptian grave site (3400 BC) with the preserved corpse surrounded by grave goods originally buried with it.

Moses's and Aaron's Sin at Meribah

Big Idea *Leaders of God's people are fallible.*

Understanding the Text

The Text in Context

Numbers here skips to the fortieth year after the Israelites left Egypt (see comments at Num. 20:1). Evidently, not much worth mentioning has happened in the intervening years. The Israelites had been condemned to forty years of wilderness wandering when they refused to enter the land of Canaan (Num. 14:33–34). By now, as predicted, most of those persons twenty years of age and older have died in the wilderness. Even the old leadership is dying off: both Miriam and Aaron die in this chapter (Num. 20:1, 28–29).

Dennis Cole sees three cycles of rebellion in Numbers:[1]

> **Rebellion Cycle A** (Num. 10:11–15:41). Rebellions over manna, Moses's marriage, and entering the land.
> **Rebellion Cycle B** (Num. 16:1–19:22). Korah's rebellion followed by teachings meant to squelch further rebellion against Aaron.
> **Rebellion Cycle C** (Num. 20:1–25:18). Rebellions that lead Moses and Aaron

to sin, God to punish the people by sending venomous snakes to bite them, and a rebellion involving idolatry and sexual immorality.

Numbers 20 begins the third rebellion cycle. In between the deaths of Miriam and Aaron is one more rebellion by the old, disobedient generation (see comments on 20:3) as the narrative transitions toward the new, better generation.

Numbers 20:2–13 echoes a similar event nearly forty years earlier in Exodus 17:1–7 before Israel had arrived at Mount Sinai. In both, the people quarrel with Moses over lack of water and express concerns that they and their livestock may die of thirst. In both, they long to be back in Egypt. In both, Moses prays to Yahweh and is commanded to take a staff to a rock. In both, he strikes the rock, after which water comes forth at a place called "Meribah." But here, Moses and Aaron are rebuked for what they do.

Historical and Cultural Background

Water still comes from rocks in the Sinai today. In the desert, rain—what little there is—can seep into the ground and spring forth from cracks at the base of mountain cliffs. On a trip to Mount Sinai (Jebel Musa) in July 1983, I visited a small oasis northeast of Jebel Musa. Water came from a spring at the base of a cliff. The Bedouin had built a basin for catching the water for people and livestock. It was easy to imagine Moses striking such a "rock" to bring forth water.

Interpretive Insights

20:1 *first month*. This is probably the fortieth year since the exodus. Aaron dies in this chapter (Num. 20:28–29), and he is

later said to have died in the "fifth month of the fortieth year after the Israelites came out of Egypt" (Num. 33:38).

Desert of Zin . . . Kadesh. Zin is on the southern border of Canaan and transitions into the Desert of Paran around Kadesh, which is an oasis also called "Kadesh Barnea" (Num. 32:8). Scouts had been sent from Kadesh into Zin to explore the land (Num. 13:21, 26).

Miriam. Concerning her rebellion, see Numbers 12:1–16. She is a prophet (Exod. 15:20) and, with her brothers Moses and Aaron, a leader of Israel (Mic. 6:4).

20:2 *there was no water*. Lack of drinking water (cf. v. 5) is the immediate threat to the people's lives and to those of their livestock (v. 4b), causing this dispute.

20:3 *If only we had died when our brothers fell dead*. "Brothers" cannot refer to their ancestors at the beginning of the journey, since ancestors would be called "fathers," not "brothers."[2] It may denote the 14,700 influenced by Korah who had died in a plague some years before (Num. 16:46–50) or, more generally,

The Israelites grumble about the lack of water when they arrive at Kadesh in the Desert of Zin. God once again provides water from an outcrop of rock. The Nahal Zin is a dry wadi (streambed) that runs through the Negev, which borders the Wilderness of Zin. Water seeping through canyon rock layers produces a water supply, even in the heat of summer. In this photo, showing part of the Ein Avdat canyon, water runs out of the rocks into the pool below. Even if the source of the water may have a natural explanation, there is no doubt that God met the Israelites' need.

to the contemporaries of these spokesmen, nearly all of whom had already perished in the desert over the last four decades.[3] The spokesmen for these grumblers would then represent the last remnant of the first generation who remained unrepentant in their complaining.

20:4 *Why did you bring the LORD's community . . . ?* The verb in Hebrew is plural, addressing both Moses and Aaron. The rabble unfairly question their motives and/or competence.

20:5 *terrible place.* Or "evil place" (ESV, KJV).

no grain or figs, grapevines or pomegranates. A steady diet of just manna contributes to their discontent (cf. Num. 11:5).

20:6 *fell facedown.* This shows the earnest humility of Moses's and Aaron's prayers.

glory of the LORD. This refers to the visible manifestation of God through a fire cloud (see Exod. 16:10; 40:34–35; Num. 9:15; 14:10; 16:42).

20:8 *Speak to that rock.* Moses and Aaron are to issue a command that the rock give water for Israel and its livestock.

20:9 *Moses took the staff.* Which staff was it: Moses's or Aaron's (cf. v. 8)? I believe that the staff taken by Moses is both Aaron's staff that had blossomed and Moses's staff by which Moses performed his miracles. Moses was to take the staff "from the LORD's presence," but a few chapters earlier Aaron's staff is said to be stored before God in the tabernacle (Num. 17:6–11). Moreover, Aaron's staff is said to be "a sign to the rebellious" (Num. 17:10), so bringing it to the confrontation with the complainers would convey an appropriate symbolic rebuke. Carrying

Aaron's staff would also symbolize that both these leaders are united in purpose against the rebels.[4] It is Aaron's staff that had turned into a snake (Exod. 7:7–12), and Aaron's staff had been used in turning the Nile into blood (Exod. 7:19–20). But Aaron's staff that became a snake had been in fact the staff given by God to Moses (Exod. 4:1–4, 17), also known as "the staff of God" (Exod. 4:20; 17:9). The staff used by Moses in Exodus 17:1–7 is called "the staff with which you struck the Nile" (Exod. 17:5), but the staff used to strike the Nile is called "your [Aaron's] staff" in Exodus 7:19. Aaron also had used this staff in the plagues of the frogs and of the gnats (Exod. 8:5, 16–17). Thus, in Exodus Moses's staff and Aaron's staff are one and the same. If this carries over into Numbers, then the staff that had blossomed and came to be stored at the tabernacle (Num. 17) is also that same staff. It is then brought out by Moses in Numbers 20:1–13 as a symbol of divine power and authority and is shown as a rebuke to the rebels.

20:10 *rock.* This term (*sela'*) refers here to a cliff or outcrop of rock rather than a boulder (see "Historical and Cultural Background" above).

rebels. This term (*morim*) comes from a root that denotes a "deliberate, willful decision to disobey."[5] The blossoming of Aaron's staff is meant to be a sign for such rebels (Num. 17:10), which is why that staff is brought on this occasion. Ironically, Aaron rebels (Num. 20:24) in conjunction with using a symbol against rebellion.

must we bring you water out of this rock? The "we" is a dreadful gaffe that contributes to God's condemnation of Moses and Aaron (see v. 12).

20:11 *struck the rock twice.* The double striking of the rock reflects Moses's anger and perhaps his unbelief (see v. 12).

20:12 *you did not trust in me.* Lack of faith may be indicated in Moses's hitting the rock not once but "twice" (v. 11), suggesting doubt about whether God will come through.

to honor me as holy. The way Moses and Aaron speak in verse 10 ("Must we bring you water out of this rock?") dishonors God by glorifying themselves. They speak as if they were Egyptian magicians performing miracles by their own powers, when instead they should have ascribed the miracle to God. Such robbing God of his glory deserves severe punishment. They also disobey God's command (cf. Num. 20:24): they have been told to assemble the congregation and address the rock; instead, Moses addresses the people and strikes the rock. For these offenses, Moses and Aaron are punished with exclusion from the land. Aaron dies in this chapter (Num. 20:28–29), and Moses dies later, before the conquest (Deut. 34).

20:13 *Meribah.* This oasis came to be called Meribah ("strife/quarreling") because the "Israelites quarreled with the LORD there." It is elsewhere called "Meribah Kadesh" (Num. 27:14; Deut. 32:51) to distinguish this site near Kadesh from the site named Meribah (also called "Massah") after an earlier quarrel at Rephidim in the Desert of Sin (Exod. 17:1–7).

proved holy. God shows himself to be holy by displaying his unsurpassed power and by expressing judgment even against his own leaders who fail to meet his high standards.

Moses "struck the rock twice with his staff. Water gushed out" (20:11). This illumination from the Northern French Miscellany (AD 1277–86) depicts the scene.

Theological Insights

Numbers 20:1–13 shows that leaders of God's people are not perfect. Even the best of leaders are still sinners who, like Aaron, Miriam, and Moses, can become guilty of unbelief, idolatry, envy, angry outbursts, rebellion, or disobedience. Sometimes their people provoke them to these sins. Even so, God holds them accountable. Offenses that seem to be minor from a human perspective can be major in God's eyes, especially when his leaders commit them.

Christian leaders can, of course, also sin. The apostle Paul worries that he might become disqualified from receiving his full prize by some bad behavior (1 Cor. 9:27). Cephas (Peter) is rebuked by Paul for shunning gentile Christians and not treating them as full siblings in Christ (Gal. 2:11–18). Apollos needs correction for his inaccurate doctrinal teaching (Acts 18:24–26). The apostle John includes himself with the "we" who sin but have an advocate in Christ

(1 John 2:1). Even spiritual leaders must take heed: "If you think you are standing firm, be careful that you don't fall!" (1 Cor. 10:12).

Teaching the Text

Even mature spiritual leaders can fall into sin. Miriam and her brothers Moses and Aaron are regarded as the leaders of Israel (Mic. 6:4). But Miriam's last recorded actions show her to be envious of Moses, and she is punished with temporary "leprosy" (Num. 12). The juxtaposition of her death with the account of Moses's and Aaron's sin suggests a connection between her sin and her not entering the land. In any case, her reputation is marred. Not only does Aaron join with Miriam in rebellion against Moses (Num. 12), but also he had helped the people in the idolatry of the golden calf (Exod. 32:1–5, 21–22). His sin at the waters of Meribah in Numbers 20:2–13 is the last straw: Aaron will not enter the land (cf. Num. 20:24).

Not even Moses is immune from sin. At Meribah Moses too is excluded from the land because he disobeys God's command, shows unbelief, and robs God of his glory (see comments at Num. 20:12; see also Deut. 32:50–52).

Psalm 106:32–33 provides commentary on this incident: "By the waters of Meribah they angered the LORD, and trouble came to Moses because of them; for they rebelled against the Spirit of God, and rash words came from Moses' lips."

There is a lesson here for us: we are never too old to mess up. Even if we are godly, mature leaders in the church, we can fall into sin. Like Moses, we might choose to disobey God's word. Or we might substitute for God's word what we would have liked God to have said. We might betray God by our unbelief. Or in pride we could give the glory to ourselves rather than to God. What Moses did might seem to us a minor rebellion, but God demands complete obedience, especially from spiritual leaders. A leader's bad example might encourage the people to be lax in their obedience to God's commands as well. So God made an example of Moses, Aaron, and Miriam. And if we are ethically and spiritually lax, we too may forfeit our blessings or ministries.

Illustrating the Text

Sadly, there are many examples of leaders falling prey to sin.

News: Moses and Aaron are not the only leaders of God's people who have had their ministries marred by sin. There are many modern examples. Here are a few.

Some years ago a president of Inter-Varsity Christian Fellowship had to resign from that position when he admitted to having an adulterous affair. In 1988 a well-known television evangelist was accused of spending time at a motel with a prostitute, which led to the revocation of his standing as a licensed minister. In 2006 a leader of the National Association of Evangelicals (NAE) admitted to having had a massage from a male prostitute from whom he also purchased methamphetamine. This led to his leaving his pastorate and resigning as leader of the NAE. In 1989 a famous television preacher went to prison for fraud.

The sins recounted above are the kinds that make for public scandal. But other sins of Christian leaders can be subtler and would not necessarily draw the attention of either law enforcement or their congregations. Moses's and Aaron's sin at Meribah was so subtle that many readers at first glance tend to say, "Huh?" when God condemns it. It was not immediately obvious what they had done wrong. And yet their sin so displeased God that they forfeited entrance into the land. So it is not merely the openly scandalous sins that can have an ill effect on Christian ministry. The subtler sins of Christian leaders can also limit God's blessings.

Our example can have a powerful impact.

Testimony: Allow your congregation to hear firsthand how people's lives are directly influenced by leaders. Consider three options:

1. Share a personal testimony, recalling a moment in your life when a teacher, coach, parent, or mentor said or did something that affected the trajectory of your life.
2. Interview one or two people during your sermon, inviting them to answer a few questions that will highlight how they have been impacted by a leader.
3. If your ministry context allows, record a video testimony from someone who shares the impact a leader had on his or her life. Consider the possibility of having pictures or even a small video segment with the leader as well.

A Failure of Leadership

Big Idea *Leaders' plans fail and leaders die, but God's work goes on.*

Understanding the Text

The Text in Context

Three things form obstacles to the goal of progress toward the promised land in Numbers 20: death, rebellion, and opposition. Numbers 20:1–13 shows that not only are there still voices of discontent and rebellion against Moses and Aaron, but also that Moses and Aaron themselves are not immune to falling into sin. As a result of their sin, they are told that neither of them will live to enter the land of promise.

Numbers 20:14–29 records the initial fulfillment of that pronouncement. The high priest Aaron dies at the end of this chapter (Num. 20:28–29), just as his sister has died at its beginning (Num. 20:1). A new leadership begins to appear as Eleazar replaces his father as high priest. Later, Joshua will be designated to replace Moses (see Num. 27:22–23). Before the death of Aaron, Moses confronts another problem: Israel's brother nation Edom is unwilling to permit Israel to pass through its territory on the way to Canaan (Num. 20:14–21).

But despite death, rebellion, and opposition, progress is made toward going to the land of promise. Israel regroups at Kadesh (Num. 20:1) and then travels to Mount Hor on the border of Edom (Num. 20:22). Along the way, God provides the people with water (Num. 20:11), and Eleazar is appointed as the new high priest (Num. 20:22–28). Thus, a new chapter of leadership for a new generation begins to unfold. Israel at long last has resumed its march toward Canaan.

Historical and Cultural Background

The Edomites who here refuse to let Israel pass through their territory are the descendants of Esau (Gen. 36:1, 5), the son of Isaac and twin brother of Jacob (Gen. 25:24–25). They were generally located south of the Zered River, south and east of the Dead Sea.

As Israel's "brother" nation, Edom holds a privileged place despite its refusal to let Israel pass through its territory in the time of Moses. The Israelites are told to be careful not to provoke the Edomites when they skirt Edom's territory (Deut. 2:3–8). God commands Israel not to despise an Edomite, since the Edomites are related to them (Deut. 23:7). Edomites can become full Israelite citizens after three generations (Deut. 23:8).

Interpretive Insights

20:14–21 These verses narrate Edom's refusal to let Israel pass through. This time Israel plans to enter Canaan not from the south but from the east, crossing the Jordan River across from Jericho. The shortest route to the territory opposite Jericho from Kadesh passes through Edom. Moses thus sends messages to request permission to pass through Edom's territory. But Edom refuses and threatens to attack Israel if it tries to pass through.

20:14 *your brother Israel*. Edom's patriarch is Esau (Gen. 36:9), the twin brother of Jacob (Gen. 25:25–26). Jacob is also known as "Israel" (Gen. 32:28), and he is the patriarch of the twelve tribes of Israel. Thus, Israel and Edom are "brother" nations.

You know about all the hardships that have come on us. Like a personal letter from a relative not seen in years, the message to Edom in Numbers 20:15–16a recounts the exodus story—Israel's long sojourn in Egypt, Egypt's oppression of Israel, Yahweh's deliverance of Israel out of Egypt in answer to Israel's prayers—to update personified Edom on its

Key Themes of Numbers 20:14–29

- Leaders of God's people can make plans that fail to work out.
- Leaders of God's people die, but God's work goes on.

"brother" nation Israel. The real purpose is to elicit sympathy before requesting passage through Edom's territory,[1] and perhaps also to evoke fear of Israel's assisting "angel."[2]

20:16 *the LORD . . . sent an angel*. This is a manifestation of divine power associated with the pillar of cloud/fire that usually precedes Israel and in the exodus serves as its rearguard against Pharaoh's chariots (Exod. 14:19). More specifically, it probably refers to God himself as manifested in the fire/cloud. The burning bush is called

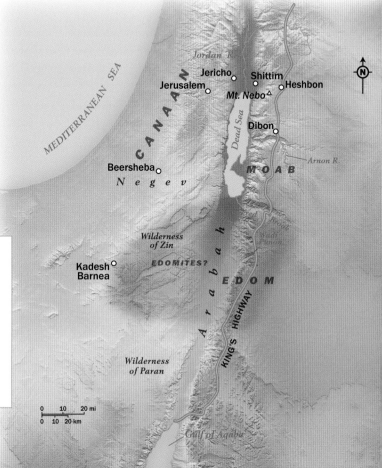

God's "angel" in Exodus 3:2. God's angel is to bring the Israelites to the land of Canaan and help them drive out its inhabitants (Exod. 23:20, 23; 32:34; 33:2).

Kadesh. Kadesh, also called Kadesh Barnea (Num. 32:8), is about fifty miles from traditional Edom, making its description as being on the edge of Edom's territory appear hyperbolic. If at that time some Edomites had come to live west of the Arabah rift valley as they did later in Edomite history, Kadesh could be literally on the edge of Edom's territory. Gordon Wenham solves the problem by suggesting that another Kadesh on Edom's border is in mind.[3] The formal request is for Israel to pass through Edom along the King's Highway (see map), the main north–south road through Edom. Moses promises the Edomites that Israel will not forage their fields or vineyards for food or drink their precious well water. But Edom refuses and threatens to attack Israel militarily if it tries to pass through.

20:19 *The Israelites replied.* A second correspondence tries to allay Edom's fears by promising to come on foot (not warhorse), to stick close to the road, and to pay for any water that the Israelites or their livestock drink from streams along the way. But Edom refuses for a second time and follows that up by dispatching its army to guard Edom's border against Israel's entry (v. 20). Because Israel does not want to fight its "brother" nation, Israel turns away from Edom, purposing to go around it instead.

20:22–29 These verses narrate the death of Aaron. Miriam dies at the beginning of this chapter (Num. 20:1). Another milestone of the end of the first generation of Israel after leaving Egypt is Aaron's death. Aaron dies in the "fifth month of the fortieth year after the Israelites came out of Egypt" at 123 years of age (Num. 33:38–39), which appears to be about four months after Miriam has died (see comments at Num. 20:1). As God has predicted, Aaron dies before leading the people to the promised land (Num. 20:12).

20:22 *Mount Hor.* The location of Mount Hor is uncertain, except that it is "near the border of Edom" (v. 23 [though see comments at Num. 33:37–39]).

20:24 *because both of you rebelled . . . at the waters of Meribah.* Neither Aaron nor Moses can enter the promised land because they have provoked God's anger by rebelling against his command at Meribah Kadesh (see Num. 20:2–13).

gathered to his people. This expression (cf. v. 26) in some contexts denotes being placed in a family tomb (e.g., Abraham buried with Sarah [Gen. 25:7–10]). But since there is no family tomb at Mount Hor, the expression here probably refers to Aaron's joining his ancestors in the afterlife.[4]

20:25 *Get Aaron and his son Eleazar and take them up Mount Hor.* Aaron is taken up Mount Hor in part to keep the uncleanness of his death away from the holy tabernacle.

20:28 *Moses removed Aaron's garments and put them on his son Eleazar.* Aaron's son Eleazar is given Aaron's high priestly garb to symbolize that he is succeeding his father. When Eleazar descends from the mountain wearing Aaron's robes, this indicates to the public that Aaron is dead and Eleazar is the new high priest.

20:29 *mourned for him thirty days.* Aaron's death is mourned for an unusually long period of thirty days, as would later be done for Moses (Deut. 34:8). This is done out of special respect for him and his office. Formal mourning periods in Israel more typically were seven days, as after the deaths of Jacob (Gen. 50:10) and of Saul (1 Sam. 31:13).

Theological Insights

In order for God's work to go on, God must pass on to new generations the responsibilities of leading his people. God hands Aaron's role over to Aaron's son Eleazar (Num. 20:22–29). Moses's role is assumed at God's direction by Joshua (Num. 27:12–22; Josh. 1:1–5). Happily, God provides new leadership for his people in each successive generation: an Elisha for Elijah (2 Kings 2:13–14), a Timothy for Paul, and the like. Otherwise, God's work would die out.

Moses removes Aaron's high priestly robes and places them on Aaron's son Eleazar. Described in detail in Exodus 28, Aaron's clothing includes a breastpiece with twelve precious stones engraved with the names of the sons of Israel. This reproduction of the breastpiece of the high priest is from the life-size tabernacle model at Timna, Israel.

Teaching the Text

1. *Leaders of God's people can make plans that fail to work out.* Even when leaders of God's people do not sin, they can still fail. An example of failure is when Moses sends a polite message to Edom requesting that it allow Israel to pass through Edom's territory (Num. 20:14–21). Moses could have hoped for a positive response from the nation descended from Jacob's twin brother, Esau. Edom is Israel's "brother" nation, more closely related to Israel ethnically than any other nation. That is why the first message to Edom is so much like a letter from a long-lost relative. But Edom's response is a flat no. Moses, however, continues in the request, trying to reason with the Edomites. He promises to pay for any resources that

Israel uses while passing through. But the response this time is a no accompanied by a large army dispatched from Edom to block any attempt by Israel to cross their border. Thus, Moses's attempt at diplomacy is a complete failure.

Why does Moses's plan fail? Is it because Moses does not ask God before making his plan? The text does not say that he prays before sending the letter. But arguments from silence are weak. Neither does the text rebuke Moses for failure to pray over this matter before sending the messengers. Is the failure of Moses's plan a consequence of his sin earlier in the chapter? That too is possible, but not clear. What we do know is that a very plausible plan by a godly leader of God's people falls flat. It seemed to have a good chance of success when it is devised, but when executed, it fails miserably. Ultimately, Moses must abandon his plan and come up with another. The new plan is much more inconvenient for Israel than Moses's original plan. It is to turn away from Edom and go around it (Num. 20:23; 21:4).

Just as Moses's plan to pass through Edom failed, so our plans, or those of our spiritual leaders, often fail as well. It may or may not have to do with any sin or failing on our part. It may result from our finite human wisdom. But if our plans fail, we should not spend a lot of time wallowing in the disappointment. Rather, we must regroup and try, with God's help, to devise new plans to accomplish God's purposes for his people.

2. *Leaders of God's people die, but God's work goes on.* Another way in which God's leaders fail has to do with their mortality. Quite simply, God's leaders die. In Numbers 20 two of Israel's three most prominent leaders die within five months of each other: Miriam and Aaron. Furthermore, Moses is again reminded that he too will die without leading Israel into the promised land to conquer Canaan (Num. 20:24; see 20:12).

But although leaders are mortal, God's work goes on. In this case Aaron's high-priestly role is assumed by his son Eleazar. This is dramatized and symbolized by the transfer of Aaron's priestly garments to Eleazar. When Eleazar descends Mount Hor wearing his father's robes, it indicates to the people that Aaron is dead and they have a new high priest.

When a really important godly leader dies, we may be tempted to despair. Who could replace such a great person? Sometimes there does not seem to be anyone of similar stature waiting in the wings to replace the leader who has passed. But we

need not be dismayed. New generations of leaders can and should take God's people where previous generations of leaders were unable to go. Moses and Aaron, as great as they were, were unable to give the people their allotment in the land of promise. Their replacements, Joshua and Eleazar, did (Josh. 14:1).

Illustrating the Text

Spiritual leaders die.

Personal Story: Three of my heroes of faith as a young Christian were the evangelist Billy Graham, the apologist Francis Schaeffer, and the British pastor and thinker John R. W. Stott. As I write these words, only Billy Graham is still alive, and he is suffering from failing health and is no longer active in ministry.

Church history records how great Christian leaders come and go. Many were and remain famous. Some are forgotten except among church historians. But God continues to raise up new leaders for each new generation. Just as Eleazar succeeded his father, Aaron, in the ministry of priesthood, so God raises up new leaders for each generation so that the work and mission of the church can go on.

Leaders die, but their work lives on.

Biography: The great civil rights leader Rev. Martin Luther King Jr. was a controversial figure who lived under constant death threats from those who opposed what he was doing.

Toward the end of his life, he could see that the tide of public opinion was turning in his direction. The trajectory of history seemed to guarantee that blacks would win the kinds of rights that King had been fighting for, though he had an ominous premonition that he would not live to see this fully achieved. This presentiment is reflected in his "I've Been to the Mountaintop" speech, delivered April 3, 1968.[5] In that speech he said,

> And then I got into Memphis. And some began to say the threats, or talk about the threats that were out. What would happen to me from some of our sick white brothers?
>
> Well, I don't know what will happen now. We've got some difficult days ahead. But it really doesn't matter with me now, because I've been to the mountaintop. And I don't mind.
>
> Like anybody, I would like to live a long life. Longevity has its place. But I'm not concerned about that now. I just want to do God's will. And He's allowed me to go up to the mountain. And I've looked over. And I've seen the Promised Land. I may not get there with you. But I want you to know tonight, that we, as a people, will get to the Promised Land!

King's premonitions were right. He did not get there with them. He never saw the full fruits of his civil rights movement. On April 4, 1968, the day after King preached these words, his life was ended by an assassin's bullet in Memphis, Tennessee.

King did not get to the "promised land" of civil rights for blacks, but the next generation did get there. Jim Crow laws were abolished. Over time blacks were widely elected to public office, and the black middle class made significant advances in many occupations. And something unthinkable in 1968 happened forty years later in 2008: the United States elected Barack Obama, the son of a black Kenyan, as president of the United States. Christian leaders may fail to reach their goals in their lifetimes, but God can work into the next generations and ensure that the work of older leaders has not been done in vain.

Victory and Serpents

Big Idea *God helps his people overcome enemies and their own mistakes.*

Understanding the Text

The Text in Context

Most of the narratives up until now in Numbers are of a negative tone, filled with rebellion and sin and death. These events include the rebellion and sin of the leaders Moses and Aaron (Num. 20:2–13) and the deaths of Miriam and Aaron (Num. 21:1, 22–29). But as the old generation disappears, the tone of the narratives becomes increasingly positive.

Numbers 21:1–9 shows progress, regress, and progress. The people are on the move, going around Edom (Num. 21:4), which has refused them passage (Num. 20:21–23), and will soon pass through Moab (Num. 21:10–20). There is a victory at Hormah, a place where the old, disobedient generation had been routed (Num. 14:45). But then there is one last rebellion that leads God to send vipers among them. But even this is mitigated by the people's expressions of remorse and repentance. Thus, this section represents movement both physically and spiritually toward the promised land.

As Dennis Olson points out, this section displays a new pattern that foreshadows Israel's later conquests.[1]

1. Israel encounters an enemy, often the aggressor.
2. Israel vows to dedicate all the booty to God if God gives it victory. This is the practice of holy war. What is done here voluntarily later becomes God's command (Deut. 7:2; 13:15; 20:17).
3. God accepts Israel's vow and delivers it victory over its enemy.
4. Israel dedicates everything to God, either by destruction or by giving it to the priests (Num. 18:14).

Historical and Cultural Background

A snake on a stick (Num. 21:9) was a symbol of healing elsewhere in the ancient world. Asclepius, the Greek god of healing, carried a rod with a snake on it, a symbol adopted in modern times by the American Medical Association. The cobra on Pharaoh's headdress (the Uraeus, symbol of the goddess Wadjet) symbolized that Pharaoh was protected from his enemies. Moses's snake similarly may have symbolized God's protection.

Some Canaanites worshiped snakes. A five-inch-long copper serpent dating to the thirteenth or twelfth century BC was found in a temple at Timna in southern

Israel, perhaps representing a Midianite snake-god. At Hazor a standard dating to the fourteenth century BC was found with a snake at the top.[2] Moses's bronze snake came to be worshiped too. It was preserved to memorialize this incident and came to be called "Nehushtan," which in Hebrew is similar to both the word for "snake" and the word for "bronze." But by the 700s BC, Nehushtan became the source of idolatry when people began offering incense to it, for which reason Hezekiah had it destroyed (2 Kings 18:4).

Austen Henry Layard's excavations at Nimrud around 1850 discovered eighth-century BC bronze bowls with West Semitic Hebrew–sounding names designating their owners. One of these depicts a winged serpent on a pole. This bowl may have belonged to a Hebrew and might portray the Nehushtan scene, though alternatively it may portray Eshmun, the Phoenician god of healing.[3]

Interpretive Insights

21:1 *Negev.* The Negev, inappropriately rendered "the South" in some versions (KJV, NKJV), is an arid region south of Beersheba.

21:3 *completely destroyed.* The word *haram* means more precisely "to dedicate [to God] for destruction." Israel's vow is the first introduction of a concept ultimately commanded for all the Canaanites (see Deut. 7:2; 13:15; 20:17; Josh. 6:18, 21).

Hormah. This name, meaning "destruction," is related to the verb *haram.* The city of Hormah,

Key Themes of Numbers 21:1–9

- Victory brings reflection on what could have been.
- A change of heart allows healing.

controlled by the Canaanite king of Arad, was north and east from Kadesh in southern Canaan, though its exact location is uncertain. Hormah was not identical with Arad, since later Hormah and Arad have different kings (Josh. 12:14). Moses perhaps is contemplating going directly north into Canaan from there. At Hormah the old generation had suffered defeat thirty-eight years earlier (Num. 14:45). Now it is the site where the new generation of Israel has its first victory in Canaan. Hormah is reoccupied shortly after Israel destroys it, so Joshua must defeat its king again. Indeed Hormah, called "Zephath" by the Canaanites, is not fully subdued until after the death of Joshua (Judg. 1:17).

21:4–5 *along the route to the Red Sea . . . around Edom.* Probably for tactical reasons, Israel prefers invading Canaan from the plains of Moab east of Jericho to invading Canaan from the south. Not wanting to fight its "brother" nation Edom (see Num. 20:14–21), Israel is forced to backtrack south along the route to the Red Sea to circumvent Edom via desert regions to Edom's south and east (v. 4a), "a detour through more than 175 miles of rather imposing landscape."[4]

grew impatient on the way . . . spoke against. Hardships again

In the ancient world, snakes were considered to have healing or protective powers. In some cultures serpents were worshiped as deities. This bronze serpent with a gilded head was found in a Midianite shrine at Timna, Israel.

lead the people to be impatient and to grumble against God and Moses, for the two are closely associated. "On the way" could be rendered "because of the journey" (cf. NASB, KJV), explaining why the people grumble.

21:6 *the LORD sent . . . venomous snakes.* The Hebrew verbal form (Piel) behind "sent" implies that God punishes the people this way repeatedly. The Hebrew word behind "venomous snakes" ("poisonous" [NRSV]), *sarap*, is from a root meaning "to burn"; hence the traditional rendering is "fiery serpents" (KJV, ESV, NASB). It denotes venomous serpents in Isaiah 14:29 and refers to angelic *serapim* ("seraphs") in Isaiah 6:2 that protect the throne of God. Angelic seraphs have either a fire-like or a snake-like appearance. "Fiery" could also be a reference to the snake's color, like the copper/bronze snake that Moses puts on a stick (see v. 9); or "fiery" may refer to the painful, burning sensation of its venom; or it may indicate the reddish inflammation of the bite wounds.[5] The snakes may have been of the genus *Echis*.[6] The carpet viper (*Echis coloratus*) is a small but aggressive animal with an extremely virulent, hemotoxic venom. The species is bronze in color and is native to the Sinai, Arabia, Jordan, Israel, and Syria. Other suggestions include the puff adder or the sand viper.

21:7 *We sinned.* Unlike the old generation, the Israelites of the new generation admit their guilt and ask Moses to pray for them.

21:8–9 *Make a snake . . . look at it . . . looked at the bronze snake.* God's remedy involves a bronze/copper model of the viper put on a pole. Verse 8 uses the common verb for "look," but "looked" in verse 9 (*nabat*)

has more the sense of "gaze at," implying that more than a casual glimpse is required for this to be effective: it requires an act of the will.[7] Bronze may have been chosen to imitate the color of the snakes (see above) and/or because in Hebrew "snake" (*nahash*) and "bronze" (*neḥoshet*), though from different homophonic roots, are similar in sound. It is ironic that the image of a snake can undo the damage done by a snake, though ancient Mesopotamians believed that apotropaic amulets worked that way, using the image of something (e.g., a demon) as a deterrent to being plagued by that same thing.[8] Though scientifically sound, it is likewise ironic that production of modern antivenom starts by using a snake's venom.

Theological Insights

Israel attributes to God things that modern people are likely to attribute to chance or circumstance. They attribute their victory at Hormah not to strength or tactics but rather to God, who has given them victory in answer to a vow (Num. 21:1–3). They also take the infestation of vipers that they encounter as an act of God in response to their rebellious grumblings (Num. 21:6–7).

God in mercy provides in a bronze snake on a pole the means of healing people from viper bites and forgiving their sin. They need only to gaze in faith and obedience upon the bronze snake (Num. 21:8–9). Jesus sees in this incident an analogy to the salvation available through faith in him and his work on the cross (John 3:14–15).

A device meant by God as something good later becomes an idol and something bad. Moses's bronze snake is destroyed by

Hezekiah because people begin to worship it (2 Kings 18:4). But it has no inherent magical power. The power is in God.

Teaching the Text

1. *Victory brings reflection on what could have been.* In Numbers 21:1–3 the Israelites experience their first victory in the promised land. They had moved north to the Negev in the south of Canaan. The king of Arad attacked and captured some of them. The Israelites respond by vowing to devote this king's cities to Yahweh—to put them under "the ban"—if he gives them victory. And Yahweh does give them victory over the king of the Arad, completely destroying his cities and renaming one of them Hormah ("destruction").

The old generation encounters a strong enemy in Numbers 13, but rather than vowing to fight, it cowers in fear. Rather than vowing the booty to God, these Israelites panic, rebel against God and Moses, and contemplate going back to Egypt (Num. 14:1–4). Then, contrary to God's command, they try to enter the land on their own. Rather than experiencing victory from Yahweh, they are defeated at the very site of victory in Numbers 21, Hormah (Num. 14:44–45). This leads to melancholy

The Lord said to Moses, "Make a snake and put it up on a pole; anyone who is bitten can look at it and live" (21:8). This plaque found at Canaanite Hazor (fourteenth to thirteenth century BC) may have been the top part of a standard used during religious processions. It pictures a figure in the middle of two snakes and may depict a deity holding a serpent in each hand.

reflections about what could have been in that old generation.

Perhaps we too can reflect on bad decisions in the past that have stopped us from achieving victories for God. Was there a time when God opened a door for us but we refused to enter it? Was there a time when we failed to achieve what God would have had us do because we were too afraid to act? Was there a time when sin reared its ugly head—whether pride or lust or envy or anger—and derailed our walk with and ministry for God? Such occasions can create profound, long-term regrets whereby we keep saying to ourselves, "What if I had handled that differently?" Israel had regrets from its earlier failings, but the nation moved on, and eventually God led it to new victories and the promised land. We too may have regrets. But often all we can do is to move on by God's grace and trust that God will give us new opportunities.

2. *A change of heart allows healing.* At the beginning of the exodus journey, the Israelites "feared the Lord and put their

trust in him and in Moses his servant" (Exod. 14:31). But that faith soon evaporated. During the next forty years, Israel constantly grumbles and complains. That bad example influences the new generation. The 175-mile detour around Edom through an inhospitable desert is the immediate cause of the Israelites' misery (Num. 21:4). That leads this new generation to complain about its hardships as the old one had done. Their words (v. 5) echo earlier complaints along the way (Num. 11:1), complaints about the threat of death in the desert (Exod. 14:11–12; Num. 20:4), lack of food and water (Exod. 15:24; 16:3; 17:2; Num. 20:2, 5), and the monotony of always eating manna (Num. 11:6). In an act of poetic justice, this generation's poisonous attitude of rebellion and ingratitude is punished by the poison of snake venom. But unlike the old generation, this generation is quick to repent. These Israelites confess their sin to Moses and ask him to pray for them (v. 7). The new generation is not perfect, but it shows signs of spiritual growth over the previous generation.

We need to recognize that we, like Israel, are ever susceptible to sin. Thus, we are in perpetual need of repentance. If our repentance is genuine and our contrition real, we, like Israel, can expect to find healing in the grace of God. God takes no pleasure in punishing sinners; rather, he longs for them to repent and live (Ezek. 33:11). There is in fact rejoicing in heaven whenever a sinner repents (Luke 15:7, 10). God is quick to provide forgiveness to the genuinely penitent, as the father receives back his prodigal son in Jesus's parable (Luke 15:11–32). Thus, though we will sin, we can take comfort in the fact that we have a God who forgives and heals those who turn to him.

Illustrating the Text

We will never know how "what might have been" can be destroyed by sin.

Film: *On the Waterfront*. In this 1954 Oscar-winning film, Terry Malloy (played by Marlon Brando) is a dockworker and a promising boxer. He has a big fight scheduled. But Terry is pressured by his mob-connected union boss, Johnny Friendly, and Terry's brother, Charley, who is Friendly's right-hand man, to throw a fight and let his opponent win so that Friendly can make money by betting on his weaker opponent. Terry complies, though he regrets it for the rest of his life. He later bemoans what might have been had Charley not convinced him to throw the fight. He tells his brother of his regrets and his resentments for what he had convinced him to do: "You don't understand! I could've had class. I could've been a contender. I could've been somebody, instead of a bum, which is what I am. Let's face it. It was you, Charley."

The older generation of Israelites also could have "been somebody." They could have taken the promised land. But just as Terry Malloy blew his chance to be somebody by cooperating in fight fixing, so the older generation lost its chance to receive the blessings of the land by disobedience, rebellion, and unbelief.

God's punishment by snake was terrible.

Literature: *Seven Pillars of Wisdom*, by T. E. Lawrence. T. E. Lawrence (1888–1935), the famous "Lawrence of Arabia," wrote about experiences with snakes in the desert that show how horrible an infestation of poisonous snakes like the one in Numbers 21:4–9 can be:

> On my dry patience they grated a little, because the plague of snakes which had been with us since our first entry into Sirhan to-day rose to memorable height, and became a terror. In ordinary times, so the Arabs said, snakes were little worse here than elsewhere by water in the desert: but this year the valley seemed creeping with horned vipers and puff-adders, cobras and black snakes. By night movement was dangerous: and at last we found it necessary to walk with sticks, beating the bushes each side while we stepped warily through on bare feet.
>
> We could not lightly draw water after dark, for there were snakes swimming in the pools or clustering in knots around their brinks. Twice puff-adders came twisting into the alert ring of our debating coffee-circle. Three of our men died of bites; four recovered after great fear and pain, and a swelling of the poisoned limb. Howeitat treatment was to bind up the part with the snake-skin plaster, and read chapters of the Koran to the sufferer until he died. They also pulled thick Damascene ankle-boots, red, with blue tassels and horse-shoe heels, over their horny feet when they went late abroad.
>
> A strange thing was the snakes' habit, at night, of lying beside us, probably for warmth, under or on the blanket. When we learned this our rising was infinite care, and the first up would search round his fellows with a stick till he could pronounce them unencumbered. Our party of fifty men killed perhaps twenty snakes daily; at last they got so on our nerves that the boldest of us feared to touch the ground; while those who, like myself, had a shuddering horror of all reptiles longed that our stay in Sirhan might end.[9]

Through Moab into the Transjordan

Big Idea *God helped Israel overcome obstacles and enemies to reach the brink of the promised land.*

Understanding the Text

The Text in Context

Rapid progress and victories follow the healing of sinful attitudes seen in preceding sections. Moses, Aaron, and the people had sinned, and Miriam and Aaron have died (Num. 20:1–13, 22–29; 21:1–9). Yet unlike the old generation, this one shows a willingness to quickly repent (Num. 21:7). Edom denies Israel easy and direct passage toward the promised land (Num. 20:14–21), but the journey toward that land proceeds around Edom. After winning a victory at Hormah (Num. 21:1–3) and traversing Edom (Num. 21:4), Israel passes through Moab (Num. 21:10–20) and engages in battle against Sihon and Og, Transjordanian kings whom they defeat (Num. 21:21–35). These victories set the stage for entering the land and beginning the conquest.

Historical and Cultural Background

Songs composed about the events described here were recorded in the now-lost hymnbook "the Book of the Wars of the LORD" (Num. 21:14), of which a snippet is quoted. The Bible elsewhere quotes from another lost hymnbook, "the Book of Jashar" (Josh. 10:13; 2 Sam. 1:18). This reminds us that other books existed in Bible times that did not become part of Scripture.

Israel ends up settling in Sihon's territory in the Transjordan (Num. 21:31). His land eventually goes to Reuben and Gad (Deut. 29:7–8; Josh. 13:15–28). Israel actually ends up with more land than God had promised it, for Sihon's land is outside Canaan.

Interpretive Insights

21:10–12 *Oboth . . . Iye Abarim . . . Zered.* Having gone south along the route toward the Red Sea to avoid passing through Edom (Num. 21:4), Israel now moves north, evidently bypassing Edom to its east. Locating the exact route is complicated by our lack of knowledge of the geography of this region (for more on which, see Num. 33). The location Oboth is unknown. The exact location of Iye Abarim (or "Iye of the Abarim"; also called "Iyim" [see Num. 33:44–45 NRSV]) is uncertain, though Abarim is a mountain range forming the rim of the Moab tableland plateau and that may form the mountainous spine of the whole country.[1] If Iye Abarim is along the Abarim, Iye must be somewhere along the far southern and eastern edge of Moab ("faces Moab from the sunrise" [v. 11b]). Zered is a valley and wadi, usually identified with Wadi el-Hesa, which drains into the south end of the Dead Sea. At times Moab extended north of the Arnon River valley east of the Dead Sea, but at this time Sihon had taken possession of their territory north of the Arnon (see v. 26 below). Hence, the Arnon formed the northern border between Moab and the Amorites (v. 13).

21:14 *Book of the Wars of the* LORD. "Book" is better rendered "Scroll" (Lexham English Bible) (see "Historical and Cultural Background" above). The quoted song recounts sites and terrain along the path (v. 15) and celebrates an occasion when at Beer (Hebrew for "well") God has Moses gather the people (an echo of Num. 20:8) and provides them with water (v. 16).

Key Themes of Numbers 21:10–35

- A new attitude can make a difference.
- God gives progress and victories.

21:18 *princes . . . nobles . . . scepters and staffs.* The tribal leaders play a prominent role in the dig using their own scepters (or singular, "scepter" [ESV]) and staffs. The KJV (similarly NKJV) renders in verse 18 "by the direction of the lawgiver, with their staves," thus finding in the singular "scepter" a reference to Moses. The Hebrew word *meḥoqeq* is used of the object "ruler's staff" in Genesis 49:10 and of God as "ruler/lawgiver" in Isaiah 33:22. In Numbers 21:18 the parallel with "staffs" suggests that the object rather than the person is in view. However, the singular "scepter" (ESV), though it might be a collective for

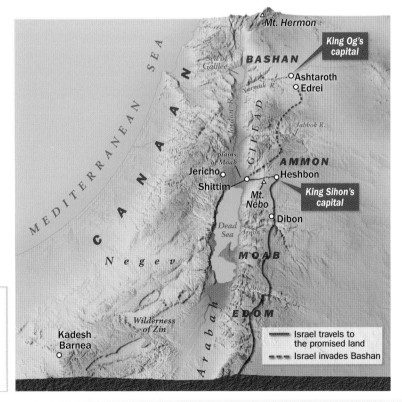

Numbers 21:10–35

"scepters" per the NIV, may well represent a focusing on Moses's ruler's staff, which, along with the staffs of the other leaders, helps dig this well. That meaning would make the parallel with Numbers 20:2–13 even stronger.

21:18–20 *Mattanah . . . Nahaliel . . . Bamoth.* None of these stations along the route can be located with certainty.

Pisgah. This is the ridge of mountains east of the northern end of the Dead Sea that includes Mount Nebo, where Moses dies (Deut. 34:1). It may refer to the northern end of the Abarim range and be the northern edge of the Moabite plateau.[2]

21:21–31 *Sihon king of the Amorites.* The Amorites are one of the groups of Canaanites who oppose Israel. The Amorites are listed as one of many Canaanite tribes, along with groups such as the Hittites and the Perizzites (Gen. 15:20–21; Exod. 3:8, 17; 23:23). Sihon lives in the Transjordan east of Canaan, but other Amorites live in the hill country of the promised land (Num. 13:29). Similar to the request made of Edom (Num. 20:17–21), Israel, which has no intention of occupying the Transjordan, asks Sihon for permission to pass through his territory toward Canaan, promising to stick to the main highway and not to forage any field or vineyard of that territory, nor to drink up its precious well water supplies (v. 22). Sihon had taken Moabite territory as far south as the Arnon River (v. 26). This victory is celebrated by the Amorite bards in a song quoted by the text to indicate how great Sihon has been in conquering Moab, whose god is Chemosh, whom Sihon has defeated as far south as the Arnon (vv. 27–30). Overconfident of his military prowess, Sihon responds to this request by dispatching troops south from his capital at Heshbon (see v. 26) and attacking Israel at Jahaz (v. 23), of uncertain location but south of Heshbon. But despite Sihon's previous victories over Moab celebrated in song, Israel proves to be his undoing. Israel counterattacks, kills him, and takes possession of both Heshbon and the rest of Sihon's territory as far north as the Jabbok River some twenty miles north of Heshbon (vv. 24–25). Israel leaves the well-fortified Ammonite territory northeast of Heshbon alone (v. 24c), land that Sihon himself probably had not possessed. Thus Israel comes to control the territory from the Arnon to the Jabbok east of the Jordan with the exception of the Ammonite lands.

21:30 *Heshbon's . . . Dibon . . . Nophah . . . Medeba.* Verse 30 is difficult to translate and may have textual corruptions. It seems to be Israel's response to the Amorite bards. Heshbon, a capital city whose king the bards celebrate, is destroyed along with other Amorite cites. Dibon is some twenty miles south of Heshbon, four miles north of the Arnon. Nophah is completely unknown as a geographic name. The NRSV emends the word following it and renders it as a verb "[until fire] spread." Medeba is about seven miles south of Heshbon.

21:31 *Israel settled in the land of the Amorites.* The victory over Sihon allows the tribes of Reuben and Gad to settle there permanently: Reuben occupies the southern part of Sihon's territory from the Arnon to Heshbon (Josh. 13:15–23), while Gad occupies the northern part of Sihon's territory, including everything south of the Jabbok River, though also farther north into Og's territory (Josh. 13:24–28) (see vv. 32–35 below).

21:32 *Jazer.* This location is uncertain, somewhere north of Heshbon.

21:33–35 *Og king of Bashan.* Once Sihon's territory south of the Jabbok is controlled by Israel, Israel comes into conflict with the territory of Og, who is called an "Amorite" (Deut. 31:4), a race of people known for their tall stature (Amos 2:9), and part of the Rephaites (Josh. 13:12), who are related to the sons of Anak, also known for their tall stature (Deut. 2:11; cf. Num. 13:33). Bashan covers what is now known as the Golan Heights, from the Yarmuk River just southeast of the Sea of Galilee to Mount Hermon in the far north. Og evidently also controls, or at least wants to control, the territory south of the Yarmuk to the Jabbok River as well. Unlike with Sihon, Israel makes no request for permission to pass through Og's territory. Israel does not actually need to have Og's

The Lord tells Moses that he will be successful in the battle with King Og of Bashan because "I have delivered him into your hands" (21:34). Other cultures in the ancient Near East also believed that the gods fought on behalf of their people and that defeat or victory depended on the strength or will of the gods. This Assyrian relief shows Ashur (see winged figure above charioteers), the Assyrian god, with bow drawn, fighting alongside Ashurnasirpal (Nimrud, 865–860 BC). The defeat of the Moabites by Sihon was blamed on their god, Chemosh, who gave up his people as fugitives and captives (21:29).

territory to invade Canaan, since the region across from Jericho has already been taken. Why, then, do the Israelites send a military expedition toward Bashan (v. 33)? Perhaps because Og's territory of Bashan, unlike Sihon's territory farther south, is considered part of the promised land and hence a legitimate target of direct attack.[3] In any case, Og responds militarily at Edrei (v. 33). Yahweh promises victory to Israel and gives them permission to do to Og what has been done to Sihon at Heshbon (v. 34).

They thus kill Og and his sons and wipe out his entire army (v. 35a). Israel takes his land (v. 35b) and eventually allots his territory to the half tribe Manasseh (Deut. 3:13), though some territory north of the Jabbok that may have been controlled by Og goes to Gad (Josh. 13:24–28).

Theological Insights

Numbers ascribes to God both the provision of water on the route (Num. 21:16) and Israel's victory over Og (Num. 21:34). These victories become the source of later theological reflection. Historical psalms reviewing these events ascribe the victories over Sihon and Og to God (Pss. 135:10–12; 136:17–21). Nehemiah's prayer of confession similarly acknowledges that God had defeated Sihon of Heshbon and Og of Bashan and given to Israel the land of these great kings (Neh. 9:22).

More generally, God is portrayed in both Testaments as a great warrior who fights for his people. Yahweh is mighty in battle (Ps. 24:8), metaphorically using a sword and a bow and arrows against his enemies (Pss. 7:11–13; 18:6–15), though any literal arrows are those shot by his people whom he empowers for war (Ps. 18:34), for he is the "God of the armies of Israel" (1 Sam. 17:45). In the New Testament Christ is portrayed as a warrior on a white warhorse, his garments sprinkled with blood as he leads the heavenly armies in slaughtering enemies. He does all this to achieve justice, vindicate his people, and establish his kingdom by punishing the beast and its wicked followers (Rev. 19:17–21; cf. Isa. 63:1–3). The concept of God as a warrior makes some Christians uncomfortable, but God's holy judgments are as attributable to God as are his acts of love. On Israel's conduct of war, see comments at Numbers 31:1–54.

Teaching the Text

1. *A new attitude can make a difference.* There are hardships along the way, but rather than being discouraged and complaining as the first generation would have, Israel now composes a song celebrating these events, a song later incorporated into its ancient (and now lost) hymnbook, "the Book of the Wars of the LORD" (vv. 14–15). Lack of water (v. 16) does not result in conflicts with Israel's leaders and rebellion against God, unlike what had happened previously (see Num. 20:2–13), but this ultimately is an occasion for another song in celebration of God's provision and Israel's leaders (vv. 17–18). The new generation is coming both physically and spiritually closer to the promised land.

Our mind-set makes a big difference in what God can do through us. Hardships in life can be the occasion of stumbling or an occasion for praise, depending on our attitude. If we approach problems with an attitude of unbelief or selfishness, then those hardships may well result in discouragement, dissension, or despair. But if we bring to our problems an attitude of gratitude and faith in God, then we often discover that many of these problems have become occasions for thanking God for helping us through them. So when we face a challenging situation, we should be mindful of our attitude.

2. *God gives progress and victories.* The story moves Israel rapidly past Edom and Moab into territory controlled by the

Amorites (vv. 10–13, 19–20). There Israel faces uncooperative, aggressive enemies. The powerful Amorite king Sihon not only refuses to allow Israel to pass through his territory but also attacks Israel militarily. Og king of Bashan, farther north in the Transjordan, attacks to try to repulse Israel (vv. 32–33). But rather than cowering in fear, Israel counterattacks and defeats Sihon and Og (vv. 21–26, 35). Amorite poets had sung of the greatness of Sihon for conquering the northern part of Moab (vv. 27–29), but now Israel can sing of having overthrown Sihon (v. 30). According to Rahab the harlot, these victories terrorize the Canaanites (Josh. 2:10–11), making future victories easier.

Like this new generation, God can work victories through us if we carefully follow "the terms of the covenant" with God (Deut. 29:7–9). If we have courage, faith, and obedience, God can turn our defeats into victories and help us overcome the obstacles and hardships, whether material or spiritual, that life presents. And as God gives us victories in such areas, these become occasions to sing songs of praise. And they can pave the way to greater victories in the future.

Illustrating the Text

When approached with the right attitude, difficult circumstances can become occasions for thanksgiving.

Spiritual Discipline: This passage from Numbers reflects how the Israelites recorded remembrances of God's provision for them in the face of opposition and difficulty. Journaling can be a powerful tool for processing challenging circumstances. In particular, we can experience a new depth of insight and intimacy with God when we take time to journal our prayers. The act of writing our thoughts down forces us to slow our pace, reflect a little more, and move from vague thoughts or repetitive words into coherent communication. In the midst of a challenging season of life, take time to journal your prayers. In particular, make an effort to reflect on at least one "reason for gratitude" each day. This practice cultivates a focus on thanksgiving. Such a focus can lead to deep, unshakable joy in the midst of any circumstance.

Our present struggles can pave the way for future victories.

Sports: Few games have been so immortalized as the so-called Miracle on Ice, which took place on Friday, February 22, 1980, at the Lake Placid Winter Olympics. When the United States ice hockey team defeated the Soviet Union, the world was stunned. Many considered it a moment that should not have been. In fact, on the eve of the game, a *New York Times* reporter wrote, "Unless the ice melts, or unless the United States team or another team performs a miracle, as did the American squad in 1960, the Russians are expected to easily win the Olympic gold medal for the sixth time in the last seven tournaments."[4] The United States team had been consistently drubbed by the Russians, year after year. However, each of those losses taught the Americans something new. The American coach, Herb Brooks, carefully trained his players to work harder, pursue a more physical game, and build stamina to last until the final buzzer. From previous defeats, they learned the key to victory.

Balak to Hire Balaam

Big Idea *God protects his people from those determined to harm them.*

Understanding the Text

The Text in Context

In Numbers 21 the Israelites move out of the desert to the western edge of Canaan. They have passed around Edom and gone through Moab into territory north of Moab claimed by Amorites Sihon king of Heshbon and Og king of Bashan, whom they defeat. Though Israel has passed by Moab without attacking, Balak king of Moab feels vulnerable. Moreover, Sihon's territory now occupied by Israel has previously been occupied by Moab (Num. 21:26), a source of resentment. Unable to confront Israel militarily, Balak seeks a Mesopotamian diviner, Balaam, to curse Israel instead (Num. 22:4–7).

Dennis Cole labels Numbers 20–25 as "Rebellion Cycle C," in which Israel, Moses, and Aaron rebel against God's commands (Num. 20:12, 24; 21:4–5; 25:1–2), representing the final collapse of the first generation that had left Egypt. After Moses falls into sin, God ironically uses another spokesman to bless his people: the idolatrous Balaam, hired by Balak to curse them (Num. 22–24).[1]

Historical and Cultural Background

Balaam was honored by non-Israelites long after his death.[2] In 1967 archaeologists discovered texts in a language similar to Aramaic, perhaps a Canaanite dialect or Ammonite. These texts at Tell Deir Alla in the East Jordan Valley had been on a plaster wall, or a stela hung on a wall, of what may have been a sanctuary dating to the mid-eighth to late-seventh century BC. The wall later collapsed, breaking the text into many fragments, and a fire burned away part of the text, which, along with confusion over the exact nature of the language, complicates the text's interpretation.

Some things in this text seem clear. In the Bible Balaam calls Israel's God *Shaddai*, "the Almighty" (Num. 24:4, 16), from whom he receives messages. The Deir Alla Inscription gives an account of Balaam the son of Beor, a seer of the gods. Balaam refers to Shaddai-gods (*Shaddayin*, plural of *Shaddai*). The text says that the gods came to Balaam by night and spoke to him a message that made him cry and refuse to eat. Evidently, the divine council asked a goddess to cover the heavens because of what was occurring on earth, which Balaam found upsetting because that would mean loss of light and life.

However reliable or unreliable the Deir Alla texts may be historically, they certainly show that the colorful character of Balaam lived on, not only in Israelite memory but also among Israel's neighbors. They also provide early extrabiblical evidence that such a person may have actually existed.

Interpretive Insights

22:1 *The plains of Moab.* Historically, this territory east of the Jordan had been Moabite until Sihon the Amorite conquered it (Num. 21:26). Moab is now confined to territory south of the Arnon River twenty-five miles to the south. Specifically, Israel is camped at Shittim (Num. 25:1).

across from Jericho. This anticipates the conquest that begins at Jericho (Josh. 6).

22:2–3 *Balak.* He is a weak king whose name ironically may mean "devastator."[3] He sees what Israel has done to the Amorites and is horrified as Israel crushes Sihon, who had crushed the northern part of Moab. The great Sihon's exploits had been celebrated in song (Num. 21:26–29). Balak is intimidated ("terrified" and "filled with dread") by Israel's even greater strength.

22:4 *elders of Midian.* Moab consults with the tribal leaders of Midian, with whom they are allied. Later, Midianite women play a major role in Balaam's plot to curse Israel (Num. 25:6, 14–18; 31:1–18).

lick up everything around us. As oxen can easily overgraze ground in this arid region and turn it into a desert, so the large horde of Israelites threaten to

- Beware of unscrupulous people who claim to know God.
- No one can thwart God's plans to bless his people.

devastate ecologically the plains of Moab and the surrounding territories.

22:5 *sent messengers to summon Balaam.* Being too weak to attack militarily, they seek a divination expert to harm Israel (see v. 7).

Pethor, near the Euphrates River. "Euphrates" is lacking in the Hebrew but implied. Pethor probably is to be identified with Pitru, of Assyrian texts, twelve miles south of Carchemish and a few miles from the Euphrates,[4] an arduous journey of about four hundred miles from Moab.

his native land. The Hebrew reads literally "the land of the sons of *his people* ['*ammo*]." A few manuscripts (the Samaritan, the Syriac, and the Vulgate) read instead "the land of the sons of *Ammon*,"

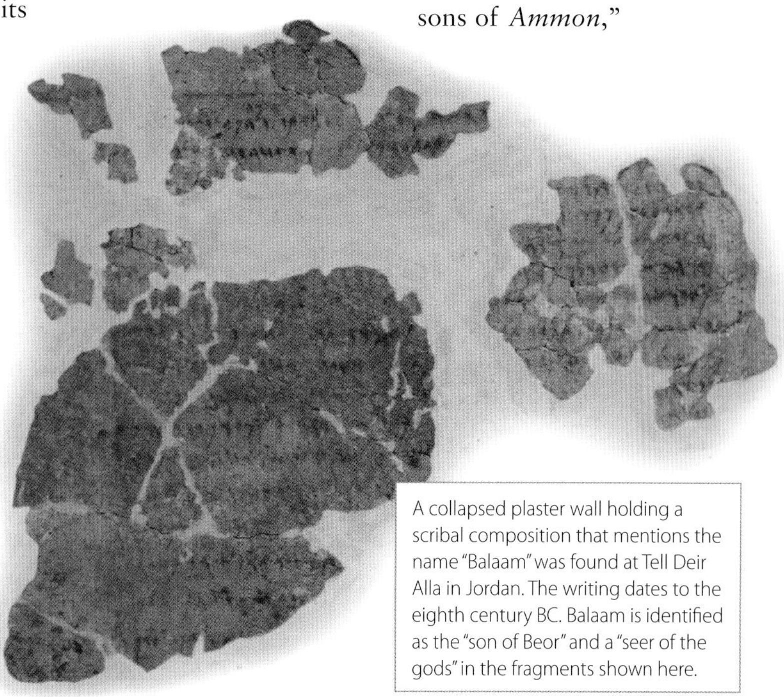

A collapsed plaster wall holding a scribal composition that mentions the name "Balaam" was found at Tell Deir Alla in Jordan. The writing dates to the eighth century BC. Balaam is identified as the "son of Beor" and a "seer of the gods" in the fragments shown here.

suggesting that the Masoretic Text accidentally omitted a letter, *nun*. This alternative reading makes sense of Balak supposing that Balaam may be willing to come since the Ammonites are nearby. It also makes sense of Balaam coming by donkey, an animal better suited for traveling short distances, and it explains why he has been celebrated at Deir Alla in Ammonite territory (see "Historical and Cultural Background" above). But the expression "the River" regularly refers to the Euphrates (so NIV), not the Jordan or Wadi Nusariyat, which flows out of Ammon, or the Jabbok, which flows north of Ammon. That Balaam comes from Mesopotamia ("Aram" [Num. 23:7]; "Aram Naharaim" [Deut. 23:4]) probably is fatal for this interpretation. A third alternative is that "his people" should be revocalized to read "the land of the sons of *Amaw*" (ESV, REB, NRSV). Amaw is mentioned in fifteenth-century BC Akkadian texts at Alalakh as a place nearby in Mesopotamia.[5] Both the traditional view and this last view seem preferable to the variant "land of the sons of Ammon."

A people has come out of Egypt. This alludes to Israel's exodus.

settled next to me. Israel is immediately north of Balak's territory.

22:6 *whoever you bless is blessed, and whoever you curse is cursed.* These words, meant to flatter Balaam, unintentionally echo and mock God's words, "I will bless those who bless you, and whoever curses you I will curse" (Gen. 12:3).

22:7 *elders of Moab and Midian.* Verse 8 calls them "princes/officials." On Midian, see verse 4.

Although in Numbers 22:9 God comes directly to Balaam, one technique diviners used to obtain information from the gods was to examine the liver or intestines of a slaughtered animal. In this Assyrian relief from the palace at Nimrud (865–860 BC), a priest, wearing the flat hat, studies the entrails of a sacrifice. The omen literature would then be consulted to receive answers to yes or no questions.

the fee for divination. "Divination" (*qesem*) can be used metaphorically for the inspired verdict/decision of a king (Prov. 16:10), but occult divination is condemned by the law (Deut. 18:10). This fee is a retainer, the balance to be paid after the deed is done (see Num. 22:37; 24:11). The Hebrew text lacks "fee for," though alternative renderings such as "instruments of divination" or "versed in divination" (NJPS) seem unlikely: Balaam surely has the tools of his own trade, and these elders are unlikely to have been experts in divination.

22:8 *the answer the LORD gives me.* On the surface, Balaam seems pious in wanting time to consult with Yahweh, though one must bear in mind that he is a pagan diviner (v. 7) who, in violation of God's law, employs sorcery (Num. 23:23; 24:1). Moses, not Balaam, is the real prophet of God. Balaam, the anti-Moses, may be merely using his divination arts to consult Israel's God to ascertain the best way to curse Israel, as Balaam might with any other god.

22:9 *God came to Balaam.* Although Balaam says that he plans to consult Yahweh, God actually initiates this encounter, probably in a dream.[6]

22:10 *Balaam said to God.* The switch from God's personal name "Yahweh" (v. 8) to his less personal title "God" (or "deity") in verses 9–10 may hint that Balaam does not in fact have a right relationship with God. For further discussion of Balaam's character, see "Teaching the Text" below and see the sidebar "Mocking Balaam" and "Teaching the Text" in the unit on Numbers 22:20–40.

22:12 *Do not go with them . . . they are blessed.* God warns Balaam not to carry out his intentions against the Israelites. The blessedness of the Israelites alludes to the patriarchal promise (Gen. 12:3; 27:33).

22:13 *The LORD has refused to let me go.* In accord with that night's revelation, Balaam dismisses his princely guests. Interestingly, he does not mention the part about Israel definitely being blessed. Does he hope that Yahweh will change his mind?

22:14 *Balaam refused to come.* The messengers abbreviate Balaam's message further by saying only that Balaam will not come, not that Yahweh the God of Israel does not let him come.

22:15–17 *Balak sent other officials.* Balak pulls out all the stops to entice Balaam, offering him wealth and power

(v. 17). The Hebrew particle *na'* in verse 16, not translated by the NIV but rendered "I beg you" by the NASB, makes the request more emphatic or urgent.

22:18 *I could not . . . go beyond the command of the LORD my God.* Balaam demurs on the grounds that he cannot go against God's command. The personal pronoun "my" claims a personal relationship with Israel's God. While Balaam does encounter God after the first envoy comes (v. 12), if he had known him intimately, he would not have thought that God could change his mind like a pagan god (cf. Num. 23:19) or that he could be persuaded to curse Israel. The rest of the Balaam cycle will show that Balaam is not a godly prophet.

Theological Insights

The Bible condemns employment of magical practices (see Deut. 18:9–14), and at times the practitioners of the magical arts seem to be mere charlatans (e.g., Dan. 2:1–11). But sometimes the experts in the occult appear to have real powers (see Exod. 7:11–12, 20–22; 8:6–7; 1 Sam. 28:7–19). The Bible certainly affirms the existence of supernatural forces besides those of God. There are "spiritual forces of evil in the heavenly realms" (Eph. 6:12), consisting (at least) of the devil and his minions.

But from where does blessing or cursing come? From God or from Balaam? From heaven or from the occult? Even if there are spiritual forces of darkness with supernatural powers, those powers are destined to be defeated (Matt. 25:41; Rev. 20:10). Dark powers can do harm for a while, but their time is short (Rev. 12:12). God prevails over all such powers in the end.

Teaching the Text

1. *Beware of unscrupulous people who claim to know God.* Balaam shows no scruples against hexing Israel. Indeed, the New Testament remarks that Balaam "loved the wages of wickedness" (2 Pet. 2:15–16) and is motivated by financial gain (Jude 11), as Balak himself believes (Num. 22:7, 37). Although he claims Yahweh as "my God" (Num. 22:18), has a genuine encounter with God (Num. 22:9), and no doubt believes that consulting with Israel's God will give him insight into cursing Israel, it seems unlikely that a pagan practitioner of magical arts condemned by the law (Deut. 18:9–13) genuinely knows the true God. If Balaam had really known God as well as he claims, he never would have considered cursing Israel.

So we today should beware of false prophets and preachers. There are those who claim to have a special intimacy with God and to speak for God. They may give some evidence that this is true, and yet their true intention is to serve themselves rather than God. We can likely detect this in their warped theology. Such persons probably do not personally know the Lord. To such preachers Christ will one day say, "I never knew you. Away from me, you evildoers!" (Matt. 7:23).

2. *No one can thwart God's plans to bless his people.* Balak is terrified of Israel (Num. 22:3), so he attempts asymmetric warfare against Israel by employing the powers of the occult.

But Balaam is told by God in no uncertain terms that it is God's will that Israel be

After defeating King Sihon, Israel controls the region from the Arnon wadi, shown here, northward. Its proximity makes Balak, king of Moab, nervous, and he thinks that if Israel were cursed, its army could be defeated.

blessed, not cursed (Num. 22:12). Balaam discovers that his powers are more limited than Balak supposes, and possibly more limited than what Balaam himself believes. Israel can be cursed if, and only if, God wills it. But it is God's will to bless instead.

Nothing can stop God from blessing his people. The New Testament puts it this way: "If God is for us, who can be against us? . . . Neither death nor life, neither angels nor demons, neither the present nor the future, nor any powers, neither height nor depth, nor anything else in all creation, will be able to separate us from the love of God that is in Christ Jesus our Lord" (Rom. 8:31, 38–39). Not even all the powers of the occult can thwart God's will to bless his people.

Illustrating the Text

Not even the devil can keep God from blessing his people.

Church History: The great Protestant Reformer Martin Luther had a sense of the reality of Satan that most of us in modern times lack. His writings make frequent reference to the devil. Legend even has it that Luther, while he was working on his German translation of the New Testament, was so tormented by demons that he threw an inkwell at one of them; though historians tell us that this story probably is the brainchild of overzealous caretakers of the room in Wartburg where he worked on his translation, who even pointed to a stain on the wall as proof of this legend.[7] But what Luther probably meant was that he figuratively threw ink at Satan; that is, he created books on theology and, most especially, produced a German translation of the Bible.

Although Luther knew of the devil and evil spirits, he knew even better the power of God, which can overcome the forces of darkness. In his great hymn "A Mighty Fortress Is Our God," Luther states clearly that God and his word trump the devil:

> And though this world, with devils
>   filled, should threaten to undo us,
> We will not fear, for God hath willed
>   His truth to triumph through us:
> The Prince of Darkness grim, we trem-
>   ble not for him;
> His rage we can endure, for lo, his
>   doom is sure,
> One little word shall fell him.

Keith Getty and Stuart Townend have expressed the same idea in the fourth verse of their contemporary hymn "In Christ Alone" (2002), exalting the power of Christ over all other powers. Nothing—not a sorcerer such as Balaam or even the devil himself—can thwart God's will to bless his people.

Balaam's Donkey

Big Idea *Speak only what the Lord says.*

Understanding the Text

The Text in Context

In Numbers 22:1–19 Balak king of Moab sends dignitaries to try to hire Balaam, a Mesopotamian diviner, to come curse Israel, who has recently come to occupy the plains of Moab. Although Balaam does not object in principle to cursing Israel, Yahweh, apparently in a dream, forbids him to go. But Balak finds Balaam's refusal unacceptable and sends the dignitaries back to persuade him further.

In Numbers 22:20–40, Yahweh once more appears to Balaam in a dream. He gives Balaam permission to go with these dignitaries, but he must speak only what God tells him to say. This is intertwined with the story of Balaam's talking donkey, a creature that appears wiser than its owner.

Interpretive Insights

22:20 *That night God came to Balaam.* God appears to Balaam for a second time (see Num. 22:8–12), presumably in a dream.

go with them, but do only what I tell you. No reason is given for God's change of orders. Perhaps God allows Balaam to

With God's permission, Balaam saddles his donkey and goes with the emissaries from Balak. Donkeys were commonly used for transportation in the ancient Near East. This plaque from 1800–1600 BC depicts a male figure riding a donkey.

go in order to display God's glory in a memorable way through Balaam and his oracles.

22:22 *God was very angry when he went.* Compare Genesis 32:22–32 and Exodus 4:24–26, where God tells Jacob and Moses to go and then intercepts them on the way and threatens to take their lives. Concerning why God is angry with Balaam for doing what God has told him to do, see "Additional Insights" following this unit.

The angel of the LORD. This arguably is a theophany or manifestation of God.[1] The "angel of the LORD" elsewhere speaks as God and seems to be identified with God (Gen. 22:15–16; 31:11; Exod. 3:2–6; Num. 22:32–35). Ironically, neither the diviner Balaam, who claims insights into the unseen spiritual world, nor his two servants are able to see any of this.

22:25 *the donkey . . . turned off the road.* This donkey (lit., a female donkey or jenny) sees the threat to which the seer Balaam is blind and veers off the path to avoid it.

22:28 *What have I done to you . . . ?* Balaam is oddly unshaken at his donkey talking, perhaps because it is a dream-vision (see "Additional Insights" following this unit) or possibly because Balaam employs omens by animal activity as known elsewhere in the ancient Near East and suggested by the Deir Alla Balaam text.[2]

22:29 *You have made a fool of me!* Alternatively, "You have abused me!" Oblivious to the sword at that very moment over his own head, Balaam wishes that he had a sword to kill his jenny. His donkey responds reasonably and articulately that she has never behaved that way before, as Balaam admits, thus showing Balaam to have been irrational in striking her. He should rather have sought the cause of her strange behavior. Three times God has threatened to kill Balaam, who is saved only by the actions of his donkey. These three events anticipate Balaam later three times blessing Israel.[3]

22:32 *Why have you beaten your donkey . . . ?* The question is an implied rebuke.

your path is a reckless one. The Hebrew word *yarat*, rendered "reckless," is of uncertain meaning ("perverse" [ESV, NRSV], "slippery"),[4] but the general sense is that Balaam's actions are wrong and can lead to his downfall.

22:34 *I have sinned.* Balaam's admission seems appropriate.

22:35 *Go with the men, but speak only what I tell you.* Balaam volunteers to go back home. Instead, God tells Balaam to go to Balak on condition that he say only what God tells him to say, echoing the words of verse 20 above. This may be the same occasion (see "Additional Insights" following this unit).

22:36 *Arnon.* This river empties into the Dead Sea about twenty miles from the sea's northern edge. The Arnon became Moab's northern border after Sihon had conquered all the Moabite territory to its north (Num. 21:26), territory now occupied by Israel.

22:37 *Why didn't you come to me?* Balak is annoyed at Balaam's initial refusal.

Am I really not able to reward you? Balak assumes that the real issue with Balaam is insufficient money at the first offer.

22:38 *I must speak only what God puts in my mouth.* Balaam superficially appears to be obeying God (see v. 35) and gives no guarantee that he can curse Israel, but he omits God's statement that Israel is definitely to be blessed (Num. 22:12).

22:39 *Kiriath Huzoth.* The location is uncertain.

22:40 *Balak sacrificed cattle and sheep.* These are fellowship offerings to make a feast in Balaam's honor. The real work begins the next day.

Mocking Balaam

The story of Balaam's donkey in Numbers 22 demeans Balaam, often using role reversals in which Balaam's jenny does what Balaam cannot:[a]

1. Balaam by reputation can subdue Israel with words alone (v. 6), but in fact he cannot even subdue his own donkey with words or a staff.
2. Balaam is thought to be a "seer" with mystical insights as a diviner (v. 7), but he cannot see divine things that his donkey sees three times.
3. Balaam becomes a mouthpiece for God, but he is matched by his donkey, which is allowed by God to speak (v. 28). God does speak though Balaam, but then God can choose to speak though any old jackass or jenny.
4. The one who would help oppress Israel with a curse is, in poetic justice, (op)pressed (against a wall) himself (v. 25). The word "press" (*lahats*) often means "oppress."
5. Balaam is very angry with his donkey, which is innocent (v. 27), but God is very angry with Balaam, who is guilty of wanting to disobey God and curse Israel (v. 22a). This God-angry-with-Balaam parallel with Balaam-angry-with-donkey suggests that the text is comparing Balaam with a donkey.
6. The one who would kill his donkey with a sword (v. 29) is in danger of being killed by the sword of the angel of the Lord.
7. Balaam's donkey sees the folly of the reckless path that Balaam is taking, but the morally blind Balaam does not.
8. Balaam complains that his donkey is making a fool of (or abusing) him (v. 29), when in fact he is making a fool of himself.
9. Balaam's donkey is faithful in serving him, but Balaam is wickedly cruel in beating his donkey with a staff (v. 27). Compare Proverbs 12:10: "The righteous care for the needs of their animals, but the kindest acts of the wicked are cruel."
10. Balaam has a reputation as a wise man, but his jenny's articulate and reasonable defense of herself (v. 30) portrays her as wiser than he.

Thus, Balaam is shown to be blinder, dumber, less articulate, less discerning, less righteous, more brutish, and less reasonable than his donkey.

[a] Way (*Donkeys in the Biblical World*, 61–62) notes that similar role reversals occur in the Deir Alla Balaam text, where weaker creatures threaten stronger ones (e.g., sparrows threaten eagles).

Theological Insights

This tale has a positive message about the power of God. Balaam loves "the wages of wickedness" (2 Pet. 2:15) that Balak is offering for cursing Israel (Num. 22:37), and he wants to use God for this evil gain. But God turns the tables on him, using this diviner instead. It is impossible for Balaam to thwart God's will to bless Israel. Instead, God uses Balaam positively to bless Israel (see Num. 23–24).

God can use the wicked for his own good purposes. He uses wicked Pharaoh to display his own power (Exod. 9:16). He uses the wicked Babylonians to punish less wicked Judah (Hab. 1:5–11), the justice of which Habakkuk himself questions (Hab. 1:12–13), though the prophet is told by God to trust that God can do this and still be just (Hab. 2:4–5). In the New Testament God uses the traitor Judas to accomplish his plan involving Jesus dying for the sins of the world (Matt. 26:24). Similarly, God uses Balaam. That God can use such persons to be a means of blessing his people, glorifying himself, or accomplishing his purposes does not mean that God condones their wicked acts. In all these cases the wicked persons whom God uses are still held accountable by God for what they do. He is not a puppeteer forcing them to do evil. Yet it speaks instead of the greatness of God that he can use people's evil choices for good (cf. Gen. 50:20).

Teaching the Text

1. *Beware of false prophets.* Does Balaam actually start out being an evil, greedy diviner intent on cursing Israel, or is he

initially honorable, perhaps even a true prophet? Balaam, despite his non-Israelite background, seems to show respect for Yahweh, the God of Israel, whom he even calls "my God" (Num. 22:18), consults (Num. 22:8, 19), and claims to obey (Num. 22:13, 18; 24:13), and whose words he speaks (Num. 23:5–12, 16–26). That said, it was common in the ancient Near East to show respect for all gods, since it was believed that any, if annoyed, could lash out. This ambiguity is clarified in Numbers 22:20–40, which ridicules Balaam (see the sidebar) in order to degrade him in the eyes of the reader, who otherwise might have thought him to be a pious gentile follower of Yahweh. Scriptural witness as a whole indicates that Balaam is greedy for gain and indifferent to the morality of cursing an innocent people for money. To the end he remains stubbornly intent on cursing Israel in defiance of the will of God. Balaam ends up being executed for continuing to try to harm Israel (Num. 31:8), fulfilling the words of the promise to Abraham: "Whoever curses you I will curse" (Gen. 12:3).

There are people today who claim to have insights into the divine, who may even say very good things about God. They can even speak words for God and be used by God, but their hearts are not in the right place. Read superficially, Balaam appears to have been a good guy. Read more carefully, he was not. Such people still exist today.

2. *God does not change his word.* The story of Balaam is a cautionary tale. Once God has told Balaam that he is definitely blessing Israel (Num. 22:12), there is no need to pray about it again or to string along Balak and his messengers with the possibility that God might change his mind. Like Balaam, some people today pray for

Balak meets Balaam at the Arnon, the northernmost boundary of his territory. The Arnon wadi flows in a westerly direction, emptying into the Dead Sea here.

Initially, it is only Balaam's donkey that sees God opposing Balaam's journey. In this oil painting by Rembrandt titled *Balaam and His Ass* (AD 1626), Balaam beats his donkey a third time as she is lying down to avoid the angel of the Lord.

God to change his word, to change some teaching of Scripture because they do not like it. There was no use in Balaam asking God a second time if it was acceptable to curse Israel. God had already spoken. If God's word clearly prohibits something, there is no reason to ask him otherwise. It is a sign of spiritual immaturity or unbelief if we ask God for permission to do what his word clearly prohibits.

Illustrating the Text

False prophets can appear true.

Popular Culture: Balaam was used by God. God spoke some wonderful things through him. But in the end, he was a pagan diviner who opposed God. He was not a true prophet of God.

In 1969 the former Beatle George Harrison wrote a song, "My Sweet Lord." To a casual hearer, the lyrics sounded Christian. It even uses the Hebrew and Christian word "hallelujah," sung by the background singers at the beginning. But as the song goes on, the background singers switch to Hindu prayers about Hare Krishna. Harrison's "Sweet Lord" was not Jesus. It was Krishna. Yet many Christians were fooled by the lyrics at the beginning.

Film: *Avatar.* This highly successful science fiction movie (2009), directed and written by James Cameron, broke many box office records. Its message was remarkable in that it had a spiritual and religious dimension. The primitive blue people of the land Pandora pay homage to Eywa, the "All Mother." Eywa is sometimes described as a network of energy, and sometimes the sum total of every living thing. Some

Christians who saw the movie identified Eywa as the equivalent of the Bible's God. But as journalist Ross Douthat correctly points out, the real theology of this movie is pantheism, a belief that everything that is, is God.[5] The Eywa in *Avatar* is an impersonal and amoral Nature with which people are supposed to become one. The Bible, in contrast, clearly distinguishes God from nature and everywhere shows him to be personal and moral. There are kernels of truth in *Avatar*'s message: greed, moral indifference, and pride can cause people to destroy the world's beauty and mysteries and lead them to abuse other people, especially if we think of them as mere savages. Cameron is right that we should be stewards of God's creation and not destroy it. But the theology that Cameron uses to defend nature is, in the end, anti-Christian. Eywa is not the God of the Bible. Cameron is more like Balaam than Moses.

The Problem of God's Anger with Balaam

Why is God angry with Balaam for doing what God, evidently, has told him to do (Num. 22:20–22)?

One solution is to say something has changed. The phrase "when he went" (v. 22) could be rendered "while he was going."[1] The Hebrew word *ki* can mean "while/when" rather than "because he went" (cf. ESV, KJV, NASB, NRSV). The participle *holek* is plausibly rendered dynamically, "was going." It was not the fact that Balaam goes—Yahweh has already permitted that—but rather what happens along the journey that arouses God's anger. That is, God reads Balaam's mind, perceiving that Balaam intends to curse Israel despite God's statement that Israel is instead to be blessed (see Num. 22:12).

I propose a different solution that sees flashback in the story. Balaam is condemned for going in verse 22 because he intends to curse Israel and has not yet been given permission to go. According to this solution, Numbers 22:22–35 is synoptic/resumptive repetition.[2] Verses 20–21 are the synoptic summary version of the dream account, stating that Balaam has a dream-vision from God that allows him to go with the dignitaries from Moab. Verses 22–35 are the resumptive-expansive version of the same story. In other words, although this argument is controversial,[3] verse 22a should be understood as a pluperfect, "[Now in that vision/dream] God *had been* very angry while he was going." The content of the dream-vision in verse 20 includes

Table 1. Comparing Numbers 22:20–21 and 22:35

Verses 20–21 ESV and MT	Verse 35 ESV and MT
[20]And God came to Balaam at night and said to him, "If the men have come to call you, rise, go with them; but only do what [lit., "do the word that"] I tell you." [21]So Balaam rose in the morning and saddled his donkey and went with the princes of Moab.	[35]And the angel of the Lord said to Balaam, "Go with the men, but speak only the word that I tell you." So Balaam went on [Hebrew text lacks "on"] with the princes of Balak.
Verse 20b–21	Verse 35b
אִם־לִקְרֹא לְךָ בָּאוּ הָאֲנָשִׁים קוּם	
לֵךְ אִתָּם וְאַךְ אֶת־הַדָּבָר אֲשֶׁר־אֲדַבֵּר	לֵךְ עִם־הָאֲנָשִׁים וְאֶפֶס אֶת־הַדָּבָר אֲשֶׁר־אֲדַבֵּר
אֵלֶיךָ אֹתוֹ תַעֲשֶׂה׃	אֵלֶיךָ אֹתוֹ תְדַבֵּר
וַיָּקָם בִּלְעָם בַּבֹּקֶר וַיַּחֲבֹשׁ אֶת־אֲתֹנוֹ וַיֵּלֶךְ	וַיֵּלֶךְ בִּלְעָם עִם־שָׂרֵי בָלָק׃
עִם־שָׂרֵי מוֹאָב׃	

the donkey story in verses 22–35, in which Balaam sees himself heading out to curse Israel but is threatened with death by God for doing so. If this view is correct, the dream in verse 20 was expanded to explain in more detail how God actually reveals to Balaam that he can go with these princes from Moab on condition that he say/do only what God says. Verse 20b and verse 35a are the same revelation given at the same time at the conclusion of Balaam's dream in verse 20a. Note the similar wording that supports that this is the same occasion (see the table). Verse 35b brings the flashback to the point of time chronologically where verse 21 has left off so that the story can again advance chronologically.

Maimonides (cited by Jacob Milgrom) previously proposed that the donkey episode was a dream. Maimonides posited this view primarily to explain the implausibility of a talking donkey. But combined with the flashback view, it can also resolve certain other exegetical difficulties. It explains why Balaam is condemned for going in verse 22 in apparent contradiction with the permission in verse 20b, since the permission in verse 20b (= v. 35a) has not yet been given. Reading this as synoptic/resumptive storytelling explains why the princes are not mentioned in the donkey narrative, though two servants are, and why the servants disappear from the subsequent narrative as Balaam continues with the princes.

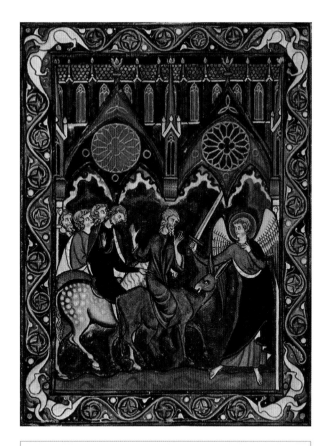

One understanding of the incident recorded in Numbers 22:22–35 and illustrated in this illumination from the Psalter of Saint Louis (AD 1258–70) is that it is a vision given to Balaam by God when God comes to him at night the second time (22:20).

This is because the dream in verses 22–34 flashes back to before he actually went with the princes, and when he went with the princes, he did not bring his servants. Being a dream-vision also explains why Balaam shows no astonishment at a talking donkey: odd things seem normal in dreams.

Balaam's First Three Oracles

Big Idea *God's will is to bless his people.*

Understanding the Text

The Text in Context

Balak king of Moab hires the sorcerer Balaam to curse Israel (Num. 22). Yahweh informs Balaam that Israel is blessed, not cursed (Num. 22:12), and that trying to curse Israel will place Balaam himself under God's judgment (Num. 22:22–38). Nevertheless, God allows Balaam to go to Balak on condition that he say nothing other than what God will tell him (Num. 22:20, 35).

What follows are three oracles. Three times the angel of the Lord has threatened to kill Balaam riding on his donkey. Now three times Balaam blesses Israel (Num.

> As Balaam describes the Israelites in his second message, he says, "They have the strength of a wild ox" (23:22). This animal is depicted on the Ishtar Gate, one of the entrances to the ancient city of Babylon (sixth century BC).

24:10).[1] Each oracle follows a similar sequence (see table 1).

Historical and Cultural Background

Balaam instructs Balak to build seven altars and offer on each a bull and a ram (Num. 23:1–2). Multiple altars in one place occur only once elsewhere in Scripture, at Elijah's contest with the prophets of Baal (1 Kings 18), with two altars for different gods. Outside the Bible, seven altars once were erected to sacrifice simultaneously to at least three deities. An Akkadian text states, "At dawn, in the presence of Ea, Shamash, and Marduk, you shall erect seven altars, you shall set seven censers of cypress, you shall pour the blood of seven sheep."[2] So, is Balaam appealing to a full pantheon of gods to assist him in cursing Israel? Or is he appealing in the fullest possible way to Israel's God, Yahweh? The latter understanding seems to fit better the verses that follow, where Balaam goes out to meet Yahweh (v. 4b).

Interpretive Insights

22:41–23:12 These verses relate the first oracle.

22:41 *Bamoth Baal.* This means "high places of Baal," implying that a Baal shrine is there. This is the Bamoth of Numbers 21:19–20.

see the outskirts of the Israelite camp. Balak evidently thinks a curse is more effective if its object is visible as the curse is pronounced.

23:1 *seven altars.* See "Historical and Cultural Background" above.

23:7 *Aram . . . the eastern mountains.* Aram (or Aram-Naharaim) is the region of Balaam's home, Pethor (Deut. 23:4; Num. 22:5). "The eastern mountains" is alternatively "the ancient hills" or "the hills of Qedem."[3] Qedem ("East") is a region of Syria mentioned in the ancient Egyptian Story of Sinuhe.[4]

denounce. The Hebrew word *za'am* connotes seething anger. Angry words were thought to make the sorcery more effective.

23:10 *the dust . . . a fourth.* "The dust" means that they are innumerable (Gen. 13:16; 28:14). "A fourth" could refer to three tribes and a clan of Levites (cf. layout of the camp in Num. 1–2).[5] Alternatively the word *roba'* may mean "dust," in parallel with the first line of the verse (NRSV, ESVmg). W. F. Albright argues that the text is corrupt and needs emendation.[6]

the death of the righteous. Balaam hopes to end his life as blessed as Israel has been, possibly alluding to its afterlife (cf. 1 Sam. 28:6–16; Ps. 73:17).

Key Themes of Numbers 22:41–24:13

- God chose us.
- God protects us.
- God blesses us.

Are There Unicorns in the Bible?

The Hebrew word *re'em* is rendered "unicorn" by the KJV in Numbers 23:22; 24:8 (and seven other times). The translators of the KJV did not know what this word meant, so they made one of the most misguided guesses in translation history. The term should rather be rendered "wild ox" or "aurochs." This ancestor of domestic cattle once inhabited a wide territory that spread into Europe, Mesopotamia, and northern Africa, though it went extinct in the seventeenth century AD. There is a Paleolithic cave painting of this creature along with other now-extinct creatures like the woolly rhino.

23:13–26 These verses relate the second oracle.

23:13–14 *Come with me to another place . . . Pisgah.* In Balak's mind the first curse may have failed because it has been attempted at the wrong place or because it is diluted by being against too large a group of people. From this site Balaam can see fewer Israelites than before. Pisgah is the ridge of mountains east of the northern end of the Dead Sea that includes Mount Nebo, where Moses later dies (Deut. 34:1).

23:19 *God.* The Hebrew word *'el* is an older term for "God" used often among the

Table 1. Balaam's Three Oracles

Sequence	First Oracle	Second Oracle	Third Oracle
1. Balak takes Balaam to observation point to view Israel.	22:41	23:13–14a	23:27–28
2. Balaam instructs Balak to offer sacrifices.	23:1	—	23:29
3. Balak sacrifices the animals as instructed.	23:2	23:14b	23:30
4. Balaam tells Balak to stand by his offering altar.	23:3	23:15	—
5. Balaam goes alone, and Yahweh reveals himself.	23:4–5	23:16	24:1–2
6. Balaam returns to Balak standing by his offering.	23:6	23:17	—
7. Balaam obeys Yahweh and speaks the oracle.	23:7–10	23:18–24	24:3–9

Note: For more on the sequence, see Cole, *Numbers*, 398.

patriarchs but less commonly later in Israelite history. Its use here suggests that the poetry is archaic, genuinely from Mosaic times.

lie . . . change his mind. "Lie" could also be "deceive" (*kazab*). On "change his mind," see "Theological Insights" below.

23:21 *No misfortune is seen in Jacob*. Alternatively, "misfortune" is "iniquity" (KJV, NKJV). This could mean that God finds nothing in them deserving of punishment,[7] though the parallelism with "misery" suggests that the meaning here is "disaster/misfortune." The first two verbs in verse 21 may be perfects of future reference ("prophetic" perfects), speaking of the future as if it had already occurred (compare NJPS: "No harm is in sight for Jacob, no woe in view for Israel").

23:22 *God brought them out of Egypt*. The Hebrew participle is better rendered as an act in progress, "God is bringing them out of Egypt" (cf. ESV, NASB, NKJV, NRSV). The process was not complete until the conquest.

they have the strength of a wild ox. This verse is obscure. The NRSV has "[God] is like the horns of a wild ox for them," which fits better with the theme of God's presence and care in verses 21cd–22a, though the NIV fits better with the lion imagery in verse 24. A predator would be reluctant to attack a wild ox, deterred by the ox's prominent horns; similarly, one dare not attack Israel, protected (or strengthened) by its God.

23:24 *devours its prey . . . drinks the blood*. God will turn Israel from prey to a predator devouring victims and drinking their blood. Those who arouse Israel will be cursed (see Num. 24:9), and Israel's enemies like Moab will themselves be defeated.

23:27–24:13 These verses relate the third oracle.

23:27 *Come . . . to another place . . . Peor*. Balak selects yet another site (cf. v. 13), Peor, another peak in the Abarim range (Num. 21:11).

24:1–2 *Balaam . . . did not resort to divination . . . looked out and saw Israel*. Balaam now realizes that his magic is useless (see Num. 23:2). Balaam looks on the totality of Israel, whereas in previous oracles he has observed only a part.[8]

24:3 *one whose eye sees clearly*. Balaam's oracle brags about his insights.

24:4 *The Almighty*. The Hebrew word *shadday* (also 24:16) occurs forty-eight times in the Hebrew Bible, mostly in Job (31x) and Genesis (6x). The use of the plural form is attributed to Balaam in the Deir Alla texts (see "Historical and Cultural Background" at Num. 22:1–19). The rendering "Almighty" is based on the Septuagint, which sometimes renders it with the Greek term *pantokratōr* ("Almighty"), and the Vulgate, which renders it with Latin *omnipotens* ("the Omnipotent") (cf. Arabic *šadid* ["strong"]).

24:5 *How beautiful are your tents*. Israel's unremarkable tents are beautiful because they are under God's blessing.

24:6 *Like valleys . . . gardens beside a river*. The Hebrew word *nahal* ("valley, torrent-valley, wadi") emphasizes Israel's vast numbers, making imagery that gently progresses from "valleys" to "gardens" to "aloes" to "cedars."[9] Alternatively, *nahal* might mean "palm groves" (ESV, NJPS, NRSV, NASBmg) rather than "valleys" based on a cognate in Arabic (*naḫl*, "date-palms"). For the garden imagery, compare the garden of Eden (Gen. 2:10).

like aloes ... cedars beside the waters. Aloe is perhaps *Aquilaria agallocha* or eaglewood,[10] which secretes aromatic resins used in ancient perfumes (Ps. 45:8; Prov. 7:17). Israel's "tents" are like these aromatic, sweet-smelling trees. Cedars were trees prominent in ancient Lebanon, so majestic that they were said to be planted by God (Ps. 104:16). They reach a height of 130 feet (40 meters), and their wood was valued for construction (2 Sam. 7:2; 1 Kings 6:9–10, 15–20). Cedars do not concentrate around streams, but Israel is majestic/strong like cedars, and it is camped near the Jordan.

24:7 *buckets.* Buckets could be made from "leather . . . with the mouth held open by cross-pieces."[11] NJPS reads "their boughs," assuming that *dal^eyaw* ("buckets") either is corrupt for *daliotayw* or is a by-form of it (cf. Jer. 11:16).

their seed will have abundant water. "Seed" means their posterity and/or their crops.

Their king . . . greater than Agag. Balaam foresees that Israel will be a monarchy (cf. Gen. 17:6, 16; 35:11). On the assumption that the text is not corrupt (Samaritan and LXX read "Gog"; Og has been proposed), "Agag" probably is a recurring title for Amalekite kings. Amalek is "first among the nations" (Num. 24:20). Israel's "king" could be predictive of David (the "star" of Num. 24:17), who fights with Amalek (1 Sam. 27:8–9), or of Saul, who defeats and executes Agag (1 Sam. 15:7–9, 32–33).

24:9 *Like a lion . . . like a lioness.* See Numbers 23:24.

May those who bless you be blessed and those who curse you be cursed! This echoes Genesis 12:3; 27:29 as a warning to Balak and Balaam. It can be rendered as a statement rather than as a wish/prayer (ESV, KJV, NASB, NKJV, NRSV).

24:10 *you have blessed them these three times.* See Numbers 23:7–10, 18–24; 24:3–9.

24:11 *the Lord has kept you from being rewarded.* Balaam leaves unpaid because Yahweh does not allow him to curse Israel.

Theological Insights

Balaam's second oracle begins with a statement about God: "God is not a human, that he should lie, nor a human being, that he should change his mind" (Num. 23:19).

Sometimes God appears to change his mind (Gen. 6:6; Exod. 32:14; 1 Sam. 15:11; Jon. 3:10), but in such cases God changes his response to people based not on ignorance of what was going to happen, but rather on their responses to him. He never capriciously changes his intentions, nor does he renege on his promises. But there can be unstated conditions on his prophetic threats and

Another image of Israel in Balaam's second message is that of a lioness much like the scene on this ivory plaque found at Nimrud (800–750 BC). "The people rise like a lioness; they rouse themselves like a lion that does not rest till it devours its prey and drinks the blood of its victims" (23:24).

promises, so promises can be forfeited by disobedience and threats can be averted by repentance (Jer. 18:7–10 and the case of Nineveh in Jonah). God appears to change his mind as he communicates his change of action to humans based on human responses, though ultimately, since he has foreknowledge of the future, he has planned beforehand to do what he does.

Essentially Balaam tells Balak, "God is not fickle like us. We do not always tell the truth. Sometimes we lie on purpose or find it impossible to do what we promised. Or we make promises and renege. But God is different from us. He never lies. He never makes a promise that he is unwilling or unable to keep. So if God promises something, he will surely bring it about."

The New Testament adds that not only does God not lie (Titus 1:2), but it is impossible for him to lie (Heb. 6:18). Lying is contrary to God's essential character.

The Bible makes all sorts of promises about salvation, heaven, and God's love for us. Are those promises reliable? Scripture teaches that God's promises are sure because they are based on the character of God, who is entirely trustworthy. God does not change his eternal purposes. Balaam comes to recognize that truth.

Teaching the Text

1. *God chose us.* Balaam's oracle recognizes the uniqueness of Israel as God's chosen people set apart from the nations (Num. 23:9). Israel is God's "treasured possession" (Exod. 19:5), chosen above all the nations (Deut. 10:15; 14:2). In the New Testament the language of Israel's election is applied to the church (Eph. 1:4; Col. 3:12; 1 Pet.

2:9). Like Israel, Christians are to be a chosen "people who live apart."

2. *God protects us.* Although Balaam and Balak try to influence God through extravagant sacrifices, they have no power to manipulate God to thwart God's protection (Num. 23:21–23). "How can I curse those whom God has not cursed? How can I denounce those whom the LORD has not denounced?" (Num. 23:8). God still protects those who put their trust in him. Christ defends and lays down his life for us, his sheep (John 10:11–18; cf. Ps. 23:1). Nothing, including angels, demons, and the powers of the occult, can separate us from the love of God (Rom. 8:38–39). We should look to God for protection.

3. *God blesses us.* God's will for Israel is to bless them (Num. 22:12). Dennis Cole writes, "The recurrent theme of the Book of Balaam [is] that God has and will continue to bless Israel. . . . God's blessing is so powerful and irrevocable that even the most renowned divination expert of the day could not counter its effectiveness. Only God could rescind his blessing upon Israel, and he would not because such an act would violate his character."[12]

Not only is Balaam unable to curse Israel, but also he recognizes that it is destined to be blessed. God blesses the Israelites with large numbers (Num. 23:10a) and allows them to be strong and flourish (Num. 24:5–9). He promises them victories over enemies (Num. 23:24). He even blesses them in death (Num. 23:10b). God through Balaam blesses Israel three times, to Balak's chagrin (Num. 24:10). By attempting to curse Israel, Balaam in fact brings curses on himself (Num. 24:9; cf. Gen 12:3; Num. 31:8, 15–16) and leaves empty-handed (Num. 24:10).

In the New Testament God has blessed Christians with every spiritual blessing in Christ (Eph. 1:3). Christians are to look to God for their blessings. God guides, protects, and blesses them with good things. Christians are not necessarily victorious in everything they try to do for God, but the book of Revelation indicates that believers will be victorious in the end, for this is God's will and promise. No one can overturn God's good plans for his people. Ultimately, it is the enemies of God's people who are cursed. God's people will be blessed.

Illustrating the Text

There are modern "cursings" of God's people.

Philosophy: Just as Balak sought to curse Israel, so many modern people "curse" Christians. Atheists and secularists do not literally curse—a curse requires a god or at least the supernatural—but they certainly speak ill of Christians. Karl Marx famously dismissed religion as "the opium of the people." In his view, religion drugs people and gives them a false sense of happiness. Friedrich Nietzsche wrote sneeringly of Christianity, "Christianity was from the beginning, essentially and fundamentally, life's nausea and disgust with life, merely concealed behind, masked by, dressed up as, faith in 'another' or 'better' life."[13]

Popular Culture: Hollywood, offended by Christian morality, goes out of its way to portray Christians negatively. While there can be positive portrayals of faithful and thoughtful Christians, movies and television shows often depict Christians as uneducated, fundamentalist, and irrelevant zealots. For instance, these movies portray

Christians negatively: *The Simpsons Movie* (2007), *License to Wed* (2007), *Saved!* (2004), *I Now Pronounce You Chuck & Larry* (2007), *Religulous* (2008), *Jesus Camp* (2006), *Hairspray* (2007), and *Juno* (2007). But then, they hated our Lord too (John 15:18).

The gods of mythology were capricious.

Mythology: The gods of mythology were known for being capricious. Take, for example, the Greek god Eurus, the "East Wind." He can be described as a "surly, treacherous fellow, striking suddenly out of the fair skies" and "a menace to shipping when his mood was foul."[14] More famously capricious was Eros, the god of amorous desire, who on a whim would strike a victim with his mischievous love arrows.

The faithful God of the Bible is different. He is not capricious. He does not lie (Num. 23:19). He does not change his mind on a whim. He always remains true to his principles.

Sin can lead us to irrational behavior.

Human Experience: A popular quote, often wrongly attributed to Albert Einstein or Benjamin Franklin, observes that insanity can be defined as "doing the same thing over and over again and expecting different results."

Balaam and Balak lived up to that definition. They kept trying to curse Israel by following exactly the same ritual. They went through the same pattern three different times for Balaam's first three oracles, hoping each time for a different result.

It is easy to mock this pagan prophet and pagan king for doing this. But sometimes we also fall into similar insane patterns of mindless repetition in life.

Balaam's Final Prophecies

The Star and the Scepter

Big Idea *God and Israel's coming king will overcome Israel's enemies.*

Understanding the Text

The Text in Context

The prophecies of Numbers 24:14–25 conclude the Balaam cycle (Num. 22–24). Three times Balak king of Moab brings the Mesopotamian diviner Balaam to a mountain height to give Israel the evil eye and curse it. Three times God makes Balaam bless Israel instead. Now Balaam foresees how Israel under its star-and-scepter king (Num. 24:17) will crush Moab and how other enemies of Israel will suffer calamity. As before, Balak goes away disappointed (Num. 24:25).

Interpretive Insights

24:16 *Most High.* This phrase renders *'elyon* (cf. *shadday* ["Almighty"] in 24:4). This title emphasizes God's exaltedness. Melchizedek refers to his and Abram's creator-God as "God Most High" (*'el 'elyon* [Gen. 14:18–22]). "Most High" and "Almighty" are shortened forms of ancient patriarchal designations for God.

24:17 *I see him, but not now . . . not near.* This introduction teases readers to draw them in. The "him" whom Balaam sees by revelation does not "now" exist, and indeed his appearance is "not near," but awaits the distant future.

A star will come out of Jacob; a scepter will rise out of Israel. This person is prominent and splendorous: he shines. Kings are sometimes referred to as stars (Isa. 14:12;

A scepter rising out of Israel refers to kingship. Shown here are two scepter heads from Israel (tenth to seventh century BC).

Rev. 22:16 [of Christ]). "Will come out" is literally "will step forth" (CJB). The Hebrew verb means to "tread, trample, march" (*darak*), suggesting military action. "Out of Jacob" indicates that this mysterious person is an Israelite. In Genesis 49:10 Israel's "scepter" or kingship belongs to the tribe of Judah.

He will crush the foreheads of Moab . . . the skulls . . . of Sheth. David conquers Moab and other groups mentioned in this passage (2 Sam. 8:1–14). This verse was taken as messianic, however, by the rabbis (e.g., *Targum Onqelos*), by the Jews at ancient Qumran, and by early Christians such as Justin Martyr (see "Additional Insights" following this unit), and this view still has defenders in modern times.[1] Its possible allusion to Genesis 49:10 lends the messianic view some support.

"Foreheads" (*pe'ah*) is literally, "the corners [of their heads]." This may indicate foreheads or temples (NIV, ESV, NASB, NKJV). Compare Leviticus 19:27, where "corner of your head" is rendered "sides of your head." This could be metaphorical for Moab's leaders.[2] Alternatively, though less likely, it may refer Moab's "corners" (KJV, NASBmg) or "borderlands" (NRSV), meaning Moab's totality ("corner to corner"). The NIV assumes that the traditional Hebrew text is corrupt and corrects the Masoretic Text's reading *qarqar* to *qodqod* ("skull"), based on the Samaritan text and the allusion to this verse in Jeremiah 48:45, both of which read *qodqod*, suggesting that the Hebrew letter *dalet* (ד) was confused with the similar-looking *resh* (ר). The corrected text makes this line parallel with "foreheads of Moab" and probably is correct. Alternatively, *qarqar* could be

Key Theme of Numbers 24:14–25

- Knowledge of God is sometimes manifested in people who do not know God.

a verb meaning "demolish" or something similar (ESV, NASB, NKJV, NIVmg) in parallel with "crush" in the previous line, or it could be taken to mean "territory" in parallel with the rendering "borders" (NRSV). "Sheth" is the same word in Hebrew (*shet*) as the name of Adam's son Seth (Gen. 4:25; 5:3), but reference to Seth seems odd, though it could be a way of saying "all humankind." It may alternatively refer to Shutu, a people group mentioned in Egyptian Execration texts dating to the nineteenth or eighteenth century BC. Perhaps "Shutu" was the Egyptian term for the Moabites.[3] Less likely is to see *shet* as a common word meaning "din, tumult" ("noisy boasters" [NIVmg]), based on an allusion to this verse in Jeremiah 48:45, where "sons of *shet*" is paraphrased as "sons of tumult," using a related cognate term.[4]

24:18 *Edom . . . Seir . . . will be conquered . . . Israel will grow strong*. Edom, south of Moab and mostly southeast of the Dead Sea, is taken by David (2 Sam. 8:12–14). Seir is a mountain range in Edom, "Mount Seir" (Gen. 14:6, Ezek. 35:15), used here as a synonym for Edom. "Will grow strong" is better rendered "does valiantly" (ESV, KJV, NASB, NKJV, NRSV).

24:19 *A ruler will come out of Jacob*. If the text is sound, this is the king of verse 17. Jacob Milgrom and Gordon Wenham suggest that the word "his enemies" (v. 18) has accidentally been misplaced and belongs to verse 19, and that there has also been an incorrect word division in verse 19a in which the preposition *mem* (מ) attached to "Jacob" should be an enclitic *mem* attached to the verb "rule." They remove "his enemies" from verse 18 and put it in verse 19 and render the latter verse, "Jacob shall rule his enemies and destroy the survivors."[5]

destroy the survivors of the city. The word *'ir* ("city") could be a collective and rendered "cities" (ESV). David's army devastates the male population of Edom (1 Kings 11:14–16). Alternatively, *'ir* might be a proper name: "destroy the survivors of Ir" (NJPS) or "Ar" (NEB [Num. 21:28]), in reference to the Moabite city Ir-Moab (Num. 22:36 NRSV). If this is a Moabite city, it should follow verse 17 about Moab.

24:20 *Amalek.* The Amalekites to the south are the "first among the nations" perhaps in the sense that they are the first enemy Israel faces after leaving Egypt (Exod. 17:8–16), or in the sense that they are the most ancient of those nations,[6] or because they are especially fierce in battle. They defeat Israel at the beginning of the wilderness wanderings (Num. 14:43–45) but are under God's curse (Exod. 17:14). Ironically, Amalek will go from "first" to last ("end"), facing "utter destruction." The Amalekites are defeated by Saul (1 Sam. 15 [see comments at Num. 24:7]) and David (2 Sam. 8:12). Subsequently, the Amalekites go into decline. Their last mention in the Bible says that in the days of Hezekiah the remnant of the Amalekites who had escaped and taken refuge in Mount Seir is defeated by the tribe of Simeon (1 Chron. 4:41–43). Thereafter they disappear from history.

24:21–22 *Kenites.* The Kenites (lit., "Kain" [ESV, KJV, NASB, NRSV]) are a Midianite tribe. Israel is not initially hostile to Kenites. Moses's in-law Hobab is a Midianite (Num. 10:29) and a Kenite (Judg. 1:16; 4:11). After a Midianite woman, in alliance with Moabite women, entices Israelite men to disobey God (Num. 25), Israel treats Midianites as enemies (Num. 31:1–10). Although they feel secure in their mountain "nest" (*qen*, which sounds like *qayin* ["Kain"]), they will be "destroyed" (lit., "burned").

Ashur. "Ashur" normally refers to Assyria, but Assyria did not invade and control the region until the eighth century. This probably refers instead to the Ashurites, a desert tribe descended from Abraham through his wife Keturah (Gen. 25:3), though there is no record of when or how the Ashurites conquered the Kenites.

24:23 *Alas! Who can live when God does this?* Compare ESV, NKJV, NRSV. Alternatively, "Alas, who can survive unless God has willed it?" (NJPS; cf. NASB).

24:24 *Ships will come from the shores of Cyprus.* The NIVmg (cf. NEB, REB) emends the Hebrew to read, "The people from the islands will gather from the north." The REB emends the Hebrew to "invaders." "Cyprus" in Hebrew is *kittim* (cf. NRSV), the descendants of Javan (Gen. 10:4), who settled in Aegean and Eastern Mediterranean islands, including Cyprus.

They will subdue Ashur and Eber. "Subdue" is literally "afflict." "Eber" is obscure. Eber is an ancestor of Abram (Gen. 11:14–27) so it could refer to the Hebrews (LXX). But a vision of Israelites being subdued after Balaam's blessings seems odd. If Ashur is Assyria, then Eber might connect with Mesopotamia, though identifying Ashur with Assyria seems unlikely in verse 21. The fulfillment of these ships

from Kittim may be the Sea Peoples' invasions of Palestine, Syria, and Anatolia in the 1200s BC, which affected wide regions of the Near East.

24:25 *Balaam . . . returned home.* Balaam either does not arrive or does not stay home. Later he is captured by the Israelites and executed for planning the events recorded in Numbers 25 (Num. 31:8, 15–16; Josh 13:22).

Theological Insights

Numbers 24:14–25 describes God as exalted ("Most High") as having the power to injure and protect ("Almighty" [see comments at Num. 24:4]), and as being able to speak and reveal messages through visions (vv. 15–16). This God brings about his prophetic predictions. He can fulfill his warning that those who curse his people will be cursed (see Num. 24:9) by punishing Moab (v. 17) and those like Edom, Amalek, and others who oppose his people (vv. 18–24). Moreover, God has a plan for Israel involving a "star" and a "scepter"—that is, a king who will help fulfill these prophecies. This messianic figure points to David, and possibly also to David's greater son (see "Additional Insights" following this unit), whom God through Balaam predicts in advance.

Teaching the Text

Knowledge of God is sometimes manifested in people who do not know God (Num. 24:15–16). Prophets are called "seers" (*hozeh*), people who see visions from God. Balaam is called a "seer" in the Deir Alla texts (see "Historical and Cultural Background" at Num. 22:1–19), and

Numbers 24:14–25

Balaam brags about being someone whose eyes see clearly spiritual truths, who hears God's word, who has knowledge from God, and who sees visions from God (Num. 24:15–16). These words are full of irony. It is true that God gives Balaam insights and his prophecies come true, but Balaam himself, as earlier chapters and the New Testament indicate, does not really know the true God. Matthew Henry, speaking of these verses, comments, "A man may be full of the knowledge of God and yet utterly destitute of the grace of God, may receive the truth in the light of it and yet be a stranger to the love of it."[7]

It is possible for us, like Balaam, to know all kinds of theological truths about God and yet not really know God himself. Some professional Bible scholars have wonderful insights into the backdrop and exegesis of the Bible, but they are atheists or agnostics religiously. All their religious knowledge does them little good spiritually. The same could be true of us. We might have knowledge—knowing the Bible inside out—but lack deep faith or the fruit of true religion, which is love (see 1 Cor. 13:2). "Head knowledge" of God is no substitute for knowing God personally.

Illustrating the Text

Sadly, it is all too easy for people who know a lot about God not to know God.

Biography: Adolf von Harnack was an enemy of Christian orthodoxy in the nineteenth and early twentieth centuries, though he did not start out that way. Harnack's father, Theodosius, taught pastoral theology in Livonia, so young Adolf grew up in an atmosphere heavy with religious reflection and was taught precious truths about God and Christ. Eventually he became a professor of church history and developed a reputation as a historian of first rank, tracing the development of Christian dogma throughout the ages. But along the way, he came to believe that many of the most-basic Christian beliefs should be tossed aside. He argued that the Apostles' Creed was no proper standard of faith, that many of the miracles in Scripture were fabricated, and that John's Gospel did not have historical value in understanding Jesus. Moreover, Harnack's "gospel" has to do with the Father and ethics but not the cross of Christ, whose deity Harnack denied. Despite his Christian upbringing and vast knowledge about the Bible and theology, from an evangelical perspective it seems doubtful that Harnack had saving faith. Sadly it is possible for people to know much about the Bible's teaching about God without really knowing God at all.

Object Lesson: Have a sample of your favorite food prepared and describe it in detail. For example, have salsa and chips displayed on a tall table. Talk about the flavor of the salsa, the consistency, the perfect contrasts of spicy peppers, biting onion, and sweet tomato. Describe how the cool salsa is best paired with a warm corn chip. Conclude the illustration by saying, "Isn't salsa great?" Walk away and then stop suddenly. "Wait a second. I missed something." Walk back. Dip a chip. Take a bite. "There is no substitute. For a lot of things, explanation can be understood only with experience."

In the same way, we can give many explanations about God. However, if we have not really experienced him, his glory and beauty, then we do not really know him.

Are the Star and the Scepter in Numbers 24:17 Messianic?

Although the most obvious identity of the star and the scepter in Numbers 24:17 is King David, both Jews and Christians have seen messianic implications here.

The Dead Sea Scrolls are the writings of a small Jewish sect, perhaps Essenes, around the beginning of the Christian era.

The *Damascus Document* (CD) of that sect understands Numbers 24:17 this way:

> The star is the Interpreter of the Law who shall come to Damascus, as it is written, *A star shall come forth out of Jacob and a scepter shall rise out of Israel* [Num. xxiv, 17]. The *scepter* is the Prince of the whole congregation, and when he comes *he shall smite all the children of Seth* [Num. xxiv, 17]. (CD-A 7:18–21)[1]

The "star" in the view of this Qumran community is the "Interpreter of the Law," and the "scepter" is the "Prince of the whole congregation," who was still to come, not David. Later the text speaks of two messiahs, the "messiah out of Aaron and of Israel" (CD-A 12:23–13:1; 14:19; CD-B 19:10–11), as if they were looking for a priestly messiah and a royal messiah. It follows that the "Interpreter of the Law" (the "star") is their priestly messiah—perhaps understood as their own leader, the Teacher of Righteousness—while their "Messiah of Israel" is the royal "scepter."[2]

In the second century of the Christian era, many Jews made a mistaken

Who is the star that will come out of Jacob and the scepter that will rise out of Israel? Many believe David is the fulfillment of Balaam's message; others look beyond David to Christ. This illumination from the opening pages of Psalms (AD 1240–50) pictures King David with his musicians seated below a depiction of Christ in Majesty.

identification of the "star" with a Jewish revolutionary, Simon Bar Kokhba. He fought in the Second Jewish War against Rome in the years AD 132–135. From letters found in caves near Qumran that he and his followers used as a hideout, his real name appears to have been "Simon Bar Kosiba," but it was changed to "Bar Kokhba" ("son of star") to associate him with the "star" of Numbers 24:17 and to identify him with the messiah.[3] Some rabbis, including the prominent Rabbi Akiba, supported the revolt and identified Simon as the messiah. Unfortunately, this revolt, like the First Jewish War with Rome (AD 66–73), was crushed by the Roman military machine.

Christians have interpreted Numbers 24:17 as messianic since at least as early as Justin Martyr, in *Dialogue with Trypho* 106:[4]

And that He should arise like a star from the seed of Abraham, Moses showed before hand when he thus said, "A star shall arise from Jacob, and a leader from Israel" [Num. xxiv. 17]; and another Scripture says, "Behold a man; the East is His name" [or, "Dayspring"; Zech. vi. 12 (according to the LXX)]. Accordingly, when a star rose in heaven at the time of His birth, as is recorded in the memoirs of His apostles, the Magi from Arabia, recognizing the sign by this, came and worshipped Him.

Justin Martyr applied the "star" of Numbers 24:17 to the star of Bethlehem, and he saw Jesus rather than David as the fulfillment of this prophecy.

It does seem a little curious that just as the pagan magician Balaam from the "east" (Num. 23:7) was led by a vision of a "star" to see ancient Israel's greatest king, so also pagan magicians (or magi) from the "east" were led by the sight of a star to the Christ child (Matt. 2:1–12), Israel's truly greatest king. Christ, like David, is called a "star" (2 Pet. 1:19; Rev. 22:16). David had splendor (star) and authority (scepter) on earth, but Jesus has heavenly glory (star) and all authority both in heaven and on earth (Matt. 28:18).[5] "Scepter" alludes to Genesis 49:10, a text often taken as messianic. The star and the scepter will defeat "all the sons of Seth/tumult" (v. 17c), an expression that could mean "all humankind" (see comments above). David never literally conquered all humankind, but every knee will bow to Christ (Phil. 2:10). Thus, even if David is the primary reference in Numbers 24:17, an indirect or typological reference to Christ remains possible, for the images and titles of David often foreshadow the kingship of Christ.

Immorality and Apostasy

Big Idea *God's people must deal with immorality and idolatry.*

Understanding the Text

The Text in Context

Numbers 25 moves from the story of the Balaam cycle to Israel's last act of rebellion in the book of Numbers: its idolatry with Baal of Peor. At first glance, this story seems unrelated to Numbers 22–24, simply picking up where Numbers 21 left off with Israel camped on the plains of Moab after defeating Sihon and Og. But that initial impression is wrong. First, this unit provides a contrast: Balaam and Balak cannot curse Israel externally, but Israel can bring on a self-inflicted curse. Second, Balaam in fact has orchestrated this whole affair in a partially successful attempt to get Yahweh to curse Israel (see Num. 31:15–18). The Moabites (Num. 25:1–2) and their Midianite allies (Num. 25:6, 14–15) have intentionally and with hostile intent "deceived" Israel (Num. 25:18).

The rebellion of this chapter forms the climatic conclusion to the story of the old generation.[1] It ends with a plague that kills twenty-four thousand (Num. 25:9), and then is followed by the census of the new generation (Num. 26). With this plague the old generation has essentially been wiped out, and a new generation has replaced it,

as was predicted about thirty-nine years earlier (Num. 14:29–35).

The story of Phinehas is a replay of the story of the golden calf (Exod. 32). Both involve idolatry. In both God sends a plague to punish Israel (Exod. 32:35; Num. 25:9). In Exodus 32 Levites assist Moses by punishing offenders and stopping idolatry. As a reward, the Levites are awarded the task of divine service (Exod. 32:26–29). In Numbers 25 the priest-Levite Phinehas assists Moses by punishing an offender to suppress idolatry. His lineage is awarded the task of high-priestly service (Num. 25:13).

Interpretive Insights

25:1 *Shittim.* This is Israel's final encampment before entering Canaan (Josh. 2:1) on the plains of Moab (Num. 22:1). The population here is still Moabite even though it has been controlled by the Amorite king Sihon (Num. 21:26). Its longer name is "Abel Shittim" (Num. 33:49), and it is probably to be identified with Tell el-Hammam.[2]

sexual immorality with Moabite women. The Hebrew word *zanah* refers to illicit sexual activity of all sorts: prostitution, adultery, and everything else prohibited by the Mosaic law. Given that they invite the Israelite men to "the sacrifices of their gods" (v. 2), perhaps these women offer the men sex on condition that they worship at pagan shrines. Or possibly they are prostitutes working in service of these shrines (cf. 1 Sam. 2:22; 2 Kings 23:7; Ezek. 8:14; Hos. 4:13), though the existence of cult prostitutes in ancient Palestine has been questioned.[3]

25:3 *Baal of Peor.* "Baal of Peor" (lit., "lord/owner of Peor") could be a title for Moab's national god, Chemosh (Num. 21:29), though it more likely refers to Baal's image at his shrine in Peor. Peor, also known as Beth Peor ("house/shrine of Peor" [Deut. 3:29]), is a mountain near the Israelites' encampment from which Balaam tries to curse them (Num. 23:28).

25:4 *Take all the leaders of these people, kill them and expose them in the broad daylight.* God commands Moses to "kill" (probably "impale" [NRSV, NJPS, ESVmg]) either the leaders or the idolaters (see comments at v. 5). The phrase "of these people" lacks "these" in the Hebrew but is an interpretive gloss that limits the killing to leaders of the idolaters ("the ringleaders" [NJPS]). Alternatively, "all the leaders [heads] of *the* people" (NASB, ESV, KJV) could indicate all the tribal leaders who heretofore have

not intervened to stop this idolatry. Leaving the bodies of those executed for public display demonstrates that these men were under God's curse (see Deut. 21:23).

25:5 *judges.* One interpretation sees "judges" as a different group than the "leaders" in verse 4, perhaps the judges initiated in Exodus 18 on advice from Jethro. These judges are to expand the punishment beyond the leaders to other Israelites worshiping Baal of Peor. An alternative interpretation (after C. F. Keil, Rashi, the Samaritan, and the targumim) is preferable. It takes the "leaders" of verse 4 to be identical with the "judges" of verse 5. These leaders/judges are to kill "them," meaning "those Baal worshipers." Taken that way, verse 5 records how Moses fulfills verse 4: he passes along the orders to these leader-judges and tells them to execute all the idolaters. This reading makes verse 5 consistent with verse 4 rather than expanding it. But before Moses can begin

Moabite women invite Israelite men to the "sacrifices to their gods" (25:2). The men sin against the Lord by bowing down to those gods and engaging in sexual acts with the women. All this most likely took place on Mount Peor, where a sacred site to Baal may have been located. This twelfth-century BC bronze model from Susa may depict a cultic site with altars, libations, water basins for purification, and sacred trees.

to carry out God's orders, a dramatic event intervenes.

25:6 *an Israelite man brought into the camp a Midianite woman.* The man, Zimri (v. 14), brings a Midianite woman literally "to his brothers," probably his family. The woman is Kozbi (v. 15). Midianites are allies of the Moabites (Num. 22:4, 7), but Moses has married a Midianite (Exod. 2:21; 3:1), and his Midianite in-law Hobab has served as a guide through the desert (Num. 10:29–32), so the Israelites are amenable to social contact with Midianites.

before the eyes of Moses and the whole assembly. That is, Zimri acts shamelessly.

they were weeping at the entrance of the tent of meeting. Others are mourning Israel's sins and seeking God's mercy while Zimri brazenly sins. Sin is even brought into the heart of the camp within eyeshot of the tabernacle. Is Zimri presenting this pagan girl to his family for marriage?[4] That he unceremoniously takes her to bed (see v. 8) suggests an immoral liaison, not a marriage.

25:7–9 *Phinehas . . . drove the spear . . . through the Israelite man and into the woman's stomach.* Phinehas means "Nubian, dark-skinned" in Egyptian.[5] He is the "son of Eleazar," who is Aaron's successor as high priest. Phinehas enters the tent and acts in accord with Moses's orders to impale offenders (vv. 4–5). The "tent" (v. 8) translates *qubbah*, a word that occurs only here in the Hebrew Bible. It may refer to an arched room within/beside a larger tent or perhaps a marriage canopy.[6] Its precise meaning is uncertain.[7] Phinehas skewers (cf. v. 4) both Zimri and Kozbi, for the two are evidently copulating. With poetic justice, the spear punishes the region of the woman's sexual organs (cf. Num. 5:21).

the plague . . . stopped . . . but those who died . . . numbered 24,000. Phinehas's action, and perhaps that of the judges (v. 5), limits God's plague. In claiming the lives of twenty-four thousand, this plague kills the last of the older generation (Num. 26:64–65). Paul, in alluding to Numbers 25, says "in one day twenty-three thousand of them died" (1 Cor. 10:8). Paul perhaps does not count those hanged by the judges, or he may reflect a tradition that most of the twenty-four thousand died on the same day, just as had happened in the similar incident of the golden calf (Exod. 32:28).

25:11 *he was as zealous for my honor . . . as I am.* Alternatively, "he was zealous with zeal for me" (cf. NRSV) or "he was zealous with my zeal" (NKJV). Phinehas's anger expresses the anger of God.

25:12–13 *covenant of peace . . . lasting priesthood.* Rendering it "a pact of friendship" (NJPS) seems weak. The Hebrew word *shalom* ("peace") has many meanings: "prosperity, success, wholeness, health, well-being, friendliness, salvation."[8] The word's root, *shlm*, can mean "to recompense, reward." Perhaps that meaning has rubbed off onto the noun: God's "covenant of *shalom*" means that God has committed himself both to "compensate" Phinehas and to bring about his "well-being."[9] Phinehas's reward is that the high priesthood will pass through his descendants (see 1 Chron. 6:50–53).

made atonement for the Israelites. Phinehas's actions appease God's anger by punishing the guilty. On "atonement," see "Additional Insights" following the unit on Leviticus 4:1–35.

25:14–15 *Zimri son of Salu . . . Kozbi daughter of Zur.* Both offenders are from prominent families. Zimri's father, Salu, is a Simeonite clan leader. Making an example of Zimri underscores that social standing does not exempt anyone from obeying God's law. The census of the next chapter indicates that Simeon suffers a large population loss (59,300 to 22,200 [Num. 2:12–13; 26:12–14]), suggesting that God's plague strikes this tribe disproportionally as a punishment. Kozbi is a Midianite princess, daughter of the tribal chief Zur, one of the "five kings of Midian" killed in battle by Israel (Num. 31:8).[10]

25:17–18 *Treat the Midianites as enemies . . . they deceived you.* See Numbers 31:1–24. Midian had "deceived" Israel on the advice of Balaam (Num. 31:8, 16–17).

Theological Insights

The Bible regards Phinehas's action against the sins of idolatry and sexual immorality to be righteous (Ps. 106:30–31). According to God's law, idolatry and immorality are inconsistent with a covenant relationship with God (e.g., Exod. 20:3, 14). Since there is no god except Yahweh (Isa. 44:8), the worship of other gods is a movement away from true religion (Rom. 1:21–23). Polytheism distorts what God is like and is tied to false value systems. Sexual expressions can be idolatrous too. Sex within marriage is a blessing from God to be enjoyed (see Song of Songs), but ideologies that see sexual activity as one's birthright and that reduce sexual morality to "whatever consenting adults decide to do together" make sexual expression into an idol that displaces God. God is the creator of sex (Gen. 1:28). He provides instructions

Sin incurs God's wrath and must be appeased. God orders the offending leaders to be punished by death and then "to expose them in broad daylight before the Lᴏʀᴅ" (25:4). This probably means that they were impaled on poles and displayed for all to see, much like the Assyrians would later do to some of the Israelites they captured at Lachish. The impalement scene shown here is from the larger Assyrian relief depicting the battle of Lachish and its aftermath (700–692 BC).

for us creatures so that we can express our sexuality in ways that please him and in the long run please us.

Teaching the Text

1. *Immorality and idolatry are ever-present dangers.* From Israel's perspective, things had been going extremely well. Israel had

emerged from the desert after forty years and won victories over Sihon and Og (Num. 21:21–35). But temptations to immorality and idolatry threaten to ruin everything, as unbelief had done at Kadesh four decades earlier (Num. 13–14). This chapter represents "a foretaste of Canaan's dangers" to which Israel unfortunately will again succumb[11] (see Judges).

Similarly, our success for God in the past does not guarantee our success in the future. Even after we have accomplished big things for and through God, sin can rear its ugly head. Idolatry and sexual immorality are dangers for us, just as they were for Israel. The two are often associated with each other (see Eph. 5:5; Col. 3:5; 1 Pet. 4:3). Like Israel, we need to be warned repeatedly against falling into these sins.

2. *God's wrath must be appeased.* This passage is one of very many in the Bible that teach us about the holiness of God and his holy hatred of sin.

First, this passage reminds us that sin deserves punishment. Immorality and idolatry make God angry and lead him to punish the offenders (cf. Num. 25:4–5, 8–9). We may presume on the mercy of God and sin freely that God's grace may abound (Rom. 6:1–2), but we do so at our own risk, for this will bring God's discipline upon us as wayward children. Still worse can be expected for those not part of God's family (Heb. 12:4–12).

Second, God mercifully limits his punishment of sin. Some look at this passage and wonder why God has killed so many. But given God's holy hatred of sin, we might instead ask why God has killed so few. More deserve to die, but God allows Phinehas's action to pacify his anger (Num.

25:8). Similarly, God in his mercy limits his punishment today. All Christians are sinners, and some are the worst of sinners, on whom God has shown mercy in salvation (1 Tim. 1:16; Titus 3:5). None of us deserves to be saved, but God in his mercy saves some from the punishment that all of us deserve.

Third, atonement can be made for sin. Phinehas is a priest, and priests in the Old Testament are in the "atonement" business. Most often atonement is made through sacrifices. This is preferable. But Phinehas makes "atonement for the Israelites" (Num. 25:13) by killing Zimri and Kozbi. God's wrath against sin will be satisfied. Our choice is to have God satisfy his wrath by punishing us as sinners or, instead, satisfy it via sacrifice by the atoning death of Christ, which we make our own through faith (Rom. 3:25).

3. *Sin among God's people must be addressed.* It was important to make an example of Zimri, who was from a prominent family, for his brazen and public flouting of God's moral standards. Otherwise, it would have undermined God's whole community. The same is true in the church today. New Testament rules of church discipline demand that flagrant, serious sin in a member first be addressed privately (Matt. 18:15–16; Gal. 6:1). If impenitent, the offender can be reproved (1 Tim. 5:20) or even excommunicated (Matt. 18:17; 1 Cor. 5:2). We are obligated to address sin in our midst. Otherwise, the whole church may suffer harm.

Illustrating the Text

True witness can be, and has been, compromised by false teaching.

Church History: In the 1970s, out of the hippie Jesus movement, arose a heterodox

Christian cult known as the Children of God (more recently known as the Family International). It was headed by David Berg, otherwise known as Moses David, or simply Mo. They spent a lot of time going around to college campuses in America and Europe, proselytizing students into their cult.

One innovation that Berg came up with in 1976 was what he called "flirty fishing." Jesus encouraged his disciples to evangelize by telling them to be fishers of men. Berg put a perverse twist on that: he sent young women from the Children of God communes to bars and nightclubs to meet potential converts, using their sexuality to seduce men into joining their cult. The women would even take these "fish" to bed in an attempt to convert them. Many of these liaisons resulted in the women getting pregnant, and the resulting babies were called "Jesus babies." This practice continued until Berg ended it in 1987, after the onset of the AIDS epidemic made the practice seem too dangerous. This was not the only deviation from biblical sexual morality that this cult practiced. Casual "sexual sharing" among members was another.[12]

What these "flirty fishers" were doing is not unlike what the Moabite women were doing. They were sexually seducing men for a religious purpose. In the case of the Moabite women, the goal was to seduce men to worship in their pagan cult. In the case of the Children of God, it was to seduce men to worship in their heretical and perverse Christian cult. Both led men astray from true worship, true morality, and the true God.

Accountability is a key part of the Christian life.

Popular Culture: Weight Watchers is an organization whose meetings help provide discipline for those trying to lose weight. The meetings include the dreaded "weigh in" to check how much weight has been lost (or gained) since the last meeting. According to the Weight Watchers website, "Many people find the accountability of being weighed by another person helpful to their weight-loss efforts and the structure of going to a Weight Watchers meeting each week is a way to keep commitment strong."

But imagine what it would do to a Weight Watchers meeting if someone came who not only had no intention of losing weight, but also insisted on eating a double cheeseburger, French fries, a jelly doughnut, and a milkshake right in front of the group. It would be totally inappropriate and disruptive. The offender probably would be asked to leave. Zimri was guilty of something similar in flagrantly and openly flouting the moral standards of God. Had he been allowed to do so unchecked, it would have undermined the discipline of all Israel.

The church, like Weight Watchers, seeks to encourage discipline (Heb. 3:13). Those who disregard its moral and theological standards might well be asked to leave (Matt. 18:15–17; 1 Cor. 5:1–5).

The Second Census

Big Idea *God's plans triumph over human frailties.*

Understanding the Text

The Text in Context

Thirty-eight and a half years after Israel had been condemned to wilderness wanderings, and shortly "after the plague" (Num. 26:1) of Numbers 25, Israel takes another census. As a result of the plague, the old generation is now gone (Num. 26:63–65). Only Moses, Caleb, and Joshua have survived to be part of this census. Thus, this genealogy marks the death of the old and the birth of the new generation. The old, rebellious generation has now been replaced by their "little ones" (Num. 14:31 NRSV), as God had predicted (Num. 14:26–35).

Israel is transitioning to new leadership. Both Miriam and Aaron are dead (Num. 20:1, 25–28), and soon Joshua will be chosen to succeed Moses (Num. 27:12–23), who will die before entering the land (Num. 20:12; Deut. 34:5). The tribal leaders also are new (Num. 34:16–29).

This is the second census in the book of Numbers (see Num. 1–2). The total number of people in this census is about the same as in the first census, though with a small decline: 603,550 versus 601,730 (Num. 1:46; 26:51). Numbers 26 has a greater focus on the land than Numbers 1–2 does because this census determines how much land each tribe will inherit (Num. 33:54). The order of this census is the same as the first except that Joseph's sons, Ephraim and Manasseh, have reversed places. See further comments at Numbers 1.

Interpretive Insights

26:1 *After the plague.* See Numbers 25:8–9.

Moses and Eleazar . . . the priest. God commands Moses and the high priest to take the census, as previously (cf. Num. 1:3).

26:2 *those twenty years old or more who are able to serve in the army.* Counting men available for military service anticipates the conquest.

26:3 *Jericho.* This is where Israel will begin the conquest (Josh. 6).

26:5–11 *Reuben . . . 43,730.* Compare Genesis 46:9; Exodus 6:14; 1 Chronicles 5:3. The 43,730[1] represents a decline of 2,770 in population during the wilderness years. The Korah incident has contributed to its decline. It is from the Pallu branch of the Reubenites that Dathan and Abiram come (v. 9); although they had joined Korah in rebellion (Num. 16:1) and died with him and his followers (Num. 16:31–35), the line of Korah survives (v. 11) as an act of God's grace. His descendants later produce Psalms 42–49; 84–88. On Nemuel (v. 9), see verse 12 below.

26:12–14 *Simeon . . . 22,200.* "Nemuel" (cf. 1 Chron. 4:24) is the same name as that of a Reubenite (v. 9 above). Earlier lists spell it "Jemuel" (Gen. 46:10; Exod. 6:15). "Ohad," found in the earlier lists, disappears; perhaps that clan has died out. "Zerah" is spelled "Zohar" in Genesis 46:10. Shaul is the son of a Canaanite woman (Gen. 46:10), an early indication of the tribe of Simeon's movement toward idolatry. Now numbering 22,200, Simeon experiences the biggest decrease among the tribes, making it the smallest tribe. This decline may relate to Zimri, the Simeonite who had provoked the actions of Phinehas (Num. 25). The plague God sends at that time may have disproportionately affected Simeon. Simeon fares poorly in the arid southland that it occupies. It assists Asa in the ninth century (2 Chron. 15:9), and

Key Theme of Numbers 26:1–65

- God's warnings and promises are sure.

Josiah acts against its idolatry in the seventh century (2 Chron. 34:6–7), but after the Babylonian exile the tribe disappears after being absorbed into Judah.

26:15–18 *Gad . . . 40,500.* In Genesis 46:16 "Zephon" appears as "Ziphion" (MT, NIVmg; NIV corrects it to "Zephon"), and "Ozni" appears as "Ezbon." The 40,500 represents a loss of 5,150 over the first census, making Gad the third-smallest tribe. No specific event helps to explain its losses.

26:19–22 *Judah . . . 76,500.* Er and Onan, who die in Canaan, act wickedly before Yahweh. Onan dies for failing to raise up an heir for his dead brother, Er, through levirate marriage (Gen. 38:1–10). Shelah, Perez, and Zerah are Judah's sons

As the Israelites are camped on the plains of Moab by the Jordan across from Jericho, the Lord tells Moses and Eleazar, now the high priest, to take a census by family of all those twenty years old or older who are able to serve in the Israelite army. Shown here are the plains of Moab viewed from the west near the region of Jericho. The Abarim Range rises behind them.

(Gen. 46:12; 1 Chron. 2:4–5). Perez and Zerah are the result of Judah's illicit union with Tamar (Gen. 38:27–30). Perez and his son Hezron are ancestors of Boaz, who is an ancestor of David (Ruth 4:18–22), who is an ancestor of Jesus Christ (Matt. 1:1, 17). Now numbering 76,500, the tribe of the star and the scepter (Num. 24:17) has increased by 1,900, making it the largest of the twelve tribes.

26:23–25 *Issachar . . . 64,300.* On Tola, Puah, Jashub, and Shimron, see Genesis 46:13 and 1 Chronicles 7:1. The name "Tola" is recycled in the judge Tola (Judg. 10:1–2), though he is not the same person. The 64,300, an increase of 9,900 from the first census, makes Issachar the third-largest tribe.

26:26–27 *Zebulun . . . 60,500.* On Sered, Elon, and Jahleel, see Genesis 46:14; they are not listed in 1 Chronicles 1–9. The 60,500 represents an increase of 3,100 from the first census.

26:28–34 *Joseph . . . Manasseh . . . 52,700.* Joseph becomes two separate tribes after Levi, the clergy tribe, ceases to be counted among the twelve. Manasseh is the firstborn, though Ephraim receives the firstborn's blessing (Gen. 48:12–20) and becomes the more prominent tribe. Makir is placed on his grandfather Joseph's knees before Joseph dies (Gen. 50:23). Makir as Manasseh's only son becomes a synonym for Manasseh (Judg. 5:14). Six subclans come from Gilead, suggesting that any other lines have died out. The region given to Makir/Manasseh (Num. 32:39–42; Deut. 3:15; Josh. 13:31) to form eastern Manasseh is named "Gilead" after Makir's son. The other half of Manasseh settles west of the Jordan. The six clans Iezer, Helek,

Asriel, Shechem, Shemida, and Hepher are, except for the first, listed in Joshua 17:2. The names "Abiezer" [= "Iezer"?], "Helek," "Asriel," "Shechem," "Shemida," and "Hepher" are geographic terms for subdivisions of Manasseh in the eighth-century BC Samaria Ostraca.[2] Part of this lineage is through an Aramean concubine (1 Chron. 7:14).[3] The mention of the daughters of Zelophehad anticipates their role in Numbers 27:1–11; 36:1–13; Joshua 17:3; 1 Chronicles 7:15. Mention of women in genealogies is rare, although we should take note of Serah (v. 46 below). The 52,700 shows that Manasseh grew by 20,500, the largest increase among the tribes.

26:35–37 *Ephraim . . . 32,500.* This is expanded with spelling and other variants in 1 Chronicles 7:20–29. Beker is a Benjamite clan (Gen. 46:21; 1 Chron. 7:6). Does it merge with Ephraim,[4] or is it displaced from the next section? The 32,500 represents a decline of 8,000, making Ephraim the second-smallest tribe. No specific event explains the losses.

26:38–41 *Benjamin . . . 45,600.* Genesis 46:21; 1 Chronicles 7:6; 8:1–2 list several names not found here, including "Beker" (cf. v. 35 above), "Gera," and "Rosh," as well as variant spellings. In Numbers 26 Arad and Naaman are said to be sons of Bela, whereas they are listed in Genesis 46:21 alongside Bela as sons of Benjamin. "Son" can mean grandson. Genesis 46:21 lists sons and grandsons without distinction. The 45,600 indicates that Benjamin has increased by 10,200 after leaving Egypt.

26:42–43 *Dan . . . 64,400.* Shuham appears as Hushim in Genesis 46:23. Dan is omitted in 1 Chronicles 1–8. The 64,400

shows an increase of 1,700, making Dan the second-largest tribe.

26:44–47 *Asher . . . 53,400.* See Genesis 46:17; 1 Chronicles 7:30. Why is the woman Serah (also in Gen. 46:17; 1 Chron. 7:30) mentioned? Nothing further is known about her. Now numbering 53,400, Asher has increased by 11,900.

26:48–50 *Naphtali . . . 45,400.* In Genesis 46:24–25; 1 Chronicles 7:13 "Jahzeel" is spelled "Jahziel." The 45,400 indicates that Naphtali has lost 8,000 since leaving Sinai.

26:51 *The total number . . . 601,730.* This is a decline of 1,820 from the first census.

26:52–56 *The land is to be allotted.* These verses give the purpose of the second census, which is the division of the land. The census of Numbers 1 measures Israel's military strength, those "able to serve in the army" (14x in chap. 1). That phrase occurs only once in Numbers 26 (v. 2). This census instead is intended to allot the land in proportion to each tribe's numbers (see Josh. 15–17). The land is to be distributed "by lot" (v. 55). This procedure for selecting each tribe's location prevents charges of favoritism on the part of the leadership. Instead the assignment of land is placed in the hands of God.[5]

26:57–62 *Levites . . . 23,000.* These verses enumerate the Levite clans, "not counted along with the other Israelites because they received no inheritance" (v. 62). See Numbers 3:17–43; 1 Chronicles 6. Numbers 3 indicates that Gershon, Kohath, and Merari are the main clans. The Libnite clan is a subclan of Merari, the Hebronite clan is a subclan of Kohath, and the Mahilite and Mushite clans are subclans of Merari. Two subclans of Levites in Numbers 3 are curiously omitted here (Shimei, Uzziel), while Izhar is included only indirectly through mention of the Korahite clan that is a subclan of Kohath through his son Izhar (Exod. 6:18, 21; Num. 3:19; 16:1). The Levites do not serve in the army, and they are not to receive an inheritance (v. 62), though they are assigned forty-eight cities to live in (Num. 35:1–8). Of note here is

Table 1. Comparing the First and Second Censuses

Tribe	First Census Numbers 1	Second Census Numbers 26	Change
1. Reuben	46,500	43,730	−2,770
2. Simeon	59,300	22,200	−37,100
3. Gad	45,650	40,500	−5,150
4. Judah	74,600	76,500	+1,900
5. Issachar	54,400	64,300	+9,900
6. Zebulun	57,400	60,500	+3,100
7. Manasseh (Joseph)	32,200	52,700	+20,500
8. Ephraim (Joseph)	40,500	32,500	−8,000
9. Benjamin	35,400	45,600	+10,200
10. Dan	62,700	64,400	+1,700
11. Asher	41,500	53,400	+11,900
12. Naphtali	53,400	45,400	−8,000
Totals	**603,550**	**601,730**	**−1,820**

the lineage of Moses, Miriam, and Aaron: Korath to Amram (married to Jochebed) to Aaron/Moses/Miriam (v. 59; cf. Num. 3:19). Amram and Jochebed appear to be Moses's parents (Exod. 6:20) rather than more remote ancestors. The lines of two sons of Aaron, Nadab and Abihu, have died out (v. 61; see Lev. 10). The 23,000 represents a 3.3 percent increase from the first census.

26:65 *the Lord had told those Israelites they would surely die.* As God had warned (Num. 14:29–32), all the Israelites have died since the first census in the Desert of Sinai (v. 64), except for Caleb and Joshua. Moses soon will die, so he is not counted with Caleb and Joshua as a survivor. Eleazar is alive, but he had been younger than twenty at the first census.

Theological Insights

Walter Kaiser maintains that the patriarchal promise of land, seed (descendants), and blessing (cf. Gen. 12:1–3) is the central theme of Old Testament theology.[6] This is why this census is so important. Numbers 26 shows that Abraham still has numerous descendants, and it prepares for the fulfillment of the land promise, in which the land will be allotted in proportion to tribal populations (Num. 26:52–56). The land promise is merely delayed

by sin, not abrogated. God's plans prevail over human frailties. Despite the sin and rebellion of the first generation leaving Egypt and God's subsequent wrath, God has preserved the Israelites in large numbers through the forty years of wilderness wanderings and is about to give them Canaan in accord with his promise-plan.

Teaching the Text

God's warnings and promises are sure. God's pronouncements come true. Just as God had warned, Israel's rebellion at Kadesh leads to forfeiture of the land for all those twenty years old and older, with the exceptions of Joshua and Caleb (Num. 14:30; 26:65). Just as God had promised, Israel's descendants are numerous (Num. 26:51). Moreover, Israel is on the plains of Moab (Num. 26:3, 63), positioned for the fulfillment of the land promise. The census is taken to allot land to each tribe proportional to its population (Num. 26:52–56) in anticipation of this promise's fulfillment in Joshua 13–20.

That God's pronouncements to his people in the past have proven true motivates us to heed God's warnings and trust in his promises today. God's warnings and promises are numerous: we are warned that sins such as unbridled

The purpose of the census is to determine the allotment of land that each tribe will receive when the Israelites enter the promised land. Distribution of land is determined by lot. Cultures of the ancient Near East, including Israel, believed that when lots were cast, their god controlled the outcome. Dice were sometimes used. This pair of dice is from the Herodian period, Jerusalem.

lust can bring punishment from God (1 Thess. 4:3–6) and that if we neglect salvation in Christ, fall away from belief, or repudiate Christ, we will face God's severe judgment (Heb. 2:1–3; 6:4–8; 10:26–29). But Christians are also promised that Christ is with us always (Matt. 28:20), that we can have his peace in this troubled world (John 14:27), that God hears and answers our prayers (1 John 5:14–15), and that we will inherit eternal life and heaven (2 Pet. 3:13; 1 John 2:25). Since God has regularly carried out his threats and kept his promises in the past, we most certainly should heed his warnings and claim his promises in the present.

Illustrating the Text

God always carries out his threats.

Human Experience: Many of us probably remember a scene like the following from our childhood. We are in the backseat of the car with a sibling. It's a family road trip. Everyone is buckled in for a four-hour drive. The first thirty minutes have gone smoothly. Bit by bit, however, relations in the backseat begin to degenerate. Battle lines are drawn. Soon, the harmony of the car is punctuated by cries of "He touched me!" or "She's looking at me!" For a time, a calm father and mother respond with, "Let's try to get along." If pressed hard enough, however, we can remember those moments when Mom or Dad would say something like, "Don't make me come back there!" Things were reaching a boiling point when the warning came: "If I have to pull this car over . . ." The unspoken consequence would hang in the air. We would fill in the blanks with various forms of discipline.

On our good days we would heed the warnings, button our lips, and get along for the rest of the ride. If we crossed the line and kept quibbling, our only hope was that the promise of parental punishment would be forgotten or go unfulfilled before we reached our destination. On our lucky days, it was. But that is never the case with God. Absent repentance, all we can expect is retribution.

God always keeps his promises.

Literature: *Pilgrim's Progress*, by John Bunyan. In this classic seventeenth-century book the protagonist, Christian, foolishly departs from the Main Highway. He has been tempted to take an apparently easier pathway, but this alternate route leads him to the land of Giant Despair, lord of Doubting Castle. The terrible giant captures Christian and begins sowing seeds of doubt about the mission that Christian has been called to pursue. At a certain point, Christian even despairs of life. At this low point, Christian's travel partner, Hope, reminds him of how God always remains faithful, as evidenced in Christian's past victories. Through prayer, the hero is encouraged and freed from the prison of doubt.

The Daughters of Zelophehad (Part 1)

Big Idea *God's people will receive their rightful inheritance.*

Understanding the Text

The Text in Context

The plague of Numbers 25 and the census of Numbers 26 mark the end of the first generation after leaving Egypt and the emergence of a new one. But how does the unit on the daughters of Zelophehad (Num. 27:1–11) fit into this sequence? One answer is that the purpose of the census of Numbers 26 is to determine allotments in the land, and this passage is related to the fair distribution of the land.[1]

But why does the narrator divide this story into two episodes, one in Numbers 27 and another in Numbers 36? Alan Kam-Yau Chan argues that the reason is structural: the first part of Numbers is bracketed by the two censuses (Num. 1–4; 26), whereas the second half (Num. 27–36) is bracketed by the two accounts of the daughters of Zelophehad (Num. 27:1–8; 36:1–13), with Numbers 26:33 ("Zelophehad son of Hepher had no sons; he had only daughters, whose names were Mahlah, Noah, Hoglah, Milkah and Tirzah") serving as the linchpin between the two sets of brackets.[2]

Also, the material between these two episodes all in some fashion looks forward to life in the land, so the last chapter, dealing with inheritance in the land by the daughters of Zelophehad, seems fitting with what comes before.[3] The story of the daughters of Zelophehad is one story in two episodes separated for literary-structural reasons.

Historical and Cultural Background

By custom, only sons inherited property at their father's death. Firstborn sons received a "double share" (Deut. 21:17)—that is, twice as much as any other brother. The same custom occurred in Assyria (Middle Assyrian Laws B ¶1). Girls typically received a portion of their father's property before the father died through the gift of a dowry at marriage.

Interpretive Insights

27:1 *the daughters of Zelophehad son of Hepher.* These five unmarried girls and their father/grandfather are mentioned in the genealogy (Num. 26:32–33) in anticipation of this story. Makir is Manasseh's son

(Gen. 50:23), the father of Gilead (Num. 26:29) and hence of the Gileadites.

Mahlah, Noah, Hoglah, Milkah and Tirzah. Four times these daughters are listed by name (Num. 26:33; 27:1; 36:11; Josh. 17:3). The etymology of each name is uncertain.

27:2 *stood before Moses, Eleazar the priest, the leaders and the whole assembly.* These girls take their case before the whole leadership structure of Israel, starting with Moses and the high priest Eleazar. The "leaders" are tribal leaders. The "assembly" is a governing body, not the whole throng of 601,730 men.

the entrance to the tent of meeting. This is where judicial decisions are made. Later in Israel's history they were made at the city gate.

27:3 *Our father . . . was not among Korah's followers . . . he died for his own sin.* Had he participated in Korah's rebellion, this might have resulted in a forfeiture of his family's inheritance rights. Compare the seizure of Naboth's fields by the state after his being (falsely) convicted of crimes (1 Kings 21:1–15). Zelophehad has at least shared in the sins of the first generation that

The daughters of Zelophehad come to Moses requesting to inherit the property that would have been assigned to their father since there are no sons to carry on the family name. Moses rules in their favor. Similar rulings can be found in the Middle Assyrian Laws, a collection of cuneiform tablets recording Assyrian legal material (ca. 1400–1000 BC). Tablet B deals with rulings on property and inheritance. Tablet A, shown here, is the best preserved and records laws pertaining to women.

Key Themes of Numbers 27:1–11

- Pray for wisdom.
- Promote God's justice for women.

left Egypt so that he dies before Israel enters the land.

27:4 *Why should our father's name disappear from his clan . . . ?* By custom, Israel is a patrilineal society in which children take the clan name of their fathers, not their

mothers, and sons, not daughters, receive inheritance. Without a son, no inheritance will be passed down in the father's name. It is assumed that the girls' mother is dead or infertile, since otherwise levirate marriage could have solved this problem (see Deut. 25:5–10).

Give us property among our father's relatives. The daughters want a share of the land to be reckoned as Zelophehad's ancestral land that will pass to their children.

27:5 *Moses brought their case before the LORD.* Moses does not know how to respond, since no law from God addresses this issue. This has also happened in earlier cases: the blasphemer, those missing Passover due to uncleanness, and the Sabbath breaker (Lev. 24:10–22; Num. 9:6–14; 15:32–36). In each of these instances, Moses brings the matter before God to determine the outcome. God, in turn, agrees with the daughters' request.

27:7–11 *Zelophehad's daughters are . . . right.* The ruling forms a precedent for the future. Although sons alone ordinarily inherit, daughters inherit if a man dies without sons. The father's brothers inherit if a man has no children at all, and if he has no brothers, then the inheritance goes to his paternal uncles; and if that fails, it goes to whoever is his nearest relative. This becomes the general law of inheritance in Israel. As Jacob Milgrom points out, an example of how this worked is found in 1 Chronicles 2:34–36. There the man Sheshan has no sons, so he gives his daughter in marriage to Jarha, his Egyptian slave. Jarha and the daughter bear a son, Attai, who ultimately inherits Sheshan's land and continues his bloodline in the genealogy.

Theological Insights

Retribution in human law involves punishing criminals in proportion with their crimes. The *lex talionis* principle of eye for eye, tooth for tooth, and so on encapsulates this concept (see Deut. 19:21). God often is the source of retribution.[4] The daughters acknowledge God's retributive justice: Korah dies because he had conspired against Yahweh, and their father dies before entering the land because of his own sin (Num. 27:3). The Bible uses an agricultural metaphor: people reap what they sow (Hos. 8:7; 10:12; Rom. 6:21–22; Gal. 6:7–8; James 3:18). If we live rightly, we will reap blessings, but if we do wrong and live carnal lives, we could receive God's punishment, such as defeat by enemies, droughts, illness, death, and consignment to the lake of fire (1 Kings 8:33–40; 1 Cor. 11:30; Gen. 2:17; Rom. 6:23; Rev. 21:8). Of course, as the book of Job teaches, not every hardship is retribution from God. Moreover, God's retribution must be balanced with God's mercy and his desire to redeem/forgive people. Thus God in his grace often does not mete out the punishments that people deserve, for which we should thank God.

Teaching the Text

1. *Pray for wisdom.* When the daughters of Zelophehad come to Israel's leaders, their request stumps even the "lawgiver" himself, Moses. Their request seems reasonable, but God has not given revelation on this particular topic. So Moses goes to God to ask for wisdom and guidance.

One of the things that one can do when confronted with an issue not directly addressed by Scripture is to do what Moses did: ask God. James gives the same advice: "If any of you lacks wisdom, you should ask God" (James 1:5). God answered Moses directly, but rarely does God do that for us. Typically, God answers a prayer for wisdom by bringing to mind relevant Scriptures to guide us (cf. John 14:26) or by helping us to think through an issue on the basis of biblical principles and circumstances.

2. *Promote God's justice for women.* When Mahlah, Noah, Hoglah, Milkah, and Tirzah talk things over with one another, it does not seem right that their father will have no inheritance in the land. So these girls do something highly irregular in a patriarchal culture: they confront the male leadership of Israel with this issue. God agrees with the women: "If a man dies and leaves no son, give his inheritance to his daughter" (Num. 27:8).

Note the many virtues of the daughters of Zelophehad. They demonstrate faith that God will in fact fulfill his land promise. They also show respect for the leadership of Moses and the others at the entrance to the tent of meeting. They are not rebels. They are not contentious. They give proper deference to the male court and its authority. Yet they are assertive and bold. They come with confidence that Moses and the other men, and ultimately God himself, will give them a fair hearing and grant them justice. They show determination and gumption. They are young and female, either of which might have deterred girls from appearing before Israel's legal dignitaries. But they have the courage to bring forth to Israel's leaders their concerns. Moreover, these women

are brutally honest. Though their father was not a bad man, these girls do not pretend that he had been perfect. He had in fact "died for his own sin" (Num. 27:3b). They clearly agree with God's justice in letting their father and others of the earlier generation die in the desert. Ultimately, they are obedient to God's word. They obey the court's injunctions and God's own command by marrying their cousins to keep the property within the clan.

These young women are unwilling to submit passively to injustice in a male-dominated society. They use the legal means available to them to seek redress of a wrong in the system. They show themselves to be quite shrewd in making legal arguments, noting how their father had been on the right side of the sons of Korah affair, and admitting that he rightly has died as a result of his sin. And God sides with them. This in turn serves as a model for how we might use the legal system to confront instances of injustice today.

Sometimes people see the Bible as being against women. But the case of the daughters of Zelophehad shows otherwise. Moses is sympathetic to their case, and God's ruling in favor of their request not only grants them rights that have not previously been allowed but also sets a precedent for other women in the future.

Biblical law is not utopian. It was given in a particular culture with certain customs, such as slavery and polygamy, that from the modern perspective are problematic. But although the Bible did not immediately eliminate all objectionable customs, it did attempt to move Israel in the right direction. In the case of Zelophehad's daughters, the law moved Israel's society in the direction of greater rights for women. We might have preferred that the law move further and more quickly in that direction. Nevertheless, the direction that this law took was clearly that of expanding rights for women, not limiting them further.

As a practical matter, that is how injustice sometimes has to be addressed today. It is rarely politically feasible to legislate a utopian vision. However, small legislative improvements repeated over time can eventually lead to large results, as they have done for women's rights in Western culture.

Illustrating the Text

God promises to pour out his wisdom for those who are willing to ask.

Popular Culture: In 2010 Warren Buffett and Bill and Melinda Gates teamed up to form The Giving Pledge and invited others to join them. These philanthropists were bound together by their net worths—at least a billion dollars each—and by their commitment to part with at least half of their net worth in their lifetimes. The list has continued to expand to include billionaires from around the globe, and it has opened up to people of all incomes. A list of signatories is published online, allowing people to view profiles for each of the generous donors. Sounds impressive, doesn't it? But such wealth and generosity cannot compare to the God we worship. His resources are infinite, and his willingness to bless is unquestionable.[5]

Christianity has played a major role in raising the status of women.

Church History: The account of Zelophehad's daughters raises the question of Christianity and the status of women.

Christianity often gets a bad rap as being oppressive of women. But this is unfair. Almost wherever Christianity has gone, it has elevated the lot of women. It has suppressed polygamy, harems, child wives, wife beating, prostitution, male promiscuity, and other cultural practices that tend to demean women.

Alvin Schmidt, in his book *How Christianity Changed the World*,[6]

The laws God set forth for Israel acknowledge women's worth and dignity. Christians have also acted to improve the welfare of women where societal practices demean or harm them. For example, Christian missionaries played a role in eliminating foot binding as an accepted practice for Chinese females. This photo shows the tiny, deformed feet—the ideal was three inches—that resulted from this procedure. Foot binding was a painful process with infection and disability as frequent consequences.

points to many ways that Christianity has elevated the role of women. He summarized these in an interview.

1. Emperor Constantine converted to Christianity. His son, Constantius (AD 337–361), ordered the segregation of jailed male and female prisoners. Pagan Romans had little regard for the welfare of women, especially for women who were no longer under the *manus* (controlling hand) of their husbands, and did not care if female prisoners were raped. That changed under Christian influence.
2. In ancient Roman society Christianity succeeded in outlawing *patria potestas*, the Roman law giving the father the right of life and death over his wife and children.
3. In India the British, influenced by Christian morality, outlawed suttee (widow burning).
4. Christian missionaries in China influenced the laws that resulted in the outlawing of Chinese foot binding, a practice that tried to artificially make the feet of women more petite and "sexy" by binding the feet of young girls, but which resulted in crippling pain, long-term medical problems, and sometimes infection and death. The practice was outlawed in 1912 under Christian influence.
5. Christians have pushed for the outlawing of female genital mutilation. Christian missionaries in Africa in the 1920s and 1930s were among the first to object to the practice.

Just as the law of Moses served to expand the rights of the daughters of Zelophehad, so Christianity has in many ways helped to improve the lot of women.

Joshua Appointed as Moses's Successor

Big Idea *God raises up new leaders for his people.*

Understanding the Text

The Text in Context

The decision allowing the daughters of Zelophehad to inherit land (Num. 27:1–10) is an appropriate occasion for God to remind Moses that he will not enter the promised land. Moses instead must appoint a successor in leadership. Moses is thus instructed about how he will soon die after viewing the land from atop the Abarim mountain range in Moab, though this foretelling is not immediately fulfilled. Moses still needs to convey the remaining laws of the book of Numbers and to deliver the speeches of Deuteronomy before his final acts on the mountain. But the time of Moses's death is quickly approaching. So in Numbers 27:12–23, at the prompting of God, Moses formally makes Joshua the heir and successor of his leadership role.

God tells Moses to view the land he has given to Israel from a mountaintop in the Abarim Range. The mountain is later identified as Mount Nebo. This is what Moses would have seen as he looked west.

Joshua has already proven himself to be a remarkable man. He is a warrior who fought the Amalekites (Exod. 17:8–16). He is one of two scouts (Caleb is the other) who believed that God could overcome their great enemies and thus encouraged the people to go ahead and enter the promised land (Num. 13–14). For decades he has been Moses's right-hand man and younger assistant (Exod. 33:11), even going partway up Sinai with Moses when Moses received the law (Exod. 24:13; 32:17).

Interpretive Insights

27:12 *this mountain in the Abarim Range.* The Abarim is a mountain range forming the rim of the Moab tableland plateau. The term appears to apply to the mountainous spine of the whole country.[1] The specific mountain is later identified as Mount Nebo (Deut. 32:49) or Pisgah (Deut. 34:1; cf. Num. 23:14). "Pisgah" and "Nebo" are either two names for the same peak or Nebo is a region of the Abarim range and Pisgah the specific peak (compare "Rocky Mountains," "Tetons," and "Grand Teton" as increasingly specific terms). Mount Nebo may be a mountain, approximately 2,600 feet or 800 meters in height, in modern-day Jordan.[2]

27:13 *After you have seen it, you too will be gathered to your people.* This is fulfilled in Deuteronomy 34:1–5. Moses is gathered to his people in the afterlife, since no family members are buried with him. On the reference to Moses's brother, Aaron, see Numbers 20:25–29.

27:14 *when the community rebelled . . . both of you disobeyed.* See comments at Numbers 20:1–13. As penalty for this disobedience, God tells Moses and Aaron,

- God seeks leaders who lead by example.
- God endows leaders spiritually for their task.
- God provides ways for leaders to be recognized.

"You will not bring this community into the land I give them" (Num. 20:12).

27:16 *God who gives breath to all living things.* This is literally, "God of the spirits of all flesh" (ESV). This expression is used in Numbers 16:22 to acknowledge that God the creator has the right to discern between human spirits so as to give or take life from his creatures as he sees fit. Here it acknowledges God's ability to discern between spirits to appoint a leader with the right spirit.

27:17 *to go out and come in before them . . . lead them out and bring them in.* This task applies metaphorically to all leaders— the young Solomon uses similar language of his leadership responsibilities ("I do not know how to come out or to go in" [1 Kings 3:7 NASB])—but the language applies literally to a military leader like Joshua.

sheep without a shepherd. These words apply to Israel when its king is killed (1 Kings 22:17) and is later applied to people lacking spiritual leadership (Matt. 9:36; Mark 6:34).

27:18 *Take Joshua son of Nun, a man in whom is the spirit of leadership.* Here God answers Moses's prayer (vv. 16–17). "Of leadership" is an interpretive paraphrase lacking in the text. Verse 16's "spirits of all flesh" (see comments there) suggests that "the spirit" here is Joshua's human spirit rather than God's Holy Spirit (against NASB, NIVmg, ESV), though the interpretations need not be mutually exclusive: personal qualities such as wisdom and counsel can come from God's Spirit (see Isa. 11:2). Joshua's spirit shows the character and leadership qualities necessary to be qualified to replace Moses, including "the spirit of wisdom" (Deut. 34:9), and strength and courage (cf. Josh. 1:7, 9). The Bible says that one whose heart has melted away in fear "has no spirit" (Josh. 2:11). Joshua has already shown a courageous spirit in fighting the Amalekites (Exod. 17:8–16), and he will show it even more in the conquest of Canaan.

lay your hand on him. This is symbolic of both recognition and transfer of authority from Moses to Joshua.

27:19 *before Eleazar the priest and the entire assembly.* Eleazar represents the authority of God, symbolizing God's approval of this selection. The members of the assembly serve as witnesses. By participating, they obligate themselves to submit to Joshua's authority.

commission him. This expression in Hebrew would ordinarily be rendered "command him" (cf. "give him a charge" [KJV]). It is sometimes used of commissioning to an office (2 Sam. 7:7; 1 Kings 1:35). Perhaps Joshua is "commanded" in the sense of being adjured on God's behalf to accept this office and to perform its duties faithfully, possibly followed by an oath by Joshua to do so.

27:20 *Give him some of your authority.* "Authority" (*hod*) sometimes refers to the "splendor" or "majesty" of kings, but here it denotes gravitas that will lead the whole Israelite community to readily obey Joshua.

27:21 *Eleazar . . . will obtain decisions for him by inquiring of the Urim.* Eleazar not only is a symbol of divine approval but also can be the source of divine counsel.

The Urim is a shortened reference to the Urim and Thummim, objects placed in the high priest's breastpiece (Exod. 28:30) and used by the high priest as a means of revelation from God. See comments at Leviticus 8:8.

Theological Insights

Numbers 27:12–23 shows God's concern that his people have leadership. Leaders are necessary "so that the LORD's people will not be like sheep without a shepherd" (v. 17).

Not all leaders of God's people are as well qualified as Joshua. In the book of Judges, God uses leaders with obvious flaws. Gideon is a reluctant farmer of no pedigree who badgers God for miracles before he will do God's bidding. Ehud is a left-handed assassin who wins by deceit and treachery. Jephthah is a son of a prostitute whose foolish vow destroys his daughter. Deborah, by the standards of her day, is a mere woman. Samson is a sex-addicted Nazirite. Later even Israel's greatest leader, David, is guilty of adultery and murder. Thus, this passage does not state minimum qualifications for leadership, even though Joshua is especially well qualified to lead. No one is perfect. God must use leaders with flaws. Some have more flaws than others.

Teaching the Text

1. *God seeks leaders who lead by example.* It is important that spiritual leaders among God's people today exhibit a commitment to obey God's word. Moses prays for God to raise up a shepherd who will "go out and in

Moses is not allowed to enter the promised land because of his disobedience at the waters of Meribah Kadesh. This sarcophagus relief from the fourth century AD depicts Moses striking the rock and water gushing forth.

spirit of wisdom, strength, and courage (Deut. 34:9; Josh. 1:7, 9). Joshua evidently also has an endowment of the Holy Spirit, as is typical among spiritual leaders (e.g., Judg. 3:10; 6:34; 11:29). Every gift or natural attribute ultimately is from God.

God's Spirit still distributes gifts to people today to edify the church. Wisdom, leadership, and offices such as prophet and teacher are among those gifts (Rom. 12:8; 1 Cor. 12:4–11, 28–29). Those whom God has called to lead his people must be endowed by God to do his work, for they will accomplish the most for God "not by might, nor by power, but by [God's] Spirit" (Zech. 4:6). If God has called someone to lead his people in some capacity, he will endow that person with the necessary gifts to do so. The job of leaders is to use the "spirit" that God has given them for his glory.

3. *God provides ways for leaders to be recognized.* Joshua is not in an enviable position. Moses has been the greatest man of God in history since Abraham. That is a tough act to follow. Any comparisons that the people might make between Joshua and Moses will be, at least at first, at the expense of Joshua. That is why God asks Moses to lay hands on Joshua publicly, symbolically transferring to Joshua Moses's leadership responsibilities and authority (Num. 27:18). The occasion is made more solemn by the presence of Eleazar the high priest (Num. 27:19), who represents God's authority and approval. All this is done to exalt the dignity and authority of Joshua in the eyes of the people so that they will in fact follow his leadership.

before them" (Num. 27:17)—that is, lead by example. But disobedience—a bad example—can disqualify us from ministry. Paul warns Timothy that leaders who fail to play by the rules might end up disqualified (2 Tim. 2:5). Even the great man of God Moses forfeits ministry opportunities by disobedience (see Num. 20:2–13). So can we.

Mediocre leaders say, "Do what I say, not what I do." Ideal spiritual leaders lead by positive example, putting into practice what they preach. They can say with Paul, "Imitate me. Do what I do" (see 1 Cor. 4:16; 2 Thess. 3:9). Can we say that?

2. *God endows leaders spiritually for their task.* It is not by chance that Joshua is chosen as Moses's successor. He has the right "spirit" (Num. 27:18), specifically a

Numbers 27:12–23

The same thing applies to any new leader of God's people today. God has led the church to practice ordination ceremonies whereby new servants of God can be publicly recognized and invested with the responsibilities and authority of their duties. Christian ordination ceremonies typically involve the solemn laying of hands by church leaders or elders on those being ordained (Acts 6:5–6; 13:2–3; 1 Tim. 4:14), publicly recognizing the call of God to those persons. Such ceremonies encourage the laity to support those new leaders and to let them take up the ministry roles to which God has called them, so that they, like Joshua, can lead their people in and out (Num. 27:21).

Illustrating the Text

Godly leaders practice what they preach.

Science: From the earliest age, we are creatures who learn by imitating. A 2013 study by researchers from the University of Washington and Temple University discovered that babies' brains are organized for imitation. When an adult touches an object with his or her hand, the part of the child's brain connected to hand motion "lights up" as the child watches the adult. The same is true for the use of feet and so forth. It is fascinating to know that we are hardwired to follow an example. The implications for leaders are readily apparent: our example communicates without a single word being spoken.[3]

Moses commissions Joshua as his successor by laying hands on him in the presence of Eleazar, the high priest, and the entire assembly of Israelites. This watercolor design drawing for a stained-glass piece depicts Joshua receiving some of Moses's authority.

Through the Holy Spirit, God gives leaders resources to serve.

Scripture: Speaking to his disciples, Jesus makes it clear that God gives his people exactly what they need to serve him: the Holy Spirit. Jesus says,

> Is there anyone among you who, if your child asks for a fish, will give a snake

instead of a fish? Or if the child asks for an egg, will give a scorpion? If you then, who are evil, know how to give good gifts to your children, how much more will the heavenly Father give the Holy Spirit to those who ask him!" (Luke 11:11–13 NRSV)

Good leadership is cultivated over time, not born in an instant.

Humor: The story is told of a tourist passing through an old village in Switzerland. He asked an elderly woman of this quaint town in the mountains, "Were great men ever born here?" The old woman replied, "No. Only babies." Joshua was not born a developed leader. Great leaders rarely start out being great. Becoming a great leader takes time. Leaders have to grow in their ministry. They have to make some mistakes. But if allowed to grow and develop, and if they are endowed with God's spirit of leadership, they can do great things.

New leaders should be recognized and supported.

History: Many of us grew up hearing tales of King Arthur and his Knights of the Round Table. We may even have played games as children, dubbing a friend with a play stick-sword. In Great Britain, the ancient tradition of conveying knighthood continues to this day. It can be assigned only by the queen (or king). The official website of the British monarchy contains fascinating information about the historical development and continued practice of knighthood (and damehood for women).[4]

Just as the words, "I dub thee Sir . . ." publicly convey a position and set of expectations, so the words of ordination communicate something important about a person called to serve in church leadership.

The Sacrifices of the Sacred Calendar

Big Idea *People can worship God through the regular cycles of life.*

Understanding the Text

The Text in Context

In the desert God prescribes a system of sacred space for Israel (Lev. 1–8), whose people camp around the tabernacle while they travel through the desert (Num. 1–4). Leviticus 23 describes the various sacred times that Israel will commemorate upon entering the land. Now in Numbers 28–29, as the conquest draws near, God reiterates the system of sacrificial worship in conjunction with Israel's sacred times around which the people are to conduct their lives.

Numbers 28–29 gives the appropriate daily sacrifices in addition to the regular daily burnt offerings for various occasions in Israel's calendar year. The first three are organized around frequency (daily, weekly, monthly), and then the rest are organized chronologically through the year (Passover, Weeks, Trumpets, Day of Atonement, Tabernacles). The establishment of these holidays sets the stage for Israel's calendar serving as a teaching device for Israel and a guide for its worship.

Historical and Cultural Background

Israel followed a lunar calendar in which the beginning of a month was at the new moon. Jewish tradition in the Mishnah indicates that new moons were announced officially by fires on hilltops and/or by messengers (Mishnah *Rosh HaShanah* 2:1–4). There were twelve or thirteen new moons per year. An intercalary month was added periodically to keep the lunar and solar calendars together.

Interpretive Insights

28:1–29:40 For an outline of the offerings of the sacred calendar, see the table "Summary of Sacrifices during Israel's Year."

28:2 *my food offerings . . . an aroma pleasing to me.* See comments at Leviticus 1:9. Burning a sacrifice produces aromas akin to cooking. Proper sacrificial worship pleases God as the smell of cooking food pleases humans.

28:3 *without defect.* See comments at Leviticus 1:3.

regular burnt offering. A morning or evening burnt offering smolders continually on the altar twenty-four hours a day, seven days a week.

28:4 *at twilight.* Literally, "between the evenings."

28:5–7 *with a grain offering . . . mixed with . . . oil from pressed olives . . . fermented drink.* Flour and drink with animal flesh round out the meal presented to God. On the pressed olives, see comments at Leviticus 24:2. On the fermented drink, see comments at Leviticus 10:9. Exodus 29:40 and Numbers 28:14 call it "wine," which may be included in the term. Alternatively, the text may be corrupt: some manuscripts of the Septuagint and the Greek translation of Symmachus, along with the Syriac and Vulgate translations, read "wine" in agreement with verse 14.

tenth of an ephah . . . quarter of a hin. These are roughly two quarts (3.5 pounds) of grain and one quart of oil/fermented drink (NIVmg).

instituted at Mount Sinai. See Exodus 29:38–41.

28:9–10 *On the Sabbath day . . . in addition to the regular burnt offering.* See comments at Leviticus 23:3 and at Numbers 28:3–7 above. The regular burnt offering is doubled on the Sabbath to sanctify it. All the other holy day offerings are in addition to the daily burnt offering.

28:11 *On the first of every month.* The first day of the month is marked by the blowing of the silver trumpets (see Num. 10:10; Ps. 81:3) and by ten burnt offerings (seven lambs, one ram, and two bulls) as well as the sacrifice of a goat for a sin/purification offering. The numerous sacrifices suggest that this was a more important holy day in Numbers than in later Judaism.

28:12–14 *three-tenths of an ephah . . . two-tenths of an ephah . . . half a hin . . . third of a hin.* Larger animals require more flour for the accompanying grain offerings (bull 3x, ram 2x, lamb 1x) and drink offerings (bull one-half, ram one-third, lamb one-fourth). On ephah and hin, see comments at Numbers 28:5–7 above.

28:16 *first month the Lord's Passover.* The list now moves to annual holy days in chronological sequence. The first month, Nisan, is March/April in our calendar. Passover celebrates the exodus. See Exodus 12–13; Leviticus 23:4–8.

Key Themes of Numbers 28:1–29:40

- We can use the regular cycles of life for spiritual purposes.
- We can give God more than the minimum.

A lamb is sacrificed both morning and evening as part of the daily burnt offering to the Lord. This illumination from a fourteenth-century AD Latin Bible manuscript is from the beginning of Leviticus and shows a sacrifice being placed on the altar.

28:17 *bread made without yeast*. At the first Passover Israel did not have time for the dough to rise (Exod. 12:39).

28:18 *sacred assembly*. Better read "sacred occasion" (NJPS) because Israel was too numerous to assemble in one place.

no regular work. This is less strict than "no work" (Num. 29:7). It applies only to the first and last days.

28:19 *Present to the LORD*. These are sanctuary offerings, not the lambs slaughtered for the household Passover meals. The grain and animal offerings are the same as for the new moon.

28:26 *On the day of firstfruits*. This is another name for the Festival of Weeks (Exod. 34:22; Deut. 16:10), the Festival of Harvest (Exod. 23:16), or Pentecost (Acts 2:1).

offering of new grain. The "day of firstfruits" derives its name from this offering of early ripening wheat to God. For other details, see Numbers 28:16–25 above and comments there.

29:1 *On the first day of the seventh month*. Later in Judaism this day is renamed "Rosh Hashanah." See more comments at Leviticus 23:23–25. The seventh month, Tishri (September/October), is special because of two major holidays in that month (Day of Atonement, Festival of Tabernacles).

hold a sacred assembly . . . sound the trumpets. On the sacred assembly, see comments at Numbers 28:18 above. This is not required for other new moons. "Sound the trumpets" is literally "a day of loud blast [of trumpet or

horn]." This could be from the silver trumpets (Num. 10:2), though the term "blast" (*t^eru'ah*) also is used of sounding animal horns (Zeph. 1:16). The offerings here are in addition to the regular new moon offerings (v. 6), making this day's offerings one bull short of doubling a regular new moon offering. For other details, see Numbers 28:16–25 above and comments there.

29:7 *On the tenth day of this seventh month*. Though not named, the holiday here is the Day of Atonement (Lev. 16; 23:27).

hold a sacred assembly. See comments at Numbers 28:18 above.

deny yourselves . . . do no work. On "deny yourselves," see comments at Leviticus 16:29–30. This probably indicates fasting (NIVmg). "Do no work" is a stronger demand than "do no regular work" (Num. 28:18, 25, 26; 29:1, 12, 35). The offerings are the same as those at the trumpet blasts (Num. 29:1–6).

29:11 *in addition to the sin offering for atonement*. See Leviticus 16:5, 9. The bull cannot be the same

The first day of the seventh month is a day to sound the trumpets, do no regular work, and hold a sacred assembly to the Lord, offering sacrifices that include a bull, a ram, and seven male lambs. This trumpet-player figurine is from eighth- to sixth-century BC Turkey.

Table 1. Summary of Sacrifices during Israel's Year (Num. 28–29)

Time	Burnt Offerings			Sin Offerings
	Lambs	Rams	Bulls	Goats
Each day (28:3–8)	2	-	-	-
Each Sabbath (28:9–10)	2	-	-	-
Each new moon (28:11–15)	7	1	2	1
Each day of Unleavened Bread (28:16–25)	7	1	2	1
Festival of Weeks (28:26–31)	7	1	2	1
Trumpets (29:1–6)	7	1	1	1
Day of Atonement (29:7–11)	7	1	1	1
Festival of Tabernacles (29:12–38)				
Day 1	14	2	13	1
Day 2	14	2	12	1
Day 3	14	2	11	1
Day 4	14	2	10	1
Day 5	14	2	9	1
Day 6	14	2	8	1
Day 7	14	2	7	1
Day 8	7	1	1	1

bull as the one Aaron offers for his own sins in preparation for the Day of Atonement ritual (Lev. 16:3, 6, 11–14), since that bull is a sin offering, whereas the one in Numbers 29:8 is a burnt offering.[1]

29:12–38 *Celebrate a festival to the LORD for seven days.* This unit concerns the Festival of Tabernacles. See more comments at Leviticus 23:1–44. As a harvest festival, this is a time of great rejoicing, which perhaps explains the large number of animals offered at this particular festival (see the table "Summary of Sacrifices during Israel's Year"). The double number of lambs on each day as compared with other festivals (fourteen versus seven lambs, two versus one ram) perhaps represents the double blessing of harvest and thus a double honoring of God.[2] The eighth day winds down the festival as the numbers are greatly reduced. The rabbis suggested that the first seventy bulls were offered for the seventy nations of Genesis 10 plus one for

Israel.[3] The command to "do no regular work" (vv. 12, 35) applies only to the first and last days of the Festival of Tabernacles.

29:39 *In addition . . . offer these to the LORD.* This postscript summarizes the unit. The earlier lists of sacrifices are not comprehensive. Individuals can add freewill burnt, grain, or fellowship offerings and offerings to complete vows. Not listed are sin and guilt offerings, which are obligatory rather than voluntary.

Gordon Wenham adds up the total annual sacrifice here as 113 bulls, 32 rams, and 1,086 lambs, more than a ton of flour, and a thousand bottles of oil and wine.[4]

Theological Insights

Why did God want Israel to keep these festivals and conduct the associated sacrifices and rituals? Israel's neighbors believed that sacrifices nourished their gods, and that "the deity needed to be cared for so that he/she could focus his/her energies on the important work of holding forces of chaos at bay."[5] In contrast, while Israel's rituals use language of feeding God—every day Israel provides God with "meals" from which God finds "an aroma pleasing"—this is strictly symbolic of gratitude and seeking fellowship with him, for God has no need for food offerings (Ps. 50:7–9). Nor do Israel's rituals help hold the universe together.

God requires these festivals not for his own benefit but for his people's. Every day is a day to seek God's favor by sacrifice (Num. 28:3–8), but psychologically people need periodic special occasions for worshiping and expressing gratitude to God. Special sacrifices underscore the sacredness of special days. All the sacrifices required by God here are atoning sacrifices, seeking God's favor despite Israel's sins and purging the sanctuary of all of Israel's impurities. Holy days served to form Israel spiritually. Holy days in the Christian calendar can do the same for us.

Teaching the Text

1. *We can use the regular cycles of life for spiritual purposes.* Although the festivals of this chapter are specifically for Israel and not the church, we can learn from them how to use today's cycles of life for spiritual enrichment.

The daily burnt offerings (Num. 28:1–8) entreat God for favor and represent the worshiper's total dedication to God (see comments at Lev. 1:1–17). We also can appeal to God through prayer, devotions, and Bible readings as we daily dedicate ourselves to him.

Israel's Sabbath days encourage Israelites to rest at least weekly and reflect on God. Sabbaths and new moons are also used to consult prophets (2 Kings 4:23). In Genesis God makes the sun and moon as "signs to mark sacred times, and days and years" (Gen. 1:14), a line that can be better rendered "signs for indicating the festival-times, both for days and years" (cf. HCSB, TEV). God has ordered the cycles of time so that we can participate spiritually. Accordingly, we can use the weekly worship services and holidays on our calendars, when we are not required to work, to pause and reflect on God, to worship, to read Christian books, or simply to rest and recuperate from labor.

The Israelites' festivals teach them to rejoice and give thanks for their blessings. The Festival of Weeks (Num. 28:26–31) and the Festival of Tabernacles (Num. 29:12–28) are agricultural festivals that express gratitude to God for the fruitfulness of the land. Similarly, we can use local harvest festivals or the holidays of Thanksgiving or New Year's Day not only for secular or family festivities but also for expressing thanks to God for his blessings.

The festivals also show us how to reflect on how God saves and forgives. The spring festival of the Passover and Unleavened Bread (Num. 28:16–25) commemorates God's greatest act of salvation in the Old Testament, Israel's deliverance from Egyptian slavery, and gives Israel the paradigm of God as its savior (Exod. 15:2). The Day of Atonement (Num. 29:7–11) shows how God purifies his sanctuary of the sins of the people so that they can continue to dwell in his midst (Lev. 16). Similarly, festival days such as Christmas, Good Friday, and Easter remind us of how God has come to save us and has provided a means of forgiveness.

If we are creative, we can find ways to employ all the special days on our calendars for God. Numbers 28–29 seems to encourage us to do so.

2. *We can give God more than the minimum.* The Israelites are reminded that they can add freewill offerings to the required offerings (Num. 29:39). Similarly, we can and should make sacrifices beyond those that are expected. We should give a portion of our income to God to support the work of God. But from time to time God may lead us to give special gifts to him that are over and above our regular offerings. We too need to be encouraged to consider making special, voluntary sacrifices to God.

Illustrating the Text

Christians can use non-Christian holidays for Christian purposes.

Popular Culture: Although Christmas can be considered a Christian holiday, the Bible does not command that we celebrate it, and it first appears historically in the fourth century AD. Some speculate that Christmas's origins lie in pagan customs in ancient Rome, such as the celebration of the winter solstice. They theorize that the holiday originated because the faithful were tempted to attend the pagan festivities at this time, so Christians created an alternative celebration that allowed the faithful to have fun without engaging in pagan debaucheries.

We are not sure whether this account is true, but even if it is, it should not bother us. Christians can and should use the special occasions on the calendar for spiritual purposes. If the early church essentially modified the winter solstice to celebrate the birth of Jesus, it was a wonderful idea.

The same sort of thing might be done for Halloween. Originally, it had a religious connection, being called "All Hallows Eve"—that is, the evening before the medieval church holiday of All Saints Day. In modern times that religious connection has been lost, but there is no reason why Christians cannot try to bring it back, since it is good to use the special days on our calendar for spiritual purposes.

Our focus should be not on giving the minimum but on giving sacrificially.

Object Lesson: Bring an unevenly cut pizza (have the pizza heated so that it will be warm and fragrant). Opening the box, show and describe what is inside. Invite six people forward to receive a free slice of pizza. Make sure that you get a giant slice of pizza and those you share with get smaller slices. Then close by holding up your piece, demonstrating that it is significantly larger (perhaps hand out the slices, "One for you, one for you . . . and one for *me*!"). Conclude with, "Now, what kind of giver am I, really?"

Keeping Promises

Big Idea *Take solemn promises and commitments seriously.*

Understanding the Text

The Text in Context

Following the first census in Numbers is a section dealing with vows, specifically Nazirite vows (Num. 6). Likewise, after the second census Numbers 30 deals with vows, especially women's vows. Why would a section on vows follow Numbers 28–29, which is on offerings made on holy days? Perhaps because holy days are occasions for completing vows. Numbers 29:39 mentions that "vows" can be completed by sacrifice on holy occasions. Another factor is the stress on women's vows here (Num. 30:3–15). This focus on women is appropriate in a unit of a book that is bracketed by the question of women's inheritance (Num. 27:1–11; 36:1–12).

The whole section is chiastically structured:[1]

A Introduction: Duty of men to keep their own vows/oaths (vv. 1–2)
  B Father's ability to void daughter's vows/oaths without penalty (vv. 3–5)
    C Husband's ability to void wife's premarriage vows/oaths (vv. 6–8)
      D Duty of widows and divorcées not under male authority (v. 9)
    C′ Husband's ability to void wife's postmarriage vows/oaths (vv. 10–12)
  B′ Husband's inability to void wife's established vows/oaths without penalty (vv. 13–15)
A′ Summary: Duty of fathers and husbands regarding female vows (v. 16)

Historical and Cultural Background

A vow is a promise to God. This "could be either positive, the suppliant promising to devote something to God (e.g., Gen. 28:20–22; Num. 21:1–3; Judg. 11:30–31), or negative, the worshiper undertaking to abstain from some comfort or, for a time, a necessity of life (e.g., Num. 6:1–21; 21:1–3; 30:13[14]; Ps. 132:2–5)."[2] Men and women under a Nazirite vow abstain from consuming wine/grapes, touching the dead, and cutting their hair (Num. 6). Typically, vows are made on condition that God will answer a prayer (Job 22:27; 1 Sam. 1:11). Sometimes a person vowed to offer a particular animal sacrifice to God (Num. 29:39). Jacob vows to worship Yahweh alone and tithe to him if God answers his prayer to give him safety on his journey to his uncle Laban (Gen. 28:20–22; cf. 2 Sam. 15:8). Jephthah vows that whatever meets him coming out of his house will be offered as a burnt offering if God gives him victory in battle (Judg. 11:30–31). Vows often are "fulfilled" by offering animal sacrifice as a votive offering (Lev. 22:21; Pss. 50:14; 116:17–18). Other vows involve giving live animals or persons to God, as Hannah gives her boy Samuel to the sanctuary in response to an answered prayer (1 Sam. 1:11, 27–28), though items or persons can be redeemed by substituting a monetary equivalent (Lev. 27).

A vow is a kind of oath. Swearing an oath involves various commitments in God's name, often using the formula "as the LORD lives" (e.g., Judg. 8:19; Ruth 3:13; 1 Sam. 14:45) or a formula like "May the LORD do X to me if I do not do Y" (cf. 1 Kings 2:23) to make the promise more solemn and to underscore the seriousness of the person making the oath. Judicial oaths place the person under divine wrath if that person is guilty of the crime of which he or she has been accused (Exod. 22:10–11; Num. 5:19–22). Other oaths are simply solemn promises. Esau swears an oath ceding his birthright to Jacob (Gen. 25:33). God swears an oath on himself (rather than another god [cf. Heb. 6:13]) to give Canaan to the patriarchs (Exod. 6:8; 32:13). Saul swears to the medium of Endor that she will not be punished for using necromancy to conjure up Samuel from the grave (1 Sam. 28:10). David swears to Bathsheba that he will make Solomon the next king (1 Kings 1:17). Solomon swears in the sense of asking God to punish him severely if he (Solomon) fails to execute Adonijah (1 Kings 2:23).

Key Themes of Numbers 30:1–16

- Keep your promises.
- Do not make rash promises.
- Do not merely reflect but transform your cultural context.

Interpretive Insights

30:1 *the heads of the tribes of Israel.* This unusual expression (used elsewhere only in 1 Kings 8:1; 2 Chron. 5:2) may be short for "the family heads of the Israelite tribes" (Num. 32:28), who relay and carry out God's instructions.

30:2 *vow . . . oath.* See "Historical and Cultural Background" above.

pledge. This is a "binding obligation" similar to a vow, except vows involve giving something to God or abstaining from something for God, while a pledge involves commitments made in God's name toward persons other than God,[3] as when Abraham's servant swears to his master not to acquire a wife for Isaac from the Canaanites (Gen. 24:9), or Saul's oath "as the LORD lives" not to harm the medium of Endor (1 Sam. 28:10).

he must not break his word. Literally, one must not "profane, desecrate" (*halal* [see comments at Lev. 21:9]) his word. A violated vow or oath constitutes "desecration" in that it involves taking God's name in vain and so putting oneself under God's judgment. Anyone who fails to fulfill a vow must offer a sin offering for the careless oath (Lev. 5:4–5).

30:3 *When a young woman still living in her father's household makes a vow . . . or . . . pledge.* An unmarried girl can make a vow or bind herself by a pledge, but since she is under the male authority of her father until marriage, he can veto any vow or pledge that she makes. But the father's veto must be done overtly and in a timely way. If he says nothing when he hears about her vow or pledge, then her act is binding. But if he objects and opposes her vow, then God will "release her" (v. 5 [lit., "forgive her"]) from her vow or oath so that she is not under threat of divine punishment for not keeping her vow or pledge.

30:6 *If she marries after she makes a vow or . . . utter[s] a rash promise.* When a girl marries, she transfers from being under her father's authority to being under her husband's authority. Thus, her husband can veto any vow she makes that he considers "rash" or "thoughtless" (ESV, NRSV), even if she makes it before marriage and with her father's approval, although, as in the case of a father, the husband's veto must be overt and timely to negate his wife's previous vow or binding pledge. The husband will likely hear about his fiancée's vows in the inchoate marriage or the betrothal stage before the marriage is actually consummated, at which point he must either negate his bride-to-be's vows or pledges or assume the obligation of keeping them.

30:9 *Any vow or obligation taken by a widow or divorced woman.* A widow or a divorced

"Any vow or obligation taken by a widow or divorced woman will be binding on her" (30:9). This ivory plaque of a robed woman was found at Megiddo (1300–1200 BC).

woman is not under male authority, so her vows cannot be vetoed and are binding.

30:10 *If a woman living with her husband makes a vow . . . a pledge.* A husband can also annul a vow or pledge of a wife made after they marry (for vows made before marriage, compare vv. 6–8). This helps him to protect the family's economic interests from unreasonable vows. If he negates her vow or pledge a long time after he knows of it, then the guilt of oath violation falls on him, not her (v. 15).

30:16 *These are the regulations . . . concerning relationships.* Curiously, the summary leaves out the case of the widow and the divorcée, suggesting that the topic is less central to the chapter's purpose than those sections discussing women under a father's or a husband's authority.

Theological Insights

Is it wrong for Christians to make vows or oaths? As this chapter shows, vows/oaths were quite common in Old Testament times. Yet the New Testament discourages the swearing of oaths. Jesus says, "Do not swear an oath at all" (Matt. 5:34 [cf. James 5:12]). This is taken by some Christians to mean that under the new covenant we are never to swear oaths, even in court. But this is a doubtful interpretation. God's swearing an oath to Abraham is portrayed positively in the New Testament (Heb. 6:13–18; cf. Gen. 22:16–17), and Paul often uses oath formulations in calling on God as his witness or charging people before God (Rom. 1:9; 2 Cor. 1:23; Gal. 1:20; 1 Thess. 2:5, 10; 5:27). When Paul condemns the "perjurer" (1 Tim. 1:10), he uses a Greek term (*epiorkos*) that pertains to "falseness in oath taking." There would be no need specifically to condemn false oath taking if all oath taking were wrong.

What "Do not swear at all" in context really means is that we must be scrupulously honest even without oaths, so that our "yes" and "no" are as good as an affirmation under oath (Matt. 5:37). This is in contrast to the sophistry of some teachers of the law who looked for loopholes (e.g., swearing without using God's name) to allow people to get out of keeping their oaths (Matt. 5:34b–36; 23:16–22). Jesus's words are thus hyperbole meant to contrast the disciples' virtue of honesty with certain deceptive Jewish practices at that time involving oaths.

Teaching the Text

1. *Keep your promises.* Since an oath in the Old Testament involved promises invoking God's name, failure to keep an oath was an offense against God. But if the oath involved another human being, its violation was likewise an offense against people.

One lesson here is that we should be people of our word. Few things are as corrosive to good relationships as dishonesty. If we make a solemn promise to someone and fail to keep it, that person will find it hard ever to trust us again. Persistent lies and deceptions can make us lose our friends, ruin our businesses, or destroy our marriages. Also, the concept of oaths reminds us that whatever promises we make, they are made before God, who will hold us accountable for our careless words (Matt. 12:36), even if they are not part of a formal oath (see "Theological Insights" above).

2. *Do not make rash promises.* Numbers 30 mentions cases of possible rash vows made by girls. Since a woman's assets and debts will become her husband's upon marriage, in practice it will be the husband's financial responsibility to fulfill his wife's vow. A rash vow can thus negatively affect the economic or marital status of the new couple. So the law grants to a new husband the authority to annul his wife's/fiancée's rash vows at the beginning of their marriage (Num. 30:6–8). But this is the exception to the rule. Even rash vows ordinarily are expected to be carried out quickly. That is why it is better not to vow at all than to vow something and not fulfill it (Prov. 20:25; Eccles. 5:5).

Since we are obligated to keep our promises, we must be careful not to promise what we cannot or should not do. To make promises that we have no intention of keeping is to lie. But to promise things that we might not be able to deliver is rash. For example, a poor man might promise his girlfriend, "Marry me, and someday we will live together in a huge mansion." The man might really mean it, but it would be foolish to make such a promise. Still worse is to swear to do something that is morally wrong, such as "If you date another man, by God, I'll kill you." It can even be wrong to promise to give lots of money to God if it means that you cannot then take care of family members whom you are morally responsible to support (Matt. 15:5–6; cf. 1 Tim. 5:8). We are obligated to keep our promises, but we need to be very careful what we promise.

3. *Do not merely reflect but transform your cultural context.* This passage largely reflects its patriarchal culture, but nonetheless it seeks to move society in a more egalitarian direction.

First, it allows women to make vows and oaths under most circumstances.[4] The law could have forbidden women from making vows at all, given that they are under male authority, but it refrains from doing so. Instead, this law allows women more freedom than they might have had under an even more strictly patriarchal system.

Second, this law protects women from male authorities who change their minds. This law limits the amount of control that the male authority has over his wife's or daughter's vow/oath to the time immediately after he hears of it.

Third, this law grants some women independence from male authority. Widows and divorced women are no longer under any male authority and so are responsible for their own vows. The law could have placed them under some other male authority—their father (if alive) or brother or nearest male relative—but it does not.

Often the Bible does not try to alter the shape of society but insists on godly behavior in society, whatever its shape. Thus, when the Bible fails to balance a patriarchal structure, accommodates slavery, operates within a system of arranged marriages with the possibility of polygamy, or promotes monarchy over other forms of government, it is working descriptively rather than prescribing those structures. All human societal structures are prone to weakness due to human frailty and sin. This passage grants Israelite women more rights than they had previously. We today can go even further in ensuring women's rights.

Illustrating the Text

In many Christian traditions vows are still taken.

Cultural Institution: One occasion for vows is that of baptism. A number of Christian traditions have candidates for baptism (or parents in the case of infant baptism) vow to "renounce the devil and all his works," a baptismal vow that goes back at least to the third century of the Christian church.[5] That vow typically is followed by the candidate's affirmation of a trinitarian confession of faith.

Another occasion of vows/oaths in Christian tradition is marriage (more of an oath than a vow in biblical usage). In traditional services ministers ask the groom something like this:

> Do you, [groom's name], take [bride's name] to be your wife, to live together after God's ordinance in the holy estate of matrimony? Will you love her, comfort her, honor and keep her, in sickness and in health, for richer, for poorer, for better, for worse, in sadness and in joy, to cherish and continually bestow upon her your heart's deepest devotion, forsaking all others, keeping yourself only unto her as long as you both shall live?

To this the groom affirms, "I will." The minister then asks the bride similar questions, and she affirms, "I will."

The high rate of divorce, even among Christians, shows that many people, unlike ancient Israelites, fail to take vows or oaths seriously. The high failure rate of marriages has led to a trend in wedding ceremonies to replace "as long as you both shall live" with words such as "for as long as we continue to love each other," or "for as long as our love shall last," or even "until our time together is over."[6] While this change represents a commendable desire of couples not to make promises that they may be unwilling or unable to keep, the change also represents a woeful lack of commitment to the marriage relationship.

It remains a Christian duty to keep solemn promises, specifically marriage vows.

Unwise oaths can be disastrous.

Mythology: Greek mythology records the rash oath made by the hero Perseus. Perseus was supposed to bring the gift of a horse to Polydectes, king of the island of Serifos, a gift that Perseus lacked. So Perseus promised instead to bring whatever else the king might demand. The king, wanting to get rid of Perseus (and to marry Perseus's mother), asked that he instead bring the head of the snake-haired monster Medusa. Medusa had been a beautiful woman, but she was cursed by the goddess Athena for thinking herself more beautiful than Athena. So Athena turned her hair into snakes and decreed that whoever looked at her would turn into stone. Perseus's vow was rash, but he was held to it. Yet with the help of Athena and the god Hermes, who gave him a shield by whose reflection he could safely see Medusa, winged sandals, and Hades's cap of invisibility, Perseus was able to behead Medusa and escape from the supernatural beings around her to deliver what he had promised to Polydectes, who himself was turned into stone when he viewed Medusa's decapitated head.

As in the case of biblical oaths, Perseus felt bound by honor to carry out the oath even at risk of his own life. In this mythological world, his imprudent oath became the occasion of a heroic act. But in the real world, unwise oaths usually lead to disaster.

> As long as a woman is under the authority of a man either as his wife or daughter, her vows or oath obligations, once discovered, can be forbidden by him and the Lord will release her from her pledge. An Egyptian family that included the priest Ptahmai, his wife, two daughters, and a son is depicted in this statue from Saqqara (1250–1200 BC).

Women's Rights and Vows

Women in ancient Israel were subject to male authority: fathers before marriage, husbands after marriage. That is why a woman's vows and oaths could be annulled by her father before marriage and by her husband during betrothal and after marriage (Num. 30:3–16). The law thus put obedience to parents and submission to husbands above voluntary religious duties such as vows.[a] The obviously patriarchal character of this troubles many modern readers.

Part of the motive here was to protect the economic status of families from rash vows. Women in this situation would commonly have just recently passed into adolescence, and the young are especially prone to act impulsively. Since so much was dependent on the woman actually bearing a child, vows often were connected to conception (e.g., Hannah in 1 Sam. 1:11). Moreover, since both child mortality and maternal mortality at childbirth were high, vows related to the preservation of life were no doubt commonplace. It made sense for the more mature father or husband to serve as a safeguard against a girl's foolish, impulsive vows. Dennis Olson remarks, "In the patriarchal society of ancient Israel, women were often economically dependent on men. In certain circumstances the ultimate responsibility for fulfilling vows made by a woman could rest on her father or husband. The laws in Numbers 30 thus protected the husband or father from the requirements to honor a woman's vow in special cases."[b]

[a] Wenham, *Numbers*.
[b] Olson, *Numbers*, 175.

War against Midian

Big Idea *God condemns the wicked but rewards his people.*

Understanding the Text

The Text in Context

Numbers 31 resumes the story of Numbers 25 in which a Midianite princess, Kozbi, and an Israelite man, Zimri, commit a flagrant act of disobedience (Num. 25:6–9, 14–15). Theirs is one of many acts of immorality and idolatry (Num. 25:1) that have brought God's wrath on Israel in the form of a plague. As a result, God tells Moses to treat the Midianites as an enemy and kill them (Num. 25:16–18).

Numbers 31 fulfills God's command to attack Midian. Among those killed are Kozbi's father, Zur, and the pagan seer Balaam (Num. 31:8). This chapter reveals that the women seducing the Israelite men to immorality and idolatry in Numbers 25 are actually part of a plot by Balaam to bring God's plague on Israel.

Interpretive Insights

31:2 *Take vengeance on the Midianites.* The Hebrew word *naqam* ("to avenge") refers not to a malicious retaliation for inflicted wrongs but rather to retributive justice to redress crimes committed.[1] The crime recorded in Numbers 25 costs the lives of twenty-four thousand Israelites (Num. 25:9).

you will be gathered to your people. This is Moses's last military act before he, like Aaron, joins his ancestors in the afterlife (cf. Num. 20:26; 27:13).

31:3 *Arm some of your men.* Alternatively, "Let men be picked out from among you" (NJPS). The translation depends on whether the Hebrew word *halats* here means "draw off" or "equip for war." Both meanings are attested.[2]

31:4–5 *a thousand men . . . twelve thousand men.* "Thousand" (*'elep*) possibly means "division, clan," making this twelve divisions of troops[3] (see "Additional Insights" following the unit on Numbers 1:1–2:34). That interpretation eliminates the inequity of requiring a higher percentage of men from smaller tribes.

31:6 *Phinehas.* See Numbers 25:6–15.

articles from the sanctuary . . . trumpets for signaling. The specifics are uncertain. The ark sometimes is brought to battles (1 Sam. 4:1–3; cf. Num. 14:44). The Urim and Thummim sometimes are used by the high priest for revelation during war (1 Sam. 28:6). This passage can refer to the vestments worn by the priest who comes to the battle with the troops and gives the troops a pep talk (Deut. 20:2–4). The "trumpets for signaling" are literally "the trumpets of the blast." This refers to the silver trumpets used to direct the troops in the battle (cf. Num. 10:8–10).

31:7 *they fought against Midian, as the* LORD *commanded.* See Numbers 25:16–18.

killed every man. According to the rules of war outside the promised land, only men are to be killed (Deut. 20:12–14). This is not genocide. It is limited to Midianite tribes allied with Moab. Other Midianites exist into the seventh century BC (Judg. 6:1–7; Hab. 3:7).

31:8 *the five kings of Midian* These "kings" are little more than tribal chieftains, which they are also called (Num. 25:15; Josh. 13:21). Their land is assigned to the Reubenites (Josh. 13:21). Among them, Zur has prostituted his daughter Kozbi as part of a plot against Israel (Num. 31:8; 25:14–15).

They also killed Balaam. Balaam is executed because he has been behind the plot of Numbers 25 (see vv. 15–16 below) and because he has practiced divination (Josh. 13:22). Balak king of Moab had dismissed Balaam to go home (Num. 24:25), but he either never makes it or does not stay there.

31:9–10 *The Israelites captured the Midianite women and children . . . herds, flocks and goods . . . burned all the towns.* In war outside

Key Themes of Numbers 31:1–54

- War is sometimes morally justifiable even though it is defiling.
- God rewards his faithful soldiers.

Canaan, women, children, and livestock can be taken as plunder (cf. Deut. 20:14). That Israel burns towns suggests that these Midianites had moved from being semi-nomadic to being sedentary.[4]

31:15–18 *Have you allowed all the women to live?* Ordinarily, non-Canaanite female and juvenile captives are spared (cf. Deut. 20:12–14). But these women are not innocent. They en masse had participated in the plan to seduce Israelite men through sexual immorality into idolatry at Peor (see Num. 25), acts that may have involved the capital offense of adultery (Lev. 20:10;

"The Israelites captured the Midianite women and children and took all the Midianite herds, flocks and goods as plunder" (31:9). A similar scenario, of an Assyrian campaign against one of their enemies, is pictured on this relief from the palace at Nimrud (865–860 BC).

Deut. 22:24). All this had been done on the advice of Balaam (v. 16). These acts had brought a plague on Israel (cf. Num. 25:9). Thus, all these women are to be executed. Also as an exception, the boys are killed (v. 17a). This permanently wipes out these specific clans and thus assures that they can never become warriors against Israel.[5] Virgin girls are clearly innocent of the offense of Numbers 25, so they are allowed to marry into Israel (v. 18).

31:19 *Anyone who has killed someone or touched someone who was killed.* On corpse contamination purification, see Numbers 19.

stay outside the camp seven days. See Numbers 5:2–3; 19:11.

on the third and seventh days . . . purify yourselves and your captives. See Numbers 19:12. The captives are presumed to have had direct or indirect contact with corpses.

31:20 *every garment . . . everything made of leather, goat hair or wood.* Objects worn or used by soldiers also require purification.

31:21 *Eleazar.* The high priest gives instructions on the rules of purity, but he is not required to administer the ashes.

31:22–23 *Gold, silver, bronze, iron, tin, lead . . . put through the fire.*

The officers of the Israelite army give their share of the gold jewelry plundered from the Midianites as an offering to the Lord, paying the ransom required for taking a head count after the battle. Armlets, bracelets, signet rings, earrings, and necklaces are presented to the Lord at the tent of meeting. The earrings and bracelets shown here are from ancient Egypt.

Items that can stand it are additionally purified by fire.

31:27 *Divide the spoils.* This is the most enjoyable part of war (cf. Isa. 9:3). It is administered by Moses, Eleazar the high priest, and the family heads. Half the spoils go to the soldiers who have fought, and half to the rest of Israel. Dividing spoils with the noncombatants is also practiced by Joshua and David (Josh. 22:8; 1 Sam. 30:24–25).

31:28 *tribute for the LORD.* The Hebrew word *mekes* ("tribute") is better rendered "levy" (ESV). In postbiblical Hebrew/Aramaic, it denotes "tolls" on bridges and "taxes, duties" on wheat.[6] One five-hundredth from the soldiers' portion goes to the priests. One-fiftieth is taken from Israel's portion and given to the Levites, ten times more than the priests (for a similar ratio, cf. Num. 18:25–32). Thus Israel acknowledges God in the division of spoils, though why a full tithe (10 percent) is not taken for God is not explained.

31:32–35 *675,000 sheep, 72,000 cattle, 61,000 donkeys and 32,000 women.* These large numbers appear fabulous, though the tribute to Yahweh that applies the ratios of 500:1 and 50:1 appears reasonable. Similar large numbers are found in royal inscriptions and the annals of Sumerian, Akkadian, and Assyrian kings, even though the general historicity of the events recorded is not in doubt.[7] See also "Additional

Insights" following the unit on Numbers 1:1–2:34.

31:49 *not one is missing.* Miraculously, not a single Israelite soldier has died in the battle, an indication of God's grace.

31:50 *gold articles . . . armlets, bracelets, signet rings, earrings and necklaces.* These are given to fulfill the law requiring a half-shekel temple tax as an atonement-ransom whenever a census is taken (Exod. 30:12–16). Thus, these articles are presented to Moses and Eleazar for use at the sanctuary.

Theological Insights

Israel is ordered to "carry out the LORD's vengeance" on Midian (Num. 31:3). How can a good and loving God exact vengeance? Vengeance among humans is often associated with the irrational and disproportionate responses of mobs, the sort of thing that escalates injustice. And yet both Testaments speak of God's vengeance (Deut. 32:35; Rom. 12:19; Heb. 10:30; Rev. 6:10; 19:2).

George Mendenhall convincingly argues that Hebrew *naqam* ("to avenge") refers not to a malicious or arbitrary retaliation for inflicted wrongs but rather to retributive justice to redress crimes committed.[8] God takes vengeance on nations for disobeying him and for abusing Israel (Mic. 5:15; Nah. 1:2). The crime punished here costs twenty-four thousand Israelites their lives (Num. 25:9). God's vengeance corresponds to the crime. Vengeance is a necessary component of God's justice. Those who rebel against God's morality and commit horrible crimes can be sure of being the objects of God's vengeance, either in this life or the next.

Teaching the Text

1. *War is sometimes morally justifiable even though it is defiling.* The conduct of war against these Midianites in Numbers 31 is brutal. At God's command all the males are killed, including all the boy children. Their villages are all burned to the ground. All the women except for the virgins are also killed.

But these things must be put in context. God condemns these Midianites because they have initiated hostilities at Peor (Num. 25:16–18). Normally, women are to be spared in war outside Canaan (Deut. 20:13–15), but these women have been part of a plot that causes the death of twenty-four thousand Israelites (Num. 25:9) (see comments at vv. 15–18 above). They have been far more effective than the Midianite men who fail to kill a single Israelite man in battle (Num. 31:49). This is why Moses insists that such women be executed (Num. 31:15–18).

Israel's actions against Midian are a necessary expression of morality to punish the Moabites for their treachery. Midian's acts are of such a heinous nature that they justify the elimination of these five clans altogether. Thus, the boys are killed, and the villages are burned. Never again will these clans attack Israel. They, along with Balaam (Num. 31:8), learn the truth of God's words spoken long ago (Gen. 12:3), echoed by Balaam himself, "Cursed is everyone who curses you" (Num. 24:9 NRSV).

And yet there is also mercy. Unlike war against the Canaanites, in which everyone is to be killed (Deut. 7:2–3; Josh. 6:21), here the thirty-two thousand virgin girls clearly innocent of the treachery recorded in Numbers 25 are spared (Num. 31:35).

Ultimately, these girls are assimilated into the people of Israel.

What lessons can we draw from Israelite war?

We must encourage governments to follow "just war" principles. Israel has such principles: (1) offering terms of peace to avoid war when possible (Deut. 20:10–11); (2) restricting the killing to the men while ordinarily sparing women, children, and animals (Deut. 20:12–14); (3) limiting ecological damage or unnecessary destruction (Deut. 20:19–20). Exceptions to these principles are made with the Canaanites and here in Numbers 31 with the Midianites only because circumstances demand it. But it is wrong to indiscriminately kill in war.

Second, we must consider all war to be defiling. War causes ceremonial uncleanness that excludes an Israelite from approaching God (Num. 31:19–24; cf. Num. 19). Moreover, God is to be associated with life, not death. Thus, we should never glory in war, even when, regretfully, it is necessary or morality demands it.

2. *God rewards his faithful soldiers.* God grants the Israelite soldiers half of the spoils captured from Midian (Num. 31:25–40). As an expression of gratitude to God, one five-hundredth from the soldiers' portion goes to the priests as a "tribute" (or "levy" [ESV]) for Yahweh, while one-fiftieth is taken from Israel's portion and given to the Levites.

We, like these Israelite soldiers, should give back to God a portion of the blessings that he grants us. It is still God who grants blessings, even if we, like these soldiers, are involved in securing the goods. When God blesses us, we should return some of that blessing to God as a way of saying thanks.

Christian workers are sometimes compared with soldiers (Phil. 2:25; Philem. 2). Being a soldier involves discipline and sacrifice (2 Tim. 2:3–4), but good Christian soldier-ministers deserve spoils for their fight for Christ—material support from other Christians (1 Cor. 9:6–7). All Christians are like soldiers for Christ, and faithful soldiers can expect to be rewarded by God for fighting the good fight (2 Tim. 4:7–8). The reward that God gave these Israelite soldiers reminds us that ultimately Christian soldiers will be rewarded by God.

Illustrating the Text

The God of the Bible does not conform to our comfort level.

Literature: The Chronicles of Narnia, by C. S. Lewis. In this series of books, C. S. Lewis has a Christ/God figure, the lion Aslan. Lewis portrays Christ as someone with whom we humans are not always comfortable. In the sixth book of the series, *The Silver Chair,*[9] the girl Jill, having been transported to the magical land of Narnia and not yet a believer in Aslan, suddenly confronts Aslan. In their conversation Jill, terrified of the lion, asks Aslan to go away so that she can drink safely from the stream. Aslan refuses, so she must take the bold step of drinking in his presence. You might want to read their conversation in chapter 2 of the book.

God is like a lion. He sometimes, as Aslan says, swallows up "girls and boys, women and men, kings and emperors, cities and realms." In Numbers 31 he commands through Moses that women and men and boys be killed and cities be burned. All this frightens and repels us about God. And yet there is nowhere else to turn to find the living waters of life (John 6:68).

So believing that our God is ultimately good and just, we, like Jill in this story, must choose to trust in the Lion of Judah and drink. And we must do so even if we do not fully understand the purposes and justifications of God's severe acts of vengeance.

Christians, no less than Israelite soldiers, are called to give back joyfully a portion of what they have received.

News: According to a recent report,[10] tithers comprise only 10 to 25 percent of families in the average church, yet they provide 50 to 80 percent of the funding for its operations. That statistic is stunning. Interestingly, these tithers are also better off financially than nontithing members—carrying less debt. Their giving, it was found, was based not on excess income but rather on commitments often formed from an early age (between childhood and their twenties). Commenting on the attitude that Christians should have about giving, Pastor Andy Stanley writes,

> Whenever we sense that hesitation, it's because we have started to view our money as our money. In those moments, we're not completely in touch with the fact that everything belongs to God, comes from Him and is dispensed by Him. In a way, we're buying into the myth that we own it and we're giving it to God.
>
> But God owns it all. So I'm really just "giving" Him what already belongs to Him. The idea that we ever "give" God anything is really just a myth.
>
> We are to honor God not with a percentage, but with all we possess. It's not 10 percent. It's 100 percent.[11]

Selfishness of the Transjordan Tribes Corrected

Big Idea *We must avoid and resolve misunderstandings among God's people.*

Understanding the Text

The Text in Context

Many dangers have been circumvented. God has thwarted Balak's attempt to use Balaam to curse Israel (Num. 22–24). God's punishment of idolatry and immorality is offset by Phinehas's bold actions (Num. 25). Balaam and his Midianite allies who have deceived Israel are killed (Num. 31). Now Numbers 32 introduces another potential crisis. The tribes of Reuben and Gad announce their desire to settle in the Transjordan rather than in Canaan. Moses fears that this could discourage the rest of Israel from taking the land. But the crisis is averted when these tribes agree to go with their sibling tribes to conquer Canaan before settling in the Transjordan.

Historical and Cultural Background

A number of the cities of Gad and Reuben are mentioned in the ninth-century BC inscription of Mesha king of Moab. Lines 10–12 state, "Now the Gadites had lived in the land of Ataroth forever and the king of Israel had built Ataroth for himself. But I fought against the city and took it, and I killed the entire population of the city, a satiation for Kemosh and Moab."[1] Mesha also practiced "holy war" against Nebo, a city rebuilt by Reuben (Num. 32:38), putting its entire population to death and "devoting" it to his god Chemosh (lines

Several Transjordan cities in the territory of the Israelite tribes of Gad and Reuben are mentioned in the ninth-century BC inscription of Mesha king of Moab, shown here.

14–18). Sihon had taken this territory from Moab (Num. 21:26), and then Israel took it from Sihon (Num. 21:24). In the ninth century Mesha retook this territory from the Israelites.

Interpretive Insights

32:5 *let this land be given to your servants.* The Reubenites and Gadites ask for land in the Transjordan area outside the promised land for their herds and flocks so that they will not have to cross the Jordan. Jazer, not far north of Heshbon, has been conquered on the way to Bashan (Num. 21:32). Gilead is north and south of the Jabbok River valley, including the Gilead Plateau east of the Jordan River between the Sea of Galilee and the Dead Sea but not as far east as Ammon.[2] Ataroth, Dibon, Jazer, and Nimrah are given to Gad (vv. 34–36); Heshbon, Elealeh, Sebam, Nebo, and Beon (another name or copyist error for "[Baal] Meon") are given to Reuben (vv. 37–38 below).

32:6 *Should your fellow Israelites go to war while you sit here?* Their request seems like a shirking of duty that will discourage others from invading the promised land, just as the scouts' negative report had discouraged Israel from entering the land

Key Themes of Numbers 32:1–42

- Selfishness can undermine God's work.
- "Your sin will find you out."
- The remedy for selfishness is living "before the Lord."

(Num. 13:28–29, 31–33). Consequently, all those adults except Joshua and Caleb have been excluded from the land (Num. 14:28–30).

32:9 *Valley of Eshkol.* There the scouts see the goodness of the land, with its huge grape clusters (Num. 13:23).

32:12 *Caleb . . . Joshua.* Caleb, son of a Kenizzite, is a descendant of Kenaz (Gen. 36:11), an Edomite clan of the Negev (Gen. 15:19) whose Jephunneh branch evidently had united with Judah before the sojourn in Egypt. Joshua is now Moses's appointed successor (Num. 27:12–23).

32:14 *brood of sinners.* Moses's fierce accusation no doubt stuns the Reubenites and the Gadites. Moses compares them to the old, now-dead sinful generation ("your fathers") who years earlier had refused to enter the land.

32:15 *you will be the cause of their destruction.* Reuben's and Gad's request could cause a chain reaction that will again lead God to exclude his people from the land.

Table 1. Transjordan Cities of Gad, Reuben, and Half Manasseh

Gad (Num. 32:34–36)	Reuben (Num. 32:37–38)	Half Manasseh (Makir) (Num. 32:39–42)
Dibon	Heshbon	Havvoth Jair
Ataroth	Elealeh	Nobah (Kenath)
Aroer	*Kiriathaim*	
Atroth Shophan	*Nebo*	
Jazer Jogbehah	*Baal Meon*	
Beth Nimrah	Sibmah	
Beth Haran		

Note: Gray italics indicate cities mentioned in the Mesha Inscription.

32:16 *women and children.* The Hebrew word *tap* often simply means "children" ("little ones" [ESV, NRSV]), though here and at Exodus 12:37 it refers to all dependents. Reuben's and Gad's counterproposal begins with leaving their livestock and families in the Transjordan. Other tribes need to bring all their families and possessions.

32:17 *arm ourselves . . . and go ahead of the Israelites.* They further volunteer to serve as Israel's "vanguard" (NRSV) or "shock-troops" (NJPS), who will be the first to engage the enemy. Only after the inheritance is secured for the other tribes will they return to the Transjordan.

32:20 *before the LORD.* This expression, used seven times in the chapter, implies that they swear an oath before God. On oaths, see "Cultural and Historical Background" at Numbers 30:1–16. Upon fulfilling their vow, they can return to the Transjordan innocent.

32:23 *your sin will find you out.* If they violate their vow, their punishment is sure.

32:25–27 *We your servants will do as our lord commands . . . fight before the LORD.* The Gadites and Reubenites show humility and respect for Moses's authority. Their oath is made in God's presence (the tabernacle?). They will fight aware that God is watching.

32:28 *Eleazar . . . Joshua . . . the family heads.* Moses will die soon (Num. 20:12; 27:12–14), so he passes instructions to leaders who will conduct the conquest: the high priest (Num. 20:28), Moses's successor Joshua (Num. 27:18–23), and the family heads (lit., "heads of the fathers of the tribes"). Eleazar takes precedence over the military leader Joshua where land allotments are concerned (Num. 32:28; 34:17; Josh. 14:1; 17:4; 19:51; 21:1). Evidently, dividing the land is considered a sacral

Moses gives the Gadites, the Reubenites, and the half tribe of Manasseh the Transjordanian territory that Israel had taken from Sihon, king of the Amorites, and Og, king of Bashan.

function.[3] If Reuben and Gad fail to show up, they will forfeit their Transjordan possessions; however, they keep their word and Joshua dismisses them to occupy the Transjordan (Josh. 4:12–13; 22:1–9).

32:31 *Your servants will do what the LORD has said.* Private negotiations with Moses are now repeated in public.

32:33 *the half-tribe of Manasseh.* Part of Manasseh, those descended from Manasseh's grandson Gilead the son of Makir (Num. 26:29), also want in on the Transjordan deal. The Gilead branch of Manasseh had led in capturing the northern part of the Transjordan from Og (v. 39; cf. Num. 21:33–35), so they request the territory that they have helped win, with which Moses concurs (vv. 40–42).

32:34–37 *The Gadites built up . . . the Reubenites rebuilt.* Part of Gad settles to the far south.[4] "Aroer" may refer to a northern site near Rabbah (Josh. 13:25) as opposed to Aroer on the Arnon given to Reuben (Josh. 13:15–16). Dibon, also called "Dibon Gad," is on a south-north itinerary between Iye Abarim in Moab and Nebo given to Reuben (Num. 33:44–47), implying that this is the Dibon near the Arnon gorge near Aroer.[5] Ataroth is in the same vicinity, likely to be identified with Khirbet Atarus.[6] Jazer is in Gilead west of modern Amman.[7] Jogbehah appears to be nearby. Atroth Shophan is uncertain in location; the KJV takes this as two places rather than one. Though some of Reuben's cities are uncertain in location,[8] they appear to be between Gad's northern and southern towns.

32:38 *Nebo . . . Baal Meon (these names were changed).* These cities are named after pagan deities: Nabu son of Marduk, and Baal. Perhaps they were changed by the Israelites temporarily, though the old names came back by the ninth century in the Mesha Inscription. Alternatively this may be an editorial comment directing readers not to read aloud the names of pagan gods in the names of these Israelite towns but to "change" them. Compare Daniel's friend Azariah, whose Babylonian name, "Abednego," is probably "changed" from "Abdi-Nabu" ("servant of Nabu"), and names that refer to the god Baal (Eshbaal, Meribbaal, Jerubbaal) where the Baal element gets changed to Bosheth, which means "shame" (compare 1 Chr. 8:33 with 2 Sam. 2:8, 1 Chr. 9:40 with 2 Sam. 4:4, and Judg. 6:32 with 2 Sam. 11:21).

Theological Insights

Gad and Reuben were in danger of falling into selfishness, which is the nature of fallen humankind. Some theologians see selfishness as the essence of sin. Augustus Strong, for example, states,

> We hold the essential principle of sin to be selfishness. By selfishness we mean not simply the exaggerated self-love which constitutes the antithesis of benevolence, but the choice of self as the supreme end which constitutes the antithesis of the supreme love of God.[9]

According to Strong, selfishness is the opposite of the love of God. He goes on to argue that every specific sin—avarice, immorality, vanity, pride—finds its root in selfishness.[10] Other theologians find sin's essence in sensuality, displacement of God, pride, unbelief, or failure to fulfill God's law,[11] but in any theology selfishness is bad. It undermines God's work in the world by ordering the world around ourselves rather than around God. It is harmful to us personally and deserves God's judgment.

Teaching the Text

1. *Selfishness can undermine God's work.* When Gad and Reuben request to settle in the land of Jazer and Gilead outside the promised land, Moses thinks that they are being selfish, lazy, disobedient, unbelieving, and cowardly like the first generation at Kadesh (Num. 32:8–15). Moreover, this request threatens to discourage the other tribes from entering the land. He rebukes them so fiercely that it may have made their heads spin.

Moses may have misinterpreted the motives of Reuben and Gad, but he was right to see potential disaster in what they were requesting. The work of God is a team sport, and all of us are players on that team. If some members of a football team play for themselves rather than carrying out the calls of the quarterback, it can wreck the whole team and lead to defeat. For us there is a danger that we will take the coward's way out. We may accept second best outside of God's promised land instead of God's first best. We may choose personal comfort rather than the rigors of the battle. We may be satisfied with what God has given us—for example, personal salvation, material blessing—but not be willing to fight to help others receive similar blessings. From time to time we need to be challenged. Are we really wholeheartedly following God's plan for the benefit of others, or are we selfishly doing things, even religious things, only for ourselves?

2. *"Your sin will find you out."* After the Gadites and Reubenites agree to join their sibling tribes in the conquest as "shock troops" (v. 17a), even though they will settle in the Transjordan, Moses accepts their proposal (vv. 20–22) but warns them that if they renege, "your sin will find you out" (v. 23). In other words, God will hold them accountable for failing to keep their commitment to help their sibling tribes.

The idea that "your sin will find you out" is a biblical concept of broad applicability. Nothing that we do escapes the eye of God, and God holds us accountable for whatever we do (1 Pet. 4:5). In context Numbers 32:23 refers to a sin of omission (not helping the other tribes) and a sin of dishonesty (breaking a promise to go), but in principle these words apply to every sin, including our secret sins, for which we will be judged (Rom. 2:16). Thus, Numbers 32:23 gives one example of a broader truth: we may seem to get away with sin for a time, but eventually it finds us out, at the last judgment if not sooner.

3. *The remedy for selfishness is living "before the LORD."* One crucial way to reduce sin is to live "before the LORD"—that is, with an awareness of God's watchful presence. This expression occurs seven times in Numbers 32 (vv. 20, 21, 22 [2x], 27, 29, 31). When I was growing up, my dog used to sneak in a nap on a forbidden couch when it was left home alone, but it would jump off it as soon as we returned. People tend to act that way too. We are more likely to do something that we know to be wrong when we think that no one is looking. But when we know that we are being watched, we usually are careful to follow the rules. But we often forget that we are always under divine surveillance. When we are conscious that God is present and

watching, it is easier to avoid sinning—we do not want to displease our heavenly Father. When we forget it, we tend to go astray.

Illustrating the Text

We must practice the presence of God.

Spiritual Biography: Brother Lawrence was a Carmelite monk who as part of his religious devotion trained his mind to be ever aware of the fact that God is present.[12] He established God's presence not only by thinking high notions about God, which naturally pushes out trivial and foolish thoughts, but also by continually conversing with God. God's presence is not limited to time in churches. It can happen at all times. For Lawrence, daily menial chores such as buying supplies or working in the kitchen were done with the awareness that it was God's business that he was doing, so he sought to do it well as an expression of his love for God. When he fell short, his awareness of God's presence would lead him quickly to beg God's mercy and seek his grace. Indeed, he considered prayer to be first and foremost an awareness of the presence of God. He sought at times to live as if there were none but him and God in the world. After falling out of proper awareness of God, Lawrence would pick himself up, set his mind aright again, and resume his practice of God's presence as if he had never fallen from it.

Just as Gad and Reuben committed to enter the land "before the LORD" aware of God's presence and will, and Brother Lawrence learned to practice God's presence in even the most trivial duties of life, so we would do well to cultivate a sense of God's presence in everything that we do. That spiritual discipline can help us to suppress sin and to live more faithfully before God.

Selfishness can be stopped when we remember that God is watching us.

Popular Culture: It seems that the stores start playing Christmas carols earlier and earlier every year. There is something fun and exciting about walking through a mall or picking up a coffee at a local shop and hearing "God Rest Ye Merry, Gentlemen" or even "Rudolph the Red-Nosed Reindeer." One Christmas classic, however, probably causes as many frowns as smiles for little boys and girls everywhere. In "Santa Claus Is Coming to Town," the jolly old man is depicted with God-like powers of perception: finding out who's naughty or nice, watching us asleep and awake, knowing who's been bad or good. A lot is riding on Santa's omniscience!

Of course, someone—God—is watching us. He sees not only what we do but also why we do it. He hears not only the words we speak but also the words that fill our mind. Our everyday thoughts, words, and deeds should be conducted with the sense that God is watching us.

Reviewing the Past

Big Idea *Reviewing God's dealings in the past helps people to keep following God in the present.*

Understanding the Text

The Text in Context

All the major events in the book of Numbers are now complete. So this seems an appropriate occasion for the book to review what has gone before by listing campsites from Egypt to Canaan, starting with Rameses in Egypt, where Israel had lived, and ending at the plains of Moab with some forty campsites in between. Verses 1–15 take us to Mount Sinai. Verses 16–36 list camps in the desert. Verses 37–49 take us through the Transjordan to the plains of Moab. This recap allows the new generation to reflect on both its recent past and those events experienced by the first generation that left Egypt. The text goes on to anticipate the future: the conquest (Num. 33:50–55) and the coming division of the land (Num. 34).

Interpretive Insights

33:1–2 *Here are the stages in the journey.* Israel's itinerary is said to be recorded by Moses himself (v. 2), implying a role for Moses in the authorship of this book (see "Introduction to Numbers"). Many of the sites are uncertain in location.[1] Some of what is known is mentioned below, with more details in the endnotes.

33:3 *Rameses.* Rameses is a store city built by the Israelites (Exod. 1:11) and from which Israel begins the exodus (Exod. 12:37).[2] Israel does not sneak out of Egypt, but leaves Rameses "boldly" (Exod. 14:8 [lit., "with a high hand"]; cf. Num. 15:30) in full view of the Egyptians, who are burying their firstborn (v. 4; cf. the tenth plague in Exod. 12:29; 13:15). Theologically, God brings judgment on the Egyptian gods (Exod. 12:12) by showing them powerless before the true God, who is incomparably greater than they (Exod. 15:11; 18:11).

33:5 *Sukkoth.* See Exodus 12:37. This is perhaps an adaptation into Hebrew script of the Egyptian city Tjeku, probably located at Tell el-Maskhuta, southeast of Pi-Rameses.

33:6 *Etham.* Etham is east of Sukkoth, though its location is not otherwise known.

33:7 *Pi Hahiroth . . . Baal Zephon . . . Migdol.* From Etham the Israelites "turned back" (Exod. 14:2), though not back to Rameses but turning either south or north to Pi Hahiroth, a site between Baal Zephon to the west, Migdol, and "the sea" (Exod. 14:2). "Migdol" is Hebrew for "tower" and may be a Semitic title for an Egyptian fort along the desert.[3] The locations of Pi Hahiroth, Baal Zephon, and Migdol are not precisely known.[4]

33:8 *through the sea.* Here the route of the exodus is obscure. The route of the present-day Suez Canal once had a series of lakes. The Bitter Lakes are some fifteen miles north of Suez on the Gulf of Suez (Red Sea). Lake Timsah ("Crocodile Lake")[5] is some eight miles north of the Bitter Lakes, and Lake Ballah is about the same distance north of Lake Timsah. Lake Timsah and Lake Ballah are connected by a canal. There are other ancient canals north from Lake Ballah to a branch of the Nile. There may have been other canals south from Lake Timsah through the Bitter Lakes to the Gulf of Suez.[6] This geography suggests that the "sea" that Israel crosses probably is not the Gulf of Suez but rather the lakes or canals that constitute an extension of the Red Sea.[7]

Desert of Etham . . . Marah. Israel moves south on the east of the present Suez Canal. The "three days' journey" (NRSV) of verse 8 echoes Moses's request to Pharaoh for Israel to be allowed to go three days into the desert to worship God (Exod. 3:18; 5:3). The Desert of Etham is also called "Desert of Shur" (Exod. 15:22). At Marah (which means "bitterness") there is no fresh water to drink, but God performs the miracle of making the bitter water sweet when Moses tosses a log into it (Exod. 15:23–25).

33:9 *Elim.* Elim is an oasis with twelve springs and seventy palm trees, making it a prime desert camping stop (Exod. 15:27; 16:1). On the assumption that Mount Sinai is near the traditional site of Jebal Musa, Elim may be the oasis at Wadi Gharandel, a bit less than forty miles southeast of Suez near the Gulf of Suez,[8] or Uyun-Musa ("Spring of Moses"), ten miles south of Suez along the eastern coast.[9]

Key Theme of Numbers 33:1–49

- God's people should reflect on what God has seen them through on the path of life.

33:10 *Red Sea.* "Red Sea" (*yam sup*) is literally "Sea of Reeds" (NIVmg). Here "Red Sea" denotes the Gulf of Suez, though the same term applies to the "sea" that Israel crosses where Pharaoh's army drowns (Exod. 15:4; Deut. 11:4; Josh. 2:10) and to the Gulf of Aqaba (1 Kings 9:26). The Gulf of Suez probably was connected by canal with the Bitter Lakes and Lake Timsah, so it could be considered part of the same body of water and be called by the same name.[10] The Gulf of Suez may have actually extended into the Bitter Lakes before

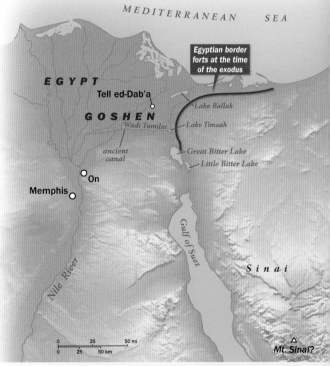

The Israelites leave Egypt and camp at Sukkoth before God delivers them one last time from their Egyptian oppressors as they cross the "sea" (33:8). Most sites mentioned on their journey to Sinai have not been clearly identified.

MEDITERRANEAN SEA

Egyptian border forts at the time of the exodus

EGYPT

Tell ed-Dab'a

GOSHEN

Lake Ballah

Wadi Tumilat

Lake Timsah

ancient canal

Great Bitter Lake

Little Bitter Lake

On

Memphis

Gulf of Suez

Sinai

Nile River

0   25   50 mi
0   25   50 km

Mt. Sinai?

silting separated the bodies, and even after that separation storm surges periodically reconnected the two.[11] For the complex debates around this term, see the discussion by James Hoffmeier.[12]

33:11 *Desert of Sin.* This is located between Elim and Mount Sinai (Exod. 16:1). "Sin" as a geographic term has nothing to do with wrongdoing; it is also unrelated to the similar-sounding Desert of "Zin" (v. 36). Its etymology is uncertain. It is possibly related to "Sinai" and could refer to the Old South Arabic and Akkadian moon-god Sin.[13]

33:13 *Dophkah . . . Alush.* The precise locations of these places are unknown. Neither is mentioned elsewhere in the Bible.

33:14 *Rephidim.* This is where Moses brings forth water from the rock (Exod. 17:1–5). It also is where the Amalekites attack Israel, though they are defeated by Israel as Moses lifts his arms in prayer (Exod. 17:6–15). It was perhaps in the vicinity of Wadi Feiran, the only oasis in the Sinai Peninsula significant enough to lead the Amalekites to fight to defend it.[14]

33:15 *The Desert of Sinai.* Here Israel receives instructions for the tabernacle. Israel camps at Sinai (Horeb) for nearly a year (see Exod. 19:1; Num. 10:11). Although some have sought the location of Mount Sinai in the northern Sinai, the far northern route seems to be precluded by Exodus 13:17, which says the Israelites avoid the road to Philistine country, even though it is the shortest path to Canaan, because it is too heavily fortified.[15] A more central Sinai route is possible, with Jebel Sin Bisher being a candidate for Mount Sinai. But the southern route seems the most likely: the campsite along the Red Sea after Israel having already crossed the sea (vv. 8a, 10 above) fits the southerly route. Since the fourth century AD, Sinai has been identified by tradition with Jebel Musa (Arabic for "the mountain of Moses") in the southern Sinai. Since it is extremely remote, it is unlikely to have been chosen arbitrarily as a "tourist" holy site. The statement that Kadesh Barnea is an eleven-day journey from Horeb (Deut. 1:2) seems more compatible with a southern Sinai route than a northern or central one. Moreover, it seems easier to find plausible sites for the various stations on the southern route than on any of the alternatives (see comments at v. 14 on Rephidim, v. 17 on Hazeroth). Even if the southern route turns out to be the correct one, it does not clinch Jebal Musa as Mount Sinai, though it is the most likely candidate.[16]

33:16 *Kibroth Hattaavah.* This means literally "graves of craving." This place was in the Desert of Paran (Num. 10:12), where God punishes Israel because of its complaints about manna and the lack of meat (Num. 11:34).

33:17 *Hazeroth.* This is where Miriam and Aaron question Moses's marriage to a Cushite woman and challenge Moses's authority (Num. 11:35–12:16).[17]

33:18–29 *Rithmah . . . Rimmon Perez . . . Libnah . . . Rissah . . . Kehelathah . . . Mount Shepher . . . Haradah . . . Makheloth . . . Tahath . . . Terah . . . Mithkah . . . Hashmonah.* These places are not mentioned elsewhere in the Bible, and their locations are unknown. "Rissah" might be identified with Rasah in the Arabah.[18] Somewhere in this sequence Israel sends scouts from Kadesh to check out the land of Canaan (Num. 13:26).

33:30–33 *Moseroth . . . Bene Jaakan . . . Hor Haggidgad . . . Jotbathah.* These places are mentioned in Deuteronomy 10:6–7 (with variation of spelling: "Moserah" for "Moseroth," "Gudgodah" for "Haggidgad"), where it states that Aaron dies and is buried at Moserah. Numbers places this event at Mount Hor (Num. 20:22–24).[19] Jotbathah is said to be a land flowing with streams of water (Deut. 10:7). The location of the first three of these sites is unknown, while the location of Jotbathah, though uncertain, may well be in the southern Arabah north of Ezion Geber.[20]

33:34–35 *Abronah . . . Ezion Geber.* Abronah is not mentioned elsewhere in the Bible. It seems to be close to Ezion Geber. Ezion Geber is adjacent to the city of Elath on the Gulf of Aqaba (Red Sea), where Solomon builds a fleet to trade with Ophir (1 Kings 9:26–28).

33:36 *Kadesh, in the Desert of Zin.* Israel moves back from the north end of the Gulf of Aqaba to the north-central Sinai, from where scouts had originally been sent out, where Miriam dies, and near where the people rebel over lack of water causing Moses and Aaron to sin (Num. 13:26; 20:1–13; 27:14).[21]

33:37-39 *Mount Hor.* Hor is "on the border of Edom" (Num. 20:23).[22] On Aaron's death, see Numbers 20:22–27. Aaron's age is not mentioned in the earlier account. The date given makes this about four

months after Miriam has died (see comments at Num. 20:1).

33:40 *Canaanite king of Arad . . . heard that the Israelites were coming.* See Numbers 21:1–3. Arad is located at Tell 'Arad, twenty miles southeast of Beersheba in the arid Negev.

33:41–42 *Zalmonah . . . Punon.* These places are not mentioned elsewhere in the Bible.[23]

33:43–44 *Oboth . . . Iye Abarim.* See Numbers 21:10–11. Some identify Oboth with 'Ain el-Weiba, eighteen miles west of Feinan (Punon?), though others prefer some site more northwest of Feinan.[24] Iye Abarim (or "Iye of the Abarim," meaning "ruins of Abarim"; also simply called "Iyim" [v. 45]) is on the border of Moab (v. 44). Its precise location is uncertain.[25]

33:45–46 *Dibon Gad . . . Almon Diblathaim.* Dibon Gad is the Dibon (Num. 21:30) that comes to be in the territory of Gad (see Num. 32:3, 34). Dibon is some twenty miles south of Heshbon, four miles north of the Arnon River. Almon Diblathaim may be the same as (or a daughter settlement of) Beth Diblathaim (Jer. 48:22; also mentioned in the Mesha Inscription), somewhere between Dibon and Nebo.[26]

Rephidim may have been located near the Wadi Feiran, which supported a large oasis, shown here, in the Sinai Peninsula.

33:47 *Mountains of Abarim, near Nebo.* Abarim is the mountain range forming the rim of the Moab tableland plateau and that may form the mountainous spine of the whole country.[27] Nebo is a city given to Reuben (Num. 32:37–38). Its location is uncertain but probably is one of the various tells (e.g., Khirbet el Mukhayyat near Jebel en Musa five miles from Hesban) near Mount Nebo, where Moses dies (Num. 34:1–5).[28]

33:48–49 *plains of Moab by the Jordan across from Jericho . . . from Beth Jeshimoth to Abel Shittim.* Beth Jeshimoth is on the border of Sihon's kingdom (Josh. 12:3) and is given to Reuben (Josh. 13:20).[29] Abel Shittim (= Shittim) is where Israel is seduced by Moabite women (Num. 25:1) and from where Joshua sends scouts to Jericho (Num. 25:1; Josh. 2:1).[30]

Theological Insights

It is good for the Israelites to recall where God has taken them, since that will help them go where God will take them in the future.

This list mentions God explicitly only a few times, but the list implicitly reminds Israel of what God has done at many places.

1. Rameses (v. 3) is where Israel has been oppressed (Exod. 1:11). God has delivered them from that oppression.
2. God parts the Red Sea (v. 8), saving Israel but drowning Pharaoh's army (Exod. 14:21–28).
3. At Marah (v. 8) God makes bitter waters sweet (Exod. 15:22–25).
4. In the Desert of Sin (v. 11) Israel receives manna and quail as food from God (Exod. 16).
5. At Rephidim (v. 14) God provides water for Israel and answers Moses's

prayer to let Israel defeat the Amalekites (Exod. 17).
6. In the Desert of Sinai (v. 15) Israel makes a covenant with God and receives the laws through Moses (Exod. 19–24).
7. At Kibroth Hattaavah (v. 16) God judges Israel for its grumbling and complaining (Num. 11).
8. At Hazeroth (v. 17) Miriam and Aaron challenge the authority of Moses, for which God strikes Miriam with leprosy (Num. 12).
9. Kadesh (v. 36) is where Israel's rebellion brings on God's punishment of forty years of wilderness wandering (Num. 13–14), and hence the many stages of the journey. Later at Kadesh Miriam dies (Num. 20:1), and Israel regroups to begin again its trek toward Canaan after the first generation has mostly died off (Num. 20:14–22).
10. God defeats enemies like "the Canaanite king of Arad" (v. 40) (Num. 21:1–3).
11. God brings Israel through the desert east of the Dead Sea to Shittim on the plains of Moab across the Jordan from the first city to conquer, Jericho (vv. 41–49). In that desert God saves Israel from viper bites (Num. 21:4–9).
12. At Shittim (v. 49) the Israelites bring God's judgment and plague on themselves when they allow themselves to be seduced into immorality and idolatry by Moabite and Midianite women (Num. 25).

Moses's list shows Israel's flaws and reminds it of the greatness of God and the wonders of his miracles. Moreover, it provides a spiritual heritage for future generations to allow them to reflect on where Israel had been spiritually and on how they need to improve.

Teaching the Text

God's people should reflect on what God has seen them through on the path of life. Moses is asked by God to write down the starting places of Israel's journey (Num. 33:1–2) and to record certain things that God has done at those places. What Moses does is a form of journaling.

Though no Scripture mandates it, journaling is a good thing for us to do as well. Donald Whitney, in his book *Spiritual Disciplines for the Christian Life*, advocates journaling: "As a Christian, your journal is a place to record the works and ways of God in your life. Your journal can include an account of daily events, a diary of personal relationships, a notebook of insights into Scripture, and a list of prayer requests."[31] The Bible gives a number of other examples of God-inspired journals: biographically and historically oriented psalms, the book of Lamentations, and the autobiographical sections of Ezra and Nehemiah. Whitney goes on to argue that journaling helps us understand and evaluate ourselves (cf. Rom. 12:3), meditate on the Lord and his word (cf. Josh. 1:8; Ps. 1:1–3), express thoughts and feelings to the Lord (cf. Ps. 62:8), remember the works of the Lord (Ps. 77:11–12) and record our spiritual heritage (cf. Deut. 6:4–7), and monitor goals and priorities (cf. Phil. 3:12–16).

Each of us has a travelogue of places where God has worked in our lives. All of us can remember the bad things that God has seen us through and the good things that God has brought our way. God had Moses do that for Israel. But we can do it for ourselves, whether formally in a journal or informally through reflection.

Illustrating the Text

It is important to remember the past.

Poetry: Sonnet XXX, by William Shakespeare. This well-known sonnet begins, "When to the sessions of sweet silent thought / I summon up remembrance of things past." Shakespeare expresses many regrets, but he also asserts, "But if the while I think on thee, dear friend, / All losses are restor'd and sorrows end." That can be true of remembering the good friends we have made throughout our lives. But it is especially true of our best friend of all, Yahweh, who has seen us through life's journey.

It is important to evaluate our present in light of the future.

Agriculture: One of the first lessons learned for driving a tractor is where to put your eyes. If one's focus is too limited and narrow, the rows will be crooked. It is important to pick a spot in the distance and consistently check back again and again to be sure that one is headed there. The discipline of journaling gives us an opportunity to look forward and look back, to watch for trends and keep our eyes focused on the future that God calls us to pursue.

Numbers 33:1–49

Making a Successful Future

Big Idea *Success requires obeying God and trusting in his promises.*

Understanding the Text

The Text in Context

Numbers 33:1–49 reviews the past: the places where Israel has gone from Egypt to the plains of Moab over the course of forty years. Now the focus moves to the future. In the immediate future Israel must carry out the conquest of Canaan, eradicating the Canaanites (Num. 33:50–55). Two and a half tribes have been assigned the Transjordan as their settlement. The text goes on to describe the coming division of the land among the nine and a half tribes not assigned to the Transjordan (Num. 34:1–15) and the names of the men who will oversee the land's division (Num. 34:16–29).

Interpretive Insights

33:50 *the plains of Moab.* This refers to the arid[1] "steppes" (NJPS) of the east Jordan valley just north of the Dead Sea opposite Jericho, the first city conquered (Josh. 6).

33:52 *drive out all the inhabitants.* Israel is to eradicate (or "dispossess" [NJPS]) the Canaanite religious culture. In battles everyone is to be killed (Deut. 20:16; Josh. 6:21), but the mandate to "drive out" (Exod. 23:28; 33:2; 34:11, 24; Num. 33:55; Deut. 4:38; 7:22; 11:23; Josh. 13:13) can be accomplished without killing everyone. The fierce tactics of Israel's armies will cause multitudes of Canaanites to flee to other lands.

Destroy all their . . . images . . . idols . . . high places. This utter destruction symbolizes Israel's radical break with the old Canaanite society and a formation of a new society.[2]

33:54 *Distribute the land by lot.* Each clan's territory is proportional to its population, but the location is decided by lot to prevent charges of favoritism.

33:55–56 *barbs in your eyes and thorns in your side.* Failure to drive out the Canaanites will have dire consequences. Israel, unfortunately, discovers this. Having failed to drive out the Canaanites (Judg. 1), Israel at times is subjugated to them (Judg. 4:2–3). The Israelites bring the punishment intended for the Canaanites upon themselves by allowing themselves to be enticed into idolatry among other Canaanite sins (Deut. 20:17–18; Judg. 2:11–13), thus making Israel liable to the judgments the Canaanites merit (Num. 33:56; see Lev. 18:24, 28). Sadly, this happens through the Assyrian and Babylonian exiles.

34:1–15 These verses lay out the borders of the land of Canaan (v. 2), named after Noah's grandson (Gen. 10:6, 15–18) who fathered the Canaanite tribes. The borders of the nine and a half tribes extend from Lebanon to the edge of the Sinai Peninsula, from the Rift Valley to the Mediterranean.

34:3–5 *southern side.* The Desert of Zin is in the northern Sinai Peninsula running against Edom's western border and then on north to the Dead (lit., "Salt") Sea. The Scorpion Pass, or "the ascent of Akrabbim" (Hebrew for "Scorpions"), is at the southern end of the Dead Sea.[3] Which specific pass is in mind is uncertain. On Kadesh Barnea, see comments at Numbers 33:36. Hazar Addar ("settlement/enclosure of Addar") is called "Addar" in Joshua 15:3. The locations of Addar and Azmon are uncertain, though northwest of Kadesh appears likely. The Wadi of Egypt (or "Brook

Key Themes of Numbers 33:50–34:29

- Future success requires eradication of evil.
- Future success builds on hope of inheritance.

of Egypt" [ESV]) is not the Nile but rather a wadi/stream forming the traditional border between Egypt and Canaan. It is either Nahal Bezor, one of the largest wadis in the Negev, which drains into the Mediterranean four miles south of Gaza, or, less likely, Wadi el-'Arish, which enters the Mediterranean about forty miles farther south.[4]

34:6 *western boundary.* The western border is the coast of the Mediterranean Sea.

34:7–9 *northern boundary.* The Mount Hor named here is not where Aaron is buried (Num. 20:22–29; 33:37–39) but rather is one of the peaks of the Lebanese range,

Mount Hor, perhaps Mount Hermon, was part of the northern boundary of the promised land. Mount Hermon, shown here, is the highest mountain in modern Israel and is at the southern end of the Anti-Lebanon mountain range.

perhaps Mount Hermon north of Dan or Jabel Akkar, a mountain east of Tripoli in north Lebanon.[5] Lebo Hamath, the northernmost place visited by the scouts (Num. 13:21), probably is Laboue (or Al Lebweh or Lebwe) in the Bekaa Valley of modern Lebanon, sixty miles north of Mount Hermon.

34:10–12 *eastern boundary.* Hazar Enan may be modern Hadr at the foot of Hermon or, more likely, Qayatein, about seventy miles northeast of Damascus and sixty miles east of Lebo Hamath (Laboue). This decision is significant: the latter view implies an 80 percent larger territory for Israel than the former.[6] That the northern border extends to the Euphrates (Gen. 15:18; Deut. 1:7; 11:24; Josh. 1:4) makes Qayatein more likely. The location of Shepham is unknown. Riblah probably is near modern Ribleh on the east bank of the Orontes River, twenty miles north of Lebo Hamath

(Laboue). The location of Ain is uncertain; it is either north near Kadesh on the Orontes River or south near the Sea of Galilee,[7] depending on whether the larger or smaller delineation of Israel's land is meant. The Sea of Galilee is literally "sea of Kinnereth" (NIVmg), this sea's older name.

34:13–15 *Nine and a half tribes . . . two and a half tribes.* The tribes of Reuben and Gad and the half tribe of Manasseh are allowed to settle in the Transjordan outside of Canaan (see Num. 32).

34:16–29 *one leader from each tribe.* These verses list ten new tribal leaders who will apportion the land once it is taken. No leader for Reuben and Gad is listed, since their land is already assigned (see vv. 13–15 above). Only Caleb remains from the old generation that left Egypt. The use of "El" and the lack of "Yahweh" in these names indicate that they are ancient (like names

Table 1. Ten New Tribal Leaders

Tribe	Name	Meaning of Name	Ancestor
Judah	**Caleb**	"Dog," perhaps metaphorical for a fierce warrior	Jephunneh, Kenizzite leader of Judah (Num. 13:6)
Simeon	**Shemuel**	Proposed meanings: "heard by God," "one who is from God," "his name is El"; same name in Hebrew as "Samuel"	Ammihud, "the Majestic One is my kinsman"; another Ammihud is an Ephraimite (Num. 1:10), and yet another is from Naphtali (see below)
Benjamin	**Elidad**	"God [El] is a friend"; variant of Eldad (Num. 11:27)	Kislon, "one of hope/trust"
Dan	**Bukki**	"tested" (?) (i.e., tried and true)	Jogli, "led into exile" (?)
Manasseh	**Hanniel**	"God is gracious to me"	Ephod, "costly garment"
Ephraim	**Kemuel**	"God . . . (?)"	Shiphtan, "judge; the just"
Zebulun	**Elizaphan**	"God has protected"; compare Zephaniah ("Yahweh has protected")	Parnach, Elamite loan word for "splendor" (?)
Issachar	**Paltiel**	"God is my rescue"; Palti (Num. 13:9) is a short form of this name (1 Sam. 25:44)	Azzan, "strong one"
Asher	**Ahihud**	"brother of majesty"	Shelomi is short for Shelomiel, "God is my friend, ally"
Naphtali	**Pedahel**	"God has redeemed"	Ammihud (see above)

in Num. 1). Later, most Israelite names become Yahwistic. For other information on these leaders and their names, see table 1.[8]

Theological Insights

Why does God call for complete eradication of the Canaanites (Num. 33:51–53)? Here are several reasons.

First, the Canaanites deserve it. It is not simply that the Canaanites are pagans but that they are especially evil ones. Among their abominations deserving eradication is human sacrifice (Lev. 18:21, 24–30).

Second, the Canaanites have been given plenty of time to repent. Genesis 15:16 states that they cannot be displaced at that time because "the sin of the Amorites [i.e., Canaanites] has not yet reached its full measure." This text indicates that in Abraham's day the Canaanites had not sinned enough to be displaced by Israel. God gives them an additional four centuries, years in which they could have turned from their evil ways, before God sends Joshua's armies to destroy them.

Third, the Canaanites, if allowed to remain, will lead Israel astray morally and cause them trouble (Num. 33:55; Deut. 20:18). Only with the utter eradication of Canaanite culture can Israel maintain the radical break with Canaanite lifestyles that God wants. When Israel fails to drive out the Canaanites completely, Israel gets caught up in Canaanite sins (see the book of Judges), and eventually God does to them

as he has planned to do to the Canaanites (Num. 33:56): he drives them from the land in the Assyrian and Babylonian exiles.

Borders of the promised land

Teaching the Text

1. *Future success requires eradication of evil.* Israel's next step is the conquest of Canaan. But there is a warning. The Canaanites and their religion must be totally wiped out. If Israel fails to do that, the Canaanites will prove to be a barb in their eye and a thorn in their side, and ultimately God will do to Israel what Israel was to do

Numbers 33:50–34:29

to Canaan (Num. 33:56): Israel itself will be driven out.

One's success in living for God depends on eradicating sin as ruthlessly as Israel was to purge Canaan. Consider Jesus's words given in the context of condemning adultery: "If your right eye causes you to stumble, gouge it out. . . . And if your right hand causes you to stumble, cut it off" (Matt. 5:29–30). These words, while not to be taken literally, show how seriously we are to act to purge sin. An inappropriate touch with the hand or a lustful glance with the eye can be the first step toward the act of adultery itself. We are to stamp such things out before they take root. Failure to root out the causes of sins will result in those sins being a barb in our eye and a thorn in our side, as the Canaanites proved to be for Israel when Israel failed to eradicate them.

2. Future success builds on hope of inheritance. God motivates the Israelites to take the land by reminding them that he has given it to them (Num. 33:53). Laying out the boundaries of the land for the Israelites (Num. 34:1–15) makes God's promise more concrete than it has been previously. They can begin to see how generous and expansive that inheritance will be. They can see the wisdom of God in planning the particulars of that inheritance. God specifies beforehand that the land be divided among the tribes according to the size of their populations (Num. 33:54) and by lot (Num. 34:13) so there would be no disputes or jostling for the territory (contrast the case of Reuben and Gad [Num. 32]). He even chooses leaders who will distribute the land (Num. 34:16–29). No longer an abstract promise, now its borders to the south and west and north and east are specified. The hope of inheritance is made quite vivid.

We too are motived by hope of inheritance. As God's children, Christians will inherit from God salvation (Heb. 1:14), eternal life (Titus 3:7), the kingdom of God (James 2:5; cf. 1 Cor. 6:9–10), blessings (1 Pet. 3:9), and heavenly rewards (1 Pet. 1:3–6; Rev. 21:7). As generous as God's promise to Israel was, the inheritance promised to Christians is even greater. Like the Israelites, we can be sure that God will distribute this inheritance wisely and fairly. As in the Israelites' case, hope of inheritance should motivate us to lay claim to our full allotment by living out the Christian life as God's children and heirs. The more we understand our inheritance, the more it motivates us to live for God.

Illustrating the Text

A vision of future possibility can motivate present action.

Personal Story: As cross-cultural missions professor at Crossroads College, Dr. Cláudio Divino often leads students on short-term mission trips. The students must commit to going, get a passport if they lack one, and raise a certain amount of funds for the trip before finally actually making the trip.

I participated in a trip to Rwanda to help an orphanage and churches in the region torn by genocide a decade and a half earlier. The trip was scheduled for July. Some students were falling a bit short of the money needed to go. Some were getting discouraged and were considering backing out. So just before the end of spring semester Dr. Divino called a meeting of everyone who initially planned to go on this trip. At that meeting he passed out the airplane tickets for the first stage of the trip to each student. He did this in order to change the idea of this trip from a fanciful dream into something very concrete in the minds of students. There before them was their boarding pass. They saw their own name on the ticket that would begin their long journey to Africa. This experience led some who had been wavering to redouble their efforts to go.

In Numbers 34 God makes the land promise more tangible by showing Israel the breadth and the length of what he is giving them. And this serves to motivate them to make this dream a reality.

Our future faithfulness is dependent on our present commitment to holiness.

True Story: Our forty-third president, George W. Bush, had to overcome some significant personal issues on his way to the White House. It must have been daunting to grow up in a family as prominent as his. He was tempted to run from responsibility, not toward it. Perhaps most importantly, he had to overcome a serious drinking problem. In an interview with Oprah Winfrey, President Bush's wife, Laura, shared openly about the president's struggle and his determination to overcome it. At the heart of his decision was a focus on the future. Looking forward, he realized that the man he would become was being determined by his actions in the present:

> "We had the wild drunken weekend and it was no different from any other weekend," Laura Bush said of the trip the couple took with friends to Colorado Springs in 1986.
>
> "George just woke up and he knew he wanted to quit," she said. "And he stopped and he was able to stop. A lot of people can't. A lot of people need help to stop. He just stopped cold turkey."
>
> In the book, she wrote: "I was not going to leave George and I wasn't going to let him leave me with twins. Our marriage was enduring, we loved each other and we were two people who did not have divorce in our DNA. But I was disappointed and I let him know that I thought he could be [a] better man. . . . He had a wife who loved him, had baby twin girls, and had a father thinking about running for president who was vice president."[9]

Focusing on where God desires to take us can give motivation to take the right step, right now.

Cities of Refuge

Big Idea *Bloodshed is an offense against humankind for which God requires expiation.*

Understanding the Text

The Text in Context

The last chapters of the book of Numbers are concerned with the division of the land. Numbers 32 describes how Reuben, Gad, and half of the tribe of Manasseh will settle in the Transjordan, and Numbers 34 describes the borders of the land of Canaan that Israel is to conquer for the nine and a half tribes who will settle there. Numbers 36, on the daughters of Zelophehad (see Num. 27:1–11), is concerned with not disturbing the tribal plan of inheritance, ensuring that Zelophehad's inheritance will not end up in the hands of another tribe or clan.

Chapter 35 deals with the Levites' inheritance. They are not to inherit a section of Canaan like the other tribes (Num. 18:23–24; 26:62). Numbers 35 provides for where the Levites can live and specifies more of their responsibilities in cases of homicide involving the Levitical cities of refuge.

Exodus 21:12–14 anticipates laws given here. It mandates the execution of murderers but then allows a place of asylum for one who has not deliberately committed murder. Numbers 35 elaborates on that distinction.

Historical and Cultural Background

Murder was punishable by death throughout the ancient Near East in Old Testament times (Laws of Ur-Nammu §1; Laws of Eshnunna §24; Laws of Hammurabi §153). Unlike in the Bible, where deliberately killing a slave is considered murder (in Exod. 21:20 "punished/avenged" [*naqam*] implies execution), killing a slave in Mesopotamia was considered damage of property, not murder (Laws of Eshnunna §23; Laws of Hammurabi §214). As in the Bible, mitigating factors such as self-defense could reduce the penalty for homicide (Laws of Eshnunna §47A; cf. Exod. 22:2–3). With negligent homicide, the killer's son/daughter could be killed instead (Laws of Hammurabi §§210, 230), something that the Bible condemns (Deut. 24:16).

Whereas the Bible forbids accepting a ransom to save the life of a deliberate murderer (Num. 35:31–32), this was an acceptable practice in Mesopotamia (Middle Assyrian Laws A §10). Murder in Mesopotamia was considered a tort or civil offense against the family rather than a crime against the state or against the gods, so the family could choose to accept ransom and not carry out the execution. The Bible allows this in cases of gross negligence homicide (Exod. 21:29–30) but not in cases of deliberate murder, for murder is a crime against God (see "Theological Insights" below).

Interpretive Insights

35:1–8 These verses describe the forty-eight cities given to the Levites to live in, six of which will be used as cities of refuge.

35:1 *the plains of Moab.* Israel has been there since Numbers 22 (Num. 22:1; 26:3; 31:12; 33:50).

35:2 *towns . . . pasturelands.* Levites have strictly limited land outside their towns for livestock.

35:4–5 *a thousand cubits . . . two thousand cubits.* 1,500 feet and 3,000 feet, respectively. Each town appears to be a square measured from the center of the city (see figure), making each city about 0.6 mile squared. These numbers have puzzled commentators since they leave little room for a town in the center. Milgrom takes the text to imply that these pastures extended one thousand cubits squared beyond the east, south, west, and north "corners" (Hebrew *pe'ah,* translated "side" by the NIV) of each town, in which two thousand measures half the circumference of the one-thousand-cubit square. [1] This interpretation allows

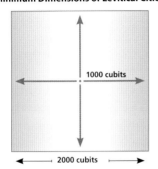

Minimum Dimensions of Levitical Cities

1000 cubits

2000 cubits

- God demands justice for killers.

towns to expand if they grow (represented by the dot in the figure). The rabbis figured the Sabbath's day journey (cf. Acts 1:12) at two thousand cubits based on these measurements (*Mishnah Erubim* 4:3).

35:6 *Six . . . cities of refuge . . . forty-two other towns.* Instead of a tribal territory, the Levites have forty-eight cities scattered equally among other tribes (see Josh. 21). "Refuge" is based on a rare Hebrew root (*qlt*) that apparently means "to take in, accept." [2] These six cities are asylums for unintentional manslayers (see vv. 9–34 below). Altars can also be used temporarily for asylum (cf. Exod. 21:14; 1 Kings 2:28), though only these cities can be used longer term. A city of refuge must be close enough for a manslayer to flee there before being killed by the avenger of blood (cf. Deut. 19:3).

35:9–34 These verses describe the cities given to manslayers as refuges.

35:12 *avenger.* Literally, "kinsman redeemer" (*go'el*). This is short for the "avenger of blood" (cf. vv. 19, 21, 24, 25, 27 below). The avenger is a relative of the person killed designated to execute the deceased's murderer. A manslayer must flee to a city of refuge quickly or else face the possibility of being killed by the avenger (Deut. 19:6). This represents a simple form of law enforcement within family clans. Middle Assyrian Laws A §10 reflects a similar practice.

stand trial before the assembly. The manslayer flees to these cities to request a trial, with Levites serving as judges.

35:13 *six towns.* Later these are specified as Bezer, Ramoth Gilead, and Golan in Transjordan (Deut. 4:43); Hebron,

cities of refuge
Levitical cities

Kedesh

Abdon
ASHER
NAPHTALI
EAST
MANASSEH
Rehob
Mishal
Sea of Galilee
Helkath
Nahalal
Kartan
Hammoth Dor
Golan
ZEBULUN
En Gannim
Jokneam
Kishion
Daberath
Yarmuk R.
ISSACHAR
Jarmuth
Taanach
Ramoth Gilead

MANASSEH
Shechem
Mahanaim
Jabbok R.
Gath Rimmon
Shiloh
GAD
EPHRAIM
DAN
Beth
Bethel
Jazer
AMMON
Eltekeh
Gezer
Horan
Geba
Mephaath
Gibbethon
Aijalon
Gibeon
BENJAMIN
Aimon
Heshbon
Beth Shemesh
Anathoth
Bezer
Holon
Libnah
Jahaz
JUDAH
Hebron
REUBEN
Kedemoth
Debir
Juttah
Dead Sea
Eshtemoa
Jattir
Arnon R.
MOAB
SIMEON
Zered Brook
EDOM

MEDITERRANEAN SEA

Jordan River

0   10   20 mi
0 10 20 km

Each Israelite tribe is to designate towns within its inheritance in the promised land for the Levites to live in. Six of those towns are to be places of safety for those who cause the death of someone unintentionally. The towns of Hebron, Shechem, Kedesh Bezer, Ramoth Gilead, and Golan become the cities of refuge. Their locations are shown on this map.

Shechem, and Kedesh west of the Jordan (Josh. 20:7–8). More can be added as required (Deut. 19:8–9).

35:15 *foreigners residing among them.* The Hebrew text actually specifies two groups: "The resident or transient alien among them" (NRSV). These rules apply equally to non-Israelites.

35:16–18 *If anyone strikes someone a fatal blow.* It is assumed that the accused has killed the victim. The question is whether it is deliberate murder. Use of certain weapons strongly suggests intentional murder. An "iron object" is perhaps a tool with iron at its end like a hammer or an ax (cf. Deut. 19:5). Rocks ("stone") or clubs ("wooden object") are more likely used by deliberate murderers.

35:20–21 *with malice aforethought.* "Malice aforethought" is literally "out of hatred" (ESV). Animosity previous to the act provides evidence that it is murder, even if no weapon is used.

shoves another or throws something at them intentionally . . . out of enmity . . . hits another. Hostility before the act provides circumstantial evidence that the act is intentional. "Enmity" (*'ebah*) is from the same root as a word for "enemy" (v. 23b). In such cases the killer is to be delivered to the avenger of blood for execution.

35:22–23 *without enmity . . . unintentionally . . . without seeing . . . not an enemy . . . no harm was intended.* Circumstances can also show that the killer has not acted deliberately. If there is no history of hostility or if there is evidence that it was an accident—a person throws a rock over a cliff unaware that someone is below—those facts can be the basis of acquittal of deliberate murder.

35:25–28 *The accused must stay there . . . until the death of the high priest.* Negligent manslaughter is nonetheless punished to a lesser degree. A person guilty of unintentional manslaughter is confined to the city of refuge until the death of the high priest. If the guilty party leaves the city before that, the avenger of blood has permission to exact lethal revenge.

35:29 *the force of law . . . throughout the generations to come.* In Numbers 35:29–32 miscellaneous other regulations are added that are abiding, not temporary.

35:30 *only on the testimony of witnesses.* There must be solid evidence to convict anyone of murder (cf. Deut. 17:6: "two or three witnesses") or any other crime (Deut. 19:15), though direct human witness may be supplemented with circumstantial evidence (vv. 16–24) to determine guilt. False witnesses who commit perjury can be punished as severely as the falsely accused would have been if found guilty (Deut. 19:16–19; cf. Prov. 19:9). If there are no witnesses, a person may be required to swear an oath of innocence, putting himself or herself under God's curse if actually guilty (Exod. 22:10–11; Num. 5:11–29), but such a person cannot be punished by the court.

35:31 *Do not accept a ransom.* Although a ransom is acceptable to save the life of a negligent owner of a goring ox (Exod. 21:29–30) and was acceptable to redeem a murderer in Mesopotamia, where the next of kin could take the culprit's property in lieu of his execution (Middle Assyrian Laws A §10), a deliberate murderer cannot under biblical law escape death by paying money. Nor can the manslayer ransom himself from confinement to the city of refuge before the death of the high priest.

35:33 *Do not pollute the land.* "Pollute" (*hanep*) is difficult to define precisely. The root is associated with "godless" people (Isa. 33:14 [parallel with "sinners"]; Jer.

23:11), corrupted people (Dan. 11:32), and "polluted" places (Num. 35:33–34 [parallel with ritual term *tame'*, "defile"]; Mic. 4:11). The pollution of the land denotes moral pollution caused by things such as murder, idolatry, and breaking God's laws/covenant (Num. 35:33; Ps. 106:38; Isa. 24:5; Jer. 3:9). The blood of the innocent cries out to God (Gen. 4:10). If not properly punished, bloodshed can cause God to break out in wrath (Joel 3:19).

except by the blood of the one who shed it. Execution of a deliberate murderer expiates God's anger. Deuteronomy 21:1–9 gives a procedure for making atonement for the land in the case of an unsolved murder by sacrificing a heifer.

Theological Insights

Mesopotamia's law was highly secular, making little reference to their gods. Executing a murderer was merely tit for tat. But the Bible has a theological basis for condemning murderers: human beings are made in the image of God, so killing a human being is in effect an attack upon God (cf. Gen. 9:6). Theologically, bloodshed "pollutes the land" morally before God (Num. 35:33–34). Bloodshed is not merely a crime against people; it is an offense against God that requires expiation either by the death of the murderer by execution or, in the case of unintentional manslaughter, the death by natural causes of the high priest.

There is an analogy here with Jesus Christ. Jesus indicates that all of us are murderers in our hearts (Matt. 5:21–22). In Numbers 35 the person guilty of killing another human can find asylum from the avenger in the city of refuge. Similarly, under the new covenant Christians find refuge from judgment in Christ. The manslayer finds redemption through the death of the high priest, after whose death he is released from the city of refuge. Christians have found redemption and release through the death of their high priest, Jesus Christ (Heb. 5:10; 6:20).

Teaching the Text

God demands justice for killers. Some of Numbers 35 is bound to its cultural context. We have no Levitical priests to serve as judges or Levitical cities to serve as courts. Cities of refuge made sense in an agrarian, sedentary culture, but not today. Nor is it reasonable today for a family member to serve as the enforcement officer and executioner of murderers. And yet there are principles of God's justice for killers here that we should apply today.

Although some Christians believe there are biblical grounds for opposing capital punishment, especially on the basis of its unfair administration or on the basis of a supposed change of law between the Testaments, Numbers 35 suggests that deliberate, premeditated murderers should be put to death. Genesis 9:6 appears to demand that murderers be executed because humans are made in God's image. This command is given to all humankind after the flood and not just to Israel, and it is not contradicted by the New Testament. Paul in fact seems to imply that the state has the right to inflict capital punishment when he speaks of the state's right given by God to "bear the sword" (Rom. 13:4). Executing murderers certainly protects society from repeat offenders and deters at least some from committing murder. Those who prefer to spare such murderers might do well to consider this talmudic proverb: "Those who are kind to the cruel will end up being cruel to the kind."

Although the Old Testament supports capital punishment for murderers, it allows it only after a trial in a regional court close enough for easy access in which sufficient, convincing evidence is presented before impartial judges (Num. 35:16–21, 24–25, 30), and only after all exculpatory evidence has been considered (Num. 35:22–23). To execute anyone without a fair trial and strong evidence is inherently unjust. Mob lynchings are always wrong. It is better to let some of the guilty escape punishment through a just, legal process than to risk wrongly condemning the innocent.

Numbers 35 also teaches us to distinguish between different kinds of homicide. The Bible condemns murder (Exod. 20:13), the taking of innocent human life. But those who commit premeditated murder are not innocent, so it is not murder to execute them. It is not wrong to engage in war if the cause and means are just. Numbers 35 suggests that those causing the death of another accidentally or unintentionally must never be executed. Exodus 22:2–3 seems to imply that killing in self-defense should not be considered murder, though killing a thief only for thievery is. To treat someone who kills a person accidentally, such as by failing to stop at a red light, the same as someone who was lying in wait to run the victim over is clearly unjust.

Numbers 35 also teaches us that even unintentional but negligent manslaughter, while not a capital offense, should not go unpunished. Thus in Numbers 35 the one guilty of negligent homicide is punished to a lesser degree by being confined to the city of refuge until the death of the high priest (vv. 22–28). So today those guilty of negligent homicide should be punished to some degree appropriate to their offense.

Any just society will distinguish between different types of killing. It will punish deliberate murderers more severely than other killers and will provide a fair, legal process whereby guilt or innocence can be established and punishments meted out. We should strive to make our society live up to these biblical standards.

Illustrating the Text

The "city of refuge" illustrates how God's law prevented unjust prosecution.

Scripture: Deuteronomy 19:5 provides an example of the "city of refuge" law at work. It was noted in the comments on Numbers 35:16–18 above that this text, when properly translated, provides an example of accidental homicide that, at first glance, appears intentional (changes from the NIV are in italics):

> For instance, a man may go into the forest with his neighbor to cut *planks of wood*, and as he swings his ax to *cut a plank of wood*, the *iron* head *slips off the plank of wood* and *finds* his neighbor *so that he dies.*

Understood this way, the case is ambiguous. Was there an accident or an intentional homicide? The scenario is that two men are cutting logs into planks, using the tool of simple carpentry, an ax. In this case, one man wields his ax at the wrong angle so that instead of sticking into and cutting the wood, it bounces (lit., "slips") off the wood and continues its swing to strike his partner, who happens to be standing too close behind in the path of the after-swing. As the deadly blow is delivered, the ax wielder is still holding the ax handle. The result is that when a relative investigates the scene, he finds his kinsman dead with an intact ax lodged in his chest. The kinsman (or other investigator) could easily jump to conclusions, decide that this was deliberate murder, and then seek blood vengeance. Only at the trial could the ax wielder's story be collaborated by the lack of any history of hostility between the two men and the ax wielder be exonerated of deliberate murder. This illustrates the kind of case where a trial at a city of refuge could come into play.

Bloodshed requires penalty.

Popular Culture: At the heart of countless blockbuster movies is a simple premise: the good guy needs to get justice by getting the bad guy. In most cases, the bad guy has stolen something or someone precious from the good guy. Often, it is the life of someone whom the good guy loved. The premise is usually simple, repeatable, and compelling. Why does this movie formula work so well? Because we humans are hardwired to understand justice. We are moral creatures with a God-given sense that bloodshed demands payment. Sadly, the payment exacted by most of the "good guys" in our movies looks more like vengeance than justice.

According to the Lord's commands through Moses, if an iron object, such as an ax, is used to administer a fatal blow, that act is murder and the punishment death. If someone is accidently killed while an ax is being used, the person who wielded the ax can find protection in a city of refuge. This iron ax head was found at Megiddo (975–925 BC).

The Daughters of Zelophehad (Part 2)

Big Idea *God's inheritance is assured.*

Understanding the Text

The Text in Context

The book of Numbers concludes by returning to the story of the daughters of Zelophehad, which begins in Numbers 27. Why does the narrator divide this story into two episodes, one in Numbers 27 and another in Numbers 36? As noted earlier, Alan Kam-Yau Chan argues persuasively that the reason is structural: the first part of Numbers is bracketed by the two censuses (Num. 1–4; 26), whereas the second half (Num. 27–36) is bracketed by the two accounts of the daughters of Zelophehad (Num. 27:1–8; 36:1–13), with Numbers 26:33 ("Zelophehad son of Hepher had no sons; he had only daughters, whose names were Mahlah, Noah, Hoglah, Milkah and Tirzah") serving as the linchpin between the two sets of brackets.[1]

Also, all the material between these two episodes in some fashion looks forward to life in the land, so the last chapter, dealing with inheritance in the land of the daughters of Zelophehad, seems to fit with what comes before.[2] More specifically, Gilead has already conquered its land (Num. 32:39–40), so clarifying God's will about the daughters of Zelophehad seems especially urgent for them. The generalized application of this ruling anticipates the conquest to come. Only after the conquest will this ruling become generally applicable.

Interpretive Insights

36:1 *The family heads . . . of Gilead . . . spoke before Moses and the leaders.* God's decision to allow the daughters of Zelophehad to inherit (Num. 27:6–7), like many precedent-setting legal decisions today, has humanly unanticipated consequences that lead to the need for another legal decision. Accordingly, the leaders of the clan of Gilead come to point out a potential problem with this decision, not only to Moses but also to the other members of his judicial counsel, "the leaders," or better "family heads" (lit., "the heads of the fathers"). This is probably the same tribal leadership group mentioned by the same name in Numbers 32:28.

36:3 *suppose they marry men from other Israelite tribes.* If these women marry outside their tribe of Manasseh, Manasseh may lose some of its inheritance in the land. According to the ruling in Numbers 27:1–11, the inheritance should theoretically stay in the line of Gilead-Makir-Manasseh-Joseph. The children borne by these women will be considered to be of the line not of their father's tribes (assuming that the father is of another tribe) but rather of the women's deceased father, Zelophehad. But the mixed tribal lineage of these children could in practice create confusion about the tribe to whom the land should belong. That confusion concerning patrilineage could result in land transferring to a different tribe. Or these women may fail to bear surviving sons, in which case the land would revert to their husbands and their tribes. This matter is somewhat urgent because Gilead has already taken possession of its territory in the Transjordan (Num. 32:39–40).

36:4 *Year of Jubilee.* This is supposed to occur every forty-nine years (see Lev. 25:8–55), though it is not clear whether Jubilee is ever actually carried out (see "Teaching the Text" at Lev. 25:1–55 for a discussion). At Jubilee all lands that have been sold will return to the original owners or their descendants. If a husband of a daughter of Zelophehad were from another tribe and he were economically forced to sell some of the land obtained from Zelophehad's daughter, this land might easily revert to his family's tribe rather than to Zelophehad's tribe at Jubilee given the confusion over tribal ownership that a mixed tribal marriage would create.

- All God's people will receive their rightful inheritance.

36:5 *the tribe of the descendants of Joseph . . . is right.* Moses, speaking for God, agreed that no inheritance in Israel is to pass from tribe to tribe, but Moses is able to ensure that this can never happen by giving God's command: the daughters of Zelophehad must marry within their own father's tribal clan. That eliminates all possibility that their land might somehow go to another tribe or clan.

36:10 *Zelophehad's daughters did as the LORD commanded.* These girls go along

Moses is God's spokesman as he guides the Israelites in understanding God's commands. Although he has the help of the tribal leaders, difficult cases are always brought directly to him. In Numbers 36, the leaders of the tribe of Manasseh are concerned about eventually losing the portion of their inheritance given to Zelophehad's daughters. They come to Moses for a ruling on the problem. A group of Israelites stands before Moses in this illumination from a French Bible (thirteenth century AD).

Manasseh's original land allotment is the area of Bashan (modern Golan Heights region), shown here, and part of Gilead, both east of the Jordan. In order to accommodate the inheritance of the daughters of Zelophehad, the tribe of Manasseh also receives an additional ten tracts of land west of the Jordan.

with this reduction of their liberty for the sake of a more general good.

36:11 *Mahlah, Tirzah, Hoglah, Milkah and Noah . . . married their cousins.* The daughters are again listed by name, though in a slightly different order. This may be the order in which they marry as opposed to their birth order. More specifically, they marry their paternal cousins (lit., "the sons of their [paternal] uncles"). The result of their choice of husbands is that the inheritance ends up going to those who would have inherited their father's property anyway had there been no daughters (Num. 27:8–11). God gives them freedom to choose any husbands within the tribal clan, so it is these girls who choose to marry

those who otherwise would have inherited the land had Moses not ruled in the girls' favor earlier. This was probably a onetime solution; the text does not generalize this case into a principle. Some elements are clearly bound by context: Israel is about to take and divide up the land, so tribal rights are especially important at that moment. Once that element ceases to exist, there will be no reason to limit inheritance within tribes. Note, however, that in the Apocrypha, Tobit 6:12–13 makes the practice of such a girl marrying her nearest relative into a "decree of the book of Moses" in which noncompliance is a capital offense, though this appears to go beyond the law itself.

36:13 *These are the commands and regulations the Lord gave.* "Commands" and "regulations" are two synonyms for God's law. The term "regulations" (Hebrew *mishpatim*, derived from the verb *shapat*, "to judge") indicates that these are verdicts from God as judge (*shophet*; cf. KJV "judgments"). The term "commands" underscores that God obligates people to keep his laws. This verse brings to an end the instructions God has given to Israel in the book of Numbers since Israel has camped at the plains of Moab (Num. 22:1), namely the laws of Numbers 27–36, by reminding God's people of the nature and source of the instructions given through Moses.

Theological Insights

The book of Numbers ends with emphasis on the need to obey "the commands and regulations the LORD gave through Moses" (Num. 36:13). Moses's granting of land to Israel and the daughters of Zelophehad is as "the LORD commanded" (Num. 36:2), and the daughters of Zelophehad "did as the LORD commanded Moses" (Num. 36:10).

The true lawgiver is not Moses but God (Isa. 33:22; James 4:12). God as lawgiver and ruler requires humans as his subjects to obey his laws. In the New Testament sin can be defined as "lawlessness" (1 John 3:4)—that is, rebellion against God's laws and correspondingly against God himself. It is true that we are not under the law but under grace (Rom. 6:14), and that many of the laws in the Old Testament are no longer in force under the new covenant; nonetheless, Christ is now our lawgiver, so we are under the "law of Christ" (1 Cor. 9:21; Gal. 6:2). Christ's law overlaps in significant ways with the Mosaic laws. That is why Jesus can say that he has not come to abolish the law (Matt. 5:17–20), and Paul can affirm that Christians do not nullify but "uphold the law" (Rom. 3:31). Indeed, Christian teaching sometimes can be described as "the sacred command" or "the command given by our Lord" (2 Pet. 2:21; 3:2), and Christians are "those who obey God's commandments" (Rev. 12:17; 14:12; cf. 1 John 5:2–3). Moreover, whoever does not keep God's commandments has not come to know God (1 John 2:3–4).

The specific commands to be obeyed have changed under the new covenant, but the need to acknowledge God as lawgiver and ruler by obeying his commands has not.

Teaching the Text

All God's people will receive their rightful inheritance. In Numbers 27:1–11 God, through Moses, grants the request of the daughters of Zelophehad to be allowed as women to inherit land so that their land can be handed down under their father's name. In Numbers 36 this ruling is narrowed to address the concern of leaders of the Gilead branch of the tribe of Manasseh to keep the inheritance of Gilead-Manasseh land within that tribe, though this does not contradict the original promise.

In some ways, the discussion may have seemed premature. Israel does not yet have the promised land to divvy up. Part of Manasseh has been allowed to settle in the Transjordan outside the original borders of the promised land (Num. 32:39–40), but the rest of Manasseh, as well as most of the other tribes, will receive their allotments only in the future in accord with God's promise. Even for the future allotments, they have faith that God will keep his promise to allot land to the various tribes so that eventually the law of Jubilee shall come into effect (Num. 36:4).

A general principle in the Bible is that God keeps his promises. He gives the land of Canaan to the Israelites, and ultimately they came to possess it. God keeps his promises to the daughters of Zelophehad, and Joshua accordingly sees to it that the daughters of Zelophehad inherit land in the territory of Manasseh east of the Jordan alongside the sons of other families of Gilead (Josh. 17:3–6). Similarly, God keeps his promises to us.

Although Christians, unlike the daughters of Zelophehad, are not promised physical land, we are promised an inheritance from God (see Eph. 1:14; Col. 3:24; Heb. 9:15). The promised land for Christians is not Canaan but a heavenly, eternal inheritance that will be given to Christians as a reward. In 1 Peter 1:3–4 it is stated this way:

> Praise be to the God and Father of our Lord Jesus Christ! In his great mercy he has given us new birth into a living hope through the resurrection of Jesus Christ from the dead, and into an inheritance that can never perish, spoil or fade. This inheritance is kept in heaven for you.

This inheritance language builds on inheritance language from the Old Testament that sees the land as a type of heaven that is the Christian's rightful inheritance. Old Testament history confirms that God keeps his promises. His eternal promise of heavenly reward for Christians is likewise assured. Like the daughters of Zelophehad and the tribe of Manasseh, Christian

As Numbers concludes, the Israelites are ready to move across the Jordan to take the land that God has promised them as their inheritance. The apostle Peter later writes about a heavenly inheritance in Christ that will "never perish, spoil or fade" (1 Pet. 1:4). This icon of Simon Peter, from a larger piece titled *Christ and Twelve Apostles*, decorated a nineteenth-century AD Orthodox church in the Antalya region of Turkey.

believers should live in the assurance of faith that God's promise of future inheritance is trustworthy for his people.

Illustrating the Text

The "family farm" meant much more than we understand in our modern, mobile society.

Human Experience: The attachment to land seen in the case of the daughters of Zelophehad is somewhat alien to modern, mobile societies, but it is still seen where family farms have been worked for many generations. There, a sentimental attachment to the land occurs that is extremely strong. Keeping the farm in the family is important.

John Ikerd, professor emeritus of agricultural economics at the University of Missouri, learned this while dealing with Georgia farmers in the farming crisis of the 1980s. Many farmers at that time were in economic distress because they had borrowed too much money at the extremely high interest rates of that era. Many were facing foreclosure and the possibility of actually losing their farms. Ikerd, himself raised on a dairy farm, was surprised by the sentimental attachment that famers had for their farms.

> In talking with these farmers, these real people, I began to understand that a family farm is much more than a business. The true family farm is part of the family and the family is part of the farm; the two are inseparable. Losing a family farm is like losing a member of the family or losing one's self; perhaps that's why so many farmers' thoughts turned to suicide at the prospect of losing their farms.[3]

To have land in the family's name was important for the daughters of Zelophehad. In a way, it would keep their father alive for them.

Heaven is our inheritance.

Human Experience: Many significant moments mark the period after a loved one has died. Of course, there is the funeral, with family and friends from all points coming to pay respects. There is the first time we dial the person's phone number, forgetting that he or she will not be on the other end. There is the first Thanksgiving, Christmas, New Year's Day, birthday. One of the moments many people remember is sitting down with a lawyer, and perhaps with other family members, and hearing the reading of the last will and testament. In that moment, what remains of the loved one's possessions is distributed. In passing, this person seeks to give us a final blessing.

As Christians, we will receive our blessing from the God of life, who will bring us into our inheritance and celebrate it with us. Here is the amazing thing: our portion will be that of coheirs with Christ.

Notes

Introduction to Leviticus

1. Walton, "Equilibrium and the Sacred Compass."
2. Longman and Dillard, *Introduction to the Old Testament*, 284; Harrison, *Numbers*, 23–24.

Leviticus 1:1–17

1. *TDOT* 15:106–7.
2. Oppenheim, *Ancient Mesopotamia*, 183–98; Walton, *Ancient Near Eastern Thought*, 131.
3. Lewis, "Covenant and Blood Rituals," 345–46.
4. Milgrom, *Leviticus 1–16*.
5. W. R. Smith, cited by Hartley, *Leviticus*; Milgrom, *Leviticus 1–16*.
6. Milgrom, *Leviticus 1–16*.
7. Ibid.; Wenham, *Leviticus*; Hartley, *Leviticus*.
8. BDB 629.
9. H. Gese and B. Janowski, cited by Hartley, *Leviticus*.
10. Image can be found in German Bible Society, *1000 Bible Images* (Bellingham, WA: Logos Research Systems, 2009) (electronic publication). For its interpretation, see Pittman, "White Obelisk."
11. George MacDonald, *The Lost Princess: A Double Story* (Grand Rapids: Eerdmans, 1992), 38.

Leviticus 2:1–16

1. *HALOT* 601.
2. H. Eising, cited by Hartley, *Leviticus*.
3. Milgrom, *Leviticus 1–16*.
4. Mathews, *Leviticus*, 34.
5. David Harding, "Boy Whose Father Died in Iraq Gives Soldier $20 He Found as a Gift, with Note Thanking Him for Service," *New York Daily News*, March 1, 2014, http://www.nydailynews.com/news/national/boy-dad-died -iraq-soldier-20-found-gift-article-1.1707274.
6. O. Henry, "The Gift of the Magi," in *100 Selected Stories*, Wordsworth Classics (Hertfordshire, UK: Wordsworth Editions Limited, 1995), 5.

7. Jacques Ellul, *Money and Power*, trans. La Vonne Neff (Downers Grove, IL: InterVarsity, 1979), 152.

Leviticus 3:1–17

1. Milgrom, *Leviticus 1–16*.
2. See John N. Oswalt, "כְּלָיָה," in Harris, Archer, and Waltke, *Theological Wordbook*, 1:440.
3. *Today in the Word* (June 1988): 13, cited at http:// www.sermonillustrations.com/a-z/j/joy.htm.

Leviticus 4:1–35

1. Milgrom, *Leviticus 1–16*.
2. Feder, *Blood Expiation*.
3. Milgrom, *Leviticus 1–16*.
4. Richard Averbeck, "חַטָּאת," *NIDOTTE* 2:98, following Kiuchi, *Purification Offering*, 124.

Additional Insights, pp. 30–31

1. *TDOT* 7:291.
2. *HALOT* 494.
3. Gane, *Leviticus, Numbers*, 278.

Leviticus 5:1–13

1. Claus Westermann, "ידה," *TLOT* 2:503.
2. Milgrom, *Leviticus 1–16*.

Leviticus 5:14–6:7

1. Roth, *Law Collections*, 44, 65, 129, 20.
2. Milgrom, *Leviticus 1–16*, 345–56; *Leviticus 17–22*, 1327.
3. *NBD*, s.v. "Weights and Measures."
4. Milgrom, *Leviticus 1–16*.
5. Ibid.
6. Kiuchi, *Purification Offering*, 31–34.
7. Motyer, *Prophecy of Isaiah*, 439.
8. Marie Louise Sjølie, "The Danish Cartoonist Who Survived an Ax Attack," *Guardian*, January 4, 2010, http://

www.theguardian.com/world/2010/jan/04/danish-cartoonist
-axe-attack.

9. Michael Muskal, "Obama Urges Florida Pastor to Drop Plan to Burn Koran on 9/11 Anniversary," *Los Angeles Times*, September 9, 2010, http://articles.latimes.com/2010/sep/09/news/la-pn-obama-koran-burning-20100910.

10. United Press International, "Protesters: Art Exhibit Shows Jesus in Sex," Oct 1, 2010, http://www.upi.com/Top_News/US/2010/10/01/Protesters-Art-exhibit-shows-Jesus-in-sex/UPI-78601285978248/.

Leviticus 6:8–7:38

1. Milgrom, *Leviticus 1–16*, 470–72.
2. Swanson, *Dictionary of Biblical Languages*, s.v. "III בַּד."
3. Milgrom, *Leviticus 1–16*.
4. Supported by Levine, *Leviticus*; Hartley, *Leviticus*; Rooker, *Leviticus*.
5. HALOT 1788.
6. Milgrom, *Leviticus 1–16*, 220.
7. Jacob Milgrom suggests that extra time is allowed to eat the vow offering because of its similarity to the freewill offering. Like the freewill offering, the vow offering is "a spontaneous offering, because it is dependent on the future fulfillment of a vow" (ibid., 220).

Additional Insights, pp. 50–51

1. Milgrom, *Leviticus 1–16*, 457–60.
2. Levine, *Leviticus*, 242.

Leviticus 8:1–36

1. *TDOT* 7:64–65.
2. Cornelis Van Dam, "אוּרִים," *NIDOTTE* 1:329–31; Van Dam, *Urim and Thummim*, 87, 224.
3. *TDOT* 7:66.
4. J. A. Davies, *Royal Priesthood*, 161.
5. M. V. Van Pelt and W. C. Kaiser, "מָלֵא," *NIDOTTE* 2:940.
6. Jeanne W. Lepper, "How Young Children Learn," http://web.stanford.edu/dept/bingschool/aboutbing_philosophy_learn.html.

Leviticus 9:1–24

1. Wenham, *Leviticus*.
2. Milgrom, *Leviticus*, 1–16.
3. Charles Haddon Spurgeon, "The Throne of Grace," http://www.spurgeon.org/sermons/1024.htm.

Leviticus 10:1–20

1. Kiuchi, *Purification Offering*, 81.
2. Hartley, *Leviticus*.
3. Hess, "Leviticus 10:1."
4. Milgrom, *Leviticus 1–16*.
5. Wenham, *Leviticus*.
6. Milgrom, *Leviticus 1–16*.
7. Ibid., 638.
8. This classic folk story is told in many variations, including button soup, wood soup, nail soup, and even ax soup.

Leviticus 11:1–47

1. N. MacDonald, *What Did the Ancient Israelites Eat?*, 33, 64–69, 72, 122n26.
2. See Edwin Firmage, "Zoology (Fauna)," *ABD* 6:1109–67.
3. *HALOT* 1646.
4. Definitions from Liddell and Scott, *A Greek-English Lexicon*.
5. Douglas, *Purity and Danger*.
6. Milgrom, "Ethics and Ritual."
7. Based on Jonathan D. Sarna, *American Judaism: A History* (New Haven: Yale University Press, 2005), 145.

Leviticus 12:1–8

1. Feder, *Blood Expiation*, 134–43.
2. Ibid., 142.
3. Pope John Paul II, "*Evangelium Vitae*: To the Bishops, Priests, and Deacons, Men and Women Religious, Lay Faithful, and All People of Good Will, on the Value and Inviolability of Human Life," http://www.vatican.va/holy_father/john_paul_ii/encyclicals/documents/hf_jp-ii_enc_25031995_evangelium-vitae_en.html.

Leviticus 13:1–59

1. For English text, see Danby, *Mishnah*, 676–97.
2. Neusner, *Principal Theological Categories*, 199.
3. Scurlock and Andersen, *Assyrian and Babylonian Medicine*, 70–73.
4. Goldman, Moraites, and Kitzmiller, "White Spots in Biblical Times."
5. Baillie and Baillie, "Biblical Leprosy"; David P. Wright and Richard N. Jones, "Leprosy," *ABD* 4:278.
6. Goldman, Moraites, and Kitzmiller, "White Spots in Biblical Times," 746.
7. Kaplan, "Biblical Leprosy."
8. Cited by Milgrom, *Leviticus 1–16*, 817.
9. Baden and Moss, "Origin and Interpretation of ṣāra'at."
10. As noted by, for example, the U.S. Department of Health and Human Services, http://www.hrsa.gov/hansensdisease/.
11. Centers for Disease Control and Prevention, "Facts about *Stachybotrys chartarum* and Other Molds," http://www.cdc.gov/mold/stachy.htm.

Leviticus 14:1–57

1. *TLOT* 1:415.
2. Milgrom, *Leviticus*, 155.
3. Ibid., 128; Wenham, *Leviticus*, 212.
4. Milgrom, *Leviticus*, 134.
5. Lew Wallace, *Ben-Hur: A Tale of the Christ* (Blacksburg, VA: Wilder, 2011), 319–20.

Leviticus 15:1–33

1. Following Milgrom, *Leviticus 1–16*.
2. Milgrom, *Leviticus 1–16*, 950–51.
3. Ibid.

4. Davidson, *Flame of Yahweh*, 334, citing S. L. Heering et al., "A Cohort Analysis of Cervical Cancer in Israeli Jewish Women," *Gynecologic Oncology* 39 (1990): 244–48; and M. Glezerman, B. Piura, and V. Insler, "Cervical Cancer in Jewish Women," *American Journal of Obstetrics and Gynecology* 161 (1989): 1186–90.

5. See Karel van der Toorn, "Prostitution (Cultic)," *ABD* 5:510–13.

6. See Sprinkle, *Biblical Law*, 101–28; Sprinkle, "Rationale of the Laws."

Leviticus 16:1–14

1. Swanson, *Dictionary of Biblical Languages*, s.v. "III בד."

Leviticus 16:15–34

1. Cowley, *Aramaic Papyri*, 114 (papyrus no. 30).

2. Arnold and Beyer, *Readings from the Ancient Near East*, 225.

3. Walton, "Equilibrium and the Sacred Compass," 300–301; figure used by permission.

4. B. J. Collins, "Puppy in Hittite Ritual."

5. Milgrom, *Leviticus 1–16*, 1078; Walton, *Ancient Near Eastern Thought*, 131–32.

6. Hartley, *Leviticus*; Milgrom, *Leviticus 1–16*.

7. Hartley, *Leviticus*.

8. Walton, "Equilibrium and the Sacred Compass," 301.

9. Gane, *Leviticus, Numbers*, 278.

10. Kaiser, *Old Testament Theology*, 118.

11. Tracey R. Rich, "Yom Kippur: The Day of Atonement," Temple Emanu-El, San Jose, CA (2008), http://www.templesanjose.org/JudaismInfo/time/yom_kippur.htm.

Leviticus 17:1–16

1. John Walton, "Equilibrium and the Sacred Compass."

2. Cited by Keel, *Symbolism of the Biblical World*, 82, 84.

3. Jack W. Vancil, "Goat, Goatherd," *ABD* 2:1040–41.

4. Keil and Delitzsch, *Pentateuch*.

5. *Kipper + b^e* is attested with the instrumental sense for the *bet* at Genesis 32:20 [MT 32:21]; Exodus 29:33; Leviticus 5:16; 7:7; 19:22; Numbers 5:8; 35:33; 1 Samuel 3:14; 2 Samuel 21:3; Proverbs 16:6; Isaiah 27:9; Ezekiel 43:22. The only usage that is not instrumental is a *bet* of location: Leviticus 6:30 [MT 6:23]; 16:17: "atonement *in* the Holy Place." *Kipper + ʿal* (Lev. 5:16; 16:30), or *kipper + le* (Deut. 21:8), or *kipper + baʿad* (Lev. 9:7) is the way in Hebrew to say, "make atonement *for* [a person]," not *kipper + b^e*.

6. Milgrom, *Leviticus 17–22*, 1478.

7. John Stott, "Why Was Blood So Important?," sermon delivered at All Souls Church, London, October 24, 1999.

8. Here is a sample of such hymns: "There Is a Fountain Filled with Blood" (William Cowper), "There Is Power in the Blood" (Lewis Jones), "Are You Washed in the Blood?" (Elisha Hoffman), "Jesus, Thy Blood and Righteousness" (Nikolaus von Zinzendorf), "Nothing but the Blood" (Robert Lowry), "Not All the Blood of Beasts" (Isaac Watts), "Redeemed by the Blood of the Lamb" (Fannie Crosby).

9. Examples include "At the Cross" (Reuben Morgan and Darlene Zschech), "Behold the Lamb" (Chris Tomlin), "In Christ Alone" (Stuart Townend and Keith Getty), and "Lead Me to the Cross" and "Worthy Is the Lamb" (Hillsong United).

10. Charles Haddon Spurgeon, "A Mighty Savior," http://www.spurgeongems.org/vols1-3/chs111.pdf.

Additional Insights, pp. 120–21

1. Levine, *Leviticus*, 112–13.

2. Kaufmann, *Religion of Israel*, 181. Contrast the view of Milgrom, *Leviticus 17–22*, 1452–53.

3. Levine, *Leviticus*, 113. Levine points out the examples that follow.

4. Lockshin, *Rashbam's Commentary*, 93n20. Also taking this view is Roy Gane: "However, the contradiction vanishes if we take seriously the differences in life situation (German *Sitz im Leben*) indicated by the two passages. Whereas Leviticus 17 applied to the desert camp, when Israelites lived close to the sanctuary, Deuteronomy 12 regulated settled life in the land of Canaan, when they spread out and many of them lived too far from the sanctuary to come there every time they wanted meat of domestic animals (Deut. 12:20–21). As a concession to this change in practical circumstances, the law of Deuteronomy allows non-sacrificial slaughter" (*Leviticus, Numbers*, 301–2).

5. Wenham, *Leviticus*.

6. Keil and Delitzsch, *Pentateuch*, 2:409.

Leviticus 18:1–30

1. Walton, "Equilibrium and the Sacred Compass."

2. Kimuhu, *Leviticus*, 113–45.

3. Stager and Wolff, "Child Sacrifice at Carthage."

4. Cornfeld and Freedman, *Archaeology of the Bible*, 52.

5. Moscati, *World of the Phoenicians*, 141–44.

6. Kaiser, "Leviticus 18:5 and Paul."

7. For a thorough, monograph-length discussion of homosexuality and the Bible, see Gagnon, *Bible and Homosexual Practice*. The discussion that follows draws on Gagnon's argument (111–46).

8. Adapted from Michael P. Green, *Illustrations for Biblical Preaching* (Grand Rapids: Baker, 1989), 333.

Leviticus 19:1–37

1. Milgrom, *Leviticus 17–22*.

2. Wilson, *"Holiness" and "Purity,"* 30.

3. Ibid., 31.

4. Ibid., 76.

5. Walton, "Interpreting the Bible," 311–12.

6. Milgrom, *Leviticus*, 236–38.

7. Walton, *Ancient Near Eastern Thought*, 138, 272.

8. Ibid., 319–24.

9. Berkhof, *Systematic Theology*, 55.

Additional Insights, pp. 134–35

1. Hoffmeier, "'These Things Happened,'" 112, citing Umberto Cassuto, *Exodus* (Jerusalem: Magnes, 1967), 112.

2. Fox, "Marked for Servitude."

3. Eisenberg, *Jewish Traditions*, 545.

Leviticus 20:1–27

1. Modified from Michael Hildenbrand, cited by Milgrom, *Leviticus 17–22*, 1728.
2. Brichto, *Problem of "Curse,"* 118–99.
3. Hartley, *Leviticus*.
4. Strouhal, *Ancient Egyptians*, 199.
5. For a discussion of why an ox that gored a person to death was executed, see Sprinkle, *Book of the Covenant*, 115–28.
6. Davidson, *Flame of Yahweh*, 332.
7. For a more detailed discussion of the relevance of the law's sanctions, see Sprinkle, *Biblical Law*, 1–27; Sprinkle, "Old Testament Civil Laws."
8. Hayes, *Moral Vision*, 382–83.
9. Westbrook, *Biblical and Cuneiform Law*, 77n156. See also Walton, *Ancient Near Eastern Thought*, 287–302.

Leviticus 21:1–24

1. Modified from Michael Hildenbrand, cited by Milgrom, *Leviticus 17–22*, 1792.
2. El-Shahawy, *Funerary Art*, 39.
3. Gane, *Leviticus, Numbers*, 374.
4. Wiersbe, *Be Holy*, 112–13.

Leviticus 22:1–33

1. Modified from Michael Hildenbrand, cited by Milgrom, *Leviticus 17–22*, 1846–47.
2. Vasholz, *Leviticus*, 275.
3. Keel, *Symbolism of the Biblical World*.
4. http://www.newadvent.org/summa/4082.htm#article5.
5. C. S. Lewis, *Yours, Jack: Spiritual Direction from C. S. Lewis*, ed. Paul F. Ford (New York: HarperCollins, 2008), 160.

Leviticus 23:1–44

1. Milgrom, *Leviticus 23–27*.

Leviticus 24:1–23

1. Finkelstein, *The Ox That Gored*, 26–28.
2. Durham, *Exodus*, 280.
3. Brichto, *Problem of "Curse,"* 118–99.
4. "Al Shabab Group Stones Man to Death," *Horseed Media: The Free Voice of Somalia*, June 17, 2011, http://horseedmedia.net/2011/06/17/somalia-al-shabab-group-stones-man-death/. Another case occurred in December 2009 in a Somalia village: "Islamic Militants Stone Man to Death for Adultery in Somali as Villagers Are Forced to Watch," *Mail Online*, December 15, 2009, http://www.dailymail.co.uk/news/article-1235763/Pictured-Islamic-militants-stone-man-death-adultery-Somalia-villagers-forced-watch.html#ixzz1QbglQfHE.

Leviticus 25:1–55

1. Westbrook, *Property and Family*, 44–50.
2. The recording is available on the National Park Service website at http://www.nps.gov/inde/photosmultimedia-soundofthelibertybell.htm.

Leviticus 26:1–46

1. Mendenhall, "Law and Covenant."
2. Milgrom, *Leviticus 23–27*.
3. Ibid., 2330.

Leviticus 27:1–34

1. Oppenheim, *Ancient Mesopotamia*, 108.
2. Wenham, *Leviticus*.

Introduction to Numbers

1. Olson, *Death of the Old*; Olson, *Numbers*.
2. Chan, "Structuring on the Book of Numbers."

Numbers 1:1–2:34

1. Milgrom, *Numbers*.
2. Wenham, *Numbers*.

Additional Insights, pp. 196–97

1. E. W. Davies, "Mathematical Conundrum."
2. Humphreys, "Number of People in the Exodus"; Milgrom, "Decoding Very Large Numbers"; McEntire, "Response to Colin Humphreys's 'The Number of People in the Exodus'"; Humphreys, "Numbers in the Exodus"; Rendsburg, "Two Recent Articles on the Number of People."
3. See *ISBE*, s.v. "Numbers, Book of."
4. According to the Central Intelligence Agency World Factbook, in 2014 the State of Israel had an estimated population of 7.8 million, https://www.cia.gov/library/publications/the-world-factbook/geos/is.html.
5. De Odorico, *Use of Numbers and Quantifications*, esp. 71–74, 174–75.
6. For further discussion, see Fouts, "Defense of the Hyperbolic Interpretation"; Vasholz, "Military Censuses."
7. Vasholz, "Military Censuses."

Numbers 3:1–4:49

1. Dozeman, "Numbers."

Numbers 5:1–31

1. Roth, *Law Collections*, 106.
2. Ashley, *Numbers*.
3. Milgrom, *Numbers*.
4. Ibid.
5. Brichto, "Case of the ŚŌṬĀ."
6. See Sprinkle, *Biblical Law*, 118–19.
7. Alan M. Dershowitz, testimony before the House of Representatives Judiciary Committee, December 1, 1988, http://www.constitution.org/lrev/dershowitz_test_981201.txt.

Numbers 6:1–21

1. Cartledge, "Were Nazirite Vows Conditional?"; Chepey, *Nazirites*, 196–97.
2. *HALOT* 928.
3. *TDOT* 11:535–36.
4. So the twelfth-century rabbi Rambam (Maimonides).

5. Milgrom, *Numbers*.

6. See *The Catholic Encyclopedia* (1911), http://www
.catholic.org/encyclopedia/, s.v. "Lay Brothers," "Monks,"
"Nuns," "Tonsure."

7. Cartledge, "Were Nazirite Vows Conditional?,"
409–10.

Numbers 6:22–27

1. Barkay et al., "Challenges of Ketef Hinnom."

2. Budd, *Numbers*.

Numbers 7:1–89

1. Wenham, *Numbers*.

2. Milgrom, *Numbers*.

3. Victor P. Hamilton, "חָנַךְ," in Harris, Archer, and
Waltke, *Theological Wordbook*, 1:301–2.

4. *HALOT* 1116–17.

5. Marvin A. Powell, "Weights and Measures," *ABD*
6:906–7; *NBD*, s.v. "Weights and Measures."

6. Driver and Miles, *Babylonian Laws*, 1:470–71.

7. Dandamaev, *Slavery in Babylonia*, 115.

8. Silver is relatively less valuable today. The ratio of
gold to silver prices in July 2013 was 65:1.

9. Milgrom, *Numbers*.

10. Allen, "Numbers."

11. *CAD* 1.1.131–34.

12. Wenham, *Numbers*, 93.

13. Jeanne Nuechterlein, "The Domesticity of Sacred
Space in the Fifteenth Century Netherlands," in *Defining the
Holy: Sacred Space in Medieval and Early Modern Europe*,
ed. Andrew Spicer and Sarah Hamilton (Burlington, VT:
Ashgate, 2005), 73–74.

Numbers 8:1–26

1. Wenham, *Numbers*.

2. Ashley, *Numbers*.

Numbers 9:1–14

1. Aryeh Kaplan, ed., *The Passover Haggadah* (New
York: Maznaim, 1982), 30–34.

2. Ibid., 68.

Numbers 9:15–10:10

1. Manniche, *Musical Instruments*, 7–13.

2. Milgrom, *Numbers*, 70.

Numbers 10:11–36

1. Wenham, *Numbers*.

2. Sarna, *Exodus*, 12.

3. Charles Haddon Spurgeon, "The March," http://www
.spurgeongems.org/vols7-9/chs368.pdf. See James Picton,
Oliver Cromwell: The Man and His Mission (London: Cas-
sell, 1889), 326.

Numbers 11:1–35

1. Shanaway, *Quail Production Systems*, 7; Burton and
Burton, *International Wildlife Encyclopedia*, s.v. "Quail."

2. Milgrom, *Numbers*.

3. Wenham, *Numbers*.

4. United Bible Societies, *Fauna and Flora*, 110–11.

5. Ibid., 96.

6. Milgrom, *Numbers*.

7. Ibid.

8. Psalm 106:15 in the MT reads "wasting disease," but
the LXX's reading, *plēsmonēn* ("fullness, plenty"), indicates
that the MT may be corrupt here.

9. Dennis Prager, *Happiness Is a Serious Problem: A
Human Nature Repair Manual* (New York: ReganBooks,
1998), 59.

10. John Perkins, *With Justice for All: A Strategy for
Community Development* (Ventura, CA: Regal Books,
1982), 29–31.

Numbers 12:1–16

1. Mentioned by Harrison, *Numbers*.

2. Milgrom, *Numbers*.

3. Ashley, *Numbers*.

4. Harrison, *Numbers*.

5. Rogers, "Moses." Another option is that Moses was
"devout" (NRSVmg), as the pious "humble, afflicted" were.

6. Milgrom, *Numbers*.

7. Harrison, *Numbers*.

8. Milgrom, *Numbers*.

9. *NBD*, s.v. "Hazeroth."

10. "Christian University 'Profoundly Sorry' for Racist
Policies," *USA Today*, November 24, 2008, http://usatoday
30.usatoday.com/news/education/2008-11-24-bob-jones
-university-race_N.htm.

11. Arthur C. Brooks, "The Downside of Inciting Envy,"
New York Times, March 2, 2014, http://www.nytimes.com
/2014/03/02/opinion/sunday/the-downside-of-inciting-envy
.html?_r=1.

Numbers 13:1–14:9

1. Wenham, *Numbers*.

2. N. MacDonald, *What Did the Ancient Israelites Eat?*,
39; Mazar and Panitz-Cohen, "Land of Honey."

3. Allan M. Harman, "נָפַל," *NIDOTTE* 3:130.

4. Milgrom, *Numbers*, 106.

Numbers 14:10–45

1. Milgrom, *Numbers*.

2. Following Keil and Delitzsch, *Pentateuch*.

3. Spieckermann, "God's Steadfast Love," 310.

4. Neusner, *Leviticus Rabbah*, 182.

5. "Stallworth Apologizes for His Actions," *ESPN*,
August 6, 2009, http://sports.espn.go.com/nfl/news/story
?id=4381138.

Numbers 15:1–41

1. Milgrom, *Numbers*.

2. Ibid.

3. Andrew Hill, "שָׁגָה," *NIDOTTE* 4:43–44.

4. Finkelstein, *Ox That Gored*, 26–27.

5. Brenner, *Colour Terms*, 145–48.

6. C. S. Lewis, *The Problem of Pain* (New York: McMillan, 1962), 118–19, 124.

7. E. Gordon Rupp, *Religion in England, 1681–1791* (Oxford: Clarendon, 1986), 297.

Numbers 16:1–50

1. Milgrom, *Numbers.*
2. Wenham, *Numbers.*
3. Ibid.
4. *NBD*, s.v. "Korah."
5. James W. Sire, *Scripture Twisting: 20 Ways Cults Misread the Bible* (Downers Grove, IL: InterVarsity, 1980).

Numbers 17:1–18:7

1. Milgrom, *Numbers.*
2. Naylor, "Numbers," 185.
3. Beale and Carson, *New Testament Use of the Old Testament*, 822.
4. Billy Graham, *Just as I Am: The Autobiography of Billy Graham* (New York: HarperCollins, 1997), 53.
5. Habibullah Kahn, "Teen Dies Saving Classmates from Suicide Bomber," *ABC News*, January 10, 2014, http://abcnews.go.com/International/teen-dies-saving-classmates-suicide-bomber/story?id=21491486.

Numbers 18:8–32

1. Ashley, *Numbers.*
2. Barna Group, "New Study Shows Trends in Tithing and Donating," April 14, 2008, http://www.barna.org/barna-update/article/18-congregations/41-new-study-shows-trends-in-tithing-and-donating.
3. Maggi Martin, "Preacher Who Fleeced Flock Gets 3 Years in Prison," October 30, 2008, *Cleveland.com*, http://blog.cleveland.com/metro/2008/10/preacher_who_fleeces_flock_get.html.

Numbers 19:1–22

1. Levine, *Numbers 1–20*, 468–79. See Charles A. Kennedy, "Dead, Cult of the," *ABD* 2:105–8.
2. Milgrom, *Numbers.*
3. Brenner, *Colour Terms*, 63.
4. Serge Schmemann, "A Red Heifer or Not?," *New York Times*, June 14, 1997, http://www.nytimes.com/1997/06/14/world/a-red-heifer-or-not-rabbi-wonders.html.
5. Brenner, *Colour Terms*, 64–65.
6. Milgrom, *Numbers.*
7. United Bible Societies, *Fauna and Flora*, 129–30; Irene Jacob and Walter Jacob, "Flora," *ABD* 2:812.
8. Milgrom, *Numbers*, 160, 438–43.
9. Milgrom, *Numbers*, 161.
10. Dozeman, "Numbers," 152.
11. Douglas, *Purity and Danger*, 51–57.
12. Levine, *Numbers 1–20*, 472.
13. David Brooks, "Cult of Death," *New York Times*, September 7, 2004, http://www.nytimes.com/2004/09/07/opinion/07brooks.html?_r=0.

Numbers 20:1–13

1. Cole, *Numbers*, 46–49.
2. Milgrom, *Numbers.*
3. Following Keil and Delitzsch, *Pentateuch.*
4. Harrison, *Numbers.*
5. *TDOT* 9:7.

Numbers 20:14–29

1. Milgrom, *Numbers.*
2. Cole, *Numbers.*
3. Wenham, *Numbers.*
4. Milgrom, *Numbers.*
5. Martin Luther King Jr., "I've Been to the Mountaintop," http://www.americanrhetoric.com/speeches/mlkivebeentothemountaintop.htm.

Numbers 21:1–9

1. Olson, *Numbers.*
2. Shanks, "Mystery of the Nechushtan."
3. Cole, "Numbers," 375–76.
4. Beitzel, *Atlas of the Bible*, 114.
5. Respectively, Milgrom, *Numbers*; Cole, *Numbers*; Ashley, *Numbers.*
6. Harrison, *Numbers.*
7. Cole, *Numbers.*
8. Saggs, *Greatness That Was Babylon*, 259–60.
9. T. E. Lawrence, *Seven Pillars of Wisdom* (1927; repr., Ware, England: Wordsworth, 1997), 261.

Numbers 21:10–35

1. Arthur J. Ferch, "Abarim (Place)," *ABD* 1:6–7.
2. Ashley, *Numbers.*
3. Milgrom, *Numbers.*
4. Dave Anderson, "'Icehockey' Russian Way," *New York Times*, February 18, 1980, C5.

Numbers 22:1–19

1. Cole, *Numbers*, 48–49.
2. See Jo Ann Hackett, "Deir 'Alla, Tell (Texts)," *ABD* 2:129–30.
3. *IDB*, s.v. "Balak."
4. *NBD*, s.v. "Pethor."
5. Henry O. Thompson, "Amaw (Place)," *ABD* 1:183.
6. Milgrom, *Numbers.*
7. See James M. Kittelson, *Luther the Reformer: The Story of the Man and His Career* (Minneapolis: Augsburg, 1986), 286.

Numbers 22:20–40

1. Rooker, "Theophany"; against W. G. MacDonald, "Christology." MacDonald argues that *mal'ak yhwh* refers not to God or Christ, but rather to an angel who serves as God's spokesperson.
2. Way, "Balaam's Hobby Horse"; Way, "Animals in the Prophetic World," 50; Way, *Donkeys in the Biblical World*, 60–67, 184–91.
3. Alter, *Art of Biblical Narrative*, 104–7.

4. *HALOT* 438.

5. Ross Douthat, "Heaven and Nature," *New York Times*, December 20, 2009, http://www.nytimes.com/2009/12/21/opinion/21douthat1.html.

Additional Insights, pp. 342–43

1. Ashley, *Numbers*.

2. For more on synoptic/resumptive storytelling, see Brichto, *Grammar of Biblical Poetics*, esp. 13–14.

3. The existence of the *wayyqtl* form to convey the pluperfect is disputed. John Cook ("Biblical Hebrew Verbal System," 298) denies that the *wayyqtl* form ever conveys a pluperfect meaning. Bruce Waltke and Michael O'Connor (*Biblical Hebrew Syntax*, 552), noting the doubts, affirm with examples that it can. Literary considerations in particular passages (e.g., Gen. 15:7; Jon. 4:5) lead me to side with the latter view.

Numbers 22:41–24:13

1. Alter, *Art of Biblical Narrative*, 104–7.

2. Largement, "Les oracles de Bile'am," 46, cited and translated by Milgrom, *Numbers*, 194, 320.

3. Milgrom, *Numbers*.

4. Hallo and Younger, *Context of Scripture*, 1:78; Pritchard, *Ancient Near Eastern Texts*, 19–21.

5. Keil and Delitzsch, *Pentateuch*.

6. Albright, "Oracles of Balaam." Albright emends *mispar* ("number") to *mi sapar* ("who can number"), based on the Samaritan and the Septuagint. He further emends *et roba'* to the word *trb't* to relate it to the Akkadian word *turbu'tu* ("dust cloud"), though this change is purely conjectural.

7. Ashley, *Numbers*.

8. Milgrom, *Numbers*.

9. Wenham, *Numbers*.

10. United Bible Societies, *Fauna and Flora*, 90–91.

11. Swanson, *Dictionary of Biblical Languages*, s.v. "דְּלִי."

12. Cole, *Numbers*, 411.

13. Friedrich Nietzsche, *The Birth of Tragedy*, 23, cited at "The Perspectives of Nietzsche," http://www.theperspectivesofnietzsche.com/nietzsche/nchrist.html.

14. Bernard Evslin, *Gods, Demigods & Demons: A Handbook of Greek Mythology* (London: I. B. Tauris, 2006), 66.

Numbers 24:14–25

1. For example, Allen, "Numbers."

2. Ashley, *Numbers*.

3. Pritchard, *Ancient Near Eastern Texts*, 329.

4. BDB 980–81.

5. Wenham, *Numbers*; Milgrom, *Numbers*.

6. Budd, *Numbers*.

7. Henry, *Commentary on the Whole Bible*, 225.

Additional Insights, pp. 356–57

1. Vermes, *Dead Sea Scrolls*, 89.

2. Juel, *Messianic Exegesis*, 70–71; J. J. Collins, *Scepter and the Star*, 78–80.

3. Schiffman, *From Text to Tradition*, 171–74.

4. Schaff, *Apostolic Fathers*, http://www.ccel.org/ccel/schaff/anf01.viii.iv.cvi.html.

5. Delitzsch, *History of Redemption*, 70–71.

Numbers 25:1–19

1. Olson, *Numbers*.

2. *NBD*, s.v. "Shittim."

3. Karel van der Toorn, "Prostitution (Cultic)," *ABD* 5:510–13.

4. Milgrom, *Numbers*.

5. *NBD*, s.v. "Phinehas." Nubia was the region south of Egypt. He may have been given this name because he was dark-skinned at birth, perhaps reflecting some Nubian ancestry.

6. Milgrom, *Numbers*.

7. Because of this incident, *qubbah* came to mean a "brothel" in later mishnaic Hebrew. See Jastrow, *Dictionary of the Targumim*, 1343.

8. *HALOT* 1506–10.

9. *TLOT* 3:134.

10. Roland Allen sees a wordplay on Kozbi's name, which as Hebrew could mean "my lie/deception," though a similar word in Akkadian (*kuzbu*) means "voluptuousness" (*IDB* 1:724).

11. Naylor, "Numbers," 190.

12. Timothy Miller, *America's Alternative Religions* (Albany: State University of New York Press, 1995), 128–29.

Numbers 26:1–65

1. Reuben's 43,730 is the only count in Numbers 26 that does not round to the nearest one hundred. Only one number in the first census does not round to the nearest one hundred, and it rounds to the nearest fifty. Some manuscripts of the Septuagint round this number to the nearest fifty: 43,750.

2. Ivan T. Kaufman, "Samaria (Ostraca)," *ABD* 5:925; M. Patrick Graham, "Shemida (Person)," *ABD* 5:1202; Adam Zertal, "Hepher (Place)," *ABD* 3:139.

3. The Masoretic Text of 1 Chronicles 7:17–19 appears to have suffered in transition. H. G. M. Williamson (*1 and 2 Chronicles*, 79) reconstructs the text to make the Aramean concubine Manasseh's wife.

4. Milgrom, *Numbers*.

5. Cole, *Numbers*.

6. Kaiser, *Old Testament Theology*.

Numbers 27:1–11

1. Olson, *Death of the Old*.

2. Chan, "Structuring on the Book of Numbers." For a similar point, made more briefly, see Sakenfeld, *Journeying with God*, 185.

3. Sakenfeld, *Journeying with God*.

4. See Patterson, "Divine Retribution"; Towner, "Retribution."

5. This illustration could be supplemented with pictures, facts, and figures by visiting http://givingpledge.org/.

6. Alvin Schmidt, *How Christianity Changed the World* (Grand Rapids: Zondervan, 2004), 43, 101, 110, 116–20. See also Schmidt, *Under the Influence: How Christianity*

Transformed Civilization (Grand Rapids: Zondervan, 2001), chapter 4 ("Women Receive Freedom and Dignity").

Numbers 27:12–23

1. Arthur J. Ferch, "Abarim," ABD 1:6–7.
2. Beitzel, Atlas of the Bible 61 (map 18).
3. Molly McElroy, "A First Step in Learning by Imitation, Baby Brains Respond to Another's Action," UW Today, October 30, 2013, http://www.washington.edu/news/2013/10/30/a-first-step-in-learning-by-imitation-baby-brains-respond-to-anothers-actions/.
4. https://www.royal.gov.uk/MonarchUK/Honours/Knighthoods.aspx.

Numbers 28:1–29:40

1. Contrary to Ashley, Numbers.
2. Cole, Numbers.
3. Milgrom, Numbers.
4. Wenham, Numbers, citing A. F. Rainey.
5. Walton, Ancient Near Eastern Thought, 130.

Numbers 30:1–16

1. Following, with modifications, Sakenfeld, Journeying with God; Wenham, Numbers.
2. Robin Wakely, "נדר," NIDOTTE 3:39.
3. Currid, Numbers, citing N. H. Snaith.
4. Evans, "Women."
5. See Everett Ferguson, Baptism in the Early Church: History, Theology, and Liturgy in the First Five Centuries (Grand Rapids: Eerdmans, 2009), 335, 366.
6. Jennifer D'Angelo, "Some Seek Alternatives to 'Till Death Do Us Part,'" Fox News, July 29, 2005, http://www.foxnews.com/story/2005/07/29/some-seek-alternatives-to-til-death-do-us-part/.

Numbers 31:1–54

1. Mendenhall, "'Vengeance of Yahweh.'"
2. BDB, s.v. חלק I" and "חלק II."
3. Ashley, Numbers; Milgrom, Numbers.
4. Milgrom, Numbers.
5. Keil and Delitzsch, Pentateuch; Ashley, Numbers.
6. Jastrow, Dictionary of the Targumim, 783.
7. Fouts, "Defense of the Hyperbolic Interpretation," 383–86.
8. Mendenhall, "'Vengeance of Yahweh.'"
9. C. S. Lewis, The Silver Chair (New York: Macmillan, 1953).
10. Melissa Steffan, "An Inside Look at Church Attenders Who Tithe the Most," Christianity Today, May 17, 2013, http://www.christianitytoday.com/gleanings/2013/may/inside-look-at-church-attenders-who-tithe-the-most.html.
11. Andy Stanley, "There's More to Tithing Than 10%," Relevant, December 23, 2013, http://www.relevantmagazine.com/life/career-money/there's-more-tithing-10.

Numbers 32:1–42

1. Translation by Kent P. Jackson, in Dearman, Mesha Inscription and Moab, 97–98.

2. Beitzel, Atlas of the Bible, 35–36.
3. Milgrom, Numbers.
4. Aharoni and Avi-Yonah, Macmillan Bible Atlas, map 68; Aharoni, Land of the Bible, 213. This separation sometimes is not shown in Bible maps. Aroer may have had a mixed Reubenite/Gadite population.
5. Dibon was three miles north of the Arnon (Wadi el-Mujib) near modern Dhiban; Aroer was also on the north slope of that valley (NIDB, s.v. "Dibon" and "Aroer"). Aroer may have had a mixed Reubenite/Gadite population.
6. NIDB, s.v. "Ataroth."
7. Perhaps Khirbet es-Sar, or Khirbet Jazzir, which seems to preserve Jazer's name (NIDB, s.v. "Jazer").
8. Heshbon is well established. Elealeh might be el-'Al, a site northeast of Heshbon. Baal Meon was north of Ataroth between the King's Highway and the Dead Sea. Kiriathaim was northwest of Baal Meon between the northern end of the Dead Sea and the King's Highway. Baal Meon is probably Khirbet Ma'in, about five miles southwest of Madaba. Sibmah is perhaps Khirbet Qarm al-Qibsh, about three miles southwest of Heshbon. See the entry for each place in NIDB; see also Dearman, Mesha Inscription and Moab, 302.
9. Strong, Systematic Theology, 567.
10. Ibid., 567–73.
11. See Erickson, Christian Theology, 2:577–80.
12. See Brother Lawrence (Nicholas Herman of Lorraine), The Practice of the Presence of God (London: Allenson, 1906).

Numbers 33:1–49

1. For a discussion of the various places, see Kitchen, Reliability of the Old Testament, 190–99, 254–63, 268–74; Hoffmeier, Israel in Egypt, 176–222.
2. Rameses was once identified with Tanis but now is to be identified with Khatana-Qantir (Tell ed-Dab'a) in the northeast delta of the east bank of the Pelusaic arm of the Nile. Short for "Pi-Rameses" (after Rameses II), "Rameses" incorporated the Hyksos capital Avaris. Edward F. Wente, "Rameses (Place)," ABD 5:617–18.
3. "Pi(r) Hahiroth" may mean "house of [the goddess] Hathor" in Egyptian, or it may be derived from a Semitic word meaning "to dig" and thus refer to a site along a canal (see comments at Num. 33:8, 10). See Hoffmeier, Israel in Egypt, 190.
4. Beitzel, Atlas of the Bible, 108.
5. Hoffmeier, Israel in Egypt, 212.
6. Kitchen, Reliability of the Old Testament.
7. If Israel moved north from Ethan (Num. 33:7), they would have been trapped against Lake Timsah or the connecting canal between it and Lake Ballah to their east. If they moved south, they would have been trapped against the Bitter Lakes to their east.
8. Kitchen, Reliability of the Old Testament, 271, 629.
9. Milgrom, Numbers.
10. So Jerome. See Hoffmeier, Israel in Egypt, 207.
11. Ibid., 208.
12. Ibid., 199–222.
13. HALOT 751.
14. Kitchen, Reliability of the Old Testament, 273–74.

15. Jebal al-Lawz in Saudi Arabia is the least likely of various proposed views and is generally rejected by biblical scholars. For discussion, see Beitzel, *Atlas of the Bible*, 110–12. The claim by the late, self-proclaimed "archaeologist" Ron Wyatt to have found remains of Pharaoh's army in the Gulf of Aqaba is the specious product of an overly vivid imagination.

16. The nearby Jebal Serbal is a possible alternative. Yet the traditional site of Jebal Musa, unlike Jebal Serbal, has a plain where Israel might have camped. See Kitchen, *Reliability of the Old Testament*, 270.

17. It might be identical to the similar-sounding "Ain Hudeirat" ("Hudhera," "Khadra," "Khodara") or this spring's wadi some forty miles northeast of Jebal Musa.

18. Levine, *Numbers 21–36*; Sidnie Ann White, "Rissah (Place)," *ABD* 5:775.

19. This suggests that Mount Hor was in the vicinity of Moseroth/Moserah. Hor Haggidgad (= Gudgodah) probably is along Wadi Ghadhaghedh. Ray L. Roth, "Hor (Place)," *ABD* 3:287.

20. *IDB*, s.v. "Jatbathah." D. Baly tentatively suggests Bir Tabā as the location (cited by Ashley, *Numbers*).

21. Kadesh is generally identified with 'Ain Qudeirat, some fifty miles south of Beersheba.

22. A possible site is Jabel Madurah, fifteen miles northeast of Kadesh, though this identification remains uncertain. Ray Lee Roth, "Hor (Place)," *ABD* 3:287.

23. Wadi Salmana is a possible identification of Zalmonah (Cole, *Numbers*), and Faynan (Greek Phaino), Jordan, twenty miles south of the Dead Sea, is a probable site for Punon. Ernst Axel Knauf, "Punon (Place)," *ABD* 5:556–57.

24. Arthur J. Ferch, "Oboth (Place)," *ABD* 5:7.

25. Gerald L. Mattingly, "Iye-Abarim (Place)," *ABD* 3:588.

26. Deleilat esh-Sherqiyeh and 'Ain ed Dib have been suggested as possible locations, among others. See Dearman, *Mesha Inscription and Moab*, 187; Randall W. Younker, "Almon-Diblathaim (Place)," *ABD* 1:161.

27. Arthur J. Ferch, "Abarim (Place)," *ABD* 1:6–7.

28. Arthur J. Ferch, "Nebo (Place)," *ABD* 4:1056; *NBD*, s.v. "Nebo."

29. Its location is uncertain, though it may be the similar-sounding "Khirber es-Suweimeh." C. Gilbert Romero, "Beth-Jeshimoth (Place)," *ABD* 1:689.

30. Shittim probably is to be identified with Tell el-Hammam. See *NBD*, s.v. "Shittim."

31. Donald S. Whitney, *Spiritual Disciplines for the Christian Life* (Colorado Springs: NavPress, 1991), 195. See his entire discussion (195–211).

Numbers 33:50–34:29

1. The area receives four to twelve inches of rain each year (Beitzel, *Atlas of the Bible*, 63 [map 19]).

2. Kang, *Divine War*, 143.

3. *NBD*, s.v. "Akrabbim."

4. Beitzel, *Atlas of the Bible*, 35, 103 (maps 27, 35); Manfred Görg, "Egypt, Brook of," *ABD* 2:321. For Nahal Bezor, see Levine, *Numbers 21–36*; for Wadi el-'Arish, see Ashley, *Numbers*.

5. Ray L. Roth, "Hor (Place)," *ABD* 3:287.

6. Gary A. Herion, "Hazar-Enan (Place)," *ABD* 3:84.

7. John L. Peterson, "Ain (Place)," *ABD* 1:131–32.

8. For several of the meanings, see Levine, *Numbers 21–36*.

9. Russell Goldman, "Laura Bush Reveals How George W. Stopped Drinking," *ABC News*, May 4, 2012, http://abcnews .go.com/Politics/laura-bush-reveals-george-stopped-drinking /story?id=10552148.

Numbers 35:1–34

1. Milgrom, *Numbers*, following Rambam (Maimonides).

2. *HALOT* 1102.

Numbers 36:1–13

1. Chan, "Structuring on the Book of Numbers."

2. Sakenfeld, *Journeying with God*.

3. John E. Ikerd, *Crisis and Opportunity: Sustainability in American Agriculture* (Lincoln: University of Nebraska Press, 2008), 229.

Bibliography

Recommended Resources

Cole, R. Dennis. *Numbers*. New American Commentary. Nashville: Broadman & Holman, 2000.

Gane, Roy. *Leviticus, Numbers*. NIV Life Application Commentary. Grand Rapids: Zondervan, 2004.

Hartley, John E. *Leviticus*. Word Biblical Commentary 4. Dallas: Word Books, 1992.

Milgrom, Jacob. *Leviticus 1–16: A New Translation with Introduction and Commentary*. Anchor Bible 3. New York: Doubleday, 1991.

———. *Leviticus 17–22: A New Translation with Introduction and Commentary*. Anchor Bible 3A. New York: Doubleday, 2000.

———. *Leviticus 23–27: A New Translation with Introduction and Commentary*. Anchor Bible 3B. New York: Doubleday, 2001.

———. *Numbers*. JPS Torah Commentary. Philadelphia: Jewish Publication Society, 1990.

Olson, Dennis T. *Numbers*. Interpretation. Louisville: John Knox, 1996.

Wenham, Gordon. *Leviticus*. New International Commentary on the Old Testament. Grand Rapids: Eerdmans, 1979.

———. *Numbers*. Tyndale Old Testament Commentaries. Downers Grove, IL: InterVarsity, 1981.

Select Bibliography

Aharoni, Yohanan. *The Land of the Bible: A Historical Geography*. Translated and edited by A. F. Rainey. 2nd ed. Philadelphia: Westminster, 1979.

Aharoni, Yohanan, and Michael Avi-Yonah. *The Macmillan Bible Atlas*. 2nd ed. New York: Macmillan, 1977.

Albright, W. F. "The Oracles of Balaam." *Journal of Biblical Literature* 63 (1944): 207–33.

Allen, Roland B. "Numbers." In vol. 2 of *The Expositor's Bible Commentary*, edited by Frank E. Gaebelein, 655–1008. Grand Rapids: Zondervan, 1990.

———. "The Theology of the Balaam Oracles: A Pagan Diviner and the Word of God." ThD diss., Dallas Theological Seminary, 1973.

Alter, Robert. *The Art of Biblical Narrative*. New York: Basic Books, 1981.

Arnold, Bill T., and Bryan E. Beyer, eds. *Readings from the Ancient Near East: Primary Sources for Old Testament Study*. Encountering Biblical Studies. Grand Rapids: Baker Academic, 2002.

Ashley, Timothy R. *Numbers*. New International Commentary on the Old Testament. Grand Rapids: Eerdmans, 1993.

Baden, Joel S., and Candida R. Moss. "The Origin and Interpretation of ṣāraʿat in Leviticus 13–14." *Journal of Biblical Literature* 130 (2011): 643–62.

Bailey, Lloyd R. *Leviticus*. Knox Preaching Guides. Atlanta: John Knox, 1987.

Baillie, Rebecca A., and E. Eugene Baillie. "Biblical Leprosy as Compared to Present-Day Leprosy." *Southern Medical Journal* 75 (1982): 855–57.

Balentine, Samuel E. *Leviticus*. Interpretation. Louisville: John Knox, 2002.

Barkay, Gabriel, et al. "The Challenges of Ketef Hinnom: Using Advanced Technologies to Recover the Earliest Biblical Texts and Their Contexts." *Near Eastern Archaeology* 66, no. 4 (2004): 162–71.

Beale, G. K., and D. A. Carson, eds. *Commentary on the New Testament Use of the Old Testament*. Grand Rapids: Baker Academic, 2007.

Beitzel, Barry J. *The New Moody Atlas of the Bible*. Chicago: Moody, 2009.

Bergen, Wesley J. *Reading Ritual: Leviticus in Postmodern Culture*. Journal for the Study of the Old

Testament: Supplement Series 417. London: T&T Clark, 2005.

Berkhof, Louis. *Systematic Theology*. 4th ed. Grand Rapids: Eerdmans, 1996.

Bonar, Andrew. *A Commentary on the Book of Leviticus.* Reprint, Grand Rapids: Baker, 1978.

Brenner, Athalya. *Colour Terms in the Old Testament.* Journal for the Study of the Old Testament: Supplement Series 21. Sheffield: JSOT Press, 1982.

Brichto, H. C. "The Case of the ŚŌṬA and a Reconsideration of Biblical 'Law.'" *Hebrew Union College Annual* 46 (1975): 55–70.

———. *The Problem of "Curse" in the Hebrew Bible.* Journal of Biblical Literature Monograph Series 13. Philadelphia: Society of Biblical Literature, 1963.

———. *Toward a Grammar of Biblical Poetics: Tales of the Prophets.* New York: Oxford, 1992.

Budd, Philip J. *Numbers.* Word Biblical Commentary 5. Waco: Word, 1984.

Burton, Maurice, and Robert Burton, eds. *International Wildlife Encyclopedia.* 3rd ed. Tarrytown, NY: Marshall Cavendish, 2002.

Cartledge, Tony W. "Were Nazirite Vows Conditional?" *Catholic Biblical Quarterly* 51 (1989): 409–22.

Chan, Alan Kam-Yau. "One More Structuring on the Book of Numbers: A Canonical Approach." Paper presented at the Annual Meeting of the Evangelical Theological Society, New Orleans, November 17, 2009.

Chepey, Stuart. *Nazirites in Late Second Temple Judaism: A Survey of Ancient Jewish Writings, the New Testament, and Other Writings from Late Antiquity.* Arbeiten zur Geschichte des antiken Judentums und des Urchristentums 60. Leiden: Brill, 2005.

Cole, R. Dennis. "Numbers." In vol. 1 of *Zondervan Illustrated Bible Backgrounds Commentary*, edited by John H. Walton, 338–417. Grand Rapids: Zondervan, 2009.

Collins, Billie Jean. "The Puppy in Hittite Ritual." *Oriental Institute News and Notes* 136 (Winter 1992): 1–6.

Collins, John J. *The Scepter and the Star: The Messiahs of the Dead Sea Scrolls and Other Ancient Literature.* New York: Doubleday, 1995.

Cook, John A. "The Biblical Hebrew Verbal System: A Grammaticalization Approach." PhD diss., University of Wisconsin, 2003.

Cornfeld, Gaalyah, and David Noel Freedman. *Archaeology of the Bible: Book by Book.* New York: Harper & Row, 1976.

Cowley, A. E., ed. *Aramaic Papyri of the Fifth Century B.C.: Edited, with Translation and Notes.* Oxford: Clarendon, 1923.

Currid, John D. *A Study Commentary on Numbers.* Evangelical Press Study Commentary. Darlington: Evangelical Press, 2009.

Danby, Herbert, trans. and ed. *The Mishnah.* Oxford: Oxford University Press, 1933.

Dandamaev, M. A. *Slavery in Babylonia: From Nabopolassar to Alexander the Great (626–331 B.C.).* Translated by Victoria A. Powell. Edited by Marvin A. Powell and David B. Weisberg. DeKalb: Northern Illinois University Press, 1984.

Davidson, Richard M. *Flame of Yahweh: Sexuality in the Old Testament.* Peabody, MA: Hendrickson, 2007.

Davies, Eyrl W. "A Mathematical Conundrum: The Problem of Large Numbers in Numbers I and XXVI." *Vetus Testamentum* 45 (1995): 449–69.

Davies, John A. *A Royal Priesthood: Literary and Intertextual Perspectives on an Image in Exodus 19.6.* Journal for the Study of the Old Testament: Supplement Series 395. London: T&T Clark, 2004.

Dearman, Andrew, ed. *Studies in the Mesha Inscription and Moab.* Society of Biblical Literature Archaeology and Biblical Studies 2. Atlanta: Scholars Press, 1989.

Delitzsch, Franz. *Old Testament History of Redemption.* Translated by Samuel I. Curtiss. Edinburgh: T&T Clark, 1881.

De Odorico, Marco. *The Use of Numbers and Quantifications in the Assyrian Royal Inscriptions.* State Archives of Assyria Studies 3. Helsinki: Helsinki University Press, 1995.

Douglas, Mary. *Purity and Danger: An Analysis of Concepts of Pollution and Taboo.* New York: Praeger, 1966.

Dozeman, Thomas B. "The Book of Numbers." In vol. 2 of *The New Interpreter's Bible*, 1–268. Nashville: Abingdon, 1998.

Driver, G. R., and John C. Miles. *The Babylonian Laws.* 2 vols. Oxford: Clarendon, 1952.

Durham, John. *Exodus.* Word Biblical Commentary 2. Waco: Word, 1987.

Eisenberg, Ronald L. *The JPS Guide to Jewish Traditions.* Philadelphia: Jewish Publication Society, 2004.

El-Shahawy, Abeer. *The Funerary Art of Ancient Egypt: A Bridge to the Realm of the Hereafter.* Cairo: American University in Cairo Press, 2006.

Erickson, Millard J. *Christian Theology.* 3 vols. Grand Rapids: Baker, 1983–85.

Evans, Mary J. "Women." In *Dictionary of the Old Testament: Historical Books*, edited by Bill T. Arnold and H. G. M. Williamson, 989–99. Downers Grove, IL: InterVarsity, 2005.

Feder, Yitzhaq. *Blood Expiation in Hittite and Biblical Ritual: Origins, Context, and Meaning.* Writings from the Ancient World Supplement Series 2. Leiden: Brill, 2011.

Finkelstein, J. J. *The Ox That Gored.* Philadelphia: American Philosophical Society, 1981.

Fouts, David. "A Defense of the Hyperbolic Interpretation of the Large Numbers in the Old Testament."

Journal of the Evangelical Theological Society 40 (1997): 377–87.

Fox, Nili S. "Marked for Servitude: Mesopotamia and the Bible." In *A Common Cultural Heritage: Studies on Mesopotamia and the Biblical World in Honor of Barry L. Eichler*, edited by Grant Frame et al., 267–78. Bethesda, MD: CDL Press, 2011.

Gagnon, Robert A. J. *The Bible and Homosexual Practice: Texts and Hermeneutics*. Nashville: Abingdon, 2001.

German Bible Society. *1000 Bible Images*. Bellingham, WA: Logos Research Systems, 2009 [electronic publication].

Gerstenberger, Erhard S. *Leviticus: A Commentary*. Translated by Douglas W. Stott. Old Testament Library. Louisville: Westminster John Knox, 1996.

Goldman, Leon, Richard Moraites, and Karl Kitzmiller. "White Spots in Biblical Times." *Archives of Dermatology* 93 (1966): 744–53.

Hallo, William W., and K. Lawson Younger Jr., eds. *The Context of Scripture*. 3 vols. Leiden: Brill, 1997–2002.

Haran, Menahem. *Temples and Temple-Service in Ancient Israel: An Inquiry into Biblical Cult Phenomena and the Historical Setting of the Priestly School*. Reprint, Winona Lake, IN: Eisenbrauns, 1985.

Harris, R. Laird. "Leviticus." In vol. 2 of *The Expositor's Bible Commentary*, edited by Frank E. Gaebelein, 499–654. Grand Rapids: Zondervan, 1990.

Harris, R. Laird, Gleason L. Archer, and Bruce K. Waltke, eds. *Theological Wordbook of the Old Testament*. 2 vols. Chicago: Moody, 1980.

Harrison, R. K. *Leviticus: An Introduction and Commentary*. Tyndale Old Testament Commentaries. Downers Grove, IL: InterVarsity, 1980.

———. *Numbers: An Exegetical Commentary*. Grand Rapids: Baker, 1992.

Hayes, Richard B. *The Moral Vision of the New Testament: Community, Cross, New Creation; A Contemporary Introduction to New Testament Ethics*. San Francisco: HarperSanFrancisco, 1996.

Henry, Matthew. *Matthew Henry's Commentary on the Whole Bible: Complete and Unabridged in One Volume*. Peabody, MA: Hendrickson, 1994.

Hess, Richard. "Leviticus 10:1: Strange Fire and an Odd Name." *Bulletin for Biblical Research* 12 (2002): 187–98.

Hoffmeier, James K. *Israel in Egypt: The Evidence for the Authenticity of the Exodus Tradition*. New York: Oxford University Press, 1996.

———. "'These Things Happened': Why a Historical Exodus Is Essential for Theology." In *Do Historical Matters Matter to Faith? A Critical Appraisal of Modern and Postmodern Approaches to Scripture*, edited by James K. Hoffmeier and Dennis R. Magary, 99–134. Wheaton: Crossway, 2012.

Humphreys, Colin. "The Number of People in the Exodus from Egypt: Decoding Mathematically the Very Large Numbers." *Vetus Testamentum* 48 (1998): 196–213.

———. "The Numbers in the Exodus from Egypt: A Further Appraisal." *Vetus Testamentum* 50 (2000): 323–28.

Jastrow, Marcus. *A Dictionary of the Targumim, the Talmud Babli and Yerushalmi, and the Midrashic Literature*. 2 vols. New York: Shalom, 1967.

Juel, Donald. *Messianic Exegesis: Christological Interpretation of the Old Testament in Early Christianity*. Philadelphia: Fortress, 1988.

Kaiser, Walter C., Jr. "Leviticus." In vol. 1 of *The New Interpreter's Bible*, edited by Leander E. Keck, 983–1191. Nashville: Abingdon, 1994.

———. "Leviticus 18:5 and Paul: Do This and You Will Live (Eternally?)." *Journal of the Evangelical Theological Society* 14 (1971): 19–28.

———. *Toward an Old Testament Theology*. Grand Rapids: Zondervan, 1978.

Kang, Sa-Moon. *Divine War in the Old Testament and the Ancient Near East*. Beihefte zur Zeitschrift für die alttestamentliche Wissenschaft 177. Berlin: de Gruyter, 1989.

Kaplan, David. "Biblical Leprosy: An Anachronism Whose Time Has Come." *Journal of the American Academy of Dermatology* 28 (1993): 507–10.

Kaufmann, Yehezkel. *The Religion of Israel: From Its Beginning to the Babylonian Exile*. Translated by Moshe Greenberg. Chicago: University of Chicago Press, 1960.

Keel, Othmar. *The Symbolism of the Biblical World: Ancient Near Eastern Iconography and the Book of Psalms*. Translated by Timothy J. Hallett. New York: Seabury, 1978.

Keil, C. F., and F. Delitzsch. *The Pentateuch*. Translated by James Martin. 3 vols. in 1. Biblical Commentary on the Old Testament. Reprint, Grand Rapids: Eerdmans, 1978.

Kellogg, S. H. *The Book of Leviticus*. 3rd ed. Reprint, Minneapolis: Klock & Klock, 1978.

Kimuhu, Johnson M. *Leviticus: The Priestly Laws and Prohibitions from the Perspective of Ancient Near East and Africa*. Studies in Biblical Literature 115. New York: Peter Lang, 2008.

Kitchen, K. A. *On the Reliability of the Old Testament*. Grand Rapids: Eerdmans, 2003.

Kiuchi, N. *The Purification Offering in the Priestly Literature: Its Meaning and Function*. Journal for the Study of the Old Testament: Supplement Series 56. Sheffield: JSOT Press, 1987.

Knight, George A. F. *Leviticus*. Daily Study Bible. Edinburgh: Saint Andrew Press; Louisville: Westminster John Knox, 1981.

Largement, R. "Les oracles de Bile'am et la mantique suméro-akkadienne." In *Mémorial du Cinquantenaire*

1914–1964, 37–50. Travaux de l'Institut catholique de Paris 10. Paris: Bloud & Gay, 1964.

Levine, Baruch A. *Leviticus.* JPS Torah Commentary. Philadelphia: Jewish Publication Society, 2003.

———. *Numbers 1–20: A New Translation with Introduction and Commentary.* Anchor Bible 4. New York: Doubleday, 1993.

———. *Numbers 21–36: A New Translation with Introduction and Commentary.* Anchor Bible 4A. New York: Doubleday, 2000.

Lewis, Theodore J. "Covenant and Blood Rituals: Understanding Exod. 24:3–8 in Its Ancient Near Eastern Context." In *Confronting the Past: Archaeological and Historical Essays on Ancient Israel in Honor of William G. Dever*, edited by Seymour Gitin, 341–50. Winona Lake, IN: Eisenbrauns, 2006.

Liddell, H. G., and R. Scott. *A Greek-English Lexicon.* Oxford: Clarendon, 1982.

Lockshin, Martin I., trans. and ed. *Rashbam's Commentary on Leviticus and Numbers: An Annotated Translation.* Brown Judaic Studies 330. Providence, RI: Brown Judaic Studies, 2001.

Longman, Tremper, III, and Raymond B. Dillard. *An Introduction to the Old Testament.* Grand Rapids: Zondervan, 1994.

Maarsingh, Berend. *Numbers: A Practical Commentary.* Translated by John Vriend. Text and Interpretation. Grand Rapids: Eerdmans, 1987.

MacDonald, Nathan. *What Did the Ancient Israelites Eat? Diet in Biblical Times.* Grand Rapids: Eerdmans, 2008.

MacDonald, William Graham. "Christology and the 'Angel of the Lord.'" In *Current Issues in Biblical and Patristic Interpretation: Studies in Honor of Merrill C. Tenney Presented by His Former Students*, edited by Gerald F. Hawthorne, 324–35. Grand Rapids: Eerdmans, 1975.

Macht, D. I. "A Scientific Appreciation of Leviticus 12:1–15." *Journal of Biblical Literature* 52 (1933): 253–60.

Magonet, Jonathan. "'But If It Is a Girl, She Is Unclean for Twice Seven Days': The Riddle of Leviticus 12.5." In *Reading Leviticus: A Conversation with Mary Douglas*, edited by John F. A. Sawyer, 144–52. Journal for the Study of the Old Testament: Supplement Series 227. Sheffield: Sheffield Academic Press, 1996.

Manniche, Lise. *Musical Instruments from the Tomb of Tut'ankhamūn.* Tut'ankhamūn's Tomb Series 6. Oxford: Griffith Institute, 1976.

Mathews, Kenneth A. *Leviticus: Holy God, Holy People.* Preaching the Word. Wheaton: Crossway, 2009.

Mays, James L. *Leviticus, Numbers.* Layman's Bible Commentary. Atlanta: John Knox, 1975.

Mazar, Amihai, and Nava Panitz-Cohen. "It Is the Land of Honey: Beekeeping at Tel Rehov." *Near Eastern Archaeology* 70, no. 4 (2007): 202–19.

McEntire, Mark. "A Response to Colin Humphreys's 'The Number of People in the Exodus from Egypt: Decoding Mathematically the Very Large Numbers in Numbers I and XXVI.'" *Vetus Testamentum* 49 (1999): 262–64.

Mendenhall, George E. "Law and Covenant in Israel and the Ancient Near East." *Biblical Archaeologist* 17, no. 2 (1954): 49–76.

———. "The 'Vengeance of Yahweh.'" In *The Tenth Generation: The Origins of the Biblical Tradition*, 69–104. Baltimore: Johns Hopkins University Press, 1973.

Milgrom, Jacob. "Ethics and Ritual: The Biblical Foundations of the Dietary Laws." In *Religion and Law: Biblical-Judaic and Islamic Perspectives*, edited by Edwin B. Firmage, Bernard G. Weiss, and John W. Welch, 159–91. Winona Lake, IN: Eisenbrauns, 1989.

———. *Leviticus: A Book of Ritual and Ethics.* Continental Commentaries. Minneapolis: Fortress, 2004.

———. "On Decoding Very Large Numbers: A Reply to Colin Humphreys." *Vetus Testamentum* 49 (1999): 131–32.

Moscati, Sabatino. *The World of the Phoenicians.* Translated by Alastair Hamilton. New York: Praeger, 1968.

Motyer, J. A. *The Prophecy of Isaiah: An Introduction and Commentary.* Downers Grove, IL: InterVarsity, 1993.

Naylor, Peter J. "Numbers." In *New Bible Commentary: 21st Century Edition*, edited by D. A. Carson et al., 158–97. Downers Grove, IL: InterVarsity, 1994.

Negev, Avraham, and Shimon Gibson, eds. *Archaeological Encyclopedia of the Holy Land.* Rev. ed. New York: Continuum, 2001.

Neusner, Jacob. *Leviticus Rabbah.* Vol. 4 of *A Theological Commentary to the Midrash.* Studies in Ancient Judaism. Lanham, MD: University Press of America, 2001.

———. *Principal Theological Categories.* Vol. 1 of *Theological Dictionary of Rabbinic Judaism.* Studies in Judaism. Lanham, MD: University Press of America, 2005.

Noth, Martin. *Numbers: A Commentary.* Translated by James D. Martin. Old Testament Library. Philadelphia: Westminster, 1968.

Olson, Dennis T. *The Death of the Old and the Birth of the New: The Framework of the Book of Numbers and the Pentateuch.* Brown Judaic Studies 71. Chico, CA: Scholars Press, 1985.

Oppenheim, A. Leo. *Ancient Mesopotamia: Portrait of a Dead Civilization.* Chicago: University of Chicago Press, 1977.

Patterson, Paige. "Divine Retribution." In *Holman Illustrated Bible Dictionary*, edited by Chad Brand et al., 434–35. Nashville: Holman, 2003.

Pittman, Holly. "The White Obelisk and the Problem of Historical Narrative in the Art of Assyria." *Art Bulletin* 78, no. 2 (June 1996): 334–55.

Pritchard, James, ed. *Ancient Near Eastern Texts relating to the Old Testament*. 3rd ed. Princeton: Princeton University Press, 1969.

Rashi. *The Pentateuch and Rashi's Commentary: A Linear Translation into English*. Translated and edited by Abraham Ben-Isaiah and Benjamin Sharfman. 5 vols. Brooklyn, NY: S. S. & R., 1949.

Rendsburg, Gary. "An Additional Note to Two Recent Articles on the Number of People in the Exodus from Egypt and the Large Numbers in Numbers I and Numbers XXVI." *Vetus Testamentum* 51 (2001): 392–96.

Rogers, Cleon. "Moses: Meek or Miserable." *Journal of the Evangelical Theological Society* 29 (1986): 257–63.

Rooker, Mark F. *Leviticus*. New American Commentary. Nashville: Broadman & Holman, 2000.

———. "Theophany." In *Dictionary of the Old Testament: Pentateuch*, edited by T. Desmond Alexander and David W. Baker, 863–64. Downers Grove, IL: InterVarsity, 2003.

Roth, Martha T. *Law Collections from Mesopotamia and Asia Minor*. SBL Writings from the Ancient World 6. Atlanta: Scholars Press, 1995.

Saggs, H. W. F. *The Greatness That Was Babylon: A Survey of the Ancient Civilization of the Tigris-Euphrates Valley*. 2nd ed. London: Sidgwick & Jackson, 1988.

———. *The Might That Was Assyria*. London: Sidgwick & Jackson, 1984.

Sailhamer, John H. *The Meaning of the Pentateuch: Revelation, Composition, and Interpretation*. Downers Grove, IL: IVP Academic, 2009.

Sakenfeld, Katharine Doob. *Journeying with God: A Commentary on the Book of Numbers*. International Theological Commentary. Grand Rapids: Eerdmans, 1995.

Sarna, Nahum. *Exodus*. JPS Torah Commentary. Philadelphia: Jewish Publication Society, 1991.

Schaff, Philip. *The Apostolic Fathers with Justin Martyr and Irenaeus*. Vol. 1 of *The Ante-Nicene Fathers*. Reprint, Grand Rapids: Eerdmans, 2001.

Schiffman, Lawrence H. *From Text to Tradition: A History of Second Temple and Rabbinic Judaism*. Hoboken, NJ: Ktav, 1991.

Scurlock, Jo Ann, and Burton R. Andersen. *Diagnoses in Assyrian and Babylonian Medicine: Ancient Sources, Translations, and Modern Medical Analyses*. Urbana: University of Illinois Press, 2005.

Shanaway, M. M. *Quail Production Systems: A Review*. New York: Food and Agriculture Organization of the United Nations, 1994.

Shanks, Hershel. "The Mystery of the Nechushtan." *Biblical Archaeology Review* 33, no. 2 (2007): 58–63.

Spieckermann, Hermann. "God's Steadfast Love: Towards a New Conception of Old Testament Theology." *Biblica* 81 (2000): 305–27.

Sprinkle, Joe M. *Biblical Law and Its Relevance: A Christian Understanding and Ethical Application for Today of the Mosaic Regulations*. Lanham, MD: University Press of America, 2006.

———. *The Book of the Covenant: A Literary Approach*. Journal for the Study of the Old Testament: Supplement Series 174. Sheffield: JSOT Press, 1994.

———. "How Should the Old Testament Civil Laws Apply Today?" *Liberty University Law Review* 2 (2008): 909–28.

———. "The Rationale of the Laws of Clean and Unclean in the Old Testament." *Journal of the Evangelical Theological Society* 43 (2000): 637–57.

Stager, Lawrence E., and Samuel R. Wolff. "Child Sacrifice at Carthage: Religious Rite or Population Control?" *Biblical Archaeology Review* 10, no. 1 (1984): 30–51.

Strong, Augustus H. *Systematic Theology*. Reprint, Old Tappan, NJ: Revell, 1979.

Strouhal, Eugen. *Life of the Ancient Egyptians*. Translated by Deryck Viney. Norman: University of Oklahoma Press, 1992.

Stubbs, David L. *Numbers*. Brazos Theological Commentary on the Bible. Grand Rapids: Brazos, 2009.

Swanson, James. *Dictionary of Biblical Languages with Semantic Domains: Hebrew (Old Testament)*. Electronic ed. Oak Harbor, WA: Logos Research Systems, 1997.

Towner, W. Sibley. "Retribution." In *Harper's Bible Dictionary*, edited by Paul J. Achtemeier, 865–66. San Francisco: Harper & Row, 1985.

United Bible Societies. *Fauna and Flora of the Bible*. 2nd ed. Helps for Translators. New York: United Bible Societies, 1980.

Van Dam, Cornelis. *The Urim and Thummim: A Means of Revelation in Ancient Israel*. Winona Lake, IN: Eisenbrauns, 1997.

Van Houten, Christiana de Groot. *The Alien in Israelite Law*. Journal for the Study of the Old Testament: Supplement Series 107. Sheffield: JSOT Press, 1991.

Vasholz, Robert I. *Leviticus*. Mentor Commentary. Fearn, Scotland: Mentor, 2007.

———. "Military Censuses in Numbers." *Presbyterion* 18 (1992): 122–25.

Vermes, Geza. *The Dead Sea Scrolls in English*. 3rd ed. Sheffield: JSOT Press, 1987.

Waltke, Bruce K., and Michael P. O'Connor. *An Introduction to Biblical Hebrew Syntax*. Winona Lake, IN: Eisenbrauns, 1990.

Walton, John H. *Ancient Near Eastern Thought and the Old Testament: Introducing the Conceptual World of the Hebrew Bible*. Grand Rapids: Baker Academic, 2006.

———. "Equilibrium and the Sacred Compass: The Structure of Leviticus." *Bulletin for Biblical Research* 11 (2001): 293–304.

———. "Interpreting the Bible as an Ancient Near Eastern Document." In *Israel: Ancient Kingdom or Late Invention?*, edited by Daniel I. Block, 298–327. Nashville: B&H Academic, 2008.

Way, Kenneth C. "Animals in the Prophetic World: Literary Reflections on Numbers 22 and 1 Kings 13." *Journal for the Study of the Old Testament* 34 (2009): 47–62.

———. "Balaam's Hobby Horse: The Animal Motif in the Balaam Traditions." *Ugarit-Forschungen* 37 (2005): 679–93.

———. *Donkeys in the Biblical World: Ceremony and Symbol.* History, Archaeology, and Culture of the Levant 2. Winona Lake, IN: Eisenbrauns, 2011.

Westbrook, Raymond. *Property and Family in Biblical Law.* Journal for the Study of the Old Testament: Supplement Series 113. Sheffield: JSOT Press, 1991.

———. *Studies in Biblical and Cuneiform Law.* Cahiers de la Revue biblique 26. Paris: Gabalda, 1988.

Wiersbe, Warren W. *Be Holy: Becoming "Set Apart" for God.* 2nd ed. "Be" Commentary Series. Colorado Springs: David C. Cook, 2010.

Williamson, H. G. M. *1 and 2 Chronicles.* New Century Bible Commentary. Grand Rapids: Eerdmans, 1982.

Willis, Timothy M. *Leviticus.* Abingdon Old Testament Commentaries. Nashville: Abingdon, 2009.

Wilson, E. Jan. *"Holiness" and "Purity" in Mesopotamia.* Alter Orient und Altes Testament 237. Kevelaer: Butzon & Bercker; Neukirchen-Vluyn: Neukirchener Verlag, 1994.

Yamauchi, Edwin M. *Foes from the Northern Frontier: Invading Hordes from the Russian Steppes.* Baker Studies in Biblical Archaeology. Grand Rapids: Baker, 1982.

Image Credits

Unless otherwise indicated, photos are copyright © Baker Publishing Group and Dr. James C. Martin. Unless otherwise indicated, illustrations and maps are copyright © Baker Publishing Group.

The Baker Photo Archive acknowledges the permission of the following institutions and individuals.

Photos on pages 48, 145, 393 © Baker Publishing Group and Dr. James C. Martin. Courtesy of the Ägyptisches Museum, Berlin, Germany.

Photos on pages 10, 12, 19, 33, 67, 131, 149, 177, 205, 301, 305, 327, 332, 347, 361, 384, 395, 396 © Baker Publishing Group and Dr. James C. Martin. Courtesy of the British Museum, London, England.

Photo on page 253 © Baker Publishing Group and Dr. James C. Martin. Courtesy of the British Museum, London, England, on loan from Berlin.

Photos on pages 84, 289 © Baker Publishing Group and Dr. James C. Martin. Courtesy of the Egyptian Ministry of Antiquities and the Museum of Egyptian Antiquities, Cairo, Egypt.

Photos on pages 42, 83, 155, 180, 282, 319 © Baker Publishing Group and Dr. James C. Martin. Courtesy of the Eretz Museum, Tel Aviv, Israel.

Photo on page 232 © Baker Publishing Group and Dr. James C. Martin. Courtesy of the Field Museum, Chicago.

Photo on page 226 © Baker Publishing Group and Dr. James C. Martin. Courtesy of the Gemaldegalerie, Bode Museum, Berlin.

Photo on page 92 © Baker Publishing Group and Dr. James C. Martin. Courtesy of the Holyland Hotel.

Reproduction of the City of Jerusalem at the time of the Second Temple, located on the grounds of the Holyland Hotel, Jerusalem, 2001. Present location: The Israel Museum, Jerusalem.

Photos on pages 76, 81, 86, 96, 119, 120, 160, 207, 229, 240, 256, 273, 350 © Baker Publishing Group and Dr. James C. Martin. Collection of the Israel Museum, Jerusalem, and courtesy of the Israel Antiquities Authority, exhibited at the Israel Museum, Jerusalem.

Photo on page 27 © Baker Publishing Group and Dr. James C. Martin. Collection of the Israel Museum, Jerusalem, and courtesy of the Israel Antiquities Authority, exhibited at the Rockefeller Museum, Jerusalem.

Photo on page 219 © Baker Publishing Group and Dr. James C. Martin. Collection of the Israel Museum, Jerusalem, and courtesy of the Israel Antiquities Authority, exhibited at the Shrine of the Book, the Israel Museum, Jerusalem.

Photo on page 244 © Baker Publishing Group and Dr. James C. Martin. Courtesy of the Italian Ministry of Antiquities: On licence Ministero per I Beni e le Attivita Culturali; Soprintendenza Archaeologica di Roma, Rome, Italy.

Photo on page 331 © Baker Publishing Group and Dr. James C. Martin courtesy of the Jordanian Ministry of Antiquities and the Amman Archaeological Museum, Jordan.

Photos on pages 122, 129, 137, 141, 151, 166, 196, 296, 359, 400 © Baker Publishing Group and Dr. James C. Martin. Courtesy of the Musée du Louvre; Autorisation de photographer et de filmer. Louvre, Paris, France.

Photos on pages 195, 198 © Baker Publishing Group and Dr. James C. Martin. Courtesy of the Neues Museum, Berlin.

Photos on pages 16, 39, 179, 390, 423 © Baker Publishing Group and Dr. James C. Martin. Courtesy of the Oriental Institute Museum, University of Chicago.

Photos on pages 52, 344 © Baker Publishing Group and Dr. James C. Martin. Courtesy of the Pergamon Museum, Berlin.

Photo on page 104 © Baker Publishing Group and Dr. James C. Martin. Courtesy of the Skirball Museum, Hebrew Union College–Jewish Institute of Religion, 13 King David Street, Jerusalem 94101.

Photo on page 428 © Baker Publishing Group and Dr. James C. Martin. Courtesy of the Turkish Ministry of Antiquities and the Antalya Museum, Turkey.

Photos on pages 62, 176 © Baker Publishing Group and Dr. James C. Martin. Courtesy of the Turkish Ministry of Antiquities and the Istanbul Archaeological Museum.

Photos on pages 4, 271, 379 © Baker Publishing Group and Dr. James C. Martin. Courtesy of the Vatican Museum, Rome.

Photo on page 368 © Baker Publishing Group and Dr. James C. Martin. Courtesy of the Wohl Archaeological Museum and Burnt House, Jerusalem.

Additional image credits

Photo on page 91 © Dr. Avishai Teicher / Wikimedia Commons, CC-BY-2.5.

Photo on page 222 courtesy of the Birmingham Museums and Art Gallery / Bridgeman Images.

Photo on page 124 © BishkekRocks / Wikimedia Commons.

Photo on page 276 © Brian Jeffery Beggerly / CC-BY-2.0.

Photo on page 159 © Brian Maudsley / Shutterstock.com.

Photo on page 110 courtesy of the British Library, Creative Commons CC0 1.0 Universal Public Domain Dedication, http://www.bl.uk/catalogues/illuminatedmanuscripts/ILLUMIN.ASP?Size=mid&IllID=46510.

Photo on page 163 courtesy of the British Library, Creative Commons CC0 1.0 Universal Public Domain Dedication, http://www.bl.uk/catalogues/illuminatedmanuscripts/ILLUMIN.ASP?Size=mid&IllID=44625.

Photo on page 238 courtesy of the British Library, Creative Commons CC0 1.0 Universal Public Domain Dedication, http://www.bl.uk/catalogues/illuminatedmanuscripts/ILLUMIN.ASP?Size=mid&IllID=49729.

Photo on page 263 courtesy of the British Library, Creative Commons CC0 1.0 Universal Public Domain Dedication, http://www.bl.uk/catalogues/illuminatedmanuscripts/ILLUMIN.ASP?Size=mid&IllID=51456.

Photo on page 292 courtesy of the British Library, Creative Commons CC0 1.0 Universal Public Domain Dedication, http://www.bl.uk/catalogues/illuminatedmanuscripts/ILLUMIN.ASP?Size=mid&IllID=49741.

Photo on page 309 courtesy of the British Library, Creative Commons CC0 1.0 Universal Public Domain Dedication, http://www.bl.uk/catalogues/illuminatedmanuscripts/ILLUMIN.ASP?Size=mid&IllID=50111

Photo on page 383 courtesy of the British Library, Creative Commons CC0 1.0 Universal Public Domain Dedication, http://www.bl.uk/catalogues/illuminatedmanuscripts/ILLUMIN.ASP?Size=mid&IllID=30330.

Photo on page 425 courtesy of the British Library, Creative Commons CC0 1.0 Universal Public Domain Dedication, http://www.bl.uk/catalogues/illuminatedmanuscripts/ILLUMIN.ASP?Size=mid&IllID=18989.

Photo on page 22 courtesy of Cornelis Pietersz. Bega, 1663/ Rijksmuseum, Amsterdam.

Photo on page 171 © David W. Leindecker / Shutterstock.com.

Photo on page 211 © De Agostini Picture Library / S. Vannini / Bridgeman Images.

Photo on page 242 courtesy of Egyptian National Museum, Cairo, Egypt / Photo © Boltin Picture Library / Bridgeman Images.

Photo on page 134 courtesy of Egyptian National Museum, Cairo, Egypt / Bridgeman Images.

Photo on page 290 © Erik Hermans (2008) (photographer), "Statue of winged deity at Ain Dara, Syria," Ancient World Image Bank (New York: Institute for the Study of the Ancient World, 2009–) <http://www.flickr.com/photos/isawnyu/5613580338/>, used under terms of a Creative Commons Attribution license (CC_BY_2.0).

Photos on pages 114, 230 © Fred Mabie.

Photo on page 269 courtesy of the Getty's Open Content Program.

Photo on page 356 courtesy of the Getty's Open Content Program. The J. Paul Getty Museum, Los Angeles, Ms. Ludwig VIII 2, fol. 11v.

Photo on page 72 © Joshua Walton, courtesy of the Tell es-Safi excavations.

Photo on page 44 courtesy of The Karnak Great Hypostyle Hall Project.

Photo on page 153 © Kim Walton.

Photos on pages 106, 303 © Kim Walton. Courtesy of the British Museum, London, England.

Photo on page 354 © Kim Walton. Courtesy of the Byzantine and Christian Museum, Athens.

Photo on page 99 © Kim Walton. Courtesy of The Chora Museum, Istanbul.

Photo on page 143 © Kim Walton. Courtesy of the Ephesus Archaeological Museum.

Photo on page 321 © Kim Walton. Collection of the Israel Museum, Jerusalem, and courtesy of the Israel Antiquities Authority, exhibited at the Israel Museum, Jerusalem.

Photo on page 112 © Kim Walton. Courtesy of the The Metropolitan Museum of Art, NY.

Photos on pages 30 © Kim Walton. Courtesy of the Musée du Louvre; Autorisation de photographer et de filmer. Louvre, Paris, France.

Photos on pages 47, 336 © Kim Walton. Courtesy of the Oriental Institute Museum, University of Chicago.

Contributors

General Editors Mark. L. Strauss John H. Walton	*Project Editor* James Korsmo
Associate Editors, Illustrating the Text Kevin and Sherry Harney	*Interior Design* Brian Brunsting William Overbeeke
Contributing Author, Illustrating the Text Adam Barr	*Visual Content* Kim Walton
Series Development Jack Kuhatschek Brian Vos	*Cover Direction* Paula Gibson Michael Cook

Index

vengeance of, 397
warnings, 368–69
as warrior, 328
wilderness, led Israel through, 240, 243
word, does not change, 339–40, 347–48
worship, appearance in, 61–62
Golan, 419
gold dish, 224
golden calf, 60–61, 270, 273, 274, 310, 358
golden lampstand, 228, 231
gold plate, 53
Good Friday, 157, 386
good Samaritan, 35, 131
good works, 175
grace, 36, 175, 220, 221, 272–73, 274, 372
Graham, Billy, 292–93, 316
grain offerings, 12–14, 24, 45, 59, 148, 206, 277, 279, 283
grapes, 155, 167, 211, 213, 265, 401
gratitude, 21, 175, 182, 277, 279, 328, 329, 386
grumbling, 252
guidance, from Word of God, 243
guilt, 39–41, 205, 208
guilt offering, 6, 38–43, 46, 130, 148, 149, 205, 208, 212, 224
　for leprous person, 88, 89–90

Haggadah, 239
Hahiroth, 406
hair
　long and unkempt, 66, 84, 144
　shaving of, 89, 211–12
Ham, 266
Hannah, dedication of Samuel, 182, 211, 389
Hansen's disease, 83, 86
hare, 71
harlotry, 272
Hazeroth, 260, 264, 408, 410
healing, 318, 321–22
health, 74, 85–86, 97–98
heaven, 428, 429
Hebron, 265, 268, 272, 419
hedonism, 126
Heidelberg Catechism, 221
hell, 139
hemophobia, 117
Henry, Matthew, 354
hepatomancy, 20
herem, 180, 295, 319
Herodotus, 18
hesed, 272–73
Heshbon, 326
Hezekiah, 319, 321
hides, 46
high-handed sinning, 280
high places, 115, 174
high priest, 55–56, 109, 144

Hittites, 266, 326
　rituals, 25, 76, 78, 110
　suzerainty treaties, 172, 175
Hobab, 248, 250, 251, 360
Hoglah, 371, 373, 424, 426
holidays, 386–87
holiness, 4, 54, 55, 89, 128, 132–33, 136–37, 152
　and cleanliness, 304
　degrees of, 201
　and grace, 272–73
　laws of, 5, 114
　learning, 157
　and love, 132
　of Nazirites, 211
　of priests, 142–46, 148–52
　and wholeness, 144, 150, 304
holiness code, 142, 148, 154, 172
holy and common, 64–65, 66, 73, 144
holy days, 4, 154–59, 388
holy of holies, 109, 225. *See also* most holy place
holy place, 109. *See also* tabernacle
Holy Spirit, 254, 377–78
　gifts, distributes, 379
　indwelling of, 243
holy things
　impurity, cleansing from, 45
　profaning of, 39
holy war, 180, 182, 295
homicide, 419, 422–23
homosexual acts, 124, 126, 138, 139, 140
honey, 14, 266
hope, 186, 189
hope of inheritance, 416
Hormah, 272, 318, 319, 320, 321
horns of the altar, 24, 26, 27
hostility from God, 174
houses
　restoration from mold-uncleanness, 90, 92
　vowed to God, 179
human impurity, before holy God, 98, 103
human sacrifice, 50, 122–23
husband
　annuls vow of a wife, 390
　jealousy of, 205–6, 208
hyperbole, in census numbers, 197
hypermenorrhea, 96
hyssop, 89, 91, 92, 302, 303

"I am the LORD," 134, 162, 172
idolatry, 60–61, 114–15, 117–18, 121, 133, 135, 136, 139, 172, 358, 361–62, 394–95
image of God, 421–22
images, 68, 129
immorality, 361–62
impurity, before holy God, 31, 97, 108, 109, 300
inadvertent sinning, 24, 59, 169, 277, 279. *See also* unintentional sins

inbreeding, 126
incense, 13, 103, 206, 224, 286
incest, 50, 122, 124, 126, 137, 140
ingratitude, 255–56
inheritance, 186, 250, 296–97, 370, 372, 416, 425–26, 427
intercessory prayer, 273–74, 275, 286
interest, 168
Israel
  blessedness of, 333
  "blood consciousness" of, 7
  brings on self-afflicted curse, 358
  camps around God, 194
  defeat of enemies, 346, 347, 351–53
  disobedience of, 176
  election of, 348
  failure of, 264, 270
  flaws of, 410
  grumbling of, 254, 255–56, 258, 260, 267, 270, 320, 322, 410
  holiness of, 207, 280
  march toward promised land, 243, 246, 249
  multiplication of, 196
  preparation for war, 194
  preservation of, 368
  rituals of, 385–86
  separateness of, 73–74, 125, 128, 278
  tents of, 346–47
  as tribal society, 191
  unfaithfulness of, 272
Issachar, 191, 192–93, 247, 366
Ithamar, 66, 102, 201
Izhar, 282

Jabbok River, 326–28
Jacob, 313, 388–89
jealousy, 165, 208
Jebusites, 266
Jephthah, 378, 389
Jericho, 331, 364, 410
Jesus Christ
  blood of, 117, 119
  as high priest, 55–56, 104, 105, 145
  name of, 151
  sacrifice of, 27, 35, 113, 304
  as star and scepter, 357
  as substitution, 202–3
Jethro, 248
Jochebed, 368
John Paul II, Pope, 80
Joseph, 191, 366
Joshua, 254, 256, 264, 266–68, 271, 368, 401, 402
  spirit of, 377–78, 379
  as successor to Moses, 312, 315, 316, 364, 376–80
Josiah, reforms of, 216–17
journaling, 411
joy, 143, 206
  in fellowship offerings, 48
  in the Lord, 21–22

Jubilee. *See* Year of Jubilee
Judah, 191, 192–93, 223, 247, 365
judges, 359
judicial oaths, 389
justice, for killers, 422
Justin Martyr, 351, 357
just war, 398, 422

Kadesh, 264–65, 273, 307, 314, 409, 410
Kadesh Barnea, 186
Kaiser, Walter, 368
Kassites, 258
Kedesh, 420
keeping, 217, 219
keeping promises, 391
Kenites, 248, 352
Kenizzites, 401
Kibroth Hattaavah, 248, 253, 255, 258, 260, 264, 408, 410
kidneys, 19–20, 26
King, Martin Luther, Jr., 316–17
kinsman redeemer, 167–68, 205, 419, 423
knowledge of God, 353–54
Kohath, 199–201, 367
Kohathites, 201, 223, 247–48, 282, 290
Korah, 188, 282–87, 288, 290, 300, 307, 364–65, 371, 372
Korahites, 283, 367
Kozbi, 360–61, 362, 394, 395

laity, 38, 44
Lake Timsah, 407
lamps, 161
lampstand, 163, 228
land
  allotment of, 167, 367, 370, 412
  flowing with milk and honey, 138, 266, 267, 268
  pollution of, 421
  Sabbath rest of, 176
  See also promised land
land animals, 70–71
law of retaliation, 162
Lawrence, Brother, 405
Lawrence, T. E., 322–23
Laws of Eshnunna, 38, 418
Laws of Hammurabi, 38, 204, 418
laying on hands
  on the Levites, 228
  as ordination, 378, 380
  on sacrifice, 8, 26, 54, 109, 228
lay Israelites, 7
leaders, 27, 57, 194, 359
  mortality of, 316
  as sinners, 309–11
leadership, 188, 376–81
  challenge of, 257
  failure of, 315–16
  as shared, 256

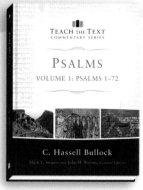